Imperial Women of Rome

Imperial Women of Rome

Power, Gender, Context

MARY T. BOATWRIGHT

OXFORD
UNIVERSITY PRESS

OXFORD
UNIVERSITY PRESS

Oxford University Press is a department of the University of Oxford. It furthers the University's objective of excellence in research, scholarship, and education by publishing worldwide. Oxford is a registered trade mark of Oxford University Press in the UK and certain other countries.

Published in the United States of America by Oxford University Press
198 Madison Avenue, New York, NY 10016, United States of America.

© Oxford University Press 2021

First issued as an Oxford University Press paperback, 2024

All rights reserved. No part of this publication may be reproduced, stored in a retrieval system, or transmitted, in any form or by any means, without the prior permission in writing of Oxford University Press, or as expressly permitted by law, by license, or under terms agreed with the appropriate reproduction rights organization. Inquiries concerning reproduction outside the scope of the above should be sent to the Rights Department, Oxford University Press, at the address above.

You must not circulate this work in any other form
and you must impose this same condition on any acquirer.

Library of Congress Cataloging-in-Publication Data
Names: Boatwright, Mary Taliaferro, author.
Title: Imperial women of Rome : power, gender, context /
Mary T. Boatwright.
Description: New York, NY : Oxford University Press, 2021. |
Includes bibliographical references and index.
Identifiers: LCCN 2020050573 (print) | LCCN 2020050574 (ebook) |
ISBN 9780190455897 (hardback) | ISBN 9780197777008 (paperback) |
ISBN 9780197567036 (epub) | ISBN 9780190455910
Subjects: LCSH: Upper class women—Rome—History. |
Upper class women—Rome—Social conditions. | Marginality, Social—Rome—History.
Classification: LCC HQ1136 .B535 2021 (print) |
LCC HQ1136 (ebook) | DDC 305.48/210937—dc23
LC record available at https://lccn.loc.gov/2020050573
LC ebook record available at https://lccn.loc.gov/2020050574

DOI: 10.1093/oso/9780190455897.001.0001

Paperback printed by Marquis Book Printing, Canada

To my family:
To those no longer with us—Boat and Billy, Bill, Jack and Dorsey,
and to the present and future—Paul, Sammy,
Joseph, Amelia, and Isaac.

Table of Contents

Acknowledgments	ix
Abbreviations	xi
Map: The World of Rome's Imperial Women	xiv
Introduction: Subjects and Sources	1
1. Rome's Imperial Women and Rome's Imperial Power	10
2. Crimes and Punishments of Imperial Women	47
3. Imperial Women within the Imperial Family	83
4. Imperial Women on Coins and in Roman Cult	119
5. Imperial Women's Mark on the City of Rome	167
6. Models and Exemplars: Statues of Imperial Women	211
7. Imperial Women Abroad, and with the Military	248
8. Conclusions: Agency and Constraints	281
Appendix 1: Imperial Women and Their Life Events	289
Appendix 2: Genealogical Tables of Imperial Families	297
The Julio-Claudian Family	298
The Flavian Family	299
The Second-Century Imperial Family	300
The Severan Family	301

viii   *Table of Contents*

Appendix 3: List of Divae   303
    Consecrated Males until 235 CE   313

Bibliography   315

Index Locorum   339

Index   355

Acknowledgments

WRITING THIS BOOK has been a great pleasure. Duke University's generous research funding enabled assistance from keen-eyed students including Melissa Huber, Adrian Linden-High, Elizabeth Needham, Evangeline Marecki, Michael Freeman, and Zihan Chu (my genealogical wizard), as well as supported the book's illustrations and maps. My department encouraged me to teach seminars that improved my knowledge and understanding specifically and generally, from Mack Zalin's exploration of Alexander Severus to the stunning team-based Claudium project by Adrian High, Katelin McCullough, Henrietta Miers, Mariangela Morelli, and Crystal Terry. Most recently, a first-year undergraduate seminar in 2019 on "Imperial Women of Rome" reminded me—yet again—of the vital importance of clarity, conviction, and absurdity.

Many others have provided support, suggested different avenues to explore, or reviewed parts of my work. Absolving all for my infelicities and omissions, I thank here Richard Talbert, Eve D'Ambra, Judith Evans Grubbs, Emily Hemelrijk, Tom McGinn, Corey Brennan, Clare Woods, Lucrezia Ungaro, Cynthia Bannon, Jeremy Hartnett, and Kent Rigsby. Stefan Vranka has been a patient and encouraging editor. Roger Ulrich generously provided the beautiful image of Sabina as Ceres from Ostia, and Susan Wood helped locate a photo of Matidia the Younger. I am grateful to countless others for guidance and interest over the years.

I profited enormously from testing select topics in papers whose lively interlocutors encouraged me to refine or broaden my arguments. At the Classical Association of the Midwest and South I presented "Domitia Longina and the Criminality of Imperial Roman Women." Signe Krag and Sara Ringsborg kindly invited me to a conference in Aarhus, Denmark, on women and children on Palmyrene funerary reliefs (part of the Palmyra Portrait Project), allowing me to focus on the exemplarity of the imperial family. At the Women's Classical Caucus panel at the Society for Classical Studies I spoke on "Imperial Mothers and Daughters in Second-Century Rome." Lucrezia Ungaro's gracious invitation to speak at "Le donne nell'età dell'equilibrio: *first ladies* al tempo di Traiano e Adriano," part of the brilliant exhibition *Trajan, Constructing the Empire, Creating Europe*, let me explore the topographical imprint of imperial women in Rome. In every case the opportunity to hear colleagues' related papers was provocative and fruitful.

Individual venues proved equally stimulating. Invitations to Minnesota allowed initial steps on my first chapter, and development of my thinking on imperial women's sculptural presence in Rome and elsewhere. Greg Bucher invited me to Creighton University to present "Family Matters: Rome's Imperial Mothers in the Spotlight"; later that year Jeremy Hartnett asked me to Wabash College, where I gave "Alma Mater? Rome and the Emperor's Mother." Roberta Stewart welcomed me to Dartmouth, to give "God-Like Power? Imperial Women and Roman Religion" as the Annual Benefactors' Fund Lecturer. The 2018 Biggs Family Residency in Classics Reunion at Washington University in St. Louis encouraged "Above the Law? Crimes and Punishments of Imperial Women." At all these fine institutions the questions of perceptive students and faculty sharpened my thinking. At the end, a talk at the Stonington Free Library (Conn.) helped me complete my manuscript. Further, the warm reception in my childhood home encouraged the hope that this project might appeal to many beyond those specializing in Rome's imperial history.

Tolly Boatwright
Durham, NC
30 June 2020

Abbreviations

FOR ANCIENT LITERARY works I follow the abbreviations of the most recent *Oxford Classical Dictionary* other than using "HA" for Historia Augusta rather than "SHA" for *Scriptores Historiae Augustae*, as the work is sometimes called. Cassius Dio poses special challenges because of the fragmented status of his text, and for convenience I use the book, chapter, and section numbering of the Loeb edition by E. Cary, *Dio's Roman History* (London and Cambridge, MA, 1914–27).

AE	*L'Année Épigraphique*, published in *Revue Archéologique* and separately (1888–).
BMCRE	British Museum Catalogue of Coins of the Roman Empire. London 1923–.
CFA	Acta of the Arval Brethren; cited *CFA* and document number as they appear in the authoritative edition of J. Scheid (with P. Tassini and J. Rüpke) (ed.), *Commentarii fratrum Arvalium qui supersunt. Les copies épigraphiques des protocoles annuels de la confrérie arvale (21 av.-304 ap. J.-C.)*, Rome 1998. For convenience the pertinent EDCS referent is also provided.
CIL	*Corpus Inscriptionum Latinarum* (1863–).
EDCS	Epigraphik-Datenbank Clauss-Slaby, http://www.manfredclauss.de/gb/index.html
FIRA	*Fontes Iuris Romani Anteiustiniani* [FIRA] 3 vol. Florence 1941–1943; reprint 1964–1968.
FOS	References to the catalogue of M.-T. Raepsaet-Charlier, *Prosopographie des femmes de l'ordre sénatorial (Ier–IIe siècles)*. Louvain 1987.
ILS	*Inscriptiones Latinae Selectae*, ed. H. Dessau. 1892–1916.
IRT	*The Inscriptions of Roman Tripolitania*, ed. J. M. Reynolds and J. B. Ward-Perkins. Rome 1952.

xii   *Abbreviations*

LTUR   *Lexicon Topographicum Urbis Romae*, ed. E. Steinby, 6 vols.
            Rome 1993–2000. Citations to this are followed by volume
            number and page, entry, and author of entry, although subse-
            quent citations to the same entry tend to be only to *LTUR* vol-
            ume and page.
MW   M. McCrum and A. G. Woodhead, *Select Documents of the
            Principates of the Flavian Emperors, A.D. 68–96*. Cambridge 1961.
OCRE   Online Coins of the Roman Empire, http://numismatics.org/
            ocre/.
PIR   *Prosopographia Imperii Romani Saeculi I, II, III,* 1st edition by
            E. Klebs and H. Dessau (1897–1898); 2nd edition by E. Groag,
            A. Stein, and others (1933–).
RDGA   *Res Gestae Divi Augusti.*
RE   *Real-Encyclopädie der klassischen Altertumswissenschaft*, ed.
            A. Pauly, G. Wissowa, and W. Kroll (1893–).
RIC   *Roman Imperial Coinage*, ed. H. Mattingly, E. A. Sydenham,
            et al. (London 1923–1967); revised edition of vol. I only, ed.
            C. H. V. Sutherland and R. A. G. Carson. London 1984.
RIC II.1²   *Roman Imperial Coinage.* Vol. II—Part 1. Second fully revised
            edition. *From AD 69–96. Vespasian to Domitian.* I. A. Carradice
            and T. V. Buttrey. General editors M. Amandry and A. Burnett.
            London 2007.
RPC   *Roman Provincial Coinage*, ed. A. M. Burnett, M. Amandry, and
            P. P. Ripollés Alegre. Paris 1992.
RRC   *Roman Republican Coinage*, 2 vols., ed. M. H. Crawford.
            London 1974.
RS   *Roman Statutes*, ed. M. H. Crawford. 2 vols. BICS Supplement
            64. London 1996.
SCPP   *Senatus Consultum de Pisone patre, CIL* II²/5, 900 = EDCS-
            46400001, cited according to the text as established by Eck,
            Caballos, and Fernández, 1996.
Smallwood   E. M. Smallwood, *Documents Illustrating the Principates of
            Nerva, Trajan, and Hadrian.* Cambridge 1966.
VDH   The edition of Fronto's letters as established by M. P. J. Van den
            Hout, *M. Cornelii Frontinis Epistulae.* Leipzig 1988.

MAP 1   The world of Rome's imperial women. © AWMC.

Introduction: Subjects and Sources

IF THE ROMAN *princeps* was first among equals, what position and visibility did an imperial woman have? Livia, Plotina, and a few other imperial women are celebrated for unwavering support of their emperor and empire;[1] Agrippina the Younger and Julia Domna are branded as impudently attempting to assert autonomy and exercise authority; a handful, most notoriously Julia the Elder and Messalina, are luridly depicted as sexually insatiable and manipulative of their exalted positions. Most, however, are more indistinct, as Faustina the Elder, a cipher despite her numerous posthumous portrait coins; Sabina, chameleon-like in her varied portrait statues and lack of presence; or Lucilla and Crispina, mere wraiths overshadowed by Commodus. Considered over time and as a whole, however, these and other women closely connected to the emperors illuminate Roman history and afford us glimpses of fascinating and demanding lives.

From its informal and gradual establishment by Augustus (30s BCE–14 CE) through the end of Severan rule (235 CE), the Roman empire oversaw Rome's far-flung and diverse peoples, religions, languages, and needs. The political system in this period essentially centered on one man, the princeps, whose eminence and authority were based on asserted Republican precedents and vaguely defined powers. Successful, evolving, and often self-contradictory, this principate was an unofficial dynastic system. The second-century Appian saw Augustus' changes as establishing "a family dynasty to succeed him and to enjoy a power similar to his own" (App. *B Civ.* 1.5), although Augustus' apparent claim to have restored the Republic was often repeated.[2] Many others similarly recognized the significance of family, and especially of the women related to the Roman princeps by blood or marriage.

---

1. For the dates and relations of these and other imperial women I discuss, see Appendix 1.

2. *RGDA* 34.1; Vell. Pat. 2.89.3; *ILS* 8393 = EDCS-60700127, lines 35–36; see Edmondson 2009, 197–202.

Imperial Women of Rome. Mary T. Boatwright, Oxford University Press. © Oxford University Press 2021.
DOI: 10.1093/oso/9780190455897.003.0001

Subject to Rome's distinctive gender norms, the wives, mothers, sisters, daughters, and others closely associated with the emperor—individuals embraced in my term "imperial women"—had no legitimate power of their own either individually or collectively. Yet they were key to the new and shifting power dynamics, they were present albeit marginally in Rome's highest circles, and they partook possibly in momentous decisions but certainly in the best resources of the empire. The investigation of these women clarifies the image and functioning of Rome's principate as well as its gender roles. At the same time my study elucidates remarkable people overlooked or diminished in ancient and modern accounts of Rome.

I use the expression "imperial women" to designate those who shared marriage or immediate family with the emperor. My term has no equivalent in Latin or Greek. It is not derived from a formal designation as is our "emperor" from the *Imperator* most Roman emperors bore as part of their name and titles.[3] The honorific title *Augusta* (*Sebaste* in Greek) was used for a wide assortment of imperial women: wives, mothers, sisters, mothers-in-law, daughters, or other cognate or agnate relatives. By the early third century Ulpian uses "Augusta" apparently to refer to the wife of the emperor, but his are general words (Ulp. 13, ad l. iul. et pap., Dig. 1.3.31; see Ch. 2). The imprecision of "imperial women" as a heuristic term corresponds to the ambiguities of these women's position and roles, as we see repeatedly in this book. Rome's empire was never a constitutional monarchy in which succession to the throne was carefully calibrated by descent, legitimacy, or some other stated criterion. Furthermore, women were barred by their gender from holding and exercising command of various sorts, the civil and military positions developed and honed through the long years of Rome's Republic and whose titles, at least, continued into the principate.

Political and military activities, and other public roles like oratory and jurisprudence, were not only considered inherently male but also those deemed noteworthy by Roman historians and other ancient observers. This reality vastly limits evidence even for women closest to an emperor. The best documented, such as Livia and some others mentioned earlier, have prompted stimulating biographies on which I draw in my research here.[4] But mine is not a series of biographies of imperial women. Instead, I aim to explore them as a whole, and to investigate

---

3. See, e.g., Hurlet 2015.

4. Cited in later chapters, they include K. Welch's forthcoming monograph on Livia with Oxford University Press.

their activities and visibility over time. These emerge more clearly from a comprehensive view spanning from the establishment of the principate in the 30s BCE by Octavian, with his sister Octavia and his wife Livia, to its violent interruption in 235 CE by the mutinous murder of Severus Alexander and his mother Julia Mamaea.

The lives and experiences of imperial women were shaped by custom and law, the exigencies and failures of the evolving new regime, and the personality, health, and luck of the individuals themselves. The last is the hardest to document and explore even for the best-attested women, although I signal such fascinating particulars in the vignettes that open each chapter. The main aim of my book, however, is to present chronologically the mores, laws, and evolving structures of the most significant functions and venues of Rome's imperial women. Ch. 1, circling around Livia, probes the powers imperial women were granted or thought to have. In Ch. 2 we turn to Roman law and its impact on imperial women. Ch. 3 inspects, within the wider context of the Roman family, the growing importance of the imperial family as an institution. Ch. 4 explores imperial women's involvement in religious activities of the principate: here, as throughout this book, I prefer the terms *divus* and *diva* to "deified" or "divinized."[5] In Ch. 5 we survey the imprint imperial women made on the capital city of Rome through their movements and presence as well as by monuments associated with them. The briefer Ch. 6 looks at a related type of public modeling, imperial women's representation through sculpture and relief. Ch. 7 explores the connections of our women to Rome's military forces and the provinces.

My substantive chapters thus begin and end with activities that Romans considered most inappropriate for women—politics and the military—ones with which imperial women's visibility was most shocking. Furthermore, as the Severan women were especially associated with Rome's armed forces, the arc of my book is generally chronological, starting with Livia and ending with the Severans. Within chapters I also tend to proceed chronologically: although Rome's deep-rooted traditionalism means that women are often presented in timeless tropes, one goal of my book is to evaluate change over time. We discuss those changes in Ch. 8, my conclusions.

As we see repeatedly in this book, imperial women's eminence was contingent on their relationship to the emperor and the imperial house. This

---

5. For the term *divus*, see, e.g., Price 1987, 77; Woolf 2008, 242. This chapter is longer than others because a traditional sphere of Roman women's activity was religious, and because it also reviews using coins as evidence.

4 IMPERIAL WOMEN OF ROME

was something new, although at first sight reminiscent of the history of some late Republican women (see Ch. 1). The principate was based on family, although—in keeping with the un- and understated power bases of the new regime—it was never an overt monarchy.[6] Around the princeps was an imperial court of family members, freedmen, close advisors, and others who controlled access to him or influenced his reaction to a petition, event, or person.[7] This court system, combined with Augustus' and later emperors' emphasis on dynastic succession (see Ch. 3), boosted the wife, mother, daughter(s), sister(s), and other women closest to the emperor. It is reflected variously in our evidence. When Cassius Dio's Livia urged Augustus to pardon Cornelius Cinna, for example, the prototypical imperial woman asserted that only a wife can be the true confidante of one who rules alone.[8] More independent documentary evidence, the *Senatus Consultum de Pisone patre* of 20 CE, affirms that even Tiberius admitted listening to his mother Julia Augusta (see Ch. 1). Later, Julia Domna is said to have given Caracalla "much excellent advice," a positive statement qualified immediately by the scandalized note that she "held public receptions for all the most prominent men, just like the emperor" (Cass. Dio 78.18.2–3).

This latter aspect, the supposed transgressions of women within the imperial house, is reflected in Livia's reported declaration that it was she who had made Tiberius emperor.[9] The last Julio-Claudian, Nero, clearly admitted the situation, at least in Tacitus' searing histories. In Nero's short accession speech to the senate paraphrased by Tacitus, the young princeps uses words for "home," household, and family three times: he promises to hear cases not "within his house" alone, to have nothing for sale or open to influence "in his household," and to keep separate

---

6. See, e.g., Hekster 2015 on emperors' erratic practices regarding dynastic genealogies.

7. See, e.g., Wallace-Hadrill 1996; Winterling 1999; Pani 2003.

8. Cass. Dio 55.16.1–2; see Adler 2011a, 145; Purcell 1986, 93; Ch. 1 below. A different perspective is provided in Vitellius' speech to the senate urging that marriage between uncle and niece (Claudius and Agrippina) be allowed because an emperor's wife helps the state by freeing his mind from domestic cares (Tac. *Ann.* 12.5).

9. Cass. Dio 57.12.3. Later, when detailing the worsening relations of Agrippina and Nero and reporting that Agrippina said to her son, "It was I who made you emperor," Cassius Dio adds "just as if she had the power to take away the sovereignty from him again" and notes she was a private citizen (61.7.3; tr. Loeb). The concept of the imperial woman as "maker of kings" may be reflected in Suetonius' note, at the beginning of both *Galba* and *Otho*, of the patronage of "Livia Augusta" for them when they were private citizens: Suet. *Galb.* 5.2, *Otho* 1.1.

Subjects and Sources

his "house" and the state (Tac. *Ann.* 13.4; see Ch. 3).[10] Although the promise was made to distinguish his future actions from those of Claudius, Nero could not keep it (see, e.g., Ch. 2).

The evolving principate meant that no emperor could be isolated from the imperial house and imperial women: even the short-lived principate of Nerva in 96–98, when the emperor was sixty-six to sixty-eight years old, saw a dedication or statue honoring his "imperial" mother (see Ch. 3). The importance of women for the imperial image and for legitimacy is reflected in other ways. Although reportedly estranged from his wife Sabina, Hadrian removed from imperial service the praetorian guard prefect Septicius Clarus, the imperial secretary (and biographer) Suetonius Tranquillus, and others, because they had interacted with Sabina more casually than reverence for the imperial court demanded. If we can believe the fourth-century source for this event, what provoked the emperor was no personal affront to Sabina or Hadrian himself, but rather the slight to dynastic courtly protocol.[11] Emphasizing a different aspect of the close-knit dynastic system of the second century, Marcus Aurelius allegedly averred that if he divorced Faustina the Younger, his wife and the daughter of his predecessor Antoninus Pius, he would have to give back her dowry—that is, the empire.[12] My book recounts many other acknowledgments of women's importance to the imperial house and imperial stability.

Yet we also see numerous criticisms of imperial women on various grounds, in fact disproportionately to the general scarcity of evidence for these women. As the above examples suggest, most literary information about imperial women is presented to illustrate imperial men and their decisions, not the women themselves.[13] Rome's patriarchal order was emphasized particularly strongly in the imperial house. A woman's failings reflected on her husband, father, or another

---

10. *non enim se negotiorum omnium iudicem fore, ut clausis unam intra domum accusatoribus et reis paucorum potentia grassaretur; nihil in penatibus suis venale aut ambitioni pervium; discretam domum et rem publicam.* When Nero acted to reduce Agrippina's power he removed her from his house (*domus*) and transferred her to the one Antonia had owned (Tac. *Ann.* 13.18).

11. HA, *Hadr.* 11.2: *familiarius se tunc egerant quam reverentia domus aulicae postulabat.* Scholars debate the particulars of this incident, usually assumed as 122 and in Britain: see esp. Birley 1997, 138–41, and 333 n.26; Fündling 2006, 581–88.

12. HA, *Marc.* 19.8–9. See Wallinger 1990, 47–51. Burrus earlier expressed the idea when trying to restrain Nero from divorcing Octavia, Claudius' daughter (Cass. Dio 62.13.2).

13. For instance, a passage emphasizing Domitian's vicious unpredictability notes incidentally that Julia, the daughter of Titus, nominated Lucius Julius Ursus as consul for 84 CE (Cass. Dio 67.4.2). Similarly, the report that Vitellius' wife Galeria Fundana saved the consul Galerius Trachalus from execution in 68 stresses not her bravery, but rather the savage volatility of the early Vitellian reign when no effective emperor had control (Tac. *Hist.* 2.60.2).

man responsible for her: for instance, Messalina's sexual escapades serve to underline Claudius' lack of control. Further, imperial women's propinquity to the most powerful man in Rome apparently caused others to view them distrustfully and, as we see in Ch. 1 and elsewhere, unusually targeted some women as peddling influence and imperial favors. Despite such biases and other source problems, discussed further later and in individual chapters, enough evidence remains for Rome's imperial women to allow us to trace, over time, the actions and roles of various ones in various contexts, and to illuminate a number of different features of the principate. Sir Ronald Syme once wrote, seemingly in remorse for the topic, "Women have their uses for historians" (Syme 1986, 169). My study, in contrast, examines imperial women as worthy subjects in themselves, as well as for the insight their reported activities provide for the history of imperial Rome as a whole.

My chapters open with a vignette about a particular imperial woman or women engaged in some activity or situation relating to that chapter's larger issues, to remind us that these were real individuals in heady circumstances and under intense scrutiny and pressure. My focus on those at the top of Rome's center of power, however, means less attention to other aspects of the principate. I cannot address fundamental topics such as the vast numbers of enslaved and freed, even those serving imperial women; imperial relations with provincials and the poor; and administrative and military hierarchies below the very highest level, especially in the provinces. Such topics appear occasionally—for example, Ch. 7 includes a section on the provincial travels of imperial women—but it would be a different, less focused book to have explored them as well as imperial women. Nonetheless, the book as a whole should contribute to our understanding of larger-scale structures and changes in the principate, even while it brings to life some of the intriguing women who witnessed Rome's history in the making even if they did not personally direct the course of events.

Tacitus and other Roman historians appear frequently in what follows, but I turn also to legal codes, coins, inscriptions, and other sources less familiar to the general reader. The literary accounts are usually inadequate and often tendentious.[14] Generally, what interested most ancient historians of the principate were the emperor, the men around him, and political and military affairs, and they were generally indifferent to women and children, especially girls.[15] Even

---

14. A further complication is the restricted access to information Cassius Dio laments for the principate (53.19).

15. The rare reports about a child usually presage the later behavior of a notable man, as when Suetonius details Nero's childhood and musical training (*Nero* 6, 20).

some of my most important information is incomplete and incidental, such as the report of Livia's enrollment "among the mothers of three children" and vote of statues as consolation for the death of her son Drusus in 9 BCE (55.2.5–55.3.1; see Ch. 1). Cassius Dio continues from this note to explain briefly that the "right of three children" could be granted to those "to whom Heaven has not granted that number of children." Writing in the early third century, he adds that formerly the senate but now the emperor made such grants—thus leaving unclear who made the grant to Livia—and that even gods could receive the privilege so as to inherit. Then he concludes, "So much for this matter," and turns back to his main theme: Augustus and what the princeps did that year.

Other literary evidence more clearly exhibits loaded rhetoric and terms. For example, Tacitus notes the dedication by Julia Augusta (Livia) and Tiberius of a statue of *divus* Father Augustus at the Theater of Marcellus in 22 CE, an act also recorded by a public calendar. Tacitus, however, uses the occasion to declare deteriorating relationships between the two and to direct blame to Julia Augusta.[16] This second-century historian and others frequently charge Rome's imperial women with "jealousy" and "envy," especially regarding other women, as well as with greed and peculation.[17] Besides obscuring the indubitable friendships and other ties among Rome's elite women,[18] each such report would repay a close feminist reading. My main focus is historical, however, not historiographical. Throughout the following pages I try to attend to the larger contexts as well as do some justice to the subtleties of the evidence.

To aid readers' comprehension, I provide numerous illustrations, plans, and a map of the empire. Other than the empire's capital city, consistently called Rome, I identify ancient sites with their modern toponym at first mention even should that be in a footnote; thereafter I refer to them by their Roman names. The two-page map of the Roman empire in my front matter locates, by ancient topynym, cities and most sites mentioned in my text, allowing the reader to trace imperial women's travels and locations outside Rome.[19] Four in-text tables summarize complicated information. The three appendices cover material useful for every

---

16. *Fast. Praen.* ad 23 April = EDCS-38000281; Tac. *Ann.* 3.64.2; discussed further in Ch. 5.

17. See, e.g., the jealousy and animosity of Livia, Agrippina the Elder toward Munatia Plancina, and Messalina: Tac. *Ann.* 2.43, 11.1, and 11.3; Cass. Dio 58.22.5; Ch. 2 below.

18. A good instance is Tac. *Ann.* 13.19: after Nero snubbed Agrippina late in 54 no one visited her other than a few women, "unclear whether from love or hate," then exemplified by a long discussion about one such visitor, Junia Silana, and her insults from Messalina and Agrippina.

19. My index also references each site by grid square on my map. I follow the same identifying principle about toponyms in Appendix 3, but cannot include all those sites on my map. In a few instances I also use modern terms, such as the Balkans.

8 IMPERIAL WOMEN OF ROME

chapter. Appendix 1, "Imperial Women and Their Life Events," notes full names and information for the imperial women discussed in my book;[20] Appendix 2 presents four genealogical trees: the Julio-Claudian Family, the Flavian Family, the Second-Century Imperial Family, and the Severan Family. Appendix 3 is a chronological list of consecrated imperial women with the major references for the cult of each, which is complemented by a short, unreferenced list of consecrated imperial men until 235 CE.

I have adopted the following conventions for dates and names. Unless otherwise remarked, all dates are CE, that is "from the Common Era," and in passages that might otherwise be confusing I note BCE (Before the Common Era) and/or CE. Other than in Appendix 1 I use the names by which my subjects are generally known, including familiar renditions such as Julia and Gaius (rather than Iulia and Caius). This can pose a challenge: for example Livia, Augustus' wife and prototypical imperial woman, had the full name "Livia Drusilla," which officially changed to "Iulia Augusta" (Julia Augusta) after Augustus' testamentary adoption of her in 14 CE. Unless the discussion might become unclear I use the name chronologically appropriate to the argument at hand, a practice I use when referring to Rome's first emperor now known as Octavian (Gaius Julius Octavianus) during his rise to power in the 40s and 30s BCE, but as Augustus (Imperator Caesar Augustus) after consolidation of that power in 27 BCE. Otherwise I use the commonly accepted names for emperors—for example, Vespasian, rather than "Imperator Titus Flavius Vespasianus Caesar," and Severus Alexander, rather than his birth name "Bassianus Alexianus," or "Imperator Caesar Marcus Aurelius Severus Alexander Augustus, son of Publius," his name often cited in inscriptions from his reign. I generally use the full name the first time an individual is mentioned in a chapter, but thereafter the person's more common referent or a shortened form. Ch. 2, for example, begins by discussing the wife of Domitian as "Domitia Longina," but then usually refers to her as Domitia. Severan women appear as Julia Domna, Julia Maesa, Julia Soaemias, and Julia Mamaea when first introduced in a chapter, but thereafter usually as Domna, Maesa, Soaemias, and Mamaea. Other than in tables where space is at a premium, I use "the Elder" and "the Younger" rather than "I" and "II" (or *maior* and *minor*).

When referring to primary sources, I quote Latin and Greek mainly when making an argument about the content, bias, or reliability of a passage. When citing inscriptions I generally provide the original reference in *Corpus Inscriptionum Latinarum* (*CIL*) or the like, supplemented whenever possible with the

---

20. Since there I also give references to FOS or another prosopographical source, I do not repeat such references when discussing an individual in the narrative.

Subjects and Sources

corresponding entry in the Epigraphik-Datenbank Clauss-Slaby or EDCS. EDCS is electronically searchable, frequently provides links that include photographs, and usually indicates more recent publications of the inscription. Thus, for example, in Ch. 2 I make a point about imperial women's occasionally ruinous identification with their husbands by citing *CIL* VIII 22689 = EDCS-24100029. Most references to coins are to the standard and easily available *Roman Imperial Coinage* or *RIC*,[21] and I almost exclusively discuss coins struck by the imperial mints predominantly at Rome and for circulation in Rome, Italy, and the West. These I call "centrally struck coins," "central coins," and "central coinage" (rather than "imperial coinage" or "official coinage").[22] Finally, whenever possible I provide information about provenance and current location for statues and busts, citing the objects according to their museum inventory numbers. Dimensions are in the metric system.

The evidence and analysis in this book reveal that many elements of imperial women's lives remained constant over the two and a half centuries I survey, but particular roles and images fluctuated. Throughout, from Octavia through Julia Mamaea, imperial women were supposed to exemplify womanly virtues, especially deference, obedience, and family support.[23] As female members of the imperial family, they represented stability and the future. Other than within the family, their most acceptable functions in Rome were religious, a traditional locus of women's activities, and the growth of imperial cult encompassed imperial women first as priests in Rome and then as objects of cult themselves. This was a development that affected women's lives throughout the empire, as we see in Ch. 4. Yet imperial women's most important roles were as acquiescent helpmeets to the emperor. Above all, they were not to act independently or flaunt their resources and proximity to power in any way. This is particularly clear in historians' denunciations of imperial women who allegedly deviated from the ideal and strove for more than was thought due to their gender and their duty. The following pages show both that roles and ideals did change over time, and that imperial women were individuals who often fit imperfectly the positions they held by marriage or birth. The investigation of these women reclaims their value as individuals even as it illuminates the times and structures in which they lived.

---

21. Metcalf 2012, 3–11, provides an excellent introduction to numismatics. *RIC* is the reference used in OCRE or Online Coins of the Roman Empire, http://numismatics.org/ocre/.

22. See, e.g., Hekster 2015, 6, 30–32. That the imperial mint for gold and silver was established first at Lugdunum (modern Lyon, France) around 14/12 BCE (Strabo 4.192) is immaterial to my argument.

23. I use the term "exemplarity" in this book to mean deliberate showcasing as a model rather than typicality or worthiness as a model.

I

Rome's Imperial Women and Rome's Imperial Power

Introduction: The power (potentia) of Julia Augusta in Rome's new principate

Among the events of 16 CE Tacitus reports to adumbrate the corrupt new regime of Rome,[1] he includes Lucius Calpurnius Piso's disgust with politics and the law that was triggered by a case Piso instigated against the prominent Plautia Urgulania (Tac. *Ann.* 2.34).[2] Piso is presented as close to Tiberius, Urgulania to Tiberius' mother Julia Augusta (Livia). Shifting from Piso's bitter complaints about Rome's degraded judicial system to details of the case against Urgulania, Tacitus himself incriminates Livia for the laws' debasement, noting "the friendship of Livia had raised [Urgulania] above the laws" (*quam supra leges amicitia Liviae extulerat*: *Ann.* 2.34.2). Urgulania withdrew to the palace (*in domum Caesaris*), but Piso insisted on pursuing the case even when Tiberius' mother—whom Tacitus now calls "Augusta"[3]—complained that she herself was being violated and diminished.[4] First Tiberius and then his mother interceded again, and at

---

1. For instance, Tacitus concludes the section with *vetus mos fuerit* (2.34), comparing Urgulania's arrogance to earlier womanly deference even of the high-placed Vestal Virgins.

2. In brief for Piso, see *PIR* 2nd ed. C 290; for Plautia Urgulania, *PIR* V 684; *RE Suppl.* 9.1868-9 (Hanslik). Her granddaughter, Plautia Urgulanilla, was Claudius' first wife, married almost certainly before 14 CE and divorced 24–27 (FOS #619). For Tacitus' passage, see, e.g., Goodyear 1981, 293–95 ad loc., and Barrett 2002, 165–67.

3. Part of her official name after her testamentary adoption by Augustus in 14. See more later.

4. *quamquam Augusta se violari et imminui quereretur.* Goodyear 1981, 293–94 clarifies the legal situation and Urgulania's provocation (had she stayed in her own house, she would have been safe from his threats); he also notes *imminuo* as "peculiarly Tacitean."

Imperial Women of Rome. Mary T. Boatwright, Oxford University Press. © Oxford University Press 2021.
DOI: 10.1093/oso/9780190455897.003.0002

last "Augusta" ordered that the disputed money be given to Piso. Two books later, when reporting a trial against Piso for *maiestas* in 24 CE (*Ann.* 4.21),[5] Tacitus recalls the incident by noting that Piso earlier "had dared to drag Urgulania into court, scorning the power of the Augusta, and to rouse Urgulania out from the house of the *princeps*" (*Ann.* 4.21.1).[6]

In these two passages Tacitus credits Julia Augusta, the prototypical imperial woman in Tacitus and others, with "power" (*potentia*, 4.21.1) as he factually reports that her friendship had raised Urgulania "above the laws" (2.34).[7] Julia Augusta's reported complaint, that she was being "violated" and diminished by Piso's actions (2.34), uses a particularly strong verb (*violare*) and echoes the language of offenses against *maiestas*,[8] an association underscored by the passages' repeated references to the imperial house (*domum Caesaris*, 2.34; *domo principis*, 4.21: see Ch. 2 and Ch. 3). Tacitus' narrative thus highlights "power" associated with this first imperial woman, even though he does not detail what that power was or how she had gained it.

Most readers of this and analogous passages of Tacitus and other Roman historians have noted the striking ways in which ancient authors remark on and narrate women's proximity and claims to power, termed *potentia, imperium, dominatio, exousia,* or some other word.[9] S. Benoist (2015), J. Ginsburg (2006), and F. Santoro L'Hoir (1994) are only a few of the many who have illuminated various ways in which ancient authors convey that *women's* power was dangerous and an inversion of proper norms. I do not need to make those arguments again. Rather, this chapter aims to distinguish the power or powers an imperial woman could and did command individually, institutionally, or both. Certainly by the beginning of the second century, when Suetonius reports Tiberius' taunt to Agrippina the Elder, "If you do not rule, my daughter, do you think you're being injured?" (Suet. *Tib.* 53.1), it was generally assumed that imperial women desired domination and would arrogate it whenever possible.

---

5. Martin and Woodman 1989, 152 ad *Ann.* 4.21.2 remark that Tacitus' term in the passage, *adversum maiestatem*, is "most unusual" and *Tiberii* is probably to be supplied.

6. *spreta potentia Augustae trahere in ius Urgulaniam domoque principis excire ausus est.*

7. For Tacitus' use of *potentia, auctoritas, dominatio,* and other such terms with women, see Santoro L'Hoir 1994. In 2.34 Tacitus credits Urgulania also with *potentia.*

8. E.g., Barrett 2002, 166 and note 65. Velleius uses *violare* and cognates when holding that Augustus' house was defiled by the adulterous Julia the Elder (2.100.4–5), and Tacitus later uses *violata maiestas* when discussing the adulteries of Augustus' daughter and granddaughter (*Ann.* 3.24.2): see Ch. 2.

9. Such as Tac. *Ann.* 12.7, his signal passage on Rome's complete upheaval by Agrippina the Younger's marriage to Claudius and devotion to domination (*dominatio*) and money: see Ch. 5.

Much of this chapter revolves around Livia, who spent over sixty years next to an emperor, first her husband and then her son. When Octavian took and consolidated power in the 30s and 20s BCE, Livia was simply his aristocratic second wife, one of a number of women known from the highest ranks of Republican Rome.[10] But she became extraordinarily eminent in Rome, as Cassius Dio remarks two centuries later while discussing Tiberius' accessibility and modesty at the time of his accession in 14 CE:

> Moreover, [Tiberius] bade his mother conduct herself in a similar manner, so far as it was fitting for her to do so, partly that she might imitate him and partly to prevent her from becoming over-proud. For she occupied a very exalted station, far above all women of former days, so that she could at any time receive the senate and such of the people as wished to greet her in her house; and this fact was entered in the public records. The letters of Tiberius also bore for a time her name and communications were addressed to both alike. Except that she never ventured to enter the senate-chamber or the camps or the public assemblies, she undertook to manage everything as if she were sole ruler. For in the time of Augustus she had possessed the greatest influence and she always declared that it was she who had made Tiberius emperor; consequently, she was not satisfied to rule on equal terms with him, but wished to take precedence over him. (57.12.1–3, tr. E. Cary; see also Suet. *Tib.* 50.2)[11]

No documented letters from Tiberius bear also her name, and no known communications are addressed to both alike.[12] It is vital to keep actual behavior distinct from alleged arrogance and assertiveness as reported by Cassius Dio, Tacitus, and others. Cassius Dio's assessment directly compares Livia to "women of former days," so we start there.

A few earlier and contemporary women are noted for direct or indirect involvement in the turbulent political events. In many cases they were held to

---

10. See Perkounig 1995. Livia maintained friendships with other women besides Urgulania, such as Mutilia Prisca (Tac. *Ann.* 4.12). In contrast, Agrippina the Younger's isolation is noted (Tac. *Ann.* 13.19).

11. Excerpts from Cassius Dio's Claudian history repeat for Agrippina a similar report, that she used to greet in public all who desired it and this was entered in the records (60.33.1). This boldness is greater than that of Julia Augusta, since Agrippina was in public. See Ch. 5.

12. The few surviving communications concerning both parties, such as the letter about religious honors from Gytheion (Gytheio, Greece), go to Tiberius, who responds that the petitioners can contact Julia Augusta (see Ch. 4).

be working for their family, something viewed as more acceptable than if they were aiming for their own power (see HA, *Heliogab.* 4.3; Jer. *Ep.* 22.16).[13] Quarta Hostilia in 180 BCE, and Cornelia the mother of the Gracchi, for example, were famous for their alleged political advancement of their sons (Livy 40.37.6; Nep. fr. 59 Marshall).[14] Caecilia Metella, Sulla's fourth wife, was said to be a mitigating influence over her violently erratic husband, called upon by the "people" wanting restoration of the exiled supporters of Marius (Plut. *Sulla* 6.12). Servilia made history during the Republic's destruction, counseling Caesar, Cicero, Cassius, Brutus, and others through her character and personal and familial ties.[15] To beg off an exceptional tax of the triumvirs, Rome's wealthy women approached the leaders' "women-folk" Fulvia (Mark Antony's wife), Mark Antony's mother (Julia Antonia), and Octavian's sister (Octavia). In Appian's rendition it was only when rudely repulsed by Fulvia that the massed women made their way to the Forum Romanum, where Hortensia's speech so incensed the triumvirs that they set the lictors to drive the women away, to the public's dismay (App. *B Civ.* 4.32–34).[16] Analogously, the now unnamed protagonist of the "Laudatio Turiae" dared address the triumvirs Lepidus and Octavian on behalf of her husband and family concerns, to be harshly forced back by Lepidus (*CIL* VI 41062 = EDCS-60700127).[17] Octavia interceded with Octavian for the eminent Tanusia (otherwise unknown) about repealing the proscription of Tanusia's husband, Titus Vinius (Cass. Dio 47.7.4–5).

Such incidents, often noted to underscore the self-annihilation of the Republic, indicate that overt political interference by women was generally inacceptable. In Ch. 7 we discuss Fulvia and some of the transgressions attributed to her. Less notorious, but similarly denounced in antiquity, are other women portrayed as inappropriately acting and meddling in men's affairs. For example, Terentia is said to have attended Cicero in his private trials of revolutionary followers of Catiline when he was consul in 63 BCE (Pseudo-Sallust, *Invective against Cicero* 3). Such charges against women were a way for male authors to denounce the men of their families, as well as to convey dramatically the inversion of norms at the end of the Republic.

---

13. Chastagnol 1979, 12, referring also to Suet. *Galb.* 5.1.

14. Dixon 1988, 168–203; Barrett 2002, 67–84; Dixon 2007. Livia's purported scheming to gain the accession of her son Tiberius squarely fits this construct.

15. Treggiari 2019 provides a full and sensitive account of Servilia.

16. Hortensia's speech (App. *B Civ.* 4.33) adduces the same incapacities of women regarding magistracies and politics as does Livy's speech of Lucius Valerius discussed later.

17. Hemelrijk 2004 explores "male" and "female" virtues and weaknesses in the speech.

Political intercession by women continued into the principate, but many fewer instances are noted for non-imperial than for imperial women. *Privatae* or non-imperial women are usually reported as acting with, and often for, other women. For example, in 16 CE prominent women (*primores feminae*) accompanied Drusus Libo in (unsuccessfully) canvassing for support in a trial (Tac. *Ann.* 2.29.1). In 20 CE Roman matrons (*clarae feminae*) publicly protested charges of adultery, poisoning, and other crimes against an Aemilia Lepida, accompanying the accused into the theater and piteously but vainly testifying to her innocence before Tiberius and the assembled crowd (Tac. *Ann.* 3.22–24; Suet. *Tib.* 49.1; see Ch. 2). The chief Vestal Virgin Vibidia tried to intercede for Messalina, Claudius' disgraced wife (Tac. *Ann.* 11.32.2 and 34.3), as earlier Vestals had for Cicero's wife Terentia (Cic. *Fam.* 14.2.2): the prestige Vestals had in Rome, and their apparent impartiality due to their unique status, made them valuable intermediaries.[18] It may well be that such "political" activity on the part of elite but non-imperial women continued throughout my period.[19] If so, it is eclipsed by the literary sources' focus on imperial women that is part and parcel of the historiographic concentration on the emperors and imperial court. Imperial women were treated as exemplary (see esp. Ch. 6). Although in fact they were seen relatively rarely in Rome and elsewhere, as Ch. 5 reveals clearly, their proximity to the emperor exposed them to charges of meddling in men's decisions—at the least behind the scenes, as we see at the end of this chapter. Thus in the principate the reports of politically active women center on Rome's imperial women.

These women, closely related to the emperor, were nearby as he faced decisions of every sort and oversaw the resources and well-being of the empire.[20] As we see especially in Ch. 3, they were central to the imperial family and house, which Tacitus trenchantly calls "dominating" (*domus regnatrix*, Tac. *Ann.* 1.4).[21] Honors to them grew in number and variety over the centuries, as we show. Yet as is clear in the following section, by law and convention Roman women were prohibited from holding power or having legal capacity, simply because of their

---

18. See DiLuzio 2016, 223–39 for the Republic; Gallia 2015, 77–87, through my period, though stressing the evidence for Vestals' continuing ties to their birth families.

19. A growing number of scholars suggest that among Rome's elite women cultural influence was not necessarily top-down, but rather went from non-imperial to imperial women or at least was reciprocal: see, e.g., D'Ambra 2013; Cooley 2013, esp. 26, 42–43; Alexandridis 2010, 193; Hemelrijk 2005a, 316–17; Fittschen 1996.

20. Millar 1977 stresses the reactive nature of the emperor's work.

21. See also Appian, *B Civ.* 1.5, quoted in the Introduction. For Livia's house after 14 CE, see Kunst 1998.

gender. Is there any evidence that Rome's imperial women went beyond these boundaries?

The evidence is sparse, indeed, and centers on Livia. Furthermore, the rights she and Octavia gained during Octavian's ascent are tied to *his* jockeying for power and drop from sight by the time he consolidates his authority and commands. Those privileges were not repeated for later imperial women, and their transience reveals that in the end the possibilities for imperial women never transcended those of other Roman women. We begin with this more general subject.

The "power" of a woman in ancient Rome

All Roman women were barred legally and conventionally from politics, legal decisions, and military commands. After the disastrous end of the Republic, the Augustan Livy has Lucius Valerius advocate for the repeal of the Oppian Law in 196 BCE by emphasizing that women could hold "no offices, no priesthoods, no triumphs, no decorations, no rewards or spoils of war" (34.7).[22] Women's exclusion from positions of power was based on a widespread conviction of their weakmindedness and fickleness of purpose,[23] and it was enshrined in law. Alexander Severus stated in an imperial decision of 224: "To act as a legal guardian is the office of a man; such business is incompatible with the weakness of a woman" (Cod. Iust. 5.35.1).[24] Around the same time Ulpian asserted as legal doctrine: "Women are separate from all civil and public duties, and for that reason cannot be judges, or hold a magistracy, or make a prosecution, or intervene for another, or be procurators" (Ulp. 1, ad sab., Dig. 50.17.2pr).[25] They were barred as pleaders in cases not related to themselves, so that they would not be involved in others' lives contrary to the sense of shame belonging to their sex, and they could not take on men's functions (Dig. 3.1.1.5).[26]

---

22. This list incidentally mirrors what Roman historians considered noteworthy.

23. See also Val. Max. 9.1.3.

24. *Tutelam administrare virile munus est, et ultra sexum feminae infirmitatis tale officium est.* Dixon 1984 remains fundamental. Ironically, Severus Alexander is censured for subservience to his mother Julia Mamaea: see Ch. 7.

25. *Feminae ab omnibus officiis civilibus vel publicis remotae sunt et ideo nec iudices esse possunt nec magistratum gerere nec postulare nec pro alio intervenire nec procuratores existere.*

26. *contra pudicitiam sexui congruentem:* see Gardner 1986, 261–63; Levick 2007, 60–61. Tiberius reportedly told his mother the same thing (Suet. *Tib.* 50.2–3). Julia Berenice of Judaea, a Roman citizen, is said to have adjudicated proceedings at which her own matters were being questioned (Quint. *Inst.* 4.1.19): Crook 1951, 169–70 admits to puzzlement about the passage.

On the other hand, Livy's Valerius stresses that since Roman women could not gain prominence through office holding or military command, they should at least be able to enjoy publicly their gold, jewels, and fine clothing subject to their menfolk's authority (34.7). His successful oration, buttressed by women's demonstrations, resulted in the repeal of the Lex Oppia. The debate discloses Roman ambivalence about women's control of wealth, and was ultimately resolved in what modern scholars might consider as a fairly liberal stance.[27]

Roman *patria potestas* was buttressed by the belief that women's innate inconstancy (*animi levitas*) made them incapable of deciding matters for themselves, and unreliable stewards of wealth and resources. Thus Roman women were supposed to be under the supervision of a guardian, either their father, husband, or another man, unless they were specifically absolved from *tutela mulierum*—obligatory guardianship of women—or declared *sui iuris*—under their own guidance, as were the Vestal Virgins (Gai. *Inst.* 1.144).[28] In the fabled past a Roman woman would pass from the *tutela mulierum* of her father into that of her husband upon marriage *cum manu*. By the first century BCE, however, many women were married *sine manu*, remaining under the guardianship of their father. At the death of a woman's guardian (and a father was likely to die before a husband), she would be assigned another tutor to oversee important legal and commercial transactions, like making a will or disposing of property.[29] But as time went on, *tutela* was for many women "little more than an inconvenience."[30] Although the second-century jurist Gaius noted that many women were more than capable of transacting sound business deals and did so sometimes despite their tutors (Gai. *Inst.* 1.190), laws and social norms persisted.

Prominent counter-examples warned imperial and other women to stay far away from exercising power. Dominant women, whether historical or mythical, were presented as transgressive, and many are non-Roman queens. Among the charges against Antony in the 30s BCE was that he had become "enslaved" to the Egyptian queen Cleopatra: he titled her "queen" and mistress, put Romans under her command as soldiers in her bodyguard, and allowed her to personally judge lawsuits, manage festivals, and envision rule over the Romans (Cass. Dio 50.5.5). In Vergil's *Aeneid* the Carthaginian queen Dido is introduced as the laudable leader of an *imperium* (e.g., *Aen.* 1.340, 364, 421–38), but her rule falters once

---

27. Milnor 2005, 154–85.

28. See Evans Grubbs 2002, 23–37.

29. See e.g. Evans Grubbs 2002, 24; Hemelrijk 1999, 102; Gardner 1986, 11–12.

30. Gardner 1986, 8. Women continued to gain more financial autonomy: Treggiari 1996, 900.

she falls in love with Aeneas and enters their "marriage," furthering threatening Aeneas' fate to establish the Roman race (e.g., *Aen.* 4.50).[31] The Briton Boudicca (sometimes called Boudica or Boadicea), queen of the Iceni, is depicted by Tacitus and Cassius Dio as uncontrolled and ultimately doomed in her attempt to lead the Britons against the Romans in 60–61 CE (Tac. *Agr.* 16, *Ann.* 14.29–39; Cass. Dio 62.1–12).[32] But this book documents many cautionary tales and opprobrious judgments of Roman imperial women: the ancient world saw a widespread distrust of women in power.[33]

The highest praise for imperial woman was for their self-restraint in the presence of power. All three citations of Julia Augusta in the *Senatus Consultum de Pisone patre* (*SCPP*) of 20 CE specifically commend her moderation and self-control (lines 132–33, 148–50, 118; see the end of this chapter). A decade later Velleius Paterculus lauds her, calling her "most exalted, and in every way more like the gods than like men," because no one ever felt her power unless they were relieved from danger or advanced politically (*potentia*, 2.130.5).[34] Some seventy years later, among Pliny's panegyrics for the new princeps Trajan is his praise of Trajan's modest wife and sister for wanting nothing from Trajan's power other than delight (*potentia, gaudium: Pan.* 83–84). Hadrian twice repeated the same idea in public venues. In his encomium of his mother-in-law Matidia the Elder, preserved in a fragmentary inscription from Tibur (now Tivoli, Italy), he states that she preferred to rejoice in his fortune than to avail herself from it; further, she was of such reserve that she never sought anything from him, frequently even things he would have wished requested (*CIL* XIV 3579 = EDCS-04800013; from 119 CE).[35] In Cassius Dio's report of Hadrian's slightly later praise of Plotina, Hadrian's adoptive mother and the wife of Trajan, Hadrian says, "Though she asked much of me, she was never refused anything," which Cassius Dio glosses as, "Her requests were of such a character that they neither burdened me nor

---

31. The mythical queen seems modeled on Cleopatra, who continues to be denigrated in the Augustan period (Verg. *Aen.* 8.685–88; Prop. 3.11.39; Hor. *Carm.* 1.37.21).

32. See, e.g., Santoro L'Hoir 1994, 7–11; Adler 2011b, 117–53; Gillespie 2018. Cartimandua is another such transgressive figure: Tac. *Ann.* 12.40.2–3.

33. E.g., the *Sibylline Oracles* predicted that the end would come when a scheming woman ruled the world (*Or.* 3.75–76): see Anagnostou-Laoutides and Charles 2015, 26.

34. *eminentissima et per omnia deis quam hominibus similior femina, cuius potentiam nemo sensit nisi aut levatione periculi aut accessione dignitatis.* We later discuss other summaries of Livia's life, such as Cassius Dio's statement that she never presumed to enter the senate-chamber, military camps, or public assemblies (57.12.3).

35. Lines 30, 28: *Gaudere fortuna mea maluit quam frui . . . post tanta modestia uti nihil umquam a me pe[tierit cre]braque non petierit quae peti maluissem.* Jones 2004, 269–70 notes parallels.

afforded me any justification for opposing them" (Cass. Dio 69.10.3a, trans. E. Cary).

Cassius Dio, whose senatorial career took place while the Severan women were markedly visible and active, is usually more nuanced than other historians when assessing imperial women. His appraisal of Julia Augusta, cited above, offsets negative criticism with some good: *despite* her unprecedented eminence—marked by receiving senators and the people in her house, managing all affairs alone, and repeatedly acting arrogantly vis-à-vis Tiberius—she "never ventured to enter the senate-chamber or the camps or the public assemblies" (57.12.1–3). In other words, she exercised some self-restraint.[36] Cassius Dio also reports the only administrative task ever credited an imperial woman: Julia Domna's supervision of Caracalla's routine correspondence. He cites this, however, to discredit the emperor:[37] Caracalla disregarded the "much excellent advice" Domna gave him, put her in charge of petitions and his correspondence in both languages, and even praised her in letters to the senate. But, Cassius Dio continues, "Need I add that she held public receptions for all the most prominent men, precisely as did the emperor?" (78.18.2–3; tr. E. Cary). Again a reference to an imperial woman mixes tribute with disapproval of her presumptuousness.[38] That Domna sometimes mediated communications with her son is corroborated by an inscribed letter from her to Ephesus offering reassurances that she would help the city get further benefits from Caracalla (*AE* 1966, 430 = *I. Ephesos* 2, 212). As B. Levick and others emphasize, however, in that letter Domna "performs no act of government nor even of administration and is in no way indiscreet."[39]

The slight praise noted above pales in comparison to the many criticisms of imperial women for greed for power, misuse of influence, or attempts to wield power or *potentia*. Literary references censure the women either directly or through various vignettes discrediting them and the males they supposedly dominated.[40] Although we cannot believe all the details, the anecdotes reflect Roman

---

36. As opposed to the Severan women; see esp. Ch. 7.

37. Tuori 2016b, 180–81.

38. Adler 2011a, esp. 134–35, discusses Dio's presentation of Livia and other strong females.

39. Levick 2007, 96, also notes the impossibility of estimating her influence on her son. Tuori 2016b discusses the passage in depth, concluding that any official or legal role for her is highly unlikely; further, any supervisory role she may have taken in adjudication would have been largely invisible. Ephesus is near modern Selçuk, Turkey.

40. E.g., Langford 2013 holds that Julia Domna was vilified to criticize Septimius Severus and Caracalla; Späth 1994, esp. 181–205, sees the literary emphasis on imperial Julio-Claudian women's power-mongering as criticism of the establishment of the principate itself.

beliefs and ideologies.[41] But we must distinguish reality from rumor. Tacitus' story at the opening of this chapter implies that the new political regime of the principate gave Julia Augusta judicial power to exonerate her friend Urgulania from Piso's charges against her in 16. Did she have this or any other actual power or right, authorized by others, to make binding decisions in law, administration, or warfare; to command others; or to enjoin or commit violence with impunity, whether for punishment or in combat? Such capacities are included in the Roman concept of *imperium*. But *imperium* is generally understood as inaccessible to Roman women.[42] (A less coercive type of "power," immunity from Roman law, is discussed in Ch. 2.)

Authorized powers for imperial women?

Did Julia Augusta have some special right of appeal, akin to what had been granted to Augustus by 18 BCE when Roman citizens' right of appeal to the *populus Romanus* was transferred to appeal to the emperor? A few literary anecdotes, some with legal implications, suggest Livia's beneficial intervention for others in sticky situations. A request from her to Augustus obtained *immunitas* for a Gaul (Suet. *Aug.* 40.3).[43] She interceded successfully with her husband for the conspirator Gnaeus Cornelius Cinna Magnus (Sen. *Clem.* 1.9.2–12; Cass. Dio 55.14–22, perhaps in the middle of his reign).[44] In 14 CE her entreaties to her son Tiberius saved the senator Quintus Haterius from death after he inadvertently tripped the new emperor (Tac. *Ann.* 1.13.4–6; cf. Suet. *Tib.* 27).[45] A similar entreaty seems behind Livia's mercy toward a group of naked men condemned to death for encountering her by accident (Cass. Dio 58.2.3ª; see more later). Cassius Dio says generally that she "saved not a few" senators (58.2.3); Velleius remarks that alleviation of danger was one way some felt her *potentia* (2.13.5, earlier); and the extraordinary *SCPP* from 20 positively notes her impact in this area (more

---

41. See Saller 1980. Wallace-Hadrill 1996, 284–85 notes that imperial authors frequently resorted to anecdotes as "a structural consequence of the retreat of politics behind closed doors."

42. See, e.g., Levick 2007, 60–61.

43. Purcell 1986, 87 remarks that in 30 CE Cleopatra supposedly thought she could turn to Livia for mercy (Cass. Dio 51.13.3; Plut. *Ant.* 83.6 mentions Octavia as well as Livia).

44. Most view Cassius Dio's rendition of Livia's speech about clemency as a literary construct, but suitable for Livia's presumed influence: see, e.g., Bauman 1992, 126–27; Adler 2011a.

45. Tacitus' rendition suggests that Julia Augusta was walking with Tiberius in the palace when the incident occurred.

later). Ovid hoped Livia would help him return from exile, but he calls upon her merely as an interlocutor with the emperor, who had the final decision about the poet's banishment (see esp. *Pont.* 3.1.114–66, and Ch. 3).[46]

Neither Livia nor any later imperial woman could legitimately exonerate a condemned person or overturn a judgment: the anecdotes we have exemplify positive influence even while demonstrating that an imperial woman alone never made a binding judicial decision. On the other hand, many more stories refer to condemnations and trials attributed to imperial women. Messalina is especially noted as interfering in trials *intra cubiculum principis* (Tac. *Ann.* 11.2.1, cf. 11.28.2, 13.4.2), and we see in Ch. 2 other convictions ascribed to Agrippina and others.[47] Political inference by an imperial woman seems to be a constant fear: even Sabina, so famously alienated from Hadrian, was liable to suspicions of intrigue and obstruction (HA, *Hadr.* 11.3; *Epit. de Caes.* 14.8). In terms of the law, appeals to imperial women had no binding significance. Although imperial women could sway an emperor to clemency, as noted particularly for the first imperial woman, Livia, they were more often feared as harmful. Velleius' approving note early in the principate that some felt Julia Augusta's *potentia* because she "eased their peril" acknowledges this deep-seated fear.

Other, more definitive evidence reveals a few initiatives toward legitimate power for imperial women. These are documented only at the inception of the principate, and although we might think grants of political and financial rights and privileges were handed down to subsequent imperial women, such special treatment drops from sight even during the Augustan era. On the other hand, conspicuous honors for women connected with the imperial house, such as the title *Augusta*, become ever more frequent with Caligula and later emperors. Honorifics took the place of legal privileges and rights, in other words. The changes correspond with the rise in importance both of the imperial family, the subject of Ch. 3, and of the imperial court, the subject of the final section of this chapter.

The earliest rights associated with imperial women date to 35 BCE, when Octavia and Livia—then merely wives of triumvirs—were assured security and protection against verbal insult similar to what was provided for the tribunes, gained the right to be honored by public statues, and were allowed to administer

---

46. The poem has been dated between 12 and 16 CE. Millar 1993 examines Livia and Ovid's exilic poetry; see also G. Williams 2002; Wood 1999, 2; Johnson 1997.

47. Osgood 2011, 147–50, 191–205; e.g., the death around 43 of Julia (the daughter of Livilla and Drusus the Younger), attributed to a "trick" by Messalina (*dolus*; Tac. *Ann.* 13.32.3).

their own affairs without a guardian (Cass. Dio 49.38.1).[48] Livia had been married to Octavian only three years, and Octavia to Antony five; Octavia had just returned to Rome from Athens and her intermittent life there with her husband. (See Ch. 7.) Although Cassius Dio suggests that as triumvir Octavian was responsible for the legislation of 35 BCE, some modern scholars argue that the senate or tribunes ratified the privileges.[49] If so, the grant indicates collective recognition that at least some women of the late Republic had capacities equal to those of men. The grants came as the triumvirs Octavian and Antony became openly estranged, discrediting Antony by enhancing the status of his repudiated wife, a Roman citizen *matrona* and Octavian's sister.[50] Never before had such rights been granted women in Rome.

Cassius Dio presents the protection against verbal insult as analogous with a traditional right of the tribunes. But this would be extremely unusual in application to two women, whose gender excluded them from the tribunate and all other civic offices.[51] What purpose could this tribunician right have served Octavia or Livia? As N. Purcell has noted, it postulates some degree of public exposure for the two: within the house both women would presumably have been protected by Octavian himself.[52] Only two possible instances, both trivial, suggest "tribunician" protection being invoked for them. We saw above that Livia's encounter with a group of naked men triggered their death sentence, which she begged off by saying that to her naked men were no different than statues (Cass. Dio 58.2.3ᵃ; see also Ch. 2). With a less happy ending, Augustus condemned to the galleys a man who besmirched Octavia's chaste reputation by claiming to be her illegitimate son and by discrediting Marcellus as not the son of Octavia's first husband, Gaius Claudius Marcellus (Val. Max. 9.15.2).[53] It seems as though the special grant was rarely used. It is also striking that the privilege the women were

---

48. It is implied that the two women would enjoy the privileges without expiry. Hemelrijk 2005a, 316 sees the privileges of 35 BCE as anticipating "the creation of a ruling dynasty;" cf. Dettenhofer 2000, 41–42, contra Flory 1996, 299 and Bauman 1981, 179.

49. Bauman 1981, 181 suggests the grant was made by a legislative act; Barrett 2002, 136, by tribunician edict.

50. See, e.g., Flory 1993, 293–95; Bauman 1981, 179. Barrett 2002, 31–32 holds that the inclusion of Livia, whose secondary mention in Cassius Dio's report indicates Octavia was the chief target of the honors, generalized the honors and possibly mitigated their novelty.

51. See Bauman 1981; cf. Purcell 1986, 85–87 and Barrett 2002, 136–37. In some ways the right prefigures the five-year grant in 23 BCE to Augustus of *tribunicia potestas* separate from the actual tenure of the office: see previous note.

52. Purcell 1986, 86.

53. See Barrett 2002, 137.

granted is one associated with the tribunate, which conveyed no *imperium*, rather than with another position in Rome's political hierarchy. Later Roman imperial women may have enjoyed some form of protection against verbal insult, but the sources never again inform us specifically about this privilege.[54]

The extension to Octavia and Livia of a right of the tribunes in 35 BCE emphasizes how the intense struggle for power and prestige at the end of the Republic subverted traditional civic rights and privileges. Julius Caesar and Octavian himself are both reported, controversially, to have received such "tribunician protection" (Caesar in 44 and Octavian in 36: Cass. Dio 44.5.3, 49.15.3–6; cf. App. *B Civ.* 5.132). Tribunician power (*tribunicia potestas*) would become one of the mainstays of the princeps' command and authority (*RGDA* 10; Tac. *Ann.* 3.56.2; Cass. Dio 53.17), although with rights enhanced from those tribunes held in the Republic.[55] The obsolescence of the two women's "tribunician protection" must have contributed to the impression of restored traditions under Augustus.

By 8 CE Livia's safeguard against verbal insult may have been subsumed under the *lex maiestatis* or treason law.[56] By then women of the imperial family were also included in the oath of allegiance sworn to the emperor and the imperial family (see Ch. 4).[57] But the safety of imperial women was probably seen to in more practical terms. Even during the triumviral period Octavia is reported as having a security detail (App. *B Civ.* 5.95).[58] A stray remark from Tacitus indicates that by the time of Nero the wife of the emperor normally had a protective guard personally assigned to her: Agrippina the Younger's had been reinforced by Germans as a special honor before the breach with her son in 54 caused Nero to dismiss them (Tac. *Ann.* 13.18.3; cf. Suet. *Nero* 34.1; Tac. *Ann.* 4.67.3).[59] The special detail was probably a normal part of an empress' life: according to Cassius Dio, after

---

54. There is no evidence for "tribunician rights" granted to later women: e.g., Barrett 2002, 137.

55. Along with *maius imperium*: see Cass. Dio 53.32.5–6. Bauman 1967, 213 briefly canvasses the scholarly opinion to that time of whether full tribunician power for life was granted Octavian in 36 (App. *B Civ.* 5.132 and Oros. 6.18.34, 20.7) or in 23 (Cass. Dio 49.15.5–6, 53.32.5).

56. Bauman 1981, 180 notes that the Narbonensis altar dedication from 11 CE (*CIL* XII 4333 = EDCS-12100286) specifies protection of the emperor's wife (*coniunx*) as well as children and family or *gens*. For the inscriptions, see Ch. 3, n.51.

57. Barrett 2002, 135–37 postulates that the tribunician protection "was perhaps seen as coming too close to the admission of women into a formal role in Rome's governance" (p. 137).

58. In Tarentum (37 BCE) Octavian "gave Octavia" a bodyguard of one thousand men, to be selected by Antony (Plutarch holds that the thousand soldiers from her brother were for her husband, *Ant.* 35.4).

59. Agrippina the Elder may also have had such a personal guard: Tac. *Ann.* 4.12.

Caracalla's death in 217 Julia Domna took as a hopeful sign that no change was made in the praetorian guard attending her in Antioch (79.23.2; Antioch is now Antakya, Turkey).

Another special grant to Octavia and Livia that Cassius Dio notes for 35 BCE was freedom from *tutela mulierum* so that they could act without a guardian in financial matters and thus control their own resources. This, too, is hard to document in subsequent generations of imperial women.[60] In part the obscurity is due to larger changes in Roman matrimonial customs, such as the growing number of women married *sine manu* at the end of the Republic and during the principate.[61] Such a marriage apparently gave a wife greater financial autonomy, perhaps because it may have been more difficult for her to consult closely with her own *paterfamilias* once she had moved from his house. A further confounding factor is the so-called marriage or social legislation of Augustus, which is associated with a privilege granted Livia in 9 BCE.

As consolation for the death of Livia's younger son Drusus the Elder in 9 BCE, the senate granted Livia the "right of three children" and more statues (Cass. Dio 55.2.5–6; the award of statuary is discussed in Ch. 6).[62] The right of three children (or *ius trium liberorum* as it is often cited) was relatively novel, associated with unusual Augustan legislation passed around 18 BCE, the *Lex Iulia de adulteriis coercendis* and *Lex Iulia de maritandis ordinibus* (Julian law against adultery and Julian law about marriage of the orders). This multifaceted legislation is not clearly outlined in the ancient sources and is further complicated by the *Lex Papia Poppaea* passed in 9 CE; the whole is sometimes called the Julian and Papian law or Augustan social legislation.[63] Together the legislation apparently aimed at encouraging the legitimate birth rate of Roman citizens especially

---

60. Späth 1994, 189 holds that after Livia all women of the imperial house were freed from *tutela* and enjoyed the right to control their own resources; this occurred independently or came because the women had earned the *ius trium liberorum*.

61. See, e.g., Treggiari 1996, 891; Barrett 2002, 137–38.

62. In addition to reasserting Livia's freedom from *tutela* (received in 35 BCE), the grant of the *ius trium liberorum* gave her the right of succession to the inheritance of her children: Barrett 2002, 124; Hemelrijk 2005a, 315 n. 39; Purcell 1986, 85. The *ius trium liberorum* specifically granted to the Vestals eighteen years later was a concession at the time of the *lex Papia Poppaea* of 9 CE (Cass. Dio 56.10.2), although the XII Tables (*FIRA* 1.37) had given them freedom from tutelage. The Vestals' right to a *lictor* is similarly dated uncertainly: see n.104 in this chapter.

63. For the *Lex Papia Poppaea* of 9 CE, see Tac. *Ann.* 3.25, 28; Cass. Dio 56.1–10; Treggiari 1991b, 60–80; McGinn 2013a. The relative novelty of the *ius trium liberorum* may account for Cassius Dio's digression when noting Livia's grant of 9 BCE (see Introduction).

among the elite (see Ch. 3), in part by stabilizing the various *ordines* or social and political ranks into which Roman citizens were being increasingly categorized.[64]

The legislation combined inducements and punishments,[65] and reflects Roman concern with marks of status. One incentive was the right of three children, by which freeborn and legitimately married couples with three children could gain various privileges such as accelerated careers in public life (for men) and relief from disabilities imposed on the childless in regards to receiving bequests (for men and women). Important to this chapter is the stipulation that bearing three children released a freeborn woman from obligatory guardianship, or *tutela mulierum*, as well as gave her the right of succession to the inheritance of her children (Gai. *Inst.* 3.44): in other words, the *ius trium liberorum* gave freeborn women autonomy—financial and otherwise.[66] But the concession was also given to childless individuals, and even to gods (Cass. Dio 55.2.7). When Augustus granted Vestal Virgins the right of three children in 9 CE (Cass. Dio 56.10.2),[67] the privilege was clearly divorced from actual childbearing. Livia herself bore three children—Tiberius and Drusus the Elder to her first husband Tiberius Claudius Nero (42 and 38 BCE), and a stillborn child to Augustus at uncertain date (Suet. *Aug.* 63.1)—but the senate's grant to her of the *ius trium liberorum* in 9 BCE was clearly honorary.[68]

It is hard to know if later imperial women had that same right, whether they had delivered three children or not. Our sole legal discussion of imperial women's privileges, Ulpian's statement in the Digest we explore in Ch. 2 (Ulp. 13, ad l. iul. et pap., Dig. 1.3.31), is excerpted from a longer discussion of the Augustan

---

64. For example, the laws ensured that children born to parents of senatorial status were ranked in the *ordo senatorius*—that is, had senatorial status and its attendant prestige simply because of their birthparents: Cass. Dio 56.7.2; Dig. 23.2.44; cf. Dig. 23.2.47 and Cass. Dio 54.16.2; Raepsaet-Charlier 1987, 1–4; Levick 1983, esp. 98. Further references will be discussed further in Ch. 3. Treggiari 1996, 886–92 provides a summary of the legislation; see also Treggiari 1991b, 60–80; in brief Barrett 2002, 123–24; McGinn 1998, 78.

65. Senatorial status for women from senatorial families correlates with increased scrutiny and penalization of their sexuality: Raepsaet-Charlier 1987, 4–7; McGinn 1998, 70–104.

66. Treggiari 1996, 889; Linderski 1988, 189. This applied to women still under their father's control (*alieni iuris*) after marriage: see Gardner 1986, 96, 20, 28 n.66. Some of the rewards started at three children for senators and equestrians in Rome, but more children were required the farther parents were from Rome and the lower they fell in Rome's status ranks: four children gave a freedwoman similar privileges. See also Treggiari 1996, 889.

67. Here Cassius Dio also notes Augustus' grant of immunity from the *lex Voconia* (see Gardner 1986, 170–78) to some *matronae* so that they could inherit more than 100,000 HS at a time.

68. Parkin has argued that the children had to be living or at least born live (e.g. 1992, 118). Later, e.g., Pliny the Younger successfully petitions Trajan for its grant to the childless Suetonius (*Ep.* 10.94, 95; see 10.2).

marriage legislation that became so complicated by exceptions such as the *ius trium liberorum*.[69] Further difficulties are posed by the troubled and incomplete history of many early imperial women. Julia the Elder amply earned the *ius trium liberorum* by bearing to Agrippa Gaius, Lucius, Julia the Younger, Agrippina the Elder, and Agrippa Postumus (as well as a son, who died in infancy, to Tiberius). She was, however, *in potestate* or under the legal supervision of her traditionally minded father, Augustus, and until his death could not own anything independently (see further in Ch. 2).[70] In the same generation Antonia the Younger, the second daughter of Octavia and Mark Antony, bore to Drusus the Elder three children who survived to maturity: Germanicus, Livilla, and Claudius.[71] When Antonia's grandson Caligula became emperor in 37 and she was granted "all the honors that Livia once had" (Suet. *Calig.* 15.2; see later), did this expressly include the *ius trium liberorum*? The right of three children is even less clear for other women of the early imperial house—such as Augustus' granddaughter Julia the Younger, whose only legitimate child was her daughter Aemilia Lepida Julia bore to Lucius Aemilius Paullus perhaps at the turn into the modern era, and for others whose unhappy vicissitudes we discuss in Ch. 2.[72]

Literary and documentary sources alike, however, indicate that whatever the basis of their economic power, imperial women could inherit and control their own wealth whether they married into the imperial family or were born in it.[73] Women deemed suitable for the imperial house came from the most elite families in Roman society; once married to an emperor they apparently kept control of their ancestral wealth and could add to it.[74] Livia owned the sumptuous villa at

---

69. See, e.g., Brunt 1977, 108; Daube 1954 [1991], 549; Levick 2014, 27.

70. Linderski 1988, with Suet. *Tib.* 50; cf. Gardner 1988, 96. Augustus' granddaughter was not in his *potestas* (Moreau 2009, 36).

71. Some other children apparently died before maturity: see Kokkinos 2002, 11–13.

72. For reasons of space and legibility, this marriage and child do not appear on the Julio-Claudian genealogical tree in Appendix 2.

73. The documentary evidence includes brick-stamps, lead pipes, and epitaphs of their slave and freed dependents: see, e.g., Granino Cecere 2010; Boatwright 1992, 25–26 on the freedmen Mindii of Matidia the Younger. For lead pipes, see e.g., Bruun 2000.

74. Dowry transferred a woman's familial wealth temporarily to her husband (Treggiari 1991b, 324–30, 445), but in some cases may have been appropriated by an imperial husband. Caracalla presumably took over Plautilla's enormous dowry after doing away with her and her family (in 202 Plautianus had given "as much for his daughter's dowry as would have sufficed for fifty women of royal rank": Cass. Dio 77.1.2). Domitia Longina may have reclaimed her extensive holdings after Domitian's assassination: Fraser 2015, 241–42.

Prima Porta from before her marriage to Octavian (Suet. *Galb.* 1),[75] and around 10 CE she inherited from Herod's sister Salome rich lands and palm groves in the East (Joseph. *BJ* 2.167, *AJ* 18.31). We do not know when or how Livia acquired the lucrative copper mine in Gaul that Pliny the Elder notes was exhausted by his day (Plin. *NH* 34.2.2–4). She inherited one-third of Augustus' estate after he specifically requested senatorial permission for her to receive such a large portion, more than the legal amount (Cass. Dio 56.32.1).[76] S. Treggiari's 1975 exploration of the inscriptions from the *columbarium* of her *familia*, the burial place of her household dependents on the Via Appia, reveals the large number and various occupational specialties of Livia's male and female slaves and freedpersons: more than four hundred epitaphs were found in situ, and Treggiari estimates that at least eleven hundred persons were originally buried there.[77] Inscriptions similarly reveal the enslaved and freed of later imperial women. For example, Poppaea had ancestral property, slaves, and freedmen in the closely set Campanian cities Oplontis, Pompeii, and Stabiae.[78] Lollia Paulina, Caligula's third wife, adorned herself in her own inherited jewels worth 40 million sesterces, which her subsequent unhappy history suggests she retained despite her divorce from the emperor (see Ch. 2). Antoninus Pius is said to have given to his daughter Faustina the Younger his private fortune (*patrimonium*; HA, *Ant. Pius* 7.9). In another example, Julia Maesa is said to have amassed a great fortune while living and traveling with the imperial Severan family; further, at the death of her sister Julia Domna in 217 the ephemeral emperor Macrinus (r. 217–218) sent Maesa back to her ancestral estates (Hdn. 5.3.2). These were almost certainly in Emesa (now Homs, Syria).

---

75. See Huntsman 2009, 137–41, 148–49; Barrett 2002, 28–29. The villa is twelve kilometers north of Rome. In Ch. 5 we discuss the building Livia sponsored on the Via Latina, whose inscription names her as "Livia, daughter of Drusus, wife of Caesar Augustus" (*CIL* VI 883 = EDCS-17301015).

76. Champlin 1991, 204 lists only three other imperial women as heirs and legatees. Antonia the Younger was named as heir of Berenice, the mother of Agrippa I (Joseph. *AJ* 18.156); Agrippina the Younger was presumably the heir of her companion Acerronia (Tac. *Ann.* 14.6.1); and Faustina the Younger was the beneficiary of a contested will of Matidia the Younger (Fronto, *ad amicos* 1.14 and *ad Ant. Imp.* 2.1, pp. 180, 95 VDH; see Champlin 1991, 71).

77. Treggiari 1975, 48 noting that only about ninety are certain members of Livia's staff. Others had been owned by her relatives or freedmen.

78. See Kragelund 2010, 565 with references, and also Tac. *Ann.* 13.45.1–2. For slaves and *liberti* of the imperial women of the Trajanic-Hadrianic period, see Boatwright 1991. Chantraine 1980 is the fundamental compilation, from Octavia to the Severans.

Rome's Imperial Women and Rome's Imperial Power

Within the *fiscus* there was no discrete category of goods reserved for imperial women, such as jewels or special robes.[79] Imperial property belonged to the emperor and the state, as did jewelry and female ornaments passed down with other imperial property (Tac. *Ann.* 13.13.4 and 14.28.2; Suet. *Nero* 28.2; Cass. Dio 72, fr.1; Claud. *Epithalamium de Nuptiis Honorii Augusti* 13–14).[80] In other words, during the principate an imperial woman did not have any unique rights to property.[81]

Paradoxically but suggestively, the least ambiguous evidence for imperial women's wealth was inconspicuous in antiquity. These are the brick stamps that now document the brickyards or *figlinae* many imperial women owned in and around Rome, but which in antiquity would have been buried in Rome's walls and other constructive elements. Brickyard ownership by imperial women is particularly marked in the second half of the second century, which also sees non-imperial men and women as proprietors.[82] Some evidence suggests that in the first century Julia Titi owned *figlinae*,[83] and her coeval Domitia Longina also had brickyards, even though some maintain that Domitia's "industrial" activity began over twenty years after the assassination of her husband Domitian.[84] In the next generation Plotina definitely owned *figlinae*. Later, Sabina is spottily attested.[85] Still later owners include Domitia Lucilla, the mother of Marcus Aurelius;[86] Faustina the Younger; and her daughter Lucilla.[87] Yet the evidence for such property would have been unobtrusive if not invisible to most contemporaries.[88]

---

79. Barrett 1996, 131–33 (referring *inter alia* to Brunt 1966) discusses the uncertain distinction of the *fiscus* (the emperor's private wealth) from the *aerarium* (the state treasure) from the beginning of the principate (see also *SCPP* line 55, the earliest attested use of *fiscus* for the private patrimony of the princeps, with Champlin 1999, 118).

80. See Temporini-Gräfin 2002, 235. Dig. 49.14.6.1 Ulp. 63 *ad Ed.* suggests that the accounts of an empress were bundled with those of the emperor.

81. I thank Cynthia Bannon for advice on this section.

82. Chausson and Buonopane 2010, 92–93, 109, noting that in the second century only Marciana, Faustina the Elder, and Crispina are not attested as brickyard owners.

83. Chausson and Buonopane 2010, 100.

84. Chausson and Buonopane 2010, 100–101; see also Fraser 2015, 241–42.

85. Boatwright 1991, 521, 523; Chausson and Buonopane 2010, 109.

86. Chausson and Buonopane 2010, 93, 109.

87. Chausson and Buonopane 2010, 93–94, 100: Lucilla was evidently the owner of the *figlinae Fulvianae.*

88. This invisibility extends to stamped lead pipes, such as those attesting the Temple of *diva Matidia*, the Lavacrum Agrippinae, and some houses of imperial women: see Ch. 5.

It is also noteworthy that this period of women's ownership of building materials does not overlap in any way with imperial women's patronage of monuments in Rome, which clusters in the Augustan period. Such architectural patronage in the capital city, discussed and mapped in Ch. 5, might correlate with imperial women's use of their own resources. Pertinent to this chapter about imperial women's autonomy is the debate about their agency, which swirls especially about buildings associated with Augustan women, such as Octavia's Porticus Octaviae (23–11 BCE) and Livia's three new or reconstructed monuments, the Porticus Liviae (6 BCE), Temple of Concord, and Temple of Bona Dea. If Octavia and Livia patronized these structures, they would not have been unique, for elite women were patronizing building in late first-century BCE Italy, and Vipsania Polla, the sister of Agrippa, undertook completion of the Porticus Vipsania along the Via Flaminia in Rome (after 7 BCE; Cass. Dio 55.8.4).[89] In any case, modern scholars disagree over whether Octavia and Livia were actually responsible, or were simply honored nominally by the "true" sponsor, Augustus. Those advocating for Augustus' agency turn to the sources from the second century and later (Suet. *Aug.* 29.4; Cass. Dio 49.43.8, 54.23.6), without taking into full account the growing historiographical animus against independent imperial women.[90] As we see in Ch. 5, post-Augustan public building in Rome sponsored by imperial women is attested only by documentary evidence. As the emperor increasingly appropriated public building in Rome, he undoubtedly suppressed building patronage there by women as well as by elite men.[91] Further, the problematic record for imperial women's building patronage in Rome even at the beginning of the principate suggests persistent unease with such visibility.

Rome frowned upon the display of wealth by women, but imperial women's expenditures seemingly aimed at nurturing family or others generally meet with little or no reproach. Again, Livia is the prototype. The *SCPP* of 20 CE speaks approvingly of Julia Augusta's "numerous and great benefactions towards men of every rank" (lines 116–17; more later).[92] At her death nine years hence she was honored by the senate because she had "saved the lives of not a few [senators],

---

89. See Cooley 2013; Boatwright 2015, 236–37. I refer to Rome's north-south artery, now traced by the Via del Corso, as the Via Flaminia rather than the often-encountered Via Lata, since the latter toponym appears first in the fourth century: *LTUR* 5.139, s.v. "Via Lata" (J. Patterson).

90. Suetonius' assertion, made to confirm Augustus' modesty in claiming building patronage (Boatwright 2013, 21–22; Horster 2001, 24–29), has led some to reject Livia and Octavia as genuine patrons with real input into the types and locations of their donations (cf. e.g., Richardson 1976, 62; Kleiner 1996, 30, 40 n.23).

91. See, e.g., Levick 2007, 19, 67.

92. See Eck et al. 1996, 226.

reared the children of many, and helped many to pay for their daughters' dowries, prompting some to call her Mother of the Country" (Cass. Dio 58.2.3).[93] Tacitus reports that she aided Augustus' granddaughter Julia the Younger in her exile until the latter's death in 28 CE, even though the historian characteristically maligns Livia as one "who ostentatiously showed pity to her tormented stepchildren, although she had secretly undermined them while flourishing" (Tac. *Ann.* 4.71.4).[94] In another act redounding to familial piety, Livia gave a million sesterces to the man who swore he had seen Augustus ascending to heaven (Cass. Dio 56.46.2).[95] Outside the bounds of her immediate family, Livia supported the senators Servius Sulpicius Galba, Marcus Salvius Otho, and Gaius Fufius Geminus (Suet. *Galb.* 5.2; Plut. *Galb.* 3.2; Suet. *Otho* 1.1; Tac. *Ann.* 5.2.2).[96]

Yet after Livia, reports are rare even of "maternal" public expenditures by imperial women, despite increasing emphasis on the imperial family. The encouragement—which may not always have included financial outlays—extended also to writers, but the evidence is somewhat spotty. Octavia helped find support for Vitruvius before he published *De Architectura* around 25 BCE (Vitr. *Arch.* 1 *praef.* 2–3), Domitia may have helped Josephus (*Vit.* 76.429), and Julia Domna aided Philostratus, and allegedly others besides (Cass. Dio 78.18.2–3; Philostr. *VA* 1.3).[97] Only in the mid-second century, which witnessed extraordinary attention to domesticity (see Ch. 3), do we find more publicized gestures, such as charities established in Rome for girls (and sometimes boys) that are called *Puellae Faustinianae*. Despite the nurturing, maternal image of imperial women advertised by these charities, almost all of them were posthumously founded by an emperor in honor of a deceased wife.[98]

---

93. It is dubious that Livia was the actual guardian for her wards, since women were not supposed to act as guardians: *CJ* 5.35.0–1, *Quando mulier tutelae officio fungi potest* (though dated to 224 CE). See above for her "saving" senators. Her unofficial title was presaged in 14 when the senate debated calling her *mater patriae* or *parens patriae* (Tac. *Ann.* 1.14.1; cf. Cass. Dio 57.12.4 and Suet. *Tib.* 50.3).

94. See Ch. 3 for more about stepmothers.

95. The apotheosis surely strengthened her new position as priest of *divus* Augustus (see Ch. 4).

96. For Livia and Galba, see further Wiedemann 1996, 261 noting the Edict of Tiberius Julius Alexander from Egypt calling Galba "Lucius Livius Galba" (*OGIS* 665 = *SEG* 8.794) and that Livia's head appears on Galba's coins. Wallace-Hadrill 1996, 303 hazards from Sen. *Consol. ad Marc.* 24.3 that Marcia's friendship with Livia secured a priesthood for her son Metilius. Purcell 1986 also emphasizes Livia's numerous connections with Rome's *matronae*.

97. For Domna see Levick 2007, 107, 112–15, with references. For the intellectual activities and patronage of imperial women in general, see Hemelrijk 1999, 104–22.

98. See Ch. 5.

IMPERIAL WOMEN OF ROME

Other ways imperial women were noted for wealth are presented more critically. Augustus had his granddaughter Julia's house torn down because of its extravagance (Suet. *Aug.* 72). When bemoaning the luxury of the imperial age, the moralistic encyclopedist Pliny the Elder excoriates Lollia Paulina, named immediately as the wife of Caligula, for flaunting emeralds and pearls in alternating rows in her hair and ears, in wreaths, and on her neck, arms, and fingers, at a private wedding dinner. Pointing out that this 40 million *sestertii* show was not even the gift of the profligate princeps (Caligula) but rather her grandfather Marcus Lollius' provincial plunder, Pliny bemoans the virile austerity of the early Republic. He scorns this "one little woman of the Empire" (*una imperii muliercula*) before turning to the even more extravagant pearls of Cleopatra (Plin. *HN* 9.117–19).[99] Pliny the Elder, Tacitus, and Cassius Dio all remark about the Fucine Lake spectacle in 52 involving Agrippina's gold *chlamys*, perhaps as much for its prodigality as for the symbolism of her appropriation of this traditionally male mantle (*HN* 33.63; *Ann.* 12.56.3; Cass. Dio 60.33.3).[100] As later Agrippina tried to retain power over Nero in the initial stages of his affair with Acte she offered to transfer to him many of her own resources, which Tacitus describes as "not much less than imperial ones" (*Ann.* 13.13.1; around 55). Slightly later Nero gave Octavia the home of Afranius Burrus and the *praedia* of Rubellius Plautus as "consolation" for their divorce in 62 (Tac. *Ann.* 14.60 calls them "unlucky gifts"). Burrus' home may have been Nero's to give—donated to the princeps by his increasingly estranged former advisor—but Plautus' goods were presumably state-owned because he had been killed on a charge of *maiestas* (treason).[101]

It may well be that Livia's right of three children granted in 9 BCE, which reinforced and augmented the freedom from tutelage she and Octavia had received in 35 BCE, became a right of imperial women after the Augustan period. Less debatable is that over time, even as early as Caligula's reign, ever less evidence attests such women's autonomous use of resources. Their prominence in the imperial family made them lightning rods for criticism for "luxury" and egotistic expenditures. We cannot know whether the women's retreat from public spending and the public eye was always their own choice. The foil of Matidia the

---

99. Lollia's subsequent history (see FOS #504) suggests she retained her wealth despite her marriage and divorce from Caligula.

100. See Ginsburg 2006, 29.

101. Barrett 1996, 132. Nero's gifts to Octavia were possible after their divorce: husband and wife could not give each other substantial gifts (see esp. Dig. 24.1; Treggiari 1981, 62). After the condemnation of his sisters Agrippina and Julia Livilla for conspiracy in 39, Caligula had their ornaments, furniture, slaves, and *liberti* sold off in Gaul (Suet. *Calig.* 39.1).

Younger is telling. She surely did not have more wealth than her younger sister Sabina, Hadrian's wife, and she never gained the honorific title *Augusta* that distinguished many imperial women. But as we see in Ch. 6, documentary evidence attests her considerable resources and high profile in Italy and the empire.[102] She plainly enjoyed more freedom than her sister at the peak of the Roman world. In sum, the unprecedented rights granted early imperial women did not become entitlements to act however they wished. We see this in much more detail in Ch. 2, on imperial women and the law.

Extraordinary distinctions for Livia in 14 CE

Augustus adopted Livia by testament into his own *gens Iulia*, in a move never repeated.[103] She was also honored by the title *Augusta* (so that her name became Julia Augusta), became a priest in the new cult of *divus* Augustus, and was granted the privilege of being accompanied by a *lictor* (Tac. *Ann.* 1.8.1; see Cass. Dio 56.46.1–2). These three honors would be repeated for later imperial women, although the most conspicuous, the priesthood and presence of a lictor, were much less frequent than the bestowal of *Augusta* by the senate—and even that title is rare until the later Neronian period. Indeed, the honors of 14 CE for Livia are unusual in the 250 years I survey in this book. This woman, who as the wife of the first princeps and mother of the second was beside imperial power for over 60 years, may seem prototypical, but the longer perspective reveals how atypical she really was. In Ch. 4 we see that her religious position was replicated by only Antonia the Younger and Agrippina the Younger, thus confined to the Julio-Claudian period. Here I discuss the right of the lictor, documented later only with Agrippina the Younger, and then the title *Augusta*.

The evidence for Julia Augusta's lictor is not straightforward, almost certainly because accompaniment by a lictor was extraordinary in Rome. The presence of a lictor, a civil servant and bodyguard indicating the distinction of the one he escorted, traditionally marked magistrates with *imperium*: Roman consuls were accompanied by twelve lictors and praetors by six, each carrying *fasces* or the insignia of a bundle of rods, with an axe inserted when the magistrate was outside

---

102. Some later imperial women are seen as patrons outside of Rome: e.g., Vibia Aurelia Sabina, a daughter of Marcus Aurelius and Faustina the Younger, was the patron of the *municipium* of Calama (now Guelma, Algeria): *CIL* VIII 5328 = EDCS-13001559.

103. Barrett 2002, 148 sees the adoption as Augustus' "attempt after his death to grant Livia what he had denied her during his lifetime, a form of institutional status."

the city of Rome. Accompaniment by a lictor also signified the religious authority of the Vestal Virgins, although the origin of having each Vestal attended by a lictor is uncertainly dated.[104] The Vestals' lictors, like others attached to priests within the pontifical college, were *lictores curiatii* of lesser status.[105] Cassius Dio ties the grant to Julia Augusta to her new position as priestess of *divus* Augustus, reporting that she could use a lictor when performing her sacred duties (56.46.2); a century earlier, however, Tacitus reports in the *Annals* that Tiberius actually refused to allow the senate to decree a lictor for Livia (Tac. *Ann.* 1.14.3).

Most scholars accept Cassius Dio's details, noting that Tacitus includes this, among other honors the senate vainly proposed after Augustus' death, as a way to show Tiberius as grudging and resentful of his mother's eminence.[106] When Agrippina the Younger was made *flaminica* of *divus* Claudius after his death in 54, she gained the honor of two lictors (Tac. *Ann.* 13.2.6; explored in Ch. 6).[107] The lictors of both these imperial priestesses must have been similar to those of the Vestals. After Agrippina, however, we never hear again of an imperial woman being accompanied by lictors (instead, as we see in Ch. 5, in the late second and early third centuries they moved through the city with the "sacred fire"), or of one being a specialized priest. Thus, particularities that had distinguished the first imperial women drop from sight. This is not so true of the honorific title *Augusta*: following a generation of desuetude after its widespread use for Livia, it ended up spreading widely for imperial women. The honor was granted by the senate. (See Table 1.1.)[108]

After 14 Livia is almost always referred to as "Julia Augusta" on official inscriptions and other centrally created documents.[109] The import of *Augusta* is as clear but as hard to pinpoint as is that of *Augustus*, the designation decreed the first princeps by the senate in 27 BCE and used as his cognomen and that of

---

104. Gallia 2015, 95 follows Plutarch in crediting Numa with the Vestals' honor (*Num.* 10.3), but also considers the date of 42 BCE, for which see Cass. Dio 47.19.4; Bauman 1981. Barrett 2002, 143–44 argues against the notion of a deliberate policy on Augustus' part to create a special connection between Livia and Vesta or the Vestal Virgins.

105. They carried bundles of rods without the axes: see DiLuzio 2016, 141; Brännstedt 2015, 42.

106. Bauman 1981, 175–77 (stressing the senate's agency); Barrett 2002, 144 and 160, exploring the grant as Tiberius' concession to Livia's right to a public role.

107. In Agrippina's case the lictors join other distinctions, such as the special guard of praetorian troops assigned to her earlier in Claudius' reign (Tac. *Ann.* 13.18.3); Barrett 1996, 152 holds that she could be accompanied by two lictors at any time.

108. See Kolb 2010a, 23–35, with sources; Kuhoff 1993; Temporini 1978, 27–35.

109. E.g., Späth 1994, 188 n.90.

Table 1.1 List of *Augustae*

Imperial women granted the honorific title *Augusta* via senatorial decree (see Kolb 2010a, 23–35, with sources; for individual references see also Kienast 2017; Kuhoff 1993; Temporini 1978, 27–35). Women posthumously granted the title are in **bold**.

1.	**Livia**, 14 CE + adoption into *gens Iulia*
2.	Antonia the Younger, 37, again 41
3.	Agrippina the Younger, 50
4.	Poppaea, 63
5.	Claudia (daughter Poppaea and Nero), 63
6.	Statilia Messalina, 66
7.	Sextilia, mother of Vitellius
8.	Julia Titi, 79
9.	**Domitilla**, wife or daughter of Vespasian
10.	Domitia Longina, 81[1]
11.	Plotina, between 100 and 105
12.	Marciana, between 100 and 105[2]
13.	Matidia the Elder, 112
14.	Sabina, 128[3]
15.	Faustina the Elder, 138
16.	Faustina the Younger, 147 (at the birth of her first child: HA, *Marc.* 6.6)
17.	Lucilla, 163
18.	Crispina, 178[4]
19.	?Flavia Titiana,[5] 193
20.	Manlia Scantilla and Didia Clara,[6] 193
21.	Julia Domna, 193
22.	Fulvia Plautilla, 202
23.	Julia Soaemias, 218
24.	Julia Maesa, 218
25.	Cornelia Paula, 219–220[7]
26.	Julia Aquilia Severa, 220
27.	Annia Faustina (or Fundania), 221
28.	Julia Mamaea, post 222
29.	Sallustia Orbiana, 225–227

---

1. *Augusta* in (e.g.) the Acts of the Arval Brethren for September 15, 81 (*CIL* VI 2060 p.509, line 46) and in *CIL* XIV 2795 of 140. See also Kuhoff 1993, 246n.11; Temporini 1978, 32.

2. Kolb 2010a, 25–26 discusses 104/105 as *terminus ante quem* for the grants to Plotina and Marciana (see *CIL* XI 1333 = EDCS-20402783); the t.p.q. of 100 is provided by Plin. *Pan.* 84.

3. Eck 1982, followed by many (e.g. Alföldy 1992, 151 n.12), argues for 119 (after death of Matidia) or 123 (after death of Plotina), but gives too much credence to unofficial titles in provincial contexts (see Chaniotis 2003). Brennan 2018, argues convincingly for 128.

4. Cass. Dio 71.33.1; HA, *Marc.* 27.8; *CIL* X 408 = EDCS-11400492, 180–185 CE.

5. HA, *Pert.* 5.4 and 6.9 indicate the title was voted, but refused by Pertinax.

6. Wife and daughter of Didius Julianus; not discussed in this book.

7. Hdn. 5.6.1.

IMPERIAL WOMEN OF ROME

almost every subsequent emperor.[110] The Latin word *augustus* signified charisma and sacred awe (see Cass. Dio 53.16.4), and its feminine form *augusta* had much the same connotations: when reporting changes attendant on Claudius' adoption of Agrippina's son Nero in 50, for example, Tacitus remarks that "Agrippina was enhanced by the cognomen *Augusta*" (Tac. *Ann.* 12.26.1; see Cass. Dio 61.33.2a).[111] Julia Augusta's new name must also have denoted her identification with her husband. In part it may have been the connection to Augustus himself that inhibited the title's spread in the Julio-Claudian period.

But the title must also have been viewed as a conspicuous distinction, to judge especially from its early history, even though it does not designate any institutional power.[112] Tacitus and others depict Tiberius as resentful of such honors for his mother (*Ann.* 1.14.3; cf. Suet. *Tib.* 50.3; and Ch. 3). After her death in 29 it did not appear again until 37, when it was offered to Antonia the Younger at her grandson Caligula's accession; she refused it, but in 41 her son Claudius, as emperor, proposed she be granted it posthumously (Suet. *Calig.* 15.2; Cass. Dio 59.3.4; Suet. *Claud.* 11.2).[113] On the other hand, that same year Claudius refused for his (third) wife Messalina the title that the senate proposed when she gave birth to Britannicus (Cass. Dio 60.12.5).[114] In 50, however, Claudius' fourth wife, Agrippina the Younger, was granted the title when Claudius adopted her son Nero: she is the first *Augusta* whose husband was ruling.[115] After that title's conferral by the senate,[116] Agrippina and Claudius were assimilated as Augusta and Augustus on coins and in other media (see Ch. 4), and as noted earlier, Tacitus remarks that "Agrippina was enhanced by the cognomen *Augusta*" (Tac. *Ann.* 12.26.1; see Cass. Dio 61.33.2a).[117] The title may also have suggested her direct

---

110. Tiberius made a point of not using Augustus for himself other than when writing to kings (Suet. *Tib.* 26.2), although Millar (1993, 15) notes that Ovid "and everyone else in the Empire" used "Augustus" to refer to Tiberius from the beginning of his reign.

111. For "Augustus," see (in brief) Hurlet 2015, 182; for "Augusta," see Barrett 2002, 322–25 (less plausibly 153–54); Flory 1988 [1997].

112. See, e.g., Kuhoff 1993, 247.

113. Eck 1993, 40; Kienast 2017, 62; Kuhoff 1993, 246 n.7: despite the refusal Suetonius cites, Antonia is called "Augusta" in the Arval *acta* of January 31, 38.

114. Levick 2014, 34 holds that by refusing the title for Messalina, Claudius was maintaining Tiberian precedent of keeping the title for mothers of living emperors (contra Flory 1988, 124).

115. Flory 1988, 113 argues that the date, coinciding with the adoption of Nero, suggests the title was originally for the mother of the emperor or heir; contra Levick 2007, 65.

116. Eck 1993, 40 points out that the sources do not make clear who conferred the title, but Tacitus' context suggests it was the senate.

117. Eck 1993, 40–41. She received "all honors" after Claudius' death in 54 (Tac. *Ann.* 13.2.3).

descendance from Augustus, a significant element of her claims to power (Tac. *Ann.* 12.37.4).[118]

In 63 the senate bestowed the title to Nero's infant daughter Claudia and her mother, Poppaea, in what Tacitus presents as a paroxysm of sycophancy (*Ann.* 15.23), and the title thereafter becomes more frequent. In the civil war following Nero's death Vitellius' mother, Sextilia, was honored with the title briefly before her death (Tac. *Ann.* 2.89). The Flavian Julia Titi gained it at her father's accession in 79, and Domitia Longina at her husband, Domitian's, accession in 81; Domitilla, Vespasian's wife or daughter, was honored as "Augusta" on coins of 79, although both women had been dead over a decade (see Ch. 3). Thereafter others were called "Augusta" in increasing numbers and based on various relationships with the emperor, to the point that some see the term transformed from a name to a title in the Trajanic period.[119]

That the title still seemed presumptuous, however, is suggested by Pliny's report that the modest Plotina and Marciana refused the honorific in 100 because Trajan had refused the title *pater patriae*, or because they considered it greater to be called simply Trajan's wife and sister (*Pan.* 84.6). Epigraphic and numismatic evidence, however, shows that they both accepted it before 105. Marciana is the first sister of an emperor to receive the title. When she died in 112 her daughter Matidia the Elder was entitled "Augusta," probably as another mark of senatorial respect for Trajan but again demonstrating the honor's diffusion.[120] Ambivalence about the title resurfaces in the next generation, however, when indeterminate evidence complicates the date at which Sabina received the title: in 119, 123, or at the ten-year anniversary of Hadrian's rule in 128.[121] Further, Sabina's older sister Matidia the Younger was never so honored.

Thereafter, however, most imperial women received the title, corresponding with the Antonine and Severan emphasis on the imperial house (see Chs. 3 and 7). Faustina the Elder became "Augusta" when her husband, Antoninus Pius, became

---

118. See, e.g., Kuhoff 1993, 247. Ginsburg 2006 explores the literary tradition for this iconic imperial woman. Rose 1997, 73 (cf. *CIL* XVI 4 = EDCS-12300209) includes among her public marks of power Nero's genealogy in official documents with patrilineal and matrilineal descent, i.e., as son of Claudius and grandson of Germanicus. Agrippina is actually not named, however.

119. E.g., Kuhoff 1993, 248. Gualerzi 2005, 219–20 sees the rapid conferral of "Augusta" to Marciana (see following note) as not only recognizing her own merits, but also signifying the restricted agency and obligatory morality of Trajanic women. But by the second century Juvenal scornfully refers to Messalina as *meretrix Augusta* (*Sat.* 6.118; see 115–32).

120. See Roche 2002, 56, referring to *BMCRE* III, Trajan nos. 658–64, 1088–89.

121. Eck 1982, with some supporters argues for 119 (after the death of Matidia) or 123 (after the death of Plotina), but see now Brennan 2018, 67–94.

emperor in 138 (HA, *Ant. Pius* 5.2);[122] her daughter Faustina the Younger, "Augusta" when she bore her first child in 147 to Marcus Aurelius, Pius' adoptive son (HA, *Marc.* 6.6). Their daughter Lucilla gained the title in 163, two years after the young teenager was betrothed to Marcus Aurelius' "brother" and co-emperor Lucius Verus and a year before their imperial wedding in Ephesus.[123] The wives of all the various contenders of the civil war of 193 were called "Augusta,"[124] as were all the Severan women, including Elagabalus' three wives in four years.[125]

The spread of *Augusta* corresponds with increasing titles for elite Roman men and women, and especially for emperors.[126] Inscriptions and other evidence show that by ca. 169 CE *clarissima femina* designated a senatorial wife; by 176 CE an unmarried senatorial daughter would be termed *clarissima puella*;[127] and by 184 a consular wife would formally hold the title of *consularis femina*.[128] On the other hand, the proliferation of *Augusta* corresponds with widening separation of the emperor and imperial family from the rest of Roman society, as we see in the next chapter.[129] By the third century Ulpian apparently uses "Augusta" as shorthand for an imperial woman (Ulp. 13 ad l. Iul. et Pap., Dig. 1.3.31; see further Ch. 2). Yet Matidia the Younger shows that not all imperial women were titled *Augusta*. *Augusta* did not originate to demarcate imperial women from others: for example, some of the women most troubled by allegations of *maiestas*—Augustus' daughter and granddaughter, Julia the Elder and the Younger, respectively (see Ch. 2)—never had the title. *Augusta* was simply a mark of honor, and its halting beginnings suggest that even that was viewed as inappropriate for a woman.

---

122. Levick 2014, 35, 71.

123. HA, *Marc.* 20.6 suggests that the status *Augusta* for mother and daughter made them reluctant to consider Tiberius Claudius Pompeianus, the son of an equestrian, as Lucilla's second husband.

124. Although Pertinax reportedly refused the title for his wife (HA, *Pert.* 5.4 and 6.9).

125. See, e.g., Kosmetatou 2002, esp. 408–12.

126. Alföldy 1991, 319.

127. See Chastagnol 1979, 9; Raepsaet-Charlier 1987, 7–8, citing epigraphic evidence as well as Dig. 1.9.8, 10, 12 (Ulpian); the use of *clarissimus* for senatorial men appears in the first century and expands under Hadrian. Marcus Aurelius seems first to regulate titles for equestrian men.

128. See Chastagnol 1979, 17–19 and Raepsaet-Charlier 1987, 9.

129. Julia Domna, for example, is entitled *Mater Castrorum, Mater Caesaris, Mater Augusti et Caesaris, Mater Augustorum, Mater Augusti* (or *Imperatoris*), and finally *Mater Castrorum et Senatus et Patriae*: Kuhoff 1993, 252–53; Kienast 2017, 152–53 provides a rough chronology.

Some other special honors and privileges for Livia and subsequent imperial women

But Julia Augusta's eminence, including for the fifteen years she lived during her son's reign, prompted other marks of status for her. Most were religious in nature, corresponding to one type of approved visibility for elite women dating back to the Republic (see Ch. 4); this familiar aspect may account for the more frequent adoption of the distinctions for later imperial women.[130] Coins suggest that she is the first imperial woman to ride in the *carpentum*, a special carriage whose use was granted apparently after she recovered from a serious illness in 22 (Tac. *Ann.* 3.64.3; see my Ill. 4.5).[131] Transport in Rome in a *carpentum* was a privilege the Vestal Virgins and a few male priests enjoyed (cf. Plin. *HN* 7.141), as well as singularly honored individuals like the matrons who contributed their gold and jewelry to Rome during the dark days of the struggle against Veii (Livy 5.25.8–9, cf. Isid. *Etym.* 20.12). In 23 Julia Augusta received another privilege shared with the Vestals: the right to sit in the special, lower seats at spectacles. The concession was all the more evident because the recent *lex Iulia theatralis* had strictly regulated where spectators could sit, relegating most women to the highest tiers.[132] Caligula's sisters and Messalina would later receive this right (Cass. Dio 59.3.4; Chs. 4 and 6). Julia Augusta's most signal honor came when Claudius sponsored her deification as *diva* Augusta in 42.[133] Honoring her thirteen years after her death in 29, however, this tribute was meaningless for Livia herself.

In sum, Livia enjoyed few institutional rights after the unique honors granted her and Octavia in the triumviral period. Most subsequent distinctions for her were clearly tied to the men in her family. The death of her son Drusus the Elder occasioned the *ius trium liberorum* in 9 BCE, and Augustus' demise and the accession of her other son Tiberius prompted an outpouring of honors. Although Tiberius resisted many of the proposals, Julia Augusta did become priest of the new *divus* Augustus, unusually gaining the use of a lictor. Distinctions traditionally tied to religious positions intensified for her in the 20s CE. But she herself never held *imperium* or any other power.

---

130. This overlap, related to Augustus' and Tiberius' conservatism, has some think that the imperial women are assimilated to Vestals. See Ch. 4 and Gallia 2015, 95–96.

131. See Ginsburg 2006, 59–60.

132. Gallia 2015, 96; E. Rawson 1987, 85. The law dates after 5 CE. Perhaps indicative of her perceived dominance at this point, Tacitus remarks that the privilege was intended to increase the Vestals' status rather than her own (Tac. *Ann.* 4.16.6): see, e.g., Bauman 1981, 175; Barrett 2002, 144.

133. Kienast 2017, 60: on 17 January 42. See *CFA* 17 = EDCS-18300757.

The influence of imperial women

As we have seen, however, Livia's influence was immense, helping to create the impression that subsequent imperial women would have the same sway. Imperial women's influence is due to their inclusion in the imperial court. Rather than repeat the excellent and recent analyses of that court,[134] Here I broaden our understanding of this key of the principate by starting with where imperial women lived, so as to understand their interactions with imperial men.

Only a few discrete houses for imperial women are mentioned by the literary sources, mostly incidentally perhaps because of the traditional association of elite houses with the conduct of quasi-public business (Vitr. *De arch.* 6.5.2).[135] Julia the Younger had a "lavish" domicile that Augustus destroyed after her disgrace (Suet. *Aug.* 72.3). With no such notoriety Livia may have maintained her own home on the Palatine in Rome, in which Cassius Dio portrays as extraordinary her reception of whomever she wanted (57.12.2, noted earlier).[136] Her house accommodated Antonia the Younger (Val. Max. 4.3.3), the widow of Livia's son Drusus the Elder (d. 9 BCE), as well as their children Germanicus, Livilla, and Claudius. Much later Antonia housed there the fatherless, teenage Caligula and probably also his sisters after their mother, Agrippina the Elder, was banished in 29 CE (Suet. *Calig.* 10.1, 24.1).[137] Agrippina the Younger also had distinct properties, although she apparently relished living in the imperial domicile first with Claudius and then with Nero. As her relationship with her son Nero deteriorated after 54, she was moved from the palace into Antonia's house (Suet. *Nero* 34.1; Tac. *Ann.* 13.18). In 59 she was invited by Nero to visit him at a villa in Campania, but her own villa near the Lucrine lake was the setting of her murder

---

134. E.g., Winterling 1999, 9–10, 195–210; Wallace-Hadrill 1996, 299, remarking that the institution of the court and changes in wealth and influence were resented "precisely because the exercise of patronage was how the elite traditionally defined its own standing."

135. I do not treat here the domiciles of imperial women not immediately related to the ruling emperor, such as that of Domitia Lepida in which she housed her young nephew Nero when his mother was exiled in 39 (Suet. *Nero* 6.3).

136. Foubert 2010, 66–67 rightly notes that no archaeological or literary evidence definitely attests a separate residence. See *LTUR* 2.130–32, s.v. "Domus: Livia" (I. Iacopi), citing Suet. *Tib.* 5 and a lead pipe with *Liviae Aug(ustae)* (*CIL* XV 7264 = EDCS-37801412). Claudius was raised in her household and imbued with her *disciplina*: *SCPP* lines 148–51; Barrett 2002, 127–29.

137. Caligula moved to Tiberius' villa in Capri in 31, when he was 19. Foubert 2010, 69–70 notes the use of Augustus' and Livia's residence as the living space of Julio-Claudian imperial *matresfamilias*. Under like circumstances Nero was raised in the home of his paternal aunt Domitia Lepida after his widowed mother was relegated in 39 (Suet. *Nero* 6.3).

Rome's Imperial Women and Rome's Imperial Power

(Suet. *Nero* 34.2; Tac. *Ann.* 14.4–5).[138] As we saw earlier, after divorcing Octavia in 62 Nero gave her separate domiciles (Tac. *Ann.* 14.60).

It may be, of course, that imperial women regularly maintained independent homes, as inferred from lead pipes found near the modern Piazza Vittorio Emanuele on Rome's Esquiline attesting property there of Matidia the Elder, Matidia the Younger, and Sabina (*AE* 1954, 62 = EDCS-13800082; *CIL* XV 7306 = EDCS-37801464; *CIL* XV 7313 = EDCS-37801377–79). The fate of Julia the Younger's house, however, suggests that an imperial woman should not appear too independent. A better image was conveyed when the imperial family lived together, under the direct influence of the emperor.

Once the imperial residences were built up and the court gained strength, the emperor's domicile apparently exerted a magnetic pull in Rome.[139] Imperial women frequently are noted as in or disappearing into the emperor's house or palace: the emperor was the obvious paterfamilias (see Ch. 3).[140] Octavia lived with her brother Octavian after her divorce from Mark Antony in 32 BCE (see Plut. *Ant.* 87, and 54.2,57.3, 35.5).[141] Claudia Livia Julia (Livilla), the sister of Germanicus and widow of Drusus the Younger, vanished into her father-in-law Tiberius' palace after her purported lover Sejanus was disgraced and executed for treason in 31 CE. There she was executed, a throwback to the earlier custom of punishing women domestically (Cass. Dio 58.11.7; see Ch. 2).[142] In 54 Claudius had all his unmarried children in his palace (Tac. *Ann.* 12. 68.2–3). Julia Titi lived in the palace of her uncle Domitian,[143] and Pliny stresses the move to Trajan's palace in 98 by his sister Marciana as well his wife Plotina (perhaps together with Marciana's daughter Matidia the Elder, and Matidia's children Matidia the

---

138. She also had *horti* in Rome, and estates in Tusculum and Antium: Tac. *Ann.* 14.3.

139. Joseph. *AJ* 19.1.15 remarks on the accretive nature of the imperial residence that grew by attaching others' houses to itself. Larger residences, like the Villa Adriana, could accommodate separate quarters for the empress, as often presumed for Sabina. The Historia Augusta frequently reports that after adoption by an emperor a young man had to move into an imperial residence (e.g., Marcus Aurelius into Hadrian's private house, *Marc.* 5.3; Lucius Verus into the *domus Tiberiana* or Tiberian palace, *Verus* 2.4).

140. Causing particular problems for Julia the Elder: Linderski 1988. Herodian (1.13.1) remarks that as the emperor's sister Fadilla had free and easy access to Commodus. Tiberius chose the husbands of Drusilla and Julia Livilla in 33: Tac. *Ann.* 6.15.1, with Syme 1986, 171–73.

141. When in 36 BCE Octavian was insisting that Octavia leave Antony, he supposedly urged her to return to Rome and go to "her own home" (Plut. *Ant.* 54.1).

142. See Lott 2012, 303. The rumor that Antonia starved her daughter Livilla to death suggests that Antonia moved to the palace after the death of Julia Augusta.

143. Cass. Dio 67.3.2; see Jones 1992, 35.

Younger and Sabina; see Plin. *Pan.* 84).[144] Julia Maesa, the sister of Julia Domna, lived in the palace while Septimius Severus and Caracalla were emperors. Only after Caracalla's assassination and Domna's death in 217 did Maesa return to her own property in Syria (Hdn. 5.3.2; Cass. Dio 79.30.3).

Growing up in the palace prepared children for politics and powerful individuals, and proximity to the emperor and his advisors facilitated imperial women's presence at decision-making events. Various scholars have compiled the evidence for Livia's patronage and political negotiations,[145] such as her swaying Augustus' favor toward foreign cities at the beginning of his rule (unsuccessfully for Samos, at first; successfully for Sparta),[146] her defense of Cornelius Cinna Magnus and others from a charge of conspiracy, and her persuasion of Augustus to a policy of leniency in the middle of his reign (Sen. *Clem.* 1.9; Cass. Dio 55.14–22),[147] and her aid to Marcus Salvius Otho in gaining senatorial status (Suet. *Otho* 1.1).[148] But the evidence for such political influence is scattered and downplayed: Livia was not to be seen as a major power broker.[149]

Just as Augustus himself became the exemplar for all subsequent emperors, Livia, the *princeps femina* (Ov. *Pont.* 3.1.125),[150] was the explicit or implicit touchstone for later imperial women. At Caligula's accession in 37 CE he at once conferred "all of Livia's rights" on Antonia the Younger, working through a single senatorial decree (Suet. *Calig.* 15.2), but she refused the title of *Augusta*. Antonia thus acted modestly, as Livia was seen to do throughout Augustus' reign.[151] In the

---

144. See Temporini 1978, 187–88. Sabina would have moved to Hadrian's house after marriage around 100.

145. Purcell 1986 remains fundamental; see also Barrett 2002.

146. See Barrett 2002, 331–32; Badian 1984, 165–70, who notes (p. 168) her hereditary Claudian ties to Samos. Intercession for Sparta came during the tour of 22–21 BCE (Cass. Dio 54.7.2).

147. For this incident, and Cassius Dio's depiction of Livia in the speech, see Adler 2011a. In Chs. 2 and 5 we return to this incident for its legal aspects and its setting.

148. For assessments of Livia at her death, see Cass. Dio (eulogy of Livia) 58.2.1–6; cf. Vell. Pat. 2.75.2–3, 2.130.5; Eck et al. 1996, 46–47, 222–28 on *SCPP.* She was eight-seven when she died.

149. Only Josephus notes Antonia's vital role in denouncing Sejanus to Tiberius (*AJ* 18.6.6). In contrast the imperial concubines Caenis and Lysistrate are pointedly reported as "selling" access to the emperor (Ch. 3).

150. This oxymoronic title must have been startling when Ovid first used it at the end of Augustus' rule (Jenkins 2009; Thakur 2014): Augustus' own title *princeps* derived from that of the *princeps senatus*, who had the right of speaking first in the senate. Within a century, however, Pliny used *princeps femina* for Ummidia Quadratilla (*Ep.* 7.24.4), further suggesting the fusion of imperial and other elite women.

151. See Bauman 1981, 177–78, likening the grants of all Livia's rights to Antonia (presumably with *uti licuit Liviae Augustae*) to what we see in the *lex de imperio Vespasiani*, where each

Rome's Imperial Women and Rome's Imperial Power

heady days after Claudius' British victory in 43, Cassius Dio reports, "Messalina was granted the same privilege of occupying front seats in the theater that Livia had enjoyed, and also that of using the *carpentum*" (60.22.1–2; see Chs. 3 and 6). By the time of Messalina, however, Livia's celebrated restraint was long in the past.

Indeed, ancient authors mark Messalina, Agrippina the Younger, and other imperial women of the mid-first century as outrageously bold and arrogant, violating traditional boundaries and interfering in men's affairs. Messalina supposedly involved herself in trials *intra cubiculum principis* (e.g., Tac. *Ann.* 11.2.1, 13.4.2) and is also said to have designated Gaius Silius as consul (Cass. Dio 60.31.3).[152] She allegedly was behind the exiles of Seneca and of Caligula's sister Julia Livilla in 41 (Suet. *Claud.* 29.1; Cass. Dio 60.8.4–5) and the deaths of Statilius Taurus and Julia, the daughter of Drusus (Tac. *Ann.* 12.59; Cass. Dio 60.18.4, cf. Tac. *Ann.* 13.32.3 and 43.2). Similarly, Agrippina was notorious for her greed, jealousy, and spitefulness that doomed many, including Lollia Paulina in 49 and her former sister-in-law Domitia Lepida in 54 (Tac. *Ann.* 12.22–23, 14.12.4; Cass. Dio 61.32.4, cf. 61.10.1; Tac. *Ann.* 12.64–65; Suet. *Nero* 7.1).[153] Agrippina reportedly also interfered in various ways with Seneca the Younger and the praetorian prefects, weighed in on senatorial decisions, and attempted to sit in the senate and take on other prominent positions (Tac. *Ann.* 12.8, 13.5.1–2, cf. 12.42).[154] Poppaea is painted by Tacitus as instrumental in the deaths of Agrippina and of Octavia (Tac. *Ann.* 14.1, 60–61).

The sources' lurid picture is not matched until stories about Julia Mamaea, the allegedly overbearing mother of Severus Alexander. One confused tradition holds that Mamaea first engineered Ulpian's promotion to praetorian prefect, then helped antagonize two other prefects to plot against him—and then suppressed the plot (Zos. 1.11.2–3). Another story holds that Mamaea, in a jealous rage, exiled her daughter-in-law Sallustia Orbiana to "Libya" (Africa; Hdn. 6.1.9–10). The tales are adduced at least in part to emphasize Severus Alexander's

---

individual power is itemized separately but then generalized by adding *uti licuit divo Augusto* to each. In Cassius Dio's presentation (59.3.4) the privileges for Antonia and for Caligula's sisters are said to be those of the Vestal Virgins.

152. Osgood 2011, 147–50, 191–205; see, e.g., the death of Julia (the daughter of Livilla and Drusus) around 43, attributed to a "trick" of Messalina's (*dolus*; Tac. *Ann.* 13.32.3). Women's interference in trials was not a new kind of charge, to judge from the rumor that Cicero, while consul in 63 BCE but with his wife in attendance, privately held trials of revolutionary followers of Catiline (Pseudo-Sallust, *Invective against Cicero* 3).

153. While vilifying Messalina in 48, Tacitus adds the note (incongruous in his general treatment of Agrippina) that her vehemence stirred pity for Agrippina (Tac. *Ann.* 11.12.1).

154. See Ginsburg 2006, esp. 62 on Agrippina the Younger and Livia.

domination by his mother,[155] but they also fit the unbounded arrogance of the later Julio-Claudian women.

Although political presumptions are foremost in Nero's accusations of his mother after her death (Tac. *Ann.* 14.11.1–2) and Agrippina certainly tried to wield power and influence more obviously than had Livia,[156] she had no more institutionalized power than her great-grandmother had enjoyed. As we see in Ch. 2 and from other instances—such as the appointment of the incompetent Gessius Florus as procurator of Judaea in 64–66 because of the friendship of Nero's Poppaea with Florus' wife Cleopatra (Joseph. *AJ* 20.252–53) and Julia Titi's supposed nomination of Lucius Julius Ursus as consul for 84 (Cass. Dio 67.4.2 and 67.3.1)[157]—imperial women's political influence was a recurrent charge. Even Plotina, usually lauded for self-effacement (e.g., Plin. *Pan.* 83.6; Cass. Dio 68.5.5), is alleged to have orchestrated the accession of Hadrian by means of influence often derided as *favor Plotinae* (HA, *Hadr.* 2.10, 4; Cass. Dio 69.1.2, 4, 69.10.3[1]).[158] The velvet-gloved discretion with which women should exert any political pressure is strikingly clear in the *Senatus Consultum de Cn. Pisone patre* (*SCPP*), the senatorial decree passed in Rome on 10 December 20 CE that has been found in multiple copies in modern Spain.[159]

Julia Augusta in the Senatus Consultum de Pisone patre

The *SCPP*, a modern designation for the senatorial proceedings following the suicide of Gnaeus Calpurnius Piso after Germanicus' mysterious death in 19 CE, refers to Livia individually three times as Julia Augusta and as Tiberius' mother.

---

155. Julia Mamaea had no power to exile anyone. J. McHugh 2017 provides a recent assessment of Severus Alexander and his reign.

156. An inscription from Corinth (*AE* 1927, 2 = EDCS-08200293) records a Gaius Julius Spartiaticus who was *procurator Caesaris et Augustae Agrippinae*, presumably jointly appointed by Nero and Agrippina, as if she were indeed openly recognized as the co-ruler of the empire. See Flower 2011, 190; Eck 1993, 42.

157. See Vinson 1989; B. Jones 1992, 40–42. The Florus appointment obviously discredits Nero's administration, although Josephus admired Poppaea for her interest in Jewish affairs (see Ch. 4).

158. See also Aur. Vict. *Caes.* 13.13; Eutrop. 8.6. Although some accept Plotina's influence in Hadrian's accession (Birley 1997, 77), Temporini 1978, 78–86, 120–59, 179 discredits with detailed arguments the idea that Plotina was working against Trajan's wishes; cf. Boatwright 1991, 530–31. See Ch. 7.

159. See Eck et al. 1996; Potter and Damon 1999; and Lott 2012: the fragments were found in the late 1980s and 1990s.

Rome's Imperial Women and Rome's Imperial Power 43

She always appears in a family context (see Ch. 3). In lines 132–33 the senate earnestly praises Julia Augusta's self-control and that of Drusus Caesar (Drusus the Younger, Tiberius' son), holding that with that virtue they imitated the justice of Tiberius.[160] Lines 148–50 comment on the laudable restraint of Germanicus' grieving children, ascribing it to the self-command of their grandfather and paternal uncle (Tiberius) and of Julia Augusta.[161] Julia Augusta shares her restraint, a virtue we earlier noted of some imperial women, with others in the imperial family.

Lines 109–20 turn to Julia Augusta and the pardon of Piso's wife Plancina, implicated in her husband's lobbying of Roman troops, insubordination toward Germanicus and Tiberius, and other un-Roman activities. We read that the senate remitted Plancina's punishment after Tiberius interceded at the request of his mother:[162]

> (109): as for what might pertain to the case of Plancina, against whom a great many and most serious charges had been laid, since [Plancina] confessed that she had her entire hope in the pity of our *Princeps* and senate, and that our *Princeps* often and thoroughly has requested from this *ordo* that the senate, content with the punishment of Gnaeus Piso *pater*, might spare [Piso's] wife just as [that of Piso's] son Marcus, and since he has interceded for Plancina at the request of his mother and that, for the matter for which his mother wished to obtain these concessions, he has heard the most just reasons laid out for him by her, the senate thought that accommodation and indulgence should be made both for Julia Augusta, who deserved the most from the republic not only for her birth of our *Princeps* but also for her many outstanding benefits towards men of every order (a woman who, although she ought justly and deservedly to have the most influence in any matter which she might request from the senate, nevertheless used that power most sparingly), and for the greatest piety of our *Princeps* towards his mother, and it decided that the punishment of Plancina be exonerated.[163]

---

160. *item senatum laudare magnopere Iuliae Aug(ustae) / Drusiq(ue) Caesaris moderationem imitantium principis nostri iustitiam.*

161. *modum probabilem, iudicare senatum referendum quidem esse acceptum maxume discipulinae avi eorum et patrui et Iuliae Aug(ustae).*

162. See Seager 2012, 51 on Livia's praise here.

163. *Quod ad Plancinae causam pertineret, qu<o>i pluruma et grauissuma crimina /* [110] *obiecta essent, quoniam confiteretur se omnem spem in misericordia{m} / principis nostri et*

44 IMPERIAL WOMEN OF ROME

Ambiguous phrasing and ponderous, indirect grammatical structure are characteristic of this document as the senate struggles both to evoke its traditional autonomy while conveying suitable deference, and to express appropriate outrage at the alleged insults against Tiberius and the imperial house (see Ch. 3). Reading between the lines, however, we can pick up that Livia repeatedly spoke to Tiberius about Plancina, bringing up numerous points to exculpate her friend (*pro Plancina rogatu matris suae . . . iustissumas ab ea causas sibi expositas*, line 113). Further, she apparently canvassed individual senators, reminding them not only of her maternal relationship to the ruling princeps but also of numerous ways in which she had helped them and others (*optume de r(e) p(ublica) meritae non partu tantum modo principis nostri, sed etiam multis magnisq(ue) erga cuiusq(ue) ordinis homines beneficis*, lines 115–17).[164] Another strength of Livia's petition for Plancina may have been its exceptionality, or so the senate implies when it explicitly acknowledges both her vast influence in the senate and her restraint in using it (*quae, cum iure meritoq(ue) plurumum posse in eo, quod a senatu petere<t>, deberet, parcissume uteretur eo*, lines 117–18).

In this official senatorial decree the senate openly albeit deferentially admits Livia's influence with Tiberius and its own rank or *ordo*, a great contrast to Tacitus' depiction of Julia Augusta with which this chapter opened.[165] Political relations between senate and the imperial house were particularly hesitant during Tiberius' reign, and a leitmotif of the *SCPP* is moderation and self-restraint on the part of the imperial house. As we saw at the opening of this chapter, reticence and self-restraint become dominant praise for imperial women.

---

senatus habere, et saepe princeps noster accurateq(ue)˙ ab / eo ordine petierit, ut contentus senatus Cn. Pisonis patris poena uxori ⌈e⌉ius / sic uti M. filio parceret, et pro Plancina rogatu matris suae depreca⌈tus⌉ s⌈it⌉ et, / quam ob rem e⌈a⌉ mater sua inpetrari uellet, iustissumas ab ea causas sibi ex- /[115] positas acceperit, senatum arbitrari et Iuliae Aug(ustae), optume de r(e) p(ublica) meritae non / partu tantum modo principis nostri, sed etiam multis magnisq(ue) erga cui- / usq(ue) ordinis homines beneficis, quae, cum iure meritoq(ue) plurumum posse in eo, quod / a senatu petere<t>, deberet, parcissume uteretur eo, et principis nostri summa<e> / erga matrem suam pietati suffragandum indulgendumq(ue) esse remittiq(ue) /[120] poenam Plancinae placere. Text from Potter and Damon 1999, 30, based on the 1996 edition of Eck et al.

164. With Eck et al. 1996, 226, we translate *cuiusq(ue) ordinis homines* as "men of every rank" rather than as "men of each rank," which would restrict her benefactions to senators and equestrians.

165. Eck et al. 1996, 88, 109–20 note the general agreement of the *SCPP*'s depiction of Livia's influence during the trial with Tacitus' rendition of it (e.g., *Ann.* 3.15.1, 17).

Imperial women's influence and the imperial court

Imperial women did not have any "constitutional" powers or rights granted them after the short-lived experiment of protection from verbal assault similar to what tribunes enjoyed. Even though their various honors expanded over time, they lacked emperors' capacities to command militarily, to enforce corporal punishments and civil penalties legally, and to make law and adjudicate disputes compellingly.[166] Such institutional powers for men, ratified for the princeps by the Senate and the People of Rome and based on Republican precedents of great esteem, had been re-forged for the imperial system. *Imperium maius* and *tribunicia potestas* were two mainstays of the military, political, and civil pre-eminence of Augustus and subsequent emperors, and during the period I discuss they were conferred by the senate and sanctioned by the people. They contributed to the princeps' religious distinction and overall authority.[167] They could be granted to other men, especially those related to the imperial family by blood or marriage.[168] They enabled political benefits (*beneficia*), such as citizenship and the *ius trium liberorum*, and accelerated advancement in the *cursus honorum*.[169]

No woman, however, could wield either tribunician power or *maius imperium*, and imperial women never had any power institutionalized in traditional military and political commands.[170] Suetonius' Tiberius repeatedly reminded his mother to keep far away from important matters that were unsuitable for women (*maioribus nec feminae convenientibus negotiis*: Suet. *Tib.* 50.3). Pliny notes that

---

166. A final "power" of Augustus and his successors, impunity, was superfluous for imperial women. Once an emperor was ratified by the senate there was no legal way to remove him without violence, which often spilled over to imperial women (Ch. 2).

167. The literature is enormous here; see, e.g., Hurlet and Mineo 2009; Levick 2010; Griffin 1997 for *imperium maius*; Bauman 1981, 182 for tribunician power. I use "authority" somewhat neutrally, as Rowe 2013.

168. And even select others like Sejanus: see esp. Tac. *Ann.* 6.8, with Hurlet 1997.

169. For such *beneficia*, see, e.g., Millar 1977, 420–34. The alleged sale of citizenship rights, military commands, procuratorships, and governorships by Messalina and Claudius' freedmen (Cass. Dio 60.17.5, 8; see Tac. *Ann.* 12.3) is a hyperbolic criticism of Claudius' "subservience" to his women and freedmen: see, e.g., Osgood 2011, 191–93, 208–9. Tacitus astutely remarks about the early Claudian principate that the emperor's growing involvement in the laws and magistracies opened the way for others to make money: *nam cuncta legum et magistratuum munia in se trahens princeps materiam praedandi patefecerat, Ann.* 11.5.1.

170. Dixon 1984. Wood 1999, 9–10 adds that Rome's essential patriarchy was never seriously challenged either by imperial women or by anyone else. Suetonius' statement that Caligula, when sick (in 37), had decided to make Drusilla the heir of his goods and the empire (or *imperium*: [*Drusillam*] *heredem quoque bonorum atque imperii aeger instituit, Calig.* 24.1) emphasizes nonsensically Caligula's mad infatuation for his sister (contra Wood 1995, 458–59).

Trajan's women would not be in any harm should they become private individuals again, since they had never presumed to power (*Pan.* 84.6). The *SCPP*, Tacitus' Urgulania incident, and other evidence, however, show that at times Livia did engage in "male" business—the *SCPP* uses *beneficia* to describe her benefits to others—but that such behavior was acceptable when connected to her family.

Conclusion

After a few extraordinary rights granted Octavia and Livia in 35 BCE that apparently became obsolete at their deaths if not before, no powers or privileges fundamentally distinct from those of other elite women in Rome were voted or approved for Rome's imperial women from the time of Augustus through the death in 235 CE of Julia Mamaea, the mother of Severus Alexander.[171] Imperial women thus demonstrated continuity with the Republic: despite *imperium maius* and other exceptional powers granted the princeps, the women of his family expressed traditional virtues, and at least during Augustus' rule they kept in the background. We see in Ch. 2 the numerous legal difficulties of some imperial women, Julio-Claudians in particular, that resulted in their disappearance even from the shadowy corridors of imperial power in Rome. In some cases, such as that of Agrippina the Younger, untraditional behavior combined with endurance to leave an indelible impression of ambition and power (see esp. Ch. 5). Nonetheless, even Agrippina had no institutional privileges. Only with the Severan women, as we see in Ch. 7, do imperial women dominate the historical narrative. Not coincidentally, the only imperial woman with a reported administrative post, Julia Domna and her supervision of imperial letters, dates from this time. Yet the evidence even for this anomalous position indicates that Domna is not the one who makes binding decisions. Although associated with imperial power by virtue of their relationships with the emperor, imperial women were always kept apart from it.

---

171. Gallia 2015 argues convincingly that the Vestal Virgins were not as cut off from their families and the norms of Roman society as often portrayed.

2

Crimes and Punishments
of Imperial Women

Introduction: The criminality of Domitia Longina

Domitia Longina's twenty-six-year marriage to Domitian, emperor from 81 until assassinated in 96, is the second-longest imperial marriage covered in this book.[1] Its endurance contrasts the turbulent, even criminal behavior ancient authors report for both consorts. Domitia is named as one of "many wives" Domitian debauched as soon as his father, Vespasian, secured imperial power in 70 (Suet. *Dom.* 1.3; Cass. Dio 65.3.4): some eighteen years old, she was already married to the well-placed Lucius Aelius Lamia Plautius Aelianus.[2] After a quick divorce from Aelius Lamia, Domitia wed Domitian probably that same year. The wedding met no obstacles despite the penalties against adultery stipulated by the *lex Iulia de adulteriis* (see later) and the notoriety of the sexual intrigue: the latter was reportedly a sore spot for Domitian, causing the death of the cuckolded Aelius Lamia when he later joked openly about it (Suet. *Dom.* 1.3 and 10.2).

For the next decade or so we know little, other than that around 73 Domitia bore a son who died before Domitian became emperor in 81 after his brother Titus. The year 81 saw remarkable honors for Domitia as well: she received both the title *Augusta* (Suet. *Dom.* 3.1) and the novel epithet *divi Caesaris Mater* (mother of *divus* Caesar) upon the divinization of their deceased son.[3] (See Ill. 3.7.) But perhaps in 83 or 84 the imperial couple separated and may even have divorced

---

1. That of Livia and Augustus lasted fifty-two years, from 38 BCE to 14 CE.

2. For Domitia, see Chausson 2003; for Aelius Lamia, *PIR*[2] A 205 and Levick 2002, 201. Other bibliography is cited later.

3. Kuhoff 1993, 246 n.11; Temporini 1978, 32; for the child, whose name is assumed as Titus Flavius Caesar, see Ch. 3, n.105, and Ch. 4.

Imperial Women of Rome. Mary T. Boatwright, Oxford University Press. © Oxford University Press 2021.
DOI: 10.1093/oso/9780190455897.003.0003

(Suet. *Dom.* 3.1, 13.1).[4] More illegal activity is reported. Domitia allegedly engaged in adultery with the famous pantomime Paris (Suet. *Dom.* 3.1; Mart. 11.13.3), and Domitian reportedly murdered Paris in a street brawl as well as engaged in an incestuous relationship with his niece Julia Titi (Cass. Dio 67.3.1–2; cf. Philostr. *Vita Apoll.* 7.7).[5] Nonetheless, Domitia returned to Domitian's palace, or rather to what her husband and emperor called his "divine couch" (*pulvinar*: Suet. *Dom.* 13.1),[6] even as Julia Titi was rumored to have continued living in the palace in a sexual relationship with her uncle (Cass. Dio 67.3.1).[7]

Some years later Domitia was implicated in Domitian's assassination. Suetonius, the closest to the event of 96,[8] states that Domitian's wife was part of the conspiracy (*Dom.* 14). Cassius Dio holds she was motivated by terror for her life, knowing that Domitian hated her (67.15.2).[9] Fourth-century epitomes suggest she was moved by love for Paris (Aur. Vict. *Caes.* 11.7; *Epit. de Caes.* 11.11). Whatever the rumors, Domitia survived until at least 127 in conspicuous wealth and respect in Rome and Italy. She owned property, including brickyards, in Rome,[10] Puteoli (Pozzuoli, Italy),[11] Peltuinum (in Italy's Abruzzi), and perhaps Gabii, east of the capital city.[12] Despite the official *damnatio memoriae* of her

---

4. Castritius 1969, 497; Jones 1992, 35–37; Chausson 2003, 122; and Roche 2002, 42 argue for the repudiation in 83; FOS #327 p.287 dates the separation "around 82."

5. Suet. *Dom.* 22 reports that Titus had offered her to Domitian in marriage (Jones 1992, 35). Bauman 1996, 94–95 considers the death of Paris (who as an actor was *infamis*: PIR 1st ed., P95 for Paris), and the divorce of Domitia, as Domitian's attempt to exemplify restored morals (Suet. *Dom.* 8.3). See also Chausson 2003, 122–23. Someone *infamis* had lost or never possessed civil rights and an honorable reputation because of status (e.g., slavery, dishonest military discharge), dishonorable profession (e.g., mime actor, tavern worker, prostitution), or condemnation (e.g., violating a partnership, bankruptcy).

6. Vinson 1989, 448, with Castritius 1969, 501–2, credits the reconciliation to Domitia's political supporters.

7. Castritius 1969, 498; Jones 1992, 35; and Roche 2002, 42 reject the allegations of incest but note Julia in the palace until her death in 87–90. On the vague words of Martial 4.3.8, cf. 6.3, some posit a second pregnancy for Domitia in 90 (see, e.g., FOS #327 p.287).

8. Suetonius' *Caesares* may have appeared in their entirety by 122 (Power 2010).

9. Collins 2009, 83–84 rejects Cassius Dio's story that Domitia found Domitian's incriminating list of future victims (67.15.3–4) as a late interpolation derived from the similar story concerning Commodus' concubine Marcia and his death (Hdn. 1.17.1–2, 7–8).

10. See, e.g., *CIL* XV 548–58.

11. *CIL* XV 555.4 = IG XIV 2404 = ICR I 517; *CIL* XV 7293.

12. *CIL* IX 3418, 3419, 3438, 3469 (15). Burns 2007, 99 has her live in Gabii. Josephus' reference to her patronage at the end of his autobiography (*Vit.* 76.429) may indicate that it came late: Den Hollander 2014, 220–21.

husband Domitian in 96, she is later attested variously as Domitia Domitiani ("Domitia, wife of Domitian") or as Domitia Augusta. For example, the shrine raised to her memory in Gabii in 140 and discussed later identifies her as Domitia Augusta and daughter of Gnaeus Domitius Corbulo.[13]

Long after Domitia's death, presumed from brick stamps not to have occurred before 127,[14] two dependents Gnaeus Domitius Polycarp and his wife Domitia Europe dedicated a shrine in Gabii "in honor of the memory of the house of Domitia Augusta, the daughter of Gnaeus Domitius Corbulo," ornamenting it with statues and "other things." The shrine is dated to April 22, 140 and called both *aedes* and *templum* on its large white marble inscribed lintel (*CIL* XIV 2795 = EDCS-05800775).[15] The fine bust of an *ignotus* found at the site has been tentatively identified as that of Domitia's father Corbulo; more unusual for a private shrine would be the imperial busts found nearby that included Tiberius, if they in fact were part of Domitia's memorial.[16] The freed husband and wife also provided for annual feasts in the honor and memory of their patron Domitia on her birthday, and their entire donation was approved by the local municipal council (lines 6–10, 15). The enduring public reverence for Domitia, and her sustained close association with the imperial house suggested by her title Domitia Augusta and the possible display of imperial busts at the shrine raised in her honor, are extraordinary in light of the alleged lawlessness and scandal of her marriage to Domitian.

Domitia's remarkable story has caught the attention of scholars, most of whom explicitly or implicitly discount the reports cited earlier.[17] Some note that her ancestors—eminent in the Julio-Claudian period and including "martyrs" like her father Corbulo, forced by Nero in 66 to commit suicide—made a Flavian

---

13. Domitia Domitiani, e.g., *CIL* IX 3469 = EDCS-14804493; *CIL* XV 548, 553, 556, see EDCS-32800185, 32800186, 32800238, and some forty similar brickstamps from 123 or undated; Domitia Augusta, e.g., *CIL* IX 3432; for the shrine, see later. Jones (1992, 37) holds that Domitia deliberately chose to be named as *Domitia Domitiani*, but Treggiari 1991b, 498 notes this as the common way to name widows; see Collins 2009, 85. Varner 1995, 202–206 dates some portraits of Domitia after 96.

14. Brickstamps suggest she lived until ca. 127 (e.g., Fraser 2015, 254).

15. 78 cm H, 355 cm W, 2–6 cm LH; MA 596, Louvre: Giroire and Roger 2007, #37.

16. Now in the Louvre: Giroire and Roger 2007, ##9, 19 (e.g., MA 1329, Tiberius); *ignotus* is Louvre MA 925. See Varner 1995.

17. Mostly in the aim of a political reading of the events. For example, Levick 2002, 203, 206, with references, accepts the adultery in 70 but discounts alleged improprieties of the separation in the 80s. See also, e.g., Castritius 1969, 2002; Fraser 2015. Alexandridis 2010; Varner 1995; Varner 2001; and D'Ambra 2013 explore Domitia's image; D'Ambra notes art historians' dependence on ancient historians' remarks to differentiate her portraits from those of Julia Titi.

marriage with Domitia opportune. Vespasian was building power after the demise of the Julio-Claudians and Titus lacked a son.[18] The apparent incongruity of the scandalous tales with her long life and posthumous veneration has drawn notice: M. Vinson, for example, holds that the stories circulated to discredit Domitian himself and were the more plausible in Rome's tradition of denigrating women, especially imperial ones.[19] On various grounds, many now discount or minimize Domitia's possible participation in her husband's assassination.[20]

My goal is not to re-sift the scattered evidence to discover the "truth" about Domitia. Rather, I move from this fascinating individual to discuss the rights, constraints, and privileges of imperial women in Roman law. Whether Domitia actually committed adultery with Domitian in 70 while married to Aelius Lamia, was unfaithful to her second husband Domitian with the pantomime Paris in the 80s, or even participated in Domitian's assassination in 96 is less important for my aims than that such stories circulated. The anecdotes, combined with her sustained resources and esteem, imply that imperial women had special legal status. We saw in Ch. 1 that Tacitus, writing the *Annals* more than a decade after the widowed Domitia Augusta left the palace, alleged that close association with Julia Augusta (Livia) placed Urgulania "above the laws" (*Ann.* 2.34.2). Urgulania was merely a friend of Livia, not herself an imperial woman. Did the principate bring impunity or other legal privileges for the emperor's wife, mother, or other female relative?

That imperial women might have special legal standing fits a more widespread notion, that emperors themselves were above the law. In an excerpt from Ulpian's writings of the early third century, the Digest notes, "an emperor is free from the laws; although an empress (*Augusta*) is not, emperors nonetheless give her the same privileges that they enjoy" (Ulp. 13, ad l. iul. et pap., Dig. 1.3.31).[21] In the following section we discuss this controversial maxim; for now, I note only D. Daube's view that although the princeps theoretically was never above the law,

---

18. Chausson 2003, 109–110 suggests that Domitia herself initiated the liaison. Domitia's father Corbulo was maternal brother to Milonia Caesonia, Caligula's last wife; Domitia's mother may have been (Cassia) Longina, daughter of Caligula's sister Drusilla or of Aemilia Lepida, great-granddaughter of Augustus. See Varner 1995, 188 n.11; cf. Vinson 1989, 439; and Fraser 2015, esp. the genealogical table on p. 216.

19. Vinson 1989 (e.g., 440–48); Jones 1992, 33–38; see also Dixon 2001, 140–53.

20. Jones 1992, 33–38; Levick 2002, 210–11; Collins 2009, 83–85, e.g., suggests "passive complicity on her part" (85). Contra Burns 2007.

21. *princeps legibus solutus est: Augusta autem licet legibus soluta non est, principes tamen eadem illi privilegia tribuunt, quae ipsi habent.* Levick 2007, 59 paraphrases the end of this: "The empress is not exempt from the law, but the emperor allows her the same privileges as he enjoys." For *Augusta*, see Ch. 1.

Domitian's reign marked the start of emperors' ever diminishing respect for legal restraints.[22] The legal standing, including impunity, of imperial women is even more difficult to assess, not least because most of the "wrong-doing" attributed to Domitia and others is sensationalist and clichéd. On the other hand, Ulpian asserts that an imperial woman *did* have some privileges, even if subject to an emperor's whim and not due to their own position.

The following section briefly surveys the use of legal sources for Roman women's history and Ulpian's statement, focusing as it does on the rights and privileges of emperors and the *Augusta*. We then turn to norms and regulations for imperial women's sexuality, particularly marriage and divorce.[23] This introduces the larger subject of crimes and punishments of imperial women, accompanied by the summary of evidence and circumstances in Table 2.1. The spectacular adultery cases and punishments of Augustus' own daughter Julia the Elder in 2 BCE and granddaughter Julia the Younger in 8 CE, both linked to treason (Tac. *Ann.* 3.24.1–2), figure here. Within the theme of imperial women's punishment, the next segment focuses on imperial women's fates at the deaths of their husband or other relative as emperor. Although Domitia Augusta long survived the assassination of Domitian, Caligula's wife Milonia Caesonia and baby daughter Julia Drusilla; Elagabalus' mother, Julia Soaemias; and Severus Alexander's mother, Julia Mamaea were slaughtered along with the ruling emperor. It is a chilling story. Throughout the chapter I focus on whatever legal information is available.

Roman law and (imperial) women

Imperial women are rarely mentioned in our remaining sources for Roman law, whether by name or as *Augusta*. Their general absence, especially in references dating to the period I survey in this book, means we lack not only any statement of their legal capacities and constraints at any one moment much less over time, but also any citation of them that might give insight into their personalities and lives or exemplify desirable behavior.[24] Scholars have stressed that wealthy and

---

22. Daube 1954 [1991], 549.

23. Although same-sex relationships were often censured for imperial men—for example, in 20 Tiberius denounced to the senate his grandson Nero (son of Germanicus) for homosexuality (Tac. *Ann.* 5.3) and Hadrian was belittled for his affection for Antinous (see Ch. 3)—we hear nothing similar about imperial women. Modern discussion of a sexual relationship between Sabina and Balbilla (to my knowledge first suggested by Bowie 1990, 62) rests only on inference from the ancient sources, which offer no condemnation of it.

24. Compare the frequent depiction of some emperors as judicious and concerned; cf. Williams 1976. I thank Cynthia Bannon for discussion; whatever errors remain are due to me.

Table 2.1 Crimes and Punishments of Imperial Women

Individual	Relation to Emperor	Date	Main Charge	Other Charge(s)	Outcome	Reference
Paradigmatic						
1. Julia the Elder	Daughter of Augustus (r. 27 BCE–4 CE), wife (11–2 BCE) of Tiberius (r. 14 CE–37)	2 BCE	Adultery—but no trial	"Treason"?	No trial, but public censure. Exile to Pandateria; death in Rhegium in 14 CE	Tac. *Ann.* 3.24.2–3; Suet. *Aug.* 25, 65; Plin. *NH* 7.46.149; Cass. Dio 55.10.12–15; Vell. Pat. 2.100.5; Sen. *Clem.* 1.10
2. Julia the Younger	Granddaughter of Augustus	8 CE	Adultery—but no trial	"Treason"?	No trial; public censure? Exile to Trimerus Island, where died in 28	Tac. *Ann.* 3.24.1–3, 4.71.4
With trials						
3. Appuleia Varilla	Great-niece of Augustus	17	*Maiestas* (treason): mocking Augustus, Tiberius, and Livia	Adultery	Tiberius dropped treason charge; Varilla convicted of adultery, Tiberius urges her to be handed over to family for punishment (relegation)	Marshall 1990b, 342, #1; Tac. *Ann.* 2.50
4. Aemilia Lepida	Fiancée of L. Caesar, thus destined to be Augustus' own granddaughter-in-law	20	*Falsum*	Adultery, poisoning, treason	Tiberius asks to drop treason charge; Lepida found guilty and punished for the others	Marshall 1990b, 343, #4; Tac. *Ann.* 3.22–23
5. Claudia Pulchra	Relative of Agrippina the Elder, thus of Augustus	26	*Maiestas* (poisoning and magic aimed at Tiberius)	*Stuprum* (illegal sexual activity)	*Maiestas* charge apparently dropped; convicted of *stuprum*	Marshall 1990b, 344, #9; Tac. *Ann.* 4.52, cf. *Ann.* 4.66.1; Cass. Dio 59.19.1

6. Agrippina the Elder	Granddaughter of Augustus; daughter of Julia the Elder	29	*Maiestas?*	After her death in 33, Tiberius said she should have also been charged with adultery	Exiled to Pandateria; mistreated; death by starvation in 33	Marshall 1990b, 345, #10; Tac. *Ann.* 5.4.2, 6.25
7. Aemilia Lepida (different from #4 earlier)	Former wife of Drusus Caesar (Caligula's brother, died in prison in 33)	36	Adultery		Public trial; Aemilia Lepida anticipates conviction by suicide	Marshall 1990b, 348, #17; Tac. *Ann.* 6.40.4
8. Agrippina the Younger	Inter alia, sister of Caligula (r. 37–41)	39	Adultery	Hints of treason? (Suet.)	Not clear if actually tried; exiled to the Pontine islands; restored in early 41	Cass. Dio 59.22.6–8; Suet. *Calig.* 24.3
9. Julia Livilla	Sister of Caligula	39	Adultery	Hints of treason? (Suet.)	Not clear if actually tried; exiled to the Pontine islands; restored in early 41	Cass. Dio 59.22.6–8; Suet. *Calig.* 24.3
10. Lollia Paulina	Married to Caligula 38–39 (divorced)	49	*Maiestas*		Convicted without being given the chance to defend herself (Tac.)	Marshall 1990b, 349, #22; Tac. *Ann.* 12.22
11. Domitia Lepida	Paternal aunt of Nero (r. 54–68), inter alia	54	Magic	Disturbing the peace	Convicted	Marshall 1990b, 354, #37; Suet. *Nero* 7.1, 34.5

(Continued)

Table 2.1 Continued

Individual	Relation to Emperor	Date	Main Charge	Other Charge(s)	Outcome	Reference
"Charged," but no public trial						
12. Livilla (Claudia Livia Julia)	Sister to Claudius and Germanicus, widow of Tiberius' son Drusus the Younger (d. 23), whom she married after first husband C. Caesar d. 4 CE (inter alia)	31	*Maiestas*? Alleged lover of Sejanus; implicated in death of Drusus the Younger		No trial; killed at home	Marshall 1990b, 353, #33; Tac. *Ann.* 4.3, 4.10; Cass. Dio 58.11.6–7, cf. 57.22.4
13. Julia Livilla (second trial)	Sister of Caligula	41 (under Claudius)	Adultery? Suet. says charge uncertain and no chance for defense		Exiled and killed (in 41?). Charges "trumped up" by Messalina (Cass. Dio)	Suet. *Claud.* 29.1; Cass. Dio 60.8.4–5
14. Messalina	Wife (38–48) of Claudius (r. 41–54)	48	*Maiestas*? Wed C. Silius while still married to Claudius		No trial; killed in imperial gardens	Tac. *Ann.* 11.26–38
15. Agrippina the Younger (second incident)	Inter alia, married since 49 to Claudius, and mother of Nero	59	Posthumous allegations of *maiestas*; no trial		No trial; killed	Tac. *Ann.* 14.1–13; Suet. *Nero* 34.1–4, cf. 39.3; Cass. Dio 61.11–17
16. Claudia Octavia	Daughter of Claudius; first wife of Nero (married in 53)	62	Adultery	Abortion, and treason	No trial; exiled; forced to suicide. Specious charges	Marshall 1990b, 354, #39; Tac. *Ann.* 14.62–64; Suet. *Nero* 35.2

17. Julia Titi	Daughter of Titus (r. 79–81), niece of Domitian (r. 81–96)	83?	Adultery with Domitian. No charges or trial		No trial, no consequences	Suet. *Dom.* 22; Cass. Dio 67.3.2.
18. Domitia Longina	Wife (70–) of Domitian	70, 82/83?, 96	Adultery (70, 82/83)	Treason (conspiracy), 96	No trials, no consequences	Suet. *Dom.* 3, 14; Cass. Dio 67.3, 15
19. Faustina the Younger	Wife (145–) of Marcus Aurelius (r. 161–180)	160, 170s	Adultery with a gladiator, among others (160)	Treason (conspiracy) with Avitus Cassius (170s)	No trials, no consequences	HA, *Marc. Aur.* 19.2–5, 7, 24.6–7, 26.5, 29.1–3; Cass. Dio 71.22.3
20. Lucilla	Daughter of Marcus Aurelius, wife of L. Verus (co-r. 161–169), sister of Commodus (r. 180–192)	Early 180s	Conspiracy (treason)	Adultery?	No trial; exiled by Commodus	HA, *Comm.* 4.1,4, 5.7, 8.3; Cass. Dio 71.1.3, 72.4.4–6; Hdn. 1.6.4, 1.8, 3–5
21. Bruttia Crispina	Wife (178–) of Commodus	191/192?	Adultery		No trial; killed by Commodus	HA, *Comm.* 5.9; Cass. Dio 71.33.1, 72.4.6
22. Julia Domna	Wife (185?–) of Septimius Severus (r. 192–211)	Early 200s	Allegations of adultery and treason?		No trial, no consequences for Domna; her accuser, Plautianus, killed by Caracalla in 205	Cass. Dio 76.15.6, cf. 78.24.1; HA, *Sev.* 18.8
23. Publia Fulvia Plautilla	Wife (202–) of Caracalla (r. 198–217)	205	Treason?		Exiled, without a trial, by Septimius Severus at downfall of her father; killed by Caracalla in 211	Cass. Dio 77.6.3, 78.1.1; Hdn. 3.13.2–3; HA, *M. Ant.* 1.8
24. Sallustia Orbiana	Wife (225–) of Severus Alexander (r. 222–235)	227	Treason?		Exiled, without a trial	Hdn. 6.1.9–10

high-status Romans often encountered preferential legal treatment,[25] which might suggest that Rome's richest and most elite women, the female relatives of the emperor, would be above the law. Yet as we see shortly, imperial women conspicuously figure in legal difficulties during the Augustan and Julio-Claudian periods, demonstrating the adherence of the princeps to Roman law. By the end of 54 CE nine imperial women had faced a public trial, and four others seem to have been charged with egregious criminal wrongdoing.[26] Many of the indictments were connected with new Augustan laws on adultery, part of Augustus' "social legislation."

The new adultery laws revolutionized Roman law and convention by facilitating women's routine appearance in public courts.[27] This was something new, since during the Republic Roman women were usually judged, and punished, within the household and by male relatives with *potestas* over them (a father with *patria potestas*, a husband in a *manus* marriage: see Ch. 1). Women's crimes, in the generalized meaning of acts punishable by a state or another authority, traditionally had not been under the jurisdiction of the Roman state or *res publica*, but were private affairs.[28] Moralists and others thought that judging women in a family court dated back to the very beginning of Rome and that infractions included a woman's adultery and even consumption of wine, with punishments as severe as death.[29]

Only a few public trials of the Republic involved women, and these were held in the Forum Romanum.[30] They concern poisoning,[31] mass indictments for *stuprum* or *probrum* (criminal sexual activity or shameful lewdness),[32] and charges associated with the "Bacchanalian" conspiracy of 186 BCE, although most of the women convicted in this crisis were executed at home.[33] A few special trials

---

25. See, e.g., Gardner 1986, 3; the classic study is Garnsey 1970.

26. For the trials, see Table 2.1, ##3–11; for the others, ##1–2, 12–13.

27. E.g., Marshall 1990b, 334–37; Robinson 1985, 534 (cf. 559–60), noting the relative rarity of women in known trials and suggesting "that women are less criminally inclined than men."

28. Bauman 1996, 32; Robinson 1985, 530–32.

29. Bauman 1996, 32; Gell. *NA* 10.23.4–5, citing Cato; Pliny, *HN* 14.14.89–90; Plut. *Rom.* 22.

30. Women's appearance here was especially abnormal: Boatwright 2011b, 112–13.

31. Livy 40.37.5–7, of Quarta Hostilia in 180 BCE: see Marshall 1990a, 53 n.24. Poisoning was considered peculiarly female: e.g., Purcell 1986, 95; Robinson 1985, 538; Ch. 1 n.106.

32. Livy 10.31.9, 295 BCE; 25.2.9, 213 BCE, both involving *aliquot matronae*, several matrons. See also Gardner 1986, 122–23.

33. Val. Max. 6.3.7; see Livy 39.18.6. Livy's rendition of the event emphasizes women's unbridled sexuality and access to poisoning.

Crimes and Punishments of Imperial Women

are documented for Vestal Virgins accused of unchastity (*incestum*),[34] and for women whose charges are now unknown.[35]

Only after Augustus consolidated power, in part through his social legislation, did women appear regularly in public trials.[36] The Augustan *lex Iulia de adulteriis* of 18 BCE established adultery as a distinct criminal offense. A permanent court, the *quaestio perpetua de adulteriis*, was set up to oversee *adulterium* and *stuprum*, capacious charges that included consensual or forced sex with a respectable married woman (*adulterium*) or a widow or unmarried free woman neither registered as a prostitute nor categorized otherwise as disreputable or disenfranchised (*stuprum*). Incest seems to have been regarded as a special type of *stuprum*.[37] Once the crime of adultery was in the public realm, others besides the offenders' families could be involved: if neither the woman's father nor her husband undertook public prosecution within sixty days of the alleged adultery or of the aggrieved husband's divorcing his wife,[38] any adult male citizen could come forward as accuser.[39] Romans designated this individual as a *delator*, a role Tacitus and others denounced (see later on Appuleia Varilla, Tac. *Ann.* 2.50). Although the *quaestio perpetua de adulteriis* has been said to have "had the longest life and the heaviest workload of any jury-court in the Principate,"[40] we hear about this public court only rarely: families of senatorial or equestrian status, those deemed noteworthy by the ancient authors, had their cases held before the senate or the

---

34. Moved from the "private sphere" of the pontifical college presided over by the Pontifex Maximus to a public trial before a secular commission appointed by a *lex* of the people in 114–113 BCE: Bauman 1996, 93.

35. Val. Max. 5.4.7. See Robinson 1985, 532–34, and Alexander 1990, whose compilation of all public trials from 149 to 50 BCE reveals that less than 5 percent involved women.

36. Robinson 1985, 535: adultery is the crime sources note for women most frequently. Marshall 1990b, 360 notes that among his twenty-nine cases of women tried in a senatorial court were eight charges of adultery and seventeen of *maiestas*.

37. McGinn 1998, 140–47; Treggiari 1996, 890; Bauman 1996, 32; Gardner 1986, 121–27; Richlin 1981. The status of the woman, especially her marital status, was crucial, although both men and women could be charged.

38. Barring the events that a father found his daughter and her lover *in flagrante delicto* in his own or his son-in-law's house, which allowed him to legally kill both adulterers together (reminiscent of Republican practice), or that the husband caught the adulterers *in flagrante delicto*, whereupon he could legally kill his wife's lover if he were *infamis*.

39. In this case the husband would also be charged for the crime of *lenocinium* (pandering or "pimping," that is abetting or consciously allowing the illicit sex), since he had not acted to punish his wife: Bauman 1996, 32–33; Gardner 1986, 128; McGinn 1998, 171–94. The normal time frame for outsiders to prosecute was four to six months, with a maximum of five years.

40. Bauman 1996, 32–34; quotation p.32.

emperor himself.[41] The imperial women I discuss here were judged in these more prestigious settings, where their fates clearly announced to Rome's elite acceptable sexual behavior and the imperial family's compliance with Roman law.[42]

Other parts of Augustus' social legislation, the "Julian and Papian law" discussed in Ch. 1 with Livia's special grant of the right of three children in 9 BCE, were not criminal but civil law. They offered political and social inducements for marriage and childbearing we return to in Ch. 3, with some penalties affecting the disposal of a person's property.[43] Rome's lack of a public prosecution system meant that private individuals could initiate prosecutions, as we saw earlier with the adultery law, and to encourage such "public-minded" accusers, successful *delatores* received a percentage of the property.[44] Tacitus decries the *Lex Papia Poppaea* as pivotal for the spread of such accusers who "subverted every household" (Tac. *Ann.* 3.25; see later).[45] His statement, though clearly hyperbolic, signals that the new laws opened Roman women to increased public scrutiny.[46] This would be particularly problematic for imperial women, given Augustus' merging of state and his own family.

Emperor and imperial family: Above the law?

The Augustan social legislation and other laws were part of the transformation of the Republic to the principate. This enormous subject cannot be fully explored here, but one element calls for treatment in this chapter: the relationship of the princeps to Roman law.[47] As we have seen, in the early third century the jurist

---

41. Gardner 1986, 135 n.26, also noting that the *quaestio* was probably superseded, perhaps at the end of the second century, by the jurisdiction of the urban prefect; McGinn 1998, 142.

42. Marshall 1990b, 335–36 stresses the novelty of women appearing before the senate in the senatorial trials; see also Talbert 1984, 466. McGinn 1998, 147 notes the law's link of social rank and acceptable sexual behavior.

43. E.g., named beneficiaries of wills had to have at least one child, or the property (thereafter considered *caduca*) would fall to another eligible person or to the imperial treasury: Treggiari 1991, 75–77, referring to *Tituli Ulpiani* 17,1; cf. Gardner 1986, 77–78. *Caduca* are testamentary dispositions made in favor of persons who, according to certain statutes, were incapable of acquiring under a will.

44. Treggiari 1991b, 76–77 notes that the unknown original percentage was reduced to 25 percent by Nero: Suet. *Nero* 10.1.

45. Woodman and Martin 1996, 335–36; see also Treggiari 1991, 77.

46. See also Harries 2007, 95–96.

47. Among the changes were that the princeps could now make law: Ulp. 1 inst., Dig. 1.4.1.1. See now Tuori 2016a.

Ulpian stated that the emperor was freed from the laws (*legibus solutus*). Cassius Dio, Ulpian's older contemporary, reported that in 24 BCE the senate released Augustus and subsequent emperors from all compulsion of the laws, ensuring that they were not bound by any of the written ordinances (53.18.1; 53.28.2).[48] Such statements, however, simplify and distort the relationship of the princeps and Roman law in and after Augustus' reign.

Ulpian's statement is excerpted from a longer discussion of the Julian and Papian law, a contested topic among the jurists.[49] Its complications for bequests surface in one of the few references to imperial women now in the Digest. By the middle of the second century jurists attended to the problem of bequests to an emperor or empress (*Augusta*) in which the recipient dies before the testator. It was decided that if a legatee emperor died before the bequest came through, it should go to the new emperor. If a legatee empress passed away—and here are cited the precedents of Hadrian ruling about Plotina and Antoninus Pius about Faustina the Elder—it would be void (Gaius 14, ad l. iul. et pap. and Mauricius 2, ad l. iul. et pap., Dig. 31.56-57).[50]

The Julian and Papian law clarified by Ulpian's statement was not criminal law. Nonetheless, his excerpted assertion has often been read out of context and as affirming that the Roman emperor was free from criminal, public, and private laws. Given Cassius Dio's presentation of Augustus' elusive powers in 27 and 24 BCE, some have dated the legal absolutism of the princeps to the Severan period.[51] The principle more likely dates to the Justinianic period, when the Digest was compiled.[52]

Legal absolutism, so incompatible with the ideology of the Republic (see, e.g., Livy 38.50.8),[53] was an insistent difficulty for emperors, senators, and others throughout the principate.[54] In the *Ad Polybium* that Seneca composed

---

48. For other statements (third century and later), and the interpretation that *solutio legibus* is tied to the emperor's capacity to make laws, see Gallo 1984, e.g. 660 (cf. n.52 in this chapter).

49. Brunt 1977, 108; Daube 1991, 549; Levick 2014, 27.

50. See Price 1987, 80. We discuss elsewhere the strong links of Hadrian and Plotina.

51. E.g., Brunt 1977, 107–16; contra, e.g., Lucrezi 1984.

52. I conclude this after generous discussion of the matter with T. A. J. McGinn, who also argues against the notion that the Severan period witnesses the exemption of the emperor from all restrictions on *caduca* originally set by the Julian and Papian law. See Gallo 1984.

53. Here is enunciated the idea that citizens should compete for glory and status so long as no one citizen becomes so preeminent that he is not accountable to the laws. I owe this reference to my colleague Jed Atkins.

54. For example, so as not to exploit his power and diminish the laws, Tiberius refused to step into a senatorial case (Tac. *Ann.* 3.69.6).

in 43 in hopes that Claudius would repeal his exile, "the ruler may do all" (*Caesari . . . omnia licent*, 7.2).[55] In contrast, in the *De Clementia*, written to advise his young ward Nero as he began to rule, Seneca notes that the emperor should act "as if" he would have to give an account to the laws (*Clem.* 1.1.4: *tamquam legibus . . . rationem redditurus sim*). Soon after Domitian's assassination and *damnatio memoriae*, Pliny stressed Trajan's voluntary submission to the laws that governed everyone (*Pan.* 65.1–2).[56] His eager note in the *Panegyricus* roughly coincides with Dio Chrysostom's more ambiguous assertion, that the emperor is "greater than the laws" even though good rulers do not exploit that position (see *Orat.* 3.10 and 62.3). When emperors acted without restraint, senators and others were endangered even if they did not suffer personally. Domitian's alleged street murder of Paris and incestuous relationship with his niece Julia were in keeping with a ruler who referred to himself as *dominus et deus noster* (Suet. *Dom.* 13.2). The lack of a Roman constitution, and the stress by Augustus and later emperors on a nebulous imperial *auctoritas* rather than on legally defined rights and privileges, meant that such misdeeds could grow ever worse (see Tac. *Agr.* 2–3).

Autocratic behavior signaled a "bad emperor": compare, for example, Caligula's reported retort to his grandmother Antonia the Younger: "You should remember that all things are lawful for me, in every way" (Suet. *Calig.* 29),[57] to the care with which the law was changed so that Claudius could marry his niece Agrippina (Tac. *Ann.* 12.5; Suet. *Claud.* 26.3; see further later). To rule effectively the princeps had to rely on senators and others equally steeped in a Republican ideology of fierce political competition among equals consistently subject to law and custom; he could not long seem to rule arbitrarily or tyrannically. Claudius had experienced the murder of his autocratic and erratic predecessor Caligula; Octavian, the later Augustus, well knew the brutal fate of Julius Caesar. Such bloody events underscored the importance of exhibiting that the princeps was *primus inter pares*, the first among equals and subject to the same Roman laws and customs as those around him.

---

55. Suetonius caps his report of Nero's many murders with Nero's boast that he, first of all the emperors, had realized the extent of imperial power: Suet. *Nero* 37.2.

56. Nonetheless, in their praises of Nero and Trajan Seneca (*Clem.* 1.1.2) and Pliny (*Pan.* 4.4), both note that the emperor's power equals that of the immortal gods.

57. See also Suet. *Calig.* 14.1. HA, *M. Ant.* 10.1–4, a fictitious discussion between Caracalla and Julia Domna supposedly before incest, has her remind him that he is the emperor and makes laws, rather than being subject to them.

Imperial women conveniently demonstrated that the emperor was not above the laws, especially in the early principate.[58] Surely Augustus did not want his daughter, and then his granddaughter, to be so unhappy in their marriages that they would engage in adultery and risk exile or worse: it would be cynical indeed to see as merely a show Augustus' public anguish and humiliation at their lapses (see, e.g., Suet. *Aug.* 65.4; later and Ch. 3). On the other hand, the two women's illicit sexual activity allowed the first princeps to demonstrate that he and his family were as accountable to the laws as any other. The information discussed here makes clear that women of the Augustan and Julio-Claudian family had no personal impunity: they were publicly shamed and conspicuously punished for infractions of the new adultery laws. Many of the cases apparently also included charges of treason, at least originally. We now turn to the crimes and punishments of imperial women, beginning with norms and charges relating to their gender and sexuality.

Licit and illicit sexuality within marriage, and divorce

Roman men and women alike, including members of the imperial family, could initiate a divorce, and remarriage was frequent in the principate.[59] Seven emperors, six of whom span from Augustus through Titus, had been married at least once by the time of their accession.[60] Seven emperors ruled while unmarried: again six of these date to the first century but now include Galba and Otho.[61] (In Ch. 3 we discuss the special cases of Vespasian and Antoninus Pius, who lived with unmarried "concubines" while emperor, Antoninus Pius during twenty years as a widower on the throne.) As we detail shortly, eight women whose husbands became emperor or were destined as such had previously been

---

58. We should also point out that male members of the imperial family also did not have personal immunity: Agrippina the Elder's sons Nero and Drusus, for example, were exiled in 29 and 30. The women's cases, however, are more infamous in the literary record.

59. If the wedding was *cum manu* the woman had no legal authority to act. For divorce generally, see Treggiari 1991a and 1991b, 435–82.

60. Augustus was said to have been wed briefly to Antony's stepdaughter Claudia in a marriage never consummated (Suet. *Aug.* 62.1) and was married to Scribonia 40–39 BCE; Tiberius (single while ruling), twice before 14 CE; Caligula once; Claudius thrice before 41; Nero to Claudia Octavia in 53; Titus twice before 79 (to Arrecina Tertulla, who died; to Marcia Furnilla, from 62 to divorce ca. 65 or 66: Gregori and Rosso 2010, 195–96); Septimius Severus once before Julia Domna, in 185 or 187, and widowed.

61. Tiberius, Galba, Otho, Vespasian, Titus, Nerva, and Caracalla.

married, all from the first century CE: Caligula's quip that he was following the precedent of Romulus and Octavian when he seized his wife Orestina (or Orestilla) from her wedding ceremony to Gaius Calpurnius Piso indicates the banality of the occurrence.[62] The phenomenon may seem odd in cultures preoccupied with virginity, but is explicable given the importance of procreation, especially for the imperial family (see Ch. 3). Indeed, when Tacitus reports discussions leading to Claudius' fourth marriage in 48 he lists as criteria for a suitable imperial wife high lineage, proven childbearing, and virtuous piety. Agrippina the Younger's advantages included that this thirty-three-year-old, still of childbearing age, had proven her fecundity (Tac. *Ann.* 12.2, 12.6; her son Nero was eleven).[63]

Women previously married before wedding an emperor or someone destined to become one include Livia (with one son and pregnant with another when betrothed to the recently divorced Octavian in 39 BCE); Julia the Elder (married twice, with five living children when she wed Tiberius in 11 BCE); Lollia Paulina (the third wife of Caligula after he "took" her from her husband Publius Memmius Regulus, in 38, childless); Milonia Caesonia (with three daughters when she married Caligula in 39/40, she reportedly bore their child Julia Drusilla on their wedding day: Suet. *Calig.* 25, 33; Cass. Dio 59.23.7); Agrippina the Younger (with eleven-year-old Nero from her first marriage when she wed Claudius, her third husband, in January 49); Poppaea Sabina (twice married before wedding Nero in 62, and with a son from her first husband); Statilia Messalina (whose previous husband Nero allegedly killed in 66 so he could wed her: Suet. *Nero* 35.1); and Domitia Longina (see earlier). Most of these previously married women already had children: only Lollia Paulina was definitely childless at the time of her imperial wedding.[64] The matter of progeny seems key, especially in the Julio-Claudian period.

In contrast, no second- or third-century wives of emperors are known to have been previously married, other than Julia Aquilia Severa when she married Elagabalus for the second time in late 221. She, however, had been a Vestal Virgin

---

62. Suet. *Calig.* 25.1; Cass. Dio 59.8.7. For Caligula's second wife Cornelia (Livia) Orestina or Orestilla, married to the emperor for only a few months, see n.73 in this chapter.

63. *deligi oportere feminam nobilitate puerperiis sanctimonia insignem.* The criteria ring ironically in Tacitus' later depiction of Agrippina. Poppaea, with a son from her first marriage to Rufrius Crispinus, reportedly flaunted her fecundity when inducing Nero to divorce Octavia in 59: Tac. *Ann.* 14.1.2.

64. On onomastic and prosographical grounds some suggest Domitia had born a son to Lamia, Lucius Fundanius Lamia Aelianus, *cos. ord.* 116, *procos. Asiae* 131/2 (PIR² A 204): Fraser 2015, 218. FOS #327 is more tentative, and most scholars omit the possibility.

before her first marriage to him in late 220.[65] Growing attention to the chasteness of imperial women may also be seen in Hadrian's public praise of his mother-in-law Matidia the Elder. She was lauded as with only one husband and living most virginally in a long widowhood after her husband's death (*castissima*: *CIL* XIV 3579, ll. 23–24), a puzzling claim in light of the strong evidence suggesting she was married twice.[66] Although one can never argue from stories about Elagabalus, it appears relevant here that he married a Vestal Virgin. After the first century, it seems, the chasteness of emperors' wives and female relatives assumed greater importance for the image of the imperial house. Charges of sexual promiscuity were a constant in attacks on women and the men connected to them, as we see with Faustina the Younger in Ch. 3. The later image of an imperial woman as *univira*, married only once and faithful to her husband, emphasized that her sexuality was controlled by the emperor alone.[67] An earlier reflection of this may be Caligula's reported prohibition of his divorced (third) wife Lollia Paulina from ever sleeping with another man (Suet. *Calig.* 25).[68]

The necessity to establish the imperial family in the early principate is reflected in the unusual circumstances of two marriages.[69] Livia, with a three-year-old son Tiberius born from her husband Tiberius Claudius Nero, was some six months pregnant and recently divorced when Octavian consulted the pontifices, Rome's highest religious college, for sanction before marrying her 17 January 38 BCE.[70] The other is Agrippina the Younger's wedding to Claudius in January 49 (her

---

65. Lucilla (daughter of Faustina the Younger and Marcus Aurelius) wed first Lucius Verus and then Tiberius Claudius Pompeianus (supposedly scorning him as not elite enough: HA, *Marc.* 20.6–7); Julia Mamaea, the daughter of Julia Maesa, had wed a consular before the equestrian Gessius Marcianus, who would be the father of her son Severus Alexander.

66. Jones 2004, 272–73 tenders that the first marriage to an unknown Mindius ended in divorce. The second-century emphasis on chastity renders less convincing modern scholarly assumptions that, despite the lack of evidence, Matidia the Younger was married (e.g., Wood 2015, 235–36).

67. Tacitus suggests Tiberius refused second marriages for Agrippina the Elder and Livilla because of political considerations (Tac. *Ann.* 4.53, 4.39–40).

68. She, Nero's (third) wife Statilia Messalina, and Domitia Longina are the only imperial divorcées to survive their ex-husbands' reigns. In 2 BCE Augustus had Julia the Elder divorced from Tiberius before her disgrace and exile (Suet. *Tib.* 10.1, 11.4; see later): Linderski 1988 convincingly argues that Julia had remained under *patria potestas*.

69. The senate passed a special decree allowing Octavia to marry Antony in October 40, sooner than the ten months required after the death of her former husband, Gaius Claudius Marcellus (Plut. *Ant.* 31.3).

70. His punctiliousness did not deter gossip (Cass. Dio 48.44); see Perkounig 1995, 46–53 and Barrett 2002, 22–27. Octavian reportedly divorced his first wife Scribonia on the very day she gave birth to his only child, Julia the Elder (Cass. Dio 48.34.3).

third marriage; his fourth). In this instance the sticking point was the blood relationship of the two: Claudius was Agrippina's paternal uncle, and Roman law forbade such marriages.[71] A senatorial decree prompted by Lucius Vitellius, Claudius' colleague in the censorship of 47/48, changed the law and confirmed Claudius as law-abiding (Tac. *Ann.* 12.5–7).[72] As we saw earlier, Agrippina's proven child-bearing capability was called pivotal in Claudius' choice of her.

In the Augustan and Julio-Claudian periods, and perhaps up to the end of the first century, imperial women and men could marry more than once; indeed, the need to establish an imperial family apparently encouraged marriage with a woman whose child-bearing capacities had already been proven in lawful marriage. On the other hand, once in place an imperial family should be stable. The four emperors from our period who divorced while ruling are all stereotypically "bad." Caligula and Elagabalus both divorced at least once while on the throne.[73] More instructive are the details about the divorces of Nero and Domitian. Nero, reportedly incited by his lover Poppaea, put his wife Octavia aside only to take her back when Rome's populace rioted in protest. Poppaea allegedly pushed him again to finally divorce Octavia in 62 and then have her killed (Tac. *Ann.* 14.1, 14.60–61; Suet. *Nero* 35.1–3). Suetonius reports that Domitian divorced but then remarried Domitia "as if the people demanded it" but really because he missed her (Suet. *Dom.* 3.1, 13.1). Popular support for stable imperial marriages may be behind Hadrian's and Marcus Aurelius' reported rejections of the very idea of divorcing their wives Sabina and Faustina, respectively (see Ch. 3). It seems clear that by the end of the first century the "imperial marriage" is more sacrosanct. The contrast could not be greater with the scandalous cases involving imperial women, adultery, and treason in the early principate, to which we now turn.[74]

---

71. Cass. Dio 60.31.8; more later.

72. When urging the senate to change the law, Tacitus' Vitellius implies Octavian and Caligula acted improperly in "carrying off" others' wives: *Ann.* 12.6.2. Only a few couples followed Claudius' example, none from the senatorial *ordo*: Eck 1993, 38; Suet. *Claud.* 26.3; Tac. *Ann.* 12.7.1; Cass. Dio 60.31.8. The new law would have allowed Domitian to marry Julia Titi, his brother's daughter, and may have covered the marriage of Lucilla to Lucius Verus, her father's adoptive brother (if adoptive relationships were considered the same as blood ones).

73. While ruling in 37–41 Caligula divorced two of his four wives: Cornelia (Livia) Orestina or Orestilla (FOS #285 doubts the legitimacy of her liaison with Caligula ~37), and Lollia Paulina, whom Caligula married in 38 but divorced in 39. While emperor in 218–222 Elagabalus married and divorced Cornelia Paula (219–220), Julia Aquilia Severa (220/221–?July 221; remarried, end 221), and Annia Faustina (or Fundania) (?July 221–end 221).

74. Wallace-Hadrill 1996, 304: since at this time "marriage was used as an official instrument . . . to mark succession and to unify potentially divergent groups, adultery represented . . . group formation out of the emperor's control."

Crimes and punishments of imperial women: Charges of adultery and maiestas for Julia the Elder and Julia the Younger?

The earliest and most notorious incidents are those of Augustus' daughter Julia the Elder in 2 BCE and his granddaughter Julia the Younger in 8 CE, with the latter complicated by the obscure exile of Ovid. The legal circumstances are far from clear, and the case of Julia the Younger is particularly poorly attested.[75] The ancient sources present differing versions of the downfall of Julia the Elder in 2 BCE, when her (third) husband Tiberius had been in Rhodes for four years. Seneca the Younger implausibly describes her having sex with droves of lovers throughout Rome, even in the Forum Romanum on the Rostra "from which her father had proposed the *lex de adulteriis*" (Sen. *Ben.* 6.32.1; cf. Cass. Dio 55.10.12; Plin. *HN* 21.9).[76] (Similarly exaggerated charges against Messalina, whose case is briefly discussed here, should also be dismissed.[77]) Suetonius and Cassius Dio describe Augustus' deep distress and anger at the news of his daughter's infidelities, which led him to notify the senate by letter and to shun others' company; Suetonius adds that he even thought about killing her (*Aug.* 25; see Cass. Dio 55.10.12). But further details are scarce and sometimes contradictory.

Between the sources we have the names of some six lovers, and the implication of treason. Cassius Dio holds that the adulterers included Mark Antony's son Iullus Antonius, who was put to death for political aims while others were relegated to islands (55.10.12–15).[78] Velleius Paterculus states that Iullus Antonius committed suicide, but that Quintus Crispinus, Appius Claudius, Sempronius Gracchus, Scipio, and others of less prominence, senators and equestrians alike, were punished under Augustus' adultery law, that is, by relegation (expulsion, but less severe than exile; 2.100.3–5).[79] Pliny the Elder links Julia's infidelity to

---

75. For Julia the Elder, see esp. Linderski 1988; Fantham 2006, 85–91, 139–46; cf. Barrett 1996, 20–21, 256 nn.30, 36. For Julia the Younger, see Fantham 2006, 109–11 and Syme 1986, 118–20, noting (p.118) that her exile is "plausibly assigned to AD 8 because of the large gap in the text of Cassius Dio." Ovid's situation is not discussed here.

76. See, e.g., McGinn 1998, 168–70; Boatwright 2011b, 128.

77. McGinn 1998, 169–70, with Plin. *NH* 10.171: by entertaining twenty-five partners in a night Messalina won a contest with a slave prostitute. McGinn aptly notes Procopius' story of Theodora's having sex with more than forty men in a night, *Anec.* 9.16.

78. Cassius Dio here includes the nicety that a tribune named among the adulterers was not tried until he had finished his term of office.

79. Bauman 1967, 198. See later, n.84 in this chapter.

her parricidal plots, but names no alleged lover (*NH* 7.46.149).[80] Seneca in his work *On Clemency* notes that although Augustus had convicted Julia's adulterers, he did not kill them; instead, he ensured their safety when they were sent away (*Clem.* 1.10.3). Macrobius, who adds a Demosthenes to the list of lovers, mentions adultery alone (*Sat.* 1.11.17). As we see later, our other witness, Tacitus, is even more complicated (Tac. *Ann.* 3.24.2–3).

The upshot, however, seems clear: after ensuring Julia's divorce from Tiberius but without a trial,[81] Augustus relegated his daughter to the Campanian island Pandateria (Ventotene, Italy), where he banned her from wine, fine foods, and visitors other than her mother Scribonia, who voluntarily accompanied her daughter to the impoverished speck of land (Suet. *Aug.* 65; Cass. Dio 55.10.14; Vell. Pat. 2.100.5). Julia was later allowed to move to Regium (modern Reggio Calabria, Italy), where she died miserably in 14.[82]

Her sorry tale has faint echoes in that of her daughter, Julia the Younger. Similarly without a trial, in 8 CE Augustus' granddaughter was disgraced and exiled to the tiny island of Trimerus off Apulia (in the Isole Tremiti, Italy).[83] Her only attested lover is Decimus Junius Silanus, whom Augustus punished merely by renouncing his friendship (Tac. *Ann.* 3.24.1). Despite Livia's support to her exiled granddaughter, Julia the Younger lived wretchedly on the remote island until her death in 28 (Tac. *Ann.* 4.71).

A common perception, deriving mostly from the cases of the two Julias, is that adultery with an imperial woman was tantamount to treason, or *maiestas* as it is called in Latin.[84] Three sources link the women's downfalls to treason: as

---

80. In this extended passage (*HN* 7.45–46.147–51) Pliny presents an extraordinary list of negatives about Augustus, many otherwise unknown.

81. Suet. *Tib.* 10.1, 11.4: see Fantham 2006, 86; Marshall 1990b, 352; Richlin 1981, 231.

82. Tac. *Ann.* 1.53, noting too the death that year of her supposed adulterer Sempronius Gracchus. Cassius Dio reports Julia was transferred to Regium after Rome's populace demanded her return (55.13.1). Linderski 1988, 195–96 suggests but rejects that Scribonia stayed with Julia to the end in Regium (4–14 CE). See also Fantham 2006, 89–91.

83. At the time she was married to Lucius Aemilius Paullus: see Syme 1978, 206–11.

84. E.g., Wood 1999, 38–39; Cogitore 2002, 165–72; Fantham 2006, 110, App. II.4b; Ginsburg 2006, 13; Hekster 2015, 6. Richlin 1981, 233–34 discusses combining charges of *maiestas* and adultery as a political weapon. Yakobson 2003 stresses the impossibility of knowing surely what the crime of *maiestas* meant. Under Augustus and Tiberius the punishment for those convicted of adultery was relegation (expulsion from Rome) and confiscation of half their dowry and a third of their other property (for women; convicted men forfeited half their property); for *maiestas* it was exile or interdiction (permanent banishment from Rome), confiscation of the goods of the convicted, and sometimes *damnatio memoriae*. See Bauman 1996, 50–64; Treggiari 1996, 890–92; Milnor 2005; cf. Dig. 48.5.30 (29), pr. 1.

Crimes and Punishments of Imperial Women   67

we saw above, Cassius Dio mentions the political aims of Iullus Antonius, one of Julia the Elder's alleged lovers (55.10.15), and Pliny the Elder holds that Julia the Elder was parricidal (*NH* 7.46.149). Perhaps more important, in a characteristically challenging and unforgettable discussion of the women's fates Tacitus uses the words "violated majesty." While reporting events at Rome in 20 CE Tacitus digresses on the "mixed luck" of Augustus. Contrasting the princeps' great political fortune to his unfortunate home life, marred by the lewdness (*impudicitia*) of his daughter and granddaughter, Tacitus goes on:

> Augustus drove the two women from Rome and punished their adulterers with death or exile. But he acted against custom, and illegally, for he overstepped the clemency of our forefathers and the scope of his own laws by identifying a failing—widespread among men and women—with the momentous charge of "infringed religious duty and violated majesty" [treason]. (Tac. *Ann.* 3.24.2–3, paraphrase mine).[85]

The whole is provoked by a general report on the misfortunes—and one "success story"—of noble families in Rome (Tac. *Ann.* 3.22–24),[86] itself part of a longer section devoted to Rome, judicial trials, and notable political events of the year 20 (Tac. *Ann.* 3.22–30).

Maintaining that Augustus exceeded legal limits when punishing his daughter and granddaughter and their adulterers, Tacitus links *maiestas*, *religio*, and sexual impropriety in Augustus' family.[87] He uses the indicative throughout for his appraisal of Augustus' actions, and he corroborates his verdict with a causal clause introduced by *nam*. Just as notably, he places this appraisal after the senatorial trial of an Aemilia Lepida on a number of charges—falsely claiming a child, adultery, poisoning, and treasonably consulting astrologers about the "house of

---

85. *ut valida divo Augusto in rem publicam fortuna ita domi improspera fuit ob impudicitiam filiae ac neptis quas urbe depulit, adulterosque earum morte aut fuga punivit. nam culpam inter viros ac feminas vulgatam gravi nomine laesarum religionum ac violatae maiestatis appellando clementiam maiorum suasque ipse leges egrediebatur.* Bauman 1967, 200 n.3 translates: "in so doing [punishing] he gave the weighty name of 'a breach of religious duty and a violation of majesty' to a common peccadillo of men and women, thus disregarding the clemency of our ancestors and going beyond the scope of his own laws." *Laesae religiones* can mean sacrilege.

86. Woodman and Martin 1996, 224 describe Tac. *Ann.* 3.24.2–3 as a "flashback." The "success" is the pardon of Decimus Silanus, whose penalty for adultery with Julia the Younger was lighter than the law demanded: Woodman and Martin 1996, 226.

87. Woodman and Martin 1996, 227 note his use of the plural *viros* and *feminas* in *Ann.* 3.24.3. Seneca had remarked that Augustus was milder than the law allowed (*Clem.* 1.10.3).

the emperor," that is, *maiestas* (Tac. *Ann.* 3.22–23; we return to this).[88] He follows his reference to the two Julias with a long analysis of law as a whole. That digression, prompted by senatorial discussion of another "social" law of Augustus (the *Lex Papia Poppaea*), covers from primitive man up to Caesar Augustus' sixth consulship (28 BCE), when Augustus abolished the emergency laws of the triumvirate and "provided laws for us to use in peace and under a *princeps*" (Tac. *Ann.* 3.25-28.2).[89]

Tacitus' forceful connection of the charge of violated *maiestas* to the adulteries of the two Julias, seemingly echoed by trials of Julio-Claudian women in which adultery and treason charges are mentioned (addressed here), has generated controversy and confusion. A. J. Woodman and R. Martin, the authors of the Cambridge Commentary on Tacitus' *Annals* 3, themselves disagree on how to interpret the explanatory clause in which *maiestas* appears. Martin holds it "to mean that in punishing the Julias and their lovers Augustus exceeded the provisions of the *lex Iulia de adulteriis* of 18 or 17 BC," thus agreeing with Cassius Dio's and Pliny's allegations of political treason.[90] Woodman, however, rejecting explanations that Augustus "trumped up the charge or that there was some 'actual' treason," posits, "T[acitus] is saying that in the Julias' cases Augustus exceeded his own law because he called adultery by the name of *laesarum religionum ac violatae maiestatis.*"[91] Arguing that *maiestas* refers to *patria maiestas*, a father's honor, and *religiones* to "obligations" attendant on that acknowledged standing, Woodman concludes that Augustus' position as princeps and head of Rome's most important family forced him to act.[92]

Arguing in a similar vein, R. Bauman examines Tacitus' words from the perspective of Rome's laws. In his fundamental investigation of the crime of treason or *crimen maiestatis*, Bauman separates the *maiestas* allegedly "violated" by the two Julias and their adulterers from the *maiestas populi Romani*, the majesty or standing of the Roman state. He sees the *maiestas* of Tacitus' *Annals* 3.24 as the "majesty" of Augustus himself, which came from Augustus' tribunician

---

88. Woodman and Martin 1996, 210–23. For Lepida's charge of *maiestas*, see *Ann.* 3.22.2, with Woodman and Martin 215 ad loc. I return to the case later.

89. For this digression, see Woodman and Martin 1996, 236–59. They note that this is the first long digression in the *Annals*, and (258) that the digression's culmination, *deditque iura quis pace et principe uteremur*, can also be translated "and he provided laws by means of which we could enjoy our peace and *princeps*" (p. 238).

90. See Woodman and Martin 1996, 225–26. Yakobson 2003, 91–92 interprets the case politically but concludes that there was no formal equation of adultery and treason.

91. See Woodman and Martin 1996, 226–27.

92. Woodman and Martin 1996, 227–28, followed by, e.g., Ginsburg 2006, 123–30.

sacrosanctity and the general patronage he gained during and after the triumviral period and that enhanced his whole *domus* or family.[93] The date of Julia the Elder's disgrace in 2 BCE is particularly important for Bauman, for that year saw Augustus honored with the title *pater patriae*.[94]

Although scholars divide between concluding that "actual" treason motivated the illicit activities of the Julias[95] or that moral considerations were paramount,[96] we must recognize the impossibility of disentangling morals from politics and the quest for power,[97] which fits the evolution of law in the principate. Distinguishing the person of the princeps from the state became ever more difficult as the emperor's persona grew to include his family (household or *domus*): by the time of the *Senatus consultum de Pisone patre* of 20 CE, the dramatic date of Tacitus' discussion of *maiestas violata* in *Ann.* 3.24, one fault leveled against Piso was his lack of respect for the *maiestas domus Augustae* (see Ch. 3).[98] In the next section we see Tacitus was not alone in confounding treason with cases of imperial women indicted for illicit sexual activity: various women connected to the imperial family by blood or marriage apparently faced the two charges together. But we also see that adultery with a woman connected to the imperial house was not treasonable in and of itself, however close those ties were.[99]

Crimes and punishments of other imperial women

It is often hard to discern concrete charges in the crimes and punishments of imperial women (see Table 2.1), since in general such women rarely went to trial.

Neither of the two Julias faced a public trial, despite their humiliation and punishment, and none of their alleged lovers underwent a public trial either. Other than the Julias, I know of nine instances of legal difficulties for imperial

---

93. Bauman 1967, 227–29. Bauman here seems overly schematic in differentiating the *maiestas populi Romani* from the *violata maiestas (principis)*.

94. Bauman 1967, 234–42, esp. 240–41, noting also the dedication of the Temple of Mars Ultor and the Forum Augustum.

95. Such as Syme, e.g., 1986, 90–92 for Julia the Elder, and 117–23 for Julia the Younger (and Ovid), in two characteristically oblique passages.

96. The references in Bauman 1967, 241 have only grown in the last half-century.

97. See, e.g., Linderski 1988, 182 n.2; Edwards 1993, 60–62; and Severy 2003, 198, noting "the lack of distinction between treason and sexual disloyalty to Augustus' family."

98. *neclecta (sic) maiestate domus Aug(ustae)*, *SCPP* ll. 32–33; Corbier 2001; Yakobson 2003.

99. Yakobson 2003, 91, who sees the idea behind the combined charges against Appuleia Varilla in 17 (see later), stresses Tiberius' rejection of the notion of adultery as treason.

women: five trials under Tiberius (r. 14–37, ## 3–7); two rather uncertain ones under Caligula (r. 37–41, ## 8–9, both his sisters); one under Claudius (r. 41–54; #10, Lollia Paulina, whom Tacitus holds was targeted by Claudius' new wife Agrippina the Younger); and one under Nero (r. 54–68; #11, Domitia Lepida, whose difficulties are also ascribed to Agrippina). Some of these trials are doubtful (## 8–9). Others are reported as heard in the senate in the presence of the emperor (##3–4, 10, perhaps 7). The ninth seems to have been heard not at a public trial at all, but *intra cubiculum*, that is only by the emperor and his advisors (#11, Domitia Lepida).[100] After Domitia Lepida's case in 54, no imperial woman is known to have been tried publicly.

Fundamental here is A. J. Marshall's 1990 investigation of women on trial in the Roman senate, where he identifies some 29 definite or possible senatorial trials of women in the first century of the principate. He notes that this number compares to 122 men in such trials recorded by Tacitus alone.[101] Imperial women are litigants in 9, perhaps 11, of Marshall's 29 possible senatorial trials of a woman. In nine of these eleven cases a charge of *maiestas* figured in the arraignment, whether an actual trial occurred or not (Table 2.1, ##1–6, 8–10). Indeed, four cases seem not to have been heard in a tribunal (##1 and 2, the two Julias; ##8 and 9, Agrippina the Younger and her sister Julia Livilla). But of the other five cases of imperial women charged with treason (*maiestas*) with or without another indictment, two saw the treason charge dropped on Tiberius' urging (##3 and 4, Appuleia Varilla and Aemilia Lepida), and a third seems also to have never heard the treason charge (#5, Claudia Pulchra).

The earliest case—of Appuleia Varilla in 17 CE, which is known only from Tacitus—opens ominously: "In the meantime, the law of treason was coming into its own" (*Ann.* 2.50). Tacitus then details the accusations of a *delator* against this woman, identified as the granddaughter of Augustus' sister [Octavia]: that she had mocked Augustus, Tiberius, and Tiberius' mother [Julia Augusta] by scandalous gossip and, although connected to the imperial house, was engaged in an adulterous affair. Tiberius refused immediately to hear the charges of *maiestas* relating to himself and his mother; he ended up dropping the *maiestas* charge entirely, although he originally said Appuleia would be punished if found to have said anything improper about Augustus.[102] When Appuleia was convicted for

---

100. Brunt 1972, 168.

101. Of these, the first twenty come under Tiberius. For the first century most of our evidence comes from Tacitus, whose *Annals* feature senatorial trials of prominent persons, including women. Marshall 1990b, 340–41, 357 notes Tacitus' moralistic rather than legally precise presentation of such trials; see also Richlin 1981, 232–34.

102. Marshall 1990b, 342 concurs with this reading. See also Yakobson 2003, 90–91.

Crimes and Punishments of Imperial Women

adultery Tiberius urged she be handed to her family for relegation from Rome. Her lover Manlius was forbidden to live in Italy or Africa.[103]

Four other trials of imperial women during Tiberius' reign are reported. The case of Aemilia Lepida, mentioned above, merits two long chapters in Tacitus' *Annals* for 20 CE (Tac. *Ann.* 3.22–23). Her charges included *falsum* for pretending to bear Publius Quirinius' child, adultery, poisoning, and *maiestas* for astrological consultation about the imperial family (*quaesitumque per Chaldaeos in domum Caesaris*). Among Tacitus' details are that Aemilia Lepida was once destined as the wife of Lucius Caesar, that is, Augustus' own daughter-in-law (when Lucius Caesar had been adopted by Augustus; Tac. *Ann.* 3.22.1 and 23.1).[104] The charge of *maiestas* was dropped on Tiberius' request, but she was found guilty and punished on the other two indictments (Tac. *Ann.* 3.22.2).[105] In a third Tiberian case involving illicit sexuality, *maiestas*, and a woman of the imperial family, the widow Claudia Pulchra, Agrippina the Elder's maternal cousin or *sobrina*, was charged in 26 with *maiestas* for magic aimed at the emperor and poisoning and for *stuprum*, criminal sexual activity (Tac. *Ann.* 4.52; cf. *Ann.* 4.66.1 and Cass. Dio 59.19.1).[106] Since Tacitus reports only the conviction of Pulchra and her alleged lover Furnius, Marshall suggests that the *maiestas* charge, which had been leveled against Pulchra alone, may not have been pursued.[107]

A few other imperial women known to have been punished may have faced conjoined charges of criminal sexuality and of *maiestas*. In 29 Agrippina the Elder was tried and exiled to the island Pandateria for what seems to have been

---

103. *Adolescebat interea lex maiestatis. et Appuleiam Varillam, sororis Augusti neptem, quia probrosis sermonibus divum Augustum ac Tiberium et matrem eius inlusisset Caesarique conexa adulterio teneretur, maiestatis delator arcessebat. de adulterio satis caveri lege Iulia visum: maiestatis crimen distingui Caesar postulavit damnarique, si qua de Augusto inreligiose dixisset: in se iacta nolle ad cognitionem vocari. interrogatus a consule quid de iis censeret quae de matre eius locuta secus argueretur reticuit; dein proximo senatus die illius quoque nomine oravit ne cui verba in eam quoquo modo habita crimini forent. liberavitque Appuleiam lege maiestatis: adulterii graviorem poenam deprecatus, ut exemplo maiorum propinquis suis ultra ducentesimum lapidem removeretur suasit. adultero Manlio Italia atque Africa interdictum est.* For Appuleia Varilla, see FOS #85.

104. Here Tacitus also provides a rare picture of women publicly supporting someone.

105. See Marshall 1990b, 343 (his case #4); Woodman and Martin 1996, 211–15, 221–23. For this Aemilia Lepida, see FOS #28.

106. In Tac. *Ann.* 4.66.1 she is also said to be the mother of Quintilius Varus, "rich and close to the emperor." For Claudia Pulchra see *PIR*[2] C 1116 and the Julio-Claudian genealogical tree in FOS, although she does not have her own entry; she does not appear in our Appendix 2.

107. *Pulchra et Furnius damnantur*; Marshall 1990b, 344. Nothing indicates Tiberius' interest, key for dropping the *maiestas* charges in the two earlier cases.

maiestas,[108] but after her death there by starvation in 33 Tiberius harshly suggested she also should have been charged with *impudicitia*, for adultery with Asinius Gallus (Tac. *Ann.* 6.25). In late 39 her daughters, Julia Livilla and Agrippina the Younger, were also exiled to Pandateria and the nearby island Pontia, respectively. They were charged with adultery with their brother-in-law Marcus Aemilius Lepidus, the widower of Caligula's favorite sister Drusilla (Cass. Dio 59.22.6–8); Suetonius adds that Caligula's humiliation of his sisters, sexually and otherwise, made it easier for him to gain their condemnation as adulteresses complicit in Lepidus' plots against the emperor (Suet. *Calig.* 24.3).[109] Both women returned to Rome in 41 when the new emperor Claudius cancelled many of Caligula's acts. By the end of the year, however, Julia Livilla was exiled again, to Pandateria. According to Suetonius, in this second crisis she faced no actual charge and had no chance of defense. Cassius Dio presents her downfall as due to charges fabricated by a jealous Messalina that included adultery, for which Seneca was also exiled (Suet. *Claud.* 29.1; Cass. Dio 60.8.4–5).[110] Julia Livilla was killed soon thereafter.[111]

Other Julio-Claudian imperial women were actual or potential litigants in trials that apparently did not combine adultery and treason. The year 36 saw the conviction, for adultery alone, of the Aemilia Lepida once married to Drusus Caesar (a different woman from the Aemilia Lepida tried in 20).[112] In another case, reputedly impelled by the jealous and grasping Agrippina the Younger in 49, Lollia Paulina, divorced from Caligula since 39, was convicted for treason alone; she was banished from Italy, deprived of her fortune, and killed (Tac. *Ann.*

---

108. Marshall 1990b, 345, his case #10; Deline 2015; FOS #812. For a while she was held in Herculaneum: Sen. *de Ira* 3.21.5.

109. Ginsburg 2006, 14 (with references) supports Suetonius' skepticism; see also Barrett 1990, 91–113; Syme 1986, 179–80. Cassius Dio calls them "unjustly exiled" (60.4.1). In 39 Agrippina was married to Domitius Ahenobarbus, and Julia Livilla to Marcus Vinicius. Barrett 1996, 69 argues Agrippina the Younger was sent to Pontia, Julia Livilla to Pandateria.

110. Barrett 1996, 69. Tac. *Ann.* 14.63.1–2 more simply blames Claudius alone.

111. Seneca's pardon came after Messalina's downfall seven years later, in 48: Levick 2015, 63–64; *Schol. Juv.* 5.109; Sen. *Cons. Ad Pol.* 13.2; Sen. *Apoloc.* 10.4; Tac. *Ann.* 12.8 and 13.42.3. Agrippina's regained power after her return reportedly caused a jealous Messalina to try to assassinate Nero as a potential rival to Britannicus (Suet. *Nero* 6.4).

112. FOS #30; Marshall 1990b, 348, his case #17; Tac. *Ann.* 6.40.4 for Drusus. The death in 43 of Drusus Caesar's daughter Julia (FOS #422; not in our Appendix 2), with allegations of adultery although no trial, is also attributed to Messalina (Cass. Dio 60.18.4, cf. Tac. *Ann.* 13.32.3 and 43.2; Syme 1986, 182).

12.22–23, 14.12; Cass. Dio 61.32.4, cf. 61.10.1).[113] In 54 Domitia Lepida, the paternal aunt of Nero, was convicted for magic and disturbing the peace in a case also attributed to the resentful and avaricious Agrippina (Tac. *Ann.* 12.64–65; Suet. *Nero* 7.1).[114] In yet another sorry instance, the "official" version of Agrippina the Younger's murder in Campania in 59 incriminated her for plotting to kill Nero—that is, for treason.[115]

Three other cases involving first-century imperial women elucidate the nexus of adultery, *maiestas*, and public trials. The first is the downfall of Livilla (Claudia Livia Julia) in 31.[116] Livilla, the daughter of Antonia the Younger and Drusus the Elder and the sister of Germanicus and Claudius, is inseparable from the *domus Augusta* in the Augustan and Tiberian periods.[117] She had married Tiberius' son Drusus the Younger after 4 CE and the death of her first husband, Gaius Caesar (one of Augustus' grandsons and adoptive sons), and she bore Drusus three children. By 22 and a special grant of tribunician power Drusus the Younger had become the heir apparent to his father and emperor (Tac. *Ann.* 3.56–57).[118] But in 23 Livilla allegedly was seduced by Sejanus (*adulterium*, Tac. *Ann.* 4.3) and engaged in all types of wrongdoing, including scheming to kill her husband (Suet. *Tib.* 62; cf. Cass. Dio 57.22.2).[119] The lack of immediate charges at Drusus' death in 23 suggests that she was not suspected at the time. Nonetheless, Tiberius

---

113. Marshall 1990b, 349, his case #22 (see FOS #504). Tacitus' report of the trial includes the information that Claudius "suppressed" her marriage to Caligula: *Ann.* 12.22. Her alleged treason was suspicious consultation of oracles and dabbling in magic.

114. A charge of *maiestas* is not reported: see Marshall 1990b, 354. This Domitia Lepida, the daughter of Antonia the Elder (thus the grandniece of Augustus) and the mother of Claudius' wife Messalina, may be the Lepida implicated in a charge of incest laid against Gnaeus Domitius Ahenobarbus but dropped at Tiberius' death (Suet. *Nero* 5.2). Neither sister appears in my Appendix 2.

115. Tac. *Ann.* 14.1–13, esp. 14.10.3–11.2; Cass. Dio 61.11–17, esp. 61.14.3; Suet. *Nero* 34.1–4, cf. 39.3. Tacitus presents her downfall as due to Poppaea's jealousy, but he and Suetonius highly sexualize her attempts to retain influence over her son in 54: Ginsburg 2006, 120–21. Flower 2011, 189–94 discusses her death and possible *damnatio memoriae*.

116. Marshall 1990b, 353, case #32.

117. She was granddaughter of Livia, grandniece of Augustus, granddaughter of Mark Antony, and niece and daughter-in-law of Tiberius. She appears in the *SCPP*, where she and her mother Antonia are said not to belong to the house (*gens Iulia*) of Julia Augusta and Tiberius: *etiam si non contingere(n)t domum eorum* (143–44). See Ch. 3.

118. See, e.g., Lott 2012, 347.

119. As Tacitus puts it in the tired cliché, *neque femina amissa pudicitia alia abnuerit*, "once having lost her virtue, a woman will refuse nothing else" (*Ann.* 4.3; see 4.10). Flower 2011, 171–82 provides a nuanced discussion of the evidence.

74 IMPERIAL WOMEN OF ROME

refused Sejanus' request to marry her in 25 (Tac. *Ann.* 4.39–40). When Sejanus was denounced and killed in 31, his former wife Apicata implicated Livilla in his crimes. Livilla was punished in the imperial palace, either by Tiberius or her own mother Antonia the Younger (Cass. Dio 58.11.6–7, cf. 57.22.4). The scandalized sources mention no official trial, much less any specific charges, although Livilla suffered a *damnatio memoriae* (Tac. *Ann.* 6.2.1).[120] The sordid tale—whatever its credibility—unmistakably sets an imperial woman's illicit sexuality in political contexts.[121]

Messalina provides the second instance. Tacitus' lurid presentation of her downfall in the *Annals* (11.26–38) is just one of the censorious literary damnations of this woman whom Juvenal dubbed "the prostitute empress" (*meretrix Augusta*, 6.118). The granddaughter of Octavia and grandniece of Augustus, Messalina married Claudius in 38 CE when she was some fourteen years old and he, twice married before, was forty-seven. The marriage, linking the Julian and Claudian branches of the imperial family, resulted in two children, Octavia (b. ~39/40) and Britannicus (b. 41), the first male child born to a ruling emperor. For whatever reason—the ancient sources credit lasciviousness as well as savagery and greed—Messalina began an open affair with Gaius Silius, the designated consul of 48. That year the two even celebrated a marriage with a witnessed contract, celebratory dinner, and "wedding night" in Rome while Claudius was in Ostia. Tacitus portrays the whole with political touches as well as moral outrage. When Claudius' freedmen broke the news to the emperor, they threatened, "If you don't act quickly, her husband holds Rome," and Claudius' shocked reaction included his repeated doubts that he still controlled the empire (see also Cass. Dio 60.31.5). The freedmen, it was later said, pushed Claudius to execute Messalina without a trial (see Suet. *Claud.* 26), so we can never know the charges.[122] In their censorious focus on Messalina's uncontrolled sexuality, Tacitus, Suetonius, and Cassius

---

120. Despite terms associated with trials and punishments in some references (*poena*, in *Octavia* 941–43; *flagitiis . . . punitis*, Tac. *Ann.* 6.2.1), Marshall 1990b, 353 persuasively holds that no senatorial trial took place; rather she was tried before the emperor's tribunal or domestically (see Suet. *Tib.* 62.1). Flower 2011, 175 notes this as the first sanctioning by the senate of a Julio-Claudian, and probably the first of any Roman woman.

121. Syme 1986, 171 has her commit suicide, and doubts her complicity. Charges of adultery with Livilla later spread: Mamercus Aemilius Scaurus was indicted in 34 for adultery with Livilla and sorcery (Tac. *Ann.* 6.29.4–7; Cass. Dio 58.24.2–3; cf. Suet. *Tib.* 61.3; Sen. *Suas.* 2.22, mentioning *maiestas* alone). See Marshall 1990b, 354, case #36.

122. Domitia Lepida, who in pity had joined her daughter Messalina when she retreated to Lucullus' Gardens, took her daughter's corpse for burial (Tac. *Ann.* 11.37–38).

Crimes and Punishments of Imperial Women

Dio occlude political motivations, rendering murkier the charge of treason.[123] Sanctions against Messalina's memory (Tac. *Ann.* 11.38.3), however, reveal the woman's political importance.[124] In any case, the record of Messalina's downfall emphasizes the impossibility of distinguishing imperial women's sexuality from politics.

The last and most pitiful case is that of (Claudia) Octavia, the daughter of Claudius and Messalina, in 62.[125] Betrothed in 49 to Nero when the eleven-year-old became her stepbrother and she was nine or ten, a further symbol of the ties of Claudius to the Julian Agrippina, Octavia married Nero in 53, the year before he became emperor. By 62 he divorced her so he could marry his mistress Poppaea, but since Poppaea reportedly resented and feared popular support for Octavia, the younger woman was killed on charges that included adultery, abortion, and treason for soliciting the fleet to support her rather than the emperor (Tac. *Ann.* 14.60–64). No trial is reported, and Tacitus indicates that all the charges were implausible fabrications. Yet Nero suffered no repercussions, just as he had survived the obviously illegal murder of his mother Agrippina in 59. Such cases chart his growing autocracy and "freedom" from laws and controls (see, e.g., Tac. *Ann.* 14.13.2). Octavia's tragic history, dramatized in the only complete historical drama to survive from Rome, underscores the perils of belonging to the imperial family despite individual innocence and purity.[126]

No imperial women after the Julio-Claudians are known to have been tried in a public court, although the literary sources incriminate a number on various charges and insinuations. Despite the stories with which this chapter began, Domitia Longina never underwent a public trial for adultery or treason. The Historia Augusta and other sources besmirch Faustina the Younger's reputation with rumors of promiscuity including Commodus' bastard descent from a gladiator, and her alleged participation in the revolt of Avidius Cassius (e.g., HA, *Marc.* 19.2–5, *Ver.* 10.1–2, *Comm.* 8.1; HA, *Marc.* 24.6–7; Cass. Dio 71.22.3; see Ch.

---

123. Tacitus' extended treatment (*Ann.* 11.26–38, with some background at 11.12) includes that two of Claudius' concubines helped convince him of Messalina's infidelity. See also Juv. 10.329–45; Suet. *Claud.* 26.2, 29.3, 36, 39.1; Cass. Dio 60.31.1–5.

124. Flower 2011, 182–89. Most modern scholars see politics as driving Messalina's liaison with Silius: e.g., Bauman 1992, 167–68; Fagan 2002, 575–79; Levick 2015, 73–75. F. Cenerini in *Claudio imperatore* 2019, 22–23 briefly surveys various political interpretations of the events.

125. Marshall 1990b, 354.

126. Emphasized in Tacitus, when a servant of Octavia avows under torture that Octavia's womanly parts were purer than Tigellinus' mouth (*castiora muliebria*: *Ann.* 14.60). For "Octavia," now agreed as post-Senecan, post-Neronian, and probably early Vespasianic, see, e.g., Boyle 2008, esp. xiii–xvi.

IMPERIAL WOMEN OF ROME

3). Nonetheless, she was never divorced, tried, or punished in any way. Lucilla, Commodus' older sister, is implicated in a conspiracy that resulted in her exile to Capri early in her brother's reign.[127] Cassius Dio insults her as "no more modest or chaste than her brother Commodus" and incriminates her sexually by naming a lover among the senatorial conspirators, but no actual charge or trial is noted (Cass. Dio 73.4.4–6; Hdn. 1.8.3–6, 8; HA, *Comm.* 4.1–4).[128] Bruttia Crispina, Lucilla's sister-in-law and Commodus' wife, was similarly exiled by Commodus, apparently for adultery (Cass. Dio 73.4.6; HA, *Comm.* 5.9). Crispina's downfall is murkier even than Lucilla's;[129] more important for my purpose here is that no trial is mentioned.

Severan imperial women, too, reportedly acted against the law, were penalized, or both. While charting the growing influence and licentiousness of the praetorian prefect Gaius Fulvius Plautianus in the early third century, Cassius Dio reports that Plautianus criticized Julia Domna violently to her husband Septimius Severus and collected "details" about her, even torturing women of the nobility for information (76.15.6, cf. 78.24.1).[130] Taken together with a generalized statement in the Historia Augusta—that Severus faithfully retained his wife although she was notorious for adulteries and even charged with conspiracy (HA, *Sev.* 18.8)—Cassius Dio's account has been construed as attesting that Plautianus charged Domna for adultery or treason.[131] In light of Domna's continued high status in the imperial court,[132] however, not to mention the illegality of torturing elite women, the report surely is vilification of Plautianus as well as of an imperial woman.[133] Plautianus' daughter Publia Fulvia Plautilla, who had been married unhappily to Caracalla since 202, was simply banished—without a trial—by Septimius Severus at her father's downfall in 205 (Cass. Dio 77.6.3,

---

127. Hekster 2002, 52–54 analyzes this conspiracy.

128. Cassius Dio holds that she wanted to destroy her colluding but despised husband, Tiberius Claudius Pompeianus; Herodian cites as motive Lucilla's jealousy of Commodus' new wife Crispina in the front imperial seat Lucilla had enjoyed at the theaters; the HA cites only her disgust at Commodus' desire to destroy the senate and his "lifestyle." HA, *Comm.* 5.7 has Commodus himself send Lucilla to Capri, and kill her there. Hekster 2002, 53 dismisses Lucilla's asserted liaisons as standard denigration of powerful women.

129. Hekster 2002, 72 n.181 surveys the evidence, plausibly suggesting a date of 191/192.

130. Levick 2007, 33, 76: ca. 202–204 CE.

131. Charged with adultery, e.g., Williams 1902, 268 and Langford 2013, 11; with treason, Levick 2007, 76, who doubts the charge of adultery (see also Levick 2007, 33).

132. Julia Domna was not implicated in Geta's "plot" of 211 (Levick 2007, 89–90).

133. Perhaps also of Septimius Severus: Langford 2013, 41–42. But see Levick 2007, 33.

Crimes and Punishments of Imperial Women

78.1.1; Hdn. 3.13.2; more later); when Caracalla gained sole rule in 211 he had her killed.[134] Finally, Sallustia Orbiana, the wife of Severus Alexander, is said to have been exiled to Libya by her jealous mother-in-law, Julia Mamaea. No other details are known (Hdn. 6.1.9–10).[135]

The apparently arbitrary exiles and deaths of imperial women in the later second and the third century, just as the brutal ends of Julia Soaemias and Julia Mamaea we discuss in the next section, evoke the principate's growing autocracy.[136] Although many first-century cases, especially in the later Julio-Claudian period, are attributed to the jealousy and greed of imperial women themselves, in the later period all but one sentence are due to the emperors. Messalina and Agrippina are portrayed as malevolently influencing Rome's legal system;[137] later imperial women appear as the victims of injustice. Some early cases involving imperial women were judged domestically by the emperor and his family, notably the two Julias and Livilla, probably to emphasize continuity with Republican customs. After the Julio-Claudian period, however, judgment of imperial women "at home" rather than in a public court reinforces the distinction of the *domus Augusta* from the rest of Roman society, something we discuss in the following chapter. In any case, the domestic "trials" of Domitia Longina and other imperial women who never came to trial despite criminal charges (the third category of Table 2.1) are obscure and filled with allegations and calumny. Four of these women, Julia Titi (#17), Domitia Longina (#18), Faustina the Younger (#19), and Julia Domna (#22), apparently escaped the criminal imputations swirling around them. The other eight were punished without the chance to face their accusers or defend themselves in a public trial. We will never know their innocence or guilt.

Imperial women clearly were not above the law, and they do not appear to have enjoyed such impunity. Their lack of special legal status is reflected in the conflicting distinction of their statues in comparison to statues of emperors. An individual's refuge to statues of emperors and *divi*, just as to emperors themselves, could convey asylum, protection from criminal proceedings. Starting at the latest in the Augustan period, an image of the emperor could provide asylum to someone accused. Bauman has explored the various references to this right of asylum, noting that during the Tiberian period the matter was discussed

---

134. See also Hdn. 3.13.3; HA, *M. Ant.* 1.8. Plautilla's brother was banished with her.

135. Julia Mamaea had no power to exile anyone. "Libya" is Africa.

136. Marcus Aurelius' virtuous clemency is signaled by his refusal to act on gossip about Faustina the Younger: HA, *Marc.* 26.5–6.

137. See too Tacitus' acerbic presentation of Julia Augusta and Urgulania and Piso (Ch. 1).

in the senate in 21 CE and was otherwise conspicuous.[138] There existed both "immovable" and "portable" asylum: "immovable" asylum aided someone fleeing to a shrine or immovable statue, and "portable" asylum protected someone grasping or brandishing a moveable object such as a statuette, medallion, or coin.[139] In both cases an image of the ruling emperor was as effective as one of a *divus*.[140] A related legal matter was that destruction or disrespect of a consecrated imperial statue was covered under the Julian Law about treason (*lex Iulia de maiestate*). Such punishable desecration included melting down or selling a consecrated statue.[141] Despite the variety of literary and juristic sources for asylum *ad statuam* and for questions concerning criminally treasonable handling of imperial statues, however, nothing suggests such special power or standing for statues or shrines of imperial women, whether the woman was deified or still alive in the court.[142] The contrast underscores the lesser status of imperial women in the law.

Imperial women's fates at emperors' deaths

In a fictional discussion Cassius Dio presents between Augustus and his wife, Livia states, "I have an equal share in your blessings and your ills, and as long as you are safe I also have my part in reigning, but if you come to any harm, (Heaven forbid!), I will perish with you" (55.16.2). This platitude expresses more than the exemplary concord of the first princeps and his wife, and more than the concept of a demure "power behind the throne." Livia's anticipated violent demise with her husband exposes the predicament of imperial women when "their" emperor died. Underlying the history of Domitia Augusta, the question is the more serious because of two fundamental facts of the principate. First is that the

---

138. See Tac. *Ann.* 3.36, 3.63.3, 4.67.6; Suet. *Tib.* 53.2, 58; Bauman 1974, 85–92, followed by later authors such as Ando 2000, 369–70. Gamauf 1999, 27 collects sources, e.g., Cass. Dio 57.12.

139. Bauman 1974, 87.

140. Bauman 1974, 71–85; Wallace-Hadrill 1986, 73. Bauman 1974, 90–92 assumes that a *senatus consultum* of 29 CE abolished the right of immovable asylum but that portable asylum continued.

141. Gamauf 1999, 32–38; Bauman 1974, 81–85; Price 1984, 191–206. Tiberius repeatedly tried to quash accusations tied to desecration of a statue: Tac. *Ann.* 1.73, 3.70. Suet. *Tib.* 58 alleges that it became a capital charge to take into a latrine or brothel Tiberius' effigy on a coin or a ring. Sen. *Ben.* 3.26 tells of a man who was almost indicted for using a chamber pot while wearing a ring with Tiberius' image.

142. References in the section of the Digest pertinent to treason and statues specify *caesaris* or *imperatoris* (48.4.4.1–48.4.6), implicitly excluding statues and images of imperial women.

Crimes and Punishments of Imperial Women

principate, which was never a constitutional monarchy, nevertheless had ever stronger familial and dynastic elements. Second is that imperial Rome lacked legal and constitutional means to rid itself peacefully of an inept, corrupt, harmful, or insane princeps.[143]

Historical patterns for the fates of imperial women at an emperor's death are hard to discern. The many emperors unmarried at their deaths include Tiberius, Galba, Otho, Vespasian, Titus, Nerva, Antoninus Pius, Commodus, Caracalla, and Severus Alexander, as well as Hadrian and Marcus Aurelius, both recently widowed.[144] If an emperor died more or less peacefully after having clearly indicated a successor, whether a birth son or adopted, the empress continued in the court. Livia, Agrippina the Younger, and Julia Domna, imperial wives whose sons succeeded their husbands, have often been called "dowager empresses," a term commonly designating a widow with a title, status, or property derived from her late husband. In Rome, however, their position had no constitutional basis (Ch. 1).[145]

Other imperial women continued in the court, especially in the second and third centuries. The women of Trajan's family continued close to Hadrian, facilitated by the marriage of Trajan's grand-niece Sabina to Hadrian around 100, and Hadrian was markedly respectful toward both his mother-in-law Matidia the Elder who was Trajan's niece, and his adoptive mother Plotina who was Trajan's wife.[146] Indeed, Plotina's close ties with Hadrian contributed to the rumors of *favor Plotinae* in his accession (Ch. 1).[147] Faustina the Younger, the daughter of Antoninus Pius, had been married to Marcus Aurelius some sixteen years when her father died in 161 and Marcus Aurelius and Lucius Verus became joint emperors. Lucilla, married after 169 to her second husband Tiberius Claudius Pompeianus, was still considered part of the imperial court when she "conspired" against her brother Commodus early in his reign (see earlier).

---

143. The timing of an emperor's designation as *hostis publicus* and his assassination is not always clear. From my period Nero (Suet. *Nero*. 49.2), Commodus, Pescennius Niger, Clodius Albinus, Geta, and Macrinus and his son were each charged as *hostis*: Varner 2001, 42.

144. I do not here treat contenders from civil strife in 193 and 217–218.

145. Agrippina's role with Nero, only sixteen when he came to the throne, might have seemed more "natural": Corbier 1995, 187–90. All three sons became estranged from their mothers.

146. See Ch. 1, Ch. 3, and the dossier of Plotina to the Epicureans in Athens discussed in my Ch. 5.

147. Hadrian's distant ties to Trajan were considered trivial in Trajan's choice of him as successor: Birley 1997, 75–76. For Matidia the Younger and the imperial house, see Ch. 6.

Less peaceful transitions endangered imperial women, perhaps seen as proxies or deemed responsible for the offenses of a hated emperor.[148] Milonia Caesonia, the wife of Caligula when he became the first assassinated emperor in 41, was butchered together with their baby daughter Julia Drusilla after her husband's murder. Josephus reports the conspirators' debate over her innocence or complicity in Caligula's misdeeds, concluding with a story that she had made him insane (*AJ* 19.2.4).[149] On the other hand, Statilia Messalina, Nero's wife of some two years, outlived her imperial husband's ignominious fall in 68.[150] As we saw at the beginning of this chapter, Domitia Longina survived the assassination of Domitian; perhaps her alleged complicity in the plot helped insulate her from Domitian's misdeeds.

Two later imperial women were not so fortunate. Julia Soaemias, the mother of Elagabalus and notorious for interfering in the senate, was murdered with her son in the praetorian camp in Rome in 222. Her body was defiled like his (see Ch. 7).[151] Her sister Julia Mamaea, the mother of Elagabalus' successor Severus Alexander and equally reviled for co-ruling with her son,[152] was cut down in 235 with her son by disaffected Roman troops near Mogontiacum (now Mainz, Germany; see Ch. 7).[153] These two imperial mothers thus were "punished" together with their insane or maladroit sons and emperors.

The common identification of imperial women with the emperor is suggested by an intriguing dedication for the safety and welfare of Marcus Aurelius, his son Commodus, and Commodus' wife Bruttia Crispina from Sabratha (now Sabratah,

---

148. *Octavia* 863–66, as interpreted by Bauman 1996, 89–90 (with Tac. *Ann.* 6.10), questions whether women could actually be charged as *hostes publicae* (see Varner 2001, 42–44).

149. Josephus' passage ends with Caesonia volunteering her throat to the assassin, much as the later Agrippina the Younger is said to have offered her womb to her murderer (Tac. *Ann.* 14.8; Cass. Dio 61.13.5). Suetonius holds that Caesonia had earlier been paraded in military costume to the troops by Caligula: *Calig.* 25.3. Lollia Paulina, Caligula's previous (third) wife, survived his assassination in 41, perhaps because she had been divorced two years earlier: see above.

150. Her close identity with Nero is suggested by the pro-Neronian Otho's intention to marry her: Suet. *Otho* 10.3. In 69 Vitellius' wife Galeria Fundana outlived the violent death of her husband, although their son was killed; she was called markedly virtuous (Tac. *Hist.* 2.64) and oversaw Vitellius' funeral. Their young daughter, also spared, became an example of Vespasian's clemency (Suet. *Vesp.* 14.1). See FOS #399 and #817.

151. For the brutal death of Julia Soaemias, which included decapitation, see HA, *Heliogab.* 18.2–3; Cass. Dio 80.20.2; Hdn. 5.8.8–10. See also Kettenhoffen 1979, 151–53 and Varner 2001, 49 for her erased inscriptions and *damnatio*.

152. HA, *Alex. Sev.* 14.7, 60.2; Hdn. 5.8.8–10, 6.1.1, 6.1.5, 6.1.10, noting also his submissiveness to his grandmother Julia Maesa.

153. HA, *Alex. Sev.* 59.6, 60.2, 63.5; HA, *Max.* 7.4; Hdn. 6.9.6–8.

Libya).[154] Lines 4–6 once held the names of Commodus and Crispina, and the inscription must have been installed between Crispina's marriage to Commodus around 178 and Marcus Aurelius' death in 180. The names of Commodus and Crispina were chiseled out, surely at Commodus' fall and *damnatio memoriae* after 192. Crispina's memory was as affected as that of Commodus, even though he had already charged her with adultery, divorced her, and had her killed (see Table 2.1, #21).[155] The rage against her name, so at odds with her personal history, suggests that by this time imperial women were completely identified with their emperors. Especially outside Rome, the women had little or no independent image. It is a startling contrast with the afterlife of Domitia Longina in Italy represented by her brickyards and honorary shrine in Gabii.

Conclusion

Perhaps more than other chapters in this book, this one reveals imperial women's limits and constraints. Rome's enduring values, reflected in laws and customs reinforced under Augustus, ensured little or no agency for even these most highly placed women. Their proximity to the princeps gave them no license, rights, or powers. Ulpian makes clear that any privileges they might enjoy were at the emperor's whim (Ulp. 13, ad l. iul. et pap., Dig. 1.3.31).[156]

Instead, inclusion in the imperial family brought women greater liability. Admittedly, ancient sources are more attentive to imperial than to other women; nonetheless, the crimes and punishments we have surveyed are strikingly insistent. Should we presume that imperial women had a higher criminal propensity? As others, they were liable to the charges of adultery and other nonnormative female sexuality criminalized by Augustan legislation. Their exalted position, however, enhanced the potential for scandal that would include gossip of a political nature

---

154. *CIL* VIII 22689 = EDCS-24100029: *[Do]minae Caelesti / [pro] salute Imp«[[p(eratorum)]]» / [M(arci) A]ureli Antonini «[[et]]» / «[[M(arci) Aureli Commodo(!)]]» / Aug«[[g(ustorum)]]» [[[e]t [Brutt]i[ae]]] / [[C[rispinae Aug(ustae)]]] / L(ucius) Aemilius Calpurni / anus Muse et Mucia / Pudentilla eius / ob honorem / L(uci) Aemili Muciani et / Q(uinti) Aemili Augurini / quondam filiorum / piissimorum d(onum) d(ederunt)*, originally reading "To Mistress Caelestis, for the health and safety of the emperors Marcus Aurelius and Commodus, Augusti, and of Bruttia Crispina Augusta. Lucius Aemilius Calpurianus Muse and his wife Mucia Pudentilla, on the occasion of honor of Lucius Aemilius Mucianus and Quintus Aemilius Augurinus, their most pious sons, gave this gift."

155. See Alföldy 1998, 43–44, and Hekster 2002, 72 n.181.

156. This is exemplified in another excerpt from Ulpian, in Dig. 1.9.12 pr. Imperial women apparently had financial autonomy, perhaps connected with the *ius trium liberorum* and thus shared with other women and men (see Ch. 1).

(see, e.g., Tac. *Ann.* 2.50, 3.24.1–3). Were they unfairly penalized by the overly high expectations famously averred by Julius Caesar, that his wife and family should be above suspicion?[157] The murkiness of most cases, worsened by the fact that most imperial women never faced a public trial, means we are left with only rumors and scandalous innuendoes. Nonetheless and especially during the Julio-Claudian period imperial women demonstrated usefully, for Rome's new rule of law in the principate, that the emperor and his family were not above the law.

---

157. Plut. *Caes.* 10.9; Suet. *Caes.* 74.

3

Imperial Women within the Imperial Family

Introduction: Faustina the Younger, model imperial woman?

Faustina the Younger has the singularity of being the daughter, wife, mother-in-law, and mother of Roman emperors. In 147 this Faustina, the daughter of the reigning emperor Antoninus Pius, was honored with the title *Augusta* when—two years into her marriage—she bore her first child to Marcus Aurelius, one of Pius' designated successors. She was then about seventeen, the only surviving child born to Pius and Faustina the Elder before Pius became emperor in 138 and her mother died in 140.[1] As a girl Faustina the Younger was engaged to Lucius Verus (HA, *Ael.* 6.9), the son of the man Hadrian had designated in late 136 as his own son and successor. After Verus' father died Hadrian adopted early in 138 Faustina's father Antoninus, who in turn adopted Marcus Aurelius and Lucius Verus (then about seventeen and seven years old, respectively) and betrothed his daughter, then perhaps eight, to Marcus Aurelius. In 145, when Faustina was about fifteen, she wed Marcus in a celebrated marriage, so that when Pius died in 161 and Marcus Aurelius and Lucius Verus became co-rulers, Faustina became the wife of one of the emperors. Her daughter Lucilla was betrothed to the other co-emperor Lucius Verus, to marry him in 164.[2] Two years after Faustina's death

---

1. See Levick 2014, 22–23, 61–63 for the connections of her elite family from Narbonensis and Baetica (modern southwestern France and southern Spain); Levick 2014, 13: birth in 130 is calculated from the dates of her marriage (145) and her last known childbirth (170; see n.8 in this chapter), but since Roman women could marry as early as twelve it could have been 131 or 132.

2. See Levick 2014, 47–53 for references. Lucilla, the second daughter of Faustina and Marcus, was born around 149.

84   IMPERIAL WOMEN OF ROME

in 175 her oldest surviving son Commodus became co-emperor with his father Marcus, to rule as sole emperor after Marcus' death in 180. Women's importance to the dynastic setup of the principate could not be clearer.[3]

Faustina the Younger lived no fairy-tale life, however. While still a child she lost a sister, two brothers, and her mother in the span of some five years, from ca. 134 to 140—that is, from when she was about five to ten years old.[4] From her immediate family remained only her father, who never remarried. We do not know if his concubine, the freedwoman Galeria Lysistrate discussed at the end of this chapter, helped nurture his sole surviving child.[5] Faustina surely had the best care money could buy, although nothing explicitly documents her nurses or other childhood attendants.[6] Her family's high mortality was not uncommon in Rome, but we know less about Roman childhood than we would like even for elite children like Faustina the Younger.[7]

Faustina the Younger bore thirteen or even fifteen children to Marcus Aurelius in some twenty-three years, from 30 November 147 when she presumably was seventeen, through 170 when she was forty.[8] She had eleven or more live births, including two sets of twins. At most six children, four females and two males, seem to have been still alive when Faustina the Younger died in 175: Lucilla, born 7 March 148/150 and dead in 182 (see Ch. 2); Annia Galeria Aurelia Faustina, born 150/151 and alive in 180; Fadilla, born in 159 and alive after 192; Cornificia, born August 160 and dead in 212; Commodus, born 31 August 161 as the twin of Titus Aurelius Fulvus Antoninus, who died age four or five; and possibly

---

3. For her dynastic importance see Hdn. 1.7.4: Commodus had "imperial ancestry through three generations of distinguished Romans; his father's family tree included a number of distinguished senators; his mother, the empress Faustina, was the daughter of Antoninus Pius, the granddaughter of Hadrian on her mother's side, and traced her ancestry to Trajan, her great-grandfather." Levick 2014, 87–89 notes the somewhat uncertain date of Faustina's death.

4. Levick 2014, 61 and Beckmann 2012a, 3, referring to the *Fasti Ostienses*, argue for Faustina the Elder's death at the end of October 140.

5. Stressing his own sexual self-restraint Marcus Aurelius thanks the gods that he was not brought up with his grandfather's concubine (*Med.* 1.17.2).

6. The small and fragmentary *CIL* VI 8941, cfr. p. 3463 = EDCS-18900008 (Rome), with a *t.p.q.* of Faustina the Elder's consecration in 140, records a nurse/wet-nurse of *diva* Faustina (*nutrix [divae F]austinae*) who lived thirty years.

7. See Laes and Vuolanto 2017.

8. The evidence includes coin imagery such as the nine portrait types of Faustina (Fittschen 1982), letters of Faustina's contemporary Fronto, the Historia Augusta, and the Exedra of Herodes Atticus at Olympia (Bol 1984); Levick 2014, 115–18 discusses the various hypotheses, relying on Ameling 1992, 161, and Birley 1993, 247–48. For my purposes the exact number and names of Faustina the Younger's children are not important.

Marcus Annius Verus, born toward the end of 162 and still alive after Lucilla's marriage to Lucius Verus in 164.[9] The birth and loss of so many children must have been physically and emotionally draining for their mother, but no such personal information survives for Faustina.[10] Much more clear is the high number of her births overall, and her own pivotal position in the transmission of Rome's imperial power.

Indeed, Faustina the Younger is essential to the history of the Antonine age, the mid-second century that is traditionally seen as the principate's high point, and she was central to the ideal of the imperial family that dominated this era. Nevertheless, she has a contested reputation we explore at the end of this chapter. Her history and reputation emphasize that for most of the principate any one woman was but a cipher and pawn in the imperial family, despite that family's undeniable significance in the Roman world. In the Severan period a series of unusually visible imperial women became active in the midst of new demographic and political conditions in Rome and elsewhere. Yet the rapid turnover of emperors in the succeeding era undermined the stability and prominence of such women and the imperial family itself. This chapter explores the imperial *domus*—house, household, family—and women's roles within it from Augustus through the Severans. As we see here, that *domus* was a cornerstone of the principate.

The importance to the principate of the family and the imperial family

The first princeps, Augustus, made Roman population issues and "the Roman family" a priority at the latest from the middle years of his rule.[11] The evidence is manifold. Suetonius notes that the first emperor read aloud and publicized for Senate and People alike an earlier oration by Quintus Metellus on increasing the

---

9. For Lucilla, see also Ch. 2. Levick 2014, 112–18 refers to ancient and modern sources. For those not in my Appendix 1: Annia Galeria Aurelia Faustina, FOS #61; *PIR*[2] A 707; Levick 2014, 116 #5, notes that FOS takes her to be the eldest daughter, born 30 November 147; Fadilla, FOS #356, *PIR*[2] F 96; Cornificia, FOS #294, *PIR*[2] C 1505; and M. Annius Verus, *PIR*[2] A 698.

10. In contrast to a few other celebrated losses. The (probably Tiberian) *Consolatio ad Liviam* speaks to the anguish of Livia when her adult son Drusus died in 9 BCE; Fronto bewails the deaths in infancy of his oldest five children and first grandson (*de nepote amisso* 2.1, 10); Quintilian laments two sons who died ages six and ten (*I.O.* 6.13); and Pliny the Younger grieved when his wife Calpurnia miscarried their first child (*Ep.* 8.10).

11. Severy 2003 argues convincingly for a lower and more detailed chronology than had most.

86   IMPERIAL WOMEN OF ROME

birth rate (*de prole augenda*: *Aug.* 89).[12] A summary of Livy's Book 59 gives more detail:

> Quintus Metellus, as censor, proposed that everybody should be compelled to marry for the sake of generating children. His speech is preserved, and when discussing the marriages of the orders Augustus Caesar read it out in the senate as if it were written for these very days. (*Per.* 59, covering 133–127 BCE)

A century and a half later than Livy, Aulus Gellius paraphrased part of Metellus' speech, which advocated thinking for the future of the Roman race and family rather than for immediate sexual satisfaction with an enslaved or other unmarried partner:

> If we could live without a wife, all of us would choose to be free from that bother, but since nature has thus decreed that is it possible neither to live easily enough with them nor without them at all, we should take thought for our enduring well-being rather than for the pleasure of the moment. (Gell. *NA* 1.6)[13]

Although Gellius' larger exposition critiques Metellus' dour severity, the speech fits the overall presentation of women by Gellius and other Roman authors: contemporary women are troublesome, expensive, and nagging, especially in comparison to Rome's legendary women.[14] The speech is directed to men, as are the critiques Gellius provides. We see women similarly elided in the instances of imperial concern with family.

The exhortations of the second-century Metellus, seconded by Cicero's recommendations that a censor should prohibit celibacy and Julius Caesar should look to increasing the birth rate (*Leg.* 3.3.7; *pro Marc.* 23), show that apprehension about Rome's birth rate was nothing new in Rome. Unease was well warranted in the absence of modern medicine and understandings of hygiene and nutrition. Throughout its history Rome was characterized both by markedly high mortality

---

12. Langlands 2014 explores Suetonius' presentation of Augustus' attention to the family within the context of exemplarity.

13. Aulus Gellius wrongly credits Metellus Numidicus with the speech he refers to as *de ducendis uxoribus* and *ad matrimonia capessenda*. The Metelli seem to have been particularly associated with natalism: see n. 24 in this chapter.

14. See Holford-Strevens 2003, 206, 308.

Imperial Women within the Imperial Family 87

rates, especially for newborns and young children, and by generally high levels of fertility.[15] One in three children died in the first year of life, many from diarrheal illnesses, and one in two children died before they reached the age of ten. Since only half of children born would survive childhood, women had to give birth five to six times for Rome's population rate to remain steady.[16] For those lucky enough to reach the age of ten, life expectancy extended another thirty-five to forty years; a forty-year-old might well live an additional twenty years.[17] This pattern of high infant mortality and a noticeably short life expectancy characterized Rome in the Republic and the Empire, extending to elite Romans with access to the best food, medicine, water, and care: the emperors, senators, and city councilors whose lives are most fully documented.[18]

How women actively understood and participated in these concerns is less known, especially for the Republican period.[19] Most apparently complied readily with the norms: marriage in their teens, and multiple anticipated births to their lawful husband.[20] There were no respectable roles other than wife and mother, and no safe contraception or abortion.[21] Roman women had very little control over their own fertility or the survival of their infants. It seems as though there was a general desire *not* to limit family size.[22] The continuing praise of *univirae*,

---

15. The following is based on Parkin and Pomeroy 2007, 44.

16. Parkin and Pomeroy 2007, 45; Bagnall and Frier 1994, 138–39, 144–45. In this book I discuss only mortality and fertility, not the important demographic factor of migration or the demographic impact of slavery (see Scheidel 2011). In modern developed nations replacement fertility—the level required to maintain a steady population—is ~2.1 or 2.2 births per woman.

17. Parkin and Pomeroy 2007, 44–45: "something like half the population would have been under the age of 25 years at any one time, and only about 7 per cent over the age of 60." Parkin 1992 goes into greater detail, and concludes (84–86) a life expectancy at birth of some twenty-five years.

18. Scheidel 1999, 263.

19. Scheidel 1999, 257 remarks on the dearth of vital statistics for wives and daughters of emperors.

20. Elite women typically married in their mid- to late teens, with men some ten years older: Shaw 1987; Treggiari 1991b, 398–403; Levick 2014, 62. Treggiari 1991b is indispensable for Roman marriage; Dixon 1988, for the Roman mother; Dixon 2016 for summary of Roman law and the family. Pliny *HN* 29.27.85 mentions a contraceptive amulet "to help those women who are so prolific that they stand in need of such a respite."

21. See Prioreschi 1995 and Kapparis 2002, e.g., 117–20 (somewhat uncritical of the ancient medical sources). Evans Grubbs 2002, 202 discusses the legal texts, Dig. 47.11.4 and 48.19.39: abortion was legal but should be decided by the paterfamilias, not the mother. The mother's lesser role is seen also in the law that children of divorce routinely went to their father's house.

22. Frier 1994, 328–29, against Riddle 1992.

88 IMPERIAL WOMEN OF ROME

women who married but once, as Antonia the Younger and purportedly Matidia the Elder, is at odds with this pro-natalist stance but reveals the significance of controlling women's sexuality.[23] Large families were praised in general,[24] and a few women are lauded for their fecundity.[25] Agrippina the Elder, for example, receives accolades in the *SCPP* of 20 CE for her many children with Germanicus who were still alive.[26] The anxiety about women's control over their own bodies and fertility expressed particularly in the early second century CE by Tacitus, Juvenal, and Favorinus may reflect the childlessness of the emperors Nerva, Trajan, and Hadrian, if it is not simply a literary trope.[27]

Nonetheless, we should not envision that most Roman marriages resembled that of Faustina the Younger and Marcus Aurelius, whose health and marital harmony resulted in at least a dozen infants in their thirty-year marriage. Generally short life expectancy, not infrequent divorce, maternal mortality,[28] and the common age gap of some ten years resulted in many elite Roman families being "blended" by serial marriages and stepchildren.[29] For imperial families, as is clear from Ch. 2 and the imperial genealogical trees in Appendix 2, this was the common pattern for the Julio-Claudians but much less notable thereafter.

What Augustus brought to long-standing concerns with Rome's birth rate was his growing authority and exemplarity. When visiting (presumably Italian) regions, he gave out a thousand sesterces for each child to ordinary people who showed him proof of sons and daughters (Suet. *Aug.* 46). In more personal

---

23. Antonia *univira* in the *SCPP* (ll. 140–42); Matidia the Elder remained chaste after her first marriage although in her prime (Hadrian's encomium, *CIL* XIV 3579 = EDCS-04800013, l. 23). For *univira*, see Lightman and Zeisel 1977; Treggiari 1991b, 232–37; Lott 2012, 302–3.

24. One of Rome's earliest funeral speeches, of Lucius Caecilius Metellus (d. 247 BCE), praises him for achieving, among the ten greatest things a wise man desires: "to leave many children" (no wife is noted; Plin. *HN* 7.139; cf. Cic. *de Or.* 3.3.12, *ad Fam.* 4.5.5.1).

25. Cornelia bore to her husband Tiberius Sempronius Gracchus twelve children, although only Tiberius, Gaius, and Sempronia reached adulthood: Plut. *Ti. Gracch.* 1.5.

26. line 139: *tot pignora edita partu felicissumo eorum, qui superessent.* These were six of the nine she had birthed: see Suet. *Calig.* 7; Tac. *Ann.* 2.71.4; Lindsay 1995.

27. Juv. 6.592–600; Tac. *Germ.* 19.5; Gell. *NA* 12.1; Treggiari 1991b, 407–9 on the tendentious stereotypes. Frier 1994, 331–33: most women linked with these topics are in nonmarital relationships (e.g., Ov. *Fast.* 1.623–24, *Am.* 2.14.3–4).

28. See French 1986; Todman 2007 (suggesting, from later comparative evidence, twenty-five deaths per thousand births); Carroll and Graham 2014, 17.

29. Bradley 1991, 125–76; Cantarella 1992, 106–107. Extended absences, usual for senators and equestrians, may have depressed fecundity, but Aulus Caecina Severus boasted in a senatorial debate of 21 that his wife, who never left Italy, bore him six children despite his forty terms of service in the provinces (Tac. *Ann.* 3.33; see also Ch. 7). I discuss the ideal of *univirae* below.

Imperial Women within the Imperial Family

displays he reinforced traditional female roles by showily requiring his daughter and granddaughters to learn spinning and weaving (Suet. *Aug.* 64.2), wearing at home garments reportedly woven and sewn by his sister, wife, daughter, or granddaughters (Suet. *Aug.* 73.1).[30] When his daughter and later his granddaughter "failed" him, he openly mourned them and publicly denounced the two women, and his perhaps disabled grandson Agrippa Postumus, as his "three boils and three ulcers" (Suet. *Aug.* 65.4). The two women fell afoul of his laws on adultery and other family concerns, and we argued in Ch. 2 that Augustus used their punishments to demonstrate that the emperor was not above the law.

Suetonius devotes a chapter of his biography of Augustus to the emperor's laws that, among other topics, concerned "adultery, chastity, and which orders should marry which," noting that the last was so hard to enforce that Augustus had to lessen penalties and increase rewards for compliance (*Aug.* 34, characteristically undated).[31] The biographer adds that as a way to quell criticism and provide an example, Augustus openly gestured at a public show to Germanicus' many children.[32] Cassius Dio reports a speech Augustus gave publicly in the Forum Romanum in 9 CE after being importuned to repeal the social legislation: in this lengthy rendition Augustus urges equestrians to marry and procreate (Cass. Dio 56.1–10). As Augustus' public gesture to Germanicus' children indicated, the laws were for all Romans.[33] The specifics of the laws, now often referred to as the Julian and Papian law, are now almost impossible to disentangle.

The laws were merely part of the growing paternalism of Augustus within the Roman state, for which he employed his own household. His familial authority was epitomized in the conferral to him in 2 BCE of the title *pater patriae* or Father of the Fatherland (see *RGDA* 35).[34] In the senatorial proposal of this title,

---

30. Later Claudius had his children dine with him sitting in old-fashioned style at the ends of the couches on which their parents reclined (Suet. *Claud.* 32).

31. Spagnuolo Vigorita 2010 argues the laws were conceptualized in the early 20s BCE.

32. Simultaneously his own grandchildren (through their mother Agrippina the Elder) and great-grandchildren (through Germanicus, son of his stepson Drusus the Elder). This was an *exemplum*: Suet. *Aug.* 34. Claudius later gauchely repeated the gesture while helping a gladiator after pleas from his four children. Claudius also cancelled Tiberius' supplement to the Papian-Poppaean law that implied men over sixty years old could not beget children (Suet. *Claud.* 21, 23).

33. We do not discuss here Augustus' prohibition of marriage for serving soldiers: see Phang 2001, e.g., 16–17, and passim; also, Ch. 7, this volume.

34. For full discussion of the term, see Alföldi 1971; for its appearance on coins, see Stevenson 2007. Bauman 1967, 235–42 interprets as a constitutional element the title *pater patriae* ("the last of the three great concepts which shaped the majesty of Augustus," p.235). See Barrett

Marcus Valerius Messalla Corvinus linked Augustus' "house" (*domus*) to the state (*res publica*), saying (in Suetonius' report),

> May this [title] be good and prosperous for you and your house, Caesar Augustus! For we think thus that we are praying for the eternal happiness of the state and good things for this [city]: the senate, together with the Roman people, hails you Father of the Fatherland. (Suet. *Aug.* 58.2)[35]

Augustus, his house, and the state were now one. In the *Res Gestae divi Augusti* he proudly notes the census figures for 28 BCE, 8 BCE, and 14 CE—respectively, 4,063,000, 4,233,000, and 4,937,000 citizens—in a chapter that ends with his claim to have "set examples of many types for posterity to imitate" (*RGDA* 8).

The women of his house, however, have a curiously muted presence during his rule. B. Severy has argued that as Augustus worked to restore order and old-fashioned morality after the violent triumviral period, keeping his female relatives out of public was one way to reassert traditional boundaries.[36] Even after women of Augustus' house began to appear publicly in person and on monuments (see Chs. 5 and 6), they were subsumed within the family, not presented as individuals. Their public imaging on coins, reliefs, and sculpture stressed their family roles and the men to whom they were linked.[37] On the Ara Pacis of 13–9 BCE, which is one of the earliest known public depictions of Livia and other imperial women, the few females appear as part of a close-knit family whose similar likenesses confound identifications.[38] (See Ill. 3.1.) Analogously, on what may be the earliest centrally struck coin to depict a historical woman, an Augustan

---

2002, 156–58, and below for the proposed title of "Mater Patriae" for Livia (not until Julia Domna is a woman officially called *mater patriae*).

35. *Quod bonum, inquit, faustumque sit tibi domuique tuae, Caesar Auguste! Sic enim nos perpetuam felicitatem rei publicae et laeta huic [urbi] precari existimamus: senatus te consentiens cum populo Romano consalutat patriae patrem*: see Moreau 2009, 37–38.

36. Severy 2003, 50–61 dates the promotion of women only to around 17 BCE.

37. We saw this in the discussion of the later *SCPP* of 20 CE (Ch. 1).

38. This is true also for the men: e.g., Torelli 1982; Fullerton 1985, 481 (linking the monument with the *gens Iulia* generally and the *domus Augusti* specifically); Brännstedt 2015, 40–41. The monument was commissioned 4 July 13 BCE to celebrate Augustus' return from Spain, and consecrated 30 January 9 BCE (Livia's fiftieth birthday) to honor established peace. In Ill. 3.1 the leftmost woman (turned to the viewer's right) has been identified as Antonia the Younger and as Vipsania (Tiberius' first wife; divorced in 11 BCE); the woman in profile as Antonia the Elder; the woman in shallow relief between them as a daughter of Antonia the Elder.

Imperial Women within the Imperial Family

ILL. 3.1 Part of the south, "historical," frieze of the Ara Pacis, with women and children. Museum of the Ara Pacis, Rome, Italy. Scala/Art Resource, NY. ART114579.

ILL. 3.2 Augustan silver denarius from 13 BCE, whose reverse includes the portrait of a woman often identified as Julia the Elder. © The Trustees of the British Museum.

silver *denarius* of 13 BCE, the woman is unidentified (Ill. 3.2). On the obverse is Augustus, clearly labeled;[39] on the reverse the bust of a woman is found between two busts of men, all looking right. Over the woman's head floats an oak crown. The encircling legend identifies not these individuals but the man responsible for

---

39. *RIC* I², Augustus no. 404: Augustus has a *lituus* behind him, and the legend AVGVSTVS (or, on variants, AVGVSTVS DIVI F).

issuing the coin, Gaius Marius, in one of the last central issues to traditionally display a moneyer's name.[40]

Livia and Octavia do not appear on any central coinage of Augustus,[41] rendering more puzzling this woman on the denarius of 13 BCE. She is usually identified as Augustus' daughter Julia the Elder: she is clearly not a deity, and her hair in the *nodus* style is seen on other women of the early Augustan family.[42] The two flanking male busts are considered by some to represent her sons Gaius and Lucius, adopted by Augustus in 17 BCE, by others Augustus himself and Agrippa, Julia's husband in the year the coin was struck.[43] Although the oak crown above her head suggests the woman's centrality to the transmission of power within the imperial family,[44] visually everything is subsumed under Augustus' authority.

Augustus' emphasis on family, legitimizing his plans for succession and supporting his authority with age-old Roman values including *patria potestas*, was a cornerstone of the principate.[45] His stress is essential for understanding Rome's imperial women. Rome's family emphasis traditionally centered on males, and that continued. In the Augustan and Tiberian periods the earliest oaths of loyalty, fragmentary as many now are, specifically mention only males: Gaius, Lucius, Tiberius, Germanicus, and others (see Ch. 4). But Augustus himself had no natural sons:[46] as the "Julia" coin of 13 BCE shows, it was women who were key to dynastic succession and the longevity of Augustus' authority and fame. Yet

---

40. III VIR C MARIVS TRO(mentina), Gaius Marius (from the voting tribe Tromentina) was one of the three officials for striking coins that year: Wallace-Hadrill 1986, 77–79. Ill. 3.2 is from the British Museum, Mus. # 1921,0612.1. *RIC* I², Augustus no. 403, struck also by Marius, depicts (rev.) Diana with a quiver over her shoulder, who is identified with Julia by some (Fullerton 1985, 475–77, 480; Wallace-Hadrill 1986, 79 n.75); contra Wood 1999, 63–64, 68.

41. Kleiner 1992, 365–66; Hekster 2015, 117. Barrett 2002, 140–41 (among others) doubts Fulvia was depicted on coinage, noting Julia the Elder as the only historical female on Augustus' official coinage (on this coin). Octavia and Cleopatra appear on coins struck in the east by Antony (*RRC* 527/1, 533/3a; 543/1): e.g., Severy 2003, 43 n.39 and Wallace-Hadrill 1986, 75.

42. Wood 1999, 63–69 provides a full discussion. In the *nodus* style a woman's hair is parted into three; the two side parts are brought back into a bun at the nape, and the middle section looped back on itself.

43. See Rose 1997, n.65; contra (e.g.) Hekster 2015, 117. The adult cast of the two male busts does accord poorly with the young ages of Gaius and Lucius in 13 BCE (seven and four years old, respectively).

44. See, e.g., Fantham 2006, 67; Severy 2003, 76–78; Kleiner and Matheson 1996, 57–58 #6; Wood 1999, 67 (oak crown); Fullerton 1985, 473, 480.

45. Severy 2003; Corbier 1995, followed by many others.

46. A point emphasized, e.g., by Corbier 1995, 179–86, 192, and Millar 1993, 11, 16–17.

Imperial Women within the Imperial Family 93

what was important was the principate itself, less so individuals and especially not individual women. In contrast to the few but formidable elite women of the late Republic—individuals like Cornelia, Servilia, and even Fulvia, who apparently acted and made decisions independently—imperial women were not to be seen apart from the emperor and other men of the family. Tiberius' well-known resentment of Julia Augusta's eminence, and Agrippina the Younger's much-criticized and unconventional liberties and visibility, reveal the sharp tensions of the new system. The significance of that new setup, however, can be seen in the spread of special designations for the imperial household, the most famous of which are *domus Augusta* and *domus divina*.[47]

Special designations for the imperial family

Singular terms for Augustus' extended family reveal its distinction from others in the Roman world, and after the demise of the Julio-Claudians such titles continued to be used by imperial families. As with so many changes and concepts of the Augustan era, it is impossible to determine whether the names originated at Augustus' initiative, in the court, or locally.[48] What is clear, however, is that the imperial house or household—no matter how designated—was never legally or constitutionally demarcated.[49]

Designations of Augustus' family including *gens*, a traditional term for a family group, generally peter out after the Julio-Claudian period.[50] *Gens Iulia*, which Augustus headed as Julius Caesar's adopted son, is found on an altar documenting a dedication by the people of Narbo to Augustus, his (unnamed) wife and children, and his *gens*, as well as to the Senate and the People of Rome and others in the Narbonese community, in accordance with a vow made in 11 CE. The dedication specifically includes a woman though not by name,

---

47. For the *domus August(i)ana*, a term appearing from the time of Tiberius into the third century to designate the buildings on the Palatine serving as the imperial residence, see Panciera 2007a.

48. Millar 1993, 3, cf. 6 and 15–16, and Moreau 2009, 39, lean toward the court and various elite families as responsible for developing the idea of the imperial house; Moreau notes the gradual development was evidenced diversely (e.g., the Narbo altar and Corinth inscription mentioned later), showing the lack of central planning. Hurlet 2015, 186 suggests Augustus' agency.

49. Winterling 2009, 79–81.

50. I do not discuss here the "Altar of the Gens Julia in the Area Capitolina," noted on diplomas as the location of their originals in the first century and cited in the Acts of the Arval Brethren (*CIL* VI 2035, line 4, with restoration in *CFA* 00019 = EDCS-21300001): *LTUR* 2.269–70, s.v. "Gens Iulia, ara" (E. La Rocca).

Augustus' wife or *coniunx* (*Imp. Caesari / divi f. Augusto . . . coniugi liberis gentique eius*).[51] *Gens Augusta*, a more unusual term but still derived from traditional ideas of family, is found on a dedication from Carthago (Carthage) of Tiberian or late Augustan/Tiberian date, as well as on one from Corinth that may date to 37 CE.[52]

Tacitus, typically precise when designating the leaders of Rome, refers to the early imperial family in broader terms: *domus Iuliorum Claudiorumque*, and *Claudia et Iulia domus* (Tac. *Hist.* 1.16, *Ann.* 6.8). These terms include cognatic kin, that is relatives the Claudian Livia brought into the family. The family is now designated *domus* or "house"/"household," rather than *gens* or family group.[53] Even earlier Augustus himself had included in his Mausoleum Marcellus, his nephew (Octavia's son) who died in 23, and Agrippa, the husband of his daughter Julia and his own collaborator, who died in 12 BCE, displaying a wide and unusual understanding of family.[54] The idea of Augustus' family was further complicated by his posthumous adoption of Livia, whose transferal into the Julian *gens* is marked by her changed name of Julia Augusta.

The term *domus Augusta* developed in the late Augustan period. It may be related to the earlier designation *gens Augusta*, as well as to the inclusive construction of family revealed in Augustus' Mausoleum. The *domus Augusta* comprised Augustus' agnate, cognate, and distant relatives.[55] Its first recorded

---

51. *CIL* XII 4333 = EDCS-12100286, esp. lines 6–8. Hurlet 2015, 186 sees the *gens Iulia* as the earliest categorization. For the inscription from Narbo (now Narbonne, France), with Augustan consular dating but in an Antonine copy, see also *FIRA* III p. 227 n.73; Fishwick 2007 (whose focus is on the *numen Augusti* mentioned elsewhere in the text); and other references in EDCS.

52. Seager 2012, 49, apparently sees as Tiberian the Carthage inscription (*AE* 1914, 87 = EDCS-16201132); Moreau 2009, 43 n.105, as late Augustan-Tiberian. The Corinthian inscription, *AE* 1922, 1 = EDCS-10300681, is very fragmentary, but *genti Augustae* at the start of line 3 is clear. Hurlet 2015, 186: "since this term [*gens Iulia*] excluded some key relatives such as Agrippa (a Vipsanius), Augustus then developed the idea of the *gens Augusta*." See also Grant 1950.

53. See Saller 1984, 345–47; Moreau 2009, 34. In a reported speech Tacitus also refers to Tiberius being raised in the "dominating house" (*in domo regnatrice, Ann.* 1.4).

54. See, e.g., Moreau 2009, 34. Inscriptions from the tomb emphasize ties with Augustus as well as identify more traditionally by filiation and *nomen*: Moreau 2009, 36; Hesberg and Panciera 1994, 91. In *Consol. ad Liviam* 65–74 the Mausoleum serves to define who was in Augustus' family.

55. See, e.g., Moreau 2009. Corbier 1994 and Dettenhofer 2000 see the *domus Augusta* as an innovation; Moreau as derivative of traditional ideas of an extended kinship group known in laws from the *lex Cincia* of 204 BCE through some of Augustus' social legislation. In legal terms *domus* (as opposed to *familia*) can include relatives through women: Saller 1984, 345–47. Seager 2012, 55 sees familial relationships as significant in references to the *domus Augusta*.

Imperial Women within the Imperial Family 95

instance, a passage of Ovid's exile poetry, dates to 13 CE. The lines invoke a prosperous rule and life for Augustus, his wife (*coniux*), his son (*filius*, to be understood as Tiberius), Germanicus and Drusus (the Younger, both named; Augustus' stepsons),[56] and the "daughters-in-law and grand-daughters and sons of grandsons and other members of the Augustan house" (*ceteraque Augustae membra . . . domus*, *Pont.* 2.2.67–74). Ovid's *domus Augusta* is extensive. In later passages of his exile poetry *domus Augusta* refers especially to Tiberius, Livia, Germanicus, Drusus, and Augustus, but can include others as well.[57] F. Millar and others have argued that from afar the exile saw, or at least depicted, all members of the imperial house as a close-knit unit.[58] In Ovid's references Livia is the only female actually named, although more often is referred to simply as "wife" or is otherwise anonymous. By this late date Livia's pivotal role was clear: her Claudian son Tiberius would inherit the *domus Augusta*, something Tacitus implies in his later references to the *domus Iuliorum Claudiorumque* and the *Claudia et Iulia domus* (see earlier).

In Tiberius' early years *domus Augusta* appears in official and documentary contexts. The Tabula Siarensis of 19 CE records the senate's installation of a marble arch honoring Germanicus, to rise next to statues earlier dedicated in the Circus Flaminius to *divus* Augustus and to the *domus Augusta* (*AE* 1984, 508 = EDCS-45500034).[59] As we see in Ch. 5, the *domus Augusta* statue group probably included Augustus, Livia, Tiberius, and Germanicus. A broader vision of the imperial family was presented by the statues on the arch projected for Germanicus. These were to be of Germanicus in triumph, his "natural father Drusus [the Elder], the brother of Tiberius Caesar Augustus," his mother Antonia (the Younger), his wife Agrippina (the Elder), his sister Livia (Livilla), his brother Claudius (the future emperor), and Germanicus' (unnamed) sons and daughters

---

56. And Tiberius' adopted and natural sons: see genealogical tree in Appendix 2.

57. See Flory 1996, 293 n.23, 301. Many have seen the *domus Augusta* embodied in the "Grand Cameo of France," whose three registers represent members of the Julio-Claudian family (arguably centering on Tiberius and Livia) and the subjugated barbarians who justify their supremacy: see, e.g., Levick 2007, 77.

58. Millar 1993, Flory 1996, 301, and Seager 2012, 43–46, 55 cite and discuss some of Ovid's various references to the "dynastic house" at *Fast.* 1.532, 1.721, 6.810; *Tr.* 3.1.41, 4.2.10; see also *Pont.* 2.2.74, written shortly before Augustus' death (Barrett 2002, 317). See also Corbier 1995, 178–93; Flory 1996, 292–93. Hekster 2015, 5 credits the growth of the concept partly to the endogamous marriages of the Julio-Claudian family.

59. = *RS* 37, fr. I, ll. 10–11. The earlier statuary probably dates to early 15 CE: Flory 1996.

(a, ll. 18–21, discussed further in Ch. 5).[60] In a later section the decree vaunts the devotion of all orders to Rome's *domus Augusta.*[61]

The *Senatus Consultum de Pisone patre* of the following year, 20 CE, both employs the term *domus Augusta* and presents a unified view of the Julio-Claudian family. The text specifies among Piso's offenses in Syria his disregard of the *maiestas* or power of the "Augustan house."[62] Other lines toward the text's end further establish that the *domus Augusta* was a well-defined notion and assimilated to the principate itself by the time of this decree six years into Tiberius' reign. In lines 159–63 the senate expresses the hope that the troops will maintain their loyalty and devotion to the *domus Augusta,* since the safety of "our empire" is in the safekeeping of that house;[63] this echoes the association of the *domus* or household of Augustus with the *res publica* and the city of Rome in Valerius Messalla's proposal of the title *pater patriae* for Augustus (Suet. *Aug.* 58.2; see earlier).[64] When the *SCPP* then commends the commanders "who most devotedly have revered the name of the Caesars, which preserves this city and the empire of the Roman people,"[65] it equates the *nomen Caesarum* ("name of the Caesars") with the *domus Augusta.*

More women are mentioned in documents of the Tiberian period than the Augustan one. In the *SCPP* they are singled out for laudable moderation, and their connections to the male relatives of Augustus and Germanicus are specified. Julia Augusta and Germanicus' brother Drusus (the Younger) are praised for their restraint that emulates Tiberius';[66] Agrippina (the Elder) is cited for having been in Augustus' high regard, as well as for her harmonious and fertile married life with Germanicus.[67] Germanicus' mother Antonia (the Younger), lauded as *univira*

---

60. *patris eius naturalis, fratris Ti. Caesaris Aug.*; The lacunose text now lacks *Agrippina uxor*: see Lott 2012, 90, ll. 18–21.

61. *pie<t=L>as omnium ordinum erga domum Augustam*: b, II.22–23.

62. *neclecta* (sic) *maiestate domus Aug(ustae)*, l. 16; see, e.g., Corbier 2001, 160–61.

63. *fidem pietatemq(ue) domui Aug(ustae) . . . salutem imperi nostri in eius domu<s> custodia posita<m> esse{t}.*

64. Seager 2012, 52; see also Wardle 2000, 480.

65. *salutare huic urbi imperioq(ue) p(opuli) R(omani) nomen Caesarum coluissent*, line 165.

66. lines 132–33; later Julia Augustus, Tiberius, and Drusus are said to model "discipline" for Germanicus' sons and Germanicus' brother Claudius (ll. 146–51).

67. For her fertility and surviving children, discussed earlier, see ll. 136–39; Lott 2012, 301–2 ad loc. She was in the family council assisting Tiberius in selecting honors: Seager 2012, 56. Tacitus has her vaunt her ties with *divus* Augustus, first when refusing to back down from the mutiny in Germany in 14 CE, and then again before Tiberius in 26 CE (*Ann.* 1.40.3, 4.52.2).

Imperial Women within the Imperial Family

(married but once), is described of such morals as to make her worthy of her close relation to Augustus (ll. 140–42);[68] Germanicus' sister Livilla is commended as so highly regarded by Tiberius and Julia Augusta alike that she could parade their esteem "even though not belonging to their house," that is even though she was a member of the *gens Claudia* and not the *gens Iulia* into which both Tiberius and Julia Augusta had been adopted.[69] Yet although women are cited as virtuous and exemplary, the many virtues of the *domus Augustus* lauded so strikingly in this ultimately public document derive from Augustus, Tiberius, and other imperial men.[70]

As the odd note about Livilla reveals, by 20 CE the *domus Augusta* comprised more than Augustus' traditional kinship group. It included his widow Julia Augusta who had been adopted into Augustus' Julian *gens* at his death, as well as his agnates or blood descendants. Adopted and blood children were traditionally part of a man's *familia*. But the *SCPP* also shows that six years into Tiberius' reign the *domus Augusta* included Augustus' "cognates"—that is, the descendants of his wife Livia, as well as individuals married to or adopted by anyone in either group.[71] *Augusta* connected the whole group to Augustus, imparting an air of sanctity much as did the term *Augustus* itself for a princeps.[72] The *domus Augusta* had survived the death of its patriarch Augustus, to continue into the rule of his adopted son Tiberius and look toward the future.[73]

The future was dependent on children—those of Agrippina and Germanicus are cited—so mothers were essential. By 20 CE imperial women of the *domus Augusta* were recognized by name, in contrast to earlier practice. But just as important as their individual names was their relationship to the princeps or other important men in the family. We see in Ch. 6 that dedications and statues for imperial women portrayed them in their family relationships, and group installations to the imperial family increased in numbers in Italy and elsewhere starting with the Tiberian period and especially noticeably with the Claudian

---

68. lines 140–42: Lott 2012, 302–3 ad loc. notes that Antonia is referred to only as Germanicus' mother, and also for participating in Tiberius' family council about honors. See above for *univirae*. For Antonia the Younger, see Kokkinos 2002.

69. *etiam si non contingere{n}t domum eorum*, ll. 143–44; Lott 2012, 304 ad loc. notes Livilla's attachment to Tiberius' *domus* by marriage to his son Drusus.

70. Cooley 1998, esp. 208.

71. See, e.g., Moreau 2009, 33.

72. See, e.g., Moreau 2009, 37; Ch. 1 on "Augusta."

73. Seager 2012. The next generation featured Germanicus (adopted by Tiberius in 4 CE) and Tiberius' son Drusus the Younger (see Ovid, *Pont.* 2.2.67–74, discussed earlier). Hekster 2015, 9 remarks that by the time of Caligula "it was not so much emperorship as leadership over the *domus Augusta* that was transferred from one *princeps* to the next."

98 IMPERIAL WOMEN OF ROME

one.[74] By the mid-first century an aqueduct in Teate Marrucinorum (modern Chieti, Italy) was rebuilt by a Dusmia Numisilla "in honor of the Augustan house," and the *flaminica domus Augustae*, or priestess of the Augustan house, Julia Laeta was commemorated in Tucci (now Martos, Spain).[75]

By the end of Tiberius' principate the term *domus divina* appears for the imperial family, indicating further distinction from other Roman families. It spreads with time.[76] Its first attested use is in 33: a dedication from a *sevir Augustalis* in central Italy's Lucus Feroniae that begins "In honor of the Divine House" (*In honorem domus divinae*).[77] Some two decades later Gaius Julius Spartiaticus, a procurator of "Caesar" [Nero] and Augusta Agrippina (the Younger) and the priest of the *domus Augusta* in Corinth, was honored for his virtue and spirited and expansive munificence toward Corinth and the Divine House (*domus divina*) (*AE* 1927, 2 = EDCS-08200293, 54–59 CE).[78] Perhaps from this same period comes a fragmentary dedication to Marcia Celsa, from Abdera (now Adra, Spain), a "perpetual priestess of the Divine House" (*sacerdos perpetua domus d[ivinae]*).[79] During the rule of Domitian, the Augustales of Puteoli made a vow for the health and well-being of Domitian, members of his family, and the whole "Divine House."[80] The Trajanic *lex Manciana* begins with a vow for the

---

74. Buonocore 2007, 76, 81–82, 86–87, 89–90; Rose 1997; Cogitore 1992; 2002, 163–64 (dating the dynastic conception to Claudius); Hurlet 1997, on Claudius; Hurlet 2015, 188–89.

75. *CIL* IX 3018 [p. 677] = EDCS-14804019, *In honorum domus Augustae*, dated 31–70 CE; Iulia C. f. Laeta, *CIL* II 1678 = EDCS-08700099, dated between Tiberius and the Flavians: Hemelrijk 2015, 425. The cult of the *domus Augusta* in third-century Baetica had both men and women as *flaminica*, *sacerdos*, and *pontifex*: Bassignano 2013, 159 no. 64.

76. Grant 1950, 96–98, 104 and Morizio 1996, 211 see this as indicating growing acceptance of the principate as a more or less hereditary monarchy already by Tiberius' rule; Cogitore 1992, 833 and Flory 1995, 134 date the change to the time of Claudius.

77. The inscription, *AE* 1988, 553 = EDCS-09200248, was raised shortly after Tiberius prohibited the senate's proposed consecration of Julia Augusta (Suet. *Tib.* 51.2; Cass. Dio 58.2.1). Some connect the appearance of the phrase and concept *domus divina* to the fall of Sejanus (see Hurlet 2015, 188–89; Flory 1996, 303; Phaedrus 5.7.35). Wardle 2000 discusses Valerius Maximus' complex understanding of the Tiberian *domus divina*. Lucus Feroniae is thirty kilometers north of Rome.

78. Nero, who praised Poppaea in her funeral oration for being the mother of a divinized child, is said by Tacitus to have been desirous of children (*liberorum cupiens*: Tac. *Ann.* 16.6).

79. *CIL* II 1978 = EDCS-05501676; Bassignano 2013, 159 no. 67.

80. Now fragmentary: *CIL* X 1632 = EDCS-11500564, from Puteoli,*]o Fulvo I[3] / [3 Augusta] les(?) qui pr[o salute] / [I]mp(eratoris) Domitian[i divi f(ilii)] / [Caes(aris) Augusti] Germ(anici) et [Domitiae Aug(ustae)] / [Domitiani A]ug(usti) et Iulia[e Augustae] / [totiusque domus] divinae [3] / [3]I et[.* See Fishwick 1987–2005, II.1, 424; Hekster 2015, 182.

health and well-being of "our emperor Imperator Caesar Trajan, the princeps, and of the whole Divine House of [Trajan] Optimus Maximus Parthicus" (*CIL* VIII 25902 = EDCS-46400965; 116–117 CE). In short, although the evidence is not copious, the concept of the divine imperial family seems widespread by the early second century CE, at least among individuals and groups connected with imperial cult and imperial administration.

By the late second and third centuries, military inscriptions often include the formula *in honorem domus divinae*, usually abbreviated *in h. d. d.*[81] Such inscriptions demonstrate both that the notion of the imperial house was no longer tied personally to Augustus—although its authority clearly derives from the first princeps—and that the concept included living individuals as well as deified ones.[82] O. Hekster has compiled seventeen datable inscriptions from Rome that include *domus divina*, remarking that one is probably Hadrianic, one from the 180s, eleven date between the reigns of Septimius Severus and Severus Alexander, and one dates after 235.[83] His evidence shows that the term *domus divina* was particularly frequent during the Severan dynasty and was used by civilians and military alike. By this time the imperial family was clearly above others: all known imperial women are granted the honorary title *Augusta*, and Severan empresses many other honorific epithets besides, usually including the term *mater*. With that note we turn to the figure of the imperial mother.

The imperial mother

What roles could women have within this "August" or "divine" household of the emperor, who was both paterfamilias and *pater patriae*?[84] The question is important in light of the small but growing numbers of apparently more independent aristocratic women in the late Republic. Especially in the early Augustan years,

---

81. See Raepsaet-Charlier 1975. This is when "familial" titles for imperial women proliferate (see later).

82. That is, we should not translate *domus divina* as "house founded by a *divus*": Hekster 2015, 182, contra, e.g., Fishwick 1987–2005, II.1 esp. 424–30, and Grant 1950, 97; cf. Wardle 2000, 483. *AE* 2001, 853 = EDCS-23800754 (151–175 CE) and *AE* 2001, 854 = EDCS-23800755 (180–200 CE) record Augustales from Liternum (in the Bay of Naples) "who gather together in worship of the *domus divina*" (*in cultu domus divinae contulerunt*). "Divine" titles for individual women, especially women who were deified, are explored in Ch. 4.

83. Hekster 2015, 182 n.47.

84. Some emperors, such as Tiberius (Cass. Dio 57.8.1; Tac. *Ann.* 2.87) and Hadrian, refused to assume the title *pater patriae* immediately upon accession.

written and visual material tends not to identify imperial women other than Livia, and she figures but occasionally.[85] But Augustus' death in 14 CE removed the obvious center of the family and destabilized the patterns his longevity had encouraged within it.

Among the many honors the senate proposed in 14 CE for Livia, now Julia Augusta after adoption into the *gens Iulia*, was the unprecedented title *Mater* or *Parens Patriae*, "Mother" or "Parent" of the Fatherland. Another senatorial decree, reportedly particularly upsetting to Tiberius, was that "son of Julia" (*Iuliae filius*) be added to his new titles. Tiberius adamantly refused such public recognition of Livia's maternal roles,[86] although he did allow the title *Augusta* (see Ch. 1). The literary sources emphasize Tiberius' rancor at his mother's proposed honors, but his aversion to her prominence is unsurprising in light of Rome's traditionally patriarchal ideology and his own moderation in the face of senatorial adulation.[87] Nevertheless, according to Cassius Dio, after Julia Augusta's death some began to call her *Mater Patriae* in gratitude for benefits that included her rearing children, paying for dowries, and "saving" individuals' lives (58.2.3). No documentary evidence verifies this alleged popular title, whose concept Tacitus twists viciously when describing Livia in 14 as "a mother dangerous for the state, and a stepmother grim for the house of the Caesars."[88] Yet when reporting in the *SCPP* the exoneration of Plancina at Julia Augusta's influence, the senate acknowledges that Julia Augusta's sway derived in part from her giving birth to "our princeps."[89]

To be a mother was the most respected function women could have in Rome,[90] and it is thus no surprise that early public images of historical women identify them as mothers. Among the first central coins to depict imperial women are the precious-metal *aurei* and *denarii* of Caligula that honor Agrippina the Elder, shown on the reverse with a profile portrait encircled by the legend "Agrippina,

---

85. Julia the Younger, despite her name Julia, seems not to belong to the *gens Iulia*: there is no trace of her adoption by Augustus, and her full name (not attested) was probably Vipsania Iulia (cf. *PIR*[2] I 635). She was treated as though she were under Augustus' *potestas* when he did not allow her baby to be acknowledged and reared (Suet. *Aug.* 65.4).

86. Tac. *Ann.* 1.14.1; Cass. Dio 57.12.3–4, 58.2.3; Hemelrijk 2012, 201–2. That Livia did not get the title *mater patriae* when Augustus assumed *pater patriae* in 2 BCE reflects Augustus' dominance in the family.

87. See, e.g., Wardle 2000 and Grant 1950, as well as the *SCPP* discussed above.

88. Tac. *Ann.* 1.10: *Livia gravis in rem publicam mater, gravis domui Caesarum noverca.*

89. Lines 109–20, esp. 115–16: *non partu tantum modo principis nostri.*

90. Dixon 1988.

ILL. 3.3 *Aureus* of Caligula from 37 CE with posthumous portrait of his mother Agrippina the Elder (rev.). Harvard Art Museums / Arthur M. Sackler Museum, Request of Frederick M. Watkins. © President and Fellows of Harvard College

Mother of Gaius Caesar Augustus Germanicus" (Ill. 3.3).[91] Similarly, Antonia the Younger is often presented publicly as Claudius' mother (*mater*), as on an honorary inscription raised to her in Herculaneum (now Ercolano, Italy).[92]

Recognition of imperial mothers reached new heights with Agrippina the Younger, whose role as Nero's mother is stressed in literature as well as documentary and visual material. The first praetorian password the new emperor Nero reportedly gave was *Optima Mater* ("Best of Mothers"), and early on he reputedly entrusted to his mother the management of all public and private business.[93] In 54 and 55 centrally struck *aurei* and *denarii* displayed portraits of Agrippina and identified her as "the mother of Nero Caesar" (Ills. 3.4 and 3.5; see also Ch. 4).[94]

---

91. Agrippina the Elder (rev.), draped and facing right, with legend AGRIPPINA MAT C CAES AVG GERM; struck in Lugdunum (*RIC* I², Gaius nos. 7–8, 13–14, 21–22). See Wood 1995, 458–60, and Ch. 4, this volume.

92. *Antoniae Augustae, matri Ti(beri) Claudi / Caesaris Augusti Germanici pontif(icis) max(imi)*, *CIL* X 1417 = EDCS-11500351, 49/50 CE; see also the inscriptions from Claudian monuments discussed in Ch. 5. Moderns often view her as a harsh mother (cf. Suet. *Claud.* 3).

93. Tac. *Ann.* 13.2; Suet. *Nero* 9; Cass. Dio 61.3.3: see, e.g., Barrett 1996, 150–52.

94. Ill. 3.4: *RIC* I², Nero nos. 1–3, struck in Rome in 54 CE: (obv.) AGRIPP AVG DIVI CLAVD NERONIS CAES MATER, with MATER below Nero's bust; (rev.) NERONI CLAVD DIVI F CAES AVG GERM IMP TR P, EX S C (In honor of Nero Caesar Augustus Germanicus Imperator, son of *divus* Claudius, with tribunician power. In accordance with a decree of the senate). Ill. 3.5: *RIC* I², Nero nos. 6–7; the bust of Nero (bare-headed and draped at back of neck) is foregrounded in this jugate presentation. Obv.: NERO CLAVD DIVI F CAES AVG GERM IMP TR P COS (Nero Caesar Augustus Germanicus Imperator, son of

ILL. 3.4 *Aureus* of Nero from 54 CE, with Agrippina the Younger on the obverse facing Nero. © The Trustees of the British Museum.

Such issues ceased as the estrangement of Agrippina and Nero widened, although even a year before her murder the Arval Brethren sacrificed on Rome's Capitoline on the occasion of the birthday of Agrippina, "mother of the emperor."[95]

Perhaps in reaction to what became notorious as Agrippina's excessive ambitions, and surely tied to historical circumstances, the identifiable figure of imperial mother becomes less prominent until Faustina the Younger, other than a brief efflorescence with Domitia Longina, celebrated on coins as "Mother of *divus* Caesar" when her husband Domitian became emperor in 81. After Nero no emperor until Marcus Aurelius either came to power while his mother was still alive, or while emperor had with his wife a son who survived childhood. Yet by the time of the Flavians the idea of imperial dynasty was set.[96] Vespasian was

---

divus Claudius, with tribunician power, consul; rev.: AGRIPP AVG DIVI CLAVD NERONIS CAES MATER EX S C (Agrippina Augusta, [wife of] *divus* Claudius, mother of Nero Caesar, in accordance with a decree of the senate), with a quadriga of elephants, left, bearing chairs with radiate figures of *divus* Claudius and *divus* Augustus. On some provincial milestones Nero is identified with filiation tracing him to *divus* Claudius, Germanicus, Tiberius, *divus* Augustus and even Caesar, e.g., *CIL* II 4719 = EDCS-05600089, *CIL* II 4926 = EDCS-05600294, *CIL* III 346 = EDCS-26600085: some take this stressing Nero's matrilinear descent (Ginsburg 2006, 74–78; Barrett 1996, 291; Rose 1997, 47), but I note that Agrippina is not named.

95. *CFA* 27 = EDCS 21300007, 6 November 58. AGRIPPINA AVGVSTA MATER AVGVSTI is found on provincial coins from Caesarea in Cappadocia, *RIC* I², Nero nos. 607–8, 610–11, 54–60 CE; Ginsburg 2006, 74–78; Barrett 1996, 152, 167–80. In contrast, games Puteoli's Augustales staged in 56 honored Nero, Agrippina Augusta (not *mater Augusti* or the like), Jupiter Optimus Maximus, and the Genius of the Colony (the names of both Nero and Agrippina were later erased: *CIL* X 1574 = EDCS-11500508; cf. Tac. *Ann.* 14.27.1).

96. Hekster 2015.

ILL. 3.5 *Aureus* of Nero from 55 CE, with jugate busts of Nero and Agrippina the Younger on the obverse. © The Trustees of the British Museum.

famous for saying in the senate, "Either my sons will succeed me, or no one will" (Suet. *Vesp.* 25; Cass. Dio 65.12.1).[97]

The women of Vespasian's family have more liminal roles, although under Titus and Domitian imperial women appear on coins, and more frequently than in the Augustan and Tiberian periods.[98] Their general insignificance compared to the males of the family, however, is reflected in the difficulties of identifying the "Domitilla" of coins and sculpture as Vespasian's wife or his homonymous daughter, both dead before he took power in 69.[99] This Domitilla appears in Flavian self-promotion under Titus and Domitian, commemorated on *sestertii* of 80–81 CE that have obverses of a *carpentum* (ceremonial carriage) with the legend "For the memory of Domitilla; the Senate and the People of Rome" (Ill. 3.6),[100] and on *aurei* of

---

97. Crook 1951, 171 and Levick 2008, 145–47, with Pliny, *Pan.* 11.1; Stat. *Silv.* 1.1.94–98; and Tac. *Hist.* 2.77. See *RIC* II.1², 52–56 and Carradice 2012, 383–85 for Vespasian's coinage featuring his sons. Alexandridis 2010, 201 remarks, "Vespasian followed republican tradition and Augustus in excluding his family's women from the public image of power."

98. Alexandridis 2010, noting also (198–99) Titus' "restoration coins" representing Agrippina the Elder (see Ch. 4, n.65), and perhaps Livia.

99. I concur with preference for identification as Vespasian's wife rather than daughter (Titus' and Domitian's sister): Palombi 2014, 195 n. 26; Wood 2010, esp. 48–51, 55; Alexandridis 2010, 197; Frei-Stolba 2008, 386–90; and Hahn 1994, 228–32, though see Kienast 2017, 103, 107 and Carradice 2012, 384–85. For Vespasian's wife, see also Barrett 2005b.

100. The *sestertius* of Ill. 3.6 is *RIC* II.1², Titus no. 262; 80–81 CE. Obverse reads MEMORIAE DOMITILLAE SPQR; reverse centers a large S C within the legend IMP T CAES DIVI VESP F AVG P M TR P P P COS VIII (Imperator Titus Caesar Augustus, son of *divus* Vespasian, Pontifex Maximus, with tribunician power, Father of the Fatherland, consul for the 8th time). We discuss the *carpentum* type for coins of imperial women in Ch. 4.

ILL. 3.6 *Sestertius* of Titus from 80–81 CE, with (obv.) a *carpentum* honoring the memory of Domitilla. Coin from Münzkabinett, Staatliche Museen, Berlin, courtesy of the American Numismatic Society.

82–83 that carry portraits of *divus* Vespasian (obverse) and *diva* Domitilla Augusta (reverse).[101] Titus' daughter Julia was honored during her father's reign, with five issues in silver and four in bronze portraying her.[102] Domitian's coinage continued dynastic themes, with *aurei* of 82–83 showing *divus* Titus Augustus (obv.) and (rev.) Julia Augusta, the daughter of *divus* Titus.[103] Eight issues in precious metal and four in *aes* honored Domitia, Domitian's wife.[104] Most important to my immediate concern are the coins struck at the beginning of Domitian's reign featuring her with the legend "Mother of *divus* Caesar." (See Ill. 3.7.) Although her son with Domitian had died in infancy sometime before Domitian came to power in 81, her fecundity was publicized as a guarantee of the continuity of the imperial family.[105]

A. Alexandridis has pointed out that many of Titus' and Domitian's coins portraying women have on their other sides not the emperor—the norm during

---

101. The *aureus* is *RIC* II.1², Domitian no. 146; see Alexandridis 2010, 197 n.32. *RIC* II.1², Domitian no. 157, Pl. 121, are *denarii* with DIVA DOMITILLA AVGVSTA (obv.) and Fortuna (rev.), 82–83 CE.

102. Alexandridis 2010, 198 terms this "prospective dynastic thinking."

103. IVLIA AVGVSTA DIVI TITI F: *RIC* II.1², Domitian no. 147. For Domitian's family coinage, see *RIC* II.1², 243.

104. Alexandridis 2010, 199–200 provides the references, remarking that the division of coinage honoring her into two phases depends on the literary depiction of her turbulent marriage with Domitian (see the opening of Ch. 2).

105. The bronze dupondius of Ill. 3.7, *RIC* II.1², Domitian no. 136, from 81/82 portrays Domitia with the legend "Domitia Augusta, wife of Imperator Caesar Domitian Augustus son of *divus* [Vespasian]" (obv.), with (rev.) Domitia (?) standing over an altar, sacrificing with a patera and holding a scepter, with the legend "Mother of *divus* Caesar, in accordance with a decree of

ILL. 3.7 Bronze dupondius of Domitian from 81/82 portraying Domitia (obv.) and "Mother of *divus* Caesar" (rev.). Courtesy of the American Numismatic Society.

the Julio-Claudian period for the few issues that did feature women—but deities and abstractions.[106] This must have contributed to the growing identification of the imperial house as the *domus divina*. In any case, under Titus and Domitian imperial women were shown more often on coins, as support for the political ambitions of those establishing a new dynasty and imperial order after the Julio-Claudians.[107] The familial roles of such women would become more complicated after the Flavians, since the next three emperors were childless; further, although Trajan and Hadrian were married when they came to power and elevated the women of their family, Nerva was not.

The motherless imperial household

How did imperial women fit into the "age of the adoptive emperors," as the period from Nerva to Marcus Aurelius is sometimes called? Ancient literary sources

---

the senate." Two other issues honoring Domitia as *mater divi Caesaris* depict a child on the reverse, either as a young boy (to whom a seated woman—Domitia?—extends a hand: *RIC* II.1², Domitian no. 132; *sestertii* 81/82) or as an infant on a globe (*RIC* II.1², Domitian nos. 152–53, 155–56, *aurei* and *denarii* of 81–82 or 82/83). See Alexandridis 2010; Varner 1995, 193–94; *RIC* II.1². As we see in Ch. 4, Poppaea had been honored as Augusta after bearing Nero's daughter, who died and was declared *diva* within months.

106. Alexandridis 2010, 198 calls it "a new step in the imperial women's public image." Cf. Table 4.2.

107. Alexandridis 2010, 201, noting also that the majority of the issues are in precious metal, suggesting that the message was aimed at the elite.

106   IMPERIAL WOMEN OF ROME

discussing imperial adoption ignore women. In Tacitus' *Histories*, written about 100–110 CE, the emperor Galba enunciates a meritorious ideology centered on adoption: "To be begotten and born of princes is mere chance and not reckoned higher, but the judgment displayed in adoption is pure" (*Hist.* 1.16).[108] Cassius Dio later reports Hadrian's adoption of Antoninus Pius that entailed Pius' adoption of Marcus Aurelius and Lucius Verus because "he had no male offspring," having Hadrian say that "a begotten son turns out to be whatever sort of person Heaven pleases," whereas an adopted son is chosen deliberately for his merits (69.20.2). The model excludes women not only as mothers of "princes," but also as unthinkable in political discussions and judgments: indeed, while eulogizing Trajan's adoption by Nerva, Pliny the Younger implicitly criticizes the adoptions of Tiberius and Nero as made "to favor a wife" (*Pan.* 7.4–8).[109]

Nonetheless, imperial women began to receive greater recognition precisely during the era of the "adoptive" emperors. They are, as usual, subsumed to their family roles, but those roles expand to include sister, mother-in-law, grandmother, and the like.[110] A harbinger of this attention may be the now-lost inscription from Rome that attests a statue or dedication to Sergia Plautilla, "daughter of Sergius Laenas and mother of the emperor Nerva Caesar Augustus": this poorly attested woman was almost certainly dead by the time her sixty-six-year-old son came to imperial power.[111] Although the dates may be due to random survival of evidence, it also seems significant that beginning in the late first century (CE) period papyri from Egypt document marriage contracts sworn in front of a statue of Julia Augusta.[112] The era's promotion of the extended imperial family correlates with continuing or even growing emphasis of the traditional Roman goal of raising legitimate children, something seen otherwise in this period in the alimentary programs initiated under Trajan.[113]

---

108. Roche 2002, 44–46. See also Tac. *Hist.* 2.77 and Hekster 2001.

109. Respectively Livia and Agrippina the Younger. This notion underlies the scandal of Plotina's alleged meddling for Hadrian's succession. See Ch. 1.

110. Roche 2002, 51 remarks that the *Panegyricus* is the first extant Latin panegyric to include praise of the subject's family, and sees that emphasis coming from a "governmental level."

111. *CIL* VI 31297 = EDCS-18700464; see FOS #704. For Nerva's accession, see Collins 2009.

112. Temporini 1978, 68–69, citing contracts of 98, 127, and 136, and one of 170 sworn in front of statues of Antoninus Pius and Faustina the Elder (BGU 252, 2/3; P.Oxy. III 496, 1, cf. 604; CPR 24.2; and P.Oxy. VI 905).

113. The *alimenta* are endlessly discussed, including whether they were begun by Nerva; for a recent overview that rightly brings out their ideological importance for Roman demography, see McGinn 2013b, 341–46.

Imperial Women within the Imperial Family

From the beginning of his rule the childless Trajan is portrayed with not only his wife Plotina, but also his (widowed) sister Marciana and her daughter Matidia the Elder.[114] In his *Panegyricus* of 100 CE Pliny celebrates Plotina and Marciana for their modesty and their reluctance to ask favors of the emperor.[115] Although repetitiously stressing the two as essential to the emperor's *domus*, Pliny identifies them not by name but with various terms for women, wife, and sister (*Pan.* 83–84).[116] Elsewhere in the same work, he ties Trajan to Rome's fecundity as he describes the crowds watching the new emperor enter the city: "At that point the greatest delight in their own fertility entered the women, when they considered the ruler for whom they had produced citizens, the commander for whom they had produced soldiers" (*Pan.* 22.3; see also 26.5-6, 27.1, 28.7).[117] This sentiment, surely odd to modern eyes, is echoed in one topic that Menander Rhetor advocates for praise of an emperor's virtues: "Because of the emperor['s moral example], marriages are chaste and fathers have legitimate offspring" (*Epid.* 2.1.396; late third century).[118]

Trajan's female relatives appeared on coins, sculpture, and other media. In some depictions such as the cameo represented in Ill. 3.8, a type of object that probably circulated among the highest elite, individuals are not labeled: in this case we can discern (on right) Trajan with his wife Plotina, facing his sister Marciana with her daughter Matidia the Elder.[119] In other likenesses, the women's relationship to the emperor and others in the imperial house is explicitly noted.[120] Statues of Trajanic women were often found in group portraits with

---

114. Boatwright 1991; Temporini 1978.

115. See Boatwright 1991; Roche 2002, 47–51; Ch. 1.

116. *mulieres, feminae, uxor, coniux, soror*, "women, women, wife, wife, sister." Pliny stresses "house" otherwise: "Great fortune has this first, that it allows nothing to be hidden or secret; truly, for emperors it opens up not only their houses, but their very bedrooms and innermost chambers, and it opens all secrets and exposes and explains them to be known to rumor" (*Pan.* 83.1).

117. See Kampen 2009, 38–63 on portrayals of the childless Trajan as a father figure.

118. See Noreña 2007, 311. Menander Rhetor's text is that edited by D. A. Russell and N. G. Wilson, *Menander Rhetor* (Oxford 1981).

119. The cameo of Ill. 3.8, in the Farnese Collection of the Naples Archaeological Museum (inv. MANN 26089), is 1.9 cm H x 3.3 cm W. Cameos may have atypical attributes and elements: Fejfer 2008, 171–72.

120. Roche 2002, 55 holds that Plotina appears on obverses in "high" numbers beginning in 112, but Marciana's "low numismatic profile while alive" went higher after her consecration in 112 (e.g., *BMCRE* III, Trajan nos. 647–55). But see Ch. 4, and also Ch. 2 and Ch. 6.

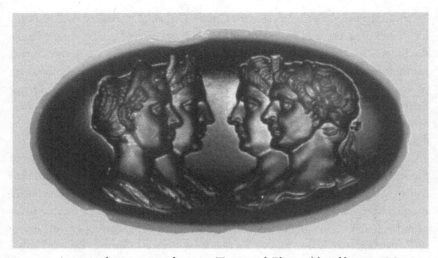

ILL. 3.8 Agate-sardonyx cameo, depicting Trajan with Plotina (r) and his sister Marciana with her daughter Matidia the Elder (behind). By permission of the Ministero per i Beni e le Attività Culturali e per il Turismo – Museo Archeologico Nazionale di Napoli.

the emperor. On a (now lost) inscription from Luna, a central, fuller text honoring Trajan and dated to ca. 104–105 is flanked by short inscriptions for Plotina Augusta and Marciana Augusta.[121] On the Arch of Ancona (Italy) of 114/115 Plotina Augusta is termed *coniux Aug(usti)* (the wife of the emperor), and *diva* Marciana Aug(usta) is titled *soror Aug(usti)* (the sister of the emperor) (*CIL* IX 5894 = EDCS-17300491). In Ch. 1 we noted Marciana as the first sister of an emperor to receive the title *Augusta*; after Marciana's death in 112 her daughter Matidia the Elder gained the title as the first woman not mother, wife, or daughter of the emperor. Despite the relative rarity of portrait coins of imperial women in the Trajanic period (see Ch. 4), gold and silver coins honored Matidia the Elder with a portrait and legend "Matidia Augusta, daughter of *diva* Marciana" (obv.), and (rev.) a female standing front and center, with her hands on the heads of two little girls and the legend PIETAS AVGVST.[122] (See Ill. 3.9.) Although we

---

121. *CIL* XI 1333 = EDCS-20402783; now Luni, Italy. This is the earliest securely dated witness for the two women's titles as Augusta.

122. MATIDIA AVG DIVAE MARCIANAE F (obv.); AVGVST (rev.) is understood either as "August[i]," which would render the latter legend as "the piety of the emperor," or as "August[a]," rendering "imperial piety." Ill. 3.9 is *RIC* II, Trajan no. 759, 115–117 CE; for *denarii* see *RIC* II, Trajan no. 761.

Imperial Women within the Imperial Family

ILL. 3.9 *Aureus* of Trajan from 115–117 CE with Matidia the Elder; the reverse image may suggest Matidia with her daughters Matidia the Younger and Sabina. © The Trustees of the British Museum.

cannot identify the two girls securely as Matidia's daughters Matidia the Younger and Sabina—in 112 both would have been over twenty-five years old—the images assert the family piety of the imperial family as they feature females rather than males. Imperial piety centered on a woman is also reflected in the consecration coins that commemorate Trajan's sister Marciana after her death in 112 (see Ill. 4.6 and Ill. 4.8). These are the earliest coins known to publicize this significant process.

The family prominence of imperial women increased through the next generation, although again the emperor, now Hadrian, was childless. One indication of Plotina's alleged influence on Trajan was the marriage of Sabina, Matidia's younger daughter and Trajan's great niece, to Trajan's distant relative Hadrian in 100 (HA, *Hadr.* 2.10).[123] As emperor after 117 Hadrian honored Plotina, now his adoptive mother,[124] his mother-in-law Matidia the Elder, and Trajan's sister Marciana on coinage, with public orations and documents, and with buildings.[125] Plotina and *divus* Trajan appeared on the opposite sides of centrally struck gold

---

123. See Ch. 1 n.158. One traditional role of women, however, had been to arrange marriages.

124. A person's adoption does not confer a legal blood relation for the wife of someone adopting another (Dig. 1.7.23); nonetheless, Hadrian calls Plotina and Trajan his *parentes* (see Ch. 5), and Matidia the Younger is termed the maternal aunt (*matertera*) of Antoninus Pius (see Ch. 6).

125. See Ch. 5 for the latter.

and silver coins from Hadrian's first year, and at the end of Hadrian's twenty-one-year reign Plotina and Trajan, now both *divi* and called "divine parents," were on the reverses of *aurei* with Hadrian on the obverse.[126] Issues from Hadrian's first year have the new emperor on the obverse and Plotina Augusta on the reverse, the first time an emperor is portrayed on a coin with the wife of his predecessor.[127] Also unusual is the aureus of 117–118 with Plotina Augusta on the obverse and Matidia Augusta on the reverse.[128]

After Matidia's death in 119 Hadrian gave a public speech mourning his "mother-in-law" and emphasizing her virtues, including that she revered her uncle Trajan "like a daughter" and was "most obedient to her mother, herself a most indulgent mother, a most dutiful relative," "by adoption cousin [to me]."[129] Although Hadrian's relationship with his own wife, Sabina, was allegedly so strained that he avowed he would have divorced her had he been a private citizen (HA, *Hadr.* 11.3), he did not separate from her.[130] Not only did he not divorce her—although Caligula, Nero, and perhaps Domitian had divorced while emperors, and Octavian had divorced Scribonia in 38 BCE allegedly for her stubbornness (Suet. *Aug.* 62.2)—but the year 128 marks a significant rise in "female coinage"—that is, coins portraying an imperial woman. Most featured Sabina. Such publicity made it clear that the women of the imperial family were essential to the image of the emperor, whether he had children or not.

Stress on family and children intensified from Antoninus Pius through the Severans. P. Weiss (2008) elucidates the important roles of marital concord

---

126. For the coins 117–118, see *RIC* II, Hadrian nos. 29–31; the *aurei* from 134–138 are *RIC* II, Hadrian nos. 232A, 232B, 387. For the date of Plotina's death and consecration, probably 123, see Appendix 1. A very rare, perhaps spurious Hadrianic *aureus* from Rome reportedly has Trajan's portrait on the obverse and Plotina's on the reverse with legends identifying each as father and mother of the emperor (DIVO TRAIANO AVGVSTI PATRI; DIVAE PLOTINAE AVGVSTI MATRI).

127. *RIC* II, Hadrian nos. 32, 32a, 33, also *aurei* and *quinarii*.

128. Matidia the Elder: *RIC* II, Hadrian no. 34.

129. Jones 2004, 268–69 provides these translations, from lines 4, 9, 25–26, 31 of *CIL* XIV 3579 = EDCS-04800013. For adoption, see Jones 2004, 273. Noreña 2007, 306 remarks this as the first funeral oration for a woman in the city of Rome in over fifty years (cf. Temporini 1978, 168–73; Jones holds it was not given in Rome), "signif[ying] Hadrian's intention to associate himself closely with the female members of his house."

130. A different concept is expressed in Marcus Aurelius' alleged retort to someone urging him to divorce or kill his "faithless" wife, that if he divorced her he would also have to return her dowry, that is, the empire (HA, *Marc.* 19.8–9).

Imperial Women within the Imperial Family

and imperial fertility (*fecunditas Augusta*) during the rules of Pius and Marcus Aurelius, and the emphasis this development gave both Faustina the Elder and Faustina the Younger (see also the conclusions to this chapter). Just as earlier marriage contracts in Egypt had been sworn in front of a statue of Julia Augusta, in 170 one was recorded as sworn in front of statues of Antoninus and Faustina the Elder.[131] A few inscriptions for imperial children of this period spell out filiation from their mother as well as father,[132] such as the later dedication from Sufetula to Marcus Annius Verus, "son of Emperor Marcus Aurelius and of Faustina Augusta [the Younger]" (*CIL* VIII 11323 = EDCS-22700718; modern Sbeitla, Tunisia).[133] As we see at the end of Ch. 6, Matidia the Younger calls herself in her building inscription from Suessa Aurunca "the daughter of *diva* Matidia Augusta, granddaughter of *diva* Marciana Augusta, sister of *diva* Sabina Augusta, maternal aunt of Imperator Antoninus Pius Augustus, father of the fatherland." The layout of the three-lined text on an architrave argues against seeing this as an ascending list; indeed, the letters of Pius' name are smaller than those of her grandmother's. Other inscriptions such as one from Ephesus follow the same "filiation," identifying her first by her imperial female relatives and then as "maternal aunt" to Pius, the adoptive son of her younger sister Sabina and Hadrian.[134] A later dedication from Auzia, Africa, identifies Geta as son of Septimius Severus and of "Julia Augusta [Julia Domna], the mother of the Caesars and of the camps," as well as brother of Caracalla (*CIL* VIII 9035 [p. 974] = EDCS-23200043, 205 CE; modern Sour El-Ghozlane, Algeria; see also *CIG* 1075).

The visibility of imperial women and family rose higher during the Severan era.[135] Again the attention on imperial family correlates with wider concerns: Septimius Severus claimed legitimacy through a fictive adoption by Marcus Aurelius (Cass. Dio 76.7), and granted to Roman auxiliaries and

---

131. Temporini 1978, 68–69. Yet we should not overstate women's influence: Marcus Aurelius' choice of Tiberius Claudius Pompeianus as Lucilla's second husband prevailed although neither Lucilla nor her mother thought him suitable (HA, *Marc.* 20.6–7; Levick 2014, 73–74).

132. Noting the mother is a marked development in a patrilinear society: Levick 2007, 63.

133. See also Titus Aelius Aurelius, "son of Marcus Aurelius Caesar and of Faustina Augusta and grandson of Antoninus Pius, emperor," commemorated in the Mausoleum of Hadrian in 161: *CIL* VI 994 = EDCS-17301105.

134. The inscription from Suessa Aurunca is EDCS-44100272, cf. *CIL* X 4745; from Ephesus, *CIL* III 7123 = EDCS-27800836.

135. For the stress on dynasty and "blood links" in the Severan period, much of which was focused on the women, see (e.g.) Rowan 2011b, 248, and Langford 2013 (on Julia Domna).

legionaries the right to conduct legal marriages while serving (Hdn. 3.8.5; see Ch. 7). Even women connected distantly to the Severan dynasty received conspicuous honors: Paccia Marciana, Septimius Severus' deceased first wife, was commemorated by the city of Cirta in Numidia, and as emperor Septimius himself raised statues to her as well as to his father, mother, and grandfather, according to the Historia Augusta.[136] More unusual may be the dedication in Palmyra to Julia Maesa, which identifies this woman as "Julia Maesa, sister of Julia Augusta" rather than in relation to the emperor.[137] Further, Julia Domna is the first imperial woman publicly depicted in religious rituals alongside the emperor, as we see in the following chapter. Along with other members of the imperial family, she also traveled with the emperor to an extent never before seen, both with Severus and later with her son Caracalla; her movements are detailed in Ch. 7, where we also explore the extraordinarily prominent roles credited to Julia Soaemias and Julia Mamaea, the mothers of Elagabalus and Severus Alexander.

A phenomenon especially connected with Severan empresses is their "maternal titles" such as "Mother of the Camps" or of some other corporate group such as the senate or the fatherland.[138] Such maternal titles echo those offered Julia Augusta after Augustus' death, particularly "Mother of the Fatherland" (Tac. Ann. 1.14.1; Cass. Dio 58.2.3; see earlier). As with the honorific Augusta, these maternal epithets proliferated in time. Domna, for example, became known as "Mother of the Emperor and the Camps and the Senate and the Fatherland" and also as "Mother of the Roman People" (mater Augusti/imperatoris et castrorum et senatus et patriae, mater populi Romani).[139] Similar designations were given to Julia Maesa, the sister of Domna and grandmother of Elagabalus and Severus Alexander, and to her daughter Mamaea, the mother of Severus Alexander,[140]

---

136. CIL VIII 19494 = EDCS-13003277, identifying her as quondam coniugi imp. Severi Aug.; modern Constantine, Algeria); HA, Sev. 14.4.

137. Yon 2012, 189 no. 192, remarking on this as unique. Palmyra is northeast of Damascus, Syria.

138. As we see in Ch. 7, the earliest appearance of mater castrorum is in 175/6, for Faustina the Younger: e.g., RIC III, Marcus Aurelius no. 753, denarius 175/6 CE. For lists (with dates) of such titles: e.g., Temporini 1978, 61–78 and Temporini-Gräfin Vitzthum 2002, 250, 276; Kuhoff 1993, 251–53; Levick 2007, 42, 93–94; Kunst 2010, 156–57. Hemelrijk 2012 explores similar titles for less elite women.

139. E.g., IRT 404; CIL VI 1035 (204 CE); CIL VI 419=30763; IGRRP 1. 577, with Ghedini 1984, 23 n.122; Kettenhofen 1979, 85–97.

140. Kienast 2017, 169 notes Maesa's titles mater castrorum and mater senatus were not official.

Imperial Women within the Imperial Family

who was even called "Mother of the Whole Human Race."[141] The titles are a clear indication of the strong familial ideology of the principate, which by this time featured imperial women as essential.[142]

Nontraditional imperial "families"

Despite the emphasis on "traditional" Roman families and childrearing endorsed by Augustus and continuing through the Severans, some emperors had conspicuously "nontraditional" families. Here I am not speaking of ephemeral liaisons and commonplace involvements between an emperor and someone not his wife, be that a male or female dependent, favorite child slave (*delicium, delicatus*), eunuch, or simply one of the helpless enslaved.[143] Rather, I focus on examples of an emperor's public, enduring relationship with someone to whom he was not married and with whom children were not expected.[144] Two of the three relationships we discuss below—Vespasian with Caenis and Antoninus Pius with Lysistrate—were with women now sometimes called concubines;[145] the other is the same-sex relationship between Hadrian and Antinous. Marriages between senators and freedwomen or between two men were not legal.[146] The three lasting involvements I treat here, however, seem to have been tolerated in their time: they did

---

141. *mater universi humani generis*: *CIL* III 7970 = *AE* 1998, 1094 = EDCS-28400655, from Sarmizegetusa (modern Varhely, Romania), 224–225 CE; *CIL* II 3413 = EDCS-05502796, from Carthago Nova (modern Cartagena, Spain), 222–235 CE.

142. Hemelrijk 2012, e.g., 202–203, underscores this within the Roman mother's highly esteemed family role in Roman society (cf. Dixon 1988); she also argues (pp. 211–12) that such titles enabled private women to have a role of authority otherwise denied them through official means. See also Nadolny 2016.

143. Domitian reportedly had a young eunuch "favorite," Earinus, even during his marriage with Domitia (Cass. Dio 67.2.3; ca. 95 CE according to Martial 9.11–13, 9.16–17, cf. 9.5, 9.7, 9.36; Statius, *Silv.* 3.4 and *Silv.* 3 praef.; Henriksén 1997). I classify among such affairs Nero's early rapport with the freedwoman Acte (contra Barrett 1996, 168–69), and omit Nero's "marriage" to Sporus in 66 or 67 (e.g., Suet. *Nero* 28.1; Champlin 2003, 144–50). The ubiquity of slaves enabled sexual liaisons with persons of lower status that were seldom seriously criticized.

144. I consider here "good" emperors, not (e.g.) Lucius Verus (whose mistress Panthea is known only from Lucian's *Eikones* and *Pro eikonibus*), Commodus (whose favorite mistress Marcia he treated "just like a legal wife": Hdn. 1.16.4 and Hekster 2002, xx), or Elagabalus (who "married" Hierocles ca. 220: Cass. Dio 79.15, cf. HA, *Heliogab.* 6.5). Treggiari 1991b, 52 stresses that concubines were not expected to bear children.

145. See Treggiari 1981, esp. 60–61, and below on Lysistrate.

146. See, e.g., Cass. Dio 54.16.2, 56.7.2; Dig. 23.2.44.

114   IMPERIAL WOMEN OF ROME

not threaten the emperor's rule,[147] and they are recorded with much less hostility than most reports of an emperor's sexual relations with married women or with boys of high status.[148]

Vespasian's Caenis and Antoninus Pius' Lysistrate, both freedwomen, are credited with illicit political influence in the court. Antonia Caenis, once the enslaved secretary (*amanuensis*) of Antonia the Younger and renowned for her prodigious memory, had a relationship with Vespasian that predated his access to power in 69 CE as a sixty-year-old widower. As emperor Vespasian kept Caenis as "his wife in all but name," and in that position she allegedly gained wealth and authority, "selling" political and religious positions and even funneling money to the emperor himself (Cass. Dio 65.14.1–4).[149] When she died before him he filled the void with a number of female sex workers (*pallacae*: Suet. *Vesp.* 21).[150] Some eighty years later another imperial freed-woman lived openly with an emperor, Galeria Lysistrate with Antoninus Pius. Lysistrate had been enslaved to Faustina the Elder, and became Pius' consort after her patron's death in 140.[151] Allegedly a guard prefect was disgraced in 158 for gaining his position through her favor (HA, *Ant. Pius* 8.9). Lysistrate is identified as "concubine of *divus* Pius" on an inscription to one of her freedmen raised after 161.[152]

---

147. Titus' years-long involvement with Berenice, sister and co-ruler to Agrippa II of Judaea and a Roman citizen, was denounced, and her repudiation by Titus in 79 is often read as appeasement of deep-seated Roman fears of "eastern" queens: Anagnostou-Laoutides and Charles 2015.

148. Citing an emperor's seduction of married women (e.g., HA, *Hadr.* 11.7) was a common way to impute abuse of power, and figures among the *topoi* for invective. See, e.g., Vinson 1989; Walentowski 1998, 233–34. Much of the animus against Hadrian's and Antinous' relationship comes from the Christian tradition, and is tied to the seriousness with which Hadrian approached it: Brennan 2018, 54–57. On the other hand, Trajan's reported penchant for young boys "harmed no one" (Cass. Dio 68.7.4; see Bennett 2001, 57–59).

149. *habuitque etiam imperator paene iustae uxoris loco*, Suet. *Vesp.* 3, cf. *Dom.* 12.3. Wallace-Hadrill 1996, 283 holds that her place in the Julio-Claudian imperial court helped Vespasian's rise.

150. An elegant funerary altar was raised to her as "Antonia Caenis, freedwoman of [Antonia] Augusta" by freedmen outside the walls of Rome near Porta Pia, *CIL* VI 12037 = EDCS-14800257. Other slaves and freedpersons of Caenis are attested in *CIL* VI 4057 = EDCS-19100262, *CIL* VI 20950 = EDCS-12201631, *CIL* VI 18358 = EDCS-10200557); a lead pipe from the Via Nomentana attests her property there (*AE* 1908, 231 = EDCS-16400411).

151. For Lysistrate, see Levick 2014, 61; Treggiari 1981, 66.

152. *CIL* VI 8972 = EDCS-18900039, *Galeriae / [Aug(ustae) liber]tae Lysistrates concubinae [. . .] divi Pii.*

The Historia Augusta, in a conventional disparagement of stepmothers,[153] explains that after the later death of Faustina the Younger Marcus Aurelius did not remarry but took a concubine instead so as not to put a stepmother over so many children (*Marc.* 29.10). Although such concern may have influenced Vespasian and Antoninus Pius as well, coming to power as mature men they may also not have desired more children; in addition, Vespasian had two adult sons. Concubines are often associated with childlessness.[154] That both Caenis and Lysistrate had been slaves before becoming imperial consorts suggests that they may have been past childbearing age. An emperor's sexual liaison that did not threaten to add children to an existing family configuration seems to have been acceptable.[155] In any case, Lysistrate's years-long open relationship with Pius did not impact the emperor's ideological promotion of Faustina the Elder. Throughout his principate an extraordinary number of coin issues memorialized his wife,[156] as did other public honors such as the Temple of *diva* Faustina in the Roman Forum (see Ch. 5). The Antonine era was a high point of family ideology.

An even more nonnormative imperial family is that of Hadrian, which openly included his young male lover Antinous from at least 128 until late October 130.[157] This same-sex relationship is renowned because of its relative longevity, candidness, and end. Antinous traveled with Hadrian and the rest of the imperial entourage. After the young man drowned in the Nile in October 130 a hero cult was established for him, with oracles allegedly initiated by the Greeks and welcomed by Hadrian (HA, *Hadr.* 14.7; Cass. Dio 69.11). Antinous is remembered in his numerous statues and busts—more now extant than for any imperial woman, and even more than for any Roman emperor other than Augustus and Hadrian. Literary sources also discussed him, especially early Christian ones that polemicized against the young man, his lover Hadrian, and the cult that posited a rebirth for him like that of Osiris, similarly drowned in the Nile.[158] Despite Hadrian's decried weakness for the "Bithynian boy," however, throughout his

---

153. Noy 1991, noting particular Roman concern about stepmothers and inheritance.

154. Treggiari 1981, e.g., 68–69; Gardner 1986, 124–25 on concubines of a senator or equestrian.

155. See, e.g., Anagnostou-Laoutides and Charles 2015, 38.

156. Beckmann 2012a. Beckmann 2011 dates the issues from 140 to at least 160 and through a die study argues that the reverse types "reacted to actual historical events [including the marriage of her daughter], as if Diva Faustina were still a figure very much alive" (p.511).

157. Antinous could have met Hadrian as early as 123: see Birley 1997, 158, 185.

158. There are more than one hundred identified representations of the youth. For recent discussions of Antinous and Hadrian, see Kampen 2007 and Brennan 2018, 106–24.

reign he notably publicized the imperial family and women within it, as we saw earlier.[159]

Vespasian, Hadrian, and Antoninus Pius alike successfully promoted the imperial family—the latter two including imperial women within the family—while simultaneously not personally modeling a legitimate Roman family. Their exceptionality reflects the unique status all emperors had; these three emperors were "good" ones, with generally positive reputations. Furthermore, although Vespasian's and Pius' concubines are criticized for "selling" imperial posts, the emperors are not charged with venality or laxness,[160] and neither woman faced legal proceedings or other repercussions. Their status as freedwomen ensured that they were strictly under the supervision and discipline of their patrons rather than of the state, as were Aemilia Lepida and other imperial women caught up in legal difficulties in the early principate. Caenis' and Lysistrate's long association with the imperial court, initially through the imperial women who owned them and then through their own positions as the emperor's partner, surely provided them with special insight and influence. Their gender made them easy targets of criticism, but their low status removed them as threats to the ruling elite and the emperors.

Scapegoating of women can also be seen in the reputation of Faustina the Younger. Her fruitful marriage to Marcus Aurelius was celebrated by coins, public sculpture, and ceremonies of the Arval Brethren and of others. Her marriage and births are associated with honorific titles and coin types. At her death an altar was set up in Rome, with silver images of her and Marcus Aurelius, where newlyweds were to sacrifice (Cass. Dio 72.31.1).[161] Marcus Aurelius lauded her in his *Meditations*, thanking the gods that he had "so obedient, affectionate, and frugal a wife" (*Medit.* 1.17.7).[162] Yet her exemplary accomplishments as wife and mother are at odds with the numerous literary accounts maligning her.

The disparagement and slander stem from Faustina the Younger's hated son Commodus, whose degenerate divergence from his revered father Marcus

---

159. Cassius Dio's puzzling note, that Hadrian was ridiculed because his excessive honors for Antinous were contrasted to a lack of funerary tributes for his sister Domitia Paulina (69.11.4), suggests a popular expectation of honors for female relatives in the imperial family by this time. My point is strengthened if Eck 1982 correctly dates to 128 the conferral of *Augusta* to Sabina; see also Ch. 4 on the rise of female coinage with Sabina in 128.

160. Cassius Dio does say, "It was even thought that [Vespasian] made money through Caenis herself as his intermediary," but that he killed no one on account of money (65.14.3–4).

161. See especially Weiss 2008.

162. See Temporini-Gräfin Vitzthum 2002, 252; Levick 2007, 59.

Aurelius became attributed to Faustina.[163] The Historia Augusta even reports rumors that Commodus was born of an adulterous relationship of Faustina, perhaps one tainted by a gladiator's blood (HA, *Marc.* 19.1–9).[164] The literary sources further vilify her by linking her with the revolt of Gaius Avidius Cassius in 175 in Egypt, Syria, and much of Asia; some hold that Faustina herself instigated him to rebel (HA, *Marc.* 24.6–7; Cass. Dio 71.22.3; cf. HA, *Avid. Cass.* 7.1).[165] The charges are implausible.[166] Faustina the Younger's wretched reputation in the literary sources emphasizes that, no matter how virtuously imperial women might fulfill the traditional roles assigned them, they could easily be condemned. Ancient authors allowed Commodus' shortcomings to overshadow the numerous positive messages exemplified by his docile and fertile mother Faustina.

Conclusion

Throughout its history Rome had intense population demands: the ancient mortality pattern of high infant mortality and a low life expectancy was aggravated by Rome's continuous military activity. The necessities must have intensified during the lifetime of Faustina the Younger, for the Antonine plague broke out in 165, desolating cities and camps, and the Marcomannic wars of 166–180 demanded ever more soldiers on the northern front.[167] These larger historical issues are the context for concentrated attention to the imperial family in the Severan period. Nonetheless, simply publicizing a "model family" could not redress Rome's demographic needs.

We can consider these questions on the microlevel through the individuals involved and their daily lives. Some pertinent information illuminates Matidia the Younger in the mid-second century, suggesting that her personal life often focused on other women and the family even though to our knowledge she herself was never married.[168] Inheritances from her mother Matidia the Elder were memorialized in various foundations bearing both women's names, permanently

---

163. Priwitzer 2009.

164. Priwitzer 2009; Boatwright 2003.

165. Boatwright 2003, 254–55.

166. See, e.g., Birley 1987, 191; Wallinger 1990, 56–60; Levick 2014, xx.

167. Harper 2017, esp. 65–118, analyzes and underscores the Antonine plague and the significant ecological changes contributing to the devastating impact of this decade-long pandemic.

168. I remain unconvinced by the speculations of Chausson 2008, that Matidia was married to one of the four consulars who lost their lives at the beginning of Hadrian's reign.

perpetuating the bonds of mother and daughter.[169] In the correspondence of Fronto, not intended for publication, Marcus Aurelius incidentally informs his teacher that Marcus' daughters are staying with Matidia in a town outside of Rome: we may envision a doting older aunt hosting her great nieces.[170] Other letters concern the disputed will of Matidia the Younger, showing that much of the woman's fortune, including a valuable pearl necklace, was destined for Faustina the Younger and her daughters and for another, unnamed female, as well as for an alimentary foundation (the "Varian protégés"). Although Fronto scorns the nameless female as an unscrupulous swindler, the discussion reinforces the glimpses we have gained of imperial and elite women associating with other women and within their extended families.[171] Extensive documentary evidence for Matidia, to which we return in Ch. 6, discloses her wide social clout in Italy and the provinces.[172] But that type of activity should not overshadow or discredit the more traditional domesticity and pleasure in female companionship that Matidia and other imperial women seem to have experienced.

This chapter has revealed that "the imperial family" was a cornerstone of the principate, but that it was difficult for imperial women to gain individual visibility within that construct. Although during his lifetime Augustus promoted "the Roman family" in various ways, his own wife, daughter, and granddaughter did not have conspicuous and enduring images. In part the unhappy histories of Julia the Elder and Julia the Younger have suppressed their traces, but their muted image may also be due to a deliberate return by Augustus to a legendary Republican ideal of women's relegation to domestic duties. Yet his family, called the *gens Iulia*, *gens Augusta*, *domus Augusta*, or another term, was the center of Rome's legal, political, and social life. At his death in 14 CE his widow was accorded extraordinary honors, including adoption into his own *gens* and the new name Julia Augusta. Six years later the *SCPP* openly acknowledged the significance of Julia Augusta, who had "given birth to our princeps." It also publicly identified as influential other women of the imperial family, lauding their virtues and emphasizing the image of a unified family. That image of the imperial family was to dominate the principate.

---

169. One in Vicetia was still providing funds in 242 CE: *CIL* V 3112 = EDCS-04202159.

170. Fronto, *ad Ant. imp.* 4.1, p. 105 VDH; Boatwright 1992, 29.

171. Fronto, *ad amicos* 1.14, pp. 179–80 VDH and *ad Ant. imp.* 4.1, p. 105 VDH. See Boatwright 1992, 29–32. Another example: Pomponia Graecina, the wife of Aulus Plautius (and in a traditional in-house trial found innocent by him of adherence to a foreign creed) was a devoted friend of Julia, Drusus the Younger's daughter killed in 43 (Tac. *Ann*. 13.32.2–3).

172. Bruun 2010.

4

Imperial Women on Coins and in Roman Cult

Introduction: Agrippina, Drusilla, and Julia (Livilla) on Caligula's coins

Central coin issues starting in the first year of the reign of Caligula depict him on one side and members of his family on the other, variously including—for the first time on Roman coinage—imperial women identified by name. The subject matter is unprecedented in imperial coinage. The coins advertise the young emperor, raised far from Rome in Tiberius' villa on Capri, as part of a strong imperial family. As we saw in Ch. 3, issues from 37/38 and later feature his (deceased) mother Agrippina the Elder on the reverse of coins with him on the obverse (see Ill. 3.3);[1] on others appears *divus* Augustus himself, the grandfather of Agrippina the Elder and great-grandfather of Caligula.[2] Other issues displaying the new emperor's siblings present him as part of a strong and fertile imperial family, the Julian *gens* at such difference from his aged and isolated predecessor, the Claudian Tiberius. For example, *dupondii* show his brothers Nero and Drusus galloping on horseback and identified as NERO ET DRVSVS CAESARES (obv.),[3] although like their

---

1. See Trillmich 1978, 38–40, 46–48; Wood 1995, 458; Wood 1999, 208.

2. Tacitus has Agrippina the Elder goad Tiberius by claiming to be the true image of *divus* Augustus, born from his heavenly blood (*Ann.* 4.52.2). In Caligula's desire to link himself with Augustus he held that his mother was born from Julia the Elder and Augustus, not Agrippa: Suet. *Calig.* 23.1. Germanicus also appears on Caligula's coins, e.g., *RIC²* I, Gaius nos. 15–18, 35, 43: Trillmich 1978, 38–40, 46–48; Ginsburg 2006, 62.

3. See Wood 1995, 460. Reverses feature a large S C surrounded by C CAESAR AVG GERMANICUS PON M TR POT: *RIC²* I, Gaius no. 34 (37 CE), no. 49 (41 CE).

Imperial Women of Rome. Mary T. Boatwright, Oxford University Press. © Oxford University Press 2021.
DOI: 10.1093/oso/9780190455897.003.0005

ILL. 4.1 *Sestertius* of Caligula from 37/38 CE, with (rev.) Agrippina, Drusilla, and Julia (Livilla) as Security, Harmony, and Good Fortune. © The Trustees of the British Museum.

mother they were long dead when Caligula came to power in 37.[4] The issues most important for my theme, however, are those showing his sisters as semidivine.

These fairly rare but higher-value *sestertii* as well as *dupondii* back Caligula's portrait, name, and titles (obv.) with an image of three standing female figures surrounded by the names AGRIPPINA, DRVSILLA, and IVLIA (Julia Livilla), with S(enatus) C(onsulto) in the exergue below.[5] (See Ill. 4.1.) Caligula's sisters had survived the diseases of youth, their father's early and suspect demise, and Tiberius' long and treacherous principate that saw their mother's tormented exile and death.[6] In 37–38 they were twenty-one or twenty-two, twenty or twenty-one, and nineteen or twenty years old, respectively. All were already wed: Agrippina the Younger to Gnaeus Domitius Ahenobarbus since 28; Drusilla to Lucius Cassius Longinus, from 33 to (probably) 37, and then to Marcus Aemilius Lepidus, perhaps in early 38; and Julia Livilla to Marcus Vinicius since 33.[7] Despite being

---

4. Nero Caesar died in 31, Drusus Caesar in 33, and Agrippina the Elder in 33.

5. *RIC*² I, Gaius no. 33 (*sestertius*), our Ill. 4.1; *RIC*² I, Gaius no. 41 (*dupondius*). Rowan 2011b, 245 n.13: in frequency estimations *RIC* holds these coins rare (only twenty, and fewer than five, examples, respectively).

6. They outlived three other siblings later commemorated by Agrippina the Younger (see Ch. 5), as well as their unfortunate brothers Nero Caesar and Drusus Caesar.

7. Controversy attends the year of Agrippina's birth and those of her sisters. With Barrett 1996, 230–32, Lindsay 1995, 8–9, and FOS #426 I infer that Agrippina was born in 15 CE and is the eldest of the surviving daughters. Caligula, born in 12 CE, was twenty-five in 37 CE. Wood 1995, 460 holds that the coins may have been "to prepare the public to accept a child born to any of the four siblings as the heir to the principate." Not all these marriages can be shown on our Appendix 2.

Imperial Women on Coins and in Roman Cult

named, the three are not portrayed as historical women or even generalized as Roman *matronae*. They appear, instead, as personified abstractions or deities. Their dress, attributes, and postures assimilate them to *Securitas*, *Concordia*, and *Fortuna*, the Roman abstractions of Security, Harmony, and Good Fortune.[8]

Their portrayal, together with Caligula's other issues depicting his family that included *divus* Augustus, alludes to the family as divine, the *domus divina* we saw acknowledged by 33. The issues, the first time that living imperial women are identified by name on centrally struck coins,[9] juxtapose explicit names to ambiguous images. The figures are hard to distinguish from one another: each wears a Greek chiton, himation, and diadem; stands facing the viewer in a *contrapposto* stance; and—in most types—cradles a large cornucopia. Only upon closer inspection can we discern distinctions and attributes. Agrippina the Younger, Security, rests her right hand and cornucopia on a pedestal, and places her left hand on the shoulder of Drusilla; Drusilla, Harmony, seems to hold a ritual bowl (*patera*) in her right hand, which she extends toward Security; and Julia Livilla, or Good Fortune, uses her right hand to govern a rudder resting on the floor.[10] The similarities of the three female figures embody the unity promised by the new princeps, a message averred also by the larger-lettered S C ("by decree of the senate").[11]

The divine aura implied for Caligula's three sisters did not ensure them secure, balanced, or fortunate lives. As others of this ill-fated family, the sisters were showily favored in the first years of Caligula's rule, including by religious innovations discussed in this chapter. But soon rumors arose about them and their increasingly erratic brother. Drusilla, reportedly incestuous with Caligula, died in 38 and was consecrated (Suet. *Calig.* 24.1–2; Cass. Dio 59.11.1–5), although her cult, to which we return, apparently vanished at his assassination in 41. In 39 Agrippina and Julia Livilla were exiled, apparently for adultery and treason after Drusilla's widower, Lepidus, was convicted on the charges.[12] Both Agrippina and Julia Livilla were recalled after Caligula's assassination brought Claudius to imperial power in 41, but their fates soon parted. Julia Livilla fell afoul of

---

8. Wood 1995, 461. For the distinctions between virtues (imperial or personified) and deities or abstract concepts, see, e.g., Wallace-Hadrill 1981, 308–10; Noreña 2007, 303.

9. For the unnamed woman, "Julia the Elder," on *RIC*[2] I, Augustus nos. 404–405, see Ch. 3.

10. Wood 1995, 461 gives an excellent visual analysis, citing *RIC*[2] I, Gaius no. 33, among others; Trillmich 1978, 39 "Typ 2," pl. 10.10. For brief overviews of these three ideals on coinage, see Noreña 2011, 130–40.

11. S C signified state guarantee of the value of bronze coins minted in Rome: Wolters 2012, 340.

12. Barrett 1990, 91–113; Cass. Dio 59.22.6–9; Wood 1995, 460; Ch. 2 in this volume. Caligula allegedly added to *maiestas* charges indictments for disrespecting Drusilla after her death: Cass. Dio 59.10.4, 11.6.

Claudius' third wife Messalina and then of Claudius himself, and was ordered to die in late 41 or early 42 (see Ch. 2). In contrast, the restored but now widowed Agrippina worked her way to imperial prominence, marrying first the wealthy Gaius Sallustius Crispus Passienus and then, widowed again, Claudius himself soon after the disgrace and death of his third wife Messalina in 48. Agrippina's status rose even higher in 54 when Claudius' death and Nero's accession made her Rome's most powerful woman: a direct descendant of Augustus, the daughter of Germanicus, the sister of Caligula, the mother of the new emperor Nero, the widow of his predecessor Claudius, and—as we discuss later in this chapter—the priest of a new imperial cult, that of *divus* Claudius. But she had no political or military position. By 55 her influence over Nero was slipping, and in 59 she suffered a spectacular death at her son's command.[13] Historical events belie the coins' assimilation of the young women to personifications and goddesses.

The coins raise many interesting questions, and in this chapter we explore two: coins as historical evidence for imperial women, and the connections of imperial women to Rome's public religion and religious culture. Coins have been cited as evidence in other chapters, and they figure prominently in discussions of imperial women and religion. They are not an easy read, however, so after brief words about Roman women and religion I include a section on numismatics. There I focus on imperial women's identification on central coinage of Rome, and their numismatic associations with goddesses, imperial virtues, and abstractions.[14] Numismatic portraiture was a singular honor, and coins' unique makeup with two signifying sides doubled the opportunities for persuasive imaging. It is generally agreed that the "collocation of an imperial portrait with a deity or personified abstraction . . . was a standard method for declaring a special rela-tionship between individual emperors and particular gods, goddesses, ideals and virtues."[15] This was true also for imperial women, even if the history of their portraiture on coins is not straightforward. In particular, we see that the women themselves determined neither their numismatic depictions, nor the choice of deity or abstraction for the reverse of a portrait coin.

In the chapter's second half we turn to religious practices actively featuring imperial women during the period up to 235 CE.[16] Women figure most nota-bly in imperial cult. Three imperial women served as imperial cult priestesses,

---

13. See Ch. 2.

14. We postpone to Ch. 6 discussion of their sculptural images in the guise of a goddess.

15. See, e.g., Noreña 2007, 302.

16. I do not discuss here imperial women's involvement with philosophy: see Hemelrijk 1999, 51–52, 123–26; earlier, Ch. 1.

fourteen were consecrated, and even more were named in the vows *pro salute*, for the good health and safety, of the emperor and members of his house that were made by Rome's Arval Brethren and others. As part of vows for the recovery of Julia Augusta from a serious illness in 22 CE, for instance, the equestrian order in Rome undertook a gift to Fortuna Equestris.[17] The collective act, and others like it, associated imperial women with divinity more than numismatic imagery.[18] Although the evidence I discuss reveals that religion is the arena in which imperial women receive the most visibility and honor, we also see that even here they had little agency and were sidelined. Their peripheral position is also perceptible in the reports linking them with Judaism and Christianity, discussed at the chapter's end.

Roman women and religion

Religious activity was traditionally the one area in which Roman women were viewed acceptably outside the home, especially during the Republic. Although women were barred legally and by custom from politics, law, the military, and other areas, gender lines were not as stark in Roman religion. Women regularly joined in public funerals, processions, and other religious occasions as mourners, observers, choral singers, and other ancillary participants.[19] A few had more prominent roles. In Rome the six Vestal Virgins and a handful of married women served religiously as active officiants and had conspicuous positions in religious processions.[20] Starting about 50 BCE inscriptions from Italy demonstrate some women were benefactors of religious buildings or served in religious roles.[21] Yet

---

17. See Ch. 1 and Ch. 5 for other events connected with her ill health that year. Tac. *Ann.* 3.71 details the problems caused by the vow, since no shrine of Fortuna with that epithet was in Rome and the gift had to be installed in a shrine in Antium.

18. See, e.g., Wallace-Hadrill 1986, 68; Price 1984.

19. Scheid 1992 and 2003b, e.g., note women's subordinate but key roles. Wives of senators and equestrians were at the funeral of Augustus in 14, and wives of senators at the consecrations and funerals of Pertinax and of Septimius Severus (Cass. Dio 56.42, 75.4.2–5.5; Hdn. 4.1–2). At funerals of regular citizens a professional female vocalist sang the dirge (Cic. *Leg.* 2.62), a role taken at Augustus' funeral by both male and female children of "leading citizens" (Suet. *Aug.* 100.2). Groups of women traditionally participated in ritual *supplicationes* (often with children: Livy 3.7.7, 27.51.9), hosted sacred banquets and sang hymns (see Severy 2003, 57–59 on the *Ludi Saeculares* of 17 BCE), and sang in choruses during apotheosis ceremonies (Hdn. 4.2).

20. For the Vestals, see Wildfang 2006; Mekacher 2006; and Gallia 2015. Hemelrijk 2005b, 137–38, and Granino Cecere 2014, 13, e.g., remark also on priestesses of Ceres, Magna Mater, and Bona Dea in the late Republic; see also Scheid 2003b and DiLuzio 2016.

21. Cooley 2013, 25–26. See further Ch. 5.

women in Republican Rome were usually inconspicuous in religious spheres as well as in other public arenas.

Their religious activity in Rome may now seem familiar because of the well-known procession scenes on the Ara Pacis (13–9 BCE; Ill. 3.1),[22] which include women and children. But the rarity of women's depictions on public monuments before that (see Ch. 6) reflects a limited acceptability of women in public even when engaged in religious activity, at least in the capital city.[23] After the Ara Pacis and the Augustan period, the visibility of imperial women in religious roles and venues slowly grew as they became priestesses of imperial cult in the Julio-Claudian period and, beginning with Drusilla in 38, were consecrated as *divae*, included in prayers, and associated with the divine on coins.[24] These changes made other women's public visibility more routine, especially when connected with religion and cult.[25] Thus, even if imperial women may not have claimed or even wanted the sacred positions and roles assigned them—other, perhaps, than Agrippina the Younger—their activities correlate with wider changes in the Roman world. Coins now most obviously link imperial women and religion.

Coins as historical evidence for imperial women

Coins are seen as Rome's closest analogy to modern mass communication and thus figure significantly in discussions of imperial ideology and culture.[26] Augustus' establishment of the principate included central reorganization of the chaotic coinage of the late Republic, and further consolidations and reforms followed, especially under the Flavians.[27] The institution of standing armies and the contemporaneous *pax Augusta* encouraged wider use of coinage for taxes, military

---

22. See Ch. 3, n.38. The monument was commissioned 4 July 13 BCE, but consecrated 30 January 9 BCE: for references see Brännstedt 2015, 40–41.

23. For the novelty of women on the monument, see, e.g., Brännstedt 2015, 40–41; Severy 2003, 62, 108–10; Kampen 1991; and Ch. 6.

24. See Chs. 1 and 5 for imperial women as patrons of religious buildings and dedications, and Ch. 5 as participants in religious processions.

25. See Hemelrijk 2007, e.g., 318–19.

26. I discuss coinage as a persuasive medium and not for its economic purposes (cf. Wallace-Hadrill 1986), avoiding the term "propaganda." Although often used, the term presumes deliberate organization, of which there is no trace (see, e.g., Levick 1982, 104–106; Duncan-Jones 2005).

27. See, e.g., Sutherland 1986, 89–90 for changes under Tiberius and later Julio-Claudians; Carradice 2012, e.g., 375, on Flavian modifications, which lasted over a century.

payments, public buildings and other imperial *beneficia*, and trade.[28] Since my work converges on Rome and the court, I focus on central coinage—that is to say, coins struck by imperial mints predominantly at Rome and for circulation in Rome, Italy, and the West.[29] The scale of this coinage was enormous. Although estimates are extremely controversial, Rome probably issued scores of millions of pieces yearly; perhaps as many as three thousand coins per day could be produced by two men at an anvil.[30] Whatever the original output was, only a tiny fraction now remains of the millions of gold, silver, bronze, and alloy coins struck in multiple copies by Rome during the principate.[31] On the other hand, extant coins probably represent most of the types that were struck.

Many factors are significant when assessing Roman coins, and I look mainly at individual designs (or "types"), and the combination of designs on both sides of a coin, the obverse ("head") and the reverse ("tail").[32] After the Julio-Claudian period the obverse is usually dominated by a portrait of the ruling emperor and frequently carries an identifying legend in the nominative.[33] The portrait conveys authority, contributing to the persuasive impact of a coin with the image of Rome's ruler.[34] Reverses, where most imperial women's images appear until 128, have a much wider range of designs.[35] First with Caligula imperial women's likenesses are found occasionally on either reverses and obverses, as we saw earlier, as were portraits of sons and other male members of the imperial family. But women,

---

28. Originally championed by Hopkins (1980; 1995/96), and contested by, e.g., Duncan-Jones 2005, 471–79; cf. Callataÿ 1995, 310–11; Howgego 1992.

29. Provincial coins, which reflected "local culture and concerns" (Rowan 2011b, 243; Howgego, Heuchert, and Burnett 2005; Harl 1987), are outside my purview. Some silver "provincial" coinage was minted not in the eastern cities in whose name they were issued, but by Rome's imperial mint; some central coinage was produced in mints elsewhere in the empire (Beckmann 2012b, 406–7; *RIC* II.1², 3–4). By the time of Nero provincial coinage circulated only in the East.

30. Figure from Walker 1988, 301–305; Callataÿ 1995, 301. Noreña 2011, 193 estimates that the Roman mint averaged ca. 22 million silver coins yearly between 64 and 235 CE, in addition to gold and bronze.

31. *RIC* 1², 11–13. See Callataÿ 1995 for debates over ancient coin production and the immense "gap . . . between the coins we have and the coins originally struck" (p. 291).

32. See, e.g., *RIC* I², 11–14, noting there is no ancient designation for obverse or reverse; Wallace-Hadrill 1986, esp. 69–70; Noreña 2007, 303.

33. *RIC* II.1², 13: starting with the Flavians obverses "more rigorously assert" the authority, the emperor ultimately guaranteeing the worth and authenticity of the issue.

34. See, e.g., Wallace-Hadrill 1986, 68–69, discussing Crawford 1983b.

35. Roman coining methods mean that reverses change more frequently than do obverses: see, e.g., Crawford 1983a, 207–11.

like males other than the emperor, were never the official minting power.[36] They had no official roles that might validate such decision-making, even if a coin's legend employed the nominative for their names.[37]

Because numismatic images feature so often in historical arguments, scholars have long debated about who determined types, the emperor or his functionaries.[38] Most cautiously concur that the emperor had nominal oversight, or at least veto power, in the choice of images—not only the imperial portrait, but also the combination of obverse and reverse images that is so important to the "message" of the double-sided coins.[39] A few ancient authors associate emperors directly with coin design (Suet. *Aug.* 94.12, *Nero* 25.2; cf. Cass. Dio 47.25.3).[40] Designs and legends suggest to some modern scholars that the Flavians were also quite deliberate about types, and Trajan and Hadrian were sometimes involved.[41] In this view the emperor, conceivably with members of his administration or court, signed off on designs and perhaps even the production size of individual issues, which varied considerably.[42] But we cannot establish a close connection between all emperors and each of the many types appearing during their reigns, especially when we consider the enormity of the production. It is tempting but often illusory to link any one type to a specific event.[43] Yet centrally issued coins can be used to evaluate the public image of the emperor and those close to him, which is what is often referred to as "imperial ideology." The designs were always flattering

---

36. Alexandridis 2010, 196 n.22. Those depicted on obverses are sometimes said to have the "right of coinage," a misleading term (Eck 1993, 41).

37. When the nominative is used with a portrait on the obverse, at times scholars refer to the issue as "in the name of." The dative appears less often.

38. Sutherland 1986 traces the development of central control of coinage "ordered from the highest level at Rome" (p. 90). Levick 1982, 107–108 finds unlikely "that the Princeps personally made the original selection" but concedes that the emperor may have been involved; she posits that mint officials divined types and presented them for approval (p. 109). Duncan-Jones 2005, 462–63 discusses some of the extensive bibliography on "the source of coinage policy," i.e., who determined designs.

39. See Noreña 2007, 302. Noreña 2011, 192 states, " these coins bore the stamp of imperial authority; . . . they carried symbols that were unambiguously official."

40. See, e.g., Wallace-Hadrill 1986, 68; Noreña 2011, 191.

41. E.g., *RIC* II.1², 13–14; Ranucci 2009, 359; Beckmann 2012b, 415.

42. To judge from coin hoards and other evidence: *RIC* I², xxi–xxii. I follow *RIC* about the commonness or rarity of issues, although these are only suggestions.

43. Duncan-Jones 2005. Some current references can be discerned, like dynastic politics or new or restored buildings in the city of Rome: see Beckmann 2011, 509–10 on coinage honoring Faustina the Elder, and Fittschen 1982 on coinage with Faustina the Younger.

to the emperor and imperial house,[44] and the inhabitants of the empire undoubtedly considered them due to the princeps.[45]

Numismatic images of imperial women may thus be understood as reflecting the preferences of the princeps or the court at the time about the public image of an imperial woman and her relationship to the emperor and Roman state, the authority for the issue. C. Rowan has argued that in a few cases, such as when a young emperor came to power, an imperial woman may have been "able to influence [her] numismatic image."[46] The extent of that influence is unknowable, however, and no literary or documentary evidence connects an imperial woman and coinage. It is sounder to use central coinage as a way to understand imperial iconography and ideology than for insight into an imperial woman's personality or preferences.[47]

The following discussion generally excludes coins that do not definitively identify an imperial woman.[48] Various issues have been said to link an imperial woman with a divinity, abstraction, or imperial virtue through assimilation: on these an imperial woman is allegedly represented "in the guise of" a goddess by being given the attributes of that goddess, including dress.[49] Without specific identifications like those for Caligula's sisters noted at this chapter's beginning, however, we cannot discuss such coins, whose identifications are unsystematic and can seem arbitrary.[50]

---

44. Levick 1982, 108 (e.g.) notes the idealization of Augustus' numismatic portraits. Even though the nine portrait types Fittschen 1982 discerns on coins struck for Faustina the Younger show her "aging" slightly between 145 and 176, they are persistently idealized.

45. Metcalf 2006, 42; Rowan 2011b, 243. Postulating ideology allows me to sidestep the question of audience, which (e.g.) Sutherland 1986 sees primarily as the army and senators, but Levick 1982, 108 as the princeps himself. Duncan-Jones 2005, 471 argues for "a lack of [Roman] interest in using coinage for communication." See also Wallace-Hadrill 1986.

46. Rowan 2011b, 244, addressing the Severan period, a suggestion also made for Agrippina the Younger (contra Ginsburg 2006, 57).

47. Keltanen 2002, e.g., reaches this conclusion.

48. Modern scholars sometimes identify earlier numismatic abstractions or goddesses as imperial women (e.g., Julia as Diana in 13 BCE, *RIC* I², Augustus no. 403; or Livia as Salus Augusta in 22 CE, discussed later), but see later discussion and Wood 1999, 63–64.

49. Matheson 1996, 182 uses this term. She makes a further distinction between association and assimilation, seeing assimilation as a more fundamental and complete identification, but association what has been described in the preceding paragraph. Such assimilations or images did not identify the imperial woman as the goddesses, however.

50. E.g., Wildwinds (http://www.wildwinds.com/coins/ric/agrippina_I/RIC_0046.jpg, accessed 13 July 2016) implausibly identifies as Agrippina the Elder the portrait of Justice (IVSTITIA) on a *dupondius* of 22–23 CE (see following note). At that date Agrippina was imprisoned and starving: Tac. *Ann.* 6.25; Suet. *Tib.* 53.2; Cass. Dio 58.22.4–5.

ILL. 4.2 *Dupondius* of Tiberus from 22–23 CE with SALVS AVGVSTA. Courtesy of the American Numismatic Society.

For instance, many have seen Livia as the female (facing right) above the legend SALVS AVGVSTA on the obverse of a *dupondius* of 22–23 (Ill. 4.2), citing this as the first time a historical woman's portrait appears on central coinage.[51] The argument depends both on the *nodus* hairstyle and features of "Salus Augusta," which strike some as those of Livia, and on the concurrence of the issue's date ascertained by Tiberius' twenty-fourth tribunician power (on the reverse) with a serious illness of Julia Augusta in 22 CE (Tac. *Ann.* 3.64.3).[52] Other authorities, including *Roman Imperial Coinage*, identify the figure simply as "Imperial Good Health," taking the legend at face value.[53] This facile assumption may have been that of those originally handling the scarce issue, if they could read the legend at all. Outside of the highest ranks in Rome, few may have seen Livia personally. L. Brännstedt has underlined the lack of evidence for Livia's public appearances in Rome. Further, Livia rarely accompanied Augustus in his trips to the

---

51. Rowan 2011b, 245 and n.12; Barrett 2002, 297; Wood 1999, 109. The identification with Livia leads some to assign the issue undue prominence, as B. Rawson in her review of B. Severy (*BMCR* 2005.05.15). Kleiner and Matheson 1996, 59–60, cat. ## 8–10, e.g., identify this, and two other *dupondii* of Tiberius from 22–23 CE, as Livia "in the guise of Salus Augusta, Iustitia, and Pietas" (contra Wood 1999, 109). The three latter images and legends again appear on the obverse of some very rare restitution *dupondii* of Titus in 80–81, where they are labeled as "Livia": *RIC* II.1², Titus nos. 405–409. See Ch. 3, n.98.

52. *RIC* I², Tiberius no. 47 (our Ill. 4.2), and nos. 50–51: (rev.) TI CAESAR DIVI AVG F AVG TR POT XXIIII around S C (Tiberius Caesar Augustus, son of *divus* Augustus, with tribunician power for the 24th time; by decree of the senate).

53. *RIC* I², Tiberius no. 47, describes the reverse as "Bust of Livia as Salus Augusta (?)."

provinces. Even by 22 CE most in the Roman world may have never seen her portrait, especially those who presumably used this low-denomination coin.[54]

The ambiguity of SALVS AVGVSTA on this centrally struck coin may be deliberate, as may be other female images on coins. Before the Augustan era Roman historical women were almost never portrayed publicly in Rome, and depictions of Livia and other imperial women mostly borrowed Hellenistic conventions for representing goddesses and abstractions.[55] The epithet *Augusta* is a further confounding element. Even during Augustus' own rule it became a common qualifier of imperial virtues, personifications, and gods and goddesses.[56] After 14 CE Livia was officially known as Julia Augusta, and many later imperial women received the honorific title *Augusta* (see Ch. 1). The numerous "Augustan" goddesses, ideals, and abstractions found on Roman coins may well have suggested Livia or another imperial woman to those handling the coins.[57] But we have no way of knowing this, and can merely point out the possible conflation of imperial women and the sacred on such coins. Other issues, however, definitely combine identified portraits with deities, personifications, and imperial virtues.

Numismatic portraits of imperial women—the "portrait type" or "empress coin"

Numismatic portraits, ostensibly real likenesses of their subjects, now often illustrate biographies and scholarship on imperial women.[58] Even at their most copious, however, from 128 through 235 CE, such portrait coins were a decided minority of the coins in circulation, at most probably only a sixth of a year's output (more later).[59] Imperial women are the only Roman historical females with portrait coins, and not all were so honored: Matidia the Younger was never

---

54. Brännstedt 2015; see Chs. 5, 7, and 6. On some provincial coinage Livia is explicitly named and at times shown in a maternal role: e.g., Barrett 2002, 139–41. Hekster 2015, 119. *RPC* 44, 46, 50 notes that cities of Asia usually distinguished larger coin denominations with portraits of the emperor, and smaller ones with portraits of his wife or mother.

55. See, e.g., Hemelrijk 2005a; Matheson 1996, 184.

56. See Panciera 2007b; Noreña 2011, 305–306.

57. In modern times this tendency is heightened when a woman's portrait is backed by the image of a goddess with the epithet AVGVSTA: e.g., the rare *aureus* with (obv.) DIVA FAVSTINA and (obverse) a standing figure of Ceres and the legend AVGVSTA (*RIC* III, Pius no. 356a) is captioned by Keltanen 2002, 127, fig. 26 as "Faustina the Elder as Ceres."

58. See, e.g., Giacosa 1977.

59. My arguments, following Duncan-Jones 2006, Rowan 2011b, and others, rest on analyses of coin hoards and a presumption of no systematic wastage or destruction of "empress coin."

named on a coin even though she was in her long maturity when such portrait coins were most abundant and her close relationship with Sabina and others of the imperial family, including Antoninus Pius, was celebrated epigraphically (see Ch. 6). Further, there is no direct correlation between the number of times an imperial woman appeared on coin issues and her position or influence.[60]

In Republican Rome, Roman women had not appeared on coins and were not portrayed publicly in sculpture. Even when men became depicted and identified on coins struck during their lifetime, a phenomenon initiating with Julius Caesar in 44 BCE and accelerating with Octavian/Augustus,[61] generations passed before living women were explicitly honored on centrally struck coins. Julia Augusta is the first living woman actually named on such a coin, on a *sestertius* depicting her privilege of a *carpentum* in 22/23 CE (Ill. 4.5; see below).[62] It took another fifteen years before living women were identified with female figures on coins,[63] when the names of Caligula's three living sisters accompanied small-scale female figures; as we saw, however, they had attributes of divine abstractions. Agrippina the Younger was the first living woman clearly portrayed and identified on a coin, on an issue struck after her marriage to Claudius in 49. Such "portrait coins" or "empress coins" present imperial women as historical personages by means of a relatively large-scale portrait on one side of a precious or base metal coin. The legend usually identifies the woman by name, often in the nominative.[64]

In terms of design, most numismatic portraits of imperial women, like those of imperial men, isolate the woman's profile view in the field. The posthumous portraits of Agrippina the Elder on Caligula's precious-metal *aurei* and *denarii* mentioned earlier depict her with the legend "Agrippina, mother of Gaius Caesar Augustus Germanicus," her son whose portrait is on the obverse (see Ill. 3.3).[65]

---

60. As we have seen, Livia was never depicted explicitly on central coinage of Augustus or Tiberius (see Barrett 2002, 140–41).

61. Wallace-Hadrill 1986, 70–71, 75.

62. *RIC* I², Tiberius nos. 50–51. See Barrett 2002, 144; Ginsburg 2006, 59–60.

63. See Hekster 2015, 112–13; Severy 2003, 43 n.39; and Wallace-Hadrill 1986, 75 for Octavia and Cleopatra on coins struck outside of Rome by Antony (*RRC* 527/1, 533/3a, *RRC* 543/1). For "Julia the Elder" on *RIC* I², Augustus nos. 404–405 (13 BCE), see Ch. 3 and Ill. 3.2.

64. See, e.g., Duncan-Jones 2006. Rowan 2011b, 247 also uses "portrait type."

65. AGRIPPINA MAT C CAES AVG GERM, from 37/38: *RIC* I², Gaius nos. 7–8, 13–14, 21–22. Wood 1999, 208 and Rowan 2011b, 245 note her inconsistent image over the four years of her son's rule. She also appears on Caligulan *sestertii* from Rome with (rev.) a *carpentum*: see *RIC* I², Gaius no. 55, 37–41 CE, and more later. She appears on commemorative *sestertii* struck 50–54 CE (*RIC* I², Claudius no. 102), and on "restoration" issues under Titus (*RIC* I.1², Titus no. 419).

ILL. 4.3 *Denarius* of Claudius from 41–45 CE, portraying Antonia the Younger and honoring her position as priest of *divus* Augustus. Courtesy of the American Numismatic Society.

Similarly emphasizing family, Claudian coins with profile portraits honored Claudius' mother Antonia throughout his reign. Some early issues in gold and silver match her portrait (obv.) to a personification of the "Steadfastness of the emperor."[66] Other early *aurei* and *denarii* couple her portrait and identifying legend (obv.) to two vertical, long, lit torches linked by ribbons and surrounded by the legend "Priest of *divus* Augustus" (rev.; see Ill. 4.3),[67] which emphasize the religious role she held briefly (discussed shortly). A third type, used for lesser-value *dupondii*, combine Antonia's portrait and identifying legend with Claudius, veiled, togate, and standing holding a *simpulum* or ritual ladle in his right hand.[68] These two early depictions of imperial women on coins both feature the deceased mother of the emperor, isolated in the field. Such a visual focus remains the norm

---

66. (Obv.) ANTONIA AVGVSTA (in nom.); (rev.) CONSTANTIAE AVGVSTI (in the dative). *RIC* I², Claudius nos. 65–66 (*aurei* and *denarii* 41–45), suggests the figure is Antonia as Constantia.

67. *RIC* I², Claudius no. 67, 68 (our Ill. 4.3), 41–45 CE: ANTONIA AVGVSTA, draped bust right, wearing crown of corn-ears (obv.); (rev.) two vertical long torches, lighted and linked by ribbons and surrounded by the legend SACERDOS DIVI AVGVSTI. Under Claudius other family members were depicted as well; the *aurei*, *denarii*, and *sestertii* honoring his father Nero Claudius Drusus (*RIC* I², Claudius nos. 69–74 [41–45 CE], no. 93 [41–50 CE], no. 109 [50–54 CE]) were more common than coins with Antonia.

68. *RIC* I², Claudius nos. 92 (from 41–50) and 104 (50–54 CE): ANTONIA AVGVSTA (obv.) and TI CLAVDIVS CAESAR AVG P M TR P IMP P P S C (rev.).

IMPERIAL WOMEN OF ROME

for an "empress coin"; similarly, depictions of the emperor overwhelmingly show him alone on the obverse.[69]

Agrippina the Younger is the first living imperial woman identified on a portrait coin, on a number of issues dating after her elevation as Augusta in 50. On *aurei* and *denarii* she appears on the reverse of coins featuring Claudius.[70] Claudius' adoption of her son Nero, then honored as "Leader of the Youth," seems reflected by the *denarii* with her on one side and the young Nero on the other,[71] Lower-value coins portray her on one side, and an honorific carriage on the other (the *carpentum*).[72] At Nero's accession in 54, extraordinary issues in gold and silver portray her, "Agrippina Augusta, [wife of] *divus* Claudius, mother of Nero Caesar," face-to-face with Nero (Ill. 3.4). Some, from 55, show her and Nero "jugate"—that is, with both busts facing the same way but overlapping (Ill. 3.5).

Portrait coins cease for Agrippina in 55, however, and remain rare for women into the second century. They become more frequent only in 128.[73] R. P. Duncan-Jones has analyzed material from Trajanic and other coin hoards to quantify what he calls "empress" (or "female") coin. He holds that during the Trajanic period, obverses of Plotina accounted for 1.9 percent of the gold coin, and reverse types for Marciana and Matidia the Elder for 0.9 percent and 1.0 percent of the gold, respectively (that is, 2 percent *in toto* for the two): in all, female coin constituted 4 percent of the gold coin from 98 to 117.[74] At Hadrian's *decennalia* in 127 and

---

69. On a smaller number of issues the field contains an imperial woman's image and one of the emperor or of the heir(s) apparent, as we see shortly.

70. *RIC* I², Claudius nos. 80 and 81, with legends AGRIPPINAE AVGVSTAE (in the dative) and TI CLAVD CAESAR AVG GERM P M TRIB POT P P, from 50–54 CE.

71. *RIC* I², Claudius no. 75, with legends AGRIPPINAE AVGVSTAE and NERO CLAVD CAES DRVSVS GERM PRINC IVVENT, from 50–54 CE.

72. *RIC* I², Claudius no. 103; *sestertius* from 50–54 CE. The single legend, AGRIPPINA AVG GERMANICI F CAESARIS AVG, "Agrippina Augusta, daughter of Germanicus, (wife of) Caesar Augustus" (nom.) suggest growing autonomy. Although Claudian coins honored his father Drusus as well as Antonia (see Ch. 5), it is tempting to see the restoration coins of Agrippina the Elder (*RIC* I², Claudius no. 102, 50–54 CE), as especially pleasing to his new wife.

73. Abdy 2014, 73 notes Sabina as the first empress honored by a sustained coinage, with ninety different types from ca. 131 to her death in 137. Alexandridis 2010, 196–201 dates to Titus the "beginning of regular mintings" for imperial women but in significantly low numbers: Julia Titi has nine types (five in silver) under Titus and five in precious metal under Domitian (Gregori and Rosso 2010, 203 count five, some with diadem); Domitia, twelve types (eight in precious metal) under Domitian.

74. Duncan-Jones 2005, 460 n.8. Duncan-Jones 2006, 223 n.5 adds that Trajanic "empress coin" in bronze and silver was "vestigial."

Imperial Women on Coins and in Roman Cult

Table 4.1 "Female coin" as a percentage of all coin, Hadrian (128–) through Commodus

Emperor	Silver	Bronze	Gold
Hadrian (128–138)	14	7	16
Antoninus Pius (138–161)	39	30	20
Marcus Aurelius (161–180)	34	42	29
Commodus (180–192)	12	15	3

Source: Duncan-Jones 2006, Table 1.

assumption of *Pater Patriae* in 128, however, the frequency of such issues rose, so that "[f]emale coinage was now ... a regular feature of mint output, not a mere after-thought."[75]

Duncan-Jones summarizes his findings in a table covering the period through Commodus, which I reproduce here as Table 4.1.[76] The high point is the Antonine period. Duncan-Jones contends that from 138 to 180 empress coin averaged about a third of all issues for precious and for base metal coins. One reason is that under Antoninus Pius appeared coins depicting Faustina the Elder (*diva* Faustina after her death in 140) as well as coins with Faustina the Younger, and under Marcus Aurelius and Lucius Verus were struck coins depicting Faustina the Younger as well as ones with her daughter Lucilla, honored as Marcus' daughter as well as Lucilla Augusta, the title she received in 163.[77] As we see later, many of these portraits of imperial women were backed by deities or abstractions.

Rowan's analogous analysis of silver coin (2011b) suggests that, after a dip under Commodus, female portrait coin rebounded in the Severan period:[78] she finds that portrait types of Julia Domna, Julia Maesa, and Julia Mamaea constitute some 18 percent, or a sixth, of the silver coinage of the principates of Septimius

---

75. Duncan-Jones 2006, 223.

76. Duncan-Jones 2006, 224 calls it a sketch. Rowan 2011a, 991: "the portrait of Faustina I graced approximately 22.5 percent of Pius' *aurei*, 30 percent of his *denarii* and 22 percent of his *aes* issues, significantly more than Sabina (who constitutes less than 10 percent of Hadrian's coinage), and slightly more than Faustina the Younger (though not on *aes* coinage)."

77. Duncan-Jones 2006, 224. Table 2 in Hekster (2015, 112, courtesy L. Claes) breaks down the percentages of different types of imperial women (e.g., [grand]mother, empress) on central coinage by emperors, also noting total coin types.

78. Duncan-Jones 2006, 224: similarly under the Severans two women were honored with coin, Julia Domna and Plautilla.

ILL. 4.4 *Aureus* of Septimius Severus from 196–211, with Julia Domna and sons Caracalla (laureate) and Geta. Bpk Bildagentur / Staatliche Museen / Art Resource: ART581546, ART581547.

Severus, Caracalla, Elagabalus, and Severus Alexander.[79] This phenomenon surely contributes to the striking visibility of the Severan women.[80]

Although exact numbers cannot be pressed too far, imperial women were prominent on centrally struck coins from 128 through the Severans. Gold and silver empress coin may have passed through fewer hands than did base metal issues, yet their valuable metal content may have made them more noteworthy.[81] Female portrait coin, especially in gold, must have contributed to the increasing awe surrounding the imperial family that was now termed the *domus divina*.

Images on the other side of empress coin fall into three main groups. The first, which we have already seen exemplified by Caligula's issues depicting his mother Agrippina the Elder (Ill. 3.3), clarifies family connections. At times a legend reinforces the importance of the imperial family to the state, as on an *aureus* with (obv.) Julia Domna and (rev.) her sons Caracalla and Geta facing one another with the legend "The eternity of empire" (Ill. 4.4).[82] This type is well represented throughout the phenomenon of empress coin.

---

79. Rowan 2011b, 246–47, suggesting that one of the six *officinae* in the city had charge of producing types for these women; cf. Hekster 2015, 112 Table 2. Nadolny 2016 notes more than three thousand different types for these three and Julia Soaemias.

80. Lusnia 1995; Rowan 2012; and Nadolny 2016, among others, focus on the coins.

81. Hekster 2003 suggests that although the evidence is uneven, gold and silver coins may have targeted senatorial and equestrian ranks and army, lower denominations the plebs.

82. *RIC* IV.1, Septimius Severus no. 540, 196–211 CE. IVLIA AVGVSTA (obv.); Caracalla, laureate and draped, face-to-face with Geta, with the legend AETERNIT(as) IMPERI (rev.). The coin shown in Ill. 4.4 is held in the Münzkabinett, Staatliche Museen, Berlin, Inv. 18203723.

ILL. 4.5. *Sestertius* of Tiberius from 22/23 CE, with *carpentum* and honors for Julia Augusta from the Senate and the People of Rome. Courtesy of the American Numismatic Society.

A second group pairs the portrait of an imperial woman with a pictorial reference to honors for her, most posthumous and almost all religious in nature (see Ill. 4.3, honoring Antonia as priest of *divus* Augustus). One signal mark of respect for a woman, the use of a special carriage or *carpentum*, is commemorated on a *sestertius* of 22–23 CE that marks the honor for Julia Augusta upon her recovery from illness in 22 (Ill. 4.5).[83] On this, the first of a notable series of issues for select imperial women, the obverse shows a richly decorated *carpentum* pulled by two mules and the legend SPQR IVLIAE AVGVST(ae) (The Senate and the People of Rome, for Julia Augusta). The reverse features a large S C (by decree of the senate) encircled by Tiberius' titulature that dates the coin.[84] From the time of Caligula the *carpentum* appears mainly on coins portraying deceased imperial women, starting with his mother Agrippina the Elder.[85] The carriage apparently denotes special funeral rites for the honored woman and repeated representation

---

83. *RIC* I², Tiberius no. 51, 22/23 CE. The issue is noted in Ch. 1.

84. TI CAESAR DIVI AVG F AVGVST PM TR POT XXIIII: Tiberius Caesar Augustus, son of *divus* Augustus, pontifex maximus, with tribunician power for the 24th time.

85. The *sestertius*, with an identified portrait of Agrippina on the obverse, shows (rev.) an ornamented funeral carriage (*carpentum*) with SPQR MEMORIAE AGRIPPINAE (*RIC* I², Gaius no. 55, 37–41 CE). Caligula's games and other honors for (his deceased mother) Agrippina the Elder included a *carpentum*: Suet. *Calig.* 45. Rose 1997, 41 notes Messalina's use of a *carpentum* in Claudius' British triumph (Suet. *Claud.* 17.2; Cass. Dio 60.22.2) denotes her extraordinary status.

ILL. 4.6. *Denarius* of Trajan for Marciana after her death and consecration in 112 CE, showing a *carpentum* (rev.). © The Trustees of the British Museum.

of her in ritual processions in Rome.[86] Such public celebrations memorably associated the honored imperial woman with religion and the divine, and were significant in Rome's popular festivals. The *carpentum* issues, such as that for Domitilla in Ill. 3.6, were permanent reminders of the events.[87]

More coin types in my second group denote an imperial woman's consecration. At times the legend CONSECRATIO accompanies an image of the woman being carried to the heavens by an eagle or a peacock, symbols of Jupiter and Juno, or graces an image of an eagle, consecration altar, funeral pyre, or even *carpentum*.[88] As on Ill. 4.6, by the time Trajan's sister Marciana died and was consecrated in 112 the *carpentum* seems to have symbolized this special honor for an imperial woman. Here we see (obv.) a portrait of Marciana Augusta with a diadem and the legend DIVA AUGUSTA MARCIANA, and (rev.) a richly

---

86. Latham 2016, 113–28 discusses the *carpentum*, the *currus elephantorum*, and carriages like the *tensa* (with a pitched rather than vaulted opening) for new imperial deities introduced into the circus procession, noting the prevalence of the barrel-vaulted *carpentum* for *divae* and the *currus elephantorum* for *divi*. The carriages apparently carried a statue of the honored individual. See also Castritius 2002, 174.

87. I look forward to exploring this topic in a future article. Here I simply list the nine women with *carpentum* or *currus elephantorum* coins: Julia Augusta, Agrippina the Elder, Antonia the Younger, Agrippina the Younger, Domitilla (probably the Elder), Julia Titi, Marciana, Faustina the Elder, and Faustina the Younger. All issues are posthumous other than those for Julia Augusta, Agrippina the Younger, and Faustina the Younger.

88. See Schulten 1979; Gradel 2002, 305–20; Noreña 2011, 192; Hekster 2015, 61–66.

Imperial Women on Coins and in Roman Cult

ILL. 4.7 Sestertius of Elagabalus from 219/220, commemorating the consecration of Julia Maesa. Courtesy of the American Numismatic Society.

decorated two-wheeled *carpentum* drawn by two mules and surrounded by the legend "Consecration."[89]

In contrast to the consecrations of some emperors memorably described by ancient historians,[90] such coins are often the best evidence we now have for the consecration of some imperial women, such as Julia Maesa. On the *sestertius* in Ill. 4.7, for instance, Maesa is portrayed on the obverse with the explicit legend DIVA MAESA AVG(usta), while the reverse shows a woman, presumably Maesa, holding a scepter and seated on a flying peacock, surrounded by the legend CONSECRATIO.[91] Although the first consecration of an imperial woman, Drusilla, was endorsed by a witness of her alleged apotheosis in 38,[92] the earliest explicit consecration coins attest Trajan's sister Marciana who was consecrated the day of her death in 112.[93] Some, as we saw on Ill. 4.6, pair *diva* Augusta Marciana with a *carpentum* and the consecration legend; others have her portrait and identification as *diva* Augusta Marciana backed by the

---

89. CONSECRATIO: *RIC* II, Trajan no. 746. The *carpentum* has an unusual pitched eave rather than the more common arched opening.

90. Cassius Dio details the obsequies of Augustus and of Pertinax, 56.42.2 and 75.4.2–5.5; Herodian 4.2, those of Septimius Severus. See Arce 2010.

91. *RIC* IV.2, Elagabalus no. 378, 219–220 CE.

92. Livius Geminius, who claimed to have seen her apotheosis, was rewarded with a huge sum (equal to one million sesterces): Cass. Dio 59.11.4, cf. Sen. *Apocol.* 1.

93. As attested by the *Fasti Ostienses*: Smallwood #22 = EDCS-20200012; Temporini 1978, 194–203. Gradel 2002, 301–302 summarizes and convincingly dismisses Bickerman's arguments

ILL. 4.8. *Denarius* of Trajan from after 112, commemorating Marciana's consecration. Courtesy of the American Numismatic Society.

depiction of an eagle about to fly, with the legend "Consecration" (Ill. 4.8).[94] The earliest known consecration coins parading a traditional apotheosis commemorate Sabina. After her death and consecration in 136/137 *aurei* and *denarii* were issued with reverses showing her on the back of an eagle as it prepares to fly skyward, with the legend "Consecration" (Ill. 4.9).[95] Faustina the Elder has a striking number of consecration issues of different types that extend unusually long after her death in 140 until her widowed husband Pius died in 161.[96] Other signifiers of consecration include a multitiered structure, often identified as a funeral pyre.[97]

The largest group of female portrait coins, however, pair the portrayed woman with an image of a goddess or an imperial virtue on the other side, suggesting a close

---

for a change in canonical procedure with Marciana's consecration. The earliest consecration coins for imperial men are those for Hadrian: Temporini 1978, 201.

94. *RIC* II, Trajan no. 743, after 112.

95. On the obverse is a diademed and veiled portrait of Sabina, with the legend DIVA AVG(usta) SABINA; the reverse has the legend CONSECRATIO: *RIC* II, Hadrian no. 418A, 136–138 CE. See Keltanen 2002, 124; Gradel 2002, 307–10. A miniature chalcedony bust now in the British Museum has been claimed to show the apotheosis of Julia Titi in the guise of a figure (winged? with a blousing mantle?) emerging from a peacock: Gregori and Rosso 2010, 207; Alexandridis 2004, 175 cat. No. 156, pl. 59.3. Alexandridis 2010, 212–13 notes this piece was for the elite.

96. Beckmann 2011. Rowan 2011a, 991: usually consecrations series were minted only briefly, at the accession of the subsequent emperor.

97. For the edifice, see Boatwright 1985.

ILL. 4.9 *Aureus* of Hadrian from 136–138, depicting Sabina's apotheosis. © The Trustees of the British Museum.

relationship between the imperial woman and the specific deity or abstraction. This may have been particularly apparent to those who handled the coins. I turn now to these issues.

Numismatic pairings of imperial women and deities

Table 4.2 presents a summary overview of the association of imperial women with deities and abstractions on empress coin,[98] although we cannot put together an analysis that discusses their nuances.[99] This table, illustrative rather than definitive, is based on *Roman Imperial Coinage*, supplemented by other research.[100] It shows how before the Flavian period imperial women are almost never portrayed on coins with deities or abstractions on the other side: if they appeared on a coin, they were almost always coupled with the emperor (e.g., Ill. 3.3).[101] Further, Table 4.2 reveals

---

98. Categories in my Table 2 are based on Keltanen 2002, although for convenience I have split them into deities and abstractions. The table cannot account, e.g., for the imaging of Agrippina the Younger, Drusilla, and Julia Livilla with which this chapter began.

99. I do not discuss details like the frequency of issues, their distribution among denominations, the placement of the woman's portrait on obverse or reverse, or the multiple numismatic links of individual imperial women to deities or abstractions.

100. Esp. Keltanen 2002; Beckmann 2011, 2012a; Lusnia 1995; Rowan 2011b; Kosmetatou 2002. I omit coins *RIC* notes as doubtful, such as the hybrids often considered a mistake.

101. Alexandridis 2010, 198 holds that Flavian women are paired with a personification or symbol, whereas Julio-Claudian women are usually with an image and/or legend of the ruling emperor.

Table 4.2 Imperial Women with Deities and Abstractions on Empress Coin

In the following table, divided for convenience into "Deities" and "Abstractions," imperial women are listed chronologically but deities and abstractions are arranged alphabetically. Without any attempt to denote frequency, X signifies simply that the deity or abstraction appears on coins portraying and identifying that particular woman. Other letters found within a column, such as L under "Diana (sometimes Lucifer)," signify that the deity appears only in that guise, i.e., as Diana Lucifer. Doublets such as X+L signify that the deity appears on that empress coin in two different guises, in this case both as Diana and as Diana Lucifer.

With Deities:

Imperial woman	Ceres	Cybele	Diana (sometimes Lucifer)	Isis	Italia	Iuno (Lu = Juno Lucina; R = Juno Regina)	Luna	Minerva	Roma	Tellus	Venus (F = Venus Felix; G = Venus Genetrix; V = Venus Victrix)	Vesta
Livia / Julia Augusta												
Agrippina I												
Antonia												
Drusilla												
Agrippina II												
Julia Livilla												
Claudia												
Poppaea												
Domitilla												
Julia Titi	X										X	X

Domitia Longina											X	
Plotina								X				X
Marciana												
Matidia I												
Sabina	X	X		X	X	X+R			X	X	X+G+V	X
Faustina I	X	X	X	X		X+Lu+R	X				X	X
Faustina II	X	X	X+L			X+Lu+R					X+F+G+V	X
Lucilla		X	XL			XLu+XR					X+XG+XV	X
Crispina	X		XL			X+XLu+XR				X	X+XF+XV	X
Julia Domna	X	X	XL	X		X+Lu+R	X?	x			X+V+G+F	X
Julia Maesa						X+R					XV	X
Julia Soaemias	(Annona)	X				X+R					X (Venus Caelestis)[1]	X
Julia Mamaea						X				X	XF+XV	X

1. This is the only time this goddess appears on central coinage; Kemezis 2016, 378 presumes it is to evoke her son Elagabalus' eastern religion.

(Continued)

Table 4.2 Continued

With Abstractions (sometimes with epithet of "Augusta," e.g., Pax Augusta):

Imperial woman	Aeternitas	Aequitas	Concordia	Constantia	Fecunditas	Felicitas	Fides	Fortuna	Genius	Hilaritas	Indulgentia	Iustitia	Laetitia	Liberalitas	Pax	Pietas	Providentia	Pudicitia	Salus	Spes	Victoria	Virtus
Livia / Julia Augusta																						
Agrippina I																						
Antonia				X																		
Drusilla			X																			
Agrippina II																						
Julia Livilla								X														
Claudia																						
Poppaea																						
Domitilla			X?					X							X?	X?						
Julia Titi			X												X				X			
Domitia Longina			X													X						
Plotina						X	X		X								X	X				

Imperial woman	Aeternitas	Aequitas	Concordia	Constantia	Fecunditas	Felicitas	Fides	Fortuna	Genius	Hilaritas	Indulgentia	Iustitia	Laetitia	Liberalitas	Pax	Pietas	Providentia	Pudicitia	Salus	Spes	Victoria	Virtus
Marciana																						
Matidia I																X						
Sabina			X				X	X			X					X	X	X	X	X		
Faustina I	X	X	X		X			X							X	X	X		X	X	X	
Faustina II			X		X			X		X	X		X		X	X		X	X	X	X	
Lucilla			X		X					X			X			X		X	X			
Crispina			X		X					X			X					X	X			
Julia Domna	X	X	X		X	X		X		X	X		X			X	X	X			X	X
Julia Maesa		X	X		X	X	X	X					X		X	X		X				X
Julia Soaemias																X		X				
Julia Mamaea		X	X		X	X	X							X	X							

both the paucity of empress coin before Sabina and Julia Domna's later saturation of the medium.

In the Greek East imperial women, beginning with Octavia and Livia, were explicitly assimilated to and worshipped as goddesses,[102] but this is not reflected on Rome's centrally struck coins. In the West, association of our women with the divine is found in inscriptions honoring imperial women "as goddesses" that may have been part of a sculptural ensemble (see Ch. 6). The phenomenon begins in the Julio-Claudian period with a statue base to "Ceres, Julia Augusta (wife of) *divus* Augustus, mother of Tiberius Caesar Augustus," which was dedicated by an imperial cult priestess soon after Augustus' death (from Gaulus, now Ghawdex, Malta).[103] Again, however, no coins associate Julia Augusta with Ceres. The statue seems to have been a spontaneous, popular dedication, not clearly tied to messages emanating from Rome.

Table 4.2 reveals that numerous female deities and abstractions, including Isis and Cybele, figured on empress coin.[104] Juno, Diana, Vesta, and Venus appear with the most imperial women, at times in different guises.[105] Most common is Venus, the goddess of fecundity. She is sometimes particularized as the legendary divine ancestor of the Julians, Venus Genetrix, and appears frequently by the Flavian period.[106] As we saw in Ch. 3, concern for imperial children and for Rome's overall birth rate was central to the principate. But many messages were embodied in the abstractions and deities paired with imperial women, attracting Rome's elite and others to the emperor and his family.[107] Coins link emperors with some of the deities and abstractions on empress coin, suggesting that some

---

102. See Hahn 1994, e.g., 359.

103. *CIL* X 7501 = EDCS-22100620. See commentary at EDR 112580 (accessed 30 June 2017).

104. Isis and Cybele, symbols of fertility, appear as early as Sabina but had long been part of Rome's public religion. Isis on Domna's coins usually has a distinct legend like "The Happiness of the Era" (SAECULI FELICITAS, e.g., *RIC* IV.1, Septimius Severus no. 577, *denarius*). Wood 1995, 481 sees a preference for "chthonian goddesses" rather than "Olympians."

105. See (e.g.) Matheson 1996; Temporini 1978, 72–76 for imperial women and Juno, Venus, Ceres, Cybele, and related goddesses; Foubert 2015, on Julio-Claudian imperial women and Vesta. As we see in Ch. 5 and the discussion of Domna's possible reconstruction of the shrine of Vesta in Rome, at times Domna's image appears with an image referring to the Vestals but with legends *Vesta Mater* (Mother Vesta) or the like: e.g., *RIC* IV.1, Septimius Severus no. 586, *aureus*. Such links are also made in literature: e.g., Ovid "reminds" Livia that he had called her the Vesta of the chaste matrons (*Pont.* 4.13.29).

106. See, e.g., Alexandridis 2010, 216–18. We may find shocking coins portraying an empress on one side and Venus Genetrix, nude to below the buttocks, on the other, but that iconography may have stressed fecundity or been understood as a type of costume.

107. Noreña 2011; Temporini 1978, 48–61 for imperial women and *Aeternitas* (Eternity) and *Providentia* (Foresight). Duncan-Jones 2006 sees abstractions as relatively infrequent.

Imperial Women on Coins and in Roman Cult   145

associations were not particularly gender-specific: issues featuring Ceres on the reverse are struck for almost every emperor, for example.[108]

In any case, evidence attesting imperial women in imperial cult, in oaths, and in prayers more clearly identifies them with the sacred. Such rituals surely encouraged the women's recognition as more than human as they involved participants viscerally, regularly, and collectively in community settings that reinforced the distinct sacredness of the occasion.

Imperial cult, and consecration of imperial women

Official consecration, or a senatorial decree of "celestial honors" (*honores caelestes*) for the deceased,[109] is crucial to imperial cult, itself a defining phenomenon of the Roman principate. Imperial women paradoxically were essential to this cult though at its margins. After Augustus died in 14 CE and was consecrated as the first emperor to receive this honor, Livia, now renamed Julia Augusta, was appointed a chief priest of the new cult. By 235 CE were consecrated fourteen imperial females, including the deceased infant daughter of Nero and Poppaea; this compares to nineteen males, including the deceased young son of Domitian and Domitia.[110] (See Appendix 3.) Some three hundred priestesses of cult for imperial women have been identified epigraphically from throughout the Roman world, attesting to the impact of imperial women on this new public religion.[111]

The difficulties of assessing imperial cult should not obscure the importance of imperial women in it. Imperial cult is inconsistent and diverse theologically and institutionally in the different spaces, practices, and personnel associated with it.[112] Official consecration differs from deific honors that Italians and

---

108. Noreña 2007 discusses the anomaly of the "Pudicitia" type for Hadrian.

109. For terminology, including *in numerum deorum referre* for the official act (e.g., *ILS* 72 = EDCS-12700639, cf. Suet. *Claud.* 45), see Eck 2016, 41. Benoist 2005, 108–109, 136–88 surveys some of the enormous bibliography.

110. Precision is difficult: e.g., in 218 the Arvals record that they made sacrifices for twenty *divi* (*CFA* 100 = EDCS-19000364). Scheid 1998, p. 300 a, line 4 suggests that the twenty include the six *divae* Julia Augusta, Poppaea, Plotina, Sabina, and the two Faustinas. Duncan-Jones 2006, 223 n.2, however, tenders Marciana, Matidia, Plotina, Sabina, and the two Faustinas. See further later.

111. See especially Hemelrijk 2015, focusing on the Latin West; Granino Cecere 2014, on Italy; Bassignano 2013, on both West and East; and van Bremen 1996 (on the Greek East). Some of these priestesses appear in Appendix 3.

112. See, e.g., McIntyre 2016, 1–4; Scheid 2003a, 675; Beard, North, and Price 1998, 1:348; Cancik and Rüpke 1997.

provincials spontaneously offered individually or collectively to an emperor or member(s) of the imperial family, often during his or her lifetime. It differs from regular funerary commemoration.[113] It is also distinct from private veneration offered by a patron's *familia*, an example of which we saw in Ch. 2 with the *aedes* in Gabii raised "in honor of the memory of the house of Domitia Augusta" by two of Domitia's freedpersons.[114] Imperial cult was not imposed from Rome: in our period neither emperor, nor court, nor senate unilaterally initiated or imposed imperial cult practices.[115] Moreover, imperial cult did not strictly demarcate "god" from "man," but rather recognized a more delicate progression of status.[116]

Combining political homage and religious awe, such veneration was essential to the cohesion of the Roman empire.[117] Women were part of it from the start. Julia Augusta was one of the first priests of *divus* Augustus, and Antonia and Agrippina the Younger later became imperial cult priests in Rome. A number of imperial women were consecrated themselves, and in Italian and provincial towns their cult was overwhelmingly served by women who thus actively participated in the public life of their own communities.[118]

Consecration in Roman imperial cult was restricted to deceased members of the imperial family, and its complicated but flexible procedures fused the senate

---

113. Even from the extraordinary honors Cicero wished to establish for Tullia that comprised an "apotheosis" and shrine (*ad Att.* 12.18.1, 45 BCE): see Cole 2013, esp. 1–6. Price 1987, 58, 62–70 discusses imperial cult's ties with "posthumous cult" and the late Republican growth of posthumous honors for powerful individuals such as Sulla.

114. See also the villa of the Volusii Saturnini family in Lucus Feronia: Boatwright 2011a.

115. Cassius Dio's problematic statement, that beginning with Augustus emperors refused cult of themselves in Rome and Italy while alive (51.20.6–8), should probably be understood as meaning that they did not force it on others here: Granino Cecere 2014, 169–73. Some presume central direction of the provincial priesthood for imperial cult because of the Vespasianic *lex de flamonio Galliae Narbonensis, CIL* XII 6038 = EDCS-09303050: Granino Cecere 2014, 14–15. Reynolds 1962 argues that provincial vows *pro salute principis* had identical Latin forms everywhere, revealing central administration. The Roman state's reactions to Christianity are not treated here, although the lack of imperial directive is supported by Pliny *Ep.* 10.96–97.

116. Gradel 2002, 27–72.

117. See, e.g., Ando 2000, esp. 373–96; Scheid 2003, 675; Gradel 2002, 101–102; Woolf 2008. Excellent scholars of imperial cult explore different parts of the empire: Fishwick 1987–2005 the Latin West; Gradel 2002 Rome and Italy; Price 1984, Friesen 1993, Burrell 2004, and Zuiderhoek 2009 the Greek East. Granino Cecere 2014, 17–19, surveys scholarship esp. for the Latin West.

118. Hemelrijk 2007, 331 notes that, except very early, "the duties of imperial priests seem to have been segregated according to gender: male priests served the cult of the emperor and his deified predecessor(s), and female priests that of the female members of the imperial family."

Imperial Women on Coins and in Roman Cult

and court.[119] A sponsor, often the emperor himself as Claudius for Julia Augusta (discussed shortly), suggested "heavenly honors." For worship of a *divus* or *diva* to become part of the public state religion then was needed the senate's official recognition of the god-like nature of the individual (thereafter referred to as *divus* or *diva*), sometimes after a witnessed apotheosis; the appointment of a priest and the establishment of a priestly college (*sodales Augustales* or some derivation thereof) to oversee worship;[120] and, apparently, the establishment of a shrine or temple at which the deified's icon could be venerated.[121] Although the senatorial *Apocolocyntosis* is quick to mock the apotheosis of Drusilla and Claudius soon after their consecrations, a generation earlier the *SCPP* of 20 unequivocally publicized its respect for Julia Augusta and other women of the imperial family (see Ch. 3). In Rome the appointed priest (*flamen* or *sacerdos*) was usually a member of the imperial family, especially in the earlier period,[122] and three imperial women were priests during the Julio-Claudian period.[123] Official consecration engaged the elite and emperor of Rome in homage to the deceased as well as positioned them in relation to the living relatives of the new *divus* or *diva*. Usually at the beginning of a new reign, consecration helped legitimize and connect the emperor, court, and senate.[124] The consecration of imperial women demonstrates how important they were to court and senate.

---

119. See, e.g., Gradel 2002, 298–304.

120. Palombi 2014, 191 lists *sodales* including *Augustales, Augustales Claudiales, Flaviales, Flaviales Titiales, Hadrianales, Antoniniani, Antoniniani Veriani, Antoniniani Marciani* or *Aureliani, Antoniniani Commodiani, Antoniniani Helviani,* and *Severiani.* Rüpke 2008, 9–10 notes different *sodalitates* existed side by side, and adds *sacerdotes domus Augustae (Palatinae).*

121. Kierdorf 1986 adds the steps of *iustitium* (public mourning with suspension of juridical activity; see Drusilla below) and *funus publicum* (public funeral), poorly attested for *divae.* See Ch. 5. The shrine is sometimes specified as a *pulvinar,* a platform or couch on which icons could be placed and venerated (Price 1987, 77–78).

122. Many (e.g., Price 1987, 78; Gradel 2002, 275) see the chief priest(s) of imperial cult (the *flamen Augustalis*) modeled on the ancient *flamines* but without traditional restrictions. Although municipal positions apparently were annual (for both prestige and income for the city; see Hemelrijk 2015), in Rome the position of a *flamen/flaminica divi* seems to have been for life.

123. Rüpke 2008 also notes male *flamines divorum: Iulianus/Augustalis* and *Claudialis* for the years 14–59 CE in his lists of "Cultus domus divinae."

124. What happened thereafter was of less concern to the state, as Tiberius made clear by deciding, in two early cases of accusations of insult to the "divine" Augustus, that such charges should be treated the same as ones against Jupiter: "Injury to the gods was the gods' concern" (*deorum iniurias dis curae*: Tac. *Ann.* 1.73.4; 15 CE). See Bauman 1974, ch. 4.

Nonetheless, their consecrations are poorly attested, as can be seen in Appendix 3 that sketches out the evidence.[125] The discrepancy is so striking that scholars infer fewer procedural steps and less apparatus for *divae* than for *divi*, concluding that *divae* had less significance overall.[126] For example, *diva* Julia Augusta never had her own temple in Rome but was worshipped in the Temple of *divus* Augustus after Claudius sponsored her consecration in 42.[127] Faustina the Elder's temple, built on the northern edge of the Forum Romanum after her consecration in 140, was used also for the cult of Antoninus Pius after his death and consecration in 161.[128] Other consecrated females, such as Drusilla, the baby Claudia Augusta, and Poppaea, may never have had a permanent shrine.

More than a half century passed after the first official consecration, that of Julius Caesar,[129] before Augustus was deified after his death in 14 CE and his widow Julia Augusta made a priest of his new cult. A quarter-century later Caligula's sister Drusilla, who died in 38, was the first consecrated woman (Cass. Dio 59.11).[130] Her cult evidently disappeared at Caligula's assassination in 41.[131] That it was not Drusilla's gender that purged her is seen in the almost immediate consecration of Julia Augusta, who had died in 29 CE but became *diva* on 17 January 42 at the prompting of her grandson Claudius, the new emperor.[132] In turn, Claudius was consecrated directly after his death in 54, bolstering the positions of his adopted

---

125. Gradel 2002, 339–47 stresses the cult's flexibility that helps explain the spotty evidence for individual *divi*. Benoist 2005, 149–73 attempts to discern a system for imperial consecrations.

126. See, e.g., Palombi 2014, 191. Hemelrijk 2015, 70 holds that in Rome cult of deified imperial women was subsumed under that of the emperors; others, beginning with Oliver 1949, call (e.g.) Matidia and Marciana "second-class *divi*" (see Benoist 2005, 154).

127. For her consecration, see Cass. Dio 60.5.2 and Suet. *Claud*. 11.2 (mentioning divine honors only). It is unclear who in Rome undertook her cult, first entrusted to the Vestal Virgins (Hemelrijk 2007, 320), nor do we know who served other *divae* in the capital city.

128. See Ch. 5, and (e.g.) Boatwright 2010, 177–80; Beckmann 2012a, 43–48. Palombi 2014, 193 lists possible cult sites in Rome for the various *divi*, noting the total absence of evidence for the more "ephemeral" *divi* like Lucius Aelius (Hadrian's first choice as successor). After Antoninus Pius' death cult *sodalitates* met in [the Temple of *divus* Pius and *diva* Faustina] (e.g., *AE* 2011, 183 = EDCS-64000102; 177–192 CE).

129. See esp. Weinstock 1971 for Caesar's deification upon senatorial decree in 42 BCE, which allowed Octavian to be termed *divi filius* and Mark Antony to serve as *flamen divi Caesaris*.

130. In this long chapter Cassius Dio condemns Caligula's abuse of power, from incest with Drusilla to political misuse of the religious eminence of his consecrated sister. Suet. *Calig*. 24.2 notes the *iustitium* granted Drusilla (see Price 1987, 63 and n.121 of this chapter).

131. Wood 1995, 465; Benoist 2005, 141 suggests it lasted until 66. See Appendix 3.

132. 17 January was also the day Livia and Octavian married and the date of the *ludi Palatini*: see Benoist 2005, 139–40; Foubert 2010, 68.

son Nero and of his widow and Nero's mother, Agrippina the Younger. In the next generation Nero's first child was deified as Claudia Augusta when she died in 63 some three months old; two years later her mother Poppaea was consecrated when she died in 65.[133] Almost from the beginning, women and even girls of the imperial family were not considered unsuitable for consecration; indeed, before the end of the Julio-Claudian dynasty four females, but only three males, had been consecrated. The *domus divina* was more than a vague term.

The fourteen imperial women consecrated up to 235 CE compare to nineteen consecrated imperial males in the same period.[134] But numbers are not everything. The evidence consistently reveals dominance by men, perhaps most clearly in Tiberius' veto of the proposed consecration of his mother.[135] Women's more marginal status may also be indicated by a report in the often-misleading Historia Augusta about Faustina the Younger's deconsecration by Caracalla after her death and consecration in 175 (HA, *M. Ant.* 11.6). Although the evidence for her cult is not as full as that for her mother's, we should probably not accept this "secularization."[136] Analogously, Suetonius notes that Claudius' cult was abandoned and abolished by Nero before being restored by Vespasian, but no other evidence indicates any disruption.[137] Before turning to the information attesting cult for imperial women in Italy and the provinces, however, which is much fuller than the testimony for their cult in Rome, I first discuss the three cases of imperial women who themselves served as priests.

*Imperial women as priests (*sacerdotes *or* flaminicae*) of imperial cult*

The earliest elevation of an imperial woman to religious prominence comes in Julia Augusta's service as a priest of Augustus' cult in Rome, apparently an

---

133. McIntyre 2013, 225–28 collects and discusses the evidence for Claudia Augusta. The routine consecration of imperial women by the second century may be implied in the thoughts Tacitus attributes to those planning Agrippina's shipwreck: "The emperor would add for the deceased a temple, altars, and other demonstrations of piety" (*Ann.* 13.3.3).

134. Many lists are provided without full ancient evidence, e.g., McIntyre 2016, 1 and Palombi 2014, 192–93. But see Bonamente 1991, 60–64, Tables 1–5.

135. See Tac. *Ann.* 1.8, 1.14; Suet. *Aug.* 101.2; Cass. Dio 56.46.1–2, 58.2.3; e.g., Wood 1999, 81. Tiberius rejected her consecration by saying that she would not have wanted it.

136. It is dismissed by, e.g., Wallinger 1990, 62. See Ch. 5 on her alleged temple.

137. Suet. *Claud.* 45: *destitutum abolitumque*; see Palombi 2014, 191. Claudius' cult temple, the Claudium, was repurposed by Nero but later restored as a shrine: see Ch. 5 and Ch. 6.

150   IMPERIAL WOMEN OF ROME

appointment for life.[138] (For clarity's sake I sometimes use "priestess" here despite the often ungendered Latin and Greek terms for the religious positions of the three women.) Her precedence was followed by Antonia the Younger and Agrippina the Younger, all members of the Julio-Claudian family. The special honors for Augustus' widow at the death of her husband of more than fifty years included adoption into Augustus' Julian *gens* and the use of *Augusta*. Among the tributes of 14 CE were two novelties: the senate's appointment of her as priest in the new cult of *divus* Augustus, and the right of being accompanied by a lictor (Cass. Dio 56.46.1–2; see Vell. Pat. 2.75.3; Ov. *Pont.* 4.9.107; see Ch. 1). The cult of *divus* Julius had been officiated by men only, just as men had traditionally held the most prominent religious positions in Rome other than those of the Vestals. Controversy about Julia Augusta's title, *sacerdos* or *flaminica*, attends this unique and poorly documented position.[139] Whatever her title, the new priesthood presumably placed her at the head of processions and in front of senators, equestrians, and the Roman populace during sacrifices on Augustus' birthday and other observances.

Nothing shows her actually serving in her unprecedented role or undertaking any priestly duties before her death in 29 CE,[140] in contrast to Julia Domna's later religious prominence. A little pertinent evidence comes from the epitaph of Julia Augusta's freedman Cnidus, *ab ornamentis sacerdotalibus* (in charge of her ceremonial dresses and outfits for religious occasions),[141] and some scholars identify statues as depicting her as *sacerdos divi Augusti,* with her head covered by the *palla* (or shawl), knotted *infulae* alongside her neck, and a crown.[142] Julia

---

138. For the lifetime tenure, see Hemelrijk 2015, 77. Rüpke 2008, 161–70 lists Julia Augusta as *flaminica divi Augusti* yearly until her death in 29.

139. Although *sacerdos* appears in Vell. Pat. 2.75.3 and Ov. *Pont.* 4.9.107 (Cass. Dio 56.46.1–2 is unclear), the presumption that the position was modeled on earlier *flaminica* positions in Rome have led many to argue for *flaminica*. See Frei-Stolba 2008, 351–52 and 359–63.

140. Brännstedt 2015, 42; Rüpke 2008, 161–70; see Ch. 5. A relief panel from Aphrodias' Sebasteion may have depicted Livia sacrificing (Smith 1987, 125–27), which Barrett 2002, 197 suggests may have been in her capacity as priestess of Augustus.

141. From the *columbarium Liviae*: *CIL* VI 8955 = EDCS-18900022, from after Livia's death: see Brännstedt 2015, 42 and 250 n.45, citing *CIL* VI 3992 as another possibility.

142. Bartman 1999, 32–53, 44, 102–105, cat. nos. 104–105. Schulten 1979, 17, followed by Hekster 2015, 120, holds that the cameo of Vienna with Livia as Ceres holding a bust of *divus* Augustus depicts her as priestess. Granino Cecere 2014, 53–59 discusses the possible distinctive clothing for local and provincial *flaminicae*, which she traces to imperial example. It may have included a *rica* (small red fringed veil), *infula tortilis* or knotted *vitta* (special cloth headbands with ends alongside the neck), and a crown. Religious poses and attributes are common for female Roman statuary: see Julia Augusta's statue from Otriculum (now Otricoli, Italy; Ill. 6.3), that depicts her in a religious pose: Rose 1997, 97, Cat. 25. See later this chapter, n.146.

Augusta's patronage of the new Temple of *divus* Augustus, undertaken together with Tiberius (Cass. Dio 56.46.3), may have been associated with her priesthood, as also her sponsorship in 15 CE of public games for *divus* Augustus (Tac. *Ann.* 1.73). On 23 April 22 and again in tandem with Tiberius, she dedicated a statue of *divus* Augustus in the Theater of Marcellus. Neither of our two sources for the act, the *Fasti Praenestini* and Tacitus, notes her religious position.[143] In any case, such dedications are echoed by earlier ones credited to her in Rome, as we see in Ch. 5.[144] Perhaps her priestly activity was mainly in the palace, as the private three-day festival she initiated there in Augustus' honor.[145] This would be in keeping with the subdued role played by this first imperial woman.

Julia Augusta's position lay vacant for eight years after she died, until in 37 CE Caligula sponsored the appointment of his grandmother Antonia the Younger as priestess of *divus* Augustus (Cass. Dio 59.3.4; see Suet. *Calig.* 15.2). Slightly more evidence attests Antonia, even though she was *sacerdos divi Augusti* for less than a year, suggesting gradual acceptance of unusual honors for imperial women. Among Caligula's initial acts as princeps to promote himself as part of the Julian *gens* was his "bestowal" to his grandmother Antonia of all the honors Livia had enjoyed, and all the privileges of the Vestals (Cass. Dio 59.3.4, with Suet. *Calig.* 15.2; see Ch. 1). These honors must have included the priesthood of *divus* Augustus. Antonia, who died at seventy-two years old within Caligula's first year (Cass. Dio 59.3.6), could have officiated but rarely. When her son Claudius assumed imperial power in 41 her position as *sacerdos divi Augusti* was celebrated on coins (see Ill. 4.3) and a monumental inscription. Epigraphy found near the Arch of Claudius, built after 51 over the busy Via Flaminia in Rome, honors "Antonia Augusta, wife of Drusus (the Elder), priest of *divus* Augustus, mother of Tiberius Claudius Caesar [Claudius]," along with other members of Claudius' family.[146] As we discuss in Ch. 5 and Ch. 6, the Arch and associated monument(s) asserted the strong legitimacy of the imperial family.

---

143. EDCS-38000281, Tac. *Ann.* 3.64; Barrett 2002, 172. Alexandridis 2004, 36 notes that the religious roles of imperial women are seldom identified on statue bases.

144. Such as the dedication of a statue of a young son of Germanicus in a Temple of Venus found on the Capitoline (Suet. *Calig.* 7.7, *Galba* 18).

145. Although this was perpetuated by "whoever is emperor" (Cass. Dio 56.46.5), not by a later priestess of the cult.

146. *CIL* VI 921; see EDCS-17301042 and *LTUR* 1.85–86, s.v. "Arcus Claudii (a. 43 d.C.)" (E. Rodríguez Almeida); Rose 1997, Cat. 42; Kokkinos 2002, 35. A small relief found near Vienne in southern France, of a young woman with a diadem and *infula*, has been tentatively identified as depicting Antonia as priestess: *Claudius imperatore* 2019, 145 no. 45.

152   IMPERIAL WOMEN OF ROME

More evidence for the position's eminence comes in information about Agrippina the Younger's priesthood of *divus* Claudius after Claudius' death and consecration in 54. According to Tacitus, in the lavish obsequies of *divus* Claudius, Agrippina emulated the magnificence of her great-grandmother Livia (Tac. *Ann.* 12.69; see Tac. *Ann.* 13.2). The senate appointed Agrippina as priest of the *flamonium* of the newly consecrated Claudius,[147] and perhaps as *flaminica* she initiated the Temple of *divus* Claudius on the Caelian.[148] This, the largest imperial cult sanctuary in Rome, may have once housed the over-life-size statue of Agrippina found on the Caelian, which portrays her in a religious pose (see Ch. 6).

Tacitus holds that Agrippina actively desired her imperial cult priesthood, whereas we hear nothing similar for Julia Augusta and Antonia. The position must have brought great renown especially in Rome, the locale of Agrippina's duties, although again no evidence attests any religious service.[149] She did not have much time at the pinnacle of power, however; her fall from Nero's favor by 55 apparently curtailed her public religious and other activity.[150] After her death in 59 no imperial woman ever became a priest of imperial cult in Rome.[151] The desuetude must be due less to the absence of imperial women for the next few decades than it is to the horrified reactions of Tacitus and other members of Rome's elite to Agrippina's demands for power and visibility.

In any case, until Julia Domna nothing documents participation by any imperial woman in ritual activities alongside men.[152] In comparison to her predecessors, however, Domna is unusually well represented in religious situations. She is recorded five times in the Acts of the *Ludi Saeculares* of 204, in four citations among other *matronae*. Three passages are complete enough to reveal her

---

147. Tac. *Ann.* 13.2.6: *propalam tamen omnes in eam* [Agrippinam] *honores cumulabantur, . . . decreti et a senatu duo lictores, flamonium Claudiale, simul Claudio censorium funus et mox consecratio.* Tacitus' *flamonium* allows us to identify her post as that of a *flaminica* (not a *sacerdos*). She also received the right of two lictors: Ch. 1.

148. Suet. *Vesp.* 9. Agrippina's patronage of this sanctuary may suggest that Julia Augusta earlier donated the *Templum divi Augusti* in her role as imperial cult priestess. See Ch. 5.

149. Tacitus does depict her calling upon Claudius the god (*consecratum Claudium*) in reported harangues to Nero (*Ann.* 13.14.3). Outside of Rome imperial cult was undertaken by local priests and priestesses.

150. Morizio 1996 explores the chronology.

151. As stressed, e.g., by Frei-Stolba 2008, 345.

152. Lusnia 2014, 66–67, cites coins illustrating (rev.) the shrine of Vesta, with either single or multiple figures sacrificing before the temple, from Pius through the Severan period (e.g., *RIC* III, Pius no. 1384), but the females depicted are not clearly imperial.

Imperial Women on Coins and in Roman Cult

in action. In two instances Domna conducts with 109 other matrons the special rites of *sellisternia* to Juno and Diana, which included sacrificing pigs, dining, and a dance (*AE* 1932, 70 and *AE* 1935, +26 = EDCS-16100321).[153] In the other, Domna, called "Mother of the Camps and Wife of the Emperor" and grouped with "matrons," was on the Capitoline hill on the festival's second day when she was approached by a procession that included her husband, two Vestal Virgins, and the specialized priests of the *quindecemviri* (the priestly board of fifteen men), after which Septimius Severus led the prayer to Juno Regina.[154] It is true that other named women participated in the *Ludi Saeculares* of 204: the two Vestal Virgins Numisia Maximilla and Terentia Flavola, and 109 senatorial and equestrian *matronae*.[155] But Domna's leading role is striking and notably contrasts with the absent Livia in the record of Augustus' *Ludi Saeculares* of 17 BCE.[156]

Domna is also the first imperial woman visually depicted at sacrificial scenes, on the relief from the east pier of the Arch of the Argentarii in Rome (204 CE) and on the northeastern attic scene from the Arch at Lepcis Magna that also dates to the early third century.[157] In the Rome relief she stands centrally behind a sacrifice performed by Septimius Severus and another figure to her left who was later chiseled off, probably Geta. Domna holds up her right hand in a praying pose. (See Ill. 4.10.) On the left side of the extant Lepcis Magna relief Domna stands, accompanied by her younger son Geta, and holds a small incense box while glancing away as Septimius Severus, Caracalla, Plautianus, and others attend the sacrifice of a bull to her left.[158] (See Ill. 4.11.) The reliefs corroborate the inference

---

153. See Rantala 2017, 89–97.

154. Here Domna is referred to in the dative, *Iuliae Aug(ustae) matri castror(um) con[iugi Aug(usti)*, *CIL* VI 32328 = EDCS-20500150.

155. See EDCS-16100321. Of these only some fifty names, including that of Domna's niece Julia Soaemias ("Iulia Suem[ia Vari Marcelli]"), can now be pieced together. See Pighi 1965, 241–43: some fourteen are equestrian.

156. Severy 2003, 57–59 and Rantala 2017, 9 nonetheless presume Livia participated in the Augustan *ludi saeculares*. We cannot know if Messalina, Domitia Longina, and Faustina the Younger were noted in the *acta* of the *ludi saeculares* of Claudius in 47, of Domitian (88), and of Antoninus Pius (148): only fragments attest the Claudian *acta*, and the other *ludi* have no epigraphic record (Pighi 1965, 76–90; 131–32 for the Claudian *acta*).

157. I do not discuss here the puzzling Altar of the Magistri Vici Sandaliari from 2 BCE, although the woman depicted to Augustus' left is sometimes identified as Livia: Alexandridis 2004, 118–19, Kat.-Nr. 9 and Pl. 2.1; Lott 2004, 124–26.

158. For the relief in Rome, see Ghedini 1984, 27–53 and her fig. 1; Kleiner 1992, 334–37; Alexandridis 2004, Cat. 224. For the relief from Lepcis Magna, see Ghedini 1984, 61–64; Alexandridis 2000, 23–24; Alexandridis 2004, Cat. 227. For other identifiable and possible images of Domna from the Arch at Lepic Magna, see Alexandridis 2004, Cat. 219–221 and 228–229. Kampen 2009, 92 (cf. Hekster 2015, 151) sees the Lepcis Arch as stressing family.

ILL. 4.10 Julia Domna shown sacrificing with Septimius Severus on the Arch of the Argentarii in Rome (204 CE). Relief in situ, Rome, Italy. DAI Rom Inst. Neg. 70.993.

from Domna's involvement in the Secular Games of 204, that imperial women's participation in Rome's public cult was now acceptable and part of the image of the princeps and the *domus divina*. This is further buttressed by the deduction that Caracalla's wife Fulvia Plautilla was originally depicted in the relief on the Argentarii Arch's (west) scene, which now shows only Caracalla sacrificing.[159]

Although in the *Ludi Saeculares* of 204 and further inscriptions, reliefs, and other media Domna has less distinction than her husband and sons,[160] she *is* shown in religious activity, something hitherto not explicitly presented for imperial women. We see in the following chapter that her buildings and statues in

---

Levick 2007, 78, 135–36 sees the two images I illustrate as suggesting "the empress's lively interest in religious ceremony."

159. Ghedini 1984, 27–53; Kleiner 1992, 334–37. See Ch. 2 for Plautilla.

160. The fragmentary document has some twenty-five references each to Septimius Severus and Caracalla, mostly with full titles, and five to Geta. The forty other extant male names can be compared with the fifty-some names extant for women in the *acta* of the *Ludi* of 204.

ILL. 4.11 Relief from the Arch of Lepcis Magna (early 3rd c.) showing Julia Domna (l) at an imperial sacrifice. Now in the National Museum, Tripoli, Libya. © Livius.org | Marco Prins.

Rome are also comparatively numerous.[161] The growth of Italian and provincial local *flaminicae* serving cult of imperial women, to which we now turn, renders the depiction of the imperial woman in state ritual less surprising than it would have been in the Julio-Claudian period.

Local priestesses for consecrated imperial women

Much of our evidence for Italian and provincial imperial cult for consecrated women comes from numerous inscriptions attesting local personnel, almost always priestesses.[162] Because many inscriptions are incomplete or imprecise— noting merely "priestess of the empress(es)" or "priestess of divinized imperial women" (especially in the Greek East), it is hard to provide exact numbers, including of priestesses of individual empresses. But in 2013 M. Bassignano came up with 150 such officiants while surveying the entire Roman empire;[163] in 2014

---

161. At least two statues were in the Forum Romanum: *CIL* VI 36932 and 36934 (see Ch. 5).

162. Hemelrijk 2007, 331. See, e.g., Appendix 3, Livia = Julia Augusta #11, #12. For maps of the geographical spread of the personnel for imperial women's cult, see the works referenced here.

163. Bassignano 2013: fifty from Italy, fifty-one from the Latin West, and forty-nine from the Greek East. She accepts only inscriptions with priestesses explicitly of imperial cult, or that include terminology exclusive to imperial cult. For honors in the Greek East to imperial women through Sabina see also Hahn 1994.

M. G. Granino Cecere listed 71 *flaminicae* and *sacerdotes* in Italy for imperial women;[164] E. Hemelrijk totaled 281 such priests in her 2015 book on elite women in the Roman West.[165] Cult was surely more widespread than these numbers suggest, since rituals for consecrated imperial women seem often to have been subsumed under those for emperors.[166]

The imperial cult priesthoods in Rome of Julia Augusta, Antonia, and Agrippina, although they served cults of *divi* or consecrated men, must have helped pave the way for citizen women outside of the capital city to serve as officiants of imperial cult.[167] Local priestesses, called *sacerdotes* and *flaminicae,* attended cult of imperial women.[168] The phenomenon emerged in the Augustan period, with *sacerdotes Iuliae Augustae* for Augustus' widow even before she was consecrated in 42.[169] Municipal priesthoods seem to have been annual positions conferred by the local senate, with the occasional epithet *perpetua* ("perpetual") designating special honor,[170] and priestesses venerated living imperial women as well as consecrated ones.[171] Some local priestesses served multiple deified empresses in two or more towns: sometime in the last quarter of the second century a now

---

164. Granino Cecere 2014.

165. Hemelrijk 2015, generally interpreting the title *flaminica* as of imperial cult unless another deity is explicitly mentioned (2015, 48–50). As do Bassignano 2013 and Granino Cecere 2014, she includes priestesses for living empresses, e.g., the *sacerdotes [Iuliae] Augustae* from Minturnae (*CIL* X 6018), Pompeii (*CIL* X 961), Vibo (*CIL* X 51), and Corfinium (*AE* 1988, 422 = EDCS-10700953).

166. As we saw, for example, with the Arval Brethren and with the lack of separate temples for many imperial women. For dates, see Bassignano 2013, 177.

167. Even the relatively few freedwomen thought to be priestesses of imperial cult seem to have been wealthy and of high social status in their towns, as Julia Helias from Lugdunum (*CIL* XIII 2181 = EDCS-10501138). Bassignano 2013, e.g., 180 discusses freedwomen as *sacerdotes*.

168. There seems to be no real difference between the terms *sacerdos* and *flaminica*: see Hemelrijk 2005b; Granino Cecere 2014, 24–30; Bassignano 2013, 142, 176–78 (with earlier references).

169. See n.165, and distributions of sweet wine and cakes to women on the birthday of "Augusta" (30 January) and similar ones to the decurions and townspeople at the dedication of statues of the emperors and of Augusta (*CIL* XI 3303 = EDCS-22500177). Julia Augusta's birthday on 30 January was celebrated publicly during her lifetime: Tac. *Ann.* 6.5.1. A vow to the Juno (or spirit) of "Livia Augusti" was fulfilled in Africa in 3 CE (*ILS* 120 = EDCS-26900659).

170. See, e.g., Hemelrijk 2015, 55–56, 81–82; Granino Cecere 2014, 30–32.

171. Granino Cecere 2014, 32, 169 presumes that at least a quarter of her seventy-one priestesses served during the imperial woman's lifetime; Hemelrijk 2015, 79–81, citing priestesses for Antonia the Younger and Agrippina the Younger during their lifetimes (e.g., *AE* 1997, 397 = EDCS-02900106 for Agrippina), holds that most priestesses "tended the cult of the living Augusta and her immediate predecessors" in the Latin West. See also Gradel 2002, 99.

anonymous woman, probably from Pollentia (now Pollenzo, Italy), was *sacerdos* of *diva* Plotina in Pollentia, of *diva* Faustina the Younger for the people of Turin, and of *diva* Faustina the Elder in nearby Concordia.[172] Such priestesses presumably honored the birthday (*dies natalis*) of the reigning empress and perhaps the anniversary of her marriage with the emperor and the birth of their children; the days of consecration for *divae*; and more local festivities, such as the dedication of a temple or cult statue of a woman of the imperial family. Duties evidently included parading in procession, attending transfers of portraits or other symbols of the *diva* or empress, care of statues, *supplicationes* (rituals of thanksgiving), offers of incense, and attendance at sacrifices.[173]

Priestesses of imperial cult were often great patrons to their towns even beyond the feasts and distributions of food, oil, or similarly useful goods noted on many inscriptions.[174] For instance, the senatorial Plancia Magna of Perge, a "priestess of the empresses," sponsored for her city in Lycia-Pamphylia a complete rebuilding of its three-story city gate around 119–122;[175] Aponia Montana of Augusta Firma gave her town in modern southern Spain circus games and a silver statue weighing 150 pounds when she was made "priestess of the divinized empresses" in the first half of the second century.[176] Cult for imperial women could make quite an impact on local communities.

Such cult was not evenly spread in Italy and the provinces from its spontaneous inception for Julia Augusta to its demise after 235 CE.[177] It is particularly well attested in the second century, when numerous Trajanic, Hadrianic, and Antonine women were consecrated,[178] but less so in the Severan period, surprising in light of Julia Domna's prominence in religious settings. Despite its overall

---

172. *CIL* V 7617 = EDCS-05400867; see Granino Cecere 2014, 30 and 131–32.

173. Granino Cecere 2014, 52–54, with previous bibliography.

174. Studies of imperial cult priestesses remark on their visibility, local status, and financial resources. Hemelrijk 2015, 390–436 and her Tables 2.11 and 2.12 note benefactions linked with imperial cult priestesses in the Latin West; Granino Cecere 2014, 44–51 and her Table 4, in Italy.

175. *Archiereia ton Sebaston*: *IK* 54, Perge, nos. 123–125. Bassignano 2013, 174, ventures she served the cults of Marciana and Matidia. See also Boatwright 1993; Trimble 2011, 230–35. Perge is fifteen kilometers east of Antalya, Turkey.

176. *Sacerdos divarum Augustarum*, *CIL* II 1162 = *CIL* II 1471 (p 702) = EDCS-08701240.

177. For its inconsistency, echoing that of cult for *divi*, see, e.g., Hemelrijk 2015, 69–82. Gradel 2002, 356–67 argues for the defunding, and thus dismantling, of imperial cult overall by Maximinus in 235–238 CE (Hdn. 7.3.5–6, in Gradel's translation).

178. For dates see, e.g., Granino Cecere 2014, 19–21. Second-century female consecrations are more than half of the non-ephemeral consecrations though six of my fourteen total *divae*.

158   IMPERIAL WOMEN OF ROME

popularity and local impact, however, it involved individual imperial women but little. The proposed involvement of Julia Augusta in determining imperial cult and honors for herself in Gytheion, Sparta's port in the southern Peloponnese, between 14 and 19 CE,[179] is unparalleled. In many cases the deified woman (or women) served by local priestesses is not named but referred to as "divine Augusta" (*diva Augusta*), *diva*, or *Augusta*, sometimes in the plural.[180] Thus the phenomenon of cult for imperial women in Rome's towns and cities accrued to the awe of the imperial family rather than to any individual, even though it was undoubtedly significant for the local priestesses and their communities.

Oaths

Imperial women's inclusion in oaths also contributed to awe for them and the imperial house. Yet women were not included in Rome's most sacred and important oaths, those undertaken collectively by the senate and the army, revealing yet again women's enduring marginality. One annual Roman oath of loyalty was derived from that to Octavian sworn in 32 BCE by "all of Italy" and the provinces of Gaul, Spain, Africa, Sicily, and Sardinia (*RGDA* 25; see also Cass. Dio 50.6.6 and Suet. *Aug.* 17.2).[181] A few later communal oaths are noted by historians or recorded on inscriptions found in modern Spain, Turkey, and elsewhere.[182] The earliest epigraphically attested, probably from Conobaria in Baetica in 6/5 BCE, specifies Augustus himself, his sons Gaius and Lucius, and his grandson Marcus

---

179. *SEG* 11.922-3 = *EJ* 102: the city offered honors to Augustus, Tiberius, Julia Augusta, Germanicus, and Drusus (the Younger) that included a *Kaisareia* festival, painted images (perhaps statues) of Augustus, Tiberius, and Julia Augusta, and sacrifices on behalf of the imperial family; Tiberius accepted the honors for Augustus, refused his own, and allowed his mother to respond for herself. Text, translation, and commentary are in Rose 1997, 142–44, cat. 74; cf. Barrett 2002, 211. In the record of Hispania Ulterior's request in 25 to set up a *delubrum* (shrine) to Tiberius and his mother on the earlier example of Asia, there is no mention of Julia Augusta's input (Tac. *Ann.* 4.37–38; the Asia example is found at *Ann.* 4.15).

180. See, e.g., Granino Cecere 2014, 29–30; Bassignano 2013, 178–79.

181. *RGDA* 25.2, *iuravit in mea verba tota Italia sponte sua* . . . is often translated as "All of Italy spontaneously swore an oath of allegiance to me." González 1988, 125 holds that *In mea verba* is military language; Cooley 2009, 215–16 *ad loc.*, that Octavian was acting as a private individual unsure of his *imperium*, and that the oath bound military and civilians (contra Herrmann 1968, 78–89). González 1988, 118 discusses similarities with the fidelity oath to Julius Caesar in 44 BCE, as well as with later oaths.

182. Herrmann 1968, 122–26, App. I quotes the six oaths then known; see Rowe 2002, especially for the Tiberian period. Brunt and Moore 1967, 67–68 *ad RGDA* 25.2 note that such oaths, which became annual in 38 CE, were taken by civilians as well as by the rank and file, binding the oath-takers to an individual man rather than to an inaugurated magistrate of the Roman people.

Imperial Women on Coins and in Roman Cult   159

Agrippa (Agrippa Postumus) (*AE* 1988, 723 = EDCS-32803827; now Las Cabezas de San Juan, Spain).[183] The Paphlagonian Oath of allegiance of 3 BCE (*OGIS* 532 = *ILS* 8781) was sworn to protect Augustus and his descendants.[184] An oath taken by the Cypriots immediately after the accession of Tiberius in 14 CE binds them to worship the household of Tiberius Caesar Augustus, and to give divine honors to Tiberius and the sons of his blood.[185] In time such oaths included all living and previous (good) emperors, to judge from Cassius Dio's note of the "catalogue of emperors whom we mention in oaths and prayers" (60.4.6, set in 41 CE).[186] But all those named individually or collectively are male.

Cassius Dio's comment applies as well to another type of political oath, that sworn yearly by the senate to uphold the acts of former and current emperors.[187] Such political oaths inherently excluded women: without the capacity for *imperium* or another means of command (see Chs. 1, 2, and 5), women could make no decisions for the state (*acta*). The absence of deified imperial women's names in annual oaths found in the Flavian municipal laws from Spain further indicates that women had no mention in such political formulations.[188] I know of no examples of the oath soldiers swore upon entering military service, to "value the safety of the emperor above everything" (Arr. *Epict. diss.* 1.14.15–17), but I doubt that this named imperial women: women could not serve or command militarily. Although imperial women had increasing visibility as part of the imperial family and *domus divina*, they must never have been a regular part of political and military oaths.

---

183. González 1988, 120 stresses the dynastic element of this oath on behalf of the safety and well-being, honor, and victory of the four; in the lacunose text Gaius' name is plausibly supplied. The text is also in Rowe 2002, 152, cf. 135–37, and see Wardle 2000, 479–80.

184. Rowe 2002, 134–49 (esp. p. 137) holds that lines 8–11 designated descendants from women as well as from Augustus, although its main concern was for male members of the family. Herrmann 1968, 43–45 underlines the lack of "precedent . . . to cover the ruler's family."

185. Flory 1995, 131, with references.

186. See also Cass. Dio 53.28.1, the senate's oath in 24 BCE to confirm and uphold Augustus' acts; Cass. Dio 59.9.1–2, the senate's oath to uphold acts of Augustus and Gaius in 38 CE; and under Claudius the senate's and emperor's oaths merely in Augustus' name (Suet. *Claud.* 11.2 and Cass. Dio 60.10.1). Brunt 1977, 115–16 notes that Clause VIII of the *lex de imperio Vespasiani* (70 CE) "suggests the kind of formula that could have been used when the senate swore to uphold the *acta* of a past emperor."

187. Cass. Dio 57.3.2 and 57.8.4–5, reporting on Tiberius; Tac. *Ann.* 4.42.3 and 13.11.1; cf. Tac. *Ann.* 1.7 and 1.34 (both *in verba* [*Tiberi Caesaris*]). Perhaps the earliest is the triumviral oath *in acta Caesaris* on 1 January 42 BCE: Cass. Dio 47.18.1–19.3. In 38 Caligula removed Tiberius from the oath: Cass. Dio 59.9.1.

188. Bonamente 1991, 71.

On the other hand, imperial women were included in some collective oaths and prayers. Caligula is again a striking innovator. Upon Drusilla's death and consecration in 38 Caligula decreed that whenever Roman women took an oath, they had to add the name of *diva* Drusilla to the vow (Cass. Dio 59.11.3; cf. Suet. *Calig.* 24.4). More unusually, he also reportedly forced the inclusion of his sisters' names along with his own in the "oaths of allegiance that were sworn to his rule" (Cass. Dio 59.3.4; Suet. *Calig.* 15.3).[189] Caligula's sisters seem to have soon dropped from the oaths;[190] after Julia Augusta's consecration in 42 Claudius decreed that women must add her name to vows whenever they took an oath (Cass. Dio 60.5.2).[191] Both emperors presumably acted in their positions as *pontifex maximus*. No examples of such personal oaths survive, so we do not know whether later consecrated imperial women similarly had their names added.

Imperial women were also included in *pro salute* vows for the emperor and his family. After Octavian consolidated power following the Battle of Actium in 31 BCE, prayers proliferated for his welfare in Rome, Italy, the provinces, and military settings, to uphold his health, safety, and well-being (*salus*).[192] The number of occasions quickly increased and the vows grew to include the imperial family.[193] The veneration apparently developed after 1 January 29 BCE, when the Roman people ratified Octavian's acts by oath and added other rights, privileges, and honors for the victorious princeps. Thereafter priests and priestesses were to pray for Octavian when praying on behalf of the Roman people and senate; Octavian's name was to be included in hymns along with the names of the gods; and those attending any public or private banquet had to pour a libation for him (Cass. Dio 51.19.7–20.1).[194]

---

189. Suet. *Calig.* 15.3 specifies *neque me liberosque meos cariores habebo quam Gaium habeo et sorores eius* and (for propositions of the consuls) *quod bonum felixque sit C. Caesari sororibusque eius*; see Scheid 2003a, 673. Wood 1995, 458 takes the information at face value.

190. See Bonamente 1991, 69, and Herrmann 1968, 107–10.

191. Frei-Stolba 2008, 381 sees these decrees as establishing and strengthening a special tie between a divinized empress and women; see also Cogitore 2000, 249.

192. Eck 2016 notes these do not denote veneration to the emperor himself.

193. As, for example, on the emperor's *dies imperii* (Plin. *Ep.* 10.52–53 and 102–103), his birthday (Plin. *Ep.* 10.89), and the like. Cooley 2009, 145 *ad RGDA* 9.1, notes several kinds of prayers for Augustus' welfare undertaken at Rome, including annual vows on 1 January (cf. Suet. *Aug.* 57.1, *ILS* 99), quadrennial vows, and vows in times of crisis.

194. For ties to earlier honors and prayers for Caesar (see App. *B Civ.* 2.16.106; Cass. Dio 44.6), see Herrmann 1968, 72–73, 108.

Imperial Women on Coins and in Roman Cult

Growing identification of Augustus with his family explains the addition of his *domus* and individual family members to such prayers and vows.[195] As we saw in Ch. 3, when Augustus was declared Pater Patriae in 2 BCE the formal decree by Valerius Messala Corvinus included prayers for the well-being and prosperity of Augustus and his family.[196] The Acts of the Arval Brethren, other inscriptions, and literary references show inclusion of the imperial house as a whole (*domus [imperatoris]*) in oaths and official vows. The Arval Acts and other evidence reveal that in time individual women also were the object of veneration or vows, particularly ones *pro salute* (for good health and safety), usually alongside others of the imperial family.[197] The consecration day of the Ara Pacis in 9 BCE coincided with Livia's fiftieth birthday, and *RGDA* 12 notes that the senate ordered magistrates, priests, and Vestal Virgins to perform an annual sacrifice at the altar. Julia Augusta was named in Arval prayers as early as 21 CE, and in 27 the Arvals are documented as undertaking vows on her birthday, 30 January.[198] After her death her birthday was celebrated by priests in Rome (Tac. *Ann.* 6.5.1). Other life events of an imperial woman, such as Julia Augusta's grave illness of 22 CE or the birth of Claudia Augusta in 63, occasioned unique public vows.[199]

The annual vow for the emperor's safety, which grew to include female members of his family, apparently became detached from the traditional vows for Rome and the state sworn on 1 January by the new consuls (see Livy 21.63.7–8).[200] With wording perhaps including "for the safekeeping of the emperor" (*pro incolumitate principis*, Tac. *Ann.* 4.17.1, cf. *Ann.* 12.68), the vow for the emperor's welfare was taken 3 January—two days later than the traditional *vota* on the kalends

---

195. The association of a man's family in an oath seems traditional, to judge from Scipio Africanus' vow of 216 BCE calling for Jupiter Optimus Maximus to wreak destruction upon him, his house, his family, and his estate if he betrays the vow: *tum me Iuppiter optimus maximus domum familiam remque mea pessimo leto adficiat*: Livy 22.53.10.

196. Cf. *ILS* 112, 12/13 CE: *quod bonum, faustum, felixque sit imp. Caesari divi f. Augusto*, and Suet. *Calig.* 15.3.

197. See also *IGRRP* 4.180 (from Lampsacus), and *IGRRP* 4.39. For the *CFA*, see Scheid 1998; Fishwick 1987–2005, II.1, 430; Fishwick 1987–2005, III.3, 249. E.g., Julia Titi was included as Iulia Augusta already in 3 January 81 (after Titus' death she remained included, but with her name behind that of Domitia Augusta, e.g., at the end of 81 and in 87: *CFA* 48–49 and 55); Domitia on 15 September 81 (*item pro salute Domitiae Aug(ustae) coniugis eius in ea verba quae*), 3 January 86, and also in 87 and 90 (see *CFA* 49 = EDCS-18700003).

198. *CFA* 4a, 5, 10. Her birthday was still celebrated in 38 (*CFA* 12 = EDCS-18200416). The longevity of cult for Julia Augusta is exceptional.

199. For events of 22 and 63, see Tac. *Ann.* 3.64, 15.23.

200. The traditional *vota* on the kalends of January were undertaken by Tiberius and later emperors, evidently as late as 66 (Tac. *Ann.* 4.70, 16.22.1). See next note.

of January—and is often referred to as the *votorum nuncupatio*.[201] But matters may not have been so distinct, and women and men of the imperial family were often honored at the same time. In the records of the Arval Brethren (*acta*), Julia Augusta is listed after Tiberius in vows of 3 January 27 CE.[202] Later in 66 the *acta* record the sacrifice of a bull to *divus* Augustus, a cow to *diva* [Julia] Augusta, a bull to *divus* Claudius, a cow to *diva* "virgin Claudia" (Nero's daughter) and a cow to *diva* Poppaea Augusta, along with a bull to the Genius of Nero and a cow to the "Juno" of Statilia Messalina, Nero's third wife.[203] *Pro salute* vows of the Arval Brethren after Titus' death in 81 included Domitian, Domitia Augusta (Domitia Longina), and Julia Titi, the closest surviving members of his imperial house.[204]

Although imperial women's inclusion in prayers and vows contributed to growing awe for the imperial family or *domus divina*, such veneration often had little to do with any woman's particular behavior. Nonetheless, from a slow beginning in the Augustan and Tiberian periods, women become more noticeable in such expressions of thankfulness for Rome's prosperity and success. Thus we find, for example, an inscription from Upper Germany for the welfare, victory, and safe return of Septimius Severus, Caracalla, Geta, and Julia Domna Augusta, "Mother of the Emperors and of the Camps" (*CIL* XIII 7417 = EDCS-11001514; Grosskrotzenburg, Germany; 208–211 CE).[205]

Imperial women and other religions

We have seen that over time imperial women become more linked to Rome's public religion. It might thus seem remarkable that some women are associated with Judaism and Christianity, two monotheistic religions outside Rome's

---

201. Tac. *Ann.* 16.22.1 notes that the reported charges against Thrasea included absenteeism both at traditional vows at the beginning of the year (*sollemne ius iurandum*), and at the *nuncupatio votorum*. Although this may be hyperbolic, the latter term is associated with the *votum pro salute principis* held on 3 January by the second century: Dig. 50.16.223.1 (Gaius): *Post kalendas ianuarias die tertio pro salute principis vota suscipiuntur* (cf. HA, *Pert.* 6.4). I thank Salvador Bartera for discussion of Tacitus' passage.

202. *CFA* 5 = EDCS-18200412. At Sejanus' peak in 29 the public offered him prayers and sacrifices, and took oaths by the Fortune of Sejanus as well as that of Tiberius: Cass. Dio 58.2.8.

203. *CFA* 30, lines 25–29 = EDCS-21300886. A Juno was the female equivalent of a man's *genius*, an individual's guardian or procreative power: see, e.g., Flory 1995, 127–28 for its association with imperial honors.

204. *CFA* 49, lines 44–48 = EDCS-18700003. McDermott and Orentzel 1978, 75; Vinson 1989, 438–50. D'Ambra 2013, 522 explains the prominence of the emperor's niece as due to dynastic concerns; cf. McDermott and Orentzel 1978, 78–79, 90.

205. See Levick 2007, 67–68. We discuss in Ch. 7 the movements of imperial women.

Imperial Women on Coins and in Roman Cult

public religion that were treated with fear and suspicion by many during during this period.[206] I treat three examples. The first-century Josephus calls Poppaea pious and god-loving (*theosebes*) as he reports her intervening with her husband Nero to decide disputes in favor of Jews and against Roman provincial authorities (around 62 CE). He also notes that he personally mediated with Poppaea in Rome, receiving from her gifts as well as a positive reply (Joseph. *AJ* 20.189–96, *Vit.* 16, in 64 CE). Domitilla, a late-first-century woman of the Flavian family, is claimed by the fourth-century Christian writer Eusebius to have been exiled at the end of the first century for her Christian faith (*Hist. Eccl.* 3.18.4).[207] Perhaps in 232, Severus Alexander's mother Julia Mamaea reportedly was so intrigued by the fame of the Christian theologian Origen that she summoned him by military escort to meet with her in Antioch. There she debated with him about divine things, according to Eusebius, who also calls her "most pious" (*theosebestate*, Euseb. *Hist. Eccl.* 6.21.3). These reports have led many to assume that Poppaea was at least a Jewish sympathizer,[208] and that the Flavian Domitilla and later Mamaea were Christians, or open to Christianity.[209]

Although I cannot explore the veracity of these links of imperial women with illicit religion, they raise pertinent points. The first is their fit with Rome's legal codes and authors in portraying women as "weak minded" and thus susceptible to exotic cults.[210] The second, more positive, is their emphasis of the role of imperial women as intermediaries. Emperors' wives and female relatives were at the sidelines of Rome's most important people and structures. Although they could never attain full power themselves, their liminality allowed them to represent

---

206. For example, the untrustworthy *Acta Hermisci* (*P.Oxy.* 1242 = Smallwood #516; Temporini 1978, 90–100), a tendentious tract written in the Hadrianic period by Alexandrian Greeks, recounts Plotina's mediation with Trajan for the Jews during an imperial hearing, so as to discredit the imperial decision made in favor of the Jews. There are, of course, various references to emperors and these two religions before 235, including reported letters from emperors referring to Christians and Jews: see, e.g., Rizzi 2010 on Hadrian's interactions with Christianity. I do not treat here the Jewish queen Berenice, Titus' consort; see Ch. 3.

207. A confounding element is the Christian cemetery named Domitilla in Rome attested by the third century CE. See Castritius 2002, 173–74.

208. The range of opinions about Poppaea have been discussed by (e.g.) Matthews 2001, 34–35 and Williams 1988.

209. For Domitilla, see FOS #369 and Jones 1992, 121–23, 131–32; for Mamaea, Brent 1995, 82–90, who treats her "kindly disposition towards Christianity" (p. 85) and reports her son's favor toward the religion (e.g., HA, *Alex. Sev.* 29.2). Williams 1904, 99, finds no support for Eusebius' claim of Mamaea's religious fervor or the later tradition of her Christianity.

210. For this *topos* see, e.g., Hemelrijk 2015, 40; Scheid 1992, 397–400; Dixon 1984.

the powerless to the all-powerful.[211] That they reportedly mediated for the most scorned religions of the Roman world highlights their potentially pivotal roles.[212] The stories also suggest that imperial women had some autonomy and in religious matters could act and believe as they wanted. If that is so, it flies in the face of the other evidence I have assessed in this chapter.

Conclusion

The principate's expansion of imperial cult to include participation of imperial women—both as officiants and as icons—had a slow start, with Julia Augusta's honors and religious veneration resisted by Tiberius, and Drusilla's apotheosis mocked in the *Apocolocyntosis*. The gradual but thorough nature of their inclusion, however, must have helped to regularize the process, apparently similar to consecration and cult for imperial men.[213] Meanwhile, they also became more visible on centrally struck coins: the difference may perhaps be best seen by comparing the "Julia the Elder" coin of 13 BCE, on which only Augustus is identified, to the coin of Julia Domna, on which only she of the three family members is identified (Ills. 3.2 and 4.4).

The involvement of imperial women themselves as priests of a *divus* intensified a process involving women in Italy by the end of the Republic, whereby women took on public roles, especially religious ones, in their communities. The imperial women's increasing associations with religion had wide effects, especially for the local women who served as their communities' priestesses of consecrated and venerated imperial women. Those *flaminicae* demonstrated their piety and virtue in their families and communities, and provided a tie to the center of power at Rome. Cults of *divae* benefited towns and cities by providing local women with respectable visibility in civic building as well as via more ephemeral patronage like the distribution of cakes and sweet wine. Such positive meanings obviously accrued to local and provincial priests of imperial cult for emperors, but those positions as *flamines* and *sacerdotes* were not as novel: Roman men always held religious positions in their communities. The religious elevation and consecration of imperial women enabled social mobility and prominence for many more than the handful of Republican women attested in Rome and Roman towns. Even if

---

211. See Kunst 2010.

212. Cassius Dio's report (72.4.7), that Commodus' mistress Marcia "greatly favored the Christians and rendered them many kindnesses, since she could do anything with Commodus," criticizes Commodus' subservience to the freedwoman (*Epit. de Caes.* 17.5).

213. We hear of no outcry as loud as that which met the divinization of Antinous (see Ch. 3).

actual numbers are not large—three imperial women as priestesses of imperial cult in Rome, fourteen consecrated imperial women, and some three hundred attested priestesses in Italy and the provinces in over two hundred years—the phenomenon demonstrates the ideologies of inclusivity, mobility, and euergetism fundamental to the consensus and longevity of the principate.

For imperial women themselves it is less easy to discern the significance. Julia Augusta, Antonia the Younger, and Agrippina the Younger must have been affected by their positions as imperial cult priests, at the least assuming the religious paraphernalia essential to priesthoods, but it is only with Agrippina that any source imputes personal desire for the position.[214] As for consecration, we might wonder if women were influenced by their predecessors' sacred status or by the hope of consecration for themselves.[215] Did Domitia Longina "pray" to her sister-in-law Julia Titi after Julia's consecration in 90? Did anyone believe that Sabina, Hadrian's wife, had really flown into the heavens at her death, as depicted on coins and the relief later associated with the Arco di Portogallo (see Ch. 5), or that *diva* Sabina could aid anyone in any way? Imperial women are never credited with direct agency for miracles, as were Vespasian and Hadrian; on the other hand, women never had an emperor's powers of life and death.[216] Nevertheless, as we saw with the allegations of Jewish or Christian sympathies, imperial women's proximity to such power may have drawn some to them as religious intermediaries.

Oaths, the growth of imperial cult, and even association with deities on coins increased the awe surrounding imperial women and thus the whole imperial family. But the women themselves gained no sacrosanctity or appreciable power. Agrippina's position as *flaminica* of *divus* Claudius did not deter Nero from having her killed in 59; perhaps more important for our purposes, her priestly status is not mentioned in any reference to her death.[217] Julia Domna's visibility in public rituals did not protect her in the aftermath of Caracalla's assassination. Julia Mamaea's status as daughter of the *diva* Julia Maesa afforded her no defense against rebellious soldiers in 235. Even Trajan's sister Marciana and niece Matidia the Elder, divinized respectively in 112 and 119 and the only two consecrated

---

214. Tac. *Ann.* 12.69.

215. We have no evidence comparable to Vespasian's quip on his deathbed, *Vae, puto deus fio!* (Suet. *Vesp.* 23).

216. That incontrovertible power makes some moderns more willing to accept ancient belief in Vespasian's "miracles" (e.g., restoring eyesight: Suet. *Vesp.* 7.2), or those associated with Hadrian (e.g., ending a five-year drought in Africa: HA, *Hadr.* 22.14).

217. See, e.g., Boatwright 2008.

imperial women not defamed with rumors of sexual scandal and other improprieties, are presented as guided by traditionally womanly and domestic virtues, not by what we might think of as religious belief or fervor.[218]

Whatever imperial women actually did in their religious roles, and no matter the more impenetrable issues of their own religious beliefs and practices, their public ties with religion in the Roman world were due to political considerations. The concerns were those of the emperor and the court. The religious eminence of imperial women accrued to the charisma of the princeps himself, bolstering the fearsome power of the imperial system. Despite the consecration and even the apotheosis of some imperial women, the prestigious religious duties of others, and the association of all with the imperial or "divine" house, Rome's imperial women remained marginalized in Roman religion just as they did in other areas of Roman life.

---

218. This contrasts with some emperors, particularly Elagabalus. For Marciana and Matidia, see Ch. 1.

5

Imperial Women's Mark on the City of Rome

Introduction: Agrippina the Younger at the Praetorian Camp in Rome

Rome's war in Britain, a long and difficult conflict Claudius pursued with great fanfare that also unusually showcased his wives, finally ended in 51 CE.[1] In Claudius' triumph of 44 for the first year's victories his wife Messalina had the unique privilege of riding in a *carpentum* behind his triumphal chariot in Rome.[2] Seven years later the great British chieftain Caratacus was brought to Rome to be triumphantly displayed; Agrippina, Claudius' new wife, figured extraordinarily in the spectacle before the people and praetorian cohorts staged in the broad plain (the campus Praetorianus) adjoining the Praetorian Camp in northeast Rome (51 CE; Tac. *Ann.* 12.36–37).[3] (See Ill. 5.1.) After recounting a dramatic interchange between Caratacus and Claudius about imperial clemency, Tacitus—and those assembled—focused on Agrippina:[4]

> And [the pardoned], freed of their chains, also venerated Agrippina, conspicuous on another platform not at all distant, with the very same

---

1. For the war, see now Osgood 2011, 87–106, including p. 101 on *CIL* VI 40416 = EDCS-00900120, the inscription of Claudius' British Victory Arch in Rome.

2. Suet. *Claud.* 17.2; Cass. Dio 60.22.2; Flory 1998, 492; Brännstedt 2015, 40. See also later in this chapter.

3. See Levick 2015, 83 for the date. The Campus Praetorianus was outside Rome's *pomerium*.

4. Tac. *Ann.* 12.37.1. Much of *Annals* 12 is devoted to the swelling importance of Agrippina, first in the court, then with Claudius, and finally in the city of Rome: see, e.g., Malloch 2013, 117–20, 123. The scene with Caratacus, two years after her marriage to Claudius, is her first depiction in public in Tacitus' extant Claudian books.

Imperial Women of Rome. Mary T. Boatwright, Oxford University Press. © Oxford University Press 2021.
DOI: 10.1093/oso/9780190455897.003.0006

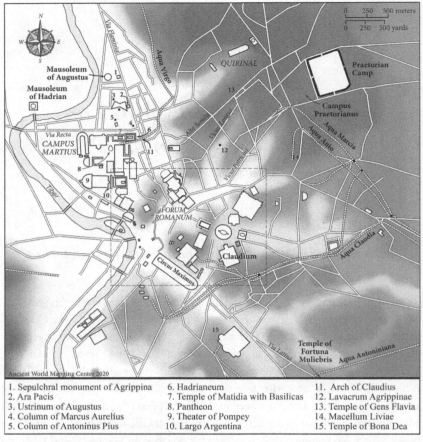

1. Sepulchral monument of Agrippina
2. Ara Pacis
3. Ustrinum of Augustus
4. Column of Marcus Aurelius
5. Column of Antoninus Pius
6. Hadrianeum
7. Temple of Matidia with Basilicas
8. Pantheon
9. Theater of Pompey
10. Largo Argentina
11. Arch of Claudius
12. Lavacrum Agrippinae
13. Temple of Gens Flavia
14. Macellum Liviae
15. Temple of Bona Dea

ILL. 5.1 Rome in the early 3rd c. CE. Area within dotted lines shown in Ill. 5.2. © AWMC.

praises and thanks with which they had honored the *princeps*. It was indisputably new and incompatible with our traditional customs for a woman to preside over Roman standards. But she herself often said that she was a partner in the empire that had been gained by her ancestors. (Tac. *Ann.* 12.37.4)[5]

Thus marking the novelty of Agrippina's public presence, the historian drops her from his narrative.

---

5. Ginsburg 2006, 26, 28–29, 114–16 discusses the passage.

Imperial Women's Mark on the City of Rome 169

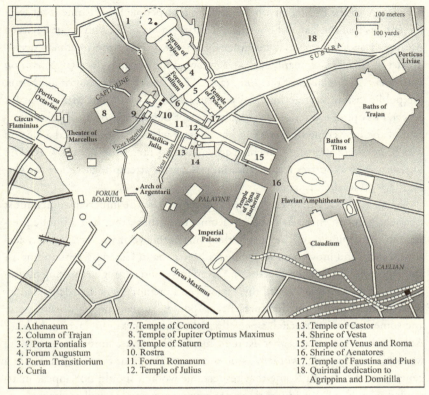

1. Athenaeum
2. Column of Trajan
3. ? Porta Fontialis
4. Forum Augustum
5. Forum Transitiorium
6. Curia
7. Temple of Concord
8. Temple of Jupiter Optimus Maximus
9. Temple of Saturn
10. Rostra
11. Forum Romanum
12. Temple of Julius
13. Temple of Castor
14. Shrine of Vesta
15. Temple of Venus and Roma
16. Shrine of Aenatores
17. Temple of Faustina and Pius
18. Quirinal dedication to Agrippina and Domitilla

ILL. 5.2 The center of Rome in the early 3rd c. © AWMC.

Tacitus' next accounts of Agrippina in public also emphasize her visibility and claims to power. Her entrance to the Capitoline in a *carpentum* in 51 allows him to comment that this was an "honor that, conceded of old to priests and sacred images, swelled the veneration of the woman who—born from a conquering general [Germanicus], and the sister, the wife, and the mother of men who would control the state—to this day is an unparalleled case" (*Ann.* 12.42.2; cf. Cass. Dio 60.33.2[1]).[6] A later event ties Agrippina's claims to power and prominence. Pliny the Elder, Tacitus, and Cassius Dio report her at the Claudian project of 52/53 to drain the Fucine Lake. All note her splendid golden mantle (*chlamys*) and seat next to Claudius at the staged naval battle on the lake some 110 kilometers east of Rome (see map in frontmatter); only Tacitus, however, explicitly connects

---

6. For the *carpentum*, see Ch. 4; see later for the Capitoline as a locus for imperial women.

her display to the capital city, by remarking that people from Rome itself were present.[7] When the lake did not drain, Tacitus' report of the ugly scene between Agrippina and the imperial freedman Narcissus includes the freedman accusing her of frenzied, womanly rage and overweening presumptions (*impotentiam muliebrem nimiasque spes*, Tac. *Ann.* 12.57.2).[8] At least for the senatorial Tacitus, the public visibility of an imperial woman in Rome correlated with grasps for power. His opinion was not unique, if we accept the account of the shocked reaction of the new emperor Nero and his advisors when she approached a dais on which they were awaiting Armenian ambassadors (Tac. *Ann.* 13.5.3; cf. Cass. Dio 61.3.4), as well as postmortem accusations of her for attempting to enter the senate house (Tac. *Ann.* 14.11.1).

As we see in this chapter, Agrippina and Livia are the imperial women most frequently documented in public in Rome, but others, too, had a public presence in the capital city. They made their marks in two main ways: by physical appearances and movement in public, as Messalina in Claudius' triumph of 44 and Agrippina before the Praetorian Camp in 51, and through enduring monuments and statues that carried their names and memory, whether dedicated by or to them. Nevertheless, their presence is sporadic, usually poorly documented, and sometimes controversial, especially with monuments of Octavia and Livia.[9] Admittedly, this reflects that Rome's historical sources simply do not note women, even imperial women, as often as they do men. Further, there was a general assumption in Rome that respectable women should not appear unattended in public.[10] Yet imperial women's own resources, as well as their prominence as part of the exemplary imperial family established by Augustus and advanced by later emperors, are at odds with what we see in this chapter: public appearances of imperial women are usually noted with opprobrium, and the women themselves have less rather than more visibility over the centuries. We can only conclude that their presence in Rome's public ceremonies and spaces was discouraged.

---

7. Tac. *Ann.* 12.56; Cass. Dio 60.33.3; Plin. *HN* 33.63. According to Tacitus so many from neighboring towns and Rome itself attended that the site "resembled a theater." Pliny calls it a *spectaculum*; Cassius Dio notes that Claudius erected stands to assemble a multitude.

8. Ginsburg 2006, 29–30: "*impotentia* connotes lack of self-control and immoderate behavior."

9. For instance, only a ninth-century pilgrim's manuscript now called the Einsiedlensis records, and hints at a location for, the sole monument Sabina is attested as dedicating in Rome (more later).

10. Gardner 1986, 117, discussing the edict *de adtemptata pudicitia*, in force by the second century CE.

Imperial Women's Mark on the City of Rome

This chapter is split into two main parts: women's public activities and visibility, arranged thematically, and the monuments that carried their names and memories to the public in Rome, arranged generally by location. The assembled evidence helps personalize imperial women, hinting at their lives and receptions by Rome's populace and nuancing interpretation of individual monuments they sponsored. Further, the evaluation of their movement through, and staging at, various locales in Rome contributes to the "spatial" study of Roman history and archaeology.[11] Imperial women's public presence in the capital city, as hard as it is to tease out, sheds new light on the complex organism that was ancient Rome. With a built-up area estimated at about fifteen square kilometers and a population ranging between some seven hundred thousand to one million persons from 35 BCE to 235 CE, Rome may have had an overall density of sixty thousand to seventy thousand persons per square kilometer at its most populous before the Antonine plague of 165.[12] Only the most well-placed and wealthy, at a maximum 20 percent in the city, had any record created either about or by them. But the fortunate few could not have existed without the anonymous masses who sustained their lives and power, and the study of Rome's imperial women in the capital city sheds some light on the now-voiceless millions who helped shaped that city and its history.

We begin the analysis of women's physical presence in the city with Rome's most important imperial rituals: public funerals, especially the *consecratio* rituals associated with the declaration of an imperial man or woman as *divus* or *diva* (see Ch. 4); the *adventus* or ceremonial procession of an emperor into the city; and the triumph.[13] Imperial women attended all three, although their presence at an *adventus* or triumph was very rare. The survey emphasizes the exceptionality of Agrippina's presence at Caratacus' submission, with which we began.

Imperial women in the public eye: Funerals

Literary evidence reports imperial women in public in Rome most often at funerals, and there they are attested more frequently as the deceased than among the mourners.[14] Public funerals centered on the Forum Romanum, giving imperial

---

11. See, e.g., Laurence 2015. Ch. 7 turns to women's travels and visibility outside of Rome.

12. See Morley 2013; Harper 2017. These are suggestive numbers.

13. Ewald and Noreña 2010, 40; Benoist 2005. I list these rituals by the frequency of women's presence in them; Benoist attends particularly to the *adventus* and *funus*.

14. For Rome's imperial funerals until the second century CE, see Benoist 2005, 103–46; for later consecrations, Benoist 2005, 147–88; cf. Wesch-Klein 1993. Cresci Marrone and Nicolini 2010 focus on funerals affecting Augustan women.

women's attendance high visibility and solemnity.[15] (See Ill. 5.2.) A few public funerals for women are known for the Republic,[16] and Octavia, the sister of Augustus, received a remarkable one after her death in 11 BCE.[17] Her state funeral featured not one but two funeral orations.[18] Augustus delivered one *laudatio funebris* for her at the Temple of Julius (Temple of *divus* Julius Caesar), where her corpse lay in state shielded by a veil.[19] Drusus the Elder, married to her daughter Antonia the Younger, gave the other at the Rostra across the Forum Romanum from the Temple of Julius (Cass. Dio 54.35.4–5). Although Augustus curtailed other honors, Octavia's body was interred in the Mausoleum of Augustus, where it joined that of her son Marcellus, who had died in 23 BCE.[20] Octavia's cortège probably moved out of the Forum Romanum by the Porta Fontinalis, then north along the Via Flaminia, and finally west to the Mausoleum. (See Ill. 5.1.) It was a solemn and exemplary affair. Others, including Augustus himself, would be honored by two funeral eulogies,[21] and the processional way must have become a familiar sight for imperial funerals during the Julio-Claudian period.

Two years after Octavia's obsequies Livia formed part of the funeral procession for her younger son Drusus the Elder, at least during the long march from northern Italy to Rome in 9 BCE. The evidence, though elusive, specifies that she did not participate in rituals in the Forum Romanum or Campus Martius, but voluntarily remained at home.[22] The implication is that Livia exemplified self-restraint and modesty by keeping away from these two areas of Rome considered

---

15. See, e.g., Arce 2010, 318; Benoist 2005.

16. Popilia in the late second century BCE (Cic. *Orat.* 2.44) is the earliest known. Julius Caesar made particular use of public funerals for women of his family (Suet. *Caes.* 6.1, 26).

17. As a boy Augustus gave a funeral oration for his grandmother (Suet. *Aug.* 8); he also had the senate vote his mother Atia a public funeral in 43 BCE (Cass. Dio 47.17.6). See Cresci Marrone and Nicolini 2010, 168–69. I know of no public funerals for non-imperial women after that for Junia in 22 CE (Tac. *Ann.* 3.76.2).

18. Wardle 2014, 557 notes that two speeches are first attested with Octavia but may have been introduced at Agrippa's funeral a year earlier (12 BCE; cf. Cass. Dio 54.28.5).

19. Benoist 2005, 123–24 notes that the veil was used also in Agrippa's public funeral, and suggests perhaps also at Atia's public funeral.

20. Cass. Dio 54.35.4–5, cf. *Consol. Ad Liviam* 442; Cass. Dio 54.35.5 (curtailing honors). Cresci Marrone and Nicolini 2010, 169–71 see the rites as canonical.

21. By Tiberius and by Drusus the Younger, Cass. Dio 56.34.

22. *Consol. ad Liviam* 49–50 makes clear that she could enter either public place: Brännstedt 2015, 38–39. Our other source is Sen. *Consol. ad Marc.* 3.2. Livia is not noted at the funeral orations for Drusus given by Tiberius in the Forum and by Augustus at the Circus Flaminius.

proper for men,[23] and the note underscores the use of the areas for imperial funerals.

Imperial women are later documented at funeral rites in the Forum Romanum and Campus Martius, the latter standing by synecdoche for the Mausoleum of Augustus.[24] The magnificent public funeral for Augustus in 14 CE included the unusual honor of his cortège passing through the Porta Triumphalis (still unlocated in the southeastern Circus Flaminius) on its way to his Mausoleum.[25] This would have brought the cortège near the Porticus Octaviae and along a route that would later feature other monuments that included female members of the Julio-Claudian family (see Ill. 5.2). Julia Augusta, the newly appointed priest of *divus* Augustus, may have joined the procession. She certainly spent five days with Rome's equestrians at his pyre or *ustrinum* on the Campus Martius (now located between the Pantheon and the Mausoleum [Ill. 5.1]),[26] where she gathered his bones to put into the Mausoleum (Cass. Dio 56.42.4). Five years later in 19, when Agrippina the Elder returned to Rome with Germanicus' ashes, she may have disembarked near that Mausoleum, which received his remains.[27] The growing association of the Mausoleum and its environs with the Julio-Claudians is suggested by the public resentment caused by Gnaeus Piso's celebrated landing there later that year.[28] At her death in 29 Julia Augusta received a funeral laudation from her great-grandson Caligula on the Rostra in the Forum Romanum before interment

---

23. See Boatwright 2011b. Severy 2003 has noted the public absence of Livia, Octavia, and other Augustan women from 32 to 13/9 BCE, roughly from Octavia's divorce from Antony to the creation of the Ara Pacis; see also e.g. Purcell 1986.

24. Panciera (in Hesberg and Panciera 1994, 72–147) lists (with discussion of evidence) those definitely and presumably interred in the Mausoleum of Augustus: "certain, non-temporary" occupants are Marcellus (23 BCE), Agrippa (12), Octavia (11/10), Drusus the Elder (9), Augustus (14 CE), Germanicus (19), Livia (29), Agrippina the Elder with her sons Nero Caesar and Drusus Caesar (37), Poppaea (65), and Nerva (98); for Agrippina the Younger and Domna, see Panciera (in Hesberg and Panciera 1994, 83, 87); Tac. *Ann.* 14.9 and Cass. Dio 79.2.3. The two Julias were barred from burial in Augustus' Mausoleum (Suet. *Aug.* 101; Cass. Dio 56.32), symbolically from Augustus' family.

25. Tac. *Ann.* 1.8.3; Suet. *Aug.* 100. Suetonius notes a witness of Augustus' apotheosis (*Aug.* 100.4), but only Cassius Dio reports Livia's award to him of a million sesterces (56.46.2).

26. Livia is not noted in the Forum or the cortège. See *LTUR* 5.97, s.v. "Ustrinum Augusti" (V. Jolivet) for location of the *ustrinum*, previously situated where Panciera now identifies the memorial created by Agrippina the Younger (for which see later).

27. See Benoist 2005, 130–32; Barrett 1996, 259 n.34 with the epigraphic evidence, *Tabula Hebana* and esp. the *Tabula Siarensis* (*AE* 1984, 508 = EDCS-45500034). Notably, Tiberius, Julia Augusta, and Antonia did not attend the funeral (Tac. *Ann.* 3.3.3).

28. Tac. *Ann.* 3.9.2: Piso had come down the Tiber, to be met at the *tumulus Caesarum* by a party of clients, Plancina, and her crowd of women.

in the Mausoleum of Augustus (Suet. *Calig.* 10; Tac. *Ann.* 5.1.4; Vell. 2.130.5): her cortège must have taken the same route proposed for Octavia.[29]

In 37 CE Caligula gathered on their islands of exile the bones of his mother Agrippina the Elder and his brother Nero Caesar, to convey them in urns up the Tiber and carry them through a crowd into the Mausoleum on a double bier (Suet. *Calig.* 15.1).[30] The note of the Tiber suggests that his route was the same as that presumed above for his mother's escort of his father Germanicus' remains eighteen years earlier. The young emperor also had his mother represented in a *carpentum* during festival games, rekindling her memory in Rome (see Ch. 4). In the next year Caligula ensured his beloved sister Drusilla had a public funeral, which involved a public eulogy delivered by her husband Marcus Lepidus, surely in the Forum, and martial processions around her tomb (Cass. Dio 59.11.1–3).[31] Poppaea's remains were interred in the Mausoleum of Augustus in 65, and her public funeral included a laudation by Nero on the Rostra in the Forum Romanum (Tac. *Ann.* 16.6). The showy funeral ceremonies for honored Julio-Claudian family members must have marked the Forum Romanum and processional route to the Mausoleum in the Campus Martius as special to the *domus divina* that increasingly recognized imperial women.[32]

Later imperial women are associated with funerals in Rome, but with ever fewer details. After her death in 91 Julia Titi was interred in Domitian's Temple of the Gens Flavia on the Quirinal Hill (Suet. *Dom.* 17).[33] Did Domitian stage an extravagant funeral for his niece to emulate earlier ones for Julio-Claudian women?[34] If Julia Titi was first eulogized in the Forum Romanum, her cortège may have moved from there through the Argiletum—whose lower part he

---

29. This is the route along which Agrippina the Younger apparently constructed a sepulchral monument: see later. Livia would also have been permanently honored by an arch in Rome, had not Tiberius thwarted the senate's vote and the record of its proposed location: Cass. Dio 58.2; cf. Tac. *Ann.* 5.2.1: Tiberius offered to pay for it, which would have made it private, not public, but he never did. Flory 1995, 132–33 sees this as part of a policy against divine honors for his family.

30. See *CIL* VI 40372 = EDCS-00900076.

31. Panciera (in Hesberg and Panciera 1994, 85) finds "unlikely" that Caligula did not bury her in the Mausoleum of Augustus. He also suggests Caligula interred Antonia the Younger there in 37 (cf., e.g., Kokkinos 2002, 28), despite disrespecting her funeral (Suet. *Calig.* 23.2–3).

32. The tomb for Lollia Paulina's ashes Nero had repatriated in 59 to increase ill will toward Agrippina (Tac. *Ann.* 14.12.6; see Ch. 2) is otherwise unattested.

33. Darwall-Smith 1996, 159–65 discusses the Temple, dating its completion to 94/95 CE; Panciera (in Hesberg and Panciera 1994, 81, 83) considers her burial there a secondary one. The temple is now usually located near the present Church of Santa Susanna, at the Largo di Santa Susanna at Via Venti Settembre (the modern street that follows the ancient Alta Semita).

34. Flavian women were linked with Julio-Claudian ones otherwise: Titus' *carpentum* issue for Domitilla assumed a motif seen on coins for Julia Augusta and Agrippina the Elder (see Ch. 4).

embellished as the Forum Transitorium—to cross to the Vicus Longus and then to the Temple of the Gens Flavia. (See Ill. 5.1.) Marciana, Trajan's sister, died and was consecrated on 28 August 112; a few days later she was honored with the special state funeral of a *funus censorium* (3 September). Her daughter Matidia (the Elder) was designated Augusta on the same day Marciana Augusta was honored as *diva*,[35] which may indicate her participation in her mother's public funeral. Although the obsequies must have started in the Forum Romanum, we do not know the site of Marciana's interment.[36]

Some five years later Plotina and Matidia the Elder, perhaps with the praetorian prefect Publius Acilius Attianus, accompanied to Rome the ashes of Trajan, who had died in Selinous while returning from the Parthian War (HA, *Hadr.* 5.9-10; Selinous is now Gazipaşa, Turkey).[37] Did Trajan's widow and niece personally attend Trajan's posthumous triumph in the capital city in 117/118? Since this procession combined elements of a state funeral with ones of a triumph its route may have gone through the Porta Triumphalis as had Augustus' before Trajan's ashes were deposited in the base of the Column of Trajan.[38] (See earlier, and Ills. 5.1 and 5.2). On the other hand, Roman women seldom appeared in triumphs; furthermore, Plotina and Matidia the Elder were notably reclusive in Rome.

Funeral honors for imperial women intensify in the second century, but are often vaguely located despite the known use of the Mausoleum of Hadrian for imperial burials after its completion by 139. Many obsequies included ceremonies in Rome's arenas and circuses. Matidia the Elder's death in late 119 was followed by public mourning and conspicuous public honors decreed by Hadrian, including gladiatorial games and donations of incense to the Roman people (HA, *Hadr.* 9.9, 19.5).[39] The remarkable inscription from Tibur with Hadrian's praise

---

35. Smallwood #22 = EDCS-20200012; Temporini 1978, 194–95, esp. n.69 on the *funus censorium* (see also Arce 2010, 321–22; Price 1987).

36. As we see later, the basilica named for her in Rome rose in the central Campus Martius, forming part of the dynastic monuments there: Boatwright 2010, 171, 178.

37. Temporini 1978, 160.

38. A triumphal chariot carried an image of Trajan: Cass. Dio 69.2.3, cf. HA, *Hadr.* 6.3. Arce 2010 and Price 1987, 69–70, e.g., note the assimilation of imperial funerals to triumphs. For the Column's sepulchral use, see Cass. Dio 68.16.3, cf. 69.2.3; Eutrop. 8.5; Panciera (in Hesberg and Panciera 1994) 81 and Ch. 5, n.42. In its vicinity were monuments of imperial women (see later). If the route did not reverse the triumphal one from the Forum Romanum to the *Porta Triumphalis*, it perhaps went clockwise from the Forum, to the vicus Iugarius, *Porta Triumphalis*, Via Flaminia, and Column.

39. The Arval Brethren's *acta* for 23 December 119 note Matidia Augusta's consecration with two pounds of perfume and fifty pounds of incense: *CFA* 69, lines 5–7 = EDCS-18900579; Jones 2004, 271. Buonocore 1985, 174 stresses the popularizing aspects of these honors.

for Matidia, his mother-in-law (*socrus*), has traditionally been understood as a funeral oration presented publicly in the Forum Romanum.[40] When Plotina died, probably in 123, she was lavishly commemorated: Hadrian dedicated hymns for her and imposed a long period of mourning (Cass. Dio 69.10.3[1]).[41] We are not told, however, where the hymns were performed, if they were paired with a funeral laudation and public funeral, or if Plotina's remains were put in the base of the Column next to those of Trajan, as some have suggested.[42] Sabina, consecrated after her death in 136/137 with an apotheosis depicted on coins and on the "Arco di Portogallo" in north-central Rome (see Ch. 4 and later), has no funeral recorded. She was buried in the Mausoleum of Hadrian in the Vatican, according to Antoninus Pius' inscription found there honoring her, *diva*, alongside Hadrian who died a year or so after her.[43]

Only with the death of Faustina the Elder in 140, some three years after Sabina's, do we get more information. Faustina was honored by a public funeral (*funus censorium*), games and circus races, the erection of gold and silver statues in the city, and the establishment, by senatorial decree, of the *Puellae Faustinianae*.[44] The funeral would have carried her remains from the Forum Romanum to the Mausoleum of Hadrian,[45] undoubtedly via the traditional funerary route through the Porta Fontinalis up the Via Flaminia, then west on the Via Recta to traverse the wide Campus Martius, and finally north-northwest to the Vatican

---

40. *CIL* XIV 3579 = EDCS-04800013. Jones 2004, 271–72 argues instead that Hadrian gave this speech to the senate while urging them to consecrate her. He suggests its location in Tibur was on the base of a statue, perhaps at a family tomb or even at Hadrian's villa. See also Panciera (at Hesberg and Panciera 1994, 83). In *CIL* Alföldy tentatively identified as a dedication to *diva* Matidia the very fragmentary *CIL* VI 40508 = EDCS-00900221 (provenance unknown; now in the Antiquarium of the Caelian Hill, NCE 4634). Nothing notes Sabina at her mother's funeral.

41. In Hadrian's absence from Rome (121–125 CE) her deification may have awaited his return and sponsorship of it to the senate: Birley 1997, 145 and Halfmann 1986, 190–92. For her consecration see Temporini 1978, 168–70 and Ch. 4.

42. Contra Claridge 2007, 92–93. I return later to Hadrian's double inscription honoring Trajan and Plotina, Hadrian's "divine parents" (*divis parentibus suis*), found near the Forum of Trajan.

43. *CIL* VI 984 = EDCS-17301095, our *terminus ante quem* for the structure. Antoninus' titulature, and the fact that Hadrian is not yet *divus*, dates the inscription before December 139.

44. Beckmann 2012a, 21–22; *Fasti Ostienses* (= EDCS-20200012) for 140 CE, with 23 October restored for her death; her *funus censorium* occurred before 13 November 140. We discuss the *Puellae Faustinianae* later.

45. Inscriptions record her burial in the Mausoleum of Hadrian, along with two sons and a daughter who died earlier: *ILS* 349 (141/142 CE)—352 = EDCS-17301098-17301101.

across the Pons Aelius (Ill. 5.1). While on the Via Recta the cortège would have skirted the rising Hadrianeum, the Temple of Matidia and basilicas of Matidia and Marciana, and the Pantheon. By this time the Julio-Claudian imprint on the central Campus Martius had been enhanced by state monuments of the second century, many of which acknowledged imperial women.[46]

The obsequies of Faustina the Elder are the last ones for an imperial woman for which we have relatively good documentation. Later imperial women— Faustina the Younger, Lucilla, Crispina, Julia Domna, Julia Soesmia, Julia Maesa, and Julia Mamaea—died far from Rome, many in disgrace or violently; to our knowledge they received no public funeral in the capital.[47] Furthermore, the scant literary sources provide no details. Even Domna, relatively well attested overall, is not mentioned in Septimius Severus' showy consecration of Pertinax in 197 (Cass. Dio 75.4.2–5.5) or in the obsequies and consecration of Severus himself in 211 (Hdn. 4.1–2), despite the fact that wives of senators are reported at both ceremonies.[48]

Imperial women in the adventus and triumph

Some little information attests imperial women "on the move," that is, in processions in the city. The scattered evidence slightly favors the Capitoline, where the processions of both *adventus* and triumph ended and where Julia Domna sacrificed to Juno Regina during the *Ludi Saeculares* of 204.

Some verses by Horace have suggested to Brännstedt that Livia and Octavia publicly greeted Augustus at his *adventus* in Rome in 24 BCE after the Spanish wars (*Carm.* 3.14.5–10).[49] Horace does not provide a location for the meeting, which may have been where the procession entered Rome's *pomerium* presumably at the Porta Fontinalis, or on the Capitoline, the climax

---

46. See, e.g., Boatwright 2010, 186–96, esp. 186–89 on the Antonine consecration altars near the Column of Antoninus Pius and the Column of Marcus Aurelius.

47. Matidia the Younger had a public funeral granted by Marcus Aurelius, but we hear of this incidentally and without details (Fronto, *ad Ant. imp.* 2.1.2, p. 95 VDH). Marcus later asked the senate to decree "honors and a temple" for Faustina the Younger (HA, *Marc.* 26.5); no evidence attests a burial in the Mausoleum of Hadrian. Some ritual may have attended Julia Maesa's interment of Domna's body in that Mausoleum after transfer from Antioch to Rome (Cass. Dio 79.2.3), but we have no information.

48. See Arce 2010. We discuss later and in Ch. 4 Domna's relatively large presence in public religious ceremonies. For Domna's own burial, see the preceding note.

49. Brännstedt 2015, 41; Thakur 2014, 191–92.

of the procession (Ill. 5.1).[50] Further, the poet does not name either woman, but simply calls them *mulier* and *soror*, "wife" and "sister."[51] His reticence downplays the two women's public appearance, which would have been very unusual at this early date.[52]

Livia's and Octavia's presence at Augustus' *adventus* would be almost without parallels. In 69 Sextilia met her son Vitellius on the Capitoline upon his arrival in Rome as princeps (Tac. *Hist.* 2.89). The encounter's location and ceremonial aspect—Tacitus notes that Vitellius here saluted his mother as *Augusta* (see Ch. 1)—must have suggested a traditional *adventus* so as to mask the son's seditious status. But no later imperial women are associated with an *adventus*. When Pliny vividly depicts Trajan's accession to Rome in 99 and shows the emperor and his followers parading through the Forum up the Capitoline, watched by men, women, and children, he does not name Plotina, Marciana, or any other female relative (*Pan.* 22–23).[53] The absence of imperial women at such events denotes their sustained political marginalization, since the *adventus* ritual signaled the new princeps to the *populus*.[54]

Some imperial women are associated with triumphs, although this, too, is rare, and their presence at the culminating ascent to the Capitoline is never specified.[55] In 17 CE five of Germanicus' children accompanied him in his triumphal chariot (Tac. *Ann.* 2.41.4): two must be Agrippina the Younger and Drusilla, still just toddlers. Similarly, although much later, Marcus Aurelius' children of both sexes, even the unmarried girls, could ride with him in his triumph over the

---

50. Benoist 2005, 25–101 discusses the development of the *adventus* and its uncertain route, which ended at the Capitoline from which the princeps could go to the Palatine (e.g., 60, 73, 90, 97–98).

51. As later Pliny does with Plotina and Marciana, *Pan.* 83–84. See Ch. 1.

52. Although other women were in crowds at public events: upon return to Rome in 30 Octavian was greeted by the Vestal Virgins, senate, and people, with wives and children (Cass. Dio 51.19.1–2); see also Trajan's *adventus* later. Brännstedt 2015, 41 n.41, focusing on Livia, holds that by not naming her Horace reveals ambivalence about mentioning her in his poetry.

53. Later Domna was either not part of Septimius Severus' entrance into the city in 193 or simply not considered noteworthy by Cassius Dio (74.1).

54. Benoist 2005, 25–101.

55. Flory 1998, 491, followed by (e.g.) Brännstedt 2015, 39–40, suggests that perhaps Livia publicly garlanded the *currus triumphales* of Augustus, Tiberius, Germanicus, and Drusus the Younger with the special laurel from her villa *ad Gallinas albas* (Prima Porta). If so, this was not repeated by another imperial woman. Although Beard 2007, 378 n.56 and Flory associate Domna with a triumph, the only evidence is her depiction on the Arch of Lepcis Magna.

Germans in 176, and could also wear triumphal dress in games decreed for the event (HA, *Marc.* 10-11).[56] In Claudius' British triumph Messalina followed his chariot in a *carpentum* (Suet. *Claud.* 17.2). To thus feature a woman was unique.[57]

Imperial women in the public eye: Other religious ceremonies

One might expect imperial women at other public ceremonies, especially because of their appearance on the southern frieze of the Ara Pacis that evidently depicts the ritual procession marking its dedication (see Ch. 3). Further, most of Rome's rituals involved religion, a traditional site of Roman women's public activity, and Julia Augusta, Antonia the Younger, and Agrippina the Younger were priests of imperial cult at its inception in the capital city. But as we saw, nothing documents these three serving in their cult roles.

Later, newlyweds undertook vows and prayers in front of Roman statues of Faustina the Elder and Antoninus Pius, and of Faustina the Younger and Marcus Aurelius. The statuary groups, usually said to have been at the Temple of Venus and Roma on the Velia (see Ill. 5.2), acknowledged the two couples' exemplary marriages (see Ch. 3).[58] But the women themselves were not there. Only Julia Domna and her niece Julia Soaemias are documented as participating in public ritual, and Soaemias only once. The two are in the record of the *Ludi Saeculares* of 204 as they process to the Capitoline to sacrifice to Juno Regina, and a relief on the Arch of the Argentarii, dated to the same year and raised in Rome's Velabrum (see Ill. 5.2), depicts Domna sacrificing together with Septimius Severus (see Ill. 4.10). The record for Domna, as sparse as it is, highlights the absence of evidence for other imperial women in religious settings in Rome.

Even less information locates imperial women while partaking of vows or other veneration. Julia Augusta's serious illness in 22 CE prompted the senate to vote circus games (*Ludi Magni*, held in the Circus Maximus) and public prayers (*supplicationes*) be undertaken by the four major priestly colleges and the *sodales*

---

56. The youngest child was about six years old, but many were older. Perhaps the "unmarried girls" were Fadilla and Cornificia. Zonar. 7.12 (12th c.) notes a triumphator's girl and infant male children could accompany him on the chariot.

57. See also Cass. Dio 60.22.2; Flory 1998, 492; Brännstedt 2015, 40. This was quite different from the exhibition of captured women in triumphs. Agrippina the Younger's later privilege of a *carpentum* at festivals (Cass. Dio 61.33) is not associated with a triumph, and Tacitus uses her entrance on the Capitoline in a *carpentum* in 51 CE to decry her overweening ambition, singular position, and visibility (Tac. *Ann.* 12.42).

58. Weiss 2008, 4–12.

Augustales in Rome (Tac. *Ann.* 3.64). Presumably in her absence the officiants prayed for her recovery at religious sites throughout the city. Later, according to Tacitus, the birth and sudden death three months later of Nero's daughter Claudia Augusta occasioned public vows, prayers, and then deification in 63; he mentions an altar and temple among the proposed honors, but they seem never to have been built (Tac. *Ann.* 15.23; Ch. 4). The vows and prayers of the Arval Brethren that included Julia Augusta and later imperial women focalized attention on them at the Arvals' various sites of worship such as the Capitoline or at the Temple of *divus* Augustus, joining the women's commemoration with that of other members of the imperial family.[59] Although the honored were not there in person, such rituals evoked imperial women and men in various spots in Rome.

On the other hand, imperial women were expressly awarded seating in Rome's theaters.[60] Their presence emphasized imperial concern for the Roman populace, and their unusual visibility was mitigated by their juxtaposition with the Vestal Virgins. In 23 CE Julia Augusta was voted, by senatorial decree, the right to sit with the Vestals in special, lower seats at the theater (Tac. *Ann.* 4.16.4–6).[61] In 37 Caligula's grandmother Antonia and his three sisters received the same privileged seating among the Vestals at the theater (Suet. *Calig.* 15.2; Cass. Dio 59.3.4); in 44 Messalina was also voted the privilege, along with the right to ride in a *carpentum* during Claudius' triumph (Cass. Dio 60.22.2). The special front-row theater seats put imperial women on display, unusual in imperial Rome. Women's general demotion to wooden seats at the rear had been recently reinforced by the *lex Iulia theatralis* that strictly regulated where spectators could sit.[62] Augustus previously allowed in the theater only Vestal Virgins, isolated and across from the praetor's tribunal; at gladiatorial games women could be seated only in the highest rows, although they had previously watched from anywhere in the audience (*promiscue*: Suet. *Aug.* 44).[63] The exceptional honor of lower seating was not extended to other women at the time, to judge from a later story in Macrobius.[64]

---

59. Though as early as 21 CE the Arval Brethren included Julia Augusta in their vows and prayers (*CFA* 4a, line 17 = EDCS-21100428), and in 27, and again in 26–40 CE, made vows for her birthday on 30 Janurary (*CFA* 5 = EDCS-18200412, lines 3 and 13, where she is called *mater eius* [Tiberius]; *CFA* 10 = EDCS-21100429). See Beard, North, and Price 1998, 195; Ch. 4. The Temple of *divus* Augustus has not yet been securely located: see later.

60. After discussing Augustus' regulations about games, Suetonius blandly notes that Augustus sometimes watched races from the pulvinar "together with his wife and children" (*Aug.* 45.1).

61. Bauman 1981, 175; Barrett 2002, 144. Nothing documents Julia Augusta using this privilege.

62. Gallia 2015, 96; Rawson 1987, 85. The law dates after 5 CE.

63. Fagan 2011, 107 argues imperial women's special seating included in the amphitheater.

64. Macr. *Sat.* 2.5.6 mentions only men in the entourages of Livia and Julia at a spectacle.

Imperial Women's Mark on the City of Rome

This may have changed over time, although the evidence is hard to parse. Among the signal marks of respect of the senate for the deceased Faustina the Younger after 175 was that, whenever the emperor was a spectator, her golden statue should be carried in a chair into the theater and placed in the special place from which she herself had been accustomed to view the games; moreover, Rome's most influential women should sit around it (Cass. Dio 72.31.2). Yet "the imperial seat at the theaters" remained extraordinary. There may have been only one such seat, to extrapolate from Herodian's note that Lucilla was jealously provoked to conspire against her brother after being ousted from the seat closest to the stage by Commodus' new wife Crispina (Hdn. 1.8.4).[65]

Two further reports from Herodian suggest that by his day imperial women were allowed at least one distinction publicly marking the emperor, the "sacred fire" or torch. Herodian reports that besides the privilege of imperial seating in the theater, Lucilla—the daughter of Marcus Aurelius and widow of Lucius Verus—had been allowed to have the "ceremonial fire" carried before her (Hdn. 1.8.3–4). Elsewhere he remarks that Marcia, Commodus' favorite mistress, was treated just like a legal wife of the emperor "apart from the sacred fire," which she was not permitted to have (1.16.4).[66] But we have no other reports of this public sign for imperial women. Nor is there now any record of other imperial women at theatrical events in Rome,[67] or involved in any incident while going to or from a theater or another spectacle building.[68]

The *carpentum*, however, allowed some imperial women to be "present" at the circus, one of Rome's most popular events.[69] (Most references are probably to the Circus Maximus [Ill. 5.1 and Ill. 5.2].) Caligula had an image of his mother Agrippina carried on a *carpentum* during the games and sacrifices he instituted in her honor after bringing her remains back to Rome (Suet. *Calig.* 15.1).[70] The

---

65. Whittaker 1969, vol. 1: 47 *ad loc.* discounts this motivation. See Ch. 2.

66. All other instances of the "ceremonial fire" I know apply only to men proclaimed emperor: Hdn. 2.3.2, 2.8.6 (where remarked as sign of emperor), 7.1.9, and 7.6.2; cf. Cass. Dio 71.35.5.

67. Agrippina is front row at the Fucine Lake celebration: Tac. *Ann.* 12.56.3; Ginsburg 2006, 115. Did Domitia Longina become smitten with the pantomime Paris after seeing him performing publicly? Jones 1992, 37 holds that Suet. *Dom.* 13.1 attests her with Domitian at the amphitheater, but the popular acclamation *domino et dominae feliciter* might have been addressed to him alone. Levick 2007, 53 assumes Domna attended the extravagant amphitheater exhibitions for Severus' *decennalia* in Rome in 203 (Cass. Dio 77.1.4–5).

68. Surely carried on litters, as Agrippina the Younger on one with Nero (Suet. *Nero* 9.1, 28).

69. Marcus Aurelius' children could watch his triumphal games (HA, *Marc.* 10–11; see earlier).

70. Ginsburg 2006, 62.

reported settings suggest that when in 22 Julia Augusta was granted the right to a *carpentum* (see earlier) the chariot represented her in the circus in her illness.[71] She may not have been much in public if she attended the earlier *ludi Palatini* she instituted in 14 CE in honor of *divus* Augustus: this three-day event, closed to the public in contrast to the *Augustalia* of 23–24 CE and other games in Augustus' honor, was held annually on the Palatine 17–19 January.[72] Finally, we hear that Agrippina, Drusilla, and Julia Livilla were in the front seats with their brother Caligula, and his fellow priests of the Augustan order, at the races celebrating the dedication of the Temple of *divus* Augustus in 37 (Cass. Dio 59.7.4). This last is yet another demonstration of Caligula's unparalleled publicity for his sisters at the beginning of his reign.

Imperial women in other public activities in Rome

A few imperial women, most obviously Livia, are also noted at banquets that were more public than typical meals at the palace. Livia had the privilege of holding a banquet with Octavian and their children at the Capitoline temple of Jupiter Optimus Maximus on the anniversary of his victory over Sextus Pompeius in 36 BCE (Cass. Dio 49.15.1; see Ill. 5.2).[73] Twenty-seven years later Livia and Julia the Elder, at once her stepdaughter and daughter-in-law as Tiberius' wife, offered a feast for the women of Rome to celebrate Tiberius' military successes in 9 BCE (Cass. Dio 55.2.4–5).[74] In 7 BCE Livia offered another banquet to celebrate Tiberius' triumph that year (Cass. Dio 55.8.2).[75] In 14 CE she planned to feast senators, equestrians, and their wives for the dedication of a statue to *divus* Augustus in her house on the Palatine, but Tiberius objected so strongly that she

---

71. See Latham 2016, 119. The eighty-year-old dowager may never have used this honor. When Claudius ensured divine honors for her, he also had a chariot (*currus*) for her in the circus procession, drawn by elephants as had been the one for Augustus; for his mother he ensured the cognomen *Augusta* and a *carpentum* paraded around her image in the Circus (Suet. *Claud.* 11.2).

72. Wiseman 1991, 55, ad Joseph. *AJ* 19.75 (cf. Tac. *Ann.* 1.73.3 and Cass. Dio 56.46.5); Foubert 2010, 68–69.

73. See Benoist 2005, 39–40. We do not know whether Livia actually attended with the young Tiberius, Julia (the Elder), and Drusus (the Elder). Other extraordinary honors for Octavian were statues and an arch surmounted by trophies.

74. Cass. Dio 55.2.4 notes that as Livia planned a banquet for women to honor her son Drusus' achievements in Germany, "the same festivities were being prepared for Drusus" but were precluded by his death. Flory 1998, 491 assumes that Antonia, Drusus' wife, was involved in the planning, as had been Julia in the feast honoring Tiberius.

75. This was the occasion for Livia and Tiberius to sponsor the Porticus Liviae discussed later.

Imperial Women's Mark on the City of Rome

entertained only the women (Cass. Dio 57.12.5; see Ill. 5.2). Although our main source for public banquets of emperors, Cassius Dio, often locates feasts on the Capitoline, for Livia's he is less precise, naming only her home and that merely for the banquet of 14.[76]

No other imperial women are known to have sponsored public or semipublic feasts in the capital city, whether on the Palatine or elsewhere.[77] But the Palatine figures in the sole public appearance—a disappearance!—of Plotina in Rome. When she entered the imperial palace at the beginning of Trajan's reign, she famously said that she wished to leave the same as she was when entering (Cass. Dio 68.5.5; see Ill. 5.2).[78] Her retiring persona in Rome, stressed also in Pliny's referring to her and Marciana in the palace simply as Trajan's wife and sister and not by name (*Pan.* 83–84), contrasts her later active presence in Athens documented by her letters about the Epicureans, the first of which dates to 121.[79]

A different kind of public feast and exposure is represented by alimentary programs named for Faustina the Elder, Faustina the Younger, and Lucilla, all central to the Antonine imperial family. Those for the two Faustinas are posthumous. Coins and medallions commemorating the *Puellae Faustinianae* program, established by the senate and Antoninus Pius for Faustina the Elder after her death, show girls receiving a benefaction under an emperor's supervision.[80] Oversight by an emperor rather than an imperial woman is true also for Marcus Aurelius' later charitable foundation honoring Faustina the Younger after her death in 175, the *Novae Puellae Faustinianae*.[81] Only the analogous honor for Lucilla, proposed by Marcus Aurelius and the senate at his daughter's marriage to Lucius Verus in 164,

---

76. Tiberius celebrated an equestrian triumph over Dalmatians and Pannonians in 9 BCE by feasting the people, "some on the Capitol and the rest in many other places" (55.2.4); in 7 BCE Tiberius feasted the senate on the Capitoline, and Livia "gave one on her own account to the women somewhere or other" (55.8.2). The Temple of Augustus and the Capitoline are noted as spots where Claudius feasted with priests (Suet. *Claud.* 33.1, 44.2).

77. Suetonius notes Claudius' frequent, grand dinner parties, often entertaining six hundred people in spacious places at one time, but does not mention his wives at them (*Claud.* 32). The feast for the Fucine Lake, at which Agrippina played such a notorious part, was outside of Rome (Tac. *Ann.* 12.56–57; earlier). Messalina's "marriage feast" for Gaius Silius was at home (Tac. *Ann.* 11.26).

78. Even G. Alföldy is tentative about assigning fragmentary dedications and other inscriptions to her, as with *CIL* VI 40507 = EDCS-00900220.

79. For the dossier, see van Bremen 2005, discussed more fully at the end of this chapter.

80. Beckmann 2012a, 22, 53–55, with reference to HA, *Ant. Pius* 8.1–2, the *Fasti Ostienses* of 140 CE, and the coins. Illustrations and a general discussion are also in Rawson 1997, 224–27. We do not know where these distributions and the others discussed here were made.

81. HA, *Marc.* 26.6, cf. *CIL* VI 10222 (p. 3907) = EDCS-19600296.

may have involved public appearances by imperial women: the relief associated with it shows young girls approaching two older women now usually identified as Lucilla and her mother Faustina the Younger.[82] Although these institutions are often cited in modern scholarship on imperial women, the recalcitrant evidence indicates primarily nominal involvement, since at least two of them were posthumous.[83] The programs apparently did not capitalize on imperial women themselves, although generally promoting the family.

A few other reports confirm that public appearance by imperial women was unusual and frowned upon.[84] Suetonius notes Tiberius' resentment when Julia Augusta once rushed to a fire near the shrine of Vesta in the Forum Romanum to help the people as she had when her husband was alive (Suet. *Tib.* 50.3; see Ill. 5.2).[85] When Cassius Dio reports Agrippina the Younger's later assistance to Claudius at a conflagration in Rome, he stresses her desire for Claudius' power and title (Cass. Dio. 61.33.12; we do not know the location of the fire). Imperial women apparently enjoyed few, if any, "spontaneous" excursions in the city of Rome.[86] The rumors about the sexual liaisons of Julia the Elder at the Rostra in the Forum, just like the stories about Messalina's lascivious nocturnal "prowling," reveal the thought that women out on their own would be out of control, disruptive, and politically dangerous.[87] Among the criticisms Cassius Dio lays against Agrippina the Younger is that she "used to greet in public all who desired it, a fact that was entered in the records" (60.33.1). The note echoes one he made about Livia but significantly moves the venue from Livia's home to Agrippina's

---

82. HA, *Marc.* 7.8. See Rawson 1997, 226. This program was for boys and girls.

83. Levick 2014, 104–106, contrasts the foundations to Matidia the Younger's more active Varian *alumni* one of 162; cf. the foundation of the two Matidias in Vicetia (*CIL* V 3112 = EDCS-04202159; Boatwright 1991, 521–22). Severus Alexander reportedly instituted the (mixed-gender) *Puellae Mammaeanae* and *Mammaeani* after his triumph over the Parthians in 227 (HA, *Alex. Sev.* 57.7); this otherwise undocumented foundation was during Mamaea's lifetime.

84. Did Livia encounter in public baths the group of naked men she pardoned (Cass. Dio 58.2.3)? (See Ch. 1.) Other references include Augustus' strictness in restricting his daughter and granddaughters from meeting strangers (Suet. *Aug.* 64.2), and Sejanus' poisonous advice that Agrippina the Elder go to the Forum to gain sympathy in 27 CE (Tac. *Ann.* 4.67.4; Boatwright 2011b, 128–30).

85. Cass. Dio 57.16.2 reports her attention to fires in 16 CE. Barrett 2005a, 306–7 sees Tiberius' resentment as stirred by the "quasi-military" nature of firefighting in Rome.

86. Other negatives about women in public are Tiberius' boast that he could have had Agrippina the Elder's corpse exposed on the Gemonian stairs (Suet. *Tib.* 53.2), and the public exposure there of a group of executed female conspirators against Claudius in 42 (Cass. Dio 60.16.1-3).

87. Julia: Sen. *Ben.* 6.32.1; Cass. Dio 55.10.12; Plin. *HN* 21.9; Messalina: e.g., Juv. *Sat.* 10.329-45. See Ch. 2.

"public."[88] Rome's imperial women are not remarked in the kind of popular canvassing or feel-good appearances of their male relatives, such as Germanicus in the camps and Hadrian in public baths in Rome (Tac. *Ann.* 2.12; HA, *Hadr.* 17.5–7). Their absence contrasts with the visibility of many modern "first ladies."

Given the acceptability of women in religious activity, however, we might presume that imperial women personally attended religious dedications they sponsored themselves and perhaps also the dedication of monuments naming them. With this we pass to the second major part of this chapter, in which I treat more permanent signs of imperial women in Rome.

Imperial women and public monuments in Rome

The loosely topographical arrangement of the following discussion should not obscure chronological distinctions, such as the much greater frequency of monuments relating to Livia than to other imperial women,[89] and the almost complete absence of commemoration of Flavian women. Starting with the lower Circus Flaminius (see Ill. 5.2), I generally circle clockwise and outward in my treatment of the scattered evidence, but ultimately return to Rome's center, the Forum Romanum and imperial fora. I can merely footnote unlocatable buildings such as the "basilica of the two Antoniae," presumably the sisters Antonia the Elder and Younger, which is known only from a freedwoman's epitaph.[90] Further, I sidestep here the question of whether Augustus himself was responsible for buildings raised in the names of his wife, sister, and sons, as Suetonius and Cassius Dio assert.[91] Strabo, much closer to the constructions, freely attributes to Augustus' wife and sister "beautiful and useful structures," particularly in the Campus Martius (Strabo 5.236). This suggests that the reservations of Suetonius

---

88. Cass. Dio 57.12.2: Livia at any time "could receive in her house the senate and such of the people who wished to greet her," a fact that was entered in the public records. See Kunst 1998.

89. I do not discuss Livia's "restorations" of the shrines of Pudicitia Patricia (Patrician Chastity) and of Pudicitia Plebeia (Plebeian Chastity): Richardson 1992, 322, s.vv. "Pudicitia Patricia" and "Pudicitia Plebeia"; Purcell 1986, 88. No real evidence supports the inference of Livia's renovations made by Palmer 1974, esp. 121–23.

90. *CIL* VI 5536 (p 3417) = EDCS-19000286: Kokkinos 2002, 53–55; *LTUR* 1.169, s.v. "Basilica Antoniarum duarum" (C. Lega). La Rocca 1994, 83 intriguingly connects the "basilica" with the Forum Augustum, the find spot of a fragmentary inscription [- - -]*o duarum Antoniaru*[m - - -] (*CIL* VI 40331 = EDCS-00900035) found in the Forum Augustum: Alföldy 1992, 35–38. I do not discuss the shrine raised to the deceased Poppaea, "the goddess Venus" (Cass. Dio 63.26.4; cf. Tac. *Ann.* 16.21.2). Sunrooms that Severus Alexander is said to have added to the palace and named for Mamaea were not public (HA, *Alex. Sev.* 26.9, cf. 26.9–10).

91. Suet. *Aug.* 29.6; cf. Cass. Dio 56.40.5 and 49.43.8; see Ch. 1.

186 IMPERIAL WOMEN OF ROME

and Cassius Dio reveal growing unease with imperial women's autonomy and visibility, just as does confusion about Livia's sole responsibility for some monuments we discuss here. For this chapter it is more important to determine which buildings were connected to imperial women and where they were in Rome. The search for imperial women's presence in the city leads me to include statues and dedications to imperial women as well as those installed by them,[92] but I omit ephemeral statues such as the golden ones of Drusilla set up in the Curia in the northwestern corner of the Forum Romanum and in a Temple of Venus (Cass. Dio 59.11.1–3—perhaps the Temple of Venus Genetrix in the Forum Julium).[93]

New finds and interpretation of older material could add to or modify my conclusions, but it is telling that the attested sites for imperial women's statues and reliefs in Rome conform with the distribution of their public statues empire-wide: Alexandridis has shown that their images appeared most frequently at honorary monuments and altars, and/or in a forum or imperial cult sanctuary.[94] In any case, the evidence assembled here can help us discern the "presence" of imperial women in the city of Rome.

The Circus Flaminius and lower Campus Martius

Monuments of Julio-Claudian imperial women were integral to the Augustan ambiance of the Circus Flaminius, just outside Rome's *pomerium* or sacred boundary and along the triumphal route.[95] (See Ill. 5.2.) Chief among them is the Porticus Octaviae that, together with its Greek and Latin library honoring Octavia's son Marcellus,[96] was dedicated at the same time as the Theater of

---

92. Such honorific statues may have required special imperial permission: Pekáry 1985, 4–12 (and see the statue to Sabina found in the Forum Julium; more later); Boatwright 2011b, 123–26.

93. And those of Octavia and Poppaea in 62 (Tac. *Ann.* 14.61.1), or those of Livilla, who was damned by senatorial decree after 31 (Tac. *Ann.* 6.2.1, with Flory 1996, 301 and Varner 2001; see Ch. 2). Others I omit below include the statue(?) attested by an inscription for Nerva's mother Sergia Plautilla (see Ch. 3, n.111), and those of Septimius Severus' first wife Paccia, perhaps installed in Rome after his accession (HA, *Sev.* 3.2 and 14.4). Alexandridis 2004, e.g., 175 Kat.-Nr. 155 includes imperial women's portraits found in Rome without context.

94. Alexandridis 2004, 32–33; and her Table 2 of a corpus of 115 statues and reliefs of imperial women, from Livia through Julia Domna, whose find-spots throughout the empire she considers at least roughly secure. Her distribution largely agrees with that of public statues for imperial men, for which see Højte 2005, 103–20.

95. See, e.g., La Rocca 1987.

96. E.g., Woodhull 2003, 14–15; *LTUR* 4.141–45, s.v. "porticus Octaviae" (A. Viscogliosi); Richardson 1992, 317. For the Greek and Latin library here, see Nicholls 2010, esp. 13.

Imperial Women's Mark on the City of Rome

Marcellus. The Porticus Octaviae dates between the aedileship of Octavia's son Marcellus in 23 BCE and her own death in 11 BCE.[97] Its complicated history, muddled by the almost identically named Porticus Octavia restored by Augustus himself (*RGDA* 19),[98] should not obscure Octavia's agency and gift. Its identification on the third-century Marble Plan of Rome as [PORTI]CUS OCTAVIAE ET FILI[. . .] (fr. 31u) designates her responsibility by the use of the genitive of her name.[99] The Porticus was multifunctional, including also a *curia Octaviae* used for senatorial meetings (Cass. Dio 55.8.1; Joseph. *BJ* 7.5.4) and other small rooms referred to as *schola* or *scholae* (Plin. *HN* 35.114, 36.22).[100] It was celebrated for its works of art that perhaps included a statue of Cornelia, the mother of the Gracchi.[101] The whole was part of the widening cultural offerings of Augustan Rome that fused education and decorous ornament with orderly administration and accessibility.[102] In its location and multiple uses, the Porticus Octaviae was a remarkably significant donation to the city. Octavia, otherwise out of the public eye after her return to Rome in 35 and divorce from Antony, here engaged in public patronage evoking the memory of her son. This was a traditional and acceptable type of female visibility.

Other imperial women contributed to the deepening Augustan imprint of the area after the death of the first princeps. Three different installations, all now lost, featured Julia Augusta, Antonia the Younger, Agrippina the Elder, Livilla (Claudia Livia Julia), and others. Two are documented by the *Tabula Siarensis* of

---

97. See Plut. *Marc.* 30.4; Suet. *De gramm.* 21; Ov. *Ars am.* 1.69–70. Richardson 1976, 61–62 also adduces Prop. 3.18.11–20 to link Octavia's patronage to Marcellus' aedileship.

98. See, e.g., Hemelrijk 1999, 105; Kleiner 1996, 32. This was confusing in antiquity: see Woodhull 2003, 24–25, citing Festus' attempt to clarify the two (Festus, 188L).

99. http://formaurbis.stanford.edu/fragment.php?slab=81&record=5. This is usually interpreted as [PORTI]CUS OCTAVIAE ET FIL[IPPI]; Richardson 1976, 63, suggested instead [PORTI]CUS OCTAVIAE ET FIL[I], "of Octavia and her son," and some simply accept that (e.g., Woodhull 2016). Ov. *Ars am.* 1.71–72 credits the structure to Octavia; cf. Livy, *Per.* 140 and Festus 188L.

100. See *LTUR* 4.141–45, s.v. "Porticus Octaviae" (A. Viscogliosi); Richardson 1992, 317–18 (Porticus Octaviae).

101. Plin. *HN* 34.31, 35.22, 35.114, 36.28–43 *passim*. Richardson 1976, 62 provides a list of works; cf. Woodhull 2003, 19–20. Artworks per se are not "feminine": e.g., Tiberius gave to the Temple of *divus* Augustus a library famous for its works of art: Suet. *Tib.* 74; *LTUR* 1.197, s.v. "Bibliotheca templi divi Augusti" (M. Torelli).

102. Nicholls 2010, 12–18; Woodhull 2003, 29; Hemelrijk 1999, 105. Its grandeur reflects the architecture that Vitruvius, who was indebted to Octavia (*Arch.* 1 *praef.* 2), holds appropriate for the new Augustan age. Different interpretations of the whole have been offered: e.g., Woodhull 2003, 23–25 sees family as prominent; Hemelrijk 1999, 105, culture.

19 CE, the senate's decree that a marble arch honoring Germanicus be installed near statues earlier dedicated in the Circus Flaminius to *divus* Augustus and to the *domus Augusta* (lines 10–11 of *AE* 1984, no. 508 = EDCS-45500034).[103] The statuary group of the *domus Augusta*, dedicated by Norbanus Flaccus probably in early 15 CE, apparently depicted Tiberius, Germanicus, Drusus the Younger, and Livia, and it was enhanced by the adjacent statue to *divus* Augustus.[104] The *Tabula Siarensis* specifies that the new Arch of Germanicus was to hold statues of Germanicus in triumph, his father Drusus (the Elder), his mother Antonia, his wife Agrippina, his sister Livilla, his brother Claudius (the future emperor), and his (unnamed) sons and daughters (EDCS 45500034, lines 18–21).[105] We do not know exactly where the arch was in the Circus Flaminius or how it accommodated presumably twelve statues.[106] Only a few years later, in 22, Julia Augusta and Tiberius dedicated another statue of *divus pater Augustus* near the Theater of Marcellus.[107] Both Tacitus and the *Fasti Praenestini* record this, suggesting that it was a public event of some moment. According to Tacitus, however, on its base Julia Augusta's name as dedicator preceded that of Tiberius, offending her son and emperor (Tac. *Ann.* 3.64.2). Although Julia Augusta was not herself depicted, the dedication memorably asserted her centrality to the imperial house.

Not far distant—perhaps a ten-minute walk in the ancient city—a fragmentary inscription plausibly reconstructed by G. Alföldy records a dedication to Sabina and Hadrian from Catana (now Catania, Sicily). It dates to 128–137 and was found in the Area Sacra di Largo Argentina at Rome (also known as the Largo Argentina; see Ill. 5.1).[108] Alföldy suggests an original location in the *Porticus ad*

---

103. = *RS* 37, fr. I. See Lott 2012, 90, and Flory 1996. These arches have not been securely located.

104. Flory 1996 on the composition of this group is now generally accepted. We do not know the date or precise location of Livia's dedicated statue of a deceased son of Germanicus (Suet. *Calig.* 7.7, *Galba* 18); see further later.

105. The lacunose text now lacks *Agrippina uxor*: see Lott 2012, 90, lines 18–21.

106. Flory 1996, 289 n.7; *LTUR* 1.94–95, s.v. "Arcus Germanici in Circo Flaminio" (E. Rodríguez Almeida). Flory 1998, 492 n.10 holds that since the honors for Drusus the Younger at his death in 23 CE "exactly imitated but also expanded on those of Germanicus" (Tac. *Ann.* 4.9.2), they included an arch with statues of his mother, grandmother, wife, sister, and other family members.

107. *Fast. Praen.* ad 23 April = A. Degrassi, *Inscr. Ital.* 13.2, p. 131, 447 = EDCS-38000281: *sig(num) divo Augusto patri ad theatrum Marc(elli) / Iulia Augusta et Ti(berius) Augustus dedicarunt.* The statue is not the (planned) one to Augustus in her house on the Palatine of 14 CE (Cass. Dio 57.12.5), and postdates that cited in the *Tabula Siarensis* (*pace* Lott 2012, 216).

108. *CIL* VI 40516 = EDCS-00900228: Alföldy 1992, 147–54. At *CIL* VI 6.8.2 p. 4314, Alföldy notes that "Sabinae" is not original to *CIL* VI 996 = EDCS-17301107, a dedication seemingly

Imperial Women's Mark on the City of Rome

Nationes that formed part of the Theater of Pompey.[109] Sabina's name and title *Augusta* appear in the left-most column of the double dedication Alföldy reconstructs.[110] Other statue dedications from communities and corporate groups to imperial women, the "Sabrathans from Africa" to *diva* Sabina and the Sextani Arelatenses to *diva* Faustina (Faustina the Elder; citizens of what is now Arles, France), have been found in this general vicinity. We return below to a dedication to Sabina found in the Forum Julium (Forum of Caesar), but here note the dedication to *diva* Faustina of 140, now lost but discovered at the Piazza Sciarra in the Campus Martius about three-quarters of a kilometer northeast of the Largo Argentina.[111] The dedications, which may have been private rather than public,[112] suggest this part of the Campus Martius was more residential and less exclusively monumental than generally assumed.[113] In any case, the lower status of the dedicants, as compared to that of the senate or the emperor, bolsters my contention in Ch. 4 about imperial women as intermediaries.

Central and northern Campus Martius

Along the northern Via Flaminia at least two monuments featured Antonia the Younger, Octavia, and Agrippina the Younger among male relatives in public celebrations of Claudius' imperial family.[114] Inscriptions found in 1562 and 1641

---

to Sabina Augusta from the *magistri* of the *fabri tignarii* (the officials of the carpentry guild) and found near the church of SS. Apostoli.

109. See Højte 2005, 405–406. A *comparandum* cited by Alföldy (1992, 151), the dedication to Hadrian from Uthina, *CIL* VI 40523 = EDCS-00900235, found near the Temple of Castor in the Forum Romanum, names only Hadrian (not Sabina). Another, but for only an imperial male, *CIL* VI 1010 = EDCS- 17400011 found in Piazza Sciarra, was raised by the *Hipponenses ex Africa* to Marcus Aurelius in 151. See Højte 2005, 532, and Filippi 2016, 185.

110. Although her identification is much more succinct than Hadrian's, this is common on imperial dedications. Alföldy 1992, 82–88, reconstructs in the Largo Argentina a honorific, statue-less base (5 or 6 CE), from the Seleucenses to Augustus and his family, perhaps including Livia.

111. Not noted on Ill. 5.1; *CIL* VI 1006 = EDCS-17400008, from Vicolo Sciarra and Vicolo della Caravita on the modern Via Lata: Filippi 2016, 85, also noting the connection of such corporate groups with dedications (cf. Boatwright 2011b, 132).

112. Daguet-Gagey 1997, 177–78 considers the dedication to Sabina to be private, identifying "Sabrathenses" not as citizens of Sabratha but merchants from that city who were stationed in Ostia or Rome. This inscription is on an extraordinarily large pedestal 180 cm H, 123 cm W, 87 cm D. See at n.190 of this chapter.

113. Noreña 2006 argues for this on different grounds.

114. Rose 1997, 113–15, Cat. #42; Flower 2011, 192; Barrett 1991.

near the Arch of Claudius on the Via Flaminia commemorate three generations of Claudius' family and can be dated to 51–54 CE. (See Ill. 5.1 for the Arch of Claudius.) The dative used for the names indicates that the texts once identified statue bases for Germanicus, Antonia Augusta "wife of Drusus, priest of *divus* Augustus, mother of Tiberius Claudius Caesar [Claudius]," Julia Agrippina Augusta "daughter of Germanicus Caesar and wife of Tiberius Claudius Caesar," Nero, Britannicus, and Octavia "daughter of Tiberius Claudius Caesar Augustus, Father of the Fatherland." Analogous inscriptions are presumed for Claudius himself and his father Drusus the Elder.[115] The whole has often, but controversially, been interpreted as the Arch's display of members of Claudius' family.[116] Complicating the picture are other fragmentary inscriptions naming Claudius and members of his family found some 500 meters northwest, at the corner of the Via dell'Impresa and the Vicolo dello Sdrucciolo (northwest of the Column of Marcus Aurelius that is indicated in Ill. 5.1). The different location of these fragments, and their use of the nominative rather than dative, show they belong to a different monument. This has recently been called the Monumentum Claudianum (51–54 CE; *CIL* VI 40420-40430).[117] Scholars reconstruct two fragments as attesting Antonia Augusta, "mother of Tiberius Claudius Caesar Augustus Germanicus," and Jul[ia Augusta Agrippina, "daughter of Germanicus Caesar, wife of Tiberius Claudius Caesar"].[118] The pronounced presence of imperial women along the upper Via Flaminia was reinforced farther north by the Ara Pacis, by Agrippina's tribute to her siblings, and by the relief depicting the Apotheosis of Sabina.

First, though, we discuss much larger memorials of imperial women west northwest of the Arch of Claudius in the Campus Martius. (See Ill. 5.1.) This area, outside Rome's sacred boundary (*pomerium*) in part because of its liability to flooding, was rendered more usable first by Agrippa and then by Hadrian. Its relative openness and proximity to the Via Flaminia, the major northern entry to Rome, made it a favorite site for imperial monuments. A remarkable one is the temple honoring Hadrian's deified mother-in-law Matidia the Elder and basilicas

---

115. *CIL* VI 921 = EDCS-17301042.

116. Rose 1997, 113–15, Cat. #42; Flower 2011, 332 n.70.

117. See Alföldy et al. 1996, pp. 4416–19; De Caprariis 1993. Legibility precludes our locating the Monumentum Claudianum on Ill. 5.1.

118. *CIL* VI 40425-26 = EDCS-00900129-00900130. Rose 1997, 114 also refers to an inscription naming Agrippina as the mother of Nero, but cites no evidence. Rejecting statues on the Arch, he proposes at least two, probably three, Julio-Claudian monuments in the Via Flaminia area.

ILL. 5.3 *Sestertius* of Hadrian from 120/121 CE, showing the Temple for Matidia. Now in the Kunsthistorisches Museum, Vienna, Inv.-No. RO 9876. Courtesy of KHM-Museumsverband.

named for her and for Marciana, her mother and Trajan's sister.[119] Hadrian's support for Matidia's consecration in 119 included a temple for her cult, whose evidence is scrappy but convincing. A sesterius of 120–121 depicts on its reverse a temple with a seated female icon and the legend "For *diva* Matidia, mother-in-law"; the porticoes to either side, perhaps the Basilicas of Matidia and Marciana, are flanked by S C (by decree of the senate).[120] (See Ill. 5.3.) The fourth-century Regionary Catalogues include in Regio IX entries for a "basilica" of Matidia and one of Marciana.[121] A lead pipe inscribed "for the temple of Matidia" was found leading west on the Via del Seminario near S. Ignazio, allowing this area and nearby sporadic finds in the Vicolo dello Spado d'Orlando to be identified with the temple.[122] The assembled evidence indicates that Hadrian's mother-in-law Matidia and her mother Marciana were honored in the vicinity of the modern Piazza Capranica by a temple for Matidia's cult, and that the temple was set back

---

119. See Boatwright 1987, 58–62; *LTUR* 3.233, s.v. "Matidia, Templum" (F. de Caprariis).

120. DIVAE MATIDIAE SOCRVI; the portrait of Hadrian on the obverse has the legend IMP CAESAR TRAIAN HADRIANVS AVG P M TR P COS III (Imperator Caesar Trajan Hadrian Augustus, pontifex maximus, with tribunician power, consul three times). Dr. K. Vondrovec, the curator of the Antike Münzkabinett, Kuntshistorisches Museum, Vienna, kindly confirms that this is a sestertius.

121. *Curiosum*: "basilicam Neptuni. Matidies. Marcianes," *Notitia*: "basilicam Matidies et Marcianes." Marciana had died and been consecrated in 112.

122. *CIL* XV 7248 = EDCS-37801396 for the pipe.

in a precinct formed by twin two-storied, flanking porticoes called the basilicas of Matidia and of Marciana.[123]

The whole is an extraordinarily open statement of the importance of Trajanic imperial women at the beginning of Hadrian's reign. Its novelty may now be obscured by the flanking structures of the Pantheon to its west and the later Hadrianeum to its east (see Ill. 5.1), all of which have figured in interpretations of the central Campus Martius as imperial and dynastic.[124] If the Temple of *diva* Matidia and its precinct opened toward the Via Recta traversing this section of the Campus Martius, it would have had the same orientation as the Pantheon to its west, opening to the major road that became used in Rome for imperial cortèges to the Mausoleum of Hadrian. In any case, the construction furthered the awesome prominence of imperial dynastic monuments for those crossing the Campus Martius.[125]

Two further monuments in the northern Campus Martius featured reliefs of an apotheosis of an imperial woman. A large relief of the Apotheosis of Sabina, the earliest known to show a woman's apotheosis in Rome,[126] was among other repurposed pieces once decorating the so-called Arco di Portogallo spanning the Via Flaminia just north of the Ara Pacis.[127] The relief, now heavily restored, measures 2.68 m H x 2.10 m W and highlights Sabina, who died in 136/137, and her husband and emperor Hadrian. (See Ill. 5.4.) Hadrian, at larger scale than Sabina, sits on a throne with a bearded man standing behind him. Both face left toward Sabina, carried by a winged, torch-bearing female figure, perhaps *Aeternitas*, above a burial pyre and a seated youth who is usually identified as the Campus Martius.[128] The relief, although originally probably not on an arch, asserted Sabina's importance in the capital city, as well the timeless piety of the imperial couple.[129] The size of the relief argues that it came

---

123. Boatwright 1987, 60–61; *LTUR* 1.182, s.v. "Basilica Marciana, basilica Matidiae" (E. Rodríguez Almeida).

124. See Jolivet 1988; Boatwright 2010, 171, 174, 186–87.

125. For the Hadrianic inscription of the Pantheon, which may have masked a Trajanic origin for the building, see Boatwright 2013.

126. Coins showing Sabina's apotheosis also are the earliest to depict a woman carried aloft: see Ill. 4.9. Gradel 2002, 165–86 (cf. Brännstedt 2015, 45) argues that the "Frieze of the Vicomagistri" from Rome may depict the consecration of Livia, but this relief is not as unambiguous as Sabina's.

127. Boatwright 1987, 226–29; *LTUR* 1.77–79, s.v. "Arco di Portogallo" (M. Torelli).

128. Boatwright 1987, 271; Alexandridis 2004, Cat. 178.

129. An ideal contradicted by the literary sources for the two, but maintained by Hadrian's decision to remain married to Sabina: see Ch. 3.

ILL. 5.4 Apotheosis of Sabina relief from the later Arco di Portogallo. Now in the Palazzo dei Conservatori, Musei Capitolini, Rome. © Vanni Archive / Art Resource, NY. ART319601.

from the environs of its reuse, near the Ara Pacis and Agrippina the Younger's funerary monument to her family. Both ensembles include commemoration of imperial women.

Within a generation of Sabina's monument came a similar statement about Faustina the Elder and Antoninus Pius, the marble relief depicting the joint apotheosis of the couple and installed after Pius died in 161, some twenty years after his wife (see Ill. 5.5). This decorated the (formerly south) side of the base of the

ILL. 5.5 Apotheosis of Faustina the Elder and Antoninus Pius on the Column of Antoninus Pius. Now in the Cortile delle Corazze of the Vatican Museums. Scala / Art Resource, NY. ART 45685.

Column of Antoninus Pius in the central Campus Martius.[130] (See Ill. 5.1.) The short dedicatory inscription on the base's original north side, proclaiming that the monument was erected to *divus* Antoninus Pius by his sons Marcus Aurelius and Lucius Verus, does not mention Faustina.[131] Although this may be one reason her name is not part of the monument's modern designation, Faustina herself is unmistakably portrayed on the opposite side of the base. The large-scale relief portrays her and Pius in apotheosis, carried by a winged genius above personifications of the Campus Martius and of Rome. Conflating the consecration of Pius with the earlier one of his wife, it emphasizes the ideal harmony of the imperial couple and the imperial house (Ch. 3).[132]

---

130. The monument, dismembered in the eighteenth century, consisted of a red granite monolith (50 RF) on a large, decorated square marble pedestal; it is known from coins struck under Marcus Aurelius in 161, drawings, descriptions, and its extant parts, particularly the pedestal in the Vatican. See Boatwright 2010, 189–91; Alexandridis 2004, Cat. 196; Kleiner 1992, 285–8; Richardson 1992, 94. The base and column, which once carried a statue undoubtedly of Pius, were surrounded by a fence.

131. *CIL* VI 1004 (cf. p. 804) = EDCS-17400006.

132. The (original) east and west sides, with the equestrian *decursio* reliefs, may represent two distinct cavalcades for Faustina the Elder, in 141, and Pius, in 161: see Kleiner 1992, 287.

The imperial house similarly features on the Ara Pacis on the Via Flaminia (see Ill. 5.1). Livia, Octavia, and other imperial women were represented on this iconic monument of 13–9 BCE, although the identities of the female figures on the historical relief have long been debated (see Ch. 3 and Ill. 3.1; Ch. 6).[133] The location and preservation of the Ara Pacis—carefully protected against flooding when the ground level in the Campus Martius was elevated during Hadrian's reign[134]—may account for the nearby siting of the Hadrianic monument with the Apotheosis of Sabina relief.

This northern part of the Campus Martius along the Via Flaminia near Augustus' Mausoleum housed yet another monument associated with an imperial woman. Agrippina the Younger is credited with building here a sepulchral memorial that Titus later enhanced (see Ill. 5.1). The monument, with travertine *cippi* ca. 66 cm high and an alabaster funerary urn, marked the cremation or funerary sites of three sons of Germanicus (Agrippina's three brothers who died as infants or children), Agrippina's sister Julia Livilla, Tiberius "Gemellus" (the son of Germanicus' brother Drusus the Younger and the Livilla who was Germanicus' sister and Agrippina the Younger's aunt), and Domitilla, wife of Vespasian.[135] Alongside the vital northern route into Rome and memorializing members of Germanicus' family who had not received burial in the Mausoleum of Augustus, this apparently plain site asserted the prominence of Agrippina and her family. Domitilla's remembrance was added later, presumably by Titus. On the funeral route from the Forum to Augustus' Mausoleum, the monument kept alive the memory of some lesser-known imperial women and others. Its construction speaks to the active role of Agrippina in Rome in her prime.[136]

Eastern Rome

Various structures linked to imperial women are also found in Rome's eastern sectors (see Ill. 5.1), which were formed by high volcanic spurs separated by valleys and primarily accommodated lower-class, dense inhabitation and imperial

---

133. For the debates, see Alexandridis 2004, 115–18, Kat.-Nr. 1-8.

134. Boatwright 1987, 66–67.

135. See Hesberg and Panciera 1994, 148–61: *CIL* VI 888–893 = EDCS-17301016-17301021, cf. Suet. *Calig.* 7. The monument must date between 49 and 55. Julia Livilla: *CIL* VI 891 = EDCS-17301019; Domitilla: *CIL* VI 893 = EDCS-17301021; *LTUR* 3.239, s.v. "Mausoleum Augusti" (M. Macciocca). Its site is near the present-day S. Carlo al Corso, at the Via della Croce.

136. Panciera in Hesberg and Panciera 1994, 161. A small bronze cuirassed trophy, found in the vicinity, has also been associated with Agrippina's monument: see *Claudio imperatore* 2019, 261 Cat. 134.

horti.[137] A *Lavacrum Agrippinae* (Bath of Agrippina) is attested by two inscribed lead pipes from near the church of San Lorenzo in Panisperna on the Viminal Hill (general find spot indicated in Ill. 5.1). Although we cannot determine if the bath, attested by the inscriptions as part of Hadrian's imperial property,[138] originally belonged to Agrippina the Younger or her homonymous mother,[139] it kept the name of Agrippina alive in this residential part of the city. The younger Agrippina is attested more unmistakably by a fragmentary inscription found nearby on the modern Via Nazionale on the Quirinal (general find spot indicated in Ill. 5.2): between 69 and 79 the imperial freedman Apollonius commemorated her, "wife of *divus* Claudius and daughter of Germanicus Caesar," together with Flavia Domitilla, wife of Vespasian.[140]

Still in Rome's northeast is the poorly attested and undated Macellum Liviae and the Porticus Liviae, two monumental structures carrying Livia's name.[141] Most scholars locate the Macellum Liviae outside the Servian Wall, north of the later Arch of Gallienus that marked the Porta Esquilina (see Ill. 5.1).[142] Archaeological remains here, indicating a rectangular open court once housing a fountain and surrounded by porticoes and shops, date later than Livia's death but may be a rebuilding. The scattered references to the market building, one of three large ones in Rome, suggest that it functioned into the fifth century CE.[143] At the foot of the Oppian Hill on the Esquiline is the better-known Porticus Liviae (Ill. 5.2), which Livia dedicated together with Tiberius on the occasion of his German

---

137. For the lead pipes found in this region that may attest domiciles of Matidia the Elder, Matidia the Younger, and Sabina, see Ch. 1.

138. *CIL* VI 29765 (p 3731) = *CIL* VI 36605 = *CIL* XV 7247, EDCS-37801374; also *CIL* XV 7311 = EDCS-37801375. Richardson 1992, 234, s.v. "Lavacrum Agrippinae," noting also statuary finds, suggests that the *Lavacrum Agrippae* of HA, *Hadr.* 19.10 be corrected to *Lavacrum Agrippinae*.

139. I omit the private Horti Agrippinae on Tiber's right bank (Sen. *de ira* 3.18.4; Philo, *leg. ad Gaium* 2.572). Perhaps near S. Pietro, these are usually attributed to Agrippina the Elder, perhaps because of *CIL* VI 4346 = EDCS-19100542, *Cydnus / Ti(beri) Germanici <servus>, supra / hortos. Narcissus / fratri merenti f(ecit)*).

140. *CIL* VI 40452 = EDCS-00900157. Both women were dead.

141. *LTUR* 3.203–204, s.v. "Macellum Liviae" (G. Pisani Sartorio); DAR, #335 (A. G. Thein; http://digitalaugustanrome.org/map/#/). The sources are late-antique, medieval, and epigraphic (a slave collar of 370 CE, *AE* 1946, 211 = EDCS-01000464). Thein corrects the assumption of *LTUR* 3.203–204 that Cass. Dio 55.8.2 refers to the Macellum Liviae rather than the Porticus Liviae (for which see later).

142. See DAR, #335 (A. G. Thein; http://digitalaugustanrome.org/map/#/rome/filter:o/ records/read/c9470891-d97f-dea3-79c1-70afcbcb869b/).

143. *LTUR* 3.203; Domínguez Arranz 2016, 82–83.

triumph in 7 BCE (Cass. Dio 55.8.2, with Ov. *Fast.* 6.639–48).[144] Controversial literary evidence and fragments of the Marble Plan of Rome attest this portico near the densely populated Subura.[145] The Marble Plan shows that its outline cut into the shops, apartment buildings, and streets around it.[146] The Porticus Liviae, adorned with plantings, symbolically reclaimed the area for Rome's inhabitants. It rose on a bequest to Augustus in 15 BCE from Vedius Pollio, whom the emperor so scorned for profligacy that he razed Pollio's opulent house when it was bequeathed to him (Cass. Dio 54.23.6; Ov. *Fast.* 6.639–48).[147] The Porticus Liviae served legal transactions and political displays: for instance, Trajan conducted trials in the Porticus Liviae as well as in the Forum Augustum (Forum of Augustus; Cass. Dio 68.10.2). As with so many other monuments in Rome, including the Porticus Octaviae completed some five years earlier, the Porticus Liviae accommodated numerous functions.

Livia's responsibility for the Porticus Liviae was disputed in antiquity: Ovid credits her alone for building the *porticus* (*Ars am.* 1.71–72), but Cassius Dio holds that together with Tiberius she dedicated the precinct (*temenisma*) named the "Livium" (an adjective from her name) in 7 BCE, on the occasion of Tiberius' triumph over the Germans (55.8.2).[148] Cassius Dio notes elsewhere that an enclosed portico (*peristoon*) was dedicated by Augustus in Livia's name (54.23.6), which would separate Livia completely from active construction. Further difficulties come from Ovid's remark that Livia dedicated a shrine (*aedes*) of Concordia to Augustus on 11 June (*Fast.* 6.637–38), although many scholars have reconciled this by identifying as a shrine (or altar) to Concord the central rectangular feature in the enclosed *quadriporticus* shown on the Marble Plan.[149]

Ovid's reference to Livia's dedication on 11 June has encouraged associations with various female deities: for example, M. Woodhull notes the proximity of the Porticus Liviae to the temple of Juno Lucina where the festival of the Matronalia

---

144. Kleiner 1996, 32 suggests that Livia was thus showing herself also as a *triumphator*.

145. See DAR, #329, s.v. "Porticus Liviae" (A. G. Thein; http://digitalaugustanrome.org/map/# accessed 25 September 2017), citing *inter alia* Plin. *HN* 14.11. Woodhull 2016, 120 presumes there were fountains in the four corners.

146. Wallace-Hadrill 2003, 193; Zanker 1988, 137–39 assumes the Porticus followed the footprint of Vedius' home.

147. Flory 1984 remains fundamental for the Porticus Liviae and Temple of Concord.

148. As we saw earlier, this remark has been wrongly linked with the Macellum.

149. *LTUR* 4.127–29, s.v. "Porticus Liviae" (C. Panella); Flory 1984, 311–12 stresses that the dedication on 11 June postdated that of the surrounding porticus by six months. Simpson 1991 has a radically different (ultimately unconvincing) interpretation, doubting the very existence of any shrine to Concord (see esp. his 449 and n.3).

was celebrated, and she also adduces the Matralia festival held 11 June by Roman mothers in honor of the fertility goddess Mater Matuta.[150] Further, ostensible design similarities of the Porticus Liviae and its shrine of Concordia to the more or less contemporary Building of Eumachia in Pompeii figure in arguments for the Porticus Liviae and other donations of Livia as "feminine space."[151] This seems overstated in the wider context and given the multipurpose nature of the Porticus.

On the other hand, Livia's restoration of the Temple of Bona Dea has a gendered aspect. The sanctuary of the "Good Goddess" was restricted to women only, and its cult was officiated by matrons married but once (*univirae*) and chosen by the Vestals.[152] The cult had been dishonored in 62 BCE, when Publius Clodius intruded on celebrations for the Bona Dea held at the house of Julius Caesar. Livia's restoration of the building may have served to reinstate Bona Dea's sanctity.[153] No remains have been securely identified with the sanctuary,[154] located by topographers either inside or outside the Servian Wall on the "Lesser Aventine." (A possible location is shown in Ill. 5.1.) Ovid, whose *Fasti* is our sole source for Livia's restoration and provides a *terminus ante quem* of 8 CE when the *Fasti* appeared, holds that her work was inspired by the building activity of her husband Augustus (Ov. *Fast.* 5.157–58).[155] The brief note furnishes no information about other motivations and repercussions of Livia's work, although the exemplary power of Augustus' activity is clear.

Southeast of Rome near the fourth milestone of the Via Latina (see Ill. 5.1), a fragmentary, inscribed white marble entablature documents Livia's responsibility for a building that the Severan family, including Julia Domna, later restored. The inscription has been plausibly reconstructed: "Livia, daughter of Drusus, wife of [Caesar Augustus] . . . The Imperial Caesars Augusti [Septimius] Severus and Antoninus [Caracalla], and most noble Caesar Geta, and Julia Augusta [Domna],

---

150. E.g., Woodhull 2016, 122. Juno Lucina oversaw childbirth. Livia's shrine of Concordia is not the same as the Temple of "Concordia Augusta" in the Forum Romanum.

151. Woodhull 2003, 2012, and 2016, 120 (the Porticus Liviae), stresses the "feminine" aspects of Livia's and Octavia's buildings; contra Cooley 2013. Cenerini 2006, 278–80, 284 is unsure.

152. Flory 1984, 317–18; Festus 348L; DAR #267, s.v. "Bona Dea" ("sub Saxo") (D. Borbonus; L. Haselberger; http://digitalaugustanrome.org/map/#/).

153. See Boatwright 1987, 212–15.

154. *LTUR* I.200–201, s.v. "Bona Dea Subsaxana" (L. Chioffi) is more certain that the sanctuary was at the site of the later S. Balbina. Hadrian apparently restored an *aedes* here (HA, *Hadr.* 19.11): Boatwright 1987, 212–18.

155. DAR #267, s.v. "Bona Dea" ("sub Saxo") (D. Borbonus; L. Haselberger; http://digitalaugustanrome.org/map/#/).

Mother of the Emperors . . . restored this."[156] The building the entablature originally embellished is usually identified as the Temple of Fortuna Muliebris ("Womanly Good Fortune"), a legendary shrine reportedly at the fourth mile of the Via Latina. It commemorated the patriotic bravery of Volumnia and Virgilia, the mother and the wife of Coriolanus who deterred him from leading the Volscian foe against Rome soon after the establishment of the Republic.[157] After some remains discovered near the Via Latina in the 1890s were identified as those of the Temple,[158] the inscription cited above, previously uncovered "not far" away, was also attributed to it. This has encouraged a long-standing identification of Livia and then Domna with the Temple of Fortuna Muliebris and exemplary Roman women.[159]

As the above shows, the basis for identifying Livia and Domna with the Temple of Fortuna Muliebris is circumstantial. Nevertheless, the inscription prompts four inferences. Even if the inscription never belonged to the Temple of Fortuna Muliebris, its size indicates that Livia was responsible for a substantial religious building: the entablature is some 61 cm high, and the letters of Livia's inscription 18 cm.[160] Second, the text gives Livia an identity other than within the imperial family, for she is identified by filiation as well as by her marriage. This is not unique in the epigraphic record outside of Rome, and it may be that her relative autonomy on this inscription is due to its origin some four Roman miles from the capital city.[161] Third, in contrast to Livia who is cited alone, Domna is listed after her husband Septimius Severus and sons Caracalla and (presumably)

---

156. *CIL* VI 883 = EDCS-17301015: *Livia [D]rusi f(ilia) ux{s}or [Caesaris Augusti 3] / Impp(eratores) C[aes]s(ares) Severus et Anto[ninus Augg(usti) et Geta nobilissimus Caesar] / et [Iulia] Aug(usta) mater Aug[g(ustorum) 3 restituerunt].* Lusnia 2014, 213 provides a detailed, rightly skeptical discussion of the evidentiary value of the finds.

157. Livy 2.40; Dion. Hal. *Ant. Rom.* 8.55; Plut. *Coriolanus* 37; Val. Max. 1.8.4 and 5.2.1; for other references and discussion, see Lusnia 2014, 212–14. Volumnia is sometimes called Veturia.

158. Lusnia 2014, 212–13 provides a lucid discussion of the finds and their interpretation.

159. Kleiner 1996, 33 notes that Dionysius of Halicarnassus' interest in the cult (8.55) may provide a *terminus ante quem* for Livia's donation, since the *Roman Antiquities* began to be published in 7 BCE. See also, e.g., Barrett 2002, 205, with reference to earlier literature.

160. As Lusnia 2014, 213 notes, the size encouraged Canina to restore the temple as tetrastyle, prostyle, and with intercolumniations of 2.6 m.

161. Four miles is about 6.4 kilometers. For comparison, the Superaequani (now Castelvecchio Subequo, Italy) raised a dedication to "Livia, daughter of Drusus, [wife] of Augustus, mother of Tiberius Caesar and [of Drusus the Elder]" between 4 and 14 CE (*CIL* IX 3304 = EDCS-14804320); a statue from Potentia (now Potenza Picena, Italy), t.p.q. 14 CE, is dedicated *Augustae Iuliae Drusi f(iliae)* (*CIL* VI 882a = EDCS-21300236). Cf. Boatwright 1991, 520; Purcell 1986, 88.

Geta and identified as "Mother of the Emperors" (*mater Aug[g(ustorum)]*).[162] Lusnia has pointed out how odd it would be that Domna is cited here only after her husband and sons if indeed "imperial women were involved in some way with the cult of Fortuna Muliebris."[163] Finally, whatever this building was, it featured Livia—and later Domna—outside the capital city, where imperial women seem to have had greater scope.

Caelian, Palatine, Forum, Capitoline

Imperial women also left impressions on the Caelian, Palatine, and Capitoline hills as well as in the valleys between them. Agrippina the Younger was prominent on and near the Caelian. In 54 she began the construction of the Claudium or Temple of *divus* Claudius on the Caelian that later was "almost totally destroyed" by Nero but refurbished and finished by Vespasian (Suet. *Vesp.* 9).[164] This huge structure, 200 m W x 180 m D, is the largest imperial cult sanctuary in Rome.[165] (See Ill. 5.1.) In Ch. 6 we discuss the over-life-size greywacke statue of Agrippina found nearby (see Ill. 6.1). This was fragmented sometime after its head ornamentation had been remodeled in the third or (more likely) fourth century, but Agrippina's face—from her third- or fourth-portrait type—is so excellently preserved that scholars have discerned it was recut after Nero's accession in 54.[166] The state of the face, and the head's evident reuse in the fourth century, suggest that Agrippina's statue was reinstalled in or near the Claudium after the Flavian restoration.[167] A statue of her had been added in 55/56 to the shrine of the Aenatores, the brass-wind instrument players of Rome, on the northeastern edge of the Palatine near the later Arch of Constantine, across from the Caelian and the later

---

162. The Severan titles give a rough date of 198–209.

163. Lusnia 2014, 214.

164. The shrine is called *Claudium* and *Templum Claudii*, respectively, by the *Curiosum* and *Notitia* of the Regionary Catalogues, Reg. II; *templum divi Claudi* in *CIL* VI 10251a = EDCS-16100479, Frontin. *Aq.* 1.20, and Suet. *Vesp.* 9; *LTUR* 1.277-78, s.v. "Claudius, Divus, Templum (reg. II)" (C. Buzzetti). See also Aur. Vict. *Caes.* 9, cf. *Epit. de Caes.* 8.8. Frontinus indicates the rebuilding was finished by the end of the first century CE. Nero's repurposing of the shrine as a nymphaeum (cf. Mart. *Spec.* 2.9–10) may date to after his mother's death and disgrace in 59 as easily as to after the Fire of 64.

165. See *Claudio imperatore* 2019, 279–82 (F. Coarelli).

166. Trillmich 2007, 45–65; Varner 2004, n.156. See Ch. 6.

167. Agrippina's rehabilitation under the Flavians is suggested also by the addition of Domitilla to her monument along the Via Flaminia and her honor with Vespasian's wife on the Quirinal.

Claudium.[168] (See Ill. 5.1; discussed further in Ch. 6.) This statue, attested only by a dedicatory inscription that was later effaced, was removed after her assassination in 59 but before the Great Fire of 64 destroyed the sanctuary. During its short display, the statue gained significance from the nearby Claudium, and both installations help us discern Agrippina's visibility in first-century Rome.

A large temple dedicated to Faustina the Younger has been located by C. Cecamore across the Colosseum valley from the Templum divi Claudi.[169] The evidence for this, passages in the Historia Augusta and possibly some fragments of the Severan marble plan of Rome, has been identified with a southern porticus some 13.5 m long uncovered in the Vigna Barberini on the northeast slope of the Palatine (Ill. 5.2):[170] Cecamore restores the whole as a temple with a double colonnade on three sides.[171] The Historia Augusta holds that Faustina the Younger was "deconsecrated" (HA, *M. Ant.* 11.6; see Ch. 4), and Cecamore has argued that the temple was repurposed by Severus Alexander first for Elagabalus (in 221) and then for Jupiter Optimus Maximus. If she is correct, Faustina the Younger had been venerated for more than a quarter century in a sanctuary dedicated to her alone and looming over a major artery of Rome. Faustina's subsequent erasure from the shrine, however, reminds us of the tenuous presence of imperial women in the capital city.

Farther west on the Palatine and probably on the southern edge of the Forum Romanum Julia Augusta sponsored or co-sponsored the Temple of *divus* Augustus (Templum divi Augusti).[172] The Temple functioned for her own cult as well after her consecration in 42, to judge from a first-century inscription naming the "Temple of *divus* Augustus and *diva* Augusta."[173] Further, coins of 158–159 attesting to the shrine's restoration by Antoninus Pius show an octastyle temple

---

168. Morizio 1996, 211; Boschung 2002.

169. See Levick 2014, 135–36.

170. HA, *Marc.* 26.5 and *M. Ant.* 11.6–7; Cecamore 1999, esp. 318–19, referring to Fr. 69–70a and b 103 of the Severan marble plan. Levick 2014, 136 and 206 n.66 sees the temple presaged by an altar to *diva* Faustina Pia (suggested by a coin; see *RIC* III, Marcus Aurelius no. 1706).

171. Cecamore 1999, 320, fig. 5, accepted by the Stanford Digital Forma Urbis Project, accessed 22 October 2018: https://formaurbis.stanford.edu/fragment.php?record=1&field0=all&searcho=103&opo=and&field1=all.

172. For this controversial temple, see *LTUR* 1.145–46, s.v. "Augustus, Divus, Templum (Novum); Aedes" (M. Torelli); Fishwick 1992.

173. "Templum divi Augusti et divae Augustae," *CIL* VI 4222 = EDCS 19100421. See Hänlein-Schäfer 1985, 87, 114 no. 6, 126–27.

with two seated over-life-size icons, presumably *divus* Augustus and *diva* Julia Augusta.[174] The Temple, still incomplete at Julia Augusta's death in 29, was not dedicated until Caligula's first year of rule.[175] It was enormously important, the site of the discharge records (*constitutiones*) for Roman auxiliary soldiers from the late first into the third century, for example.[176] It has never been securely located, and I find persuasive M. Torelli's suggestion of a site near the Vicus Tuscus, Vicus Iugarius, the Temple of Castor, Basilica Julia, and the structures at Santa Maria Antiqua.[177] (See Ill. 5.2.) The shrine would thus be in the southeastern part of the Forum, Rome's traditional political center, and at the foot of the Palatine that was increasingly appropriated by the imperial family (see Joseph. *AJ* 19.1.15). The location is apt for Julia Augusta's own position in Augustan and Tiberian Rome. As often with imperial women's patronage in the city of Rome, however, the sources are unclear about her agency. Pliny credits Livia alone for the original building (Plin. *HN* 12.94), but two centuries after the fact Cassius Dio reports that Julia Augusta and Tiberius together erected the shrine voted by the senate (Cass. Dio 56.46.3).[178]

Another public expression of Livia's devotion to her imperial family was her dedication of a statue of a young son of Germanicus, who died before his time, in a Temple of Venus found on the Capitoline (Suet. *Calig.* 7.7, *Galba* 18). We can pinpoint neither date nor location of the statue on the hill. If it dates early in Tiberius' reign, when the Circus Flaminius area saw both the installation of a statuary group of *domus Augusta* that probably included images of Julia Augusta and Germanicus, and the Arch of Germanicus with its many images of the imperial family (see earlier), Livia's statue of the boy underscored the piety and interrelations of the developing imperial house. In any case, its record counters the tradition of Livia's resentment against Germanicus and his family that Tacitus helped establish (e.g., *Ann.* 1.32).[179]

---

174. Torelli in *LTUR* 1.146 cites the coins (see *LTUR* 1, Fig. 79); also Boatwright 2010, 180–81.

175. Torelli in *LTUR* 1.145, adduces Tiberius' "evident aversion to imperial cult" for the delay.

176. Torelli in *LTUR* 1.145; the earliest known "diploma" or copy of a record placed "on the wall behind the Temple of divus Augustus, at (the Temple of) Minerva," dates to 90. Julia Augusta's inclusion in the temple, although not on the formulaic diplomas, fits the diplomas' stress on the grant of *conubium*, the right of lawful marriage, to their recipients: see Ch. 3.

177. See *LTUR* 1.145–46.

178. Neither author calls her priest of *divus* Augustus, though she may have undertaken the temple as part of her new position. See later on Agrippina the Younger and the Templum divi Claudii.

179. Purcell 1986, 89.

Faustina the Elder, who died in late 140, sponsored no building in Rome before or during the two years she lived as the wife of the ruling emperor, Pius.[180] On the other hand, she is honored in one of Rome's most notable cult buildings for an imperial woman, the Temple of *diva* Faustina that is still largely extant on the Forum Romanum (see Ill. 5.2). On a high podium on the northeast side of the central Forum, the shrine towered over the Regia and the shrine of Vesta.[181] Its constricted location in the traditional heart of Rome is emphasized by the placement of its altar on its wide frontal staircase. A prostyle design with *cippollino* columns 48 Roman feet (14.2 m) high ensured visibility throughout the Forum, including from the Palatine and Capitoline. The original dedication, incised on the temple's architrave, reads "To *diva* Faustina, in accordance with a decree of the Senate."[182] The senate's initiative is also claimed on coins from Pius' reign that depict the temple with a statue of Faustina and the legend S C, "By a Decree of the Senate."[183]

As most temples for imperial women in Rome, other than that claimed for Faustina the Younger on the Palatine already discussed, the Temple of *diva* Faustina [the Elder] firmly places her within her imperial family. Nothing now suggests whether the uppermost frieze of the temple, on which was inscribed the dedication to Pius at his death and consecration in 161, was left smooth and unembellished for two decades above the original inscription for Faustina.[184] Some scholars have presumed that expanding the building's consecration to include Pius was an afterthought; others, that such a large building in this prestigious location was always planned to honor Pius as well when his time came.[185] Large-scale temples dedicated solely to a *diva* were unusual in the capital city: the only ones known are to Matidia the Elder and to Faustina the Younger. As we saw, the former was adjacent to other monuments to members of the imperial family. That the Temple of Faustina the Elder was always destined for her husband as

---

180. Beckmann 2012a, 83–87 discusses memorials and statues of Faustina the Elder in Rome.

181. For details, see Beckmann 2012a, 42–48, 66–68 (especially on the coins), and Boatwright 2010, 177–80 (the date of Faustina's death there should be corrected to 140).

182. *Divae Faustinae Ex S C, CIL* VI 1005 = EDCS-17400007, corroborating HA, *Ant. Pius* 6.7.

183. *RIC* III, Pius no. 1115; Schulten 1979: 36, 38.

184. *Divo Antonino et,* with larger letters than those used for Faustina's dedication: *CIL* VI 1005, 31224 = EDSC 17400007. Along the temple's sides the frieze, richly decorated with griffins and candelabra, surmounts a standard architrave with two *fasciae.*

185. Claridge 1998, 107 and Richardson 1992, 11 suggest the frieze originally extended across the front; see Beckmann 2012a, 46–48. His careful study of coins depicting the temple in 143–144 and at its tenth-year anniversary in 150 (2012a, 66–68) suggests alteration of the temple's plans.

well accords with the marked emphasis on family in the second century, and on the publicized accord of Faustina and Pius on the relief of their apotheosis and in statues to the two (below).

A few imperial women were honored in the Forum Romanum itself by scattered statues and dedications.[186] An under-life-sized statue to Faustina the Younger was dedicated by the *viatores* or "runners" (minor officials) of the supervising quaestor of the public treasury at the Temple of Saturn, according to its small, inscribed base found between the Temple of Vespasian and the Temple of Concord on the Forum's west side.[187] Two installations honored Julia Domna jointly with Septimius Severus, one dedicated by minor functionaries, the *kalatores pontificum et flaminum* who served two of Rome's priestly colleges, and the other now too battered to reveal details.[188] Silver images of Faustina the Elder and Antoninus Pius, installed after 140, and an adjacent set of statues in precious metal to Faustina the Younger and Marcus Aurelius, installed after 175, were prominent near the Temple of Venus and Roma. They were used for sacrifices by newlyweds in Rome.[189] All the statues, except that of the "runners" to Faustina the Younger, honored imperial women together with their husbands.

Imperial fora area

A cluster of imperial women's monuments is found around the westernmost imperial fora (see Ill. 5.2). In 138 the "Sabrathans from Africa" raised a dedication to *diva* Sabina in front of the temple of Venus Genetrix in the Forum Julium (mentioned earlier).[190] The large marble pedestal (180 cm H, 123 cm W, 87 cm D) once carried a statue. The handsome text honoring Sabina is accompanied on the pedestal's left side by a less finely lettered inscription, which specifies that on Hadrian's order the site was granted by the supervisors of public works. Although this complicates the question of responsibility for locating dedications to an

---

186. I do not try to locate these on Ill. 5.2. Lusnia 2014, 61–68 convincingly discredits the argument that Domna rebuilt the shrine of Vesta after the fire of 191, a suggestion made on the basis of coins (see Gorrie 2004, 65–66).

187. *CIL* VI 1019 = EDCS-17400018: see Boatwright 2011b, 130–31. The Temple of Vespasian, just southwest of the Temple of Concord, is not identified on Ill. 5.2.

188. *CIL* VI 36932 = EDSC-19800507 and *CIL* VI 36934 = EDSC-19800509, respectively.

189. Weiss 2008, 4–12. See Ch. 3.

190. *Sabrathe[nses] / ex Afr[ica]*, *CIL* VI 40528 = EDCS-00900240, consular date of 13 December 138.

Imperial woman,[191] it suggests Hadrian's public concern for his recently consecrated spouse.[192] The location links Sabina with Venus, a common association on coins for imperial women that we have already noted.

Another inscription from the area documents the only monument Sabina is known to have sponsored in Rome, and its text also records a restoration by Julia Domna. The inscription, known only from the ninth-century Einsiedlensis manuscript that indicates a provenance near or in the Forum of Trajan (see Ill. 5.2),[193] notes Sabina Augusta's dedication of something to or for Rome's elite women or *matronae*, with a later restoration by Domna: "Julia Augusta [Domna], Mother of the Emperors and of the Camps, restored [this] for the Matrons; Sabina Augusta [made/dedicated this] for the Matrons." The titles of the two women date Sabina's act between her designation as *Augusta*, probably in 128, and her death in 136/137; Domna's restoration dates to 209–211.[194] The inscription has been understood as commemorating an original building benefaction and its restoration.[195] The imperial women's benefactions for Rome's *matronae* are often associated with two (or one) shadowy assemblies of women known only from late and suspect evidence mentioning the "assembly of the matrons" (or "the matrons' place") and "the little senate, that is the senate of the womenfolk" on the Quirinal.[196] Some speculate that first Sabina built, and then Domna restored, an assembly room or *schola* for Rome's matrons near the Forum of Trajan at the Quirinal's foot.[197] Although such a benefaction would be at odds with Sabina's muted profile in Rome, other imperial women are clearly associated with Rome's *matronae*.

---

191. Daguet-Gagey 1997, 177–78 considers this a private dedication.

192. Brennan 2018, 311–13, pointing out as well that the installation of the monument postdates Hadrian's death. The inscription is one of many for Hadrian's family in this central area of Rome, where Hadrian's Athenaeum likewise complemented Trajan's distinct imprint.

193. *Iulia Aug(usta) mater Augg(ustorum) et castrorum / Matronis restituit / Sabina Aug(usta) / Matronis*: See Walser 1987, 74–75 and discussion at *CIL* VI 997; also *CIL* VI pp. 3777 and 4314.

194. *CIL* VI 997 = EDCS-17301108. The late date for Domna's restoration generally fits that of the restoration of the Via Latina shrine.

195. Horster 2001, 32 n.86; Boatwright 2013, 22–23. The verb used with Domna's benefaction, *restituit* (restored), argues strongly that Sabina's benefaction was something architectural or decorative. In this inscription the earlier text is below; most other rebuilding inscriptions (e.g., as on "Fortuna Muliebris," or the Pantheon) display the earlier text above the restoration one.

196. *conventus matronarum* or *matronalis*, and *senaculum, id est mulierum senatum*. For the *mulierum senatus*, see HA, *Heliogab.* 4.3–4, *Aurel.* 49.

197. E.g., Gorrie 2004, 71–72; Lusnia 2014, 66 n.263; cf. Hemelrijk 1999, 13–14, 226 n.24, and Purcell 1986, 100 n.33. Straub 1966 discusses the HA passages; see also Richardson 1992, 348.

The Forum of Trajan itself has furnished various images of imperial women, including three statues of Matidia the Elder, Marciana, and another unidentifiable Trajanic female. The three are slightly larger than life size and of the same Greek marble, indicating that they were part of an ensemble.[198] These "Loggia dei Lanzi" statues are joined by an enigmatic colossal head, also from the Forum, that resembles portraits of Agrippina the Younger. L. Ungaro is currently investigating the "Agrippina" head, which some hold represents the poorly attested mother of Trajan.[199] Despite the wider context of growing dedications to imperial women traced in this chapter, the statues of imperial women from Trajan's Forum are the only ones known from an imperial forum.[200] Tempering the famed militaristic male impact of the Forum of Trajan,[201] the depictions of imperial women that were also found there underscore the importance of female members of the second-century imperial family.

Plotina, Trajan's wife, is attested by a spectacular inscription from this area. After her death and consecration in 123, she was honored together with *divus* Trajan by an enormous double inscription raised by Hadrian "to his parents" in accordance with a senatorial decree.[202] Fragments of the inscription were found near the Forum of Trajan and have been associated with Trajan's Column. The twin inscriptions, which once carried bronzed metal letters, were an outstanding 5.77 m L by 1.44 m H. S. Orlandi suggests a date of 125–127 for this striking commemoration of Hadrian's piety toward his adoptive father and mother.[203] As we have seen, the stress on family characterizes and may even excuse most other instances of imperial women's "presence" in Rome, especially those of the second century.

---

198. See Alexandridis 2004, 177–79, nos. 163–65; Boatwright 2000, 61–64.

199. I thank Dr. Ungaro for generous discussion of this piece; see also Boschung and Eck 1998.

200. Although a gilded statue of Cleopatra was in the Temple of Venus Genetrix: Cass. Dio 51.22.3, App. *B Civ.* 2.102.

201. See Boatwright 2000, 61–64.

202. *E]x s(enatus) c(onsulto) divi[s Tr]aiano Parthico et [Plotinae] / [Im]p(erator) Caes[ar di]vi Traiani Parthici [f(ilius)]] divi N[ervae] / [nepos Traia]nus Hadrianus Aug(ustus) pont(ifex) max(imus) / [trib(unicia) pot(estate) 3] co(n)s(ul) III parentibus suis.* CIL VI 31215 = EDCS-17301081. Although Plotina's name is not preserved, her inclusion is certain from *divi[s]* (l. 1).

203. Orlandi 2013, 55 for the date. Plotina was not Hadrian's "parent," since adoption affected only the relationship of the male adopter and the one adopted (Dig. 1.7.23). The inscription may hint that Plotina's remains were in the base of Trajan's Column. Barrett 1991, 9–10 discusses other duplicated inscriptions, associating them with triumphal arches.

Conclusion

The assembled evidence indicates that imperial women were not much in public in Rome, either in person or associated with buildings and statuary. As we saw in this chapter's first half, almost every appearance was tied to court rituals and is noted in only a few locales. The most numerous reports inform us about imperial women at funerals, a traditional milieu for Roman women out of the house. Julia Augusta was notable for her public grief and rituals at Augustus' funeral pyre in the Campus Martius. Even earlier Octavia's public funeral helped establish a processional route for imperial obsequies from the Forum Romanum to Augustus' Mausoleum in the northern Campus Martius. After the completion of the Mausoleum of Hadrian Sabina may have been the first to be honored by a procession that marked a new ceremonial route for imperial funerals, this one leaving the Via Flaminia to cut across the widest part of the Campus Martius before crossing the Tiber on the Pons Aelius. But other than Julia Augusta, imperial women at public funerals tend to be the honored dead.

More active participation in the city comes in the involvement of a few Julio-Claudian imperial women in triumphs and the *adventus*. After Agrippina's veneration by Caratacus at his submission in front of the Praetorian Camp in 51, however, no other imperial woman is attested in military and political civic celebrations. We lack evidence even for the Severan women, who were criticized for intruding into armed conflict and politics (Ch. 7). Despite state rituals' significance to the imperial presence and authority in Rome, later women apparently were kept far from such city-wide processions showcasing the emperor. Livia and a few other Augustan women are noted at public banquets, although Livia's sponsorship of all-female feasts seems to have been more proper. Imperial women's privilege of front-row seating at the theater and other spectacles was modulated by their placement with the Vestals. Other public sorties of imperial women, including "unscripted" appearances in the city, are reported but rarely and with opprobrium.

Over two and a half centuries in Rome, the most visible imperial women are Livia and Agrippina the Younger, both wives and then mothers of emperors.[204] Most of Livia's activity, both in person and more permanently through monuments, comes after Augustus' death,[205] and it was notoriously opposed by Tiberius. Agrippina had a greater presence not only during and just after

---

204. Thakur 2014, 180–85, and Barrett 2002, 199–205, e.g., credit Livia with greater patronage than I find attested.

205. See Severy 2003 and Purcell 1986.

Claudius' reign. Even after her murder and disgrace her imprint remained on the city: we saw that the only two large-scale epigraphic tributes to a Flavian woman, Domitilla, were part of structures honoring Agrippina and her family. In Rome Flavian and second-century imperial women may have kept out of public to avoid the criticism Tacitus and others leveled at Agrippina, her husband Claudius, and her son Nero, for her presumptuous intrusion into traditionally male spheres. Furthermore, images of Flavian and later imperial women became more scarce, and they are often dedicated by corporate entities and seldom in the traditional heart of Rome, the Forum Romanum.[206] The frequent location of imperial women's monuments in residential areas may have contributed to the deepening ideology of the "first family" in the city,[207] but it kept the memory of those women out of Rome's most prestigious locales.

Some have argued that imperial women's buildings and presence in Rome have a gendered "femaleness," such as Livia's restorations of the Temple of Bona Dea and Temple of Fortuna Muliebris, or pronounced cultural aspects, as the Porticus Octaviae.[208] Certainly some construction and appearances are linked with Rome's *matronae* and other eminent women, such as Livia's banquets for women, empresses' special seating with the Vestals in the theater, and Sabina's dedication for the *matronae*, restored by Domna.[209] But most buildings in Rome's dense cityscape served multiple functions, as we saw with the Porticus Octaviae and the Porticus Liviae, and neither the Julio-Claudian cluster in the Circus Flaminius nor the Trajanic-Hadrianic grouping near the Forum of Trajan seems particularly "feminine." Further, the few dedications to second- and third-century imperial women come not from women but from collective groups like the citizens of Sabratha or the "runners" of the Treasury of Saturn.

It is more important to recognize the dampened presence of imperial women in Rome itself.[210] This may be seen most clearly by comparing Plotina's reserve in Rome to her visibility in Athens.[211] In the capital city she is noted as disappearing

---

206. Boatwright 2011b; see also Alexandridis 2004, 32 n.305.

207. See Wallace-Hadrill 2003.

208. See, e.g., Kleiner 1996, 33; Bartman 1999, 79. See above for doubts about Fortuna Muliebris.

209. Purcell 1986, esp. 83–85, stresses Livia's ties to women and matrons in Rome.

210. The records and suggestions of greater architectural patronage outside of Rome by imperial women such as Antonia the Younger and Julia the Elder (Kokkinos 2002, 146–57; Domínguez Arranz 2016, 93–94) contrast their indistinctness in Rome.

211. In Ch. 6 we explore Matidia the Younger's remarkable visibility in Suessa Aurunca and other Italian and provincial cities: Bruun 2010 and Cascella 2013. Between 211 and 217 Julia Domna recommended a sophist to the chair at Athens: Philostr. *VS* 622.

Imperial Women's Mark on the City of Rome

into the palace at the beginning of her husband's rule (Plin. *Pan.* 83–84; Cass. Dio 68.5.5), and her only other traces are Hadrian's honors for her after her death. In Athens, however, a long, now incomplete inscription on Pentelic marble, found west of the Tower of the Winds near the Roman Agora, records a purposeful exchange of letters between the widowed Plotina and Hadrian.[212] The inscription, like others recording decisions of the emperor, consists of various parts, grouped in this case into two dossiers distinguished by letter forms. The first is less fragmentary than the second, and also includes texts in Latin as well as Greek.[213]

The first dossier now begins with the scrappy end of what seems to be a letter in Greek, followed by a consular date of 121 CE in Latin. Then comes a three-line request, in Latin, from Plotina to Hadrian concerning succession to the leadership of the Epicurean School. This is followed by Hadrian's ten-line response, also in Latin but directed to the head of the school and granting Plotina's request. The final element of this dossier is a long letter in Greek by Plotina, inscribed with slightly larger letters. Addressed to "all her friends," Plotina expresses joy in the benefaction and offers advice on how to implement it.[214] The second dossier, with a consular date of 125 CE and seemingly consisting of two letters in Greek, is much more fragmentary.[215] Van Bremen, who reinvestigated the entire inscription in 2005, stresses Plotina's intervention, maintaining that the second letter was written by Plotina herself before her death in 123.[216]

The whole documents Plotina's successful appeal to Hadrian for the Epicureans of Athens, a school of philosophers who had met regularly since Epicurus' own lifetime in the early third century BCE. Plotina requests Hadrian's permission for the Epicureans' leader to draw up his testament in Greek, and for his successor to be chosen from a wider group than only Roman citizens. The tone is warm, frank, and respectful on both sides: although she addresses Hadrian as

---

212. For location, see Wilhelm 1899, 270, and *Archaiologica Ephemeris* 1890, 141.

213. Such decisions are often grouped together as *beneficia*. The first dossier, ? H and 98 cm W, is EM 10404; the second, recut into two capitals now 51 and 42 cm H, is EM 12386 and EM 8385: van Bremen 2005. Letter height for the first dossier is 0.8–1 cm (Latin), and 1.2–1.5 cm (Greek), with no headings; for the second dossier, 0.8–1.2 cm, with interlineal space 0.5–0.9 cm.

214. Van Bremen 2005, 500, following Williams 1976, notes this is not a true rescript, since it is not directed to the petitioner.

215. The original inscription was cut into two Byzantine column capitals, and the relationship of the two pieces was long confused. Van Bremen 2005, 502 suggests that the two dossiers were displayed side by side, perhaps originally on a single stone.

216. Van Bremen 2005, 513 n.26 discusses the difficult dating of Plotina's death, but decides on 123. For the lapse of two years between her death and the publication of the letter, Van Bremen 2005, 512–13.

"lord," in her language and expressions Plotina demonstrates greater familiarity with Epicureanism than does Hadrian himself.[217] This is remarkable not only in light of Hadrian's notorious competitiveness (e.g., Cass. Dio 69.3.4; HA, *Hadr.* 15.10). Given what we have seen about imperial women's presence in Rome, it seems unthinkable that such an inscription could have been raised in the capital city. In Rome the emperor was always to be dominant.

Imperial women had roles in Rome indeed, but those roles were all in the family. Moreover, they were usually evident when the women themselves were dead and out of sight.

---

217. Van Bremen 2005, 512–22.

6

Models and Exemplars: Statues of Imperial Women

Introduction: Agrippina the Younger on the Caelian Hill

The Claudium or Temple of *divus* Claudius on the Caelian Hill, although the largest imperial cult sanctuary in Rome, has been as overlooked by Roman historians and topographers as it is by modern commuters rushing past the nearby Colosseum (see Ill. 5.1 and Ch. 5). The intriguing history and vestiges of the Temple of *divus* Claudius, however, feature Agrippina the Younger in extraordinary roles.[1] Remains of an over-life-size female standing statue in greywacke, fragmented into forty-one pieces, were found by R. Lanciani on the Caelian in 1885 in a semicircular late-antique wall northeast of the Claudium.[2] More than a century later, R. Belli Pasqua recognized that the statue fit with a greywacke head of Agrippina the Younger that the Ny Carlsberg Glyptotek of Copenhagen has held since purchase in Rome in the late nineteenth century. That head, originally with a diadem and a veil, is from the third or fourth portrait type for Agrippina,[3] and its cast has been added to the reconstructed statue in the latter's permanent display in Rome's Centrale Montemartini Museum.[4] (See Ill. 6.1.) The whole is of greywacke,[5] a dense and prestigious green-gray stone from Wadi Hammâmât in

---

1. For Agrippina, see Ginsburg 2006; Barrett 1996; Eck 1993; Ch. 1.

2. Along with other finds such as the "Victory of the Symmachi": Pavolini 2007, 310.

3. See Trillmich in Moltesen and Nielsen 2007, 45–65; Varner 2004, n.156 (fourth type).

4. Musei Capitolini, Centrale Montemartini I.N. 1882; the head is Ny Carlsberg Glyptotek, Copenhagen, I.N. 753. See Alexandridis 2004, Cat. 106 for the statue, reconstructed with a copy of its head in 2007.

5. The basalt stone is also called *grovacca* or basanite; when polished it resembles patinated bronze and it contrasts more commonly encountered white marble statues. Its quarries were

---

Imperial Women of Rome. Mary T. Boatwright, Oxford University Press. © Oxford University Press 2021.
DOI: 10.1093/oso/9780190455897.003.0007

ILL. 6.1 Statue of Agrippina the Younger in the Musei Capitolini, Centrale Montemartini (I.N. 1882), with a cast of a portrait head now in the Ny Carlsberg Glyptotek, Copenhagen (I.N. 753).

Egypt's eastern desert, and measures over 2 m H.[6] It is commanding for its large size, open gesture, and voluminous robes.

Agrippina's portrait statue underwent various changes over the years. The head was recut twice. The first modification assimilated her face more closely

---

under imperial control, and it may have been the prerogative of the imperial house in the first c. CE: Belli Pasqua 1995, esp. 56–58.

6. 0.30 m H (head), 1.80 m H (statue body). Rose 1997, 74 notes that imperial statues of the Julio-Claudian period were usually 2.00 to 2.20 m H, slightly over life-size.

(a)

(b)
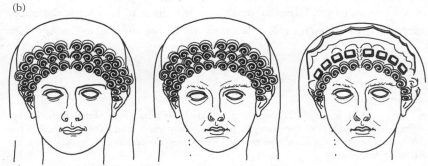

ILL. 6.2 (A) Agrippina's portrait in the Ny Carlsberg Glyptotek (I.N. 753, © Ny Carlsberg Glyptotek, Copenhagen). (B) The various phases of the portrait, in a drawing by Thora Fisker (l to r): original; the first recutting, altering the face; the second, modifying the diadem. Courtesy of M. Moltesen.

to that of the young princeps Nero, in particular by refashioning the mouth to have more cupid's-bow lips, indicating a date during Agrippina's short time as "imperial mother" from 54 to 59 CE. A second alteration, when the diadem was scalloped on top and cut to accommodate the insertion of large gems, apparently

214IMPERIAL WOMEN OF ROME

came in the third or, more likely, fourth century CE.[7] (See Ill. 6.2 A and B.) The statue type of the female body still remains uncertain, however. Earlier reconstructions of the fragments suggested the *orans* type, in which the woman lifts both hands in a praying gesture that raises a thick swath of her mantle above her front midsection. This is a conventional type, as can be seen from a posthumous statue of Livia *orans* from Otriculum in central Italy (Ill. 6.3).[8] But more recent restorations better fit the fragments and assimilate the statue to the "Hip-Swath" Type, in which the sculpted women's lowered arms allow a thick fold of the mantle to fall around the hip section. This type, too, is often encountered; a good example of it is another posthumous statue of Livia with the Hip-Swath Body Type that was found in Veleia in northern Italy.[9] (See Ill. 6.4, and further later.) Both types are common for priestesses,[10] thus appropriate for Agrippina as *flaminica* of the newly deified Claudius (Tac. *Ann.* 13.2.6; Ch. 4). It may be, in fact, that this image of Agrippina does not follow any one type at all but is unique, albeit incorporating identifiable religious elements.[11] Sometime after its head was recut to accommodate jewels, the statue was deliberately damaged in the neck, back of the head, mid-thoracic region, and forward left hip areas, yet the face remained unmarked.[12]

The statue and its find spot raise numerous questions about public statuary for Agrippina the Younger and for other imperial women. According to Tacitus, Agrippina emulated the majestic grandeur of her great-grandmother Livia while moving quickly from Claudius' death and deification to his spectacular public funeral.[13] In assuming the role of *flaminica* for the new *divus* Claudius Agrippina

---

7. Moltesen in Moltesen and Nielsen 2007, 139–48; Fisker's drawing is Moltesen and Nielsen 2007, 147. The addition of jewels may be fourth-century rather than third (as Moltesen tenders), since jewelry on female portraiture seems post-Constantinian: Schade 2016, 251; Alexandridis 2004, 72.

8. For this statue, often dated to the second half of the first century CE and found in Otricoli in 1778–1779, see Alexandridis 2004, Cat. 33.

9. For the statue shown in Ill. 6.4, from Veleia (now Velleia, Italy) and currently in the Museo Nazionale di Antichità in Parma, Italy, see Alexandridis 2004, Cat. 30.

10. Moltesen in Moltesen and Nielsen 2007, 123–36.

11. Talamo 2011 identifies traces on the statue's head of pomegranate twigs entwined with a (white) wool thread, a symbolic decoration used by priestesses.

12. Moltesen in Moltesen and Nielsen 2007. That Agrippina's face was untouched contrasts the usual post-antique destruction of statues that focused on the face (see Gregory 1994, 97).

13. *aemulante Agrippina proaviae Liviae magnificentiam*: Tac. *Ann.* 12.69.

ILL. 6.3 Statue of Livia *orans* (praying), now in the Galleria dei Busti, Museo Pio-Clementino, Vatican Museums, Inv. no. 637. © Vanni Archive / Art Resource, NY, ART359089.

was surely cognizant of the example of Livia,[14] who had been made priest of *divus* Augustus after her husband's death in 14 CE and whose portrait statues include ones in religious poses. (See Ills. 6.3 and 6.4.) Further, according to one of the scarce literary witnesses for the imperial cult sanctuary for Claudius, Agrippina herself initiated its construction; the building then was destroyed by Nero, to

---

14. Agrippina's right to be accompanied by two lictors (Tac. *Ann.* 13.2.6) was a greater honor than the single lictor granted in 14 CE to Livia as priest of *divus* Augustus: see Ch. 1 and Ch. 4.

ILL. 6.4 Statue of Livia, with a Hip-Swath Body Type. Now in the Museo Nazionale di Antichità, Parma, Italy, Inv. no. 1952.828. Photo: Eric Vandeville / akg-images.

be refurbished and finished by Vespasian (Suet. *Vesp.* 9; Ch. 5).[15] These tantalizing scraps of evidence, as well as the statue's find spot near the precinct and Agrippina's praying stance, strongly suggest that it was originally installed in the shrine to *divus* Claudius.[16] If so, it was probably outside the *aedes* proper, perhaps

---

15. If Agrippina were striving to outdo Livia by building in Rome, she succeeded: the Claudium's size (200 m W x 180 m D) almost doubles that of the similarly rectangular Porticus of Livia on the Esquiline (95 m W x 120 m D). See Ill. 5.2.

16. See Varner 2004, n.136. We return later to the probable original location of the statue.

Models and Exemplars: Statues of Imperial Women

in the *pronaos* or somewhere in the precinct since it represented a living person and not the deity to which the temple was consecrated.[17] Perhaps, to venture into pure speculation and to attribute extraordinary agency to Agrippina, the first recutting of the statue's face that rendered Agrippina's lips more like those of Nero was meant to remind the new emperor of his debt to his mother, and to reassert her control.

What happened to the statue after Agrippina's assassination in 59, when Nero repudiated his mother and imputed her death to her treacherous schemes? In the *Octavia*, a play probably dating soon after Nero's own death in 68, Agrippina's ghost charges that Nero "went wild against the name of his mother . . . destroyed my statues and inscriptions throughout the world" (*Oct.* 609–12; see also Tac. *Ann.* 14.12.1 and Cass. Dio 62.16.2). This would suggest a *damnatio memoriae* for her.[18] Scholars have argued, however, that even within Rome such obliteration may have been undertaken only halfheartedly, and that no such sanctions were undertaken systematically outside of the capital city.[19] Even in the city, as we saw in the previous chapter, Agrippina was represented by monuments and installations; in contrast, nothing now documents Livilla, the first imperial woman to suffer a *damnatio memoriae*.[20] Further, A. Alexandridis' catalogue of extant identifiable portraits of imperial women has Agrippina as the second most frequently represented woman, with twenty likenesses as compared to thirty-six for Livia.[21] Nonetheless, it is implausible that Agrippina's striking greywacke statue remained visible in the enormous cult sanctuary, especially since Nero's route into Rome late in 59 CE passed by the shrine when he returned from Campania triumphally celebrating his escape from Agrippina's alleged conspiracy.[22] E. Varner has suggested that it and other statues of Agrippina were "warehoused" after her death.[23]

---

17. Højte 2005, 120; cf. the statue of Augustus that Agrippa wanted to put in the Pantheon, but ended up placing in the porch (Cass. Dio 54.27.3).

18. Kragelund 2007, 34; contra Varner 2004, 98–99.

19. Kragelund 2007, 27; Flower 2011, 189–94.

20. See Ch. 2; Flower 2011, 175; and Varner 2001.

21. Alexandridis 2004 Table 1. Next highest numbers are seventeen for Sabina, and sixteen for Julia Domna. Ginsburg 2006, 79 identifies fifteen statue groups with Agrippina.

22. The "triumph" (see Champlin 2003, 212–13, 219–21) perhaps prompted removing Agrippina's statue from the shrine of the Aenatores (more later), even closer to the route. Yet the hurried proceedings missed at least one statue of Agrippina, later used to shame Nero: Cass. Dio 62.16.2.

23. Varner 2004, 99, citing also two bronze statues from Herculaneum similarly in priestly guise.

The vicissitudes of Agrippina's greywacke statue are difficult to trace. If warehoused, it would have more easily survived the city's devastation in the Fire of 64,[24] as well as Nero's transformation of at least the eastern part of the Claudian precinct into a *nymphaeum* for his Golden House. When Vespasian rebuilt and completed the Temple of *divus* Claudius (Suet. *Vesp.* 9), marking respect for his former commander and the imperial system overall even while conspicuously rejecting Nero's wastefulness, did the first Flavian emperor reinstall Agrippina's statue in the precinct? Did the statue's history include exhibition in some other spot on the Caelian? Some have suggested that it embellished a shrine to Isis on the hill;[25] others, a great Antonine palace there now identified as the home of Commodus (see HA, *Comm.* 16.3).[26] Its recutting that accommodated inset gems in its diadem indicates its display around the fourth century, but we have no way of knowing whether that was in a public setting.

Agrippina's magnificent statue from the Caelian opens discussion about the imaging of imperial women, especially in the capital city of Rome. What was the status of imperial women's statues? How were they viewed? How distinctive and special were they? In antiquity statues of an emperor were viewed as powerful, but statues of imperial women apparently less so. As we saw in Ch. 2, legal asylum was associated with fleeing to the statue of an emperor or *divus* but not to an imperial woman's statue. On the other hand, statues and images of imperial women were harmed officially, or spontaneously by Rome's masses, if a woman herself fell from favor, whether for her own actions or those of another.[27] This resembles the defacing of an image of an emperor or another prominent man through Rome's official censure of *damnatio memoriae*. Such sanctions were undertaken against the statues and memory of Livilla in 31,[28] and Poppaea's statues in Rome were toppled by the angry Roman populace at news of Nero's divorce of Octavia in 62,

---

24. The fire started close to the Caelian and swept through the region (Tac. *Ann.* 15.38.2; Suet. *Nero* 38), severely damaging the shrine rededicated by Rome's Brass-Wind Instrument Players (the Aenatores) to the imperial family in 55/56 near the Claudium (see later).

25. Pavolini 2007, 311 n.16, and Alexandridis 2004, 158 Cat. #106, n.3, suggest the Isaeum, a shrine originating in the end of the Republic.

26. Talamo in Moltesen and Nielsen 2007, 95–111, suggests this location for both it and the "Victory of the Symmachi" statue also found in the wall.

27. Josephus, writing in Rome, strikingly illustrates the identification of female statues with their models: at the death of King Herod Agrippa I (in 44 CE) the people stormed his palaces in Caesarea and Sebaste and dragged off statues of his three daughters (then at ages sixteen, ten, and six), which they "placed on the roofs of brothels and abused indecently" (Joseph. *AJ* 19.357).

28. Tac. *Ann.* 6.2.1. Flower 2011, 175 notes this as the first sanctioning by the senate of a Julio-Claudian, and probably the first of any Roman woman; see Ch. 2.

Models and Exemplars: Statues of Imperial Women

only to be replaced and those of Octavia removed by imperial order (Tac. *Ann.* 14.61.1). Under less hostile circumstances many imperial and non-imperial statues were recut and repurposed, some after being removed from original locations and stored for safekeeping.[29] How recognizable and authoritative the original image may have been when repurposed is unknowable.[30] The gems and ornamental cuttings applied to Agrippina's diadem three centuries or more after her death in 59 did not alter her physiognomy, but must have marked the portrait—iconic as it is to us—as that of someone different. Indeed, the following discussion argues for the interchangeability and lack of distinction of most imperial women's images.

In contrast to the previous chapter, in which we examined the topographical context of known statues and reliefs representing imperial women in Rome, this chapter turns to the modeling and presentation of the face and body of sculpted representations of imperial women. My underlying goal is to explore the functions and messages of those statues and busts.[31] I admit the speculative nature of this investigation undertaken so far from the circumstances in which these images were determined, shaped, installed, and perhaps reinstalled: the Agrippina from the Caelian demonstrates some difficulties. My goals in part derive from remarks of Tacitus and Suetonius about Claudius' posthumous honors. As we saw earlier, when presenting the deified emperor's funeral ceremony Tacitus specifically notes Agrippina's emulation of Livia as well as the two women's familial ties.[32] Suetonius' account brings out the performance Nero put on at the time.[33] The ancient authors—who detailed these earlier events as emblematic—encourage

---

29. Varner 2004, 2, with review by Brilliant 2005. Højte 2005, 56–64 cites reused imperial statue bases (and statues), noting that not all can be attributed to *damnatio memoriae*.

30. Brilliant 2005, 634. The transformed image may seem jarring, like the 3rd-c. placement of a portrait head of Marcus Aurelius on a draped female body in a statue from Cyrene now in the British Museum: Varner 2008, 201 fig. 10.

31. I do not here discuss vocabulary, noting only that some hold *imago* to refer to a likeness of living emperor and *simulacrum* to a statue (or likeness) of a consecrated *divus/diva*, and others see *statua* and *simulacrum* as referents to statues of *privati*, but *imago* and *effigies* used for imperial likenesses on cameos, gems, coins, medallions, statues, busts, and portrait heads (see Gamauf 1999, 35). Stewart 2003, 24–26 adds that *signum* often designates the representation of a god; for Greek terms see Price 1984, 176–79. Inscriptions with dative for members of the imperial family, including deified members, do not necessarily indicate a cultic context but may be simply honorific: Eck 2016, 53.

32. Tac. *Ann.* 12.69. Tacitus often stresses competitiveness between imperial women, and between imperial and private women (e.g., Tac. *Ann.* 2.43). But evaluative comparisons of individuals must have been constant: see, e.g., Macr. *Sat.* 2.5.6 on Livia and Julia the Elder.

33. *ostentatio*, although neglecting Agrippina's part in Claudius' funeral, and her emulation of Julia Augusta: Suet. *Nero* 9.

me to explore the exemplarity and emulation of imperial women of Rome, especially through the medium of statues and other sculpted images.

Imperial women as exemplars

A well-known passage in Tacitus, in which he identifies the emperor Vespasian as instrumental in restoring modest and honorable mores in Rome after the extravagance of the Neronian period (*Ann.* 3.55), expresses well the exemplarity of emperors in the Roman world. This idea has been extended to Roman portraiture, particularly in the idea of the *Zeitgesicht*, or "period face," which holds that the official depiction of the emperor was so dominant and even charismatic that private individuals in Rome, Italy, and the empire chose to have themselves represented in ways reminiscent of imperial portraits.[34] The images of imperial women have also been noted as reflecting and setting expectations concerning the imperial house, as well as for reproducing and contributing to gender norms in Rome: we see this reflected in later discussion of two statues from Perge.[35] But the information considered below shows that representations of imperial women, even of any one imperial woman, were much less distinct than those of imperial men. This conclusion rests partly on the slighter evidence for statues of imperial women than of imperial men: for example, even the highest estimate for known portraits of Livia, whose sculpted likeness is more common than that of other imperial women, is about 110,[36] whereas the number of extant statues and busts of Augustus is calculated as some 250, with those of Hadrian about 150.[37] Most statues are no longer extant, and the portraits of imperial women from Livia through

---

34. See Zanker 1982, with discussion by, e.g., D'Ambra 2013, 518 and Fejfer 2008, 270–279. The concept is that in their portraits non-imperial individuals mimicked imperial hairstyles, facial hair, and other physiognomic details such as treatment of the eyes and set of the mouth.

35. E.g., Davies 2008; Dolansky 2012, 261–62, 282–86 on dolls from Rome and *Zeitgesicht*, that of Crepereia Tryphaena with the coiffure of Faustina the Elder (and of Faustina the Younger after 150), and the ivory doll with Julia Domna coiffure, from the tomb of the Vestal Cossinia.

36. Bartman 1999, 146–87 catalogues 88 stone portraits for Livia (with three more listed as of uncertain identity), Alexandridis 2004, Tab. 1, only 36; Brännstedt 2015, 44 posits about 110 extant portraits, with epigraphic testimony for about 80 more now lost; Jessen 2013, 3, 51 extant portraits and 68 inscribed statue bases that she holds were produced during Livia's lifetime, of which 54 have known display contexts and 116 have known cities of origin.

37. Højte 2005 counts over two hundred statue bases for Augustus and over four hundred for Hadrian. M. Pfanner estimates that perhaps some ten thousand portraits overall were made of Augustus (*JDAI* 104, 1989). In general for the proliferation of statues in urban contexts, see Stewart 2003, 118–56.

Julia Domna assembled in Alexandridis' 2004 book emphasize the haphazard nature of survival.[38]

This chapter, however, suggests that other factors also contribute to the indeterminacy of portraits of imperial women. We focus on imperial statues and images exhibited for public viewing, whether officially sponsored statues installed on public ground, as presumably was the over-life-size Agrippina statue in greywacke, or dedications by individuals or corporate groups, such as Agrippina's now lost statue dedicated by Rome's Aenatores (Brass-Wind Instrument Players) discussed later.[39] In imperial Rome itself, as G. Lahusen, W. Eck, and others underscore, public statuary was under imperial control despite being nominally the prerogative of the senate.[40] Many portraits seem to have been displayed in spaces that were, strictly speaking, neither public nor private.[41] I focus on works in various types of marble and other hard and costly stone,[42] fully recognizing that the imaging and effect of any sculpted representation are dependent on factors often unknown, such as the final display context, desires of the patrons, and skills of the artisans. Full-body portraits are usually analyzed by heads and body type, with both categories including attributes and dress.

Since Alexandridis and scholars such as S. Wood, E. Bartman, C. B. Rose, and K. Fittschen have already published excellent studies of portraits of imperial women or of a single woman—individually, within their physical contexts, or both[43]—I address myself to select themes pertinent to this volume. I have drawn

---

38. Alexandridis 2004, 3–4, 11 n.99, stresses that the numbers of extant portraits, statue bases, or dedications do not correlate with the actual or even perceived power of the commemorated woman (contra, e.g., Bartman 1999, xxi, xxiii, 72, 88, and Wood 1999, 130–31, 222).

39. Fejfer 1985, 136 n.1 restricts her analysis to "official portraits," "an imperial portrait erected on official ground."

40. Lahusen 1983; Eck 1992 and Eck 1984; Pekáry 1985, 4–12.

41. The distinction was hard to make: treason charges against Granius Marcellus in 15 included accusations of disrespecting imperial statues in his gardens (Tac. *Ann.* 1.74), and Pliny the Younger felt he needed Trajan's permission to transfer, from his private property to a town, imperial statues he had accumulated by gift and other means (*Ep.* 10.8). See Ch. 2. Neudecker 1988, Rose 1997, and Stewart 2003, 223–60 note that individual statues and "family galleries" have been found in imperial and private villas, *horti*, and palaces. These would have been the locales of most Roman women of property and status.

42. Stone sculptures, especially white or light marble and limestone, were usually colored; bronze portraits could be enlivened by inlaid eyes and gilding (e.g., Fejfer 2008, 162–63). Højte 2005, 43 notes painted images as one of the commonest ancient types of public and private portrait.

43. Fejfer 1985, e.g., stresses assessing context: statue bases' physical composition and texts, provenance, exhibition conditions and setting, date, and the like.

most of my examples from the city of Rome, where virtually all of the female statues in the cityscape were of imperial women.[44] Yet the image of an imperial woman or women was difficult to identify definitively. The practice of representing historical women began late in the capital city and when in 35 BCE Octavia and Livia were specifically allowed to be portrayed publicly, Rome had no tradition of individual portraiture for women as it did for men (see more later).[45] As presumably for Cornelia's statue discussed shortly, models for historic women's portraiture were those of Greek and Hellenistic goddesses and abstractions.[46] Further, most extant statues, of women and men alike, have been found without a statue base or manifest identification.[47] Identifications, typologies, styles, and chronologies for Roman portraiture have been established by comparison of sculpted objects with imperial coin portraits, since the latter are often named as well as dated by the subject's titles. As we saw in Ch. 4, however, identified depiction of imperial women on coins begins only under Caligula. In Claudius' reign Agrippina the Younger becomes the first identified living woman with a numismatic portrait, and imperial women's portraits on coins remain fairly rare until 128. There are simply fewer portraits of women than of men, imperial and otherwise.

Complicating my discussion of imperial women's sculpted images are considerations of body types and of facial and head modeling. Imperial women's sculpted depictions come in numerous, diverse body types, in contrast to statues of imperial men, which were made almost exclusively standing, sitting, or riding in three basic types and one variant. Some male statue types in public settings seem almost exclusively for imperial men,[48] whereas all female body types were used also for private women. Alexandridis identifies twenty-six types, but notes six standing types as by far most frequent: the Greater Herculaneum Woman, the Lesser Herculaneum Woman, Ceres, the Hip-Swath Type (discussed briefly

---

44. See, e.g., Hemelrijk 2005a, 317; Fejfer 2008, 101 (noting also the relative scarcity of such statues). The imperial city hosted a limited number of non-imperial male statues.

45. Smith 1981 provocatively discusses the individualism of late Republican male portraiture.

46. Portraiture of Hellenistic queens, such as Cleopatra, may have had connotations best to avoid, but Hekster 2015, 117 remarks that the "recognized importance of women in royal rule and succession" "may well have influenced Augustan—or at least Julio-Claudian—practice."

47. For statue bases (of emperors), see Højte 2005.

48. Such as statues wearing a toga (*togata*), to emphasize his civic roles, or with the toga pulled up to cover his head (*togata capite velato*) so as to denote his position as *pontifex maximus* and head of Roman religion; in a cuirass (*loricata*) and other military garb, designating his status as chief commander; and as nude or semi-nude, representing him in a heroic pose or in the guise of a god: see, e.g., Fejfer 2008, 338–39; Højte 2005, 43; Rose 1997, 74–77.

Models and Exemplars: Statues of Imperial Women

earlier), Pudicitia, and the Shoulder-Swath Type.[49] These were common for imperial and private women alike.[50] A final consideration is that even hairstyles once deemed indicative of an imperial woman, such as the high frontal crest of curls (the *toupet*) associated with Flavian women, were also used for non-imperial women and have a long chronological range.[51] In sum, as J. Fejfer argues, "The empress did not have either a specific portrait typology, nor a strong physiognomy, nor particular statuary types that were used only by her. There were only very few attributes reserved for her, and this practice was confined to the early imperial period."[52] The indeterminacy of imperial women's images underscores the essential lack of choice of even these highly placed women.[53]

Public portraits and statues of historical women, including imperial women

Republican Rome and Italy had no tradition of public female statuary, although starting in the fourth century BCE portraits of women are known from private contexts such as funerary precincts. Cassius Dio provides a date of 35 BCE for the inception of public statues for women in Rome when, while listing extraordinary honors for Octavia and Livia that year, he notes the right to be honored by public statues (Cass. Dio 49.38.1; see Ch. 1). Public portraits for women—an honor allegedly resisted by Cato the Elder and others (Plin. *HN* 34.31)—may have been made more acceptable by having two women thus exalted together rather than one alone.[54] We should be cautious about such precise dating for what is surely a cultural trend, since some statues of women in public places in Italian municipalities may date from about 50 BCE.[55] On the other hand, we have seen repeatedly in this book that the transformation of Octavian to Augustus involved

---

49. Alexandridis 2004, 294–306, subdividing these into more specific variants and subtypes. See also Davies 2013, 176.

50. Wood 2015, 242 notes as the most popular type for both imperial and non-imperial women the Large Herculaneum Woman (with more than 200 replicas), followed by the Small Herculaneum Woman (at least 157 statues). See also Trimble 2011 and Dillon 2010.

51. See D'Ambra 2013.

52. Fejfer 2008, 356–57.

53. Contra Bartman 1999, 23, who suggests Livia "was instrumental in the process" of creating portrait types, and (xxi) sees those types as "a new visual language of female power."

54. Flory 1993, 294.

55. Hemelrijk 2005a, 310 n.6; Cooley 2013.

224 IMPERIAL WOMEN OF ROME

the women connected to him. Women were essential to the image of the new princeps.[56]

In the Republic the Roman senate had controlled both the occasion and the location of public statuary, awarding it for meritorious and virtuous activity that directly benefited the state and usually locating it in the Forum Romanum or another administrative and religious center (see Plin. *Pan.* 55.6).[57] Such activity was almost exclusively administrative or military in nature, and thus forbidden to women. Males increasingly competed for honorific visibility, and from the fourth century BCE ever more statues and portraits were on public display in Rome.[58] In contrast, only a handful of women's statues are cited before the imperial period, and for most of these the human or female nature of the subject—or both—has been challenged.[59] Modern skepticism derives from the paucity of female portraiture in Rome and from the ambivalent or negative literary references to women's portraiture. The very existence of a female statue seems to have been destabilizing: for example, Seneca maintains that a togate, equestrian statue of Cloelia on the edge of the Forum Romanum publicly shamed the effete men of his own time because it posited a woman as exemplary of superior virtue (Sen. *Consol. ad Marc.* 16.2).[60]

The situation differed slightly in Rome's eastern provinces, where from around 100 BCE Roman women were publicly portrayed in statue groups alongside their husbands or fathers who were then serving as provincial governors or in another official capacity.[61] The practice was anathema in Rome, according to Pliny the Elder, who reports its denunciation by Cato the Elder. In the same passage, however, Pliny also avers that Cornelia, the mother of the Gracchi, was honored by a public image in Rome:

> There still are extant strident protests of Cato, made during his censorship [184 BCE] against statues being erected to Roman women in the provinces; nonetheless, he could not prevent statues also being

---

56. E.g., Dettenhofer 2000, 41–42 and Corbier 1995 note honors for Augustus' female relatives earlier than when the term *domus Augusta* shows up in the exile poetry of Ovid (Ch. 3).

57. Flory 1993; Boatwright 2011b, 120–21.

58. Plin. *HN* 34.24. Fejfer 2008, 20–21 argues that public honorific portraits even of men were rare until the time of Sulla; others, e.g., Lahusen 1983, 18–22, date the phenomenon earlier.

59. See Plin. *HN* 34.25. Hemelrijk 2005a, 309, e.g., argues that all female statues attested before 35 BCE "were probably statues of goddesses or perhaps even of young men."

60. Boatwright 2011b, 120–22.

61. Kajava 1990.

Models and Exemplars: Statues of Imperial Women

raised to women in Rome, such as to Cornelia the mother of the Gracchi, who was the daughter of the elder Scipio Africanus. It represents her seated and is remarkable because of the strapless sandals: it stood in the public colonnade of Metellus, but is now in the buildings of Octavia.[62] (*HN* 34.31)

A marble base found in the Porticus Octaviae near the Circus Flaminius is inscribed "Cornelia, daughter of [Scipio] Africanus, [mother] of the Gracchi."[63] Its letter forms are Augustan. Many contend, convincingly, that the statue of Cornelia that Pliny described and to which the base apparently belongs was an Augustan reworking of a Greek bronze statue of a seated goddess, or possibly of a Hellenistic queen portrayed as a goddess, originally installed in Rome ca. 100 BCE in the Porticus of Metellus.[64] Thus a pre-existing Greek statue would have been repurposed as a portrait of a Roman historical woman.[65]

Although that rendering of Cornelia is long lost, extant public images of Octavia and Livia are suggestive. Even for some decades after the "grant of the right of portraits" to Octavia and Livia in 35 BCE, portraits of the two seem to have been scarce in Rome and the Latin West.[66] Other than on the Ara Pacis and a statue group from Veleia (near Piacenza, Italy), through 13 BCE even imperial group portraits are not known to have included women.[67] Bartman, for example,

---

62. See also Plut. *C. Gracch.* 4.3: "Later [than 123 BCE] they [i.e., the people] erected a bronze statue of her with the inscription 'Cornelia, mother of the Gracchi.'" The "buildings of Octavia" are the Porticus Octaviae, for which see Ch. 5.

63. *Cornelia Africani f(ilia) / Gracchorum <mater>*: CIL VI 31610 (= 10043) = EDCS-19200313.

64. Hekster 2015, 114; Hemelrijk 2005a, 313–15; Coarelli 1978; Flory 1993, 292; *LTUR* 4.357–59, s.v. "Statua: Cornelia" (L. Chioffi).

65. Hemelrijk 2005a, 315–16 suggests Augustus palliated the innovation of public statues of women by "restoring"—or creating—public statues of other exemplary Roman women in Rome.

66. Flory 1993, 294, 301 and Severy 2003, 232–34 argue for very few statues and portraits in Rome before 9 BCE (contra Bartman 1999, 72–101); Rose 1997, 60 notes that Livia had a number of commemorations in the Greek East even in this early period (cf. Wood 1999, 92–108). The earliest known image of Livia is attested by an inscribed base for her and Octavian (ca. 31 BCE, Eleusis): Rose 1997, 140–41 no. 71; Wood 1999, 92; Bartman 1999, 64. Portraits of Octavia, who died in 11 BCE, are rare (Wood 1999, 27–28). Bartman 1999, 80 suggests Octavia's importance may have begun to wane with the death of Marcellus in 23 BCE.

67. Hekster 2015, 117–18. That the portrait identified as Livia on the south frieze of the Ara Pacis (13–9 BCE) has no known counterpart in statuary or relief suggests fluidity for her image and the "ease" with which types could be swapped (Wood 1999, 91–92).

notes that only twenty-six inscriptions of certain Augustan date attest statues for Livia, and of these, nineteen are from the East. More than half of the twenty-six inscriptions make her connection to Augustus explicit, either by specifying her as his wife or by using the genitive form of his name. Livia's ties to others in Augustus' family and in her own Claudian *gens* became key to her sculpted image in other ways. She typically appeared in statuary ensembles with members of the imperial family, helping to constitute what began to be called the *domus Augusta* before the death of Augustus (see Ch. 3).[68]

Bartman and others have pointed out the modest demeanor of early images of Livia and other Augustan women. With no sculpted indication of jewelry, the heads are presented with idealized, youthful faces with no deep cuttings, and the women's hair, pulled back, is usually controlled in the *nodus* style.[69] (See Ill. 6.5.) Only a few tendrils escape the severe styling, and even these are placed symmetrically in front of the ears and as a short fringe behind the ears.[70] The occasional sculpted veils, floral wreaths, and other embellishments for the head may have suggested religious activity.[71] The stark hairstyles denote self-restraint, even though the intricacy of the hair knots, orderly fringes, curls, and braids would have necessitated skilled hairdressers.[72] The harmoniously similar physiognomies and hairstyles of these women, which changed but little over time,[73] evoke steadfastness and dutifulness. These women of the imperial house were shown with few individual traits that might detract from the image of collective support for their family.

---

68. Bartman 1999, 72–73, noting that in the Greek East multiple statues and inscriptions were often installed on one long base, allowing better preservation of the texts than in the West where individual statue bases could more easily be moved and repurposed. Such group portraiture may have been reinforced after the death of Drusus the Elder in 9 BCE, which occasioned more public statues and the *ius trium liberorum* as consolation for Livia's great loss (Cass. Dio 55.2.5). But no extant Augustan statue base calls her the Mother of Drusus: Barrett 2002, 46.

69. The portrait of Ill. 6.5 is 49.46 cm x 42.32 cm. This earliest type for Livia was used throughout the Augustan period: Bartman 1999, 9–11, 36 for modesty; Winkes 1995; Hemelrijk 2005a, 315–16. Barrett 2002, 138 posits that early types were probably the Marbury Hall type, his fig. 14. For the *nodus* style, see, Ch. 3, n.42.

70. Bartman 1999, 72–110 argues (76) that Octavia's images "recall traditional republican images of the nobility with their sometimes harsh realism." See also Bartman 2012. Alexandridis 2004, 137–38 Cat.-Nr. 52 hesitates to accept any extant portrait as of Octavia.

71. Alexandridis 2010, 210–11 sees wreaths as confined to the Julio-Claudian women.

72. Thus the hairstyle could signal wealth and status, subsumed to matronly virtue and simplicity. For hairdressers in Livia's *columbarium*, see Treggiari 1975, 52.

73. See Matheson 1996; Wood 1999, 118; Boschung 2002, 190–92, discussing other imperial women as well.

Models and Exemplars: Statues of Imperial Women

ILL. 6.5 Early portrait of Livia, now in the British Museum. © The Trustees of the British Museum.

Even some attributes that apparently distinguished early representations of imperial women become more widespread over time. Sculpted diadems and *infulae* (woolen fillets, usually beaded and worn by women somewhat like modern headbands but often with ends hanging to either side of the neck), grace some imperial women's heads after the reign of Caligula. They have been understood as signaling that the person represented had attained a status encompassing human and divine realms. The diadem was traditionally used for goddesses and personifications, and the attributes suggest a "general aura of sanctity."[74] By the end of

---

74. Rose 1997, 76–77; Wood 1995, 473–74, 478–79, on *infulae* (quote 479).

the first century, however, the diadem also appears on portraits of private women, where they apparently signify simply respectability and piety.[75] Perhaps to compensate for the diminished prestige of the diadem original to the Agrippina statue from the Caelian, in the later Roman period gems were added to the impressive portrait.

Body types of women's portrait statues

As previous mentioned, six standing types are by far the most numerous for imperial and private women alike: the Greater Herculaneum Woman, the Lesser Herculaneum Woman, Ceres, the Hip-Swath Type, Pudicitia, and the Shoulder-Swath Type. These were types conventionally used to depict female divinities and personifications in the Greek East, and some scholars, like Rose, have noted the popularity of statuary types for Julio-Claudians who were connected to Ceres and Venus, that is, fertility.[76] Others venture that the frequency of the Greater and Lesser Herculaneum types may lie in identification of the types as those of Demeter and Kore: these chthonic deities were appropriate to funerary contexts, the presumable provenance of many women's statues.[77] G. Davies remarks that the extant statues of imperial women found in the West tend to be of the "more open poses," that is the Ceres, Shoulder-Swath, and Hip-Swath types. She contrasts those to the other three most frequent types, the Large and the Small Herculaneum Woman, and Pudicitia. These latter three feature not only heavy drapery over the body, but also arms crossed "almost defensively" and face turned down or to the side.[78]

Although I do not illustrate each of the most frequent types, we examine a few images of Sabina to illustrate the range and presumable effects of some different body types. The Baths of Neptune in Ostia furnish a fine, over-life-size statue of Sabina, who holds in her left hand Ceres' attributes, poppies and wheat. Although Sabina's head is covered by a veil, that cloth adheres fairly closely to the back of her head, individualizing her face. The open placement of the arms and the lifted position of the head of this statue give Sabina an

---

75. D'Ambra 2013, e.g., 519–20, argues that the diadem "was not exclusively worn by imperial women [although it] signified the imperial affiliation of its wearer to earlier generations of scholars," and appears only sporadically (cf. Alexandridis 2010, 210–12).

76. Rose 1997, 75–76; see also Foubert 2015.

77. See, e.g., Wood 1995, 481–82. Pudicitia is also often found in a funerary context, especially during the late Republic and early Augustan period: Davies 2013, 172.

78. Davies 2013, 196; and her chart, 177.

ILL. 6.6 Sabina as Ceres, from Ostia. Now in the Museo Ostiense, inv. 25. Image courtesy of R. Ulrich, RBU2011.7274. Parian marble, from the Palaestra of the Baths of Neptune, 2nd c. CE, Ostia Antica, Italy.

open pose. (See Ill. 6.6.) Davies sees this pose as suggesting "someone who takes a more active and leading role";[79] although visually this seems right, it diverges from all other evidence for Sabina.[80] We may contrast a statue found in Perge that is usually identified as Sabina since a statue base for Sabina was

---

79. Davies 2013, 196. Sabina's statue, in Parian marble and found in the Palaestra of Ostia's Baths of Neptune, is Alexandridis 2004, Cat. 172.

80. See Brennan 2018, 27–30 for Sabina's muted presence.

ILL. 6.7 Statue of a woman, possibly Sabina, from Perge. Now in the Antalya Archaeology Museum, Turkey, Inv. no. 3066-3086. Alamy Stock Photo.

found nearby (Ill. 6.7).[81] Here the statue is posed in the Greater Herculaneum Woman type. The dragged fold of the outer mantle and heavy clothing underneath conceal the body from the viewer, and the upturned face is somewhat overshadowed by the female's head veil, hair, and diadem.

---

81. The general area for both finds is the city gate of Perge that was refurbished by Plancia Magna: see later. The idealized face is difficult to recognize as that of Sabina: Alexandridis 2004, 239 A.12 identifies this (Antalya Mus. Inv. A 3086, A 3066) as a private portrait of the late Hadrianic–early Antonine period; Carandini 1969, 167–68 accepts it as Sabina; Trimble 2011, 179 accepts it as Sabina but with hesitation.

ILL. 6.8 Statue of Plancia Magna from Perge. Now in the Antalya Archaeology Museum, Turkey, Inv. no. 3459. Alamy Stock Photo.

Perge presents a striking instance of the assimilation of imperial and private female statues. The statue often identified as that of Sabina was part of a costly refurbishing of Perge's City Gate undertaken in the Hadrianic period by Plancia Magna, a local woman of illustrious Roman descent.[82] Near the Gate was later installed a statue of Plancia Magna herself, also in the Greater Herculaneum

---

82. Boatwright 1993.

type (Ill. 6.8).[83] Plancia Magna's statue was dedicated by one of her freedmen and placed near her lavish civic donation; her crown with imperial busts on it, which emerges from her veil and denotes her position as an imperial cult priest, helps to identify this generous local patron. As the comparison of the two statues makes clear, the similarities of the two female's statue bodies make the statues almost interchangeable, despite the differences in the heads. The similarity must have influenced viewers' understandings of the two women and their relationship. It also suggests the exemplarity of imperial women themselves and the enduring bonds of imperial and other elite women. In Italy and the provinces, from afar some statues of imperial women may not have been immediately distinguishable from those of other elite Roman women embellishing a city's public sites and funerary spaces.

Even this brief discussion shows that the female imperial image was decidedly more indeterminate than that of imperial men. The concept of *Zeitgesicht* is not as appropriate for Roman female portraiture as it is for portraits of men. Scholars have begun to suggest reciprocal influence for style and portraits of imperial and private women.[84] This should not be surprising: other than Julia the Elder, Antonia the Younger, Julia the Younger, Livilla, Agrippina the Younger, and Faustina the Younger, the wives of emperors and of "princes" were from the senatorial elite, not an imperial family. After the Julio-Claudians very few imperial women were "born in the purple" or brought up "in the palace": Julia Titi, perhaps Sabina and her sister Matidia the Younger,[85] Faustina the Younger, Lucilla and other daughters of Faustina the Younger and Marcus Aurelius, and Julia Soaemias and Julia Mamaea. But we can glimpse the association of imperial women with women outside the imperial family, from Urgulania through the poet Balbilla, who accompanied her "mistress the beautiful Sabina" on the imperial trip to Egypt in 130. Imperial women had no special powers or rights that might distinguish them from matrons and senatorial women. Another consideration is that imperial portraiture for women gains frequency only in the reign of Caligula or Claudius, whereas public commemorations of private women in Italy are now traced back to the mid-first century BCE, a century earlier.[86]

---

83. For this statue, see Alexandridis 2004, 239 A.14.

84. See, e.g., Fittschen 1996; D'Ambra 2013; Hemelrijk 2005a, 317 n.43.

85. Temporini 1978, 187–88 assumes that Marciana was accompanied by her daughter Matidia the Elder and granddaughters Matidia the Younger and Sabina when she moved into the imperial palace with Plotina at the beginning of Trajan's reign.

86. Hemelrijk 2005a, 310 n.6; Cooley 2013. In Italy honorary inscriptions, and presumably public statuary, for non-imperial women become more common after the middle of the first

Imperial women's statues

And yet the women I investigate were connected to Rome's highest power by marriage or another familial tie, and the known contexts of many of their representations emphasize their importance to the imperial image and family. Many statues were displayed in imperial portrait groups, with their inscriptions foregrounding the relationship of the portrayed woman (or women) to the emperor.[87] More than half of the attested statues of Livia, as we saw earlier, specify her relationship to Augustus,[88] and the "Domus Augusta" group near the Circus Flaminius, discussed in Ch. 5 and probably featuring Livia, Tiberius, Germanicus, and Drusus the Younger, was definitely located next to a statue to Divus Augustus.[89] Ch. 5 also showed how rarely dedications in Rome mentioned imperial women alone. Group displays presented the imperial family as a close-knit, natural unit, much as do the literary and documentary references like Ovid and the *SCPP*. Women were essential to the developing imperial power.[90]

The physiognomies of portrayed imperial women could also emphasize familial relationships. Some portraits liken imperial women's physical traits and characteristics to those of their husband or family. Livia's most frequent portrait type during Augustus' lifetime was the Fayum type, named from a portrait apparently found in Fayum, Egypt, with other imperial portraits and now in the Ny Carlsberg Glyptotek (Ill. 6.9). The marble portrait has been dated to 4 CE or

---

century CE: Forbis 1990, 498, noting a peak at the end of the second century. Forbis' earliest datable inscription is from 79 CE (*CIL* X 7 = EDCS-11400094).

87. Bartman 1999, 72, calls this the "dynastic matriarch" type. Other relationships, such as wife, daughter, or sister, were also emphasized (e.g., Alexandridis 2004, 37): see the end of this chapter for Matidia the Younger, called the maternal aunt (*matertera*) of Antoninus Pius.

88. Even the unusual inscription from the "Temple of Fortuna Muliebris," which identifies her as the daughter of Drusus, immediately adds "wife of Caesar Augustus," specifying *uxor* (*CIL* VI 883 = EDCS-17301015).

89. In Ch. 7 we discuss a statuary group of Julia the Elder, Agrippa, and others at Thespiae.

90. See also Boschung 2002, 197–98 for the Augustan and Julio-Claudian period. Bartman 1999, 73, 78–81 argues that a small number of statuary ensembles installed by locals portrayed Livia with one or two other imperial woman but no men, citing Thasos (*IGRRP* 1.835b; in Greece) and Roman Noricum (UEL 6694, 6695, 6696, dated ca. 10–9 BCE; Magdalensberg, Austria). The discovery in Magdalensberg in 1997 of a matching inscription, probably attesting honors to Augustus (UEL 14766), weakens her argument. A base from Cillium (Kasserine, Tunisia), recording the dedication of statues (*statuae*; marble and full size?) of Antoninus Pius, Marcus Aurelius, and Lucius Verus, and of a silver *imago* (probably a bust) of Faustina the Younger, suggests that in some statue groups of the imperial family females were in smaller scale or otherwise distinguished from their male relatives: Højte 2005, 54 with Antoninus Pius 154: *AE* 1957, 77 = EDCS-13600160; see also Rose 1997, 74.

ILL. 6.9 Livia (Fayum type). Now in the Ny Carlsberg Glyptotek (I.N. 1444). © Ny Carlsberg Glyptotek, Copenhagen.

later and is considered modeled on an original from 27–23 BCE; it presents Livia with a characteristically Julian triangular face like Augustus' own. In contrast, her portraits dating to the reign of her son show her with a broader face, wide forehead, and more sharply tapering chin, as in Ill. 6.10. The face of this life-sized seated statue found in Paestum, Italy, is more characteristic of images of her son Tiberius, a similarity that must have been the more forceful because her statue was displayed together with an image of Tiberius.[91] (See Ill. 6.10.) Fittschen has noted something similar for the Antonine imperial women.[92] The first alteration of the Agrippina statue from the Caelian, in which her mouth was recut to correspond more closely to the cupid's-bow mouth of the young Nero, fits this phenomenon.

---

91. Both imperial statues are dated to the early Tiberian principate. See, e.g., Wood 1999, 14–15; Boschung 1993. Alexandridis 2004, Cat. 17 discusses the portrait from the Ny Carlsberg Glyptotek (I.N. 1444; Ill. 6.9); Alexandridis 2004, Cat. 23 that from Madrid (Ill. 6.10).

92. Fittschen 1999.

Models and Exemplars: Statues of Imperial Women

ILL. 6.10 Face of Julia Augusta from a statue found in Paestum, Italy. Now in Madrid, Museo Arqueológico Nacional. Inv. 2737. Enrique Sáenz de San Pedro.

The discussion of the statue of Matidia the Younger from the theater of Sinuessa Aurunca, with which this chapter ends, suggests how restricted the options were for portraits of imperial women in the capital city. But we first return to Agrippina the Younger, whose physical presence in Rome is documented in the material and literary record more thoroughly than that of other imperial women. This relative abundance allows us to add detail and nuance to our discussion here. We discuss three lost statues of her, all now recognized through their inscriptions, before turning again to her greywacke image from the Caelian.

Agrippina's statue from the Caelian, reconsidered

The locations of the three lost statues of Agrippina the Younger discussed here were treated in Ch. 5, where we also pointed out the relatively high visibility of Agrippina in the capital city.

Agrippina the Younger is one of the imperial women now most attested by identified statues and reliefs, twenty in Alexandridis' lists. Many of the extant portraits obviously or presumably came from group installations. Rose has emphasized the centrality of Agrippina to statuary displays produced during the Claudian period,[93] something we see here in the detailed discussion of two monuments near Rome's Via Flaminia and one near the later Colosseum. In the material record as well as in her own reported opinion (Tac. *Ann.* 12.37.4), Agrippina was key to the perpetuation of the Julio-Claudian dynasty and the principate itself.

The first monument, from north-central Campus Martius, is closely associated with Claudius. It is attested by inscriptions on multiple bases, with a *terminus post quem* of 50, that were found near the Britannic Arch of Claudius on the Via Flaminia.[94] The well-cut but fragmentary texts name, in the dative and with letters ranging from 8.6 to 4.3 cm H, three generations of Claudius' imperial family: his brother Germanicus, their mother Antonia the Younger, his wife Agrippina the Younger, his son Nero (adopted in 50), and his son and daughter Britannicus and Octavia. The inscriptions, which exhibit Claudius' famed archaic orthography, surely designated statues once above them (*CIL* VI 921 and 922 = EDCS-17301042-43; see *CIL* VI 923 = EDCS-17301044). Additional inscriptions and statues are presumed for Claudius himself and for Drusus the Elder, Claudius' father.[95]

Agrippina's inscription, which identifies her as "Julia Augusta Agrippina, daughter of Germanicus Caisar, wife of Tiberius Claudius Caisar Augustus Father of the Fatherland,"[96] is at least the fourth on one incomplete base that now measures 2.20 m W x 0.70 m H.[97] Hers was flanked by statues of Antonia—identified as "Antonia Augusta, wife of Drusus [the Elder], Priest of *divus*/Augustus, Mother of Tiberius Claudius Caisar Augustus Father of the Fatherland"—and of Nero (see later). To Antonia's right a dedication and statue of Germanicus are presumed from the few letters remaining on the broken tablet; on Agrippina's left Nero was honored as "Nero Claudius Caisar Drusus Germanicus, Son of

---

93. Rose 1997, 42–45. The majority date to, and immediately after, her marriage with Claudius in 49 and Claudius' adoption of Nero a year later. Nine honor Agrippina and Claudius together.

94. The t.p.q. of 50 is about that for the Arch itself (*CIL* VI 40416 = EDCS-00900120): see *LTUR* 1.86, s.v. "Arcus Claudii (a. 43 d.C.)" (E. Rodríguez Almeida). We discussed this monument briefly in Ch. 5.

95. Rose 1997, 113–15, Cat. #42; Flower 2011, 332 n.70; Osgood 2011, 94–96.

96. Rose 1997, 42 remarks that the first, larger-lettered line of Agrippina's dedication reads *Iuliai Aug(ustae)*, establishing "an immediate titular connection between Agrippina the Younger and Livia" [called Julia Augusta, 14 CE–29 CE].

97. The base is now in the Museo Nuovo of Rome's Capitoline Museums.

Augustus [Claudius], Pontifex, Augur, *XVvir sacris faciundis, VIIvir epulonum*, Consul Designate, Leader of the Youth."

The inscriptions, like the Britannic arch itself, pose many difficulties. Barrett proposed that the statues were on the Britannic arch, but Rose has pointed out how difficult it would be to combine a set of seven statues with the arch.[98] Further, the relatively small size of the letters on this base indicates that the texts were not placed high above viewers. It remains unclear how this installation of statues relates to the arch, although surely the adjacent monuments gained significance from each other. Looking at a different problem, the baffling lag time between the celebrated victory of Claudius over the Britons in 43 and the arch's date of 51, H. Flower has suggested that this site may have housed an earlier arch whose honors included Messalina. This third wife of Claudius had followed his Britannic triumph in a *carpentum* (in 44; see Ch. 5), tying her uniquely with that celebration. After Messalina's fall and Agrippina's ascent, the known arch and the monument attested by the extant inscriptions would have been installed to honor Agrippina and Nero, along with Claudius' birth family, and traces of Messalina suppressed.[99] In any case, after 51 Agrippina was conspicuous in this dynastic display at a nodal point in Rome's most important road from the north. She appeared with others of Claudius' family, including his mother and daughter. If Flower's attractive suggestion is correct, Claudius' new wife Agrippina replaced Messalina, who was erased from the installation.

Not far away a second sculptural ensemble honored Agrippina the Younger within the Claudian family, again including Antonia the Younger and Octavia but also others of the larger Claudian *gens*. This latter group display, sometimes called the Monumentum Claudianum, is known from a number of very fragmented inscriptions on marble and scrappy excavations in the northern Campus Martius near the area now occupied by the Palazzo Verospi.[100] The enigmatic installation seems to have been built at the same level and placement relative to the Via Flaminia as was the Ara Pacis, some hundred meters north of it, suggesting rough contemporaneity with the famed Augustan monument.[101] The fragmentary inscribed texts are in the nominative, do not use Claudius' archaizing

---

98. Barrett 1991, 7–9; Rose 1997, 113–15.

99. Flower 2011, 186–87.

100. See especially De Caprariis 1993; Alföldy et al. 1996, 4416–19 on *CIL* VI 40420-40430. The texts are now in Museo Nazionale Romano in Rome. We discussed this briefly in Ch. 5.

101. By Hadrian's day this area of the northwest Campus Martius had been raised to a higher level: see Boatwright 2010, 186–87. De Caprariis 1993, 100–102, 106–108 considers insoluble the identity of this Monumentum Claudianum.

238 IMPERIAL WOMEN OF ROME

spellings such as "Caisar," and have some letters as high as 12 cm. The three features argue that this group display is distinct from the one just discussed.[102]

Some texts or *tituli* from the Monumentum Claudianum are on discrete plaques; others were grouped together on one marble slab or another. In all, the numerous fragments are generally agreed to have once honored Tiberius; Tiberius' son Drusus the Younger; Antonia Augusta, "Mother of Tiberius Claudius Caesar Augustus Germanicus" (i.e., of Claudius); Agrippina the Younger (Ju[lia Augusta]); her son and Claudius' adopted heir Nero Caesar; perhaps the emperor Claudius Augustus himself; and Claudius' brother and two children, Germanicus, Britannicus, and Octavia.[103]

The display was not created at one time, and Claudius' additions include honors for Agrippina. Fragmentary consular dating on the text for Tiberius (*CIL* VI 40420) indicates this emperor's inscription and presumable statue date to 22, earliest in the installation. Another incomplete inscription suggests a date between 41 and 43 for an initial restoration of the site by Claudius (*CIL* VI 40421, cf. *CIL* VI 40423). The inclusion of Agrippina and Nero Caesar provides a *terminus post quem* of 50–54 CE, and the juxtaposition, on one plaque, of the inscriptions for Drusus and Nero, which are additionally inscribed with the same hand, suggests that Drusus' inscription was recut when Nero was honored in what seems to be at least a second restoration by Claudius. Scholars suggest a complicated but plausible history: Tiberius originally installed here a monument for the Claudian *gens* when his son Drusus the Younger was awarded tribunician power in 22; Claudius restored that Claudian monument at the beginning of his rule, perhaps to distinguish himself from the Julian Caligula; and after 50, now wed to Agrippina and having adopted Nero, Claudius enhanced the whole with statues of his fourth wife and adopted heir.[104] In the now lacunose record Agrippina is one of three imperial women honored at the display alongside numerous male members of the imperial family.

The third installation in Rome I discuss differs in significant ways from the two other monuments: it was raised not by an emperor but by a corporation (or *collegium*), in this instance the Aenatores or Brass-Wind Instrument Players, who were minor functionaries in Rome's official celebrations. This memorial dates

---

102. Alföldy et al. 1996, 4416 remark that the nominative likens the texts to *elogia*.

103. In order of citing above: *CIL* VI 40420 = EDCS-00900124; *CIL* VI 40424 = EDCS-00900128; *CIL* VI 40425 = EDCS-00900129; *CIL* VI 40426 = EDCS-00900130; *CIL* VI 40424 = EDCS-00900128; *CIL* VI 40423 = EDCS-00900127; *CIL* VI 40427-28 = EDCS-00900131-32.

104. Alföldy et al. 1996, 4416; De Caprariis 1993, 105; apparently accepted by Flower 2011, 186, and Osgood 2011, 61–62.

Models and Exemplars: Statues of Imperial Women

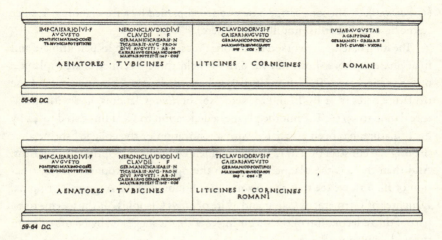

ILL. 6.11 Reconstruction of the final two phases of the statue base dedicated by the Brass-Wind Instrument Players of Rome. From Morizio in Panella 1996, Fig. 180; courtesy of C. Panella.

originally to the Augustan period and was repeatedly revamped. Agrippina seems to have been the only woman honored in it, and evidence suggests strongly that her representation there was suppressed after her fall from Nero's favor in 55/56.

Remains of a small shrine with inscribed bases for statues were found in the low area between the Palatine and Caelian hills in the vicinity of the later Claudium or Temple of *divus* Claudius. (See Ill. 5.2.) In the early imperial period, perhaps 12 BCE, the Brass-Wind Instrument Players built an enclosed sanctuary at a spot near the later southwestern pier of the Arch of Constantine. After numerous renovations, the shrine was destroyed in the Fire of 64, to be covered when the area was leveled for later buildings. The monument's complicated history has been reconstructed from the material found in situ, including a five-meter-long statue base faced with three marble plaques that were reworked more than once.[105] (See Ill. 6.11.) The long base has on its vertical face individual dedications to members of the imperial family. Spanning the base but below the imperial dedications was an inscription in larger letters identifying those responsible for the whole, the Roman Brass-Wind Instrument Players. Collectively called the *Aenatores Romani*, the minor functionaries are additionally specified in three groups according to their individual instruments, the Trumpet Players (*Tubicines*), Reeded-Trumpet Players (*Liticines*), and Curved-Trumpet Players

---

105. Morizio 1996.

(*Cornicines*).[106] The long statue base was accompanied by a freestanding, smaller statue base for Tiberius (not illustrated here).[107]

The long base was reworked numerous times, and in both its penultimate and final phases—those shown on Ill. 6.11—it held three inscribed marble plaques on its vertical face. The left-most plaque bears dedications to Augustus, whose titulature dates to 12 BCE, and to Nero, "son of *divus* Claudius" and with titulature dating to 55/56. The middle plaque, a dedication to Claudius dated to 42 by his titulature, has been associated with a renovation of the collegial shrine after the original construction in 12 BCE documented by the inscription of Augustus. And then there is the plaque farthest to the right. In the topmost reconstruction of Ill. 6.11, we see that this plaque once honored "Julia Augusta Agrippina, Daughter of Germanicus Caisar and Wife of *divus* Claudius." It thus seems to be part of the redecoration of the shrine in 55/56 that is suggested by Nero's titles on the middle plaque.[108]

As implied by the second reconstruction of Ill. 6.11, however, which represents this part of the shrine before destruction of the whole in the Great Fire of 64, sometime between 55/56 and 64 the marble plaque inscribed for Agrippina was plastered over or flipped to efface the dedication to her. This caused the word *Romani*, the last element of the shared inscription identifying the dedicants in 55/56, to be (re)inscribed on the second slab under *Liticines* and *Cornicines*.[109] Removal of Agrippina's inscribed honor and the presumable statue above it surely occurred after her murder and official disgrace in 59. To judge from the iteration of *Romani*, put on a lower line on the second slab, a void was left on the front and doubtless also on the top of this long base that had earlier honored (from left to right) Augustus, Nero, Claudius, and Agrippina.[110] Agrippina was eliminated from the shrine, although the removal of her honors left a conspicuous mark.[111]

The empty space in this small monument helps illuminate the spectacular rise and fall of Agrippina. V. Morizio, who published the inscriptions in 1996,

---

106. *CIL* VI 40307 = EDCS-00900007.

107. Tiberius' base: *CIL* VI 40334 = EDCS-00900038.

108. Morizio 1996, 211; Boschung 2002. The spelling of "Caisar" preserves Claudius' archaic orthography. The 55/56 renovation likely included the entire shrine.

109. Morizio 1996.

110. Fejfer 2008, 82 notes that a portrait head that cannot be identified with any of the members of the Julio-Claudian family was also found in the area.

111. Flower 2011, 193 and Varner 2004, 98–99 see this as a kind of *damnatio memoriae*; memory sanctions often left obvious marks. See the space left after (presumably) Geta's image was removed from the relief of the Arch of the Argentarii (Ill. 4.10).

Models and Exemplars: Statues of Imperial Women

argues that despite literary depictions of steadily worsening relations between Agrippina and Nero between her zenith in 54 and her nadir and death in 59 (e.g., Tac. *Ann.* 14.1–13; Suet. *Nero* 34.1-4), the shrine's history suggests a *modus vivendi* that acknowledged her part in Nero's rise to power.[112] Morizio does not discuss the nearby Claudium. The enormous cult precinct towering over the brass instrumentalists' shrine must have emphasized the specific ties to *divus* Claudius that the inscriptions to Nero and Agrippina proclaimed.[113] Further, as opposed to other installations with Agrippina in Rome, this shrine remarkably includes Agrippina as its only woman. It thus reflects the singular position Agrippina is said herself to have claimed (e.g., Tac. *Ann.* 12.37.4, 12.42).

These three lost Roman statues of Agrippina, and the overall history of imperial women's portraits, allow us to provide more context for the remarkable greywacke statue of Agrippina with which we began. Just like the relatively modest shrine of the Roman Brass-Wind Instrument Players, the huge Temple of *divus* Claudius nearby must have similarly housed numerous statues of the imperial family. One must have been of Nero, under whom the senate decreed Claudius' deification. The Temple doubtlessly also displayed statues of Augustus and of Julia Augusta, whose consecration Claudius had sponsored at the beginning of his reign. (See Ch. 1 and Ch. 4.) Can we presume also a statue of Antonia the Younger, mother of Claudius and grandmother of Agrippina the Younger, posthumously granted the title *Augusta* at Claudius' accession? Statues of Claudius' brother Germanicus and father Drusus the Younger, as well as of other members of the Julio-Claudian family? Agrippina's statue in the massive sanctuary, 180 by 200 m and overlooking much of Rome from its high platform, would thus be much less singular than it might now appear. On the other hand, its fine artistic treatment, large size, open gestures, and striking material may have distinguished her image from others in the sanctuary. She herself reportedly strove continually to surpass her predecessors and others, whom she saw as rivals.

Matidia the Younger at Suessa Aurunca

A recent find from central Italy, an extraordinary statue of Matidia the Younger, provides further context for understanding the imaging of imperial women as well as shows how much there is still to learn about female Roman portraiture. Archaeological materials including thirty-five hundred marble fragments have

---

112. Morizio 1996, 204–6.

113. For Agrippina's role as Claudius' *flaminica*, see Ch. 4. The *Apocolocyntosis* emphasizes the brass wind players during Claudius' funeral: Sen. *Apocol.* 12.1.

ILL. 6.12 Statue of Matidia the Younger, from the theater at Suessa Aurunca. Photo courtesy of S. Castellani.

been recently reinvestigated at the Roman theater in Suessa Aurunca, modern Sessa Aurunca that lies sixty kilometers north of Naples and east of Minturnae, Italy.[114] Among other finds, scholars have pieced together a freestanding, over-life-size statue of Matidia the Younger (Ill. 6.12), Sabina's older (half-)sister who survived the empress almost thirty years.[115]

---

114. See Cascella 2013, 73–75 for the theater's excavations and town history of Suessa Aurunca.

115. The statue, 2.6 m H x 1.5 m W, is now in the Sessa Aurunca Museum, inv. no. 297048. Cascella 2013, 76 Table 1 gives Matidia the Younger's dates as 85–162 CE but in adjoining text dates her death to 165. See my Appendix 1 for her dates of b. before 85, d. ca. 165.

Through painstaking work S. Cascella and other excavators have established that Matidia the Younger's statue once adorned the central *aedicula* in the theater's *scaenae frons*. Matidia, who had extensive holdings in this area, rebuilt this Augustan monument after an earthquake, according to a very fragmentary inscription from an architrave over one of the entrances to the theater.[116] Still enigmatic in certain points, the three-line inscription, with large letters 16.5 to 20 cm H, establishes Matidia (the Younger) as the monument's patron by naming her in the nominative. It also makes clear her relations to her mother, grandmother, and sister, each specified as *diva* and *Augusta*, and to the ruling emperor, Antoninus Pius. The text has been reconstructed as, "Matidia, Daughter of *diva* Matidia Augusta, Granddaughter of *diva* Marciana Augusta, Sister of *diva* Sabina Augusta, Maternal Aunt of Imperator Antoninus Pius Augustus Father of the Fatherland, restored the theater, collapsed because of an earthquake, and likewise the adjoining portico, with her own money."[117] Other than Antoninus Pius. all individuals named on this grandiose inscription are female: the donor Matidia (the Younger), her mother Matidia (the Elder), her grandmother Marciana, and her sister Sabina.[118]

Matidia the Younger, whose portrait type is found in six other sculptural replicas that previously had no secure identification,[119] is represented as a flying goddess without wings, an *Aura*. The composite statue uses smooth white marble from Aphrodisias for the arms, shoulders, and head, including its tightly controlled hair. The drapery, however, is rendered in dark *bigio morato* marble from Göktepe in the Taurus mountains (modern Turkey).[120] Matidia's arms are open and her stance a bit akilter as she is shown alighting from above, but her

---

116. The height of the inscription is 80 cm. Wood 2015, 237 suggests its original location as above the doorway between the large southeast basilica and the southern *parados* of the theater.

117. *[Matidia divae Matidiae] Aug(ustae) fil(ia) diva[e] Marci[anae Aug(ustae) neptis] / [divae Sabinae Aug(ustae) sor]or [I]mp(eratoris) Antonin[i] Aug(usti) Pii [p(atris) p(atriae) matertera] / [theatrum terrae motu con]laps[u]m item porticu[m c]oniunc[tum 3]*: EDCS-44100272; see also *CIL* X 4745. The end of line 3 apparently once indicated a rebuilding, but cannot be completed with confidence: Chausson 2008, 256 fig. 7, 8. The earthquake probably dates before 139: Cascella 2013, 78.

118. The stressed connections with women are echoed in other inscriptions for her, as on a statue base from Ephesus: *CIL* III 7123 = EDCS-27800836. Women could not legally adopt; Antoninus Pius had no legal familial relationship with Sabina and Matidia the Younger (see this chapter n.126 and Ch. 3, n.124).

119. See Wood 2015, 235 n.3; uncertainty was due to the lack of numismatic portraits.

120. Wood 2015, 237 for the marbles; see also Cascella 2013. A contemporaneous interest in color, floating robes, and contrasts can be seen in Lucian, *Portraits* 7–8, apparently a description of Panthea, the mistress of Lucius Verus.

expression is placid and the hair unruffled in its neat coiffure in a style popular in the 130s.[121] The composed face and body contrast the disturbed sensuality conveyed by the drapery, which swirls around the woman's body, slips off her left shoulder, and clings to her thighs and belly. Given the stark distinction of the two marble hues, perhaps the statue's "skin" was only delicately colored.[122]

Wood has recently underlined the extraordinary nature of this portrait statue, which is unparalleled for any historical woman, much less an imperial one.[123] She confirms that the head is original to the body since the pieces fit together closely, and that it was never reworked. The over-life-size sculpture, therefore, is an original, undoubtedly made for the place archaeologists have determined it originally graced: a small templelike structure framed in highly colored marble columns (*giallo antico* and *pavonazzetto*) and surmounting the central entrance of the *scaenae frons*. The statue must have been a focus for the theater's audience. Wood evocatively describes how, during theatrical spectacles, Matidia the Younger may have sat in the seat of honor at the center of the lowest seating directly across from her extraordinary statue and further aligned with a small imperial cult shrine behind her in the upper tiers.[124]

The sensual depiction of Matidia is exceptional. The closest known parallels for the body type come from the Greek East (especially Asia) and depict dancers, or are associated with Victories and statues of Isis. The statue from Suessa Aurunca is astonishing in its implications for Matidia the Younger. Wood suggests that the piece was created with at least some input from Matidia herself.[125]

If so, Matidia had more agency for her over-life-size, permanent, and atypical depiction than other imperial women seem to have had for their representations. Yet Matidia's imperial connections are spelled out on the inscription she had put on the theater, including her identification as Pius' *matertera* or maternal aunt: this claim depends on Pius' adoption by Hadrian, the husband of Matidia the Younger's younger sister Sabina.[126] The embellishment of the *scaenae frons* also included statues of other imperial relatives, probably in first-story niches.

---

121. Wood 2015, 237.

122. Other sculptures of the theater show evidence of original coloration: Wood 2015, 240.

123. Wood 2015, esp. 237.

124. Wood 2015, 240.

125. Wood 2015, 254.

126. Some ten other inscriptions found in Campania and elsewhere similarly calling her *matertera*. She could not technically be Pius' *matertera*, since adoption did not mean that the wife of the adopter was in the position of a mother to the adopted son: Dig. 1.7.23 (Paulus libro trigensimo quinto ad edictum). I thank Tom McGinn for this reference.

Models and Exemplars: Statues of Imperial Women 245

Archaeologists have identified Hadrian, Sabina, Matidia the Elder, and possibly Trajan from the statue fragments found there. Display of members of the imperial family and emphasis on the connections between them is typical, as we have seen in this chapter. Matidia the Younger's unusual, voluptuous depiction, however, is not.

Her depiction also contrasts what we previously knew about her, at least from most other sources. She never received the title *Augusta*; she was never portrayed or identified on coins. Fronto's slight evidence, discussed in Ch. 3, emphasizes her domestic roles and female companionship.[127] C. Bruun has pointed out, however, the extensive evidence for Matidia's landholdings and connections from Augusta Vindelicum in Raetia, Aequum in Dalmatia, Delphi, Athens, Ephesus, and Cuicul (now Djémila, Algeria), not to mention Vicetia in Cisalpine Italy and Suessa Aurunca, Minturnae, and Sinuessa in central Italy. In the area of Suessa she apparently donated a water supply, a bridge, a local road, a library, basilica, and other buildings besides the theater. Such patronage, Bruun argues, let Matidia function as a representative of sorts of the imperial family, even though she lacked official marks of status that elevated her mother, (half-)sister, and many other imperial women.[128] Wood, Cascella, F. Chausson, and others have gone further. Noting that all her datable inscriptions come from Antoninus Pius' reign, they suggest that Matidia was a persona non grata during the Hadrianic period,[129] but later "encouraged" by Antoninus Pius to a more public role that would highlight his connections with the previous dynasty. Such interpretations overlook Matidia the Younger's sensual self-presentation, so at odds with the demure and even suppressed persona of other second-century imperial women, as well as the prominence given her female relatives in her renovated theater in Suessa Aurunca. It may also reveal modern inabilities to accept the cultural and political norms of the Romans.

Conclusion

Perhaps more than any other chapter, this one on large sculpted portraits of imperial women underlines women's connections with other females sharing a privileged background. The absence of an independent tradition of representations of

---

127. See Boatwright 1992.

128. Bruun 2010. Dalmatia, not identified on my map, is the coastal region of Illyricum.

129. Chausson 2008 has even speculated, unconvincingly, that Matidia was married to one of the four consulars who lost their lives at the beginning of Hadrian's reign. Wood 2015 retreats to the HA and psychological discussion of Hadrian's suspicious nature.

historical women in the city of Rome meant that portraiture of imperial women was slow to start there, despite the privilege of public imaging granted Octavia and Livia in 35 BCE. Sculptors' apparent recourse to Greek models of deities and Hellenistic queens certainly contributed to an awesome image for these and subsequent imperial women. On the other hand, such models must have seemed inherently presumptuous in late Republican and Augustan Rome, where customs and laws continued to segregate women from politics and prominence despite slightly growing numbers of independently wealthy and authoritative women (as we saw in Ch. 1). This tradition may have contributed to the relative infrequency in Italy and Rome of documented images of imperial women until after the reign of Tiberius.

The similarities of many images of imperial women to ones of elite but "private" Roman women, typified by the statues of Sabina and Plancia Magna, suggest the exemplarity of members of the imperial family particularly after the Julio-Claudian period. On the other hand, and despite detailed scholarship on Roman iconography, imperial women's depictions have a certain indeterminacy. In part this is due to the number of body types used for their and other women's statues. Scholars have pointed out that at least some elements of an imperial woman's depiction—hairstyles, in particular—may have been influenced by those of portraits of women not of the imperial family. This is the very milieu from which imperial women came. As opposed to the iconic image of an emperor, conveyed by coinage as well as the dissemination of official portraits, the image of a woman or women in his family was less unmistakable. Their roles as supportive household members were traditional ones common to all women in the Roman world, even those whose individual circumstances may have made them "heads of households."

Blandness and homogeneity characterize many of the identified portraits of imperial women. Most of these would have been found in settings that also featured others of the imperial family, with whom the imperial women's consistency would have resonated. Our review of statues of Agrippina the Younger known from inscriptions found in Rome argues that even the striking, over-life-size greywacke portrait of her from the Caelian, with which we began, was originally exhibited with other statues portraying Claudius' family. What was important was not any one woman's individuality, attributes, or experience, but rather her contributions to the imperial family.

Further, the constraints imposed by imperial women's propinquity to power can be demonstrated by the vicissitudes of Agrippina's statues and commemorations discussed in this chapter. Her effacement at the shrine of Rome's Brass-Wind Instrument Players between the Caelian and the Palatine hills suggests that in Rome even corporate bodies such as *collegia* were sensitive to changes at the

Models and Exemplars: Statues of Imperial Women   247

court, quick to obliterate disgraced and discarded imperial women and thus hamper later generations' abilities to learn about them.[130]

All this makes the more extraordinary Matidia the Younger's depiction from Suessa Aurunca. Although the statue itself reminds us that new archaeological information can always overturn assumptions, the findings in this book argue that her sensuous portrait statue could have been exhibited only outside of Rome. The visibility and image of imperial women were limited in the capital city.[131] Matidia's matchless statue and singular patronage in the little Campanian town demonstrate the resources and social standing of elite women in the Roman world. But the free-flying Matidia may be the exception that proves the rule: once women became closely tied to the emperor they had little agency or scope for independence in the capital city, including the determination of how they would be represented to contemporaries and posterity.

---

130. The proposed suppression of Messalina at the imperially sponsored Claudian monument near the Britannic Arch is somewhat akin to this, but at a different level (n.99 of this chapter).

131. We might compare the prominence of Domitia Augusta [Longina] in Gabii: Ch. 2.

7

Imperial Women Abroad, and with the Military

Introduction: The Severans, the most warlike imperial women?

The latest imperial women of this book, those in the Severan dynasty that controlled Rome from 193 to 235 (see Appendix 2), are the most aberrant in the contexts of our previous discussions. Literary sources peculiarly associate Rome's military with Julia Domna, the wife of Septimius Severus and mother of Caracalla, her sister Julia Maesa, and Julia Soaemias and Julia Mamaea, Maesa's daughters who bore Elagabalus and Severus Alexander, respectively. For instance, Maesa, Soaemias, and sometimes Mamaea as well, are said to have intrigued directly with the army in Syria to bring Elagabalus to power in 218.[1] Four years later Maesa and Mamaea reportedly convinced Rome's praetorian guard to assassinate Elagabalus and his mother Soaemias so Severus Alexander could take his cousin's place.[2] The two youths, each of whom came to power at the ages of only fourteen or fifteen,[3] are said to have granted their mothers unprecedented access to the military and the senate, Elagabalus to his grandmother Maesa as well.[4] We hear that Mamaea so dominated Severus Alexander throughout his thirteen-year reign that she

---

1. Hdn. 5.3.10–11, 5.5.1; HA, *Macrinus* 9.1–4, 10. Cassius Dio attributes the coup to two men: see Schöpe 2014, 197–98. Kemezis 2016, 373–74 discusses the dramatic presentations.

2. HA, *Heliogab.* 15; Hdn. 5.7.3, 5.8.3, 5.8.10. His acclamation was on 13 March 222: Kienast 2017, 171. Agrippina the Younger had a strong but ultimately ineffectual connection with the praetorians: Tac. *Ann.* 12.41.6–42.1, 13.14.5, 14.7.5, 14.11.1; Barrett 2005a, 308–9.

3. See, e.g., Kienast 2017, 165, 171.

4. E.g., HA, *Heliogab.* 4.1–2, 12.3; Cass. Dio 80.17.2. HA, *Heliogab.* 18.3 reports that women were banned from entering the senate after the assassination of Elagabalus and Soaemias.

Imperial Women of Rome. Mary T. Boatwright, Oxford University Press. © Oxford University Press 2021.
DOI: 10.1093/oso/9780190455897.003.0008

Imperial Women Abroad, and with the Military

was responsible for her son's military setbacks, including the mutiny that killed him as well as her in 235 in his military headquarters in Mogontiacum.[5] Literary depictions of these women as close to Rome's rank and file are echoed by other evidence, such as the honorific epithet Mother of the Camps (*mater castrorum*) given at least Domna and Mamaea on coins and inscriptions (see later in this chapter and Ch. 4). Further, at least five inscriptions from Roman camps and barracks document sculptures of Domna, such as one in the *praetorium* of the legionary camp at Bonna (modern Bonn, Germany).[6] She is the only imperial woman now attested with statues in such locations.[7]

My purpose here is neither to investigate the veracity of the literary accounts nor to recount the histories of the late emperors to whom these women are connected;[8] rather, I explore the implications of the women's reported associations with Rome's military, and the related issue of their movements abroad. Romans considered military skills and discipline of paramount importance, and they generally held that women should be far away from men organized for war and military purposes. The prevailing view was that women's minds were weak and fearful. Women were thought so incapable of controlling themselves that simply their presence would corrupt men and erode obedience and purpose.[9] Yet the key importance of women to the princeps and imperial family complicated

---

5. For submissiveness, see Hdn. 6.8.3, 6.9.5; *Epit. de Caes.* 24.4–5; HA, *Alex. Sev.* 14.7; contra HA, *Heliogab.* 2.1. For the mutiny and military debacle, see Hdn. 6.8–9; cf. HA, *Max.* 7.4–5 and *Alex. Sev.* 63.5; HA, *Alex. Sev.* 60.5.

6. Fejfer 1988, 296 lists five: *CIL* XIII 12042 = EDCS-12800064 (from Bonna); *CIL* XIII 6531 = EDCS-11000558 (Roman camp at modern Murrhardt, Germany); *AE* 1958, 232 = EDCS-13500278 (Porolissum, Dacia; now Moigrad, Romania); *AE* 1929, 1 = EDCS-16200025 (Samum, Dacia; now Caseiu, Romania); and one from Spain. Fejfer 1985, 130 counts six; her nos. 40, 43, 47, 48, 65, and the Ostian one in the Caserma dei Vigili (= Alexandridis 2004, #1).

7. Alexandridis 2004, 32 considers the context plausible also for images of Faustina the Younger. But the title *mater castrorum* did not mean that images of a woman so honored would be installed and venerated in *praetoria*: see Nadolny 2016, 48, with earlier references.

8. The literary sources are inconsistent: e.g., Aur. Vict. *Caes.* 23 reports Elagabalus' accession without mentioning his female relatives (cf., e.g., HA, *Macrinus* 9.1–4, 10.1, and *Heliogab.* 1.4). For Cassius Dio's history of the Severan period, see now Scott 2018. Severus Alexander's thirteen-year rule (see McHugh 2017) seems to have been stable in Rome, beneficial to the senate and equestrians, and remarkably sober and frugal in comparison to the preceding four-year rule of Elagabalus (for which see Kemezis 2016; Arrizabalaga y Prado 2010). Most see the Severan period as distinctively stressing military and autocratic power: e.g., Noreña 2011, 242, 320.

9. E.g., Sen. *Med.* 42; Val. Max. 9.1.3 (whose *imbecillitas* echoes in the *imbecillus* appearing twice in the debate about Roman women accompanying their husbands to the provinces and military: Tac. *Ann.* 3.33–34, discussed later). In general, see Phang 2001, 344–45, 350–83.

ILL. 7.1 Bronze sword sheath from the Rhine area, often said to depict Livia and her two sons. Bonn, Rheinisches Landesmuseum, Inv. No. 4320, courtesy of the museum.

this sharp division. Even the prototypical imperial woman Livia, whom Cassius Dio praises explicitly for never entering a military camp (57.12.3), may be portrayed on a plaque for a sword sheath found in the Rhine region. (See Ill. 7.1.) On the weapon the unnamed woman appears between two young men; the trio have been identified by their hairstyles as Livia and her sons Drusus the Elder (left) and Tiberius (right). Although here the context is military, the anonymity of the three, like the purported Julia coin of 13 BCE (Ill. 3.2), stresses that Rome's prowess depended on the imperial family, not an imperial woman herself.[10] The two interwoven themes of this chapter make clear that the visibility of imperial women abroad or with Rome's military was gradual. No continuous, intentional development can be discerned.[11]

The essential background is the pronounced bias against any women's connection with Rome's armed forces, explored below. This bias extends to women's

---

10. If Drusus is depicted, the *repoussé* piece dates before his death in 9 BCE: Barrett 2002, 264; Rose 1997, pl. 10; Severy 2003, 87 fig. 4.1. Severy, 87–89 and fig. 4.2 maintains that a drinking cup from Vetera (modern Xanten, Germany) is engraved with busts of Augustus and Livia atop columns (Bonn, Rheinisches Landesmuseum 22534a [photo neg. 383/72 or 7693]), but the female is less distinctive.

11. Severy 2003, 87–89, Kettenhofen 1979, 80, and some others see this more linearly, starting in the Augustan era.

Imperial Women Abroad, and with the Military

accompaniment of men in their service outside of Rome in provincial administration, which always combined civil and military duties. Nonetheless, and intensifying over time, women are sporadically attested in more purely military settings such as camps and barracks, and even in armed conflict. In traveling with emperors and "princes" in the provinces, imperial women were not unique: others, notably wives of commanding officers, did the same. On the other hand, the exemplarity of imperial women gave their real and their symbolic presence among Rome's armed men a significance far surpassing that of other women. The map in the front matter includes the spots that imperial women visited, in part to help impress the reader of the breadth of their presence.

Women and Rome's military

Women could not serve in Rome's armed forces and were deemed antithetical to military strength and discipline.[12] Augustus' reorganization of the Roman army included a ban on soldiers contracting legally binding marriages.[13] An obvious symbolic difference of Romans from "barbarians" was that "barbarian" women either led Rome's foes in the field, as Boudicca during Britain's revolt against Rome in 60–61 CE (see Ch. 1), or participated otherwise in armed conflict, as did the German women who from the sidelines shamed and goaded their men into fiercer fighting (Tac. *Germ.* 7.3–4).[14] Rare literary reports of Roman women appearing as combatants in warfare, as when raining down roof tiles on an invading army, mark great struggles and dramatic breakdowns of customary order.[15]

Archaeologists' discovery of small leather sandals and shoes at Vindolanda and other Roman fortresses, however, has led to a reexamination of evidence and the conclusion that women (and children) were present inside Roman military installations during the principate, thus tempering the literary depictions. This

---

12. Phang 2001, esp. 344–83. Slaves also were considered improper for serving in war: e.g., Plin. *Ep.* 10.39–40.

13. This lasted until Septimius Severus' reforms mentioned later: Phang 2001, 115–33.

14. For the *dux femina* (a term of opprobrium for Roman women who transgress boundaries), see McHugh 2012, 75; Ginsburg 2006, 112–16; and Santoro L'Hoir 1994, 17–24. Tacitus notes that the Britons fatally invited their wives to witness what they thought would be the final, successful battle of Boudicca's rebellion: *Ann.* 14.34.

15. Barry 1996, esp. 72; cf. Livy 5.21.10. The report that partisan women had been killed at the battle of Cremona in 69 emphasizes the terrible vicissitudes of the civil war (Tac. *Hist.* 3.32); see Triaria later. Women gladiators were deemed freaks: Tac. *Ann.* 15.23; Juv. 6.82–113, 246–67.

IMPERIAL WOMEN OF ROME

seems to have been true for women of all ranks of life,[16] not merely the wives of commanders whose presence with their actively serving husbands is indicated by information including a well-known passage of Tacitus discussed later (*Ann.* 3.33–34). This conclusion provides important background for the investigation of imperial women and the military. Despite the difficulties of discerning relative influence—did imperial women's activities and public personae reflect those of other women in the Roman world, or guide them?—the wider context gives the discussion greater significance.

The ferocious brutality of Rome's constant belligerence and armed conflicts unquestionably affected noncombatants, especially women, as well as the male officers and soldiers who were engaged in battles and maneuvers.[17] The numerous descriptions by historians of Roman warfare and the capture and destruction of cities frequently at least allude to the rape and enslavement of women and young men, despite victims' desperate attempts to protect themselves.[18] Human rights do not seem to be the historians' concern; instead, the topic of rape is raised to inspire Romans and their allies to more zealously defend their own against the foe. We hear much less about Romans' rape of their opponents' women and children.[19] At times a Roman's treatment of women in war serves historians as a way to portray a male combatant. For example, if a leader declines to sexually exploit a beautiful female captive, as Scipio Africanus with the Spanish maiden at the fall of Carthago Nova (Livy 26.41–51), the story emphasizes the man's self-control and self-denial for Rome's greater good.[20]

---

16. See, e.g., Greene 2014; Allison 2013, 319–43; Allason-Jones 1999; Driel-Murray 1997. Contra: E. L. Wheeler in his *CJ* 2015 review of I. Haynes, *Blood of the Provinces: The Roman Auxilia and the Making of Provincial Society from Augustus to the Severans* (2013): https://cj.camws.org/node/456, and the references collected by James 2002, 11.

17. Phang 2001, 251–61 investigates insightfully Roman soldiers' rape and sexual harassment of civilians; Gaca 2016, although not focusing on Rome, argues for a recurrent pattern of martial rape and enslavement of war-captive women and girls in antiquity.

18. The danger occurs in foreign or civil war. Some elite women fled to their husbands abroad, as Caecilia Metella (with her children) to Sulla in Greece in the 80s (Plut. *Sulla* 22.1); the *Laudatio Turiae* (*ILS* 8393 = EDCS-60700127; see Hemelrijk 2004, 185) admiringly reports a woman's courageous public actions during the triumviral period. In some victim blaming, Valerius Maximus (3.8.6) notes that sedition, violence, and civil unrest can overturn ancestral custom and a woman's proper restraint (*verecundia*).

19. The *topos* is especially pointed in narratives of violence against Romans during civil strife and slave revolts: see, e.g., Tac. *Hist.* 2.12.2, 2.56.1, 4.1.3; Diod. *Sic.* 34/35.2.12. Sallust's Caesar dismisses the enumeration of rape and atrocities in sacked cities as mere rhetoric: *Cat.* 51.9–10.

20. See Chaplin 2010.

Imperial Women Abroad, and with the Military 253

Self-control was critical and—as mentioned before—women were thought to essentially lack it. They were believed to weaken the discipline and nerve of Rome's soldiers and military leaders, "unmanning" and feminizing them when "virtuous" masculinity was needed most.[21] Fulvia, decried for her presence in military situations, is a conspicuous example from the end of the Republic.[22] At times her activity serves specifically to censure a husband. Her first husband Clodius Pulcher, for example, was scorned for "the dagger clinging to Fulvia's robe" that "subordinated military dignity to feminine authority" (Val. Max. 3.5.3); her third husband, Mark Antony, was disparaged for having her in the camp at Brundisium in 44 BCE (Cic. *Phil.* 5.22, 13.18; Brundisium is modern Brindisi, Italy). Fulvia was reviled for helping orchestrate the Perusine War of 41–40, a failed uprising against Octavian in Italy.[23] When in a siege Fulvia "girded herself with a sword, gave the watchword to the soldiers, and frequently harangued them" (Cass. Dio 48.10.3–4), she epitomized the destabilizing inversions of the Republic's end.[24]

This background helps explain alike Cassius Dio's point that Livia never entered a military camp (57.12.3), and some aspects of Augustus' reforms of Rome's military. In his reorganization of the armed forces the first princeps evidently disallowed legally binding marriages for serving soldiers, and he discouraged commanding officers from home visits during winter (noncombat) months (Suet. *Aug.* 24.1).[25] When later reporting Septimius Severus' "indulgences" to soldiers, which included the right to conduct a legal marriage while serving, Herodian emphasized, "All these things are normally considered alien to military discipline and efficient readiness for war" (Hdn. 3.8.4).[26] Women should stay away from soldiers, and in the domestic realm.

Such attitudes against women extended beyond the strictly military sphere, however. Rome's administration of the provinces was inextricable from military

---

21. See Phang 2001, e.g., 366–72; Debrunner Hall 1994; Marshall 1975, 110–13. Pertinent literary passages include Pseudo-Quintilian (ca. 100 CE) *decl.* 3.12; Pliny, *Ep.* 6.31.4–6; Tac. *Hist.* 1.48.

22. See Hallett 2015; Marshall 1975, 112–13.

23. Hemelrijk 2004, 192–93; Hallett 2015, 247. Other references include Plut. *Ant.* 10.3; Cass. Dio 45.12–13; *CIL* XI 6721, nos. 3–5, 14 = EDCS- 47900407-9, 24900051. The war resulted in Fulvia's final rift from Mark Antony.

24. Hallett 2015. Velleius criticizes Fulvia for having nothing womanly but her body (2.74.2).

25. For the Augustan context, see Phang 2001, esp. 115–33, 344–83. Limited home visits might encourage a woman to attend her husband abroad, as Octavia with Mark Antony (see later). Wardle 2014, 187–88 argues against a "ban" by Augustus on wives visiting the provinces.

26. Campbell 1978, 165: conservatism helped maintain the ban on serving soldiers' *conubium.*

supervision, especially at the beginning of the principate.[27] We can see this reflected in the most extended discussion about Roman women accompanying husbands to the provinces, a senatorial discussion Tacitus reports for the early Tiberian period (*Ann.* 3.33–35).[28] In 21 Aulus Caecina Severus proposed that no magistrate should take his wife with him to his province. Caecina praised his own marriage and fertile wife, declaring that during his forty stints of service she bore him six children while never leaving Italy. He then expatiated about women's innate incompatibility with Roman provincial rule and with the Roman military, addressing usurpations of men's military and civil roles. The reported speech concluded with the ascending tricolon: "Women rule at home, in the courts, and now in the army!" (Tac. *Ann.* 3.33).[29]

Despite his stirring rhetoric, Caecina's words met with little approval in the senate (Tac. *Ann.* 3.34.1). Valerius Messalinus retorted that times had changed and the provinces were now peaceful; husbands—not the law—should control wives; long separations were too hard on marriages (Tac. *Ann.* 3.34.2–5). When Drusus the Younger, Tiberius' son and heir apparent, agreed with Messalinus and asserted that he had traveled with his "dearest wife" (*carissima uxor*) to Illyricum (the western and upper Balkans) and that Livia had often traveled with Augustus to the west and the east, Caecina's proposal was dropped (Tac. *Ann.* 3.34.6).

The opinion of Drusus and Messalinus prevailed that day in the senate, although Drusus' statement about Livia is suspect (see discussion later) and men's discomfort about women's presence among Roman provincial administrators persisted.[30] In the early third century, while Cassius Dio noted Livia's persistent separation from the camps Ulpian opined, "While it is indeed better that a proconsul go to his province *without* his wife, he can also do so with her." The jurist was commenting on a *Senatus Consultum* of 24 CE determining

---

27. Military activity was supposed to occur only outside Rome's sacred boundary or *pomerium* (Beard, North, and Price 1998, 1:177–81): women's presence with men serving outside of Rome might thus have suggested involvement in military affairs.

28. See Woodman and Martin 1996, 289–99. Among others, Santoro L'Hoir 1994, 13–14 remarks on Tacitus' intertextuality with Livy's debate on repealing the lex Oppia (Livy 34.1–7).

29. This crescendo recalls the grievance of Tacitus' Tiberius against Agrippina, *Ann.* 1.69.3–4: see below, and Woodman and Martin 1996, 295–96. The senatorial debate surely reflected the scandal of Munatia Plancina, whose attendance at cavalry and infantry exercises contributed to her husband Gnaeus Piso's charges a few years earlier (Tac. *Ann.* 2.55.6; later here and Ch. 1).

30. Marshall 1975, 113–16 discusses benefits and disadvantages of wives staying at home; on 119 and 126, he links greater acceptance of women with their husbands in the provinces to Tiberius' extension of service for governors abroad. Barrett 2005a argues that *animus* against women in the provinces (and in military situations) is particularly Tiberian, not Roman.

Imperial Women Abroad, and with the Military

magistrates abroad to be as liable for their wives' misdeeds as they were for their own (Ulp. 1 *de off. procons.*; Dig. 1.16.4.2; emphasis mine).[31] Wives, children, and even mothers accompanied magistrates, including imperial men, as they toured or administered Rome's provinces.

Criticism of "trailing spouses" could be harsh, especially if the women became linked with the military. Even in Tacitus' rendition of the debate of 21, the conciliatory Messalinus had agreed that women should not be with their husbands in actual military settings. His concession, "Men in armor, to be sure, should be the ones to go to war; but for men returning after their toil, what is more honorable than the relaxation of a wife's companionship?" (Tac. *Ann.* 3.34.2), maintains the separation of women from actual combat.[32]

Roman women's association with the military continued problematic at least into the second century CE, despite what may seem an increasingly routine incidence of women with their high-ranking male relatives in provinces and Rome's forts.[33] A notorious example is Munatia Plancina, implicated in the death of Germanicus in 19 CE. She had accompanied her husband Gnaeus Calpurnius Piso to his province Syria in 18.[34] There, according to Tacitus, Cassius Dio, and the implications of the *SCPP* of 20 CE (Tac. *Ann.* 2.71; Cass. Dio 57.18.9; Ch. 1), Plancina actively colluded with her husband to undermine and then destroy Germanicus, also in the east but with extraordinary powers greater than those of Piso. Among the charges Tacitus reports is that Plancina "transgressed proper female behavior" by partaking in cavalry and infantry maneuvers (Tac. *Ann.* 2.55.6).[35] Although in the senatorial proceedings of 20 Julia Augusta's intercession absolved the accused woman, in 33 Plancina was charged again on "hardly mysterious indictments" and committed suicide (Tac. *Ann.* 6.26; cf. Cass. Dio 58.22.5).

Later Roman women, and their male relatives, are also criticized for military intrusions. In 39 CE Cornelia, the wife of Calvisius Sabinus, was indicted because "she made the rounds of the sentries and watched the soldiers at drill" during her husband's governorship of Pannonia.[36] Among Caligula's scandalous

---

31. Ulpian mistakenly dates the *Senatus Consultum* to 20 CE: see Tac. *Ann.* 4.20.4 and Gardner 1986, 264.

32. *bella plane accinctis obeunda: sed revertentibus post laborem quod honestius quam uxorium levamentum?* See Boatwright 2003, 264; Woodman and Martin 1996, 303.

33. See, e.g., Marshall 1984.

34. For Plancina, see FOS #562.

35. *Nec Plancina se intra decora feminis tenebat, sed exercitio equitum, decursibus cohortium interesse....* The notorious case must be behind the senatorial debate of 21 already discussed.

36. Cass. Dio 59.18.4; Tac. *Hist.* 1.48.2; cf. Plut. *Galba* 12; FOS #273; and Phang 2001, 368–69.

acts reported by Suetonius is that the emperor often displayed to the soldiers his wife Caesonia, riding by his side in armor (*Calig.* 25.3).[37] An even more flagrant example in Tacitus is that of Triaria, the wife of Lucius Vitellius and sister-in-law of Aulus Vitellius who was emperor briefly in 69. Triaria is adduced early in 69 as "ferocious beyond female" as she pushed her husband to murder (*ultra feminam ferox*, Tac. *Hist.* 2.63–64); she later appears charged with actually entering civil strife girded with a sword, proudly partaking in Tarracina's brutal sack in 69 (Tac. *Hist.* 3.77.6–7).[38] In a later incident, Pliny the Younger reports that Gallitta, the bride of a military tribune, had committed adultery with a centurion in an unnamed province.[39] Pliny, who assisted Trajan at deliberations in 107, remarks that considerations of a woman's involvement with a Roman soldier, as well as the husband's reluctance to divorce his wife, gave the case greater than usual significance. Trajan made sure to mention military discipline in his judgment (Plin. *Ep.* 6.31.4–6). Similarly, among Juvenal's vilified women in the public sphere figures one who dared to speak as an equal to uniformed generals (*Sat.* 6.400–401).

Unquestionably the presence of unarmed relatives at or near the front could distract a commander and soldiers: for example, in the Parthian campaign of 62 Lucius Caesennius Paetus dangerously thinned Roman forces by assigning troops to protect the fort in which he had hidden his wife and son.[40] Yet such considerations, and the literary censure of women among troops, did not prevent women from accompanying their male relatives abroad. M.-Th. Raepsaet-Charlier (1982) counts eighty-nine senatorial women with Roman administrators and others in the first and second centuries CE, split almost equally between eastern and western provinces, and in 1950 H.-G. Pflaum counted twenty-seven equestrian women in the provinces between 150 and 300 CE.[41] Many of those women must have lived innocently while their husbands served Rome abroad, for we know of them mainly through perfunctory honorary inscriptions or incidental

---

37. See Woods 2014, 27–34 on the puzzling and uncorroborated note.

38. The reports discredit Aulus Vitellius (Benoist 2015, 273–74), and stress the perversion of civil war, as do the other women noted in Tacitus' narrative of this strife. Verulana Gratilla, who was caught up in the siege of the Capitoline in Rome, is said to "have followed the call to war rather than her children or her family" (Tac. *Hist.* 3.69). For Triaria, see FOS #765. Tarracina is now Terracina, Italy.

39. See also FOS #400; Shelton 2012, 173–75, although she does not focus on military aspects.

40. Tac. *Ann.* 15.10.3. Cassius Dio reports an incident in which Roman troops were imperiled by having women and children with them: 56.20.2 and 56.22.2. See Phang 2001, 363.

41. Pflaum 1950, 303–306; see also Marshall 1975, 121 n.63.

Imperial Women Abroad, and with the Military

references.[42] The ideal is exemplified by the unnamed wife of a prefect of Egypt, a woman Seneca the Younger lauds as never seen in public, never admitting a provincial into her house, never asking anything of her husband, and never allowing anything to be sought from her—in short, leaving no imprint whatsoever on the province Seneca claims she lived in for sixteen years with her husband (*Helv.* 19.6).[43] Such restraint and reserve are the lauded virtues of Matidia the Elder and other imperial women (see Ch. 1). Yet such a life may strike modern observers as lonely and tedious. Wooden tablets from Vindolanda attest a charming exchange between two women living with their officer husbands in northern Britain. This includes a birthday party invitation around 100 from Claudia Severa, the wife of a commander of a military unit presumably along Britain's Stanegate road, to her friend Sulpicia Lepidina, the wife of the prefect of a cohort at nearby Vindolanda (near modern Bardon Mill in northern England). The obvious warmth of Severa's words suggests the regular seclusion of Roman women in such settings.[44]

The varied evidence leads E. Phang to argue that, by the middle of the second century, women were more or less accepted in military situations.[45] This seems plausible in fact. The mother of Pertinax accompanied him to Germany when he was the commander of the German fleet in the late 160s (HA, *Pert.* 2.3; her name is unknown). The wife and sons of Clodius Albinus, the governor of Britain and one of the contenders in the civil war after Commodus' assassination on the final day of 192, reportedly were with Albinus in 197 in his final battle against Septimius Severus in Lugdunum. There they were killed and thrown into the Rhône (HA, *Sev.* 11.9). Although these anecdotes come from the notoriously unreliable Historia Augusta, they do suggest that elite women routinely went abroad with their serving male relatives. If Phang's understanding of the wider context is correct, military associations for imperial women in the late second and early third centuries were not as disreputable as reported. But traditional prejudices echoed even in this period, as we saw earlier in the words of Cassius Dio, Herodian, and Ulpian. Militarism and war were tremendously important throughout Roman history and even more so in the Severan period. It is instructive to see how imperial women figured in this historical and cultural evolution.

---

42. For example, Suet. *Calig.* 25 notes Lollia Paulina was with her husband Publius Memmius Regulus in his province Moesia (much of modern eastern Europe) when Caligula recalled and married her (Ch. 2). Syme 1986, 177 discusses Memmius' position.

43. See Raepsaet-Charlier 1982, 60.

44. See https://romaninscriptionsofbritain.org/inscriptions/TabVindol291 and its links.

45. Phang 2001, 142–96, canvassing some two thousand soldiers' epitaphs from the Latin West, finds the rate of commemoration of "de facto" marriages increasing in the second century.

The following discussion of imperial women's travel outside Rome is chronologically arranged. Although clearly Julia Mamaea, the latest imperial woman I discuss, was harshly criticized for "meddling" with the army, the scarce evidence leaves unclear whether the *Augustae* occasioned more opprobrium than others venturing outside the capital with husbands, sons, or fathers. In any case, the survey reveals that over time ever more imperial women accompanied their husbands and other male relatives on trips outside of Italy.

Julio-Claudian women and the first century of the principate

Explaining the rarity of women on imperial journeys in the Augustan and early Julio-Claudian periods, H. Halfmann argued that although the reasons and means for Roman emperors to travel outside of Italy did not differ from those of Hellenistic kings and Republican Roman administrators, traveling in the provinces in the company of wives and children did break with Republican tradition.[46] Epigraphic evidence tempers his statement, revealing that a dozen or so Roman women were publicly portrayed in statue groups alongside their husbands or fathers (or both) who served as provincial governors or some other official in Rome's eastern provinces. The dated examples begin about 100 BCE.[47] As we saw earlier, however, Halfmann is right in pointing to women's travels and activities abroad as a source of tension.

Octavia, the sister of Octavian and (fourth) wife of Mark Antony, is an interesting instance of that tension. Octavia traveled numerous times to Athens to be with Antony after they wed in fall 40, and she is even reported as participating in military negotiations. In contrast with Fulvia, Antony's third wife, Octavia had an unsullied reputation.[48] Octavia spent the winters of 39/38 and 38/37 with Antony in Athens, and returned to that city for part of 35 (App. *B Civ.* 5.76; Plut. *Ant.* 33). Heralded as a bridge between her husband and her brother, two of the triumvirs, in 35 Octavia improved their relationship before finally returning to Italy with all Antony's children.[49] Antony's respectable pretext for sending Octavia "home" was to keep her from danger as he went to the Parthian War; the

---

46. Halfmann 1986, 90.

47. Hemelrijk 2005a, 309; Rose 1997, 7; Kajava 1990; Marshall 1975, 115.

48. See, e.g., Cluett 1998, esp. 83–84. Octavia received extraordinary tributes in Athens, as on what seems to be an altar honoring her and Antony as benefactors (see Kajava 1990, 104–109).

49. See Plut. *Ant.* 31, 64; App. *B Civ.* 5.93–95; Cass. Dio 58.54.3; Plut. *Ant.* 35. For the traditional role of women as mediators, see, e.g., Cluett 1998, 78–79 with references.

Imperial Women Abroad, and with the Military   259

rumors held that he wanted to devote himself to the foreign queen Cleopatra (Cass. Dio 58.54.5). Once back in Rome Octavia withdrew from public, despite the grant to her and Livia in 35 that included the right of public statues (see Ch. 1 and Ch. 6). She lived first in Antony's home. Upon her divorce in 32 she transferred to her brother's household, to die there in 11 BCE. Were her early prominence and boldness abroad, which included her presence even in a military camp, effaced by her later domestic devotion and retreat from the public eye for the last two decades of her life?[50]

Livia, some ten years younger than Octavia, has a less definite presence outside of Rome.[51] Little supports the bland statement by Tacitus' Drusus cited earlier, that Livia often traveled with Augustus to the west and the east (Tac. *Ann.* 3.34.6). Seneca the Younger places her with Augustus in Gaul when she urged him to declare clemency for the conspirator Cornelius Cinna (Sen. *Clem.* 1.9.2–6). Seneca's vague chronology suggests a date between 16 and 13 BCE, when Augustus is attested otherwise in the province. Cassius Dio's version of this event, however, both suggests that the conversation took place in Rome and differs otherwise from Seneca's briefer report (Cass. Dio 55.14.1).[52] Another journey with Augustus, in 9 BCE to Ticinum in northern Italy (modern Pavia), was familial, since they went to meet the funeral cortège of her son Drusus the Elder as it moved from Gaul to Rome (Sen. *Consol. ad Marc.* 3.2). The assembled evidence is so slight that many scholars doubt that Livia accompanied Augustus on official trips outside of Rome and Italy.[53]

Nor does Livia have distinct connections with the military. Other than her possible and unnamed depiction between what may be Tiberius and Drusus the Elder on the repoussé bronze sword sheath from the Rhine (Ill. 7.1), Livia's visual images do not connect her with the military.[54] Some have inferred that in

---

50. For the Porticus Octaviae (23–11 BCE) see Ch. 5. Octavia's obsequies may express her double image: although she received two funeral orations in the Forum Romanum, a curtain hid her corpse from public view while displayed in the Temple of Julius: Cass. Dio 54.35.4–5.

51. Although she went to Sicily and Greece with her first husband Tiberius Claudius Nero in 40–39 BCE: Tac. *Ann.* 5.1.1; Suet. *Tib.* 6.2.

52. See Adler 2011a, esp. 135–38; Barrett 2002, 318–19; Halfmann 1986, 162.

53. E.g., Badian 1984, 167–68; Halfmann 1986, 90; Brännstedt 2015. Barrett 2002, 36–38, however, tenders that Livia joined Augustus on his eastern trip of 22–19 BCE to Sicily; Sparta, Athens, Delphi; Samos; Pergamum, Ilium, and elsewhere in Asia; and Syria. Her marriage advice to Salome, Herod the Great's sister (Joseph. *AJ* 17.1.1), does not have to show the two women met personally in the East.

54. Barrett 2002, 258–65 conveniently compiles nonsculptural images of her.

Rome she publicly garlanded the triumphal chariots of men in her family,[55] but the evidence is much clearer for her hosting elite women and sometimes men at banquets for Tiberius' victories in 9 and 7 BCE. The feasts would be far from the actual triumphal route and its thronged soldiers.[56] As mentioned earlier, Cassius Dio stresses in his obituary of Livia that she never entered a camp, or the senate or public assemblies, even though she tried to run everything by herself (Cass. Dio 57.12.3).[57] We have already discussed and dismissed Drusus' report of her travel with Augustus, which in the context of the senatorial debate implied her accompaniment of her husband also in military zones.

Younger Julio-Claudian women are better attested in the provinces with male relatives, perhaps because many trips occurred before their husbands (or sons) became emperor. Julia the Elder, Augustus' daughter, traveled with her husband Agrippa for at least part of his eastern tour from about 16 to 13 BCE. One story from that trip, that she was left nearly to drown in the flooding Scamander River by the negligent citizens of Troy (Roman Ilium, Greek Ilion; modern Hisarlik, Turkey), indicates the danger travel could pose even for an imperial woman.[58] A number of statuary installations in the Greek East honor Agrippa, Julia, and sometimes their children as well. For example, at Thespiae (near modern Thespies, Greece) a statue group featured Julia, Agrippa carrying the baby Agrippina [the Elder], Gaius, and Lucius. Yet Livia was also portrayed in the group sculpture, and no one assumes she also traveled with the family.[59] After Agrippa's death in 12 and Julia's ensuing marriage to Tiberius, Julia went north to be near her new husband as he campaigned in the Balkans. She apparently stayed in Aquileia, the port city on the Adriatic far from the fighting where she bore a son who died in infancy (Suet. *Tib.* 7.3).[60] Antonia the Younger similarly accompanied her husband Drusus the Elder, Tiberius' brother, as Drusus supervised Gaul after 13

---

55. Flory 1998, 491; Brännstedt 2015, 39–40; Thakur 2014, 199. Contra Barrett 2002, 35.

56. Cass. Dio 55.2.4–5 and 55.8.2; see Ch. 5.

57. See HA, *Heliogab.* 12.3, where Elagabalus is said to bring his grandmother (Maesa) with him every time he entered the camp or the senate house. The author stresses that never before had a woman entered the senate so that she might be called upon to give her opinion.

58. Nicolaus of Damascus, *FGrH* 2 A no. 90 Fr. 134; Levick 2007, 55.

59. Rose 1997, 13–14 and his Cat. No. 82; see Halfmann 1986, 163–66, and Fantham 2006, 61–63. Livia's presence suggests to Fantham (2006, 62) that the children were not with their parents abroad.

60. Probably around 10 BCE: Fantham 2006, 82–83.

BCE. Antonia may have stayed in the city of Lugdunum, where she gave birth to Claudius in 10 (Suet. *Claud.* 2.1; Sen. *Apocol.* 6).[61]

The presence of imperial women with their husbands helped represent the entire imperial family in the provinces. Much of the evidence notes their giving birth abroad: as we saw in Ch. 3, such events were cause for state celebration. The close-knit imperial family is idealized in Drusus' remarks that Tacitus reports in the senatorial debate of 21. Drusus the Younger extols his own marriage and "dearest wife," the mother of their many children, and stresses the novel necessity for leaders (*principes*) to visit the far reaches of the empire more frequently (Tac. *Ann.* 3.34).[62] In pursuit of that ideal Drusus evidently stretches the truth when he off-handedly exclaims about Livia's frequent travels with Augustus to the east and the west.

Nonetheless, the example of Germanicus' wife Agrippina the Elder suggests the ambivalence with which imperial women's travel and activity in the provinces could be viewed, at least in the capital city.[63] Agrippina accompanied Germanicus in 14 CE when he went to the Rhine region with special authority. There she gave birth to Agrippina the Younger in Oppidum Ubiorum (now Cologne, Germany).[64] Around that time their son Caligula, only two or so years old, was sent from Rome by Augustus to join the family abroad (Suet. *Calig.* 8). Slightly later, pregnant again, Agrippina was essential in Germanicus' suppression of a rising mutiny of the soldiers: to shame the insurgents, Germanicus put his pregnant wife and toddler son on show to the troops before sending them away, weeping and surrounded by other wives (Tac. *Ann.* 1.40–44).[65] In this scene Tacitus' objectification of Agrippina the Elder as her pregnant abdomen underlines the importance of fertility in the new dynastic rule (*uterum*, Tac. *Ann.* 1.40.3).[66]

---

61. This was the trip on which Drusus died (see earlier on Livia at Ticinum). Kokkinos 2002, 13 speculates from an inscription that Antonia was with Drusus in Spain 14–13 BCE.

62. *de matrimonio suo; nam principibus adeunda saepius longinqua imperii . . . ab uxore carissima et tot communium liberorum parente.* As often with Tacitus, the words ring hollow in light of later history: see Ch. 2 on Livilla.

63. McHugh 2012 argues that Tacitus deliberately presents Agrippina ambiguously. Agrippina may have followed the example of her mother Julia with Agrippa in 15–13 BCE.

64. In Agrippina the Younger's honor Claudius had the site renamed Colonia Claudia Ara Agrippinensium: Tac. *Ann.* 12.27.1.

65. Tacitus' note of the pitiful crowd of friends' wives escorting Agrippina corroborates my earlier point about the presence of wives with their commanding husbands. Cassius Dio 57.5.5–7 less plausibly has the insurgent soldiers seize Agrippina and Caligula and retain the boy before experiencing a change of heart.

66. The couple's second surviving daughter, Drusilla, was born in the territory of the Treviri on the lower Moselle River: Suet. *Calig.* 8.

Although Agrippina the Elder did not return to the scene of that mutiny despite the remorseful soldiers' pleas, she did stay in the province.[67]

In a later famous incident now known only from Tacitus,[68] Agrippina the Elder stopped panicked Roman soldiers from destroying the Rhine bridge at Vetera. Here she reportedly was alone while distributing clothing and medicine to Roman troops fleeing Arminius' forces to the north. Tacitus replicates Tiberius' reactions to news of her control at the rout: "These were not simple concerns.... There was nothing left for generals, when a woman visited the maniples, approached the standards, attempted handouts, carried around the son of the commander in a soldier's garb—as if no intent! . . . Agrippina was now more powerful among the army than legates, than commanders; an insurgency, which the name of the emperor had not thwarted, had been checked by a mere woman!" (Tac. *Ann.* 1.69).[69] Here the mention of the commander's son outfitted as a common soldier accentuates the inversion of norms.

Despite the criticism of Agrippina's field activities attributed to Tiberius,[70] shortly later she accompanied Germanicus on a voyage east in an extraordinary command after 17 where he similarly combined military and civil duties. She and their children were presumably with Germanicus on his meandering voyage that included Dalmatia, Nicopolis (near the site of the Battle of Actium), Athens and Euboia (in modern Greece); the island Lesbos; the Asian cities and sites Assos,[71] Perinthos, Byzantium, Ilium, Colophon, and Klaros, with excursions to the Black Sea and the north Aegean island Samothrace; Rhodes; Syria, Armenia, Cappadocia, Commagene, and Cyrrhus (in Syria); and the Egyptian Alexandria, Canopus (twenty-five kilometers east on the coast of Egypt), Memphis, and Thebes (near Luxor).[72] On Lesbos Agrippina the Elder gave birth to Julia Livilla,

---

67. Tacitus reports Agrippina's proud assertion to Germanicus that she was descended from *divus* Augustus and equally ready for perils (*Ann.* 1.40.3). Germanicus dissuaded her because of her pregnancy and the winter season, although Caligula remained in the camp (Tac. *Ann.* 1.44.1). See also Suet. *Calig.* 8.3 and Cass. Dio 57.5.6. Severy 2003, 86 interprets some glass-paste military decorations as portraying Agrippina the Elder (her fig. 9.3, from the Musée romain d'Avenches), and Germanicus with three small children (her fig. 9.2, from Vienna, Kunsthistorisches Museum AS.XI.b.8).

68. Tacitus cites Pliny the Elder for the information.

69. In the same chapter Tacitus notes she took on the tasks of a leader (*munia ducis*).

70. I am less interested in attributing the thoughts to Tacitus or Tiberius (as, e.g., McHugh 2012, 77; Barrett 2005a, 306) than in the unease they reveal about women with the army.

71. Halfmann 1986, 169, citing *IGRRP* 4.251 (= *I.Assos* 26) that documents Caligula was first with Germanicus in the city (modern Behramkale, Turkey).

72. For this itinerary, see Halfmann 1986, 168–70. Our map omits Armenia, east of Cappadocia.

Imperial Women Abroad, and with the Military

her youngest daughter (Tac. *Ann.* 2.54.1).[73] In 19 she was at Germanicus' death-bed in Antioch, Syria, whence she accompanied his ashes back to Italy and Rome (Tac. *Ann.* 2.70–72, 2.75).

As opposed to her time in Germany, Agrippina's eastern trip in 17–19 occasioned no reproach.[74] Similarly, we hear no criticism of her sister-in-law Livilla for traveling with Drusus the Younger in Illyricum; instead, as we have seen, Drusus idealizes her company in his senatorial speech of 21 (Tac. *Ann.* 3.34.6). A decade later Julia Livilla, the third surviving daughter of Germanicus and Agrippina the Elder, may have been with her husband Marcus Vinicius when he was governor of Asia, but the oblique evidence suggests no criticism of it.[75]

Although Halfmann assumes that the senatorial debate of 21 smoothed the way for the wife of an emperor to join him on trips outside Italy, he notes only one later example from the first century, Statilia Messalina.[76] Her travels with Nero to Greece in 66–67 are known merely by the Arval Brethrens' sacrifice for the safety, well-being, and return of Nero and "his wife Messalina."[77] The overall picture is complicated by historical circumstance: Caligula, Claudius, and Nero traveled outside Rome only briefly or infrequently,[78] and Galba, Otho, Vespasian, Titus, and Nerva were unmarried while ruling. Given both the importance Domitian accorded the military, and his wife Domitia's filiation from the renowned general Gnaeus Domitius Corbulo, it may seem surprising that she is not attested with Domitian in Germany in 83 and 88/89, or in an area near but safe from fighting when he went to Dacia in 85/86, perhaps in 89, and again in 92–93. Halfmann has stressed, however, the poor documentation for Domitian's travels.[79]

---

73. See Rose 1997, 25 n.55. Halfmann 1986, 168 dates the birth to early 18.

74. In part this may be because Munatia Plancina has the reprehensible role with the military (Tac. *Ann.* 2.55.6). Marshall 1975, 112 notes Agrippina the Elder as the only "military" woman who escapes direct censure.

75. *I.Pergamon* 497 = OGIS 474, suggesting 37–39.

76. Halfmann 1986, 91.

77. *pro salute et reditu*: Halfmann 1986, 91, 173–77; *CFA* 30 = EDCS-21300886. Levick 2007, 55 questions Statilia Messalina's presence on this trip.

78. I do not infer from Cass. Dio 59.22.8, as Halfmann 1986, 92 (cf. 170–77), that Caligula's sisters Agrippina and Julia Livilla were with him in Gaul and Germany in 39/40.

79. For the Dacian trip of 85/86, see Cass. Dio 67.6.3. In 92–93 the emperor may have stayed in Carnuntum, modern Petronell, Austria. Halfmann 1986, 181–84 notes that the Carnuntum stay is assumed from the epitaph of an imperial litter-bearer named Titus Flavius Celsus (*CIL* III 4497 = EDCS-28800238). Domitia was apparently estranged from her husband in 82–83: see Ch. 2.

264   IMPERIAL WOMEN OF ROME

Yet the increasing significance of a woman's presence with her imperial husband outside of Rome may clarify an event involving Aulus Vitellius, one of the imperial contenders during the civil strife of 68–69. In 69 Vitellius' wife Galeria Fundana left Rome with her young son to meet her husband after the first battle of Bedriacum (near Calvatone, northern Italy).[80] Although by then Vespasian had been acclaimed as emperor by troops in the east, the victory over Otho's troops seemed to herald Vitellius as the new emperor of Rome and Italy. Galeria Fundana's presence with Vitellius, with their young son as well, may have symbolized a return of imperial order after the chaotic ten months following Nero's suicide.[81]

Imperial women on tour during the second century

Much better data attest imperial women outside of Rome in the second century, and near its end Faustina the Younger is specifically linked to the military as well. But we should not overstate the evidence, since armed forces and travels were not integral to imperial women's reputations until the Severan women of the third century.

The women of Trajan's family were meaningful for his rule (see, e.g., Ill. 3.8), celebrated although not named in Pliny's *Panegyricus* originally delivered in 100 (*Pan.* 83–84), and with even greater prominence after 112, when Trajan's sister Marciana was consecrated immediately at her death and her daughter Matidia the Elder honored as *Augusta*.[82] Plotina and Matidia the Elder are attested with Trajan abroad in the latter part of his reign.[83] When he went east for the Parthian War of 113–117 his wife and niece were with him, to judge from their presence in Selinous when he died in 117 while returning to Rome.[84] Plotina's attendance at Trajan's deathbed is key to her alleged orchestration of Hadrian's succession (see

---

80. Tac. *Hist.* 2.60, 64; 3.70; Cass. Dio 65.1.2ᵃ, 65.4.2, 65.22.1. For Galeria Fundana see FOS #399. The son was about seven years old.

81. A similarly symbolic gesture by Vitellius may have been greeting his mother, Sextilia, as *Augusta* as soon as he entered Rome in 69, even before his acclamation as Augustus (Tac. *Hist.* 2.89–90; Kuhoff 1993, 247 discounts Sextilia as Augusta; contra FOS #715; Kienast 2017, 99).

82. In late August 112: Temporini 1978, 194–202. See Ch. 1.

83. Temporini 1978, 189, however, doubts that Plotina and his sister Marciana were with Trajan during the Dacian Wars of 101–102 and 105–106.

84. HA, *Hadr.* 4.10 and 5.9; Cass. Dio 69.1.4. For the route to Syria, from Rome via Brundisium to Athens, then to Asia, then Antioch, see Birley 1997, 65, 68. For the return in 117, when Plotina, Matidia, and the praetorian prefect Attianus transported Trajan's remains from Selinous to Antioch for inspection before going to Rome, see Birley 1997, 79–80. Birley 1997, 79–80 and Temporini-Gräfin Vitzthum 2002, 202–203 assume that Matidia the Elder's two

Imperial Women Abroad, and with the Military

Ch. 1). The many rumors of *favor Plotinae* even include her suborning someone to pretend to be her husband, whose death was not yet known, so as to announce the imperial adoption of Hadrian from Trajan's sickbed in Selinous (HA, *Hadr.* 4.10). Did Plotina's freedom outside of Rome's "proper" confines encourage such rumors?[85] If the stories were of that period, they had no effect, however: after her return to Rome with Trajan's ashes she lived there blamelessly or at least unnoted, and in the early 120s her authority with Hadrian was publicized in Athens in a dossier of letters concerning the Epicurean school (see Ch. 5).

Less controversy marks the voyages of Sabina with Hadrian. Sabina, Trajan's grand-niece through Matidia the Elder, wed Hadrian around 100 when she was probably in her mid-teens and he a decade older. Over time their marriage reportedly soured.[86] Their rumored discord seems not to have inhibited Sabina from accompanying Hadrian on his two long provincial trips.[87] The evidence is not overwhelming for the first trip, across the Roman world in 121–125. The *Historia Augusta* places, apparently in Britain, the minor scandal of Suetonius' and Septicius Clarus' excessive familiarity with the emperor's wife (*Hadr.* 11.3), and Hadrian is attested in the province in 122.[88] If we can conclude from this that Sabina was in Britain and the incident took place while abroad, it may be that the unpredictability of travel encouraged greater informality within the entourage, or rendered such rumors more plausible.[89] The evidence is much stronger for her with Hadrian during his long trip of 128–132 that was spent chiefly in Rome's eastern provinces. In 130 Sabina had inscribed on the left foot of one of the Colossi of Memnon in upper Egypt that she twice heard it "sing." Her companion Julia Balbilla attests to at least two visits there with Sabina in three charming and erudite poems also engraved on the Colossus. In one Balbilla refers to

---

daughters, Matidia the Younger and Sabina (both older than twenty-five), were also present, Sabina perhaps with her husband Hadrian.

85. I note, though, that similar "deathbed" rumors attend the transfers of power connected with Tanaquil, Livia, and Agrippina the Younger (Bauman 1994), all occurring in Rome or Italy.

86. See Ch. 4, and Brennan 2018, esp. xvi–xvii, 32.

87. For Hadrian's journeys overall, see Halfmann 1986, 188–210. Birley 1997, 63–64, 85 assumes that Sabina was with Hadrian in Athens in 111/112 (before his accession), and again possibly in Byzantium in 118.

88. Birley 1997, 115, 139; on p. 170 he cites an inscription from near Smyrna (modern Izmir, Turkey) that may suggest Sabina was with Hadrian here in 124, at the end of the journey.

89. Birley 1997, 125 sees Sabina's travel with Hadrian "advisable" because "she could have posed a threat if she had been left at Rome, the focus of potential intrigue."

266 IMPERIAL WOMEN OF ROME

her as "fair Sabina," a "queen" with a "lovely form."[90] Less clear evidence, Sabina's image on two Palmyrene *tesserae* (banquet entry tickets, which do not usually depict historical persons), hints that Sabina accompanied Hadrian to Palmyra in 129 or so.[91] Hadrian's attention to court protocol, attested both in the dismissal of Suetonius and Septicius Clarus and in his reported statement that he would have divorced Sabina had he not been emperor (HA, *Hadr.* 11.3), suggests that by now imperial women were expected to be part of the court abroad.

Imperial women figure in travels of Marcus Aurelius and Lucius Verus,[92] but not during the reign of Antoninus Pius. Pius, who is famous for not leaving Italy while emperor, reportedly said that the entourage of an emperor, no matter how sparing, burdened the provincials (HA, *Ant. Pius* 7.11). Other imperial concerns came to the fore after he died in 161 and his successors became involved in wars to the east and north. In 164 Lucilla, the daughter of Faustina the Younger and Marcus Aurelius, was sent from Rome to Asia to marry Lucius Verus, then leading another Roman war against the Parthians (HA, *Verus* 7.6). As the fourteen-year-old Lucilla traveled east from Rome she was accompanied by an older woman, perhaps Verus' sister Ceionia, as well as by Marcus Vettulenus Civica Barbarus, the half-brother of Verus' father. Verus traveled west from the front along the Euphrates to wed her in Ephesus.[93] This is our only known instance of an imperial woman traveling without husband or father, although the Historia Augusta stresses that Marcus Aurelius accompanied her until malicious gossip, that he wanted to conduct the war himself, turned him back (HA, *Marc.* 9.5). His familial affection may also account for the presence of other children, including at least one girl, with him in Pannonia in the early Marcomannic wars between 169 and 172.[94]

90. Bernand and Bernand 1960, no. 32 (Sabina); nos. 29–31, cf. 28, for Balbilla's poems. See Brennan 2018, 125–37 for this episode. Hadrian seems not to have been with them at the statue.

91. See Birley 1997, 231.

92. Levick 2007, 54–56 and Temporini-Gräfin Vitzthum 2002, 253 assume that in 178 Marcus was joined on the Danube by his daughter Lucilla and her second husband, Tiberius Claudius Pompeianus; Marcus' son Commodus and new wife Crispina; and Marcus' great-niece Annia Faustina and her husband. Contra, e.g., Hekster 2002, 39.

93. HA, *Verus* 7.7 and *Marc.* 9.4; Levick 2014, 70–71; Birley 1987, 131. Levick's note, that Marcus Aurelius wrote to Asia's proconsul and others not to come meet his daughter, may suggest financial concerns.

94. See *AE* 1964, 181 = EDCS-12800323, and Halfmann 1986, 92. According to Levick's calculation of the number, order, and dates of birth (and death) of the children (2014, 115–18), this may be Vibia Aurelia Sabina. Augustus sent Caligula to join his father and mother on the German front when the boy was two.

Imperial Women Abroad, and with the Military   267

Faustina the Younger, Marcus Aurelius' wife, spent most of her adult life pregnant or with young children; although such circumstances had not inhibited Agrippina the Elder, Faustina is not attested outside of Italy with her husband until late in her life. The military setting of both her known trips, however, may seem surprising for someone so identified with domesticity and the family (see Ch. 3). In 174 Faustina and a three-year-old daughter were with Marcus Aurelius in winter quarters at Sirmium (now Sremska Mitrovica, Serbia); informed there about a complicated case against the sophist and Athenian senator Tiberius Claudius Herodes Atticus, mother and daughter alike sided with Herodes' opponents (Philostr. *VS* 2.1.11; the case was not resolved).[95] (This northern trip is also associated with her title *mater castrorum*, as we shall see.) In 175 Faustina went with Marcus Aurelius to quell the revolt of Avidius Cassius in Syria and Egypt, but fell ill and died in Halala in southern Cappadocia (near the Cilician Gates in Turkey). The city was renamed Faustinopolis in her honor (HA, *Marc.* 26.4, 26.9).[96] Slightly later Aelius Aristides prides himself for giving a speech before the emperor and the "princesses" in Smyrna (*Or.* 42, p. 338 Keil or K, 14). If Halfmann's date of late summer 176 for the stop in Smyrna is correct, Faustina was already dead.[97]

Faustina the Younger is also the first imperial woman to receive the official honorific title Mother of the Camps (*mater castrorum*).[98] According to the Historia Augusta, Marcus Aurelius gave her the title because she had been with him in the summer camp during the Marcomannic Wars (HA, *Marc.* 26.8). Cassius Dio's more dramatic notice ties the epithet to a hard-fought Roman victory over the Quadi during those wars, even though it does not place Faustina at or even near the fighting. The extant text credits divine intervention for the Roman success, a torrential rainstorm often called "The Miracle of the Rain God' after which Marcus received a seventh imperial acclamation from his troops and Faustina was given the title Mother of the Camps (Cass. Dio 71.10.5). The battle is usually dated to 174.[99] Her honorific epithet appears perhaps on an inscription, and more definitely on coin issues centrally struck during her lifetime and posthumously.

---

95. The event is dated to 174 by Fittschen 1999, 5. See also HA, *Marc.* 26.8; Cass. Dio 71.10.5.

96. For the date, see Levick 2014, e.g., 135. For the journey, evidently directly from the Danube, see Levick 2014, 87; Hekster 2002, 37. Levick's sympathetic account of Faustina's death (87–89) discounts allegations of Faustina's complicity in the revolt. Cf. Hekster 2002, 34–36.

97. Halfmann 1986, 92, 213.

98. Levick 2014, 78–79 downplays the innovation of Faustina's title. Hemelrijk 2012 explores "maternal" titles for non-imperial women.

99. For the literary accounts, see Boatwright 2003, 258–59.

ILL. 7.2 *Aureus* of Marcus Aurelius from 176–80, depicting Faustina the Younger, Mother of the Camps. © The Trustees of the British Museum.

The posthumous issue illustrated in Ill. 7.2 shows (obv.) a portrait of Faustina and the legend "For *diva* Faustina Pia," backed by the image of a veiled female on a low chair holding a scepter and (in her right hand) a globe surmounted by a phoenix. She looks toward three standards, and the legend "For the Mother of the Camps" completes the scene.[100] The seated figure is identified as Faustina the Younger, and the coins demonstrate the publicity accorded this novel acclamation for an imperial woman. The title Mother of the Camps aptly evokes Faustina's domestic and maternal role as well as Rome's increasing military pressures.[101] The unease about her being in both camps, so to speak, may be seen in her rumored connection to the revolt of Gaius Avidius Cassius, discussed and dismissed in Ch. 3.

Third-century imperial women: The Severans

Military associations are more pronounced for Severan imperial women,[102] although the poor quality of much of the evidence in this period makes it difficult

---

100. Ill. 7.2 is *RIC* III, Marcus Aurelius no. 751: DIVAE FAVSTINAE PIAE and MATRI CASTRORVM. Issues of *aurei* and *sestertii* were struck late in her life (*RIC* III, Marcus Aurelius nos. 1659–62); others, in *aurei*, *denarii*, and *sestertii*, are posthumous (*RIC* III, Marcus Aurelius nos. 1711–12, nos. 742 and 748–49, nos. 751–53). For discussion, including of the controversial inscription from Carnuntum, see Boatwright 2003, 257–58.

101. Speidel 2012, esp. 128, emphasizes the latter topic.

102. Commodus' wife Crispina is called *mater castrorum* on one centrally struck issue (*BMCRE* IV, Commodus no. 418). She is not known to have traveled outside Rome during her unhappy and childless marriage from 178 to ~192, and Commodus himself did not travel after returning from Pannonia to Rome in 180: Halfmann 1986, 216.

Imperial Women Abroad, and with the Military

to discern developments clearly. The literary sources center on emperors and usurpers and do not often specify women.[103] Other material is often undated or mutilated because of the *damnatio memoriae* accorded Plautilla, Julia Soaemias, Julia Maesa, and Julia Mamaea.[104] Yet as we see, the Severan women often traveled outside Rome in the company of the emperor. Further, the honorific Mother of the Camps (*mater castrorum*) is frequently found on inscriptions and coins naming Julia Domna and/or Mamaea, with some three hundred examples for Domna.[105] When first awarded Domna in the mid-190s, the title probably heralded the close association to the Antonines that Septimius Severus claimed.[106] It has unmistakable military overtones, however.[107] General acceptance of these imperial women's association with Rome's rank and file may be suggested by a fragmentary votive inscription originally raised by an army unit in Lambaesis, Numidia, in 218.[108] Although the remaining text was violently altered by chiseling out Maesa's and Soaemias' names, presumably after the murder of Elagabalus and the *damnatio memoriae* of Soaemias, Maesa's title of "Mother of the Camps and of the Senate" was left undamaged. This is the more striking because, as we discover, Maesa may never have been granted the title officially.

Julia Domna, the earliest of the Severan women, clearly broke with earlier imperial women who had generally not traveled with their consorts, and her example was followed by other women of her family. Domna accompanied her husband Septimius Severus on trips throughout his reign, even close to war zones

---

103. E.g., Levick 2007, 39 notes that Domna has no mention in the long description Cassius Dio gives of Severus' way of life (77.17.1–3).

104. See Kettenhofen 1979 and Nadolny 2016. Sanctions against Maesa and Mamaea lasted only from 235 to 238 (Kienast 2017, 169 and 174), but damaged inscriptions were not repaired.

105. Kettenhofen 1979, 79–83, 154. For coins see, e.g., *RIC* IV.1, Septimius Severus nos. 563A, 567, 569 (*aurei*), 563B, 567–68 (*denarii*), 860 (*sestertius*), 880–81, 884 (*asses, dupondii*); see also *RIC* IV.1, Septimius Severus nos. 648A (*denarius*), and 650 (medallion). Langford 2013, 36–37, however, stresses that very few such coins were found in military contexts.

106. See Levick 2007, 42–45 and figs. 3.3 and 3.4.

107. See, e.g., Ghedini 1984, 7. Against the argument that the title was not aimed at the soldiers (Langford 2013, e.g., 21), see Nadolny 2016, 45–46, with references.

108. *CIL* VIII 2564 = ECDS-69500195: *[Pro salute d(omini) n(ostri) Imp(eratoris) Caes(aris)] / [M(arci) Aureli Antonini] / [Pii Fel(icis) Aug(usti) pont(ificis) max(imi)] / p(atris) p(atriae) trib(unicia) pot(estate) co(n)s(ulis) [3] / procons(ulis) divi Magni / Antonini fil(ii) divi Pii / Severi nepot(is) et [[I[ulia]e]] / [[Maesae [Aug(ustae) avi]ae Aug(usti)]] / [[n(ostri)]] matris castrorum / et senatus [[[et Iuliae So]]] / [[[aemiadis Bassianae]]] Aug(ustae) /Augusti [[n(ostri)]] / dupl(ic)ari(i) leg(ionis) III Aug(ustae) P(iae) V(indicis) [[Anto]] / [[ninianae]] devoti Numini / maiestatique eorum / regressi de expedition / ne felicissima orien/tali /.* The apparently gratuitous damage to the record of Maesa's familial identification echoes that of Crispina at Commodus' death, noted in Ch. 2. Lambaesis is eleven kilometers southeast of Batna, Algeria.

270   IMPERIAL WOMEN OF ROME

(193–211),[109] and she continued the practice with her son Caracalla while he was sole emperor (211–217).[110] In the latter guise she is said even to have assumed supervision of Caracalla's correspondence (Cass. Dio 77.18.2; see Ch. 1). Further, Domna's sister Maesa and Maesa's two daughters Soaemias and Mamaea were integral to the imperial court, with Maesa explicitly said to have "lived in the palace" the whole time Domna was *Augusta*. That note, and other evidence discussed here, indicate that the three women went abroad with Domna and her husband and sons.[111]

Closely allied with husband and son, Domna shares the military reputation of Septimius Severus and Caracalla, renowned for their attention to the army and warfare (e.g., Cass. Dio 76.15.2). Most well known is her title Mother of the Camps (*mater castrorum*), awarded her after Septimius Severus crushed his rival Pescennius Niger in 193 and moved belligerently against the Parthians.[112] For his exploits he earned his fifth through seventh acclamations as Triumphing General or *Imperator*, and by 196 and her return to Rome Domna received the honorific title Mother of the Camps.[113] Domna later received other grandiloquent titles, such as Mother of the Senate and the Fatherland, which frequently appear with Mother of the Camps on inscriptions dating after Septimius Severus' death in 211.[114]

Rather than narrate the travels of Julia Domna with Septimius Severus and Caracalla,[115] I simply list the locales Domna is attested as visiting and at what date. In no case other than at the death of Caracalla in 217 is Domna known

---

109. As a new bride she reportedly joined Septimius Severus as he governed Gallia Lugdunensis, giving birth to Caracalla in Lugdunum in 188 (HA, *Sev.* 3.8–9) and to Geta in Mediolanum in 189 (modern Milan, Italy; HA, *Geta* 3.1). See earlier for wives abroad with serving husbands.

110. After Septimius Severus' death in 211 Caracalla, Geta, and Domna went together from Eboracum (York, England) to Rome, where they stayed until after Geta's death later that year. See Halfmann 1986, 216–19 for the voyages of Septimius Severus; 223–25 for Caracalla. Birley 1999, 169, with Levick 2007, 54. Levick 2007, 41 notes for Domna's travels: "Wherever she went, her presence stressed the dynastic aspect of Severus' rule, and so its permanence."

111. The extended house is reminiscent of that of Trajan and Hadrian. See earlier and Ch. 3.

112. When Severus went on the offensive over the Euphrates, Levick 2007, 41 assumes that Domna remained in Syria, and "very likely [went] to her home town [Emesa]."

113. For the date, see Nadolny 2016, 45–47 and Levick 2007, 42; *BGU* 2, 362, 13, lines 15–16 shows it was bestowed on 14 April and celebrated annually.

114. E.g., *mater senatus et patriae et castrorum.* For the dating, see Kettenhofen 1979, 86–97; Langford 2013, 134–36. *CIL* XIV 2255 = EDCS-05800221, from Albanum outside Rome (now Albano Laziale), dates to 198–211 CE.

115. Levick 2007, 35–56 well describes the travels.

Imperial Women Abroad, and with the Military

to have journeyed without the men of her family, even though she presumably would not have been at the front during armed conflict. I have put into brackets the more uncertain trips.[116]

- Summer 197: east to the Parthian War, sailing from Brundisium to Syria.[117] Levick (2007, 48) presumes that Domna (and the children) stayed in Syria, perhaps visiting her home city Emesa.
- 199: Seacoast of Syria Palaestina; Pelusium; Alexandria.[118]
- 200–202: Syria, including Antioch by early 202 (HA, *Sev.* 16.8).
- 202: back to Rome by April 202 via Tyana (modern Kemerhasar, eastern Turkey), Nicaea (modern Iznik, Turkey), Thrace, Moesia, and Upper and Lower Pannonia.[119]
- Late 202 or early 203: to Africa with Caracalla's wife Plautilla and her father Plautianus, perhaps wintering in Lepcis Magna, the ancestral home of Septimius Severus (now Khoms, Libya); more securely in Thamugadi (about thirty-five kilometers east of Batna, Algeria) and Lambaesis (not far away).[120]
- Late 203–208: in Rome.[121]
- 208–211: in Britain; based in Eboracum from 209. Our only insight into her pastimes is her reported and surely fictitious conversation with the wife of the Caledonian Argentocoxus, comparing Roman and British sexual mores (Cass. Dio 77.16.5).

---

116. Levick 2007, 46 sees as probable Domna joining Septimius Severus north against Clodius Albinus, a journey that would have taken them through Pannonia, Noricum, and Raetia up to Upper Germany before to Lugdunum to the decisive battle against Albinus on 19 February 197.

117. HA, *Sev.* 15.2.

118. Levick 2007, 49–50 and 183 n.93 discusses the difficult evidence, including HA, *Sev.* 17.1–4 and Cass. Dio 75.13.1. On the precedent of Sabina and Hadrian, Levick assumes that Domna and the boys accompanied her husband up the Nile to the border of Ethiopia.

119. Levick 2007, 51, remarking that the route through the Balkans is uncertain other than Viminacium (near modern Kostolac, in eastern Serbia); it may have included Carnuntum.

120. Levick 2007, 51; *AE* 1954, 153 = EDCS-20100195 (Thamugadi; names of Plautilla, Plautianus, and Geta chiseled out; Domna entitled *mater castrorum*); *AE* 1957, 123 = EDCS-13600193 (Lambaesis, a votive for the health and safety of Septimius Severus and Domna); *CIL* VIII 2557 = EDCS-20600003 (Lambaesis, a vow for the imperial family; names of Plautilla, Plautianus, and Geta chiseled out; Domna entitled *mater castrorum*). Levick 2007, 51–53 cf. HA, *Sev.* 18.3 presumes that she did not assist the fighting against "most warlike tribes."

121. In 203 the emperor's ten-year anniversary (*decennalia*) was celebrated; in 204, the *Ludi Saeculares* in which Julia Domna and her niece Julia Soaemias participated (see Ch. 4). In 205 Plautilla was repudiated at the fall of her father Plautianus (Hdn. 3.10.8; see Ch. 2).

272 IMPERIAL WOMEN OF ROME

- 211: back to Rome after Septimius Severus' death in Eboracum.[122]
- [213: north with Caracalla to Germany.][123]
- 214–216: with Caracalla to the east; attested in Perinthos (on the European coast of the Propontis) and the coast of Bithynia and Asia;[124] then inland to Galatia, Cappadocia, and the Cilician Gates; then to Tarsus some twenty kilometers inland from the Mediterranean;[125] back to Antioch and Laodicea (now Latakia, Syria), with a side trip to Pelusium and Alexandria.[126]
- April 217: in Antioch, where she learned of the accession of Macrinus as emperor after her son's murder by troops between Carrhae and Edessa (now Harran and Urfa, Turkey).[127] She died in Antioch soon after; her body was later transferred to Rome and interred by her sister Julia Maesa in the Mausoleum of Hadrian (Cass. Dio 79.2.3).

Reminiscent of the Trajanic era but significantly different in that the ties were now through the empress rather than the emperor, other imperial women lived "in the palace." They presumably were widowed when they became part of the imperial entourage. Julia Maesa participated in the imperial court during much of her sister Domna's supremacy.[128] Maesa's two daughters, Julia Soaemias and Julia Mamaea, apparently also traveled with the court along with their sons.[129] They were together in Syria when Caracalla was assassinated in 217 (see, e.g., Hdn.

---

122. Levick 2007, 85–86, linking the imperial trip with a renovated road system in Gaul.

123. Williams 1902, 288; Levick 2007, 100, arguing from the *acta* of the Arval Brethren and a relief in Warsaw. For Caracalla's trips overall, see Halfmann 1986, 223–25.

124. The evidence is often merely suggestive, as the bases of statues set up for the emperor and his mother in 214 at Pergamum (but see Højte 2000), and thus debatable: Schöpe 2014, 191 places in Nicomedia an event noted by Cassius Dio (78.18.3), but Levick 2007, 95 in Rome.

125. Levick 2007, 101–102; for the bases, see Habicht 1969, 33–38, nos. 12–16.

126. In 215 and 216: Cass. Dio 77.20.1, 77.22–23; Hdn. 4.8.6–9.8, 4.9.3–8; HA, *M. Ant.* 6.2–3; Levick 2007, 102; Halfmann 1986, 224–25.

127. Levick 2007, 102–104, with Cass. Dio 79.23.1 for Antioch; Caracalla had been farther east for about a year: Halfmann 1986, 225, with HA, *M. Ant.* 7.1, Hdn. 4.13.3–8; *Epit. de Caes.* 21.6.

128. See Hdn. 5.3.2 and Cass. Dio 79.30.3 for "the palace." We might recall the scandal surrounding Julia Titi's life in Domitian's palace (Ch. 2).

129. Close ties among Severan women seem corroborated by Soaemias' participation in the Ludi Saeculares of 204 as *clarissima femina* (Ch. 4) and by the statue of "Julia Maesa, sister of Julia Augusta," attested with ones for Septimius Severus and his sons (presumably also Domna) and erected 198–211 CE by the Palmyrenes at an entrance to their agora: Yon 2012, 189 no. 192.

5.7.3).[130] Their presence in the court was so well known, according to Herodian and the Historia Augusta, that in 218 Maesa could plausibly tell the eastern troops that while the family all lived in the palace Caracalla had sex with both of her daughters, alike fathering Elagabalus and Severus Alexander (then fourteen and ten years old; Hdn. 5.3.10; see HA, *Macrinus* 9.1–10).[131]

Perhaps because of constant attendance on Septimius Severus and Caracalla, both so frequently at war, the Severan women are also reported in the presence of Rome's armed men. All accounts of Elagabalus' accession depict Maesa turning directly to the troops in Syria in 218 in her plot to bring her older grandson to power (see earlier). Cassius Dio reports that Maesa and Soaemias, Elagabalus' grandmother and mother, were in the actual skirmishes precipitating Macrinus' death and Elagabalus' acclamation:

> [The insurgents against Macrinus were fighting weakly and were about to turn tail,] had not Maesa and Soaemias, who were already with the boy [Elagabalus], leaped down from their chariots and, rushing among the fleeing men, held them back from further flight by their lamentations, and had not the boy himself been seen by them [the rebels against Macrinus] dashing along on horseback. (Cass. Dio 79.38)

Although not "girt with a sword" themselves, the two women are depicted as had been Fulvia (Cass. Dio 48.10.3–4), another woman key in Rome's political and military upheavals. The story is suspect[132]—inter alia, Elagabalus is never noted otherwise in battle—but it emphasizes the women's incursion into male spheres.

---

130. Kienast 2017, 168: Maesa was in Rome when Caracalla died 8 Apr 217. This would make more implausible the stories of her involvement in Elagabalus' accession (16 May 218): Orbis (http://orbis.stanford.edu/orbis2012/#; accessed 26 June 2018) calculates the fastest summer route from Rome to Emesa as just under a month.

131. To use the names by which they are now known; Herodian calls them Bassianus and Alexianus (e.g. 5.3.3). Cassius Dio generally credits two men with the revolt (n.1 of this chapter). Analyzing two inscriptions, Arrizabalaga y Prado 2010, 230 holds that Elagabalus was born in or near Rome; if so, this supports the whole family's presence in the court. The women's attachment to the imperial house was informal, to judge from the fact that at Domna's death Macrinus sent Maesa from Antioch to her ancestral estates (presumably in Emesa) rather than confiscating her wealth and goods (Hdn. 5.3.2): Schöpe 2014, 185.

132. See Kettenhofen 1979, 28, and Scott 2018, 97, who remarks that "the inversion of gender and age roles in Dio's account highlights the perversity of Elagabalus' impending accession."

274 IMPERIAL WOMEN OF ROME

After the eastern legions acclaimed Elagabalus emperor in 218, the family made its way back to Rome with the new princeps. The journey took a year.[133]

Maesa and Soaemias thereafter are not attested outside of Rome, but Elagabalus himself did not leave the capital city during his short and tumultuous reign. Instead, the sources emphasize the two women's assumption of Elagabalus' political duties, and their appearance in unusual spaces:[134] for example, Maesa and Soaemias flanked Elagabalus as he adopted his cousin Severus Alexander, presumably in the senate (Cass. Dio 80.17.2). Military associations resurface only in the location at the Praetorian Camp of the murders of Soaemias and Elagabalus in early March 222, implying that she entered the camp with her son for a last appeal to the guard. Soaemias' corpse reportedly endured many of the same humiliations as her son's, and both she and he suffered a *damnatio memoriae*.[135] Maesa survived, presumably because she had helped orchestrate the coup that brought Severus Alexander to power. She lived some two years into the reign of this grandson, and the circumstances of her death are unknown.[136]

Although some scholars hold that both Maesa and Soaemias were acclaimed Mother of the Camps, close examination of the wretched data convinced E. Kettenhofen in 1979 either that the titles are unofficial (appearing, e.g., on Alexandrian but not centrally struck coins), or that they never actually existed but have merely been inferred on fragmentary inscriptions.[137] He knew of only one document unequivocally attesting the title for Maesa, a votive inscription raised in 218 by troops of the Third Legion Augusta for the new emperor Elagabalus, his grandmother, and his mother upon return from the Parthian war (the inscription from Lambaesis mentioned earlier).[138] On the stone the title Mother of the

---

133. June 218–July/August 219. See Halfmann 1986, 230–31: besides Antioch, other known stops are in Prusias ad Hypium (near modern Düzce, Turkey) and Nicomedia (modern Izmit, Turkey), after which the route went through Thrace, Moesia, and the two Pannonias.

134. HA, *Heliogab.* 4.1–4, 12.3, 15.6. Kettenhofen 1979, 63–68 notes the (inconsistent) stress of the HA on women: HA, *Heliogab.* 4.1 and 18.3 recount that Soaemias accompanied Elagabalus into the senate; HA, *Heliogab.* 12.3 and 15.6 name Maesa instead. Kettenhofen thus discounts the reports entirely, arguing for Soaemias' slighter influence over Elagabalus than Maesa's.

135. Cass. Dio 80.20.2 and 80.21.3; Hdn. 5.8.8–10; HA, *Heliogab.* 17. Kemezis 2016, 363 notes that the HA does not place Soaemias at the praetorian camp. Varner 2001, 48–49 discusses memory sanctions.

136. Kienast 2017, 169 proposes tentatively that she died before 3 August 224. Kemezis 2016, 378 discusses the confused links of Maesa to Elagabalus' death and Severus Alexander's accession.

137. Kettenhofen 1979, 146–48 (Maesa), and 152–55 (Soaemias). Accepted by, e.g., Nadolny 2016, 45 and Kienast 2017, 169, who also holds (as Kettenhofen) that Maesa was never officially titled Mother of the Senate (*mater senatus*).

138. *CIL* VIII 2564 = EDCS-69500195.

Imperial Women Abroad, and with the Military

Camps was used for Maesa but not for Soaemias. Kettenhofen argued, however, that the inscription's votive character and unique status discount it as evidence for an official grant of the title to Maesa.[139] Two years later a second mutilated inscription surfaced in Africa attesting Maesa as Mother of the Camps. Its now incomplete list of names includes Julia Maesa Augusta, "Mother of the Camps and of the Army and Mother of the Augusta [Soaemias] and Grandmother of our Emperor [Elagabalus]."[140] Although we cannot unequivocally prove Maesa was officially titled Mother of the Camps, the two inscriptions suggest she had a military image as well as a maternal one. Notably, the second stone calls her "Mother of the Camps and of the Army" (*mater castrorum et exercitus*).[141]

Julia Mamaea, Maesa's second daughter, is the last imperial woman we treat in this chapter.[142] Since her son Severus Alexander ruled for thirteen years, from 222 to 235, and is typically depicted as a "mother's boy,"[143] more evidence attests her than her mother or sister Soaemias. Much of it is hostile, and her death and *damnatio memoriae* from 235 to 238 make it difficult to obtain an accurate picture. Even so, she has more clear ties to Rome's military than did previous imperial women.

Sometime after the accession of her son but before the death of Maesa in 224 Mamaea officially received the title Mother of the Camps,[144] and this and related titles appear on coins and inscriptions.[145] Three inscriptions label her Mother of the Army.[146] No literary source explains the grant of such

---

139. Kettenhofen 1979, 145–46.

140. *AE* 1981, 902 = EDCS-09001607: *mater castrorum et exercitus et (mater) Augustae et avia Augusti nostri*, with Thamugadi as its find spot; EDH005477 has its find spot between Thamugadi and Lambaesis. The (restored) names of Alexander Severus, his mother, and his wife date the inscription between 225 and 227. Speidel 2012, 137 accepts Maesa as *mater castrorum*.

141. Speidel 2012, 137 stresses the differences between *castra* and *exercitus*.

142. No data for Sallustia Orbiana, Severus Alexander's wife from 225 to 227 (Ch. 2), pertain to this chapter. For Mamaea, see Kosmetatou 2002 (credulous of the literary sources).

143. E.g., Hdn. 6.1.10; HA, *Alex. Sev.* 14.7, 26.9, 60.2.

144. Kettenhofen 1979, 157; see, e.g., *CIL* VI 32544 = EDCS-18500063.

145. Kettenhofen 1979, 156 counts 120 epigraphic attestations, of which 25 are honorary ones; only a third can be dated. See also *RIC* IV.2, Severus Alexander no. 690 (an *as*; Julia Mamaea Augusta with rev. *mater castrorum*) and no. 691.

146. *CIL* XIII 8017 = EDCS-11100242 (Bonna), *mater eius* [Severus Alexander] *et exercitus*; *AE* 1934, 33 = EDCS-16000564 (Lambaesis), *mater Augusti nostri, castrorum et exercitus*; *AE* 1972, 682 = EDCS-09700373 (Gholaia, now Abu Nujaym, Libya) *mater exercitus*: see Speidel 2012, 137 n.42, who also lists three inscriptions honoring Octacilia Severa, the wife of Philip (r. 244–245), as *mater castrorum et exercitus*.

276 IMPERIAL WOMEN OF ROME

titles to her. This contrasts with Faustina the Younger and Domna, whose parallel honorific is linked to proximity to their husbands' military exploits (see earlier). After Mamaea's *damnatio memoriae* in 235 her name but not her title *mater castrorum* was often erased from inscriptions, as in a statue base from the camp Ulcisia Castra in Pannonia Inferior (modern Szentendre, Hungary).[147] This, like the spread of the honorific to include "Mother of the Army," suggests growing acceptance of a martial persona for imperial women. A further indication of Mamaea's "military" identity is the honorific name "Mamiana Severiana Alexandriana" for the Seventh Cohort of Rome's paramilitary firefighters.[148]

Mamaea reportedly dominated her son's reign (e.g., Hdn. 6.1–2), and in 229 her title expanded to "Mother of the Emperor and the Camps and the Senate and the Fatherland" (*mater Augusti et castrorum et senatus et patriae*).[149] By 231 she set off with Alexander Severus for the Persian War.[150] Mamaea is the first imperial woman who is reported as actively influencing military decisions in a war zone:[151] according to Herodian, she deterred her son from personally going into the field against the Persians, and this set back morale and the war itself (Hdn. 6.5.9). Although she must have returned to Rome with Severus Alexander to witness his "false" triumph in 233 (HA, *Alex. Sev.* 56.1), there is no record of her personal participation in the procession. She is noted later with her son on campaign against German threats. Again she is credited with active interference in military decisions, fatally this time. Her push to conclude the German war allegedly triggered a mutiny in which disloyal soldiers hunted down mother and son in the camp's imperial quarters.[152] By spring 235 Mamaea and Severus Alexander had been murdered in Mogontiacum in the violence that brought Maximinus Thrax to power and ended the Severan dynasty. Mother and son suffered a *damnatio memoriae*, although Mamaea's was rescinded in 238.[153]

---

147. *CIL* III 3639 = EDCS-26600561, raised in 229 by the Cohors I Milliaria Nova Severiana Surorum Sagittaria. Her name is wholly or partly erased in most of the 120 examples in Kettenhofen 1979, 156.

148. See *CIL* VI 3008 = EDCS-19400008. Williams 1904, 74 notes this as a unique distinction.

149. Kettenhofen 1979, 159–60.

150. For the evidence, see Halfmann 1986, 231.

151. For Tiberius' anxiety about Agrippina the Elder in a war zone, see earlier in this chapter.

152. Mutiny: HA, *Max.* 7.5 and *Alex. Sev.* 63.5; deaths: Hdn. 6.9.6–8, cf. HA, *Max.* 7.4.

153. Kienast 2017, 174.

Conclusion

The crescendo of information for military involvement by Domna, Maesa, Soaemias, and Mamaea should not obscure other questions. What were some of the effects of imperial women's travel with their husbands, to peaceful or to militarized locations? Literary sources explicitly or indirectly blame the women for undermining Roman martial virtue and success at sites of armed conflict. Mamaea's "meddling" sparked military setbacks and a mutiny deadly for herself and her son the emperor; the presence of Maesa and Soaemias in battle led to the accession of Elagabalus, Rome's most reviled emperor. Two centuries earlier, Agrippina the Elder's stand at the Rhine bridge kept Tiberius up at night although it had halted Rome's panicking troops. But little beyond such dramatic scenes attests imperial women among armed soldiers. Imperial women could not fight or give military orders: their presence in camps must have been more worrisome than comforting to the emperors, no matter what Tacitus' Drusus averred in the senate in 21 (Tac. *Ann.* 3.34.6). If women were near conflicts fought far from Rome, Italy, or a safe city, troops could be diverted and Roman military advantage lost, if not destroyed.[154] While traveling with husbands in the extended imperial Augustan and early Julio-Claudian family, Julia the Elder, Antonia the Younger, and Agrippina the Elder bore children in sites away from the front.

We have more illuminating information about imperial journeys to peaceful areas, though little of it directly notes women.[155] In some known instances, as for Hadrian's visit to Egypt in 130,[156] arrangements began a year in advance, with locals lining up donkeys and other pack animals, suckling pigs and grown ones, wine and water, dates, barley, oil, olives, and other goods. In addition to food and drink, security had to be assured: during the visit in ca. 129 to Palmyra of Hadrian and possibly Sabina, the arrangements overseen by the clerk (*grammateus*) Malês included ones for the army.[157] The emperor and his entourage, traveling by horse- or mule-drawn vehicles, would usually be accommodated in villas and houses of

---

154. We noted earlier Caesennius Paetus' dangerous thinning of Roman forces by protecting the fort in which he had hidden his wife and son in the Parthian campaign of 62 (Tac. *Ann.* 15.10.3).

155. Millar 1977, 28–40, surveys from the late Republic into the fourth century. Van Minnen and Sosin 1996 discuss Egyptian preparations for a planned visit by Severus Alexander and Mamaea.

156. Millar 1977, 44, with earlier references.

157. Yon 2012, 153–55, no. 145 = *IGRRP* 3.1054.

278

the local elite (see Cass. Dio 69.7.4).[158] The advent and departure of the imperial train were important events at which the local population and visitors from farther afield could see the emperor.[159] Games and displays were staged for imperial entertainment, as when Aelius Aristides spoke before Marcus Aurelius and his "princesses" in Smyrna, probably in 176.[160] Lavish sacrifices impressed the gods, the imperial court, and cities' inhabitants and visitors.[161] No wonder Antoninus Pius is said to have considered the entourage of an emperor burdensome to provincials, no matter how parsimonious it was (HA, *Ant. Pius* 7.11).

Imperial travel in the provinces accomplished many purposes, most importantly making "Rome" accessible and visible to those under Rome's rule. Just as an emperor on the move could hear more petitions and personal pleas from Romans and others than one in Rome,[162] imperial women could manifest in person to Roman citizens and subjects the strength and continuity of the imperial family. Within fifteen years of Augustus' consolidation of power his daughter Julia accompanied her husband Agrippa in the East. A few years later the same woman, Augustus' only child, traveled north with her third husband Tiberius, to give birth in Aquileia. Although the child died in infancy, Julia's precedent would be followed by Antonia the Younger, who gave birth to Claudius in southern France in 10 BCE, and by Agrippina the Elder, who bore children in Gaul, Germany, and the Aegean islands a generation later. Their presence helped establish the novel imperial regime outside of Italy. Livia seems not to have traveled with Augustus to the provinces, perhaps remaining at home according to traditional gender norms. Despite such conventions, inscriptions and other documentary evidence reveal growing numbers of non-imperial women with their husbands and other family relatives as they served abroad.

By the second century, when Trajan, Hadrian, and other emperors themselves hailed from outside of Italy, imperial women attended emperors abroad without obvious censure. Sabina's travels with Hadrian are a particular high point, with the relatively abundant documentary evidence of the era attesting her even at leisure at the Colossi of Memnon. The mounting military demands besetting Marcus Aurelius, Lucius Verus, and later emperors meant that Faustina

---

158. Millar 1977, 30; 32 notes especially for the third century and later stopping-houses (*mansiones*). We should not assume that princeps and wife were in the same house, much less the same bedroom.

159. Millar 1977, 31.

160. Marcus Aurelius also heard Hadrianus of Tyre in Athens: Philostr. *VS* 2.19.

161. Millar 1977, 36.

162. See, e.g., Millar 1977, 31, 36–38.

Imperial Women Abroad, and with the Military

the Younger, Lucilla, and others who accompanied their imperial husbands and other relatives ventured farther abroad, a few even into contact with the troops. By the time of Julia Mamaea, the ideal separation of women from the military and armed conflict Caecina advocated so strongly in the senate in 21 was long forgotten. Septimius Severus had rescinded the ban against soldiers contracting legally binding marriages. Nonetheless, as with Mamaea, a women's alleged meddling with Rome's soldiers still provided a convenient scapegoat for defeats and setbacks.

The paltry evidence mostly discloses imperial women in the company of other women: Sabina and Balbilla, Domna and the wife of the Caledonian chieftain. But the few glimpses we get of imperial women at courtly events, like Faustina the Younger overhearing Herodes Atticus or "the princesses" listening with Marcus Aurelius to a brilliant speech by Aelius Aristides, suggest that travel enabled imperial women to make contacts with men as well as women. Was Plotina so deeply interested in the Epicurean sect in Athens, for which she intervened with Hadrian in the early 120s, because she had actually spent time with its adherents when in Athens en route with Trajan to the Parthian war in 113/114?[163] Did Julia Domna have a personal contact in Athens from an otherwise unattested stop there with Septimius Severus in 197, so that a later embassy from the city found a ready ear when petitioning her in the imperial court in Syria?[164]

Nonetheless, imperial women abroad have few reported roles other than Domna's supervision of Caracalla's correspondence and the cluster of derogatory references for Severan women interfering with soldiers and strategic plans. Many continued their "wifely duties" in the provinces by giving birth and offering comfort to their husbands. An essential female role is stressed by the development of the honorific titles of Mother of the Camps and Mother of the Army. Imperial women could offer a discreet but ready ear when an emperor was distressed or simply annoyed by a problem or a petitioner, as allegedly Livia to Augustus about Cinna, or Faustina the Younger to Marcus Aurelius about Herodes Atticus. Sabina in Egypt, and undoubtedly others there and elsewhere, participated in sightseeing.[165] Most, however, must have performed courtly duties: appearing at banquets, sacrifices, and processions.[166] At such functions, to extrapolate from

---

163. See Ch. 5 and van Bremen 2005.

164. See Kettenhofen 1979, 109; Levick 2007, 49.

165. See, e.g., Levick 2007, 49, 180.

166. As perhaps Sabina in Palmyra, if I interpret correctly her image on the Palmyrene *tesserae* as denoting her presence at a festive meal in the city.

our evidence, imperial women appeared alongside their officiating husbands, fathers, or sons, but never served as proxy for the emperor himself.

Overall, the growing ritual of the imperial court, the increasing importance of the imperial family as a whole, and the mounting necessity for the emperor personally to inspect the provinces and armies encouraged imperial women to travel more as the principate evolved. Regardless of discomfort and danger, such as the flooding Scamander River that Julia the Elder experienced, provincial travel with the imperial court offered excitement, a change of scene, and new conversations. Given how restricted imperial women's movements were in Rome, the opportunity may have been welcome.

8

Conclusions: Agency and Constraints

MY INVESTIGATION OF Rome's imperial women did not end as I had anticipated. I had hoped that the process of assembling and analyzing the scattered evidence about the women at the emperor's side would reveal fresh material and unusual angles about individuals from Octavia and Livia, Octavian's sister and the wife he married in the 30s BCE, to Julia Mamaea, Severus Alexander's mother murdered with him in 235 CE. Given the legendary intrusiveness of the Severan imperial women, I also imagined tracing over time increasing visibility and influence for imperial women that would resonate or contrast with the evolution of the principate itself. But no new evidence has come to light. Moreover, no simple development can be traced: the prominence and apparent authority of imperial women varied in different eras and even within lifetimes, as for Livia. Nonetheless, at its conclusion my comprehensive treatment clearly does provide novel perspectives on imperial women and the principate.

A particularly persistent problem has been the inadequate documentation, which for my subjects is more biased even if slightly more copious than for other women in the Roman world. The complete lack of first-person memoirs now complicates disentangling personal agency and historical contingency. Is Sabina now so colorless because she bore no child to Hadrian? Because she conformed to the retiring model of her mother Matidia the Elder, great-aunt Plotina, and other women of the Trajanic court? Was she simply introverted, or incompatible with her husband, the center of attention? In a different example, had Julia Maesa, Julia Soaemias, and Julia Mamaea not lost or divorced their husbands early, would we hear that they advanced Elagabalus and Severus Alexander so boldly? Without new data about individuals' personal choices it is important to assess imperial women within the history of the entire principate. This can render less idiosyncratic any one act noted by an ancient author or documentary source.

Imperial Women of Rome. Mary T. Boatwright, Oxford University Press. © Oxford University Press 2021.
DOI: 10.1093/oso/9780190455897.003.0009

The varied material and their contexts surveyed in this book do allow some conclusions. The evidence as a whole reveals imperial women's general powerlessness and silence that starkly contrast with the numerous arresting anecdotes emphasizing their abuse of resources, influence, power, and privilege. It is true that Octavia and Livia were granted distinct privileges in 35 BCE. But these were dependent on Octavian's struggle for supreme power in the late Republic. Further, the most unusual—some protection from insult like that traditionally granted to Roman tribunes—did not outlast the Augustan era. The other two—the right of public statuary in Rome that had previously been strictly inhibited for women, and special financial dispensations allowing the two more control of their wealth than the average woman—soon were widespread among the elite, although we cannot discern exactly how they spread.

The "tribunician" protection, the privilege most like a political right exercised by men, is barely attested even for Octavia and Livia, and it is never cited for a later imperial woman. The second permission, of public statues, corresponded with cultural trends developing in Italy and already evident in the Greek East, where for generations Hellenistic queens and—since around 100 BCE—even Roman women had been identifiably depicted with their families. Nonetheless, as discussed in Chs. 4 and 6, statues, busts, and other identifiable portraits of imperial women seem to have been created and disseminated slowly, with relatively few known before the reign of Caligula. Further, throughout the principate images of imperial women were usually exhibited with ones of the emperor and the imperial family, not in isolation. This was as true for freestanding and large-scale relief images in bronze and marble as it was for numismatic portraits of living women, for the latter at least until the Flavian period. Finally, imperial women's images often lack distinct individual traits, although that impression is tempered by the variety of standardized body types used for female portrait statues, by the modeling of Roman female portraits on Greek deities and Hellenistic queens, and by low numbers of surviving identifiable large-scale portraits of imperial women.

The third right awarded Octavia and Livia in 35 BCE, bolstered for Livia by a senatorial grant of the right of three children in 9 BCE, gave these first two imperial women financial autonomy. Although these are recorded as special grants, they coincide with Roman women's greater de facto control of their own resources apparent already in the late Republic. The new legal capacity associated with the *ius trium liberorum*, or "right of three children," was part of Augustan social legislation. We never hear specifically that later imperial women had the right of three children, although varied documentary evidence reveals their vast possessions. Imperial women had their own conveniences and separate domiciles, such as the Baths of Agrippina on the Viminal Hill and the domiciles of Matidia the Elder, Matidia the Younger, and Sabina also in Rome's northeast quarter. Ownership of brickyards seems especially productive for Domitia Longina, Faustina the Younger, and others of the late first and second centuries. Some women are known to have enjoyed lavish estates in the provinces, as Julia Maesa in "Phoenicia" (that is, Syria) where she went after the death of her sister Julia Domna in 217.

It is just as important to note, however, imperial women's reported use of their wealth. At the beginning of the principate they more obviously displayed their resources, not only in Lollia Paulina's self-adornment of emeralds, gold, and pearls worth 40 million sesterces so roundly condemned by Pliny the Elder, but also in public donations in Rome. Octavia and Livia are associated with a number of large, functional structures in the capital city: the Porticus Octaviae, Porticus Liviae, Temple of Concord, Macellum Liviae, Livia's restoration of the Temple of Bona Dea, and her co-sponsored Temple of *divus* Augustus. These were complemented by smaller donations of statues and public games for *divus* Augustus, at least by Livia. The scope of such munificence is impressive. But the phenomenon of public building is not restricted to these imperial women. Evidence is mounting that elsewhere in Italy wealthy women had already begun to finance public buildings, and in Rome itself Agrippa's sister Vipsania Polla completed the spacious Porticus Vipsania along the Via Flaminia after 7 BCE. Notably, controversy attends Octavia's and Livia's public works in Rome. Strabo, whose lifetime spanned Livia's own, straightforwardly attributes to Augustus' wife and sister "beautiful and useful structures" in the city, particularly in the Campus Martius (Strabo 5.236), and their contemporary Ovid holds that in restoring the Temple of Bona Dea Livia was emulating Augustus (Ov. *Fast.* 5.157–58). By the next century, however, Suetonius and other authors credit Augustus with the buildings, relegate Livia to a subordinate role, or obscure women's responsibility in some other way.

The inference that women's public use of their own resources was increasingly frowned on finds support. When Tacitus notes Tiberius' deep resentment of Julia Augusta's name above his own on their dedication of a statue of *divus* Father Augustus in 22 CE (Tac. *Ann.* 3.64.2), are we hearing anxiety that imperial women's public works might eclipse those of the emperors? It is almost exclusively documentary evidence, not historians or other writers, that reveals public building in Rome by women after Octavia and Livia. After the Julio-Claudians, it seems, lavish displays of imperial women's wealth and agency were considered inappropriate and perhaps even subversive. Tellingly, our best testimony for the wealth of late first- and second-century imperial women are the brickstamps attesting their ownership of brick factories on the outskirts of Rome. Who could see those stamps once built into a wall?

No imperial women after Octavia and Livia are known to have received any special political or legal grants or powers. As Ulpian put it in the early third century, "An emperor is free from the laws; although an empress (*Augusta*) is not, emperors nonetheless give her the same privileges that they enjoy" (Ulp. 13, ad l. iul. et pap., Dig. 1.3.31). His comment was made on the topic of the Julian and Papian law that enabled women to inherit and make decisions about their resources. It exposes the significance of Augustus' social legislation for women, but also exposes that the princeps controlled an imperial woman's privileges. He undoubtedly structured her other activities as well.

In the new Augustan principate various factors tempered the prominence Octavia and Livia accrued from their special rights of 35 and 9 BCE and from the esteem of their public donations in Rome. Octavia's professed home life and maternal duties kept her "at home." Other than possibly meeting Augustus at his *adventus* in Rome in 24 BCE, neither she nor Livia appeared in the expanding imperial public ceremonies like the celebration of the *Ludi Saeculares* of 17 BCE. Neither were named on central coins, and they were rarely depicted in statuary. Was their (self-)effacement encouraged by Augustus as a way to emphasize the revival of traditional values and roles? Or was it their own choice and predilection, or that of the growing imperial court? Later imperial women are hardly ever observed in Rome's public rituals other than imperial funerals; those noted, especially Messalina and Agrippina the Younger, are remarked upon disparagingly.

The establishment of the principate precluded any return to the good old days, even if such an idealized past ever existed in the volatile and self-contradictory late Roman Republic. The new political regime developed under Augustus and his collaborators, so clearly centered in the imperial house that was known by 14 CE as *domus Augusta* and by 33 as *domus divina*, undeniably increased the standing of the women integral to that family. The importance and visibility of the imperial family—and imperial women—continued to rise. The honorific *Augusta* was accorded ever more frequently. Women like Poppaea, Domitia Longina, and Faustina the Younger were celebrated for fecundity even if their children died before their time. By the reign of Hadrian, sisters, nieces, and mothers-in-law of emperors were consecrated by the senate. The Antonine and Severan imperial families were even more celebrated in public life, with first Faustina the Elder and Antoninus Pius and then Faustina the Younger and Marcus Aurelius exemplifying Roman conjugal harmony. Faustina the Younger was honored as Mother of the Camps; later imperial women more frequently had this and other "maternal" titles.

Julia the Elder, Antonia the Younger, Livilla, and other wives of Augustus' and Tiberius' stepsons and sons accompanied their husbands on their service to Rome outside of Italy. The women's presence helped manifest the imperial house

Conclusions: Agency and Constraints   285

in the provinces and at the front, but it also opened the women to unusual circumstances, like the mutiny Agrippina the Elder courageously faced in Germany. Such travel had apparently been suspect. From Caligula through Nerva imperial women stopped traveling with their emperor (if he himself even left Italy), even though non-imperial Roman women continued to accompany husbands to service abroad. Imperial women's journeys resumed in the second and early third centuries, when spiraling concerns took emperors outside of Italy much more frequently than in the early principate. Imperial women were part of the stately entourages abroad, even along the borders. How fraught their presence was, especially when among the military, is reflected in the stories of Plotina's orchestration of Trajan's "deathbed" adoption of Hadrian, of Faustina the Younger's encouragement of Avidius Cassius' revolt, and of the rebellion Maesa and Soaemias triggered so as to bring the young Elagabalus to the throne.

Opportunities seem much more restricted in the capital city. The relative lack of information for imperial women's activities in public in Rome is surprising even in the general indifference of literary sources. The counterexamples are Julia the Elder and Messalina, whose purported wanderings in the city correspond with their indictments of outrageous lack of sexual self-restraint. Less opprobrious evidence for imperial women in public attests to mostly the Julio-Claudians, with Livia and Agrippina the Younger particularly noted. Livia, the prototypical imperial woman, is shown a few times, often in funerary venues. But Cassius Dio and other sources maintain she demurred from entering the senate house, military camps, the Forum Romanum, and even the popular Campus Martius. In banquets and other appearances Livia's connections with elite women are stressed, an undercurrent of much of the documentation about her. Agrippina the Younger, in contrast, is noted—usually disapprovingly—in multiple areas and activities aberrant for a woman: going up the Capitoline Hill in a special carriage, seated on a dais near Claudius while being venerated by a captive Briton chief, and moving to join the young emperor Nero as he was about to receive Armenian ambassadors. In such scenes Agrippina is the only one of her sex, not only accentuating her transgression but also fitting the malignant jealousy she reportedly exhibited toward Lollia Paulina, Domitia Lepida, and other women. Later imperial women are almost never noted or shown in public in Rome, other than Julia Domna and Julia Soaemias, who are reported in religious functions. In light of women's traditional concerns with religion it is striking that earlier imperial women do not appear in such activity, not even Julia Augusta, Antonia the Younger, or Agrippina the Younger while priests of imperial cult in the capital city.

The history of imperial women's involvement with the law exposes their difficulties and dangers, especially during the Augustan and Julio-Claudian periods. Many were exiled and otherwise punished. In numerous cases, most strikingly those of Augustus' own daughter and granddaughter, we do not even know exactly what law or laws the women violated. Charges often included adultery but shaded into treason and sorcery. As with Caligula's sister Julia Livilla, Domitia Lepida, and some others, the responsibility for the legal difficulties is assigned to the jealousy and greed of Messalina or Agrippina the Younger, muddying the picture. A number of women were not even tried in a public court, but rather "domestically" by the emperor and head of family, their paterfamilias, further obliterating accusations and pleas. Overall, however, the trials demonstrated that the princeps—or at least his family—was not above the laws. The sorry histories of Julia the Elder and Julia the Younger, Agrippina the Elder, Julia Livilla, and others also suggest the constant anxiety surely afflicting early imperial women. What were their proper roles? How could they have so few functions and so little freedom of action, when their father, brother, or another close male relative enjoyed apparently limitless power?

Rome's imperial women had to learn the lessons of moderation—as the *SCPP* puts it—and of keeping "in their place" at home with the family and out of public business. The most decisive message seems to have come with the murder and denunciation of Agrippina the Younger, brought to ruin in spite of her unparalleled status as a woman descended "from an acclaimed *imperator* and the sister, wife, and mother of one who would control the state" (Tac. *Ann.* 12.42.2). Flavian and subsequent imperial women largely kept out of legal difficulties, despite Domitia Longina's notorious marriage to Domitian and alleged link to his assassination, and despite Faustina the Younger's rumored infidelity and ties to the revolt of Avidius Cassius.

Questions again arise of historical contingency and personal agency. On the one hand, after the Julio-Claudians and until the Antonines there were fewer imperial women, particularly ones who spanned imperial generations as had Livia and Agrippina the Younger. From Julia Titi and Domitia through Faustina the Elder women connected to the imperial house either were childless or bore no male children who reached adulthood. Further, Vespasian, Titus, and Nerva were unmarried while ruling. Vespasian and Antoninus Pius, the latter widowed within two years of taking office, both took concubines rather than remarry. On the other hand, Plotina, Sabina, and other imperial women of the early second century CE were remarkably modest and praiseworthy for self-restraint, and Faustina the Younger modeled the prolific and submissive wife. Did these women internalize as well as exemplify the gender norms of Rome's principate? Or did they simply prefer a domestic, retiring life and the company of other women?

It does not seem coincidental that women became enmeshed again in legal difficulties under Commodus and the increasingly autocratic emperors after him. This late period coincides with growing pressure and difficulties for the Roman

Conclusions: Agency and Constraints

state (Cass. Dio 72.36.4). It also sees increased visibility for imperial women, markedly when accompanying the emperor abroad. Nonetheless, especially after the Julio-Claudian period and the obvious ascendency of the principate over the Republic, Rome's imperial women generally demonstrated that the authority of the princeps was responsible for stable hierarchies and gender norms. This image was particularly emphatic in Rome. The muted presence of imperial women there contrasts glimpses of their dynamism outside of the capital city, as seen in Plotina's letter to the Epicureans of Athens, Sabina's lively visit to the Colossi of Memnon in Egypt, and Matidia the Younger's statue and manifold activities at Suessa Aurunca and elsewhere in Italy and abroad.

The whole may strike readers as depressing, if not oppressive. A slightly different take is provided if we focus on religion in Rome. Here imperial women served ideological purposes, especially promotion of the imperial family that included them in the *domus divina* and oaths. This had repercussions besides reinstating alike the male dominance of the emperor and his functionaries, and women's submissiveness and lack of independence. Roman women's most public roles had always been religious, and the new principate enabled more such positions. When at his death the first emperor Augustus was declared *divus* by the senate, gaining celestial honors and veneration at shrines in Rome and throughout the empire, his widow Livia, renamed Julia Augusta, became one of his priests in Rome. Public responsibility for imperial cult was thus created for women. Julia Augusta's position was repeated by Antonia the Younger in 37 and echoed by Agrippina the Younger's priesthood for *divus* Claudius in 54. Although in Rome no later imperial women served as priests of imperial cult, by the time Agrippina became *flaminica* of *divus* Claudius in Rome imperial women themselves had already been consecrated: Drusilla in 38 and, more lastingly, Julia Augusta herself in 42.

Ultimately, in the period I survey, 14 imperial women were consecrated, against 19 imperial men. More importantly, the priests of imperial women's cults in Italy and the provinces, with over 250 attested in the Latin West alone, were almost exclusively female. Individual women are documented as serving their cities and regions, giving benefactions, and gaining public prestige as priests of imperial women's cults. Whether anyone "believed" in the divinity of Rome's *divae* or not, cult for imperial women had demonstrable social and cultural significance. Even during her own lifetime Julia Augusta had been especially honored in Italy and the provinces, often by women. Such homage, like the later papyri witnessing wedding vows before statues of Julia Augusta in Egypt, indicate a kind of popularity for Livia and other imperial women we might easily miss when reading the literary accounts. Imperial women's prominence and exemplarity had widespread effects; although those effects replicated Rome's characteristic euergetism and reinforced the status of municipal elites, at least those participating were increased and diversified.

Imperial women themselves always had a fundamentally liminal status, at the center of power because of their propinquity to the emperor but only at the edges of that power because of their gender. They were undoubtedly seen as intermediaries by many, especially those less grand. Some are denounced for unwarranted influence, a complaint often voiced by the privileged who feel cheated of their assumed due. Less hostile accounts note some imperial women interacting with Jews and Christians, Poppaea with Josephus and Julia Mamaea with Origen. Both cases present markedly atypical views of these two women, suggesting again that the usual sources have tended to flatten and simplify imperial women. But without new evidence we cannot know.

If the Roman princeps was "first among equals," what position did imperial women have? Certainly no official status higher than that of any freeborn Roman citizen male. Yet their close ties to the princeps put them in a novel and unique place in the Roman world. Many, but not all, imperial women of the Augustan and Julio-Claudian periods apparently struggled as they explored their new position and tested its limits. Later imperial women seem to have fulfilled their public roles as exemplars of domesticity and deference less imperfectly. In either case, their support of the imperial family contributed to the emperor's charisma, and to the stability of the principate he headed. The fact that imperial women could never order others into battle, make binding administrative or economic decisions, or convict or absolve another in a legal proceeding does not invalidate their lives, even in the context of ancient Rome. They deserve to have their own stories told, as best as we can discover them in the historical realities of their general restrictions, frequent resentment, and usual absence from the public scene.

Various questions related to my study remain, including the following: What was the relationship between imperial women and their guards, especially the praetorians, over time? Can we trace their enslaved and freed dependents other than for Livia? What was the extent and effects of the activities and presence of imperial women in Italy and the provinces, so tantalizingly suggested by Plotina in Athens and Matidia the Younger in Suessa Aurunca? Most important, perhaps, is a question that can never be answered: What could the Roman empire have achieved had it valued and made use of its imperial, and other, women as well as its men?

APPENDIX I

Imperial Women and Their Life Events

Imperial women discussed in this book are found here in rough chronological order with dates whenever possible, and a standard proposographical reference.[1] The appendix covers the women's important life events: birth, marriage, children who survived to adulthood or who notably died young, widowhood/divorce, death; at times consecration, or a significant death in their family; and notable titles. (For *Augusta* see also Table 1.1.) Relevant incidents of individuals' lives are considered in my text. The name by which the woman is commonly known is in SMALL CAPITALS before her proper name, if that is different; SMALL CAPITALS are also used when a person in this appendix is cited in other entries. For ease of consultation I distinguish dynasties by spacing.

All dates are CE unless otherwise noted or in an entry such as OCTAVIA that falls before the Common Era. Abbreviations other than common male *praenomina* include: b = born; m = married; da = daughter; div = divorced; gmo = grandmother; ww = widowed; d = died; ca = circa. Some uncertainty is noted by a ?, and ?? means a totally unknown year. ** after an entry indicates some form of posthumous condemnation.[2]

OCTAVIA (*RE*, Vol. 17.2, 1859–68, no. 96): b 69 BCE, older sister of Octavian/Augustus; by 54 BCE m C. Claudius Marcellus; da: Marcella the Elder, b?; da: Marcella the Younger, b?; son: M. Claudius Marcellus, b 42; ww 40; m Mark Antony (Oct.)

---

1. Bibliography here is minimal; references, checked with Kienast 2017, give ancient sources, earlier bibliography, and details. I omit some transient imperial women such as Scribonia, the first two wives of Claudius, the first two of Gaius, most others divorced before their husbands became emperor, Flavia Titiana the wife of Pertinax, and most wives of contestants in civil wars.

2. Varner 2001, 41, 44.

290   *Appendix 1*

40; da: ANTONIA THE ELDER, b 39; da: ANTONIA THE YOUNGER, b ca 37; div 32 BCE (wintered in Athens with Antony 39/38 & 38/37; 37–35 in Italy without Antony; 35 to Athens and then back to Rome); 23 death of Marcellus; d 11 BCE. After 35 raised her own children and Marcus and Iullus Antonius (Antony's sons by Fulvia); Alexander Helios, Cleopatra Selene, and Ptolemy Philadelphus (Antony's children by Cleopatra); and perhaps Antonia (Antony's daughter from early marriage to cousin Antonia).[3]

LIVIA Drusilla (*RE*, Vol. 13.1, 900–24, no. 37): b 58 BCE; m Ti. Claudius Nero 43, son: Tiberius, b 42; in exile with Claudius Nero 40–39; div 39; son: Drusus (the Elder), b 38; m Octavian in 38 after birth of Drusus; stillborn son/da with Augustus; renamed Julia *Augusta* and appointed priest of *divus* Augustus 14 CE; d 29 CE (age eighty-six/eighty-seven); consecrated 17 January 42.[4]

JULIA THE ELDER, or Iulia (FOS #421): b 39 BCE, da of Octavian (later Augustus) and Scribonia; 25 BCE m M. Claudius Marcellus, ww 23; 21 BCE m M. Vipsanius Agrippa, son: Gaius Caesar, b 20, son: Lucius Caesar, b 17; da: Vipsania Iulia (JULIA THE YOUNGER), b 19?, ~16?; da: Vipsania Agrippina (AGRIPPINA THE ELDER), b ~14 in Athens;[5] son: Agrippa Postumus, b 12; ww 12; 11 BCE m Tiberius, son, b 10 who died; exiled to Pandateria, 2 BCE; transferred to Rhegium, 3 CE; d 14 CE. **

ANTONIA THE ELDER, or Antonia (*RE*, Vol. 1.2, 2640, no. 113): b 39 BCE to OCTAVIA and Mark Antony; 37 engaged to L. Domitius Ahenobarbus, m post 30; da: DOMITIA LEPIDA, son: Cn. Domitius Ahenobarbus who married AGRIPPINA THE YOUNGER in 28 CE; d 32 CE.

ANTONIA THE YOUNGER, or Antonia (FOS #73): b 31 January 36 BCE to OCTAVIA and Mark Antony; 16 BCE m Drusus (the Elder), son: Germanicus, b 16/15, da: LIVILLA, b 14–11, son: Claudius, b 10 in Lugdunum; ww 9 BCE; priest of *divus* Augustus 37; *Augusta* 37, 41; d 1 May 37 CE.

JULIA THE YOUNGER, or (Vipsania) Iulia (FOS #813): da to JULIA THE ELDER & Agrippa, b ~16? BCE; ~3 BCE m L. Aemilius Paullus; da: Aemilia Lepida (FOS #29); exiled 8 CE; son b thereafter prohibited by Augustus from being raised; d 28. **

AGRIPPINA THE ELDER, or (Vipsania) Agrippina (FOS #812): da of JULIA THE ELDER & Agrippa, b ~14 BCE; 4 CE m Germanicus; son: Nero, b 5, son: Drusus, b 8, son: Gaius (Caligula), b 12, da: AGRIPPINA THE YOUNGER, b

---

3. Bradley 1991, 133–35.

4. Levick 2015, 51, n. 13 explains the discrepancy between Cassius Dio's date of 41 and other evidence.

5. For the uncertainty of the relative or absolute ages of the sisters JULIA THE YOUNGER and AGRIPPINA THE ELDER, see Fantham 2006, 108–109.

Appendix 1 291

15, da: DRUSILLA, b 16, da JULIA LIVILLA, b 18 (on Lesbos), and three others who died as infants;[6] 19 ww; 29 exiled to Pandateria; 33 d in exile; defamed by Tiberius; 37 rehabilitated by Caligula ** After her death her birthday was added to days of ill omen (Suet. *Tib.* 53.2) and her images may have been removed from public view.[7]

LIVILLA, or (Claudia) Livia Iulia (FOS #239): da to ANTONIA THE YOUNGER and Drusus the Elder, b 14–11 BCE, grandda to LIVIA, niece and also daughter-in-law to Tiberius, grand-niece to Augustus, grandda to OCTAVIA and Mark Antony; sister to Germanicus and Claudius: 1 BCE m Gaius Caesar, 4 CE ww; m Drusus the Younger (son of Tiberius), whom accompanied at least during his campaigns in Illyricum; da: JULIA, b 7? (FOS #422), and male twins, b ~19 CE; one twin and hus Drusus d 23; thereafter Sejanus vainly asked Tiberius for her hand. After Sejanus' fall in 31 his wife Apicata accused Livilla of Drusus' murder; Livilla executed by Tiberius or perhaps Antonia. *Damnatio memoriae.* **

JULIA, or Iulia (FOS #422): da to LIVILLA and Drusus the Younger, b 3 CE; 20 m Nero Caesar, who was condemned 29; ww in 31; 33 m C. Rubellius Blandus, son: Rubellius Plautus, son: Rubellius Drusus, da: Rubellia Bassa (FOS #667); d ~43.

AGRIPPINA .THE YOUNGER, or Iulia Agrippina (FOS #426): da to AGRIPPINA THE ELDER and Germanicus, b probably 6 November 15 CE;[8] sister to Caligula, DRUSILLA, and JULIA LIVILLA; m Cn. Domitius Ahenobarbus 28, son: Nero 37; exiled to Pontia 39, recalled by Claudius 41; ww 40; m C. Sallustius Passienus Crispus (formerly married to Domitia, the elder sister of Cn. Domitius Ahenobarbus), by 44; ww ~47/48; m Claudius ~1 January 49; *Augusta* 50; *flaminica* of *divus* Claudius 54; d 13 March 59. **

DRUSILLA, or Iulia Drusilla (FOS #437): da to AGRIPPINA THE ELDER and Germanicus, b probably 16 CE;[9] m L. Cassius Longinus, 33; div ~37; m M. Aemilius Lepidus ~38; d 10 June 38; consecrated *Diva Drusilla* 23 September 38.

JULIA LIVILLA, or Iulia Livilla (FOS #443): da to AGRIPPINA THE ELDER and Germanicus, b ~17 CE,[10] betrothed to Quintilius Varus; m M. Vinicius 33; exiled to Pandateria 39, recalled by Claudius 41; exiled again to Pandateria in late 41 on charges of adultery with Seneca; d ~42. **

LOLLIA PAULINA (FOS #504): b ca 15 CE, grandda to M. Lollius (consul 21 BCE); m P. Memmius Regulus; "stolen" from husband by Caligula, 38; m Caligula 38, div 39; after death of MESSALINA in 48 contender for marriage to Claudius; exiled and killed 49.

---

6. See Lindsay 1995 for the children's birthdates.

7. Varner 2001, 62.

8. Barrett 1996, 230–32, contra Humphrey 1979 and Lindsay 1995.

9. Humphrey 1979: 15 February.

10. If born on Lesbos, b in 18.

292   *Appendix 1*

CAESONIA, or Milonia Caesonia (FOS #550): da to Vistilia (FOS #814), b ~5 CE; mother of three girls when pregnant with Caligula's child, m Caligula end 39/early 40; da: JULIA DRUSILLA (40–41); d with Caligula 41. **

JULIA DRUSILLA (FOS #438): da to CAESONIA and Caligula, b 40; d with Caesonia 41.

DOMITIA LEPIDA (FOS #326): da to ANTONIA THE ELDER and L. Domitius Ahenobarbus, grandda to OCTAVIA, grand-niece to Augustus, b ?; aunt to Nero and raised him when AGRIPPINA THE YOUNGER was in exile; m (Valerius) Messalla Barbatus, da: MESSALINA; m Faustus Cornelius Sulla, son: ?; m C. Appius Iunius Silanus; d 54.

MESSALINA, or Valeria Messalina (FOS #774): da to DOMITIA LEPIDA and Messalla Barbatus, thus paternal and maternal great-grandda to OCTAVIA, b at latest in 24; ?39 m Claudius, da: OCTAVIA (?39/40–62), son: Britannicus (41–55); "m" C. Silius 47; d 47. **

OCTAVIA, or Claudia Octavia (FOS #246): da to MESSALINA and Claudius, b ?39/40; betrothed to L. Junius Silanus Torquatus; betrothed in 49 to Nero; m Nero 53; div 62; d 62. **

POPPAEA, or Poppaea Sabina (FOS #646): da to Poppaea Sabina (the Elder) and T. Ollius, b 32 or before; m Rufrius Crispinus, so: Rufrius Crispinus who was later killed by Nero; m M. Salvius Otho (r. 60); div ~58; m Nero 62, da: CLAUDIA AUGUSTA 63; *Augusta*, 63; d 65; consecrated. **

CLAUDIA AUGUSTA, or Claudia (FOS #213): da to POPPAEA and Nero, b 63; *Augusta* 63; d 63; consecrated.

STATILIA MESSAL(L)INA, or Statilia Messalina (FOS #730): b ?; m Atticus Vestinus; ww 65; m Nero ~66; *Augusta* 66; Otho intended to marry her in 69, and bequeathed her all his goods.

SEXTILIA (FOS #719): m L. Vitellius (cos. III), sons: A. Vitellius (r. 69) and L. Vitellius; *Augusta* 69; d 69.

GALERIA FUNDANA (FOS #399): m A. Vitellius, da: Vitellia (FOS #817), so: b 62, and ordered killed by Mucianus in 70; GALERIA FUNDANA survived and lived on the Aventine.

DOMITILLA, or Flavia Domitilla (the Elder) (FOS #367): m Vespasian, so: Titus, b 39, da: DOMITILLA (the Younger), so: Domitian, b 51; d before 69; *Augusta*, 81/82?; consecrated, 81/82?[11]

DOMITILLA, or Flavia Domitilla (the Younger) (FOS #368): da to DOMITILLA (the Elder) and Vespasian; sister to Titus and Domitian; d before 69.

---

11. For the difficulties of distinguishing the homonymous mother and daughter, see Ch. 3.

Appendix 1

JULIA TITI, or (Flavia) Iulia (FOS #371): da to (perhaps) Arrecina Tertulla (FOS #93) and Titus, b 60–64; offered in marriage to Domitian; *Augusta* 79; m Flavius Sabinus before 81; d 87–90, perhaps 89;[12] consecrated 90/91.

DOMITIA LONGINA (FOS #327): da to (Cassia?) Longina (FOS #196) and Cn. Domitius Corbulo, b 11 February ??; m L. Aelius Lamia Plautius Aelianus; div 70; m Domitian ~70, so: died young and consecrated as *divus* Caesar in 81; *Augusta* 81; estranged from Domitian ~83?, reconciled; ww 96; d post 127.

PLOTINA, or Pompeia Plotina (FOS #631): b ~58?; m Trajan probably after 70; *Augusta* 100–105; d 123;[13] consecrated.

MARCIANA, or Ulpia Marciana (FOS #824): sister to Trajan; b between 44 and 62, perhaps ~50; m C. Salonius Matidius Patruinus, da: MATIDIA THE ELDER; *Augusta* 100–105; d 29 August 112, consecrated the same day.[14]

MATIDIA THE ELDER, or Salonia Matidia (FOS #681): da to MARCIANA and C. Salonius Matidius Patruinus, b before 68;[15] m (? L. Mindius), da: MATIDIA THE YOUNGER, b ?80; m L. Vibius (Sabinus?), da: SABINA, b ca 85; ww young; *Augusta* 112; d 119; consecrated.

MATIDIA THE YOUNGER, or Mindia? Matidia (FOS #533): da to MATIDIA THE ELDER (and ?L. Mindius), b probably ~80, and elder sister of SABINA[16]; d before 161.

SABINA, or (Vibia) Sabina (FOS #802): da of MATIDIA THE ELDER and L. Vibius (Sabinus ?), b ~85,[17] m Hadrian ~100;[18] *Augusta* 128; d 136/137;[19] consecrated.

FAUSTINA THE ELDER, or Annia Galeria Faustina (FOS #62): da to Rupilia Faustina (FOS #674) and M. Annius Verus, b ~97?; m Antoninus Pius before 120, of two sons and two daughters only FAUSTINA THE YOUNGER lived past 138; *Augusta* 138 at accession of Antoninus Pius; d 140;[20] consecrated.

---

12. Gregori and Rosso 2010, 194; for the disputed identification of her mother, 195–96.

13. Van Bremen 2005, 512–13 discusses the uncertain date of Plotina's death, settling on 123.

14. *Fasti Ostienses* for 112: Smallwood #22, p.32 = EDCS-20200012. Vidman 1982, 122, holds that Marciana was buried on the twelfth day after her death.

15. Gualerzi 2005, 216–17, holds that she was born in Italy not Spain.

16. Chausson 2008, 234 proposes unconvincingly that Sabina is older.

17. Temporini 1978: ca 86.

18. Jones 2004, 273: ca 101.

19. Kienast 2017, 126: not before latter half of 136, but probably December 137; Brennan 2018, 299: latter part of 137.

20. Beckmann 2009, 21–22: *Fasti Ostienses* (= EDCS-20200012) for 140 CE; 23(?) October restored.

294 *Appendix 1*

FAUSTINA THE YOUNGER, or Annia Galeria Faustina (FOS #63): da to FAUSTINA THE ELDER and Antoninus Pius and cousin of Marcus Aurelius, b ~130; betrothed 136 to Lucius Verus by Hadrian and in 138 to Marcus Aurelius; m Marcus Aurelius 145; *Augusta* 147; *mater castrorum* 174; d 175;[21] consecrated. Children include: da: Domitia Faustina, b 30 November 147 (d by 161, perhaps in 150 or 151); ?twins T. Aelius Aurelius and T. Aurelius Antoninus, b 149 and d 149; da: LUCILLA, b 7 March 148/150; da: Annia Galeria Aurelia Faustina, b 150/151, d post 180/181; son: T. Aelius Antoninus, b 152; son: dead as infant late 157 or early 158; da: Fadilla, b 159, d post 192; da: Cornificia, b August 160, d post 212; male twins: L. Aurelius Commodus and T. Aurelius Fulvus Antoninus, b 31 August 161, d (Fulvus) ca 165/166 and (Commodus) 192; son: M. Annius Verus, b ~end 162 d post 165; son: Hadrianus, b 161/163 d 180; da: Vibia Aurelia Sabina, b post 161.

LUCILLA, or Annia Aurelia Galeria Lucilla (FOS #54): da to FAUSTINA THE YOUNGER and Marcus Aurelius, b 7 March 148/150; betrothed to Lucius Verus in 161; *Augusta* 163; m Lucius Verus 164, da: Aurelia? (FOS #133), b 166?; ww 169; m Ti. Claudius Pompeianus, children but unknown; d ~182. **

CRISPINA, or Bruttia Crispina (FOS #149): da to L. Fulvius Rusticus C. Bruttius Praesens Laberius Maximus (cos. 180), b ?; m Commodus 178; *Augusta* 178; d 191/192.[22] **

JULIA DOMNA, DOMNA, or Iulia Domna (FOS #436): da to ? and (Iulius) Bassianus, b ~160, and sister of JULIA MAESA; m Septimius Severus 185 or 187, son: Caracalla, b 188, son: Geta, b 189; *Augusta* 193; supervisor of *cura epistularum Graecarum et Latinarum et libellorum* for Caracalla post 212; d suicide Apr 217; consecrated.

JULIA MAESA, MAESA, or Iulia Maesa (FOS #445):[23] da to ? and (Iulius) Bassianus, b 7 May(?) ?, sister to JULIA DOMNA; m C. Iulius Avitus Alexianus, da: JULIA SOAEMIAS, da: JULIA MAMAEA; gmo to Elagabalus and Severus Alexander; ww ??; *Augusta* 30 May 218;[24] d before 3 Aug 224?; consecrated post 7 Nov 224(?); *damnatio memoriae* March 235; annulment of *damnatio memoriae*, ca May/June 238.

PLAUTILLA, or Publia Fulvia Plautilla (PIR² F 564): da to ? and C. Fulvius Plautianus, sole praetorian prefect since 200, b ?; betrothed to Caracalla 200, m 202; *Augusta* 202; div 205 and banished to Lipara, where executed 212 after Caracalla became sole emperor. **

---

21. Levick 2014, 135.

22. Hekster 2002, 72 n.181.

23. See also Kienast 2017, 168–69.

24. *CFA* 100 = EDCS-19000364.

Appendix 1 295

JULIA SOAEMIAS, SOAEMIAS, or Iulia Soaemias Bassiana (FOS #460): da to JULIA MAESA and C. Iulius Avitus Alexianus, b 175/180?, older sister to JULIA MAMAEA; m 193/194(?) Sex. Varius Marcellus; son: Elagabalus, b 203/204; other children unknown; 204 in *ludi saeculares* as *clarissima femina*; ww 210s;[25] *Augusta* 218; d 11 March 222; *damnatio memoriae.* **

JULIA MAMAEA, MAMAEA, or Iulia Avita Mamaea (PIR[2] I 649): da to JULIA MAESA and C. Iulius Avitus Alexianus, b 14/29 August??, younger sister to JULIA SOAEMIAS; m unknown consular; div or ww; m equestrian Syrian procurator Gessius Marcianus;[26] son: Severus Alexander, b 1 October 208?; two other children, unknown; May/June 218, declared *hostis publica*; *Augusta* post 14 March 222; *mater castrorum* 224?; *mater senatus* 226?; d February/March 235 with Severus Alexander; *damnatio memoriae* 235; annulment of *damnatio memoriae*, ca May/June 238.

CORNELIA PAULA, or Iulia Cornelia Paula (PIR[2] I 660): da to (Cornelia) and Julius Paulus; m Elagabalus 219; *Augusta* 219–220; repudiated (September?) 220.[27]

JULIA AQUILIA SEVERA, or Iulia Aquilia Severa (PIR[2] I 648): Vestal virgin; m Elagabalus late 220; *Augusta* 220; di? July 221?; remarried Elagabalus late 221.

ANNIA FAUSTINA, or Annia Aurelia Faustina (or Fundania) (PIR[2] A 710): grandda to Marcus Aurelius; m Pomponius Bassus; ww; m Elagabalus (his third wife), July 221?; *Augusta* 221; repudiated late 221. **

SALLUSTIA ORBIANA, or Gnaea Seia Herennia Sallustia Barbia Orbiana (PIR[1] S 252): da to ? and L. Seius Herennius Sallustius Macrianus, b?; m Severus Alexander; *Augusta* 225–227; banned to Africa 29 August? 227.

---

25. Kemezis 2016, 351.

26. Kosmetatou 2002, 400–401.

27. Whittaker 1969, 2:47 n.3; cf. Cass. Dio 79.9.1–3.

APPENDIX 2

Genealogical Tables of Imperial Families

Although selective, these family trees include individuals discussed in the text and provide the fairly certain pertinent dates (see also Appendix 1). Names in *italics* are those normally used for the men concerned. Emperors' names are in CAPITALS. Dates BCE are in **boldface**.

The abbreviations b. and d. signify "born" and "died"; ~ indicates a fairly certain but approximate date. = signifies a marriage; the figure above = gives the date of the marriage, when known. The figure in parentheses immediately before or after the name of an individual who married more than once specifies the marriage's place in the sequence. The dashed line below HADRIAN in The Second-Century Imperial Family tree signifies his adoption of designated successors, first L. Aelius Caesar and then ANTONINUS PIUS.

THE JULIO-CLAUDIAN FAMILY

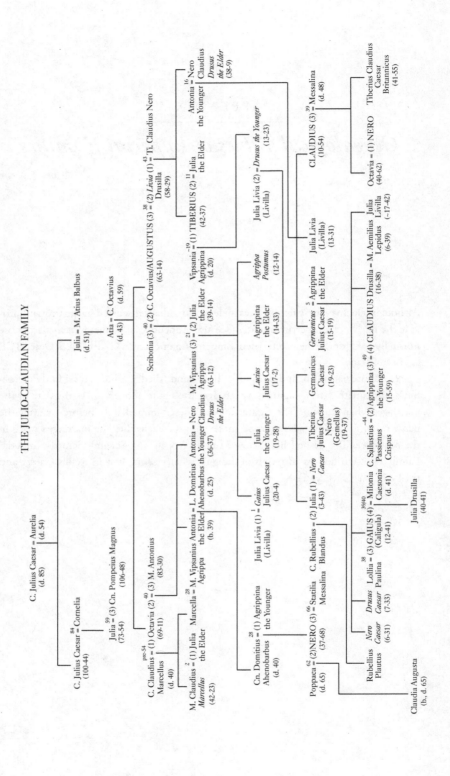

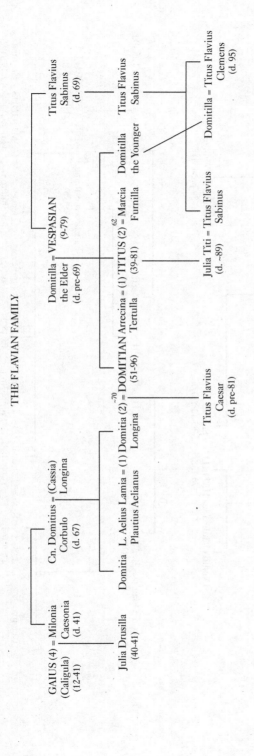

THE FLAVIAN FAMILY

THE SECOND-CENTURY IMPERIAL FAMILY

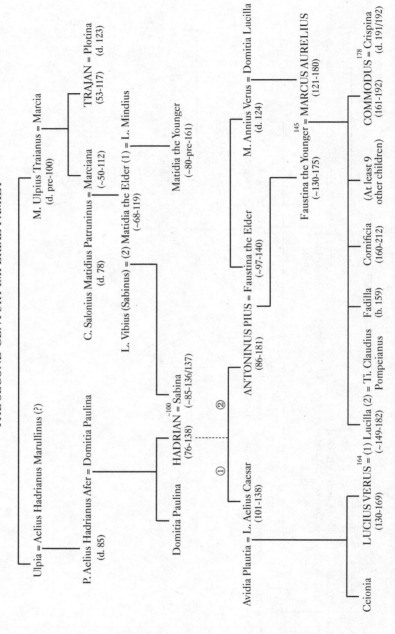

THE SEVERAN FAMILY

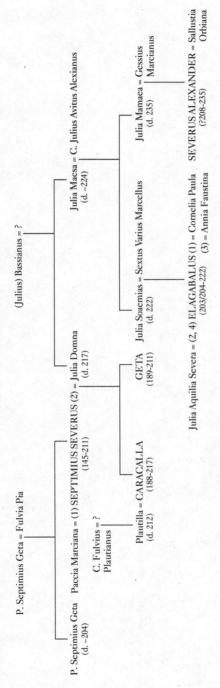

APPENDIX 3

List of *Divae*

1. Drusilla, consecrated after death in 38.[1] The senator Livius Geminus claimed to have witnessed her apotheosis, and was rewarded with an enormous sum (Cass. Dio 59.11.4–6, cf. Seneca's ridicule of the apotheosis and claim to have witnessed it, *Apocol.* 1).[2] Cassius Dio reports male and female priests were appointed for her and her new title was Panthea ("Universal Goddess," Cass. Dio 59.11.2–3), but the latter is not attested epigraphically. Venus figures large among her multiple assimilations: one statue of her was set up in the "Temple of Venus in the Forum" (Cass. Dio 59.11.1–5, esp. 2–3; Suet. *Calig.* 24.2; perhaps the Temple of Venus Genetrix in the Forum Julium),[3] and surviving inscriptions from Cyzicus and Mytilene identify her with Aphrodite.[4] Celebrations of her birthday were modeled on the Megalesia in

---

1. For lists of *divae* (usually lacking detailed references), see, e.g., Granino Cecere 2014, 187–92; Palombi 2014, 190; Woolf 2008, 242; Varner 2001, 43 (counting nineteen in all, as compared to the twenty-four condemned imperial women who are his main concern); Price 1987, 57. I do not include here references for presumed cult for living or nonconsecrated women, such as for Julia Mamaea inferred from the fragmentary (and partially erased) *AE* 1967, 93 = EDCS-09800066 = EDR 074693 with a *sacerdos [[[Iuliae Mamaeae?]]] Augustae* in Herdonia (now Ordona, Italy). My list relies on EDCS, so favors evidence from the Latin West.

2. For the date of her death, see also *CIL* XIV 244 (p 481, 773) = EDCS-20200012 (*Fasti Ostienses*). Apotheosis, witnessed also for Augustus (Suet. *Aug.* 100), is not documented for Claudius' deification (see Tac. *Ann.* 12.69.3, 13.2.3), which Palombi 2014, 190 notes as a decisive innovation in the procedure.

3. Wood 1995, 460 suggests it was as large as the icon of Venus Genetrix there.

4. Wood 1995, 460, with references including Mytilene inscription *IG* XII, pt. 2, 53 no. 172. In Olympia's Heraion, Drusilla (not identified as *diva*) is honored as "the new Charis" (*IG* XII, pt. 6, 1 no. 411).

304   *Appendix 3*

honor of Cybele in Rome (Barrett 1990, 88; Cass. Dio 59.11.3). Epigraphic witnesses
of her consecration and cult include:

1) *CIL* XIV 3576 = *ILS* 196 = *InscrIt* 4.1.76 (Tibur [Tivoli, Italy]: *[Di]vae
    Drusillae sacrum [C(aius) R(ubellius) C f Blandus [q(uaestor)] divi Aug(usti), tr
    pl, pr(aetor), cos, [pr]ocos, pontif(ex).*[5]

2) *CIL* V 7345 = EDCS-05400594 (Forum Vibii Caburrum [Cavorre, Italy];
    38–64 CE, recording a dedication by a *[flam]inica divae Drusilla*).

3) *CFA* 12 = EDCS-18200416 (38 CE)

4) *CFA* 14 = EDCS-18300755 (40 CE)

5) *CFA* 16 = EDCS-20500161 (37–41 CE)

6) *CIL* XI 1168 = EDCS-20402618 (Veleia [Velleia, Italy]; 38–41 CE).

7) *CIL* XI 3598 = EDCS-22600412 (Caere [Cerveteri, Italy]; 38–41 CE)

8) *CIL* XIII 1194 = EDCS-10500071, Avaricum [Bourges, France])

9) ?EDCS-64800533 (very fragmentary; Tarquinii [Tarquinia, Italy]; 38–54)

10) EDCS-60300305 (Valeria [Las Valeras, Spain])

11) EDCS-67000011 (Brixia [Brescia, Italy]; 37–41 CE)

12) EDCS-04900064 (Pinna Vestina [Penne, Italy]; 38–41 CE)

13) EDCS-07000504 (Collegno, Italy; dedication for *diva* Drusilla and *diva*
    Augusta)

14) *IG* IV² 1, 600 (a *hiereia* of *diva* Drusilla in Epidaurus, Greece)

15) *CIL* XII 1026 = EDCS-08500705 (Avennio [Avignon, France])

2. Iulia Augusta = Livia, consecrated 17 January 42 (*CFA* 17 = EDCS-18300757, see
Suet. *Claud.* 11), within a year of Claudius' assumption of the principate. Later historians held that the senate had wanted to consecrate her at her death in 29, but
Tiberius refused, stating that it was against her wishes (Tac. *Ann.* 5.2.1; Suet. *Tib.*
51.2; Cass. Dio 58.2.1). Various coin issues commemorate DIVA AVGVSTA, including *dupondii, RIC* I², Claudius no. 101, with DIVVS AVGVSTVS S C (with portrait) on obverse, DIVA AVGVSTA on reverse (Livia seated on ornamental throne,
with corn-ears in r. and long torch in l.); numerous *aurei, denarii*, and *sestertii* with
DIVA AVGVSTA and a standing or seated female figure (rev.) issued under Galba in
68–69:[6] e.g., *RIC* I², Galba nos. 142–43, 150–53, 184–89, 223–24. *Aurei, denarii*, and
lower-denomination issues (many from 157–158 CE) commemorating Antoninus
Pius' restoration of the Templum divi Augusti depict the octastyle temple with twin
icons within, i.e., *divus* Augustus and *diva* (Julia) Augusta, such as *RIC* III, Pius nos.
124, 143, 144, 272A, 272B, 289A–C, 290A–C, 305Aa–b, 755, 787, 795A–B, 1061.

---

5. See Eck 2016, 51.

6. See Suet. *Galba* 5. A number of issues of all denominations (but all apparently rare) struck
after Galba reached Rome also attest AVGVSTA, with the same standing or seated figure: e.g.,
RIC I², Galba nos. 331–38, 432.

Appendix 3 305

Epigraphic witnesses of the consecration and cult for *diva* Julia Augusta, sometimes termed *diva* Julia or *diva* Augusta,[7] include:

1) *AE* 2008, 1339, 1340 (probably for Livia: see Eck 2016, 52–53).

2) *CIL* VI 3945 = EDCS-19900643 (epitaph for M. Julius Agatopos, *div(ae) Aug(ustae) l(ibertus)*, from the *columbarium Liviae* in Rome).

3) *CIL* VI 8949 = EDCS-18900016 (Rome; epitaph for a *liberta divae Iuliae Aug(ustae) obstretix*).

4) *CIL* VI 18038 = EDCS-10200234 (Rome; epitaph for a *liberta divae Iuliae Aug(ustae)*).

5) *CIL* VI 33736 = EDCS-24100326 (Rome; epitaph for a *libertus tabul(arius) castrensi<s=P> a[diut(or?) a rationibus divae Iul[iae] August[ae]*).

6) *CIL* X 6638 = EDCS-37700257 (a *l(ibertus) divae Augustae, medicus*; Antium [Anzio, Italy], 51 CE).

7) Corinth-08-03, 00153[8] = EDCS-32001655 (poetry and contests of "virgins" established in Corinth *ad Iulia]m diva[m Au]g(ustam)*.

8) *AE* 1991, 01428 = EDCS-23800550 (three *sacerdotes divae Augustae* [Livia] in Philippi [Filippoi, Greece], 42–100 CE).[9]

9) *AE* 1975, 289 = AE 1995, 367 = EDCS-10701378, with further bibliography (*liberta Iuliae divai (sic) Augusta* in Regium Iulium [Reggio Calabria, Italy]).[10]

10) *CIL* III 14712 = *ILS* 7160 = ILJug-01, 00124 = *AE* 1902, 60 = *AE* 2009, +01014 = EDCS-31300306 (a very rare male *flamen Iuliae Augustae*, the equestrian L. Anicius Paetinas of Salona [near Solin, Croatia], dated 25–54).[11]

11) *CIL* X 7501 = *ILS* 121 = EDR 112580 (better than the erroneous EDCS-22100620) (another very rare male *flamen Iuliae Augustae*, married to a *sacerdos Augustae*, from Gaulus [modern Gozza near Malta and Sicily], 14–29 CE).

12) *AE* 1964, 173 = EDCS-12800317 (wife of procurator C. Crepereius Gallus and presumed priestess of *diva Iulia Augusta* in Pisidian Antioch [Yalvaç, Turkey]; 51–100 CE).

13) *CIL* II² 5, 421 = EDCS-08700442 (a *sacerdos divae Augustae* from modern Torreparedones, Baetica, 42–100 CE).

---

7. The last two terms are imprecise, and in this list identification with *diva* Julia Augusta (= Livia) has been made on chronological grounds.

8. J. H. Kent, *Corinth. Results of excavations conducted by The American School of Classical Studies at Athens 8, 3. The inscriptions 1926–1950* (Princeton 1966) 70–73, Nr. 153; pl. 14,153.

9. See also P. Pilhofer, *Philippi 2. Katalog der Inschriften von Philippi* (2. Aufl. Tübingen 2009) 283–87, Nr. 226, and HD048077.

10. See Linderski 1988; Gardner 1988.

11. Hemelrijk 2007, 231: except in the very early period, "the duties of imperial priests seem to have been segregated according to gender: male priests served the cult of the emperor and his deified predecessor(s), and female priests that of the female members of the imperial family."

306   *Appendix 3*

14) See Matidia #8 (later in list).

15) Various entries in *CFA* (see, e.g., *diva* Claudia Augusta).

3. Diva Claudia Augusta, daughter of Nero and Poppaea. Besides Tac. *Ann.* 15.23.4, which reports that at her death in 63 the three-month-old was voted a *pulvinar*, temple, and *sacerdos*, epigraphic witnesses of her consecration and cult include:

1) *CFA* 30 = EDCS-21300886, from 66 CE. Once Galba consolidates power in 68 mention of Claudia drops from the *CFA*.

2) *CIL* XI 6955 = *ILS* 8902 = *AE* 1989, 312 = *AE* 1991, 652 = *AE* 2000, +00251 = *AE* 2000, +00553 = *AE* 2001, +00958 = EDCS-20700412 (dedication *d[ivae Claudiae] N[eronis Augusti filiae] v[irgini(?)* from Luna [Luni, Italy], by the important equestrian L. Titinius Glaucus Lucretianus; 63 CE).

4. Diva Poppaea Augusta, consecrated in 65.[12] Besides Tac. *Ann.* 16.21–22, Cass. Dio 63.26.3, and information in *CFA* (see earlier for Claudia Augusta), epigraphic witnesses of her consecration and cult include:

1) *CIL* XI 1331a = *ILS* 233 = EDCS-20402781 (dedication *divae Poppaeae Augustae* by the *flamen Romae et Aug(ustorum)* in Luna, 65, in conjunction with *pro salute* vows for Nero).

2) *AE* 2009, 284 = EDCS-45600023 (dedication *[di]vae Poppaea [Augustae]* by a now anonymous *sacerdos eius*, Pinna Vestina; 65–68 CE).

3) *CIL* VI 40419 = *CIL* VI 3752 (pp. 3071, 3778) = *CIL* VI 31290 = EDCS-00900123 (fragmentary dedication *[divae] Poppae[ae] [A]ugustae*, Rome; 65–68 CE).

5. Diva Domitilla, either the mother or sister of Titus and Domitian.[13] Besides coins from 80–81[14] and again from 90, consecration and cult are attested epigraphically:

1) *AE* 1962, 272 = *AE* 1963, 83 = EDCS-13400117 (dedication of a public building *[---? divae] Domitil[lae Augustae ---]*, on an architrave in Ferentium [Ferento, Italy]; uncertain date).

2) *CIL* V 2829 = *ILS* 6692 = EDCS-04201876 (a *sacerdos divae Domitillae* in Patavium [Padua, Italy]; 90–100 CE).

3) EDCS-66500313 (a dedication, *Memoriae divae Domitillae,* from Nursia [Norcia, Italy]; uncertain date).

6. Julia Titi, or *diva* Julia (Augusta), consecrated after her death and burial in the

---

12. Kragelund 2010 argues that the temple of "Venus-Poppaea" referred to by Cassius Dio (63.26.3) as officially inaugurated by Nero in spring 68 was dedicated in Campania, not Rome.

13. I favor identification as Vespasian's wife: see Ch. 3. Domitia Longina was not divinized but had, from an act of private devotion from her two liberti, a "temple" at Gabii: see Ch. 2.

14. Although without portrait: *RIC* II, Titus nos. 153–54; *RIC* II, Titus nos. 69–73.

Appendix 3

Temple of the Gens Flavia before 3 January 90.[15] Besides coins,[16] epigraphic witnesses of her consecration and cult include:

1) *AE* 2005, 440 = EDCS-36400278 (a *libertus divae Iuliae T(iti) Imp(eratoris) filiae Aug(ustae)* from Reate [Amatrice, Italy]; uncertain date).

2) *CIL* V 6514 = *AE* 2004, +00344 = EDCS-05101679 (a *flaminica divae Iuliae No[var(iae)* [Novara, Italy], who was also *flaminica divae Sabinae* at Ticinum [Pavia, Italy] and apparently married to a *flamen divi Hadriani* who was also *flamen divorum Vespas(iani) et [Traian(i)*; 101–200 CE).

3) *CIL* III 13524 (p. 2285) = EDCS-14600331 (twin honorific inscriptions on marble to *divae Iu[l]iae* and to *Domitiae [Aug(ustae)]*, perhaps statue bases, from Celeia [Celje, Slovenia]; 90–96 CE).

4) *CIL* IX 1153 (p. 695) = *ILS* 6487 = *AE* 2000, +00352 = EDCS-12400657 (a *sacerdos flaminica divae Iuliae Piae Augustae et Matr(is) deum M(agnae) Id(aeae) et Isidis Regin(ae)*, in Aeclanum [Avellino, Italy]; 90–100 CE).

7. Marciana, died 29 August 112 and consecrated the same day. Besides numerous consecration coins (see Ill 3.9 and Ch. 4), epigraphic witnesses of her consecration and cult include:

1) EDCS-20200012 (*Fasti Ostienses*): *[Marciana Aug]usta excessit diva(que) cognominata* (3 September 113).

2) *CIL* IX 5894 (p. 690) = *ILS* 298 = EDCS-17300491 (Arch of Ancona, with dedication to *divae Marcianae Aug. sorori Aug(usti)*, at Ancona [Italy]; 114–115 CE).

3) *AE* 2006, 317 = *AE* 2008, +00389 = *AE* 2010, +00045 = EDCS-44100272 (dedication to Matidia the Younger, identified as *divae Matidiae] Aug(ustae) fil(ia) diva[e] Marci[anae Aug(ustae) neptis] [divae Sabinae Aug(ustae) sor]or*, Suessa Aurunca [Sessa Aurunca, Italy]; 138–161 CE. See Ch. 7.).

4) *CIL* III 5807 = EDCS-27100324 (dedication to Matidia the Younger, *divae Mat[idiae] [A]ug(ustae) fil(iae) di[vae] Marciana[e Aug(ustae)] [ne]pti divi [Tra][ia]ni abne[pti] divae Sab[inae] [Aug(ustae)] so[rori*, from Augusta Vindelicorum [Augsburg, Germany]; 136–160 CE).

5) *CIL* III 6070a = *CIL* III 7123 = IK-12, 00283 = IK-59, 00126 = *ILS* 00327 = EDCS-27800836 (dedication to Matidia the Younger, *divae Marcianae [A]ug(ustae) nepti divae Matidiae Aug(ustae) f(iliae) divae Sabinae Aug(ustae) sorori Imp(eratoris) Antonini Aug(usti) Pii materterae*, from Ephesus, 138–161 CE).

---

15. See Frei-Stolba 2008, 377 n.177. Gregori and Rosso 2010, 202 suggest (with references) 89 CE, and note that Julia is the first niece divinized. She is also the daughter of a divinized emperor.

16. See *RIC* II, Domitian nos. 400 (*sestertii* of 91–92) and 205, no. 411 (*sestertii* of 92–94); also *RIC* II, Domitian nos. 219–20 (*aurei* of 90–91).

308 *Appendix 3*

6) CIL X 4744 = EDCS-19800273 (dedication to Matidia the Younger, *divae Marcianae Aug(ustae) nepti, divae Sabinae Aug(ustae) sorori, Imp(eratoris) Antonini Aug(usti) Pii p. p. materterae,* from the Suessani [Sessa Aurunca]; 138–161 CE).

7) CIL X 4745 = EDCS-19800274 (dedication to Matidia the Younger, *divae Marcianae Aug(ustae) nepti, divae Sabinae Aug(ustae) sorori, Imp(eratoris) Antonini Aug(usti) Pii p. p. materterae,* from Minturnae [Minturno, Italy]; 138–161 CE).

8) *CIL* V 3111 = EDCS-04202158 (dedication to Matidia the Younger, *[divae Matidiae Aug(ustae)] [filiae] [divae Sabinae Aug(ustae)] sorori divae Marcianae [Aug(ustae)] nepti,* from the *collegium centonariorum* of Vicetia [Vicenza, Italy; 136–170 CE).

8. Matidia the Elder,[17] consecrated before 23 December 119. Besides numerous coins and *CFA*, epigraphic witnesses of her consecration and cult include:

1) *AE* 1986, 148 = EDCS-07600127 (dedication to Matidia the Younger, *divae Matidiae Aug. fil. Divae Sabinae Aug. sorori,* from Suessa Aurunca; t.p.q. 136). See also *AE* 2006, 317 = EDCS-44100272, Marciana #3 earlier.

2) *AE* 1988, 1038 = EDCS-07000883 (dedication *divae Matidiae* by Plancia Magna at Perge [Aksu, Turkey]; 119–122 CE).

3) *CIL* III 2731 = EDCS-28300056 (dedication *divae Matidiae* from Aequum [Citluk, Croatia]; 119–200 CE).

4) See Marciana, #4 earlier.

5) See Marciana, #5 earlier.

6) See Marciana, #8 earlier.

7) *CIL* V 5647 = EDCS-05100801 (a *sacerdos divae Matidiae* from Erba [near modern Como, Italy]; 119–200 CE).

8) *CIL* XI 415 = *ILS* 6658 = EDCS-24600987 (a *sacerdos divae Aug(ustae) et divae Matidiae Aug(ustae)* from Ariminum [Rimini, Italy]).

9) *AE* 1927, 31 = EDCS-08800336 (dedication *divae Matidiae* by the municipium Volubilitanum, from Volubilis [Oualili and Ksar Pharaoun, Morocco]; t.p.q. 119 CE).

10) IK-53, 19 = *AE* 1973, 515 = EDCS-03200004 (dedication *divae Matidiae Aug(ustae) filiae divae Marcianae Aug(ustae) sororis divi N[e]rvae Traiani Aug. Germanici Dacici Parthici,* from Alexandreia Troas [Turkmenli, Turkey]; 119–150 CE).

11) *AE* 1991, 492 = EDCS-05000115 (a *sacerdos divae Matidiae* from Brixia).

---

17. See Gualerzi 2005, and *AE* 1954, 62 = EDCS-13800082.

Appendix 3   309

9. Plotina: d. after 1 January 123,[18] ? buried in socle of Trajan's Column. Date of consecration is uncertain.[19] Besides consecration coins and *CFA*, epigraphic witnesses of her consecration and cult include:

1) *CIL* V 7617 = *ILS* 6750 = *AE* 1982, 376 = EDCS-05400867 (now unnamed wife of a *consul designatus*, who served as *sacerdos* of *diva Plotina* at Pollentia [Pollenza, Italy], of *diva Faustina* at Augusta Taurinorum [Torino], and of *diva Faustina maior* in Concordia [near Venice, Italy]; 175–200 CE).

2) *AE* 1997, 562 = EDCS-06300055 (a *flaminica divae Plotinae Augustae* from Pollentia; 123–150 CE).

3) *CIL* V 4387 = EDCS-04203439 (a *sacerdos divae Plotinae* in Brixia).

4) *CIL* V 4485 = EDCS-04203537 (a *sacerdos divae Plotinae* in Brixia; 123–200 CE).

5) *CIL* VIII 993 (p. 2440) = *CIL* VIII 12454 = *ILS* 04433 = EDCS-17700486 (*flaminica divae Plotinae*, at Karpis [El Merissa, Tunisia]).

6) *CIL* XI 407 = *ILS* 6657 = EDCS-24600985 (*sacerdos divae Plotinae* at Ariminum and nearby Forum Semproni; 123–200 CE).

7) *AE* 1958, 184 = EDCS-13500267 (a *libertus divae Plotinae* from Rome; 123–150 CE).

8) *AE* 1991, 811 = *AE* 2001, 1060 = EDCS-41901172 (a *sacerdos divae Plotinae Augustae*, from Verona [Italy]; 123–200 CE).

10. Sabina, consecrated after death in 136/137. Epigraphic witnesses of her consecration and cult include:

1) *CIL* V 6514 = *AE* 1999, 763 = *AE* 2004, +344 = EDCS-05101679 (*flaminica divae Iuliae Novar(iae)* [see Julia Titi #2, earlier], who was also *flaminica divae Sabinae* at Ticinum [and who seems to have been married to a *flamen divi Hadriani* who was also *flamen divorum Vespasiani et Traiani*], 101–200 CE).

2) *CIL* VIII 8929 (p. 1953) = EDCS-25100027 (dedication to *diva Sabina Aug(usta)* from Saldae in [Bejaia, Algeria]; t.p.q. 136 CE).

3) *CIL* VIII 17847 = EDCS-24500265 (dedication *divae Sabinae Aug(ustae)* at Thamugadi [near Batna, Algeria]; t.p.q. 136 CE).

4) *CIL* VI 984 = *CIL* VI 31220a1 = *ILS* 322 = *AE* 2003, +267 = EDCS-17301095 (dedication at Mausoleum of Hadrian in Rome from Antoninus Pius to Hadrian and *diva* Sabina, *parentibus suis*, 138–139 CE, before Hadrian's consecration).

---

18. Date of death is debated; though it is often put as 121 or 122, brickstamps (*CIL* XV 691 and 692) suggest she was alive in 123. I use 123 as van Bremen 2005, 512–13 who summarizes earlier arguments.

19. Birley 1997, 145 speculates that she was deified only after Hadrian returned to Rome in 126 from his second, long trip; Temporini 1978, 167, followed by most, presumes that the absent Hadrian sponsored her consecration by letter soon after her death.

5) *CIL* X 4746 = EDCS-19800275 (dedication to Matidia the Younger, *divae Sabinae Aug(ustae) sorori, Imp(eratoris) Antonini Aug(usti) Pii p. p. materterae*, from a freedman procurator Agathemerus at Suessa Aurunca; 138–161 CE).

6) *CIL* X 4747 = EDCS-19800276 (dedication to Matidia the Younger, *divae Sabinae Aug(ustae) sorori, Imp(eratoris) Antonini Aug(usti) Pii p. p. materterae*, from an imperial freedman in Suessa Aurunca; 138–161 CE).

7) *CIL* XI 408 = *AE* 2013, +194 = EDCS-20401846 (a *sacerdos divae Sabinae* at Ariminum).

8) *AE* 1991, 492 = EDCS-05000115 (dedication or building inscription of Matidia the Younger, identified as *divae Sabinae soror, Imp. Antonini Aug. Pii p. p. matertera*, from Suessa Aurunca; 138–161 CE).

9) See Matidia the Elder, #1 earlier.

10) *CIL* X 3833 = EDCS-17800446 (dedication to Matidia the Younger, identified as *divae Sabina soror, Imp. Antonini Aug. Pii p. p. matertera*, from the citizens of Sinuessa [Modragone, Italy]; 138–161 CE).

11. Faustina the Elder, consecrated as *diva* Faustina on the same day she died at the end of October 140 (*Fasti Ostienses*, EDCS-20200012). Besides many consecration coins, the report of HA, *Ant. Pius* 6 that priestesses were appointed for her, and the Temple of *diva* Faustina and *divus* Antoninus in the Roman Forum (and its many references), epigraphic witnesses of her consecration and cult include:

1) EDCS-05400867 (see earlier, Plotina #1: a *sacerdos* of *diva Plotina* at Pollentia, of *diva Faustina* at Augusta Taurinorum, and of *diva Faustina maior* in Concordia; married to a *consul designatus*, from Pollentia; t.p.q. 175).

2) *AE* 1904, 41 = EDCS-16700071 (dedication to *diva Aug. Faustina* at Volsinii [Bolsena, Italy]; 140–161 CE).

3) *AE* 1954, 152 = EDCS-13800141 (dedication t.p.q. 140 CE to *diva Faustina Aug(usta)* from Thamugadi; perhaps to Faustina the Younger).

4) *AE* 1956, 19 = EDCS-13600367 (*libertus* of *diva Faustina Antonini*, from the area of Naples or the Phlegraean fields; 140–161 CE).

5) *AE* 1995, 01292 = EDCS-03300771 (lead seal impressed with *diva Faustina Aug(usta)*, from Apulum [Alba Iulia, Romania]; t.p.q. 140).

6) *CIL* II 4096 (p. 972) = EDCS-05503128 (statue base dedicated to *diva Faustina*, from Tarraco [Tarragona, Spain]; t.p.q. 140).

7) *CIL* III 14243,6 = *AE* 2007, 1098 = EDCS-32201062 (statue base for *diva Faustina Augusta* from Salona, though perhaps for Faustina the Younger; t.p.q. 140).

8) *CIL* VI 987 = *ILS* 349 = EDCS-17301098 (dedication to *diva Faustina Augusta* from Mausoleum of Hadrian, Rome; t.p.q. 140).

9) *CIL* VI 1006 (p. 4315) = EDCS-17400008 (dedication in Rome to *diva Faustina Aug.* from the Sextani Arelatenses [Arles, France], better than Faustina the Younger; t.p.q. 140).

10) *CIL* VI 3756 = *CIL* VI 31317 = *ILS* 5160 = EDCS-19800498 (honorary inscription to *diva Faustina Aug.* from Rome; 140 CE).

Appendix 3   311

11) *CIL* VI 8941, cf. p. 3463 = EDCS-18900008 (*nutrix [divae F]austinae* from Rome, perhaps to be connected to Faustina the Younger; t.p.q. 140 CE).

12) *CIL* IX 5428 = *ILS* 5652 = EDCS-16100778 (*sacerdos divae Faustinae* in Falerio Picenus [Falerone, Italy]; 140–161 CE).

13) *CIL* X 5656 = EDCS-20403132 (*sacerdos divae Faustinae* in Fabrateria Vetus, modern Ceccano, Italy; 140–161 CE).

14) *CIL* VI 10139 = *CIL* XI 870 = EDCS-20402307 (a lutist, or *psaltria*, *divae Faustinae*, from Mutina [Modena, Italy], perhaps Faustina the Younger; t.p.q. 140 CE).

15) *CIL* XI 6323 = EDCS-23200615 (statue base for *diva Faustina Augusta*, perhaps Faustina the Younger, erected *d(ecreto) d(ecurionum)* at Pisaurum [Pesaro, Italy]; 140–180 CE).

16) *CIL* XI 6500 = EDCS-23200796 (dedication for *diva Faustina Augusta* in Sassina [Sarsina, Italy]; 140–161 CE).

17) *CIL* XI 7279 = EDCS-21000203 (dedication in honor of *diva Faustina, d. d.,* at Volsinii; 140–161 CE).

18) *CIL* XII 4343 = EDCS-09301508 (dedication to *diva Faustina Augusta* in Narbo [Narbonne, France]; 140–161 CE).

19) *CIL* XIV 5326 = *AE* 2008, 46 = EDCS-12000319 (dedication to Antoninus Pius and *diva* Faustina *d. d.,* including altar at which female and male newlyweds in Ostia can sacrifice, Ostia, Italy; 140–141 CE).

20) *AE* 1923, 17 = EDCS-08800341 (dedication for *diva* Faustina from the Volubilitani in Volubilis; 140–144 CE).

21) *AE* 1956, 232 = *AE* 2011, 945 = (*flaminica divae Faustinae* of Aquileia and Iader, from Iader [Zadar, Croatia]; 140–170 CE).

22) *IRT* 20 = EDCS-06000019 (dedication to *diva Faustina* at Sabratha [Sabratah, Libya]; 140–161 CE).

23) *IRT* 380 = EDCS-06000370 (dedication to *diva Faustina* from the Lepcitani of Lepcis Magna [Al-Khums, Libya]; t.p.q. 140 CE).

24) EDCS-08000610 (dedication to *diva Aug. Faustina*, found at Augusta Taurinorum; t.p.q. 140 CE).

25) *AE* 1988, 188 = EDCS-07000162 (a *flaminica divae Faustinae* at Ostia; t.p.q. 140 CE).

26) *IG* XIV 1390; *IGRom* I, 193–196: The "Triopion" at the third milestone outside of Rome on the Via Appia, perhaps at Regilla's family home. An inscribed dedicatory poem suggests that this round building, with twin columns inscribed to Demeter, Kore, and the Chthonic deities, originally contained a shrine with statues of Demeter and *diva* Faustina as Old and New Demeter.[20]

---

20. Gleason 2010, 142–56, with further references.

Appendix 3

12. Faustina the Younger, consecrated after her death in Halala in early summer(?) 175,[21] and whose epithet Pia often distinguishes her from her mother. Besides numerous consecration coins, epigraphic witnesses of her consecration and cult include:

1) EDCS-05400867 (see earlier, Plotina #1: the *sacerdos* of *diva Plotina* at Pollentia, *diva Faustina* at Augusta Taurinorum, and *diva Faustina maior* in Concordia).

2) *CIL* VI 33840 = EDCS-24100613 (a *collegium arkarum divarum Faustinarum Matris et Piae* in Rome; 227 CE).

3) *AE* 1922, 27 = EDCS-16201146 (dedication to *diva Faustina* from Thurburbo Maius [Henchir el-Kasba, Tunisia]; t.p.q. 175 CE).

4) *CIL* VI 1019 (pp. 3777, 4316) = *ILS* 382 = EDCS-17400018 (honorary inscription to *diva Pia Faustina* from the *viatores quaestorii ab aerario Saturnini*, Rome; t.p.q. 175).

5) *CIL* VI 10222 (p. 3907) = *ILS* 6065 = *AE* 2007, +00190 = EDCS-19600296 (an enrollée in the grain distribution of *diva Faustina Iunior*, in Rome; t.p.q. 175 CE).

6) *CIL* XIII 527 = EDCS-10400695 (statue base for *diva Faustina*, from Lactora [Lectoure, France]; 175–200 CE).

7) *AE* 1974, 348 = EDCS-09401077 (a *flaminica divae Faustinae Piae* and perhaps also *flaminica divae Faustinae* [the Elder], from Mediolanum [Milan, Italy]; last quarter of the second century CE).

13. Julia Domna, consecrated with sponsorship from Elagabalus a year or more after her death in 217.[22] Besides numerous consecration coins,[23] epigraphic witnesses of her consecration and cult include:

1) *CIL* VIII 26225 = *ILS* 08920a = *AE* 1899, 00056 = EDCS-25500066 (dedication from the Gillitani of Gillium [Henchir el-Frass, Tunisia], to *diva Iulia Domna*; t.p.q. 217 CE).

2) *CIL* XIII 12042 = *ILS* 9083a = *AE* 1910, 125 = EDCS-12800064 (dedication to *diva Iulia* from *Legio I Minervia pia fidelis* in *praetorium* of the castra at Bonna, modern Bonn, Germany; 218–222 CE).[24]

14. Julia Maesa, consecrated apparently after 7 November 224 (with her death possibly before 3 August 224): Hdn. 6.1.4.[25] Besides numerous consecration coins,[26] consecration and cult for *diva* Maesa Augusta (as *diva* Iulia Augusta) are attested epigraphically:

---

21. Caracalla allegedly deconsecrated Faustina the Younger (HA, *M. Ant.* 11.6–7): see Ch. 4.

22. Bonamente 1991, 73.

23. E.g. *RIC* IV.2, Elagabalus nos. 715, 716, Schulten 1979, nos. 304 d, 305, 305a.

24. Gilliam 1969, 286–87.

25. Kienast 2017, 169 for dates; Benario 1962 argues for her death in 223.

26. *RIC* IV.2, Severus Alexander nos. 377–80, 712–14.

Appendix 3 313

1) *AE* 1917/18, 9 = *AE* 1917/18, +97 = EDCS-16201685 (dedication *divae Iuliae/ Aug(ustae) aviae d(omini) n(ostri)/Imp(eratoris) M(arci) Aur(eli) Seve/ri [[Al[exandri]]]* by municipality of Tutugi [Galera, Spain]).

Consecrated Males until 235 CE

1. Caesar[27]
2. Augustus
3. Claudius
4. Vespasian
5. Titus
6. *Divus* Caesar Domitiani (son of Domitian and Domitia)
7. Nerva
8. Trajan
9. Lucius Aelius Caesar
10. Hadrian
11. Antoninus Pius
12. Lucius Verus
13. Marcus Aurelius
14. Pertinax
15. Commodus
16. Septimius Severus
17. Geta
18. Caracalla
19. Alexander Severus

---

27. See Bonamente 1991, 60–64 for ancient evidence for Caesar and other *divi*.

Bibliography[1]

Abdy, R. A. 2014. "Chronology of Sabina's Coinage at the Roman Mint." *RN* 171: 73–91.

Adler, E. 2011a. "Cassius Dio's Livia and the Conspiracy of Cinna Magnus." *GRBS* 51: 133–54.

Adler, E. 2011b. *Valorizing the Barbarians: Enemy Speeches in Roman Historiography.* Austin.

Alexander, M. C. 1990. *Trials in the Late Roman Republic, 149 BC to 50 BC.* Toronto.

Alexandridis, A. 2004. *Die Frauen des römischen Kaiserhauses: Eine Untersuchung ihrer bildlichen Darstellung von Livia bis Iulia Domna.* Mainz am Rhein.

Alexandridis, A. 2010. "The Other Side of the Coin: The Women of the Flavian Imperial Family." In *Tradition und Erneuerung: Mediale Strategien in der Zeit der Flavier*, ed. N. Kramer and C. Reitz, 191–237. Berlin and New York.

Alföldi, A. 1971. *Der Vater des Vaterlandes im römischen Denken.* Darmstadt.

Alföldy, G. 1991. "Augustus und die Inschriften: Tradition und Innovation. Die Geburt der imperialen Epigraphik." *Gymnasium* 98: 289–324.

Alföldy, G. 1992. *Studi sull'epigrafia augustea e tiberiana di Roma.* Rome.

Alföldy, G. 1998. "Commodus und Crispina in einer Inschrift aus Sabratha." *Faventia* 20.1: 39–47.

Alföldy, G., A. Kolb, and S. Panciera, eds. 1996. *Corpus Inscriptionum Latinarum. VI.8.2. Titulos imperatorum domusque eorum thesauro schedarum imaginumque ampliato.* Berlin.

Allason-Jones, L. 1999. "Women and the Roman Army in Britain." In Goldsworthy and Haynes 1999, 41–51.

Allison, P. M. 2013. *People and Spaces in Roman Military Bases.* Cambridge.

Ameling, W. 1992. "Die Kinder des Marc Aurel und die Bildnistypen der Faustina Minor." *ZPE* 90: 147–66.

Anagnostou-Laoutides, E., and M. B. Charles. 2015. "Titus and Berenice: The Elegiac Aura of an Historical Affair." *Arethusa* 48: 17–46.

---

1. *AJP* formatting, with journal titles formatted as *L'Année Philologique*.

Ando, C. 2000. *Imperial Ideology and Provincial Loyalty in the Roman Empire*. Berkeley, London, and Los Angeles.

Arce, J. 2010. "Roman Imperial Funerals *in effigie*." In Ewald and Noreña 2010, 309–23.

Arrizabalaga y Prado, L. de. 2010. *The Emperor Elagabalus: Fact or Fiction?* Cambridge.

Badian, E. 1984. "Notes on Some Documents from Aphrodisias Concerning Octavian." *GRBS* 25: 157–70.

Bagnall, R. S., and B. W. Frier. 1994. *The Demography of Roman Egypt*. Cambridge.

Barrett, A. A. 1990. *Caligula: The Corruption of Power*. New Haven.

Barrett, A. A. 1991. "Claudius' Victory Arch in Rome." *Britannia* 22: 1–19.

Barrett, A. A. 1996. *Agrippina: Sex, Power, and Politics in the Early Empire*. New Haven.

Barrett, A. A. 2002. *Livia: First Lady of Imperial Rome*. New Haven.

Barrett, A. A. 2005a. "Aulus Caecina Severus and the Military Woman." *Historia* 54: 301–14.

Barrett, A. A. 2005b. "Vespasian's Wife." *Latomus* 64: 385–96.

Barry, W. D. 1996. "Roof Tiles and Urban Violence in the Ancient World," *GRBS* 37: 55–74.

Bartman, E. 1999. *Portraits of Livia: Imaging the Imperial Woman in Augustan Rome*. Cambridge.

Bartman, E. 2012. "Early Imperial Female Portraiture." In *A Companion to Women in the Ancient World*, ed. S. L. James and S. Dillon, 414–22. Malden, MA.

Bassignano, M. S. 2013. "Culto imperiale al femminile nel mondo romano." In *L'indagine e la rima: scritti per Lorenzo Braccesi*, ed. F. Raviola et al., 141–88. Rome.

Bauman, R. A. 1967. *The* Crimen Maiestatis *in the Roman Republic and Augustan Principate*. Johannesburg.

Bauman, R. A. 1974. *"Impietas in principem": A Study of Treason against the Roman Emperor with Special Reference to the First Century A.D.* Munich.

Bauman, R. A. 1981. "Tribunician sacrosanctity in 44, 36 and 35 B.C." *RhMus* 124: 166–83.

Bauman, R. A. 1992. *Women and Politics in Ancient Rome*. London and New York.

Bauman, R. A. 1994. "Tanaquil-Livia and the Death of Augustus." *Historia* 43: 177–88.

Bauman, R. A. 1996. *Crime and Punishment in Ancient Rome*. London and New York.

Beard, M. 2007. *The Roman Triumph*. Cambridge, Mass.

Beard, M., J. North, and S. Price. 1998. *Religions of Rome*. 2 vols. Cambridge.

Beckmann, M. 2011. "The Coinage of Diva Faustina I." In *Proceedings of the XIVth International Numismatic Congress, Glasgow, 2009*, vol. I, ed. N. Holmes, 509–13. Glasgow.

Beckmann, M. 2012a. *Diva Faustina: Coinage and Cult in Rome and the Provinces*. New York.

Beckmann, M. 2012b. "Trajan and Hadrian." In Metcalf 2012, 405–22.

Bibliography

Belli Pasqua, R. 1995. *Sculture di età romana in "basalto."* Rome.

Benario, H. W. 1962. "The Date of the *Feriale Duranum*." *Historia* 11: 192–96.

Bennett, J. 2001. *Trajan: Optimus Princeps*. 2nd ed. Bloomington and Indianapolis.

Benoist, S. 2005. *Rome, le prince et la cité: Pouvoir impérial et cérémonies publiques (Ier siècle av.—début du IVe siècle apr. J.-C.)*. Paris.

Benoist, S. 2015. "Women and *Imperium* in Rome: Imperial Perspectives." In *Women and War in Antiquity*, ed. J. Fabre-Serris and A. Keith, 266–88. Baltimore.

Bernand, A., and E. Bernand. 1960. *Les inscriptions du Colosse de Memnon*. Cairo.

Birley, A. R. 1993. *Marcus Aurelius: A Biography*. Rev. ed. New Haven.

Birley, A. R. 1997. *Hadrian, the Restless Emperor*. London and New York.

Birley, A. R. 1999. *Septimius Severus: The African Emperor*. London.

Boatwright, M. T. 1985. "The 'Ara Ditis-Ustrinum of Hadrian' in the Western Campus Martius, and Other Problematic Roman Ustrina." *AJA* 89: 486–97.

Boatwright, M. T. 1987. *Hadrian and the City of Rome*. Princeton.

Boatwright, M. T. 1991. "Imperial Women of the Early Second Century A.C." *AJP* 112: 513–40.

Boatwright, M. T. 1992. "Matidia the Younger." *EMC* 26, n.s. 11: 19–32.

Boatwright, M. T. 1993. "The City Gate of Plancia Magna in Perge." In *Roman Art in Context: An Anthology*, ed. E. D'Ambra, 189–207. Englewood Cliffs, N.J.

Boatwright, M. T. 2000. "Just Window Dressing? Imperial Women as Architectural Sculpture." In *I, Claudia*, 2, ed. D. E. E. Kleiner and S. B. Matheson, 61–75. Austin, Tex.

Boatwright, M. T. 2003. "Faustina the Younger, *Mater Castrorum*." In *Les femmes antiques entre sphère privée et sphère publique*, ed. R. Frei-Stolba, A. Bielman, and O. Bianchi, 249–68. Bern.

Boatwright, M. T. 2008. "Tacitus and the Final Rites of Agrippina: *Annals* 14, 9." In Vol. XIV of *Studies in Latin Literature and Roman History*, Collection Latomus vol. 315: 375–93.

Boatwright, M. T. 2010. "Antonine Rome: Security in the Homeland." In Ewald and Noreña 2010, 169–97.

Boatwright, M. T. 2011a. "The *Elogia* of the Volusii Saturnini at Lucus Feroniae, and the Education of Their Domestic Service." In *L'écriture dans la maison romaine*, ed. M. Corbier and J.-P. Guilhembet, 99–112. Paris.

Boatwright, M. T. 2011b. "Women and Gender in the Forum Romanum." *TAPA* 141: 105–41.

Boatwright, M. T. 2013. "Hadrian and the Agrippa Inscription of the Pantheon." In *Hadrian: Art, Politics and Economy*, ed. T. Opper, 19–30. London.

Boatwright, M. T. 2015. "Visualizing Empire in Imperial Rome." In *Aspects of Ancient Institutions and Geography: Studies in Honor of Richard J. A. Talbert*, ed. L. L. Brice and D. Slootjes, 235–59. Leiden.

Bol, R. 1984. "Das Statuenprogramm des Herodes-Atticus-Nymphäums." *Olympische Forschungen* 15: 31–45.

Bibliography

Bonamente, G. 1991. "Il canone dei *divi* e la *Historia Augusta.*" In *Historiae Augustae Colloquium Parisinum*, ed. G. Bonamente and N. Duval, 59–82. Macerata.

Boschung, D. 1993. "Die Bildnistypen der iulisch-claudischen Kaiserfamilie." *JRA* 6: 39–79.

Boschung, D. 2002. *Gens Augusta: Untersuchungen zu Aufstellung, Wirkung und Bedeutung der Statuengruppen des julisch-claudischen Kaiserhauses.* Mainz am Rhein.

Boschung, D., and W. Eck. 1998. "Ein Bildnis der Mutter Traians? Um Kolossalkopf der sogenannte Agrippina Minor vom Traiansforum." *AA* 3: 473–81.

Bowie, E. L. 1990. "Greek Poetry in the Antonine Age." In *Antonine Literature*, ed. D. A. Russell, 53–90. Oxford.

Boyle, A. J. 2008. *Octavia: Attributed to Seneca.* Oxford.

Bradley, K. R. 1991. *Discovering the Roman Family: Studies in Roman Social History.* New York.

Brännstedt, L. 2015. "Livia on the Move." In *The Moving City: Processions, Passages and Promenades in Ancient Rome*, ed. I. Östenberg, S. Malmberg, and J. Bjørnebye, 37–46. London.

Brennan, T. C. 2018. *Sabina Augusta: An Imperial Journey.* Oxford.

Brent, A. 1995. *Hippolytus and the Roman Church in the Third Century: Communities in Tension before the Emergence of a Monarch-Bishop.* Leiden and New York.

Brilliant, R. 2005. "Roman Portraits Re-Carved: 'Now You See Him/Her, Now You Don't.'" *JRA* 18: 631–34.

Brunt, P. A. 1966. "The 'Fiscus' and Its Development." *JRS* 56: 75–91.

Brunt, P. A. 1972. Review of P. Garnsey, *Social Status and Legal Privilege in the Roman Empire* (1970). *JRS* 62: 166–70.

Brunt, P. A. 1977. "Lex de Imperio Vespasiani." *JRS* 67: 95–116.

Brunt, P. A., and J. Moore, eds. 1967. *Res Gestae divi Augusti. The Achievements of the Divine Augustus.* Oxford.

Bruun, C. 2000. "Senatorial Owners of What?" *JRA* 13: 498–506.

Bruun, C. 2010. "Matidia die Jüngere—Gesellschaftlicher Einfluss und dynastische Rolle." In Kolb 2010b, 211–33.

Bruun, C., and J. Edmondson, eds. 2015. *The Oxford Handbook of Roman Epigraphy.* Oxford.

Buonocore, M. 1985. "Munera e venationes adrianei nel 119 d.C." *Latomus* 44: 173–77.

Buonocore, M. 2007. "Le iscrizioni ad Augusto e alla sua *domus* nelle città dell'Italia centro-appenninica (regio IV)." In *Contributi all'epigrafia d'età Augustea*, ed. G. Paci, 31–90. Tivoli.

Burns, J. 2007. *Great Women of Imperial Rome: Mothers and Wives of the Caesars.* New York.

Burrell, B. 2004. *Neokoroi: Greek Cities and Roman Emperors.* Leiden and Boston.

Callataÿ, F. de. 1995. "Calculating Ancient Coin Production: Seeking a Balance." *NC* 155: 289–311.

Bibliography

Campbell, B. 1978. "The Marriage of Soldiers under the Empire." *JRS* 68: 153–66.

Cancik, H., and J. Rüpke, eds. 1997. *Römische Reichsreligion und Provinzialreligion.* Tübingen.

Cantarella. E. 1992. "Famiglia romana e demografia sociale." *Iura* 43: 99–111.

Carandini, A. 1969. *Vibia Sabina: Funzione politica, iconografia e il problema del classicism Adrianeo.* Florence.

Carradice, I. 2012. "Flavian Coinage." In Metcalf 2012, 375–90.

Carroll, M., and E.-J. Graham, eds. 2014. *Infant Health and Death in Roman Italy and Beyond.* Portsmouth, R.I.

Cascella, S. 2013. "Matidia Minor and Suessa Aurunca." In *Hadrian: Arts, Politics and Economy*, ed. T Opper, 73–88. London.

Castritius, H. 1969. "Zu den Frauen der Flavier." *Historia* 18: 492–502.

Castritius, H. 2002. "Die flavische Familie: Frauen neben Vespasian, Titus und Domitian." In *Die Kaiserinnen Roms. Von Livia bis Iulia Domna*, ed. H. Temporini-Gräfin Vitzthum, 164–86. Munich.

Cecamore, C. 1999. "'*Faustinae aedemque decernerent'* (*SHA, Marcus* 26). Les fragments 69–70 de la Forma Urbis et la première dédicace du temple de la Vigna Barberini." *MEFRA* 111.1: 311–49.

Cenerini, F. 2006. "Spazi pubblici femminili: teoria o realità?" In *Misurare il tempo, misurare lo spazio: atti del colloquio AIEGL, Borghesi, 2005*, ed. M. G. Angeli Bertinelli and A. Donati, 275–86. Faenza.

Champlin, E. 1991. *Final Judgments: Duty and Emotion in Roman Wills, 200 BC–AD 250.* Berkeley, Los Angeles, and Oxford.

Champlin, E. 1999. "The First (1996) Edition of the '*Senatus Consultum de Cn. Pisone Patre*': A Review." In *AJP* 120: 117–22.

Champlin, E. 2003. *Nero.* Cambridge, Mass.

Chantraine, H. 1980. "Freigelassene und Sklaven kaiserlicher Frauen." In *Studien zur antiken Sozialgeschichte. Festschrift Friedrich Vittinghoff*, ed. W. Eck, H. Galsterer, and H. Wolff, 389–416. Cologne and Vienna.

Chaplin, J. 2010. "Scipio the Matchmaker." In *Ancient Historiography and Its Contexts. Studies in Honour of A. J. Woodman*, ed. C. S. Kraus, J. Marincola, and C. Pelling, 60–72. Oxford and New York.

Chastagnol, A. 1979. "Les femmes dans l'ordre sénatorial: titulature et rang social à Rome." *RH* 262: 3–28.

Chausson, F. 2003. "Domitia Longina: reconsidération d'un destin impérial." *JSav*: 101–29.

Chausson, F. 2008. "Une dédicace monumentale provenant du théâtre de *Suessa Aurunca*, due à Matidie la Jeune, belle-soeur de l'empereur Hadrien." *JSav*: 233–59.

Chausson, F., and A. Buonopane. 2010. "Una fonte della ricchezza delle *Augustae*—Le *figlinae* urbane." In Kolb 2010b, 91–110.

Chaniotis, A. 2003. "Livia Sebaste, Iulia Sebaste, Caius Caesar Parthikos, Domitian Anikeitos Theos: Inofficial Titles of Emperors in the Early Principate." *AAntHung* 43.3–4: 341–44.

Claridge, A., et al. 1998. *Rome: An Oxford Archaeological Guide*. Oxford and New York.

Claridge, A. 2007. "Hadrian's Lost Temple of Trajan." *JRA* 20: 54–94.

Claudio imperatore. Messalina, Agrippina e le ombre di una dinastia—Catalogo della mostra Ara Pacis 2019. 2019. Rome.

Cluett, R. G. 1998. "Roman Women and Triumviral Politics." *EMC* 17: 67–84.

Coarelli, F. 1978. "La statue de Cornélie, mère des Gracques, et la crise politique à Rome au temps de Saturninus." In *Le dernier siècle de la république romaine et l'époque augustéenne*, ed. H. Zehnacker, 13–28. Strasbourg.

Cogitore, I. 1992. "Séries de dédicaces italiennes à la dynastie julio-claudienne." *MEFRA* 104: 817–70.

Cogitore, I. 2000. "Les honneurs italiens aux femmes de la famille impériale de la mort de César à Domitien." In *Les Élites municipales de l'Italie péninsulaire de la mort de César à la mort de Domitien entre continuité et rupture*, ed. M. Cébeillac-Gervasoni, 236–66. Rome.

Cogitore, I. 2002. *La légitimité dynastique d'Auguste à Néron à l'épreuve des conspirations*. Rome.

Cole, S. 2013. *Cicero and the Rise of Deification at Rome*. Cambridge.

Collins, A. W. 2009. "The Palace Revolution: The Assassination of Domitian and the Accession of Nerva." *Phoenix* 63: 73–106.

Cooley, A. E. 1998. "The Moralizing Message of the *Senatus Consultum de Cn. Pisone Patre*." *Greece & Rome* 45: 199–212.

Cooley, A. E., ed. 2009. *Res gestae divi Augusti: Text, Translation and Commentary*. Cambridge and New York.

Cooley, A. E. 2013. "Women beyond Rome: Trend-Setters or Dedicated Followers of Fashion?" In *Women and the Roman City in the Latin West*, ed. E. A. Hemelrijk and G. Woolf, 23–46. Leiden.

Corbier, M. 1994. "La maison des Césars." In *Épouser au plus proche. Incest, prohibitions et stratégies matrimoniales de la Méditerranée*, ed. P. Bonte, 243–91. Paris.

Corbier, M. 1995. "Male Power and Legitimacy through Women: The *Domus Augusta* under the Julio-Claudians." In *Women in Antiquity: New Assessments*, ed. R. Hawley and B. Levick, 178–93. New York.

Corbier, M. 2001. "*Maiestas domus Augustae*." In *Varia epigraphica: atti del colloquio internazionale di epigrafia: Bertinoro, 8–10 giugno 2000*, ed. M. G. Angeli Bertinelli and A. Donati, 155–99. Faenza.

Crawford, M. 1983a. "Numismatics." In *Sources for Ancient History*, ed. M. Crawford, 185–233. Cambridge.

Crawford, M. H. 1983b. "Roman Imperial Coin Types and the Formation of Public Opinion." In *Studies in Numismatic Method: Presented to Philip Grierson*, ed. C. N. L. Brooke, B. H. I. Stewart, J. G. Pollard, and T. R. Volk, 47–64. Cambridge.

Cresci Marrone, G., and S. Nicolini. 2010. "Il principe e la strategia del lutto—Il caso delle donne della *domus* di Augusto." In Kolb 2010b, 163–78.

Bibliography

Crook, J. A. 1951. "Titus and Berenice." *AJP* 72: 162–75.

Daguet-Gagey, A. 1997. *Les "opera publica" à Rome: 180–305 ap. J.-C.* Paris.

D'Ambra, E. 2013. "Mode and Model in the Flavian Female Portrait." *AJA* 117: 511–25.

Darwall-Smith, R. H. 1996. *Emperors and Architecture: A Study of Flavian Rome.* Brussels.

Daube, D. 1954 [1991]. "Princeps legibus solutus." *L'Europa e il diritto romano: Studi in Memoria di Paolo Koschaker*, 2: 463–65. Milan. Reprinted in 1991 in *Collected Studies in Roman Law*, ed. D. Cohen and D. Simon, 1: 549–51. Frankfurt.

Davies, G. 2008. "Portrait Statues as Models for Gender Roles in Roman Society." In *Role Models in the Roman World: Identity and Assimilation*, ed. S. Bell, 207–20. Ann Arbor, Mich.

Davies, G. 2013. "Honorific vs. Funerary Statues of Women: Essentially the Same or Fundamentally Different?" In *Women and the Roman City in the Latin West*, ed. E. A. Hemelrijk and G. Woolf, 171–99. Leiden.

Debrunner Hall, M. 1994. "Eine reine Männerwelt? Frauen um das römische Heer." In Dettenhofer 1994, 207–28.

De Caprariis, F. 1993. "Un monumento dinastico tiberiano nel Campo Marzio settentrionale." *BCAR* 95: 93–114.

Deline, T. 2015. "The Criminal Charges against Agrippina the Elder in A.D. 27 and 29." *CQ* 65.2: 766–72.

Den Hollander, W. 2014. *Josephus, the Emperors, and the City of Rome: From Hostage to Historian*. Leiden.

Dettenhofer, M. H., ed. 1994. *Reine Männersache? Frauen in Männerdomänen der antiken Welt*. Cologne.

Dettenhofer, M. H. 2000. *Herrschaft und Widerstand im augusteischen Principat. Die Konkurrenz zwischen res publica und domus Augusta*. Stuttgart.

Di Leo, B. 1989. "Basalt." In *Radiance in Stone: Sculptures in Colored Marble from the Museo Nazionale Romano*, ed. M. L. Anderson, A. Giuliano, and L. Nista, 56–63. Rome.

Dillon, S. 2010. *The Female Portrait Statue in the Greek World*. New York.

DiLuzio, M. J. 2016. *A Place at the Altar: Priestesses in Republican Rome*. Princeton.

Dixon, S. 1984. "*Infirmitas Sexus*: Womanly Weakness in Roman Law." *RHD* 52: 343–71.

Dixon, S. 1988. *The Roman Mother*. London and Sydney.

Dixon, S. 2001. *Reading Roman Women: Sources, Genres and Real Life*. London.

Dixon, S. 2007. *Cornelia, Mother of the Gracchi*. London and New York.

Dixon, S. 2016. "Family." In *The Oxford Handbook of Roman Law and Society*, ed. P. J. du Plessis, C. Ando, and K. Tuori, 461–72. Oxford.

Dolansky, F. 2012. "Playing with Gender: Girls, Dolls, and Adult Ideals in the Roman World." *ClAnt* 31: 256–92.

Domínguez Arranz, A. 2016. "Entre mujer y diosa: Matronazgo cívico de la emperatriz romana." In *Matronazgo y arquitectura: de la Antigüedad a la Edad Moderna*, ed. C. Martínez López and F. Serrano Estrella, 65–112. Granada.

Driel-Murray, C. v. 1997. "Women in Forts?" *Pro Vindonissa*: 55–61.

Duncan-Jones, R. P. 2005. "Implications of Roman Coinage: Debates and Differences." *Klio* 87: 459–87.

Duncan-Jones, R. P. 2006. "Crispina and the Coinage of the Empresses." *NC* 166: 223–28.

Eck, W. 1982. "Hadrian als *pater patriae* und die Verleihung des Augustatitels an Sabina." In *Romanitas—Christianitas. Untersuchungen zur Geschichte und Literatur der römischen Kaiserzeit*, ed. G. Wirth, K.-H. Schwarte, and J. Heinrichs, 217–29. Berlin and New York.

Eck, W. 1984. "Senatorial Self-Representation. Developments in the Augustan Period." In *Caesar Augustus: Seven Aspects*, ed. F. Millar and E. Segal, 129–67. Oxford.

Eck, W. 1993. *Agrippina die Stadtgründerin Kölns. Eine Frau in der frühkaiserzeitlichen Politik*. Cologne.

Eck, W. 2016. "Der Senat und der Herrscherkult." In *Kaiserkult in den Provinzen des römischen Reiches. Organisation, Kommunikation und Repräsentation*, ed. A. Kolb and M. Vitale, 37–56. Berlin.

Eck, W., A. Caballos, and F. Fernández. 1996. *Das senatus consultum de Cn. Pisone patre*. Vestigia 48. Munich.

Edmondson, J., ed. 2009. *Augustus*. Edinburgh.

Edwards, C. 1993. *The Politics of Immorality in Ancient Rome*. Cambridge and New York.

Evans Grubbs, J. 2002. *Women and the Law in the Roman Empire: A Sourcebook on Marriage, Divorce and Widowhood*. London and New York.

Evans Grubbs, J., and T. Parkin, eds., with R. Bell. 2013. *The Oxford Handbook of Childhood and Education in the Classical World*. Oxford and New York.

Ewald, B. C., and C. F. Noreña, eds. 2010. *The Emperor and Rome: Space, Representation and Ritual*. Cambridge and New York.

Fagan, G. 2002. "Messalina's Folly." *CQ* 52: 566–79.

Fagan, G. 2011. *The Lure of the Arena: Social Psychology and the Crowd at the Roman Games*. Cambridge and New York.

Fantham, E. 2006. *Julia Augusti, the Emperor's Daughter*. New York.

Fejfer, J. 1985. "The Portraits of the Severan Empress Julia Domna. A New Approach." *AnalRom* 14: 129–38.

Fejfer, J. 1988. "Official Portraits of Julia Domna. Ritratto ufficiale e ritratto privato." In *Atti della II Conferenza internazionale sul ritratto romano, Roma 26–30 settembre 1984*, ed. N. Bonacasa and G. Rizza, 295–301. Rome.

Fejfer, J. 2008. *Roman Portraits in Context*. Berlin and New York.

Filippi, F., ed. 2016. *Campo Marzio. Nuove ricerche. Seminario di Studi*. Rome.

Fishwick, D. 1987–2005. *The Imperial Cult in the Latin West: Studies in the Ruler Cult in the Western Provinces of the Roman Empire*. 3 volumes in 8 parts. Leiden and New York.

Fishwick, D. 1992. "On the Temple of Divus 'Augustus.'" *Phoenix* 46: 232–55.

Fishwick, D. 2007. "Numen Augustum." *ZPE* 160: 247–55.

Fittschen, K. 1982. *Die Bildnistypen der Faustina minor und die Fecunditas Augustae*. Göttingen.

Fittschen, K. 1996. "Courtly Portraits of Women in the Era of the Adoptive Emperors (AD 98–180) and Their Reception in Roman Society." In Kleiner and Matheson 1996, 42–52.

Fittschen, K. 1999. *Prinzenbildnisse antoninischer Zeit*. Mainz.

Flory, M. B. 1984. "*Sic Exempla Parantur*: Livia's Shrine to Concordia and the Porticus Liviae." *Historia* 33: 309–30.

Flory, M. B. 1988 [1997]. "The Meaning of 'Augusta' in the Julio-Claudian Period." *AJAH* 13: 113–38.

Flory, M. B. 1993. "Livia and the History of Public Honorific Statues for Women in Rome." *TAPA* 123: 287–308.

Flory, M. B. 1995. "The Deification of Roman Women." *AHB* 9.3/4: 127–34.

Flory, M. B. 1996. "Dynastic Ideology, the *Domus Augusta*, and Imperial Women: A Lost Statuary Group in the Circus Flaminius." *TAPA* 126: 287–306.

Flory, M. B. 1998. "The Integration of Women into the Roman Triumph." *Historia* 47: 489–94.

Flower, H. I. 2011. *The Art of Forgetting: Disgrace and Oblivion in Roman Political Culture*. Chapel Hill, N.C.

Forbis, E. P. 1990. "Women's Public Image in Italian Honorary Inscriptions." *AJP* 111: 493–512.

Foubert, L. 2010. "The Palatine Dwelling of the *Mater Familias*: Houses as Symbolic Space in the Julio-Claudian Period." *Klio* 92: 65–82.

Foubert, L. 2015. "Vesta and Julio-Claudian Women in Imperial Propaganda." *AncSoc* 45: 187–204.

Fraser, T. E. 2015. "Domitia Longina: An Underestimated Augusta (c. 53–126/8)." *AncSoc* 45: 205–66.

Frei-Stolba, R. 2008. "Livie et aliae: le culte des divi et leurs prêtresses: le culte des divae." In *Égypte, Grèce, Rome. Les différents visages des femmes antiques*, ed. F. Bertholet, A. Bielman Sánchez, and R. Frei-Stolba, 345–95. Bern.

French, V. 1986. "Midwives and Maternity Care in the Roman World." *Helios* 13.2: 69–84.

Frier, B. W. 1994. "Natural Fertility and Family Limitation in Roman Marriage." *CPh* 89: 318–33.

Friesen, S. J. 1993. *Twice Neokoros: Ephesus, Asia, and the Cult of the Flavian Imperial Family*. Leiden and New York.

Fullerton, M. D. 1985. "The Domus Augusti in Imperial Iconography of 13–12 B.C." *AJA* 89: 473–83.

Fündling, J. 2006. *Kommentar zur Vita Hadriani der Historia Augusta*. Bonn.

Gaca, K. L. 2016. "Continuities in Rape and Tyranny in Martial Societies from Antiquity Onward." In *Women in Antiquity, Real Women across the Ancient World*, ed. S. L. Budin and J. M. Turfa, 1041–56. London.

Gallia, A. B. 2015. "Vestal Virgins and Their Families." *ClAnt* 34: 74–120.

Gallo, F. 1984. "Per il riesame di una tesi fortunata sulla *solutio legibus*." In *Sodalitas: scritti in onore di Antonio Guarino,* 2, 651–82. Naples.

Gamauf, R. 1999. *"Ad statuam licet confugere": Untersuchungen zum Asylrecht im römischen Prinzipat.* Frankfurt am Main.

Gardner, J. F. 1986. *Women in Roman Law and Society.* Bloomington and Indianapolis.

Gardner, J. F. 1988. "Julia's Freedmen: Questions of Law and Status." *BICS* 35: 94–100.

Garnsey, P. 1970. *Social Status and Legal Privilege in the Roman Empire.* Oxford.

Ghedini, F. 1984. *Giulia Domna tra Oriente e Occidente.* Rome.

Giacosa, G. 1977. *Women of the Caesars. Their Lives and Portraits on Coins.* Milan.

Gillespie, C. C. 2018. *Boudica: Warrior Woman of Roman Britain.* Oxford and New York.

Gilliam, J. F. 1969. "On Divi under the Severi, II." In *Hommages à Marcel Renard,* ed J. Dumortier-Bibauw, 284–89. Brussels.

Ginsburg, J. 2006. *Representing Agrippina: Constructions of Female Power in the Early Roman Empire.* Oxford and New York.

Giroire, C., and D. Roger. 2007. *Roman Art from the Louvre.* New York.

Gleason, M. W. 2010. "Making Space for Bicultural Identity: Herodes Atticus Commemorates Regilla." In *Local Knowledge and Microidentities in the Imperial Greek World,* ed. T. Whitmarsh, 125–62. Cambridge.

Goldsworthy, A. K., and I. P. Haynes, eds. 1999. *The Roman Army as a Community.* Portsmouth, R.I.

González, J. 1988. "The First Oath *pro Salute Augusti* Found in Baetica." *ZPE* 72: 113–27.

Goodyear, F. R. D. 1981. *The Annals of Tacitus,* vol. II *(Annals 1.55–81 and Annals 2).* Cambridge.

Gorrie, C. 2004. "Julia Domna's Building Patronage, Imperial Family Roles and the Severan Revival of Moral Legislation." *Historia* 53: 61–72.

Gradel, I. 2002. *Emperor Worship and Roman Religion.* Oxford.

Granino Cecere, M. G. 2010. "Proprietà di *Augustae* a Roma e nel *Latium vetus*." In Kolb 2010b, 111–27.

Granino Cecere, M. G. 2014. *Il flaminato femminile imperiale nell'Italia romana.* Rome.

Grant, M. 1950. *Aspects of the Principate of Tiberius.* New York.

Greene, E. M. 2014. "If the Shoe Fits: Style and Function of Children's Shoes from Vindolanda." In *Life in the Limes: Studies of the People and Objects of the Roman Frontiers,* ed. R. Collins and F. McIntosh, 29–36. Oxford.

Gregori, G. L., and E. Rosso. 2010. "Giulia Augusta, figlia di Tito, nipote di Domiziano." In Kolb 2010b, 193–210.

Gregory, A. P. 1994. "'Powerful Images': Responses to Portraits and the Political Uses of Images in Rome." *JRA* 7: 80–99.

Griffin, M. 1997. "The Senate's Story." *JRS* 87: 249–63.

Bibliography

Gualerzi, S. 2005. "Una matrona sul confine: Matidia Maggiore." In *Actas del II Congreso internacional de Historia Antigua: La Hispania de los Antoninos (98–180)*, ed. L. Hernández Guerra, 213–34. Valladolid.

Habicht, C. ed. 1969. *Die Inschriften des Asklepieions*. Berlin.

Hahn, U. 1994. *Die Frauen des römischen Kaiserhauses und ihre Ehrungen im griechischen Osten anhand epigraphischer und numismatischer Zeugnisse von Livia bis Sabina*. Saarbrücken.

Halfmann, H. 1986. *Itinera principum: Geschichte und Typologie der Kaiserreisen im Römischen Reich*. Stuttgart.

Hallett, J. 2015. "Fulvia: The Representation of an Elite Woman Warrior." In *Women and War in Antiquity*, ed. J. Fabre-Serris and A. Keith, 247–65. Baltimore.

Hänlein-Schäfer, H. 1985. *Veneratio Augusti: Eine Studie zu den Tempeln des ersten römischen Kaisers*. Rome.

Harl, K. W. 1987. *Civic Coins and Civic Politics in the Roman East AD 180–275*. Berkeley.

Harper, K. 2017. *The Fate of Rome: Climate, Disease, and the End of an Empire*. Princeton.

Harries, J. 2007. *Law and Crime in the Roman World*. Cambridge.

Hekster, O. 2001. "All in the Family: The Appointments of Emperors Designate in the Second Century." In *Administration, Prosopography and Appointment Policies in the Roman Empire*, ed. L. de Blois, 35–49. Amsterdam.

Hekster, O. 2002. *Commodus: An Emperor at the Crossroads*. Amsterdam.

Hekster, O. 2003. "Coins and Messages: Audience Targeting on Coins of Different Denominations?" In *The Representation and Perception of Roman Imperial Power*, ed. L. de Blois, 20–35. Amsterdam.

Hekster, O. 2015. *Emperors and Ancestors: Roman Rulers and the Constraints of Tradition*. Oxford.

Hemelrijk, E. A. 1999. *Matrona docta. Educated Women of the Roman Élite from Cornelia to Julia Domna*. London.

Hemelrijk, E. A. 2004. "Masculinity and Femininity in the *Laudatio Turiae*." *CQ* 54: 185–97.

Hemelrijk, E. A. 2005a. "Octavian and the Introduction of Public Statues for Women in Rome." *Athenaeum* 93: 309–17.

Hemelrijk, E. A. 2005b. "Priestesses of the Imperial Cult in the Latin West: Titles and Function." *AC* 74: 137–70.

Hemelrijk, E. A. 2007. "Local Empresses: Priestesses of the Imperial Cult in the Cities of the Latin West." *Phoenix* 61: 318–48.

Hemelrijk, E. A. 2012. "Fictive Motherhood and Female Authority in Roman Cities." *EuGeStA* 2: 201–20.

Hemelrijk, E. A. 2015. *Hidden Lives, Public Personae: Women and Civic Life in the Roman West*. Oxford.

Henriksén, C. 1997. "Earinus: An Imperial Eunuch in the Light of the Poems of Martial and Statius." *Mnemosyne* 50: 281–94.

Bibliography

Herrmann, P. 1968. *Der römische Kaisereid. Untersuchungen zu seiner Herkunft und Entwicklung*. Göttingen.

Hesberg, H. von, and S. Panciera, eds. 1994. *Das Mausoleum des Augustus. Der Bau und seine Inschriften*. Munich.

Højte, J. M. 2000. "Imperial Visits as Occasion for the Erection of Portrait Statues?" *ZPE* 133: 221–35.

Højte, J. M. 2005. *Roman Imperial Statue Bases: From Augustus to Commodus*. Aarhus.

Holford-Strevens, L. 2003. *Aulus Gellius: An Antonine Scholar and His Achievement*. Oxford.

Hopkins, K. 1980. "Taxes and Trade in the Roman Empire (200 B.C.–A.D. 400)." *JRS* 70: 101–25.

Hopkins, K. 1995–96. "Rome, Taxes, Rents and Trade." *Kodai* 6-7: 41–75.

Horster, M. 2001. *Bauinscriften römischer Kaiser. Untersuchungen zu Inscriftenpraxis und Bautätigkeit in Städten des westlichen Imperium Romanum in der Zeit des Prinzipats*. Stuttgart.

Howgego, C. J. 1992. "The Supply and Use of Money in the Roman World." *JRS* 82: 1–31.

Howgego, C. J., V. Heuchert, and A. Burnett, eds. 2005. *Coinage and Identity in the Roman Provinces*. Oxford.

Humphrey, J. 1979. "The Three Daughters of Agrippina Maior." *AJAH* 4: 125–43.

Huntsman, E. D. 2009. "Livia before Octavian." *Ancient Society* 39: 121–69.

Hurlet, F. 1997. *Les collègues du prince sous Auguste et Tibère*. Rome.

Hurlet, F. 2015. "The Roman Emperor and the Imperial Family." In Bruun and Edmondson 2015, 178–201.

Hurlet, F., and B. Mineo, eds. 2009. *Le Principate d'Auguste. Réalités et représentations du pouvoir. Autour de la "Res publica restituta."* Rennes.

Huskinson, J. 1996. *Roman Children's Sarcophagi. Their Decoration and Its Social Significance*. Oxford and New York.

James, S. 2002. "Writing the Legions: The Past, Present, and Future of Roman Military Studies in Britain." *AJ* 159: 1–58. https://doi.org/10.1080/00665983.2002.11020514

Jenkins, T. E. 2009. "Livia the Princeps: Gender and Ideology in the *Consolatio ad Liviam*." *Helios* 36: 1–25.

Jessen, K. E. 2013. "Portraits of Livia in Context: An Analysis of Distribution through Application of Geographic Distribution Systems." PhD thesis, University of Iowa.

Johnson, P. J. 1997. "Ovid's Livia in Exile." *CW* 90: 403–20.

Jolivet, V. 1988. "Les cendres d'Auguste: Note sur la topographie monumentale du Champ de Mars septentrional." *Arch. Laz.* 9: 90–96.

Jones, B. W. 1992. *The Emperor Domitian*. London and New York.

Jones, C. P. 2004. "A Speech of the Emperor Hadrian." *CQ* 54: 266–73.

Kajava, M. 1990. "Roman Senatorial Women and the Greek East. Epigraphic Evidence from the Republican and Augustan Period." In *Roman Eastern Policy and Other*

Studies in Roman History. Proceedings of a Colloquium at Tvärminne, 2–3 October 1987, ed. H. Solin and M. Kajava, 59–121. Helsinki.

Kampen, N. B. 1991. "Between Public and Private: Women as Historical Subjects in Roman Art." In *Women's History and Ancient History*, ed. S. B. Pomeroy, 218–48. Chapel Hill, N.C.

Kampen, N. B. 2007. "What Could Hadrian Feel for Antinoos? Emotional Possibilities in a Story of Sexual Passion." In *Geschlechterdefinitionen und Geschlechtergrenzen in der Antike*, ed. E. Hartmann, 199–209. Stuttgart.

Kampen, N. B. 2009. *Family Fictions in Roman Art*. Cambridge and New York.

Kapparis, K. 2002. *Abortion in the Ancient World*. London.

Keltanen, M. 2002. "The Public Image of the Four Empresses—Ideal Wives, Mothers and Regents?" In *Women, Wealth and Power in the Roman Empire*, ed. P. Setälä et al., 105–46. Rome.

Kemezis, A. 2016. "The Fall of Elagabalus as Literary Narrative and Political Reality." *Historia* 65: 348–90.

Kettenhofen, E. 1979. *Die syrischen Augustae in der historischen Überlieferung: ein Beitrag zum Problem der Orientalisierung*. Bonn.

Kienast, D. 2017. *Römische Kaisertabelle: Grundzüge einer römischen Kaiserchronologie*. 6th ed., with W. Eck and M. Heil. Darmstadt.

Kierdorf, W. 1986. "*Funus* und *consecratio*. Zu Terminologie und Ablauf der römischen Kaiserapotheose." *Chiron* 16: 43–69.

Kleiner, D. E. E. 1992. *Roman Sculpture*. New Haven, Conn.

Kleiner, D. E. E. 1996. "Imperial Women as Patrons of the Arts in the Early Empire." In Kleiner and Matheson 1996, 28–41.

Kleiner, D. E. E. 2000. "Now You See Them, Now You Don't: The Presence and Absence of Women in Roman Art." In *From Caligula to Constantine: Tyranny and Transformation in Roman Portraiture*, ed. E. R. Varner, 45–57. Atlanta.

Kleiner, D. E. E., and S. B. Matheson, eds. 1996. *I, Claudia: Women in Ancient Rome*. Austin, Tex.

Kokkinos, N. 2002. *Antonia Augusta: Portrait of a Great Roman Lady*. 2nd ed. London.

Kolb, A. 2010a. "*Augustae*: Zielsetzung, Definition, prosopographischer Überblick." In Kolb 2010b, 11–35.

Kolb, A., ed. 2010b. *Herrschaftsstrukturen und Herrschaftspraxis 2: Augustae. Machtbewusste Frauen am römischen Kaiserhof? Akten der Tagung in Zürich 18.–20.9.2008*. Berlin.

Kosmetatou, E. 2002. "The Public Image of Julia Mamaea: An Epigraphic and Numismatic Inquiry." *Latomus* 61: 398–414.

Kragelund, P. 2007. "Agrippina's Revenge." In Moltesen and Nielsen 2007, 27–43.

Kragelund, P. 2010. "The Temple and Birthplace of Diva Poppaea." *CQ* 60: 559–68.

Kuhoff, W. 1993. "Zur Titulatur der römischen Kaiserinnen während der Prinzipatszeit." *Klio* 75: 244–56.

Kunst, C. 1998. "Zur sozialen Funktion der Domus. Der Haushalt der Kaiserin Livia nach dem Tode des Augustus." In *Imperium Romanum. Studien zu Geschichte und Rezeption. Festschrift für Karl Christ zum 75. Geburtstag*, ed. P. Kneissel and V. Losemann, 450–71. Stuttgart.

Kunst, C. 2010. "Patronage/Matronage der *Augustae*." In Kolb 2010b, 145–161.

Laes, C., and V. Vuolanto, eds. 2017. *Children and Everyday Life in the Roman and Late Antique World*. Abingdon and New York.

Lahusen, G. 1983. *Untersuchungen zur Ehrenstatue in Rom: Literarische und epigraphische Zeugnisse*. Rome.

Langford, J. 2013. *Maternal Megalomania: Julia Domna and the Imperial Politics of Motherhood*. Baltimore.

Langlands, R. 2014. "Exemplary Influences and Augustus' Pernicious Moral Legacy." In *Suetonius the Biographer: Studies in Roman Lives*, ed. T. Power and R. K. Gibson, 111–29. Oxford and New York.

La Rocca, E. 1987. "L'adesione senatoriale al consensus." In *L'Urbs: Espace urbain et histoire (I s. ap. J.C.)*, ed. C. Pietri, 347–72. Rome.

Latham, J. A. 2016. *Performance, Memory, and Processions in Ancient Rome: The Pompa Circensis from the Late Republic to Late Antiquity*. Cambridge and New York.

Laurence, R. 2015. "Towards a History of Mobility in Ancient Rome (300 BCE to 100 CE)." In *The Moving City: Processions, Passages and Promenades in Ancient Rome*, ed. I. Östenberg, S. Malmberg, and J. Bjørnebye, 175–85. London.

Levick, B. M. 1982. "Propaganda and the Imperial Coinage." *Antichthon* 16: 104–16.

Levick, B. M. 1983. "The *Senatus Consultum* from Larinum." *JRS* 73: 97–115.

Levick, B. 2002. "Corbulo's Daughter." *Greece & Rome* 49: 199–211.

Levick, B. M. 2007. *Julia Domna, Syrian Empress*. London and New York.

Levick, B. M. 2008. "Vespasian." In *Lives of the Caesars*, ed. A. A. Barrett, 131–54. Malden, Mass., and Oxford.

Levick, B. M. 2010. *Augustus: Image and Substance*. Harlow and New York.

Levick, B. M. 2014. *Faustina I and II: Imperial Women of the Golden Age*. Oxford.

Levick, B. M. 2015. *Claudius*. 2nd ed. London and New York.

Lightman, M., and W. Zeisel. 1977. "*Univira*: An Example of Continuity and Change in Roman Society." *ChHist* 46: 19–32.

Linderski, J. 1988. "Julia in Regium." *ZPE* 72: 181–200.

Lindsay, H. 1995. "A Fertile Marriage: Agrippina and the Chronology of Her Children by Germanicus." *Latomus* 54: 3–17.

Lott, J. B. 2004. *The Neighborhoods of Augustan Rome*. Cambridge.

Lott, J. B. 2012. *Death and Dynasty in Early Imperial Rome. Key Sources, with Text, Translation, and Commentary*. Cambridge.

Lucrezi, F. 1991. "Al di sopra e al di sotto delle leggi." In *Sodalitas. Scritti in onore di Antonio Guarino*, 2, 683–90. Naples.

Bibliography

Lusnia, S. S. 1995. "Julia Domna's Coinage and Severan Dynastic Propaganda." *Latomus* 54: 119–40.

Lusnia, S. S. 2014. *Creating Severan Rome: The Architecture and Self-Image of L. Septimius Severus (A.D. 193–211)*. Brussels.

Malloch, S. J. V., ed. 2013. *The Annals of Tacitus. Book 11*. Cambridge.

Marshall, A. J. 1975. "Roman Women and the Provinces." *AncSoc* 6: 109–27.

Marshall, A. J. 1984. "Ladies in Waiting: The Role of Women in Tacitus' *Histories*." *AncSoc* 15–16: 167–84.

Marshall, A. J. 1990a. "Roman Ladies on Trial: The Case of Maesia of Sentinum." *Phoenix* 44: 46–59.

Marshall, A. J. 1990b. "Women on Trial before the Roman Senate." *EMC* 34: 333–66.

Martin, R. H., and A. J. Woodman. 1989. *Tacitus, Annals. Book IV*. Cambridge.

Matheson, S. B. 1996. "The Divine Claudia: Women as Goddesses in Roman Art." In Kleiner and Matheson 1996, 182–93.

Matthews, S. 2001. *First Converts: Rich Pagan Women and the Rhetoric of Mission in Early Judaism and Christianity*. Stanford, Calif.

McDermott, W. C., and A. E. Orentzel. 1978. *Roman Portraits: The Flavian-Trajanic Period*. Columbia, Mo.

McGinn, T. A. J. 1998. *Prostitution, Sexuality, and the Law in Ancient Rome*. Oxford and New York.

McGinn, T. A. J. 2013a. "*Ius liberorum*." In *Encyclopedia of Ancient History*, ed. R. S. Bagnall, K. Brodersen, C. B. Champion, A. Erskine, and S. R. Huebner, 3557–59. Malden, Mass.

McGinn, T. A. J. 2013b. "Roman Children and the Law." In Evans Grubbs and Parkin 2013, 341–62.

McHugh, J. S. 2017. *Emperor Alexander Severus: Rome's Age of Insurrection*. Barnsley.

McHugh, M. R. 2012. "*Ferox Femina*: Agrippina Maior in Tacitus's *Annales*." *Helios* 39.1: 73–96.

McIntyre, G. 2013. "Deification as Consolation: The Divine Children of the Roman Imperial Family." *Historia* 62: 222–40.

McIntyre, G. 2016. *A Family of Gods: The Worship of the Imperial Family in the Latin West*. Ann Arbor, Mich.

Mekacher, N. 2006. *Die vestalischen Jungfrauen in der römischen Kaiserzeit*. Wiesbaden.

Metcalf, W. E. 2006. "Roman Imperial Numismatics." In *A Companion to the Roman Empire*, ed. D. S. Potter, 35–44. Malden, Mass.

Metcalf, W. E., ed. 2012. *The Oxford Handbook of Greek and Roman Coinage*. Oxford.

Millar, F. 1977. *The Emperor in the Roman World*. London.

Millar, F. 1993. "Ovid and the *Domus Augusta*: Rome Seen from Tomoi." *JRS* 83: 1–17.

Milnor, K. 2005. *Gender, Domesticity, and the Age of Augustus: Inventing Private Life*. Oxford.

330   *Bibliography*

Moltesen, M., and A. M. Nielsen, eds. 2007. *Agrippina Minor. Life and Afterlife = liv og eftermæle, Meddelelser fra Ny Carlsberg glyptotek.* Copenhagen.

Moreau, P. 2009. "Domus Augusta: l'autre maison d'Auguste." In *L'expression du pouvoir au début de l'Empire. Autour de la Maison Carrée à Nîmes,* ed. M. Christol and D. Darde, 33–43. Paris.

Morizio, V. 1996. "Le dediche ad Augusto e ai giulio-claudi." In *Meta Sudans* I: *un area sacra* in Palatio *e la valle del Colosseo prima e dopo Nerone,* ed. C. Panella, 201–16. Rome.

Morley, N. 2013. "Population and Social Structure." In *The Cambridge Companion to Ancient Rome,* ed. P. Erdkamp, 29–44. Cambridge and New York.

Nadolny, S. 2016. *Die severischen Kaiserfrauen.* Stuttgart.

Neudecker, R. 1988. *Die Skulpturen-Ausstattung römischer Villen in Italien.* Mainz am Rhein.

Nicholls, M. 2010. "*Bibliotheca Latina Graecaque*: On the Possible Division of Roman Public Libraries by Language." In *Neronia VIII: Bibliothèques, livres et culture écrite dans l'empire romain de César à Hadrien,* ed. Y. Perrin and M. de Souza, 11–21. Brussels.

Noreña, C. F. 2006. "Water Distribution and the Residential Topography of Augustan Rome." In *Imaging Ancient Rome: Documentation, Visualization, Imagination,* ed. L. Haselberger and J. Humphrey, 91–105. Portsmouth, R.I.

Noreña, C. F. 2007. "Hadrian's Chastity." *Phoenix* 61: 296–317.

Noreña, C. F. 2011. *Imperial Ideals in the Roman West: Representation, Circulation, Power.* Cambridge.

Noy, D. 1991. "Wicked Stepmothers in Roman Society and Imagination." *Journal of Family History* 16: 345–61.

Oliver, J. H. 1949. "The *Divi* of the Hadrianic Period." *HThR* 42: 35–40.

Opper, T. 2008. *Hadrian: Empire and Conflict.* London.

Orlandi, S. 2013. "Le testimonianze epigrafiche." *Bollettino di Archeologica On Line* 4.2-3-4: 45–59. (www.archeologia.beniculturali.it)

Osgood, J. 2011. *Claudius Caesar: Image and Power in the Early Roman Empire.* Cambridge.

Palmer, R. E. A. 1974. "Roman Shrines of Female Chastity from the Caste Struggle to the Papacy of Innocent I." *RSA* 4: 113–59.

Palombi, D. 2014. "*Inter divos relatus est.* La divinizzazione nella famiglia imperiale." In *Apoteosi da uomini a dei: Il mausoleo di Adriano,* ed. L. Abbondanza, F. Coarelli, and E. Lo Sardo, 188–99. Rome.

Panciera, S. 2007a. "Domus Augustana." In *Res Bene Gestae. Ricerche di storia urbana su Roma antica in onore di Eva Margareta Steinby,* ed. A. Leone, D. Palombi, and S. Walker, 293–308. Rome.

Panciera, S. 2007b. "Umano, Sovrumano o Divino? Le divinità auguste e l'imperatore a Roma." In *The Representation and Perception of Roman Imperial Power: Proceedings*

Bibliography

of the Third Workshop of the International Network Impact of Empire (Roman Empire, c. 200 B.C.–A.D. 476), Netherlands Institute in Rome, 20–23 March 2002, ed. L. de Blois et al., 215–29. Amsterdam.

Pani, M. 2003. *La corta dei Cesari fra Augusto e Nerone.* Bari.

Parkin, T. G. 1992. *Demography and Roman Society.* Baltimore.

Parkin, T. G., and A. J. Pomeroy. 2007. *Roman Social History: A Sourcebook.* London and New York.

Pavolini, C. 2007. "L'*Agrippina-Orante* di Villa Casale e la politica religiosa degli imperatori sul Celio." In *Res Bene Gestae. Ricerche di storia urbana su Roma antica in onore di Eva Margareta Steinby,* ed. A. Leone, D. Palombi, and S. Walker, 309–34. Rome.

Pekáry, T. 1985. *Das römische Kaiserbildnis in Staat, Kult und Gesellschaft dargestellt anhand der Schriftquellen.* Berlin.

Perkounig, C.-M. 1995. *Livia Drusilla—Iulia Augusta: Das politische Porträt der ersten Kaiserin Roms.* Vienna, Cologne, and Weimar.

Pflaum, H.-G. 1950. *Les procurateurs équestres sous le Haut-Empire romain.* Paris.

Phang, S. E. 2001. *The Marriage of Roman Soldiers (13 B.C.–A.D. 235): Law and Family in the Imperial Army.* Leiden.

Pighi, G. B. 1965. *De ludi saecularibus populi romani Quiritium. Libri sex.* 2nd ed. Amsterdam.

Potter, D. S., and C. Damon, eds. and trans. 1999. *The* "Senatus Consultum de Cn. Pisone patre." *AJP* 120: 13–42.

Power, T. J. 2010. "Pliny, *Letters* 5.10 and the Literary Career of Suetonius." *JRS* 100: 140–62.

Price, S. R. F. 1984. *Rituals and Power: The Roman Imperial Cult in Asia Minor.* Cambridge and New York.

Price, S. 1987. "From Noble Funerals to Divine Cult: The Consecration of Roman Emperors." In *Rituals of Royalty: Power and Ceremonial in Traditional Societies,* ed. D. Cannadine and S. Price, 56–105. Cambridge.

Prioreschi, P. 1995. "Contraception and Abortion in the Greco-Roman World." *Vesalius* 1.2: 77–87.

Priwitzer, S. 2009. *Faustina minor, Ehefrau eines Idealkaisers und Mutter eines Tyrannen: Quellenkritische Untersuchungen zum dynastischen Potential, zur Darstellung und zu Handlungsspielräumen von Kaiserfrauen in Prinzipat.* Bonn.

Purcell, N. 1986. "Livia and the Womanhood of Rome." *PCPS* 32: 78–105.

Raepsaet-Charlier, M.-T. 1975. "La datation des inscriptions latines dans les provinces occidentales de l'Empire Romain d'après les formules '*in h(onorem) d(omus) d(ivinae)*' et '*deo deae.*'" *ANRW* II.3: 232–82.

Raepsaet-Charlier, M.-T. 1982. "Epouses et familles de magistrats dans les provinces romaines aux deux premiers siècles de l'empire." *Historia* 31: 56–69.

Raepsaet-Charlier, M.-T. 1987. *Prosopographie des femmes de l'ordre sénatorial (Ier–IIe siècles).* Louvain. (References to her catalogue are cited only as FOS.)

Rantala, J. 2017. *The Ludi Saeculares of Septimius Severus: The Ideologies of a New Roman Empire*. Abingdon, Oxon, and New York.

Ranucci, S. 2009. "La monetazione dei Flavi. Caratteri generali e aspetti tipologici." In *Divus Vespasianus. Il bimillenario dei Flavi*, ed. F. Coarelli, 358–67. Rome.

Rawson, B. 1997. "The Iconography of Roman Childhood." In *The Roman Family in Italy: Status, Sentiment, Space*, ed. B. Rawson and P. Weaver, 204–32. Canberra and Oxford.

Rawson, E. 1987. "*Discrimina Ordinum*: The *Lex Julia Theatralis*." *PBSR* 55: 83–114.

Reynolds, J. M. 1962. "Vota pro salute principis." *PBSR* 30: 33–36.

Richardson, L. 1976. "The Evolution of the Porticus Octaviae." *AJA* 80: 57–64.

Richardson, L. 1992. *A New Topographical Dictionary of Ancient Rome*. Baltimore.

Richlin, A. 1981. "Approaches to the Sources on Adultery at Rome." *Women's Studies* 8: 225–50.

Riddle, J. M. 1992. *Contraception and Abortion from the Ancient World to the Renaissance*. Cambridge, Mass.

Rizzi, M., ed. 2010. *Hadrian and the Christians*. New York.

Robinson, O. F. 1985. "Women and the Criminal Law." In *Raccolta di scritti in memoria di Raffaele Moschella*, ed. B. Carpino, 527–60. Perugia.

Roche, P. A. 2002. "The Public Image of Trajan's Family." *CPh* 97: 41–60.

Rose, C. B. 1997. *Dynastic Commemoration and Imperial Portraiture in the Julio-Claudian Period*. Cambridge.

Rowan, C. 2011a. "Communicating a 'Consecratio': The Deification Coinage of Faustina I." In *Proceedings of the XIVth International Numismatic Congress, Glasgow 2009*, ed. N. Holmes, 991–98. Glasgow: University of Glasgow. https://www.scribd.com/document/305602139/Communicating-a-consecratio-the-deification-coinage-of-Faustina-I-Clare-Rowan

Rowan, C. 2011b. "The Public Image of the Severan Women." *PBSR* 79: 241–73.

Rowan, C. 2012. *Under Divine Auspices: Divine Ideology and the Visualization of Imperial Power in the Severan Period*. Cambridge.

Rowe, G. 2002. *Princes and Political Cultures: The New Tiberian Senatorial Decrees*. Ann Arbor, Mich.

Rowe, G. 2013. "Reconsidering the Auctoritas of Augustus." *JRS* 103: 1–15.

Rüpke, J. (with A. Glock, tr. D. M. B. Richardson). 2008. "*Fasti sacerdotum*": *A Prosopography of Pagan, Jewish, and Christian Religious Officials in the City of Rome, 300 BC to AD 499*. Oxford.

Saller, R. 1980. "Anecdotes as Historical Evidence for the Principate." *G&R* 27: 69–83.

Saller, R. P. 1984. "*Familia, Domus* and the Roman Conception of the Family." *Phoenix* 38: 336-55.

Santoro L'Hoir, F. 1994. "Tacitus and Women's Usurpation of Power." *CW* 88: 5–25.

Schade, K. 2016. "Women." In *The Last Statues of Antiquity*, ed. R. R. R. Smith and B. Ward-Perkins, 249–58. Oxford.

Scheid, J. 1992. "The Religious Roles of Roman Women." In *A History of Women in the West*. I: *From Ancient Goddesses to Christian Saints*, ed. P. Schmitt Pantel, 377–408. Cambridge, Mass.

Scheid, J. (with P. Tassini and J. Rüpke), ed. 1998. *Recherches archéologiques à la Magliana. Commentarii fratrum Arvalium qui supersunt: les copies épigraphiques des protocoles annuels de la confrérie arvale (21 av.–304 ap. J.-C.)*. Paris. (References to the Acta of the Arval Brethren are to this authoritative version, citing the document number after *CFA*.)

Scheid, J. 2003a. "Religion, institutions et société de la Rome antique." Coll. "Leçons inaugurals du Collège de France" 166: 663–76. http://www.college-de-france.fr/media/john-scheid/UPL18440_38.pdf

Scheid, J. 2003b. "Les rôles religieux des femmes à Rome: un complément." In *Les femmes antiques entre sphère privée et sphère publique*, ed. R. Frei-Stolba, A. Bielman, and O. Bianchi, 137–51. Bern.

Scheidel, W. 1999. "Emperors, Aristocrats, and the Grim Reaper: Towards a Demographic Profile of the Roman Élite." *CQ* 49.1: 254–81.

Scheidel, W. 2011. "The Roman Slave Supply." In *The Cambridge World History of Slavery*. Vol. 1: *The Ancient Mediterranean World*, ed. K. Bradley and P. Cartledge, 287–310. Cambridge.

Schöpe, B. 2014. *Der römische Kaiserhof in severischen Zeit (193–235 n. Chr.)*. Stuttgart.

Schulten, P. N. 1979. *Die Typologie der römischen Konsekrationsprägungen*. Frankfurt.

Scott, A. G. 2018. *Emperors and Usurpers: An Historical Commentary on Cassius Dio's Roman History Books 79(78)–80(80) (A.D. 217–229)*. New York.

Seager, R. 2012. "Perceptions of the *domus Augusta*, AD 4–24." In *The Julio-Claudian Succession. Reality and Perception of the "Augustan Model*," ed. A. G. G. Gibson, 41–57. Leiden and Boston.

Severy, B. 2003. *Augustus and the Family at the Birth of the Roman Empire*. New York.

Shaw, B. D. 1987. "The Age of Roman Girls at Marriage: Some Reconsiderations." *JRS* 77: 30–46.

Shelton, J.-A. 2012. *The Women of Pliny's Letters*. New York.

Simpson, C. J. 1991. "Livia and the Constitution of the *Aedes Concordiae*: The Evidence of Ovid *Fasti* I. 637ff." *Historia* 40: 449–55.

Smith, R. R. R. 1981. "Greeks, Foreigners, and Roman Republican Portraits." *JRS* 71: 24–38.

Smith, R. R. R. 1987. "The Imperial Reliefs from the Sebasteion at Aphrodisias." *JRS* 77: 88–138.

Späth, T. 1994. "'Frauenmacht' in der frühen römischen Kaiserzeit? Ein kritischer Blick auf die historische Konstruktion der 'Kaiserfrauen.'" In Dettenhofer 1994, 159–205.

Spagnuolo Vigorita, T. 2010. *Casta domus: un seminario sulla legislazione matrimoniale augustea*. 3rd ed. Naples.

Bibliography

Sparreboom, A. 2014. "Wet-Nursing in the Roman Empire." In Carroll and Graham, 2014, 145–58.

Speidel, M. A. 2012. "Faustina—*mater castrorum*. Ein Beitrag zur Religionsgeschichte." *Tyche* 27: 127–52.

Stevenson, T. 2007. "Roman Coins and Refusals of the Title *Pater Patriae*." *NC* 167: 119–41.

Stewart, P. 2003. *Statues in Roman Society: Representation and Response*. Oxford.

Straub, J. 1966. "Senaculum, id est mulierum senatus." *Bonner Historia-Augusta-Colloquium* 3 (1964–65): 221–40.

Sutherland, C. H. V. 1986. "Compliment or Complement? Dr Levick on Imperial Coin Types." *NC* 146: 85–93.

Syme, R. 1978. *History in Ovid*. Oxford.

Syme, R. 1986. *The Augustan Aristocracy*. Oxford.

Talamo, E. 2011. "Statua di Agrippina Minore come orante." In *Ritratti. Le tante facce del potere*, ed. E. La Rocca and C. Parise Presicce, 230–31. Rome.

Talbert, R. J. A. 1984. *The Senate of Imperial Rome*. Princeton.

Temporini, H. 1978. *Die Frauen am Hofe Trajans*. Berlin and New York.

Temporini-Gräfin Vitzthum, H., ed. 2002. *Die Kaiserinnen Roms: von Livia bis Theodora*. Munich.

Thakur, S. 2014. "*Femina Princeps*: Livia in Ovid's Poetry." *EuGeStA* 4: 175–213.

Todman, D. 2007. "Childbirth in Ancient Rome: From Traditional Folklore to Obstetrics." *Australian and New Zealand Journal of Obstetrics and Gynaecology* 47.2: 82–85. doi:10.1111/j.1479-828X.2007.00691.x

Torelli, M. 1982. *The Typology and Structure of Roman Historical Reliefs*. Ann Arbor, Mich.

Treggiari, S. 1975. "Jobs in the Household of Livia." *PBSR* 43: 48–77.

Treggiari, S. 1981. "Concubinae." *PBSR* 49: 59–81.

Treggiari, S. 1991a. "Divorce Roman Style. How Easy and How Frequent Was It?" In *Marriage, Divorce, and Children in Ancient Rome*, ed. B. Rawson, 31–46. Canberra and Oxford.

Treggiari, S. 1991b. *Roman Marriage. Iusti Coniuges from the Time of Cicero to the Time of Ulpian*. Oxford.

Treggiari, S. 1996. "Social Status and Social Legislation." In *CAH*, 2nd ed., X, 873–904. Cambridge.

Treggiari, S. 2019. *Servilia and Her Family*. Oxford.

Trillmich, W. 1978. *Familienpropaganda der Kaiser Caligula und Claudius: Agrippina Maior und Antonia Augusta auf Münzen*. Berlin.

Trillmich, W. 2007. "Typologie der Bildnisse der Iulia Agrippina." In Moltesen and Nielsen, 45–65.

Trimble, J. 2011. *Women and Visual Replication in Roman Imperial Art and Culture*. Cambridge.

Bibliography

Tuori, K. 2016a. *The Emperor of Law: The Emergence of Roman Imperial Adjudication.* Oxford.

Tuori, K. 2016b. "Judge Julia Domna? A Historical Mystery and the Emergence of Imperial Legal Administration." *Journal of Legal History* 37.2: 180–97. doi: 10.1080/01440365.2016.1191590

Van Bremen, R. 1996. *The Limits of Participation: Women and Civic Life in the Greek East in the Hellenistic and Roman Periods.* Amsterdam.

Van Bremen, R. 2005. "'Plotina to all her friends': The Letter(s) of the Empress Plotina to the Epicureans in Athens." *Chiron* 35: 499–532.

Van Minnen, P., and J. D. Sosin. 1996. "Imperial Pork: Preparations for a Visit of Severus Alexander and Iulia Mamaea to Egypt." *AncSoc* 27: 171–81.

Varner, E. R. 1995. "Domitia Longina and the Politics of Portraiture." *AJA* 99: 187–206.

Varner, E. R. 2001. "Portraits, Plots, and Politics: 'Damnatio Memoriae' and the Images of Imperial Women." *MAAR* 46: 41–93.

Varner, E. R. 2004. *Mutilation and Transformation: Damnatio Memoriae and Roman Imperial Portraiture.* Leiden and Boston.

Varner, E. R. 2008. "Transcending Gender: Assimilation, Identity, and Roman Imperial Portraits." In *Role Models in the Roman World: Identity and Assimilation*, ed. S. Bell and I. L. Hansen, 185–205. Ann Arbor, Mich.

Vidman, L. 1982. *Fasti Ostienses: edendos, illustrandos, restituendos.* Prague.

Vinson, M. P. 1989. "Domitia Longina, Julia Titi, and the Literary Tradition." *Historia* 38: 431–50.

Walentowski, S. 1998. *Kommentar zur Vita Antoninus Pius der Historia Augusta.* Bonn.

Walker, D. 1988. "The Roman Coins." In *The Temple of Sulis Minerva at Bath.* Vol. 2. *The Finds from the Sacred Spring*, ed. B. Cunliffe, 279–358. Oxford.

Wallace-Hadrill, A. 1981. "The Emperor and His Virtues." *Historia* 20: 298–323.

Wallace-Hadrill, A. 1986. "Image and Authority in the Coinage of Augustus." *JRS* 76: 66–87.

Wallace-Hadrill, A. 1996. "The Imperial Court." In *CAH*, 2nd ed., X, 283–308.

Wallace-Hadrill, A. 2003. "The Streets of Rome as a Representation of Imperial Power." In *The Representation and Perception of Roman Imperial Power: Proceedings of the Third Workshop of the International Network Impact of Empire (Roman Empire, c. 200 B.C.–A.D. 476)*, ed. L. de Blois et al., 189–208. Amsterdam.

Wallinger, E. 1990. *Die Frauen in der Historia Augusta.* Vienna.

Walser, G. 1987. *Die Einsiedler Inschriftensammlung und der Pilgerführer durch Rom (Codex Einsidlensis 326).* Stuttgart.

Wardle, D. 2000. "Valerius Maximus on the *domus Augusta*, Augustus, and Tiberius." *CQ* 50: 479–93.

Wardle, D. 2014. *Suetonius: Life of Augustus.* Trans., with Introduction and Historical Commentary. Oxford.

Weinstock, S. 1971. *Divus Julius.* Oxford.

Bibliography

Weiss, P. 2008. "Die vorbildliche Kaiserehe. Zwei Senatsbeschlüsse beim Tod der älteren und der jüngeren Faustina, neue Paradigmen und die Herausbildung des 'antoninischen' Prinzipats." *Chiron* 38: 1–45.

Welch, K. *Livia and the Women of Rome*. Forthcoming from Oxford University Press.

Wesch-Klein, G. 1993. *Funus publicum: Eine Studie zur öffentlichen Beisetzung und Gewährung von Ehrengräbern in Rom und den Westprovinzen*. Stuttgart.

Whittaker, C. R., tr. 1969. *Herodian*. 2 vols. Cambridge, Mass.

Wiedemann, T. E. J. 1996. "From Nero to Vespasian." In *CAH*, 2nd ed., X, 256–82.

Wildfang, R. L. 2006. *Rome's Vestal Virgins: A Study of Rome's Vestal Priestesses in the Late Republic and Early Empire*. London and New York.

Wilhelm, A. 1899. "Ein Brief der Kaiserin Plotina." *JÖAI* 2: 270–75.

Williams, G. 2002. "Ovid's Exilic Poetry: Worlds Apart." In *Brill's Companion to Ovid*, ed. B. W. Boyd, 337–81. Leiden.

Williams, M. G. 1902. "Studies in the Lives of Roman Empresses. I. Julia Domna." *AJA* 6: 259–305.

Williams, M. G. 1904. "Studies in the Lives of Roman Empresses. II. Julia Mamaea." In *Roman Historical Sources and Institutions*, ed. H. A. Sanders, 67–100. New York and London.

Williams, M. H. 1988. "'Θεοσεβὴς γὰρ ἦν'—The Jewish Tendencies of Poppaea Sabina." *JThS* 39: 97–111.

Williams, W. 1976. "Individuality in the Imperial Constitutions: Hadrian and the Antonines." *JRS* 66: 67–83.

Winkes, R. 1995. *Livia, Octavia, Julia. Porträts und Darstellungen*. Archaeologia Transatlantica XIII. Providence, R.I.

Winterling, A. 1999. Aula Caesaris. *Studien zur Institutionalisierung des römischen Kaiserhofes in der Zeit von Augustus bis Commodus (31 v. Chr.–192 n. Chr.)*. Munich.

Winterling, A. 2009. *Politics and Society in Imperial Rome*. Chichester.

Wiseman, T. P. 1991. *Flavius Josephus: Death of an Emperor*. Exeter Studies in History 30. Exeter.

Wolters, R. 2012. "The Julio-Claudians." In Metcalf 2012, 335–55.

Wood, S. 1995. "Diva Drusilla Panthea and the Sisters of Caligula." *AJA* 99: 457–82.

Wood, S. 1999. *Imperial Women: A Study in Public Images, 40 B.C.–A.D. 68*. Leiden.

Wood, S. 2010. "Who Was Diva Domitilla? Some Thoughts on the Public Images of the Flavian Women." *AJA* 114: 45–57.

Wood, S. 2015. "Women in Action: A Statue of Matidia Minor and Its Contexts." *AJA* 119: 233–59.

Woodhull, M. L. 2003. "Engendering Space: Octavia's Portico in Rome." *Aurora: Journal of the History of Art* 4: 13–33.

Woodhull, M. L. 2012. "Imperial Mothers and Monuments in Rome." In *Motherhood in Greece and Rome*, ed. L. H. Petersen and P. Salzman-Mitchell, 225–51. Austin, Tex.

Bibliography

Woodhull, M. L. 2016. "Mujeres construyendo Roma: Género y ciudad imperial desde la época de Augusto a la antonina." In *Matronazgo y arquitectura: de la Antigüedad a la Edad Moderna*, ed. C. Martínez López and F. Serrano Estrella, 113–40. Granada.

Woodman, A. J., and R. H. Martin, eds. 1996. *The Annals of Tacitus: Book 3*. Cambridge.

Woods, D. 2014. "Caligula Displays Caesonia (Suet. Calig. 25.3)." *RhM* 157: 27–36.

Woolf, G. 2008. "Divinity and Power in Ancient Rome." In *Religion and Power: Divine Kingship in the Ancient World and Beyond*, ed. N. Brisch, 235–51. Chicago.

Yakobson, A. 2003. "*Maiestas*, the Imperial Ideology and the Imperial Family: The Evidence of the *senatus consultum de Cn. Pisone patre*." *Eutopia* N.S. 3 (1–2): 75–107.

Yon, J.-B. 2012. *Inscriptions grecques et latines de la Syrie, Palmyre*, tome XVII—fascicule 1. Beirut.

Zanker, P. 1982. "Herrscherbild und Zeitgesicht." *Wissenschaftliche Zeitschrift der Humboldt-Universität zu Berlin. Gesellschafts—und sprachwissenschaftliche Reihe.* 31.2/3: 307–12.

Zanker, P. 1988. *The Power of Images in the Age of Augustus*. Ann Arbor, Mich.

Zuiderhoek, A. 2009. *The Politics of Munificence in the Roman Empire: Citizens, Elites and Benefactors in Asia Minor*. Cambridge and New York.

Index Locorum

Acta Hermisci 163n206
Aelius Aristides, *Orationes*
 (Or.) 42 267, 278,
 279
L'Année Épigraphique
 (AE)
 1908, 231 114n150
 1914, 87 93n42
 1922, 1 93n42
 1927, 2 42, 98
 1929, 1 249n6
 1932, 70 153
 1934, 33 275n146
 1935, +26 153
 1946, 211 196n141
 1954, 62 39
 1954, 153 271n120
 1957, 77 233n90
 1957, 123 271n120
 1958, 232 249n6
 1964, 181 266n94
 1966, 430 18
 1972, 682 275n146
 1981, 902 275n140
 1984, 508 95–96,
  173n27, 188
 1988, 422 156n165
 1988, 553 98n77
 1988, 723 159
 1998, 1094 113n141

2001, 853 99n82
2001, 854 99n82
2011, 183 148n128
Appian (App.), *Bella
 civilia (B. Civ.)*
 1.5 1, 14n21
 2.16.106 160n194
 2.102 206n200
 4.32–34 13
 4.33 13n16
 5.76 258
 5.93–95 258n49
 5.95 22
 5.132 22, 22n55
Arrian (Arr.), *Epicteti
 dissertationes
 (Epict. diss.)*
 1.14.15–17 159
Aulus Gellius (Gell.),
 *Noctes Atticae
 (NA)*
 1.6 86
 10.23.4–5 56n29
 12.1 88n27
Aurelius Victor (Aur. Vict.),
 Caesares (Caes.)
 9 200n164
 11.7 48
 13.13 42n158
 23 249n8

*Berliner Griechische
 Urkunden (BGU)*
2, 362, ll. 15–16 270n113
252, 2/3 106n112
*British Museum Catalogue
 of Coins of the
 Roman Empire
 (BMCRE)*
III, Trajan nos.
 647–645 107n120
III, Trajan nos.
 658–664 35n120
III, Trajan nos.
 1088–1089 35n120
IV, Commodus no.
 418 268n102
Cassius Dio
 2.13.5 19
 44.5.3 22
 44.6 160n194
 45.12–13 253n23
 47.7.4–5 13
 47.17.6 172n17
 47.18.1–19.3 159n187
 47.19.4 32n104
 47.25.3 126
 48.10.3–4 253, 273
 48.34.3 63n70
 48.44 63n70
 49.15.1 182

Index Locorum

Cassius Dio (*cont.*)
49.15.3–6 22
49.15.5–6 22n55
49.38.1 21, 223
49.43.8 28, 185n91
50.5.5 16
50.6.6 158
51.13.3 19n43
51.19.1–2 178n52
51.19.7–20.1 160
51.20.6–8 146n115
51.22.3 206n200
52.19 6n14
53.16.4 34
53.17 22
53.18.1 59
53.28.1 159n186
53.28.2 59
53.32.5 22n55
53.32.5–6 22n55
54.7.2 40n146
54.16.2 24n64, 113n146
54.23.6 28, 197
54.27.3 217n17
54.28.5 172n18
54.35.4–5 172, 172n20, 259n50
54.35.5 172n20
55.2.4 182n74, 183n76
55.2.4–5 182, 260n56
55.2.5 226n68
55.2.5–6 23
55.2.5–55.3.1 7
55.2.7 24
55.8.1 187
55.8.2 183n76, 196n141, 197, 260n56
55.8.4 28
55.10.12 65, 184n87
55.10.12–15 52*t*, 65
55.10.14 66

55.10.15 67
55.13.1 66n82
55.14–22 19, 40
55.14.1 259
55.16.1–2 4
55.16.2 78
56.1–10 23n63, 89
56.7.2 24n64, 113n146
56.10.2 23n62, 24
56.20.2 256n40
56.22.2 256n40
56.32 173n24
56.32.1 26
56.34 172n21
56.40.5 185n91
56.42 123n19
56.42.2 137n90
56.42.4 173
56.46.1–2 149n135, 150, 150n139
56.46.2 29, 32, 173n25
56.46.3 151, 202
56.46.5 151n145, 182n72
57.3.2 159n187
57.5.5–7 261n65
57.5.6 262n67
57.8.1 99n84
57.8.4–5 159n187
57.12 78n139
57.12.1–3 12, 18
57.12.2 38, 185n88
57.12.3 4n9, 17n34, 260
57.12.3–4 100n86
57.12.4 29n93
57.12.5 183, 188n107
57.16.2 184n85
57.18.9 255
57.22.2 73
57.22.4 54*t*, 74
58.2 174n29
58.2.1 98n77
58.2.1–6 40n148

58.2.3 29, 100, 100n86, 112, 149n135, 184n84
58.2.3ᵃ 19, 21
58.2.8. 162n202
58.11.6–7 54*t*, 74
58.11.7 39
58.22.4–5 127n50
58.22.5 7n17, 255
58.24.2–3 74n121
58.54.3 258n49
58.54.5 259
59.3.4 37, 41n151, 151, 160, 180
59.3.6 151
59.7.4 182
59.8.7 62n62
59.9.1 159n187
59.9.1–2 159n186
59.10.4 121n12
59.11 148
59.11.1–3 174, 186
59.11.1–5 121
59.11.3 160
59.11.6 121n12
59.18.4 255n36
59.19.1 52*t*, 71
59.22.6–8 53*t*, 72
59.22.6–9 121n12
59.22.8 263n78
60.4.1 72n109
60.4.6 159
60.5.2 148n127, 160
60.8.4–5 41, 54*t*, 72
60.10.1 159n186
60.12.5 34
60.16.1–3 184n86
60.17.5 45n169
60.17.8 45n169
60.18.4 41, 72n112
60.22.1–2 41
60.22.2 135n85, 167n2, 179n57, 180

Index Locorum

60.31.1–5 75n123
60.31.3 41
60.31.5 74
60.31.8 64n71, 64n72
60.33.1 12n11, 184
60.33.3 30, 170n7
60.33.2[1] 169
61.3.3 101n93
61.3.4 170
61.7.3 4n9
61.10.1 41, 73
61.11–17 54*t*, 73n115
61.13.5 80n149
61.14.3 73n115
61.32.4 41, 73
61.33 179n57
61.33.2a 34
61.33.12 184
62.1–12 17
62.13.2 5n12
62.16.2 217, 217n22
63.26.4 185n90
65.1.2a 264n80
65.3.4 47
65.4.2 264n80
65.12.1 103
65.14.1–4 114
65.14.3–4 116n160
65.22.1 264n80
67.2.3 113n143
67.3.1 42, 48
67.3.1–2 48
67.3.2 39n143, 55*t*
67.3.15 55*t*
67.4.2 5n13, 42
67.6.3 263n79
67.15.2 48
67.15.3–4 48n9
68.5.5 42, 183, 209
68.7.4 114n148
68.10.2 197
68.16.3 175n38

69.1.2 42
69.1.4 42, 264–265n84
69.2.3 175n38
69.3.4 210
69.7.4 278
69.10.3a 17–18
69.10.31 42, 176
69.11 115
69.11.4 116n159
69.20.2 106
71.1.3 55*t*
71.10.5 267, 267n95
71.22.3 55*t*, 75, 117
71.33.1 33*t*n4, 55*t*
71.35.5. 181n66
72, fr.1 27
72.4.4–6 55*t*
72.4.6 55*t*
72.4.7 164n213
72.31.1 116
72.31.2 181
72.36.4 287
73.4.4–6 76
73.4.6 76
74.1 178n53
75.4.2–5.5 123n19, 137n90, 177
75.13.1 271n118
76.7 111
76.15.2 270
76.15.6 55*t*, 76
77.1.2 25n74
77.1.4–5 181n67
77.6.3 55*t*, 76
77.16.5 271
77.17.1–3 269n103
77.18.2 270
77.20.1 272n126
77.22–23 272n126
78.1.1 55*t*, 77
78.18.2–3 4, 18, 29
78.18.3 272n124

78.24.1 55*t*, 76
79.2.3 173n24, 177n47, 272
79.15 113n144
79.23.1 272n127
79.23.2 23
79.30.3 40, 272n128
79.38 273
80.17.2 248n4, 274
80.20.2 80n151, 274n135
80.21.3 274n135

CFA (Acta of the Arval Brethren)
4a 161n198, 180n59
5 161n198, 162n202, 180n59
10 161n198, 180n59
12 161n198
17 37n133
19 93n50
27 102n95
30 162n203, 263n77
48 161n197
49 161n197, 162n204
55 161n197
69 175n39
100 145n110

Cicero (Cic.)
ad Atticum (ad Att.)
  12.18.1 146n113
ad Familiares (ad Fam.)
  4.5.5.1 88n24
  14.2.2 14
de Legibus (Leg.)
  2.62 123n19
  3.3.7 86
de Oratore (de Or.)
  3.3.12 88n24
Orationes Philippicae (Phil.) 5.22, 13.18 253
Orator ad M. Brutum (Orat.) 2.44 172n16

Cicero (Cic.) (*cont.*)
  pro Marcello (pro
    Marc.) 23 86
Claudianus (Claud.),
    Epithalamium de
    Nuptiis Honorii
    Augusti 13–14 27
Codex Iustinianus (Cod.
    Iust.) 5.35.1 15
  Consolatio ad Liviam
    (Consol. ad
    Liviam) 85n10;
      49–50 172n22
    65–74 94n54
    442 172n20
Corpus Inscriptionum
    Graecarum (CIG)
  1075 111
Corpus Inscriptionum
    Latinarum (CIL)
  II 1162 157n176
  II 1471 157n176
  II 1678 98n75
  II 1978 98n79
  II 3413 113n141
  II 4719 102n94
  II 4926 102n94
  III 346 102n94
  III 3639 276n147
  III 4497 263n79
  III 7123 111n134, 243n118
  III 7970 113n141
  V 3112 118n169, 184n83
  V 7617 157n172
  VI 6.8.2 188n107
  VI 419 112n139
  VI 882a 199n161
  VI 883 199n156, 233n88
  VI 888–893 195n135
  VI 891 195n135
  VI 893 195n135
  VI 921 151n146, 190n115,
      236

VI 922 236
VI 923 236
VI 984 176n43
VI 994 111n133
VI 996 188n107
VI 997 205n193, 205n194
VI 1004 194n131
VI 1005 203n182,
    203n184
VI 1006 189n111
VI 1010 189n109
VI 1019 204n187
VI 1035 112n139
VI 2035 93n50
VI 2060 33*t*n1
VI 3008 276n147
VI 3777 205n193
VI 4057 114n150
VI 4222 201n173
VI 4314 205n193
VI 4346 196n139
VI 5536 185n90
VI 8941 84n6
VI 8955 150n141
VI 8972 114n152
VI 10222 183n81
VI 10251a 200n164
VI 12037 114n150
VI 18358 114n150
VI 20950 114n150
VI 29765 196n138
VI 31215 206n202
VI 31224 203n184
VI 31297 106n111
VI 31610 225n63
VI 32328 153n154
VI 32544 275n144
VI 36605 196n138
VI 36932 155n161,
    204n188
VI 36934 155n161,
    204n188
VI 40307 240n106

VI 40331 185n90
VI 40334 240n106
VI 40372 174n30
VI 40416 167n1
VI 40420 238, 238n103
VI 40420–40430 190
VI 40421 238
VI 40423 238, 238n103
VI 40424 238n103
VI 40425 238n103
VI 40425–26 190n118
VI 40426 238n103
VI 40427–28 238n103
VI 40452 196n140
VI 40507 183n78
VI 40508 176n40
VI 40516 188n107
VI 40523 189n108
VI 40528 204n190
VI 41062 13
VIII 2557 271n120
VIII 2564 269n108,
    274n138
VIII 5328 31n102
VIII 9035 111
VIII 11323 111
VIII 19494 112n136
VIII 22689 9, 81n154
VIII 25902 99
IX 3018 98n75
IX 3304 199n161
IX 3418 48n12
IX 3419 48n12
IX 3432 49n13
IX 3438 48n12
IX 3469 48n12, 49n13
IX 5894 108
X 7 233n86
X 51 156n165
X 408 33*t*n4
X 961 156n165
X 1417 101n92
X 1574 102n95

Index Locorum

X 1632 98n80
X 4745 111n134, 243n117
X 6018 156n165
X 7501 144n103
XI 1154 156n165
XI 1333 33t2
XI 3303 156n169
XI 6721 253n23
XII 4333 94n51
XII 6038 146n115
XIII 2181 156n167
XIII 6531 249n6
XIII 7417 162
XIII 8017 275n146
XIII 12042 249n6
XIV 2255 270n114
XIV 2795 33tn1
XIV 3579 17, 63, 88n23,
    110n129, 176n40
XV 548 49n13
XV 548–58 48n10
XV 553 49n13
XV 555.4 48n11
XV 556 49n13
XV 7247 196n138
XV 7248 191n122
XV 7264 38n136
XV 7293 48n11
XV 7306 39
XV 7311 196n138
XV 7313 39
XVI 4 35n118
Corpus Papyrorum Raineri
    (CPR)
24.2 106n112

Digest (Dig.)
1.3.31 2, 24–25, 36,
    50–51, 81, 284
1.4.1.1 58n47
1.7.23 206n203,
    244n126
1.9.8 36n127

1.9.10 36n127
1.9.12 36n127, 81n156
1.16.4.2 255
3.1.1.5 15
23.2.44 24n64,
    113n146
23.2.47 24n64
24.1 30n101
31.56–57 59
47.11.4 87n21
48.4.4.1–48.4.6
    78n142
48.19.39 87n21
49.14.6.1 27n80
50.16.223.1 162n201
50.17.2 15
Dio Chrysostom,
    Orationes (Orat.)
    3.10 and 62.3 60
Diodorus Siculus
    (Diod. Sic.) 34/
    35.2.12 252n19
Dionysius of
    Halicarnassus,
    *Antiquitates
    Romanae*
    8.55 199n157

Einsiedlensis manuscript
    170n9, 205
*Epitome de Caesaribus
    (Epit. de Caes.)*
8.8 200n164
11.11 48
14.8 20
17.5 164n213
21.6 272n127
24.4–5 249n5
Eusebius (Euseb.), *Historia
    ecclesiastica
    (Hist. eccl.)*
3.18.4 163
6.21.3 163

Eutropius (Eutrop.)
8.5 175n38
8.6 42n158

Fasti Ostienses 84n4,
    137n93, 176n44,
    183n80, 303n2, 307,
    310
Fasti Praenestini 7n16,
    151, 188
Festus (Fest.)
    188L 187nn98–99
*Fontes Iuris Romani
    AnteIustiniani
    (FIRA)*
1.37 23n62
III 227 n.73 94n51
Frontinus (Frontin.),
    *de Aquae ductu
    urbis Romae* (Aq.)
    1.20 200n164
Fronto, *Epistulae
    ad amicos* 1.14 26n76,
    118n171
    *ad Antoninum
    imperatorem (ad Ant.
    imp.)*
    2.1 26n76
    2.1.2 177n47
    4.1 118nn170–171
    de nepote amisso 2.1,
    10 85n10

Gaius, *Institutiones (Inst.)*
1.14.4 16
1.190 16
3.44 24

Herodianus (Hdn.)
1.6.4 55t
1.7.4 84n3
1.8 55t
1.8.3–4 184

344 Index Locorum

Herodianus (Hdn.) (cont.)
1.8.3–6 76
1.8.4 181
1.8.8 76
1.13.1 39n140
1.16.4 113n144
1.17.1–2 48n9
1.17.7–8 48n9
2.3.2 181n66
2.8.6 181n66
3–5 55*t*
3.8.4 253
3.8.5 112
3.10.8 271n121
3.13.2 77
3.13.2–3 55*t*
3.13.3 77n134
4.1–2 123n19, 177
4.2 137n90
4.8.6–9.8 272n126
4.9.3–8 272n126
4.13.3–8 272n127
5.3.2 26, 40, 272n128, 273n131
5.3.3 273n131
5.3.10 273
5.3.10–11 248n1
5.5.1 248n1
5.6.1 33*t*n7
5.7.3 248n2, 272–273
5.8.3 248n2
5.8.8–10 80n151, 80n152, 274n135
5.8.10 248n2
6.1–2 276
6.1.1 80n152
6.1.5 80n152
6.1.9–10 55*t*, 77
6.1.10 80n152, 275n143
6.5.9 276
6.8–9 249n5

6.8.3 249n5
6.9.5 249n5
6.9.6–8 80n153, 276n152
7.1.9 181n66
7.3.5–6 157n177
7.6.2 181n66

Historia Augusta (HA)
Aelius (Ael.) 6.9 83
Alexander Severus (Alex. Sev.)
3.2 186n93
14.4 186n93
14.7 80n152, 249n5, 275n143
18.8 55*t*, 76
26.9 185n90, 275n143
26.9–10 185n90
29.2 163n209
56.1 276
57.7 184n83
59.6 80n153
60.2 80n152, 80n153, 275n143
60.5 249n5
63.5 80n153, 249n5, 276n152
Antoninus Pius (Ant. Pius)
5.2 36
6.7 203n182
7.9 26
7.11 266, 278
8.1–2 183n80
8.9 114
Aurelian (Aurel.)
49 205n196
Avidius Cassius (Avid. Cass.) 7.1 117
Commodus (Comm.)
4 55*t*
4.1 55*t*

4.1–4 76
5.7 55*t*, 76n128
5.9 55*t*, 76
8.1 75
8.3 55*t*
16.3 218
Geta 3.1 270n109
Hadrian (Hadr.)
2.10 42, 109
4 42
4.10 265, 264–265n84
5.9 264–265n84
5.9–10 175
6.3 175n38
9.9 175
11.2 5n11
11.3 20, 110, 265, 266
11.7 114n148
14.7 115
15.10 210
17.5–7 185
19.5 175
19.10 196n138
19.11 198n154
22.14 165n216
Heliogabalus (Heliogab.)
1.4 249n8
2.1 249n5
4.1 274n134
4.1–2 248n4
4.1–4 274n134
4.3 13
4.3–4 205n196
6.5 113n144
12.3 248n4, 260n57, 274n134
15 248n2
15.6 274n134
17 274n135
18.2–3 80n151
18.3 248n4, 274n134

M. Ant. (Caracalla)
  1.8 55*t*, 77n134
  6.2–3 272n126
  7.1 272n127
  10.1–4 60n57
  11.6 149, 201
  11.6–7 201n170
Macrinus
  9.1–4 248n1, 249n8
  9.1–10 273
  10 248n1
  10.1 249n8
Marcus Aurelius
  (Marc.)
  5.3 39n139
  6.6 33*t*, 36
  7.8. 184n82
  9.4 266n93, 266n94
  9.5 266
  10–11 179, 181n69
  19.1–9 117
  19.2–5 55*t*, 75
  19.7 55*t*
  19.8–9 5n11, 110n130
  20.6 36n123
  24.6–7 55*t*, 75, 117
  26.4 267
  26.5 55*t*, 177n47,
    201n170
  26.5–6 77n136
  26.6 183n81
  26.8 267, 267n95
  26.9 267
  27.8 33*t*n4
  29.1–3 55*t*
  29.10 115
Maximini (Max.)
  7.4 80n153, 276n152
  7.4–5 249n5
  7.5 276n152
Pertinax (Pert.)
  2.3 257

  5.4 33*t*n5, 36n124
  6.4 162n201
  6.9 33*t*n5, 36n124
Severus (Sev.)
  3.2 186n93
  3.8–9 270n109
  11.9 257
  14.4 186n93
  15.2 271n117
  16.8 271
  17.1–4 271n118
  18.3 271n120
  18.8 55*t*, 76
Verus
  2.4 39n139
  7.6 266
  7.7 266n93, 266n94
  10.1–2 75
Horace (Hor.), *Carmina*
    (Carm.)
  1.37.21 17n31
  3.14.5–10 177–178

IK 54, Perge,
    123–125 157n175
Inscriptiones Graecae
    ad res romanas
    pertinentes
    (IGRRP)
  1.577 112n139
  1.835b 233n90
  3.1054 277n157
  4.39 161n197
  4.180 161n197
  4.251 262n71
Inscriptiones Romanae
    Selectae (ILS)
  72 145n109
  99 160n193
  112 161n195
  120 156n169
  349–352 176n45

  8393 1n2, 252n18
  8781 159
Inscriptions of Roman
    Tripolitania (IRT)
  404 112n139
Isidore of Seville (Isid.),
    Etymologies
    (Etym.) 20.12 37

Jerome (Jer.), *Epistulae*
    (Ep.) 22.16 13
Josephus (Joseph.)
  Antiquitates Judaicae
    (AJ)
  17.1.1 259n53
  18.6.6 40n149
  18.31 26
  18.156 26n76
  19.1.15 39n139
  19.2.4 80
  19.75 182n72
  19.357 218n27
  20.189–96 163
  20.252–53 42
  Bellum Judaicum (BJ)
  2.167 26
  7.5.4 187
  Vita (Vit.)
  16 163
  76.429 29, 48n12
Juvenal (Juv.), *Satires*
    (Sat.)
  6.82–113 251n15
  6.115–132 35n119
  6.118 35n119; 74
  6.246–67 251n15
  6.400–401 256
  6.592–600 88n27
  10.329–45 184n87

Laudatio Turiae 13,
    252n18

Index Locorum

Livy
  Ab Urbe Condita Libri
    2.40 199n157
    3.7.7 123n19
    5.21.10 251n15
    5.25.8–9 37
    10.31.9 56n32
    21.63.7–8 161
    22.53.10 161n195
    25.2.9 56n32
    26.41–51 252
    27.51.9 123n19
    34.1–7 254n28
    34.7 15, 16
    38.50.8 59
    39.18.6 56n33
    40.37.5–7 56n31
    40.37.6 13
    59 86
  Periochae 140 187n99
Lucian, *Portraits*
    7–8 243n120

Macrobius (Macr.),
      Saturnalia (Sat.)
    1.11.17 66
    2.5.6 180n64, 219n32
Marcus Aurelius,
      Meditations (Med.)
    1.17.2 84n5
    1.17.7 116
Martial (Mart.)
  Epigrams
    4.3.8 48n7
    6.3 48n7
    9.5 113n143
    9.7 113n143
    9.11–13 113n143
    9.16–17 113n143
    9.36 113n143
    11.13.3 48

Spectacula (Spec.)
    2.9–10 200n164
Menander Rhetor,
      Epideictae
    2.1.396 107

Nepos, *fr.* 59 13
Nicolaus of Damascus,
      FGrH 2 A no. 90
    Fr. 134 260n58

Octavia (play)
    609–12 217
Orosius (Oros.)
    6.18.34 22n55
    6.20.7 22n55
Ovid
  Amores (Amor.)
    2.14.3–4 88n27
  Ars amatoria (Ars am.)
    1.69–70 187n97
    1.71–72 187n99, 197
  Epistulae ex Ponto
      (Pont.)
    2.2.67–74 95, 97n73
    2.2.74 95n58
    3.1.114–66 20
    3.1.125 40
    4.9.107 150, 150n139
    4.13.29 144n105
  Fasti (Fast.)
    1.532 95n58
    1.623–24 88n27
    1.721 95n58
    5.157–58 198, 283
    6.637–38 197
    6.639–48 197
    6.810 95n58
  Tristia (Tr.)
    3.1.41 95n58
    4.2.10 95n58

Oxyrhynchus Papyri
      (P.Oxy.)
    III 496 106n112
    III 604 106n112
    VI 905 106n112
    X 1242 163n206

Philo, *Legatio ad Gaium*
      (leg. ad Gaium)
    2.572 196n139
Philostratus (Philostr.)
  Vita Apollonii (VA)
    1.3 29
    7.7 48
  Vitae sophistarum (VS)
    2.1.11 267
    2.19 278n160
    622 208n211
Plato, *Phaedrus*
    5.7.35 98n77
Pliny the Elder (Plin.),
      Historia naturalis
      (HN)
    7.45–46.147–51 66n80
    7.46.149 52t, 65–66, 67
    7.139 88n24
    7.141 37
    9.117–119 30
    12.94 202
    14.11 197n145
    14.14.89–90 56n29
    21.9 65, 184n87
    29.27.85 87n20
    33.63 30, 170n7
    34.2.2–4 26
    34.24 224n58
    34.25. 224n59
    34.31 187n101, 223,
      224–225
    35.22 187n101
    35.114 187, 187n101

36.22 187

36.28–43 187n101

Pliny the Younger (Plin.)

Epistulae (Ep.)

6.31.4–6 253n21, 256

7.24.4 40n150

8.10 85n10

10.2 24n68

10.8 221n41

10.39–40 251n12

10.52–53 160n193

10.89 160n193

10.94 24n68

10.95 24n68

10.102–103 160n193

Panegyricus (Pan.)

4.4 60n56

7.4–8 106

11.1 103n97

22–23 178

22.3 107

26.5–6 107

27.1 107

28.7 107

55.6 224

65.1–2 60

83–84 17, 107, 178n51, 183, 209, 264

83.1 107n116

83.6 42

84 33*t*n2

84.6 35, 45–46

Plutarch (Plut.), *Vitae Parallelae*

Antonius (Ant.)

10.3 253n23

31 258n49

31.3 63n68

33 258

35 258n49

35.4 22n58

35.5 39

54.1 39n141

54.2 39

57.3 39

64 258n49

83.6 19n43

87 39

Caesar (Caes.) 10.9 82n157

Coriolanus 37 199n157

Gaius Gracchus (C. Gracch.) 4.3 225n62

Galba (Galb.)

3.2 29

12 255n36

Marcellus (Marc.)

30.4 187n97

Numa (Num.)

10.3 32n104

Romulus (Rom.)

22 56n29

Sulla

6.12 13

22.1 252n18

Tiberius Gracchus (Ti. Gracch.) 1.5 88n25

Procopius, *Anecdota (Anec.)* 9.16 65n77

Propertius (Prop.)

3.11.39 17n31

3.18.11–20 187n97

Pseudo-Quintilian, *declamationes (decl.)* 3.12 253n21

Pseudo-Sallust, *Invective against Cicero* 3 13, 41n152

Quintilian, *Institutio oratoria (Inst.)*

4.1.19 15n26

6.13 85n10

Res Gestae divi Augusti (RGDA)

8 90

9.1 160n193

10 22

12 161

19 187

25 158

25.2 158n181, 158n182

34.1 1n2

35 89

Roman Imperial Coinage (RIC)

I², Augustus no. 403 127n48

I², Augustus no. 404 91n39, 92n40

I², Augustus nos. 404–405 121n9, 130n63

I², Claudius nos. 65–66 131n66

I², Claudius no. 67 131n67

I², Claudius no. 68 131n67

I², Claudius nos. 69–74 131n67

I², Claudius no. 75 132n71

I², Claudius no. 80 132n70

I², Claudius no. 81 132n70

I², Claudius no. 92 131n68

I², Claudius no. 93 131n67, 131n68

I², Claudius no. 102 130n65

I², Claudius no. 103 132n72

Roman Imperial Coinage (RIC) (cont.)

I², Claudius no.
104 131n68

I², Claudius no.
109 131n67

I², Gaius nos.
7–8 101n91

I², Gaius nos.
13–14 101n91

I², Gaius nos.
15–18 119n2

I², Gaius nos.
21–22 101n91

I², Gaius no. 33 120n5, 121n10

I², Gaius no. 34 119n3

I², Gaius no. 35 119n2

I², Gaius no. 41 120n5

I², Gaius no. 43 119n2

I², Gaius no. 49 119n3

I², Gaius no. 55 130n65, 135n85

I², Gaius nos
7–8 130n65

I², Nero nos. 1–3 101n94

I², Nero nos.
6–7 101n94

I², Nero nos.
607–8 102n95

I², Nero nos.
610–11 102n95

I², Tiberius no.
47 128nn52–53

I², Tiberius nos. 50–51 128n52, 130n62

I², Tiberius no.
51 135n83

I², Titus no.
419 130n65

II, Hadrian nos.
29–31 110n126

II, Hadrian nos. 32, 32a, 33 110n127

II, Hadrian no.
34 110n128

II, Hadrian nos.
232A–232B 110n126

II, Hadrian nos.
387 110n126

II, Hadrian no.
418A 138n95

II, Trajan no. 743 138n94

II, Trajan no. 746 137n89

II, Trajan no.
759 108n122

II, Trajan no.
761 108n122

II.1², Domitian no.
132 105n105

II.1², Domitian no.
136 104n105

II.1², Domitian no.
146 104n101

II.1², Domitian no.
147 104n103

II.1², Domitian nos.
152–153 105n105

II.1², Domitian nos.
155–156 105n105

II.1², Domitian no.
157 104n101

II.1², Titus no.
262 103n100

II.1², Titus nos.
405–409 127–128nn50–51

II.1², Titus no.
419 130n65

III, Marcus Aurelius no.
742 268n100

III, Marcus Aurelius nos.
748–49 268n100

III, Marcus Aurelius no.
751 268n100

III, Marcus Aurelius nos. 751–53 268n100

III, Marcus Aurelius no.
753 112n138

III, Marcus Aurelius nos.
1659–62 268n100

III, Marcus Aurelius no.
1706 201n170

III, Marcus Aurelius nos. 1711–12 268n100

III, Pius no. 356a 129n57

III, Pius no. 1115 203n183

III, Pius no.
1384 152n152

IV.1, Septimius Severus no. 540 134n82

IV.1, Septimius Severus no. 563A 269n105

IV.1, Septimius Severus no. 563B 269n105

IV.1, Septimius Severus no. 567 269n105

IV.1, Septimius Severus nos. 567–568 269n105

IV.1, Septimius Severus no. 569 269n105

IV.1, Septimius Severus no. 577 144n104

IV.1, Septimius Severus no. 586 144n105

IV.1, Septimius Severus no. 648A 269n105

IV.1, Septimius Severus no. 650 269n105

IV.1, Septimius Severus no. 860 269n105

IV.1, Septimius Severus nos.
880–881 269n105

Index Locorum

IV.1, Septimius Severus
no. 884 269n105
IV.2, Elagabalus no.
378 137n91
IV.2, Severus Alexander
no. 690 275n145
IV.2, Severus Alexander
no. 691 275n145
Roman Republican
Coinage (RRC)
527/1 92n41, 130n63
533/3a 92n41, 130n63
543/1 92n41, 130n63
Roman Statutes (RS)
37, fr. I 95n59,
188n103

Sallust, Bellum
Catilinae (Cat.)
51.9–10 252n19
Scholia in Juvenalum
(Schol. Juv.)
5.109 72n111
Senatus Consultum de
Pisone patre
(SCPP) 4, 19, 42–
44, 46, 69, 233,
255, 286; 16 96
32–33 69n98
55 27n79
109–120 43–44, 100n89
113 44
115–116 100n89
115–117 44
116–117 28
117–118 44
118 17
132–133 17, 96n66
136–139 96n67,
97n68
139 88n26
140–142 88n23, 97

143–144 73n117, 97n69
146–51 96n66
148–50 17, 43
148–51 38n136
159–163 96
165 96n65
302–303 97n68
Seneca the Elder (Sen.)
Suasoriae (Suas.)
2.22 74n121
Seneca the Younger (Sen.)
Apocolocyntosis
(Apocol.) 164
1 137n92
6 261
10.4 72n111
12.1 241n113
de Beneficiis (Ben.)
3.26 78n141
6.32.1 65, 184n87
de Clementia (Clem.)
1.1.2 60n56
1.1.4 60
1.9 40
1.9.2–6 259
1.9.2–12 19
1.10 52t
1.10.3 66, 67n87
de Consolatione ad
Helviam (Helv.)
19.6 257
de Consolatione ad
Marciam (Consol. ad
Marc.)
3.2 172n22, 259
16.2 224
24.3 29n96
de Consolatione ad
Polybium (Cons. ad
Pol.)
7.2 59–60
13.2 72n111

de Ira
3.18.4 196n139
3.21.5 72n108
Medea (Med.)
42 249n9
Sibylline Oracles
3.75–76 17n33
Smallwood
22 137n93, 175n35,
293n14
516 163n206
Statius (Stat.), Silvae
(Silv.)
1.1.94–98 103n97
3 praef. 113n143
3.4 113n143
Strabo
4.192 9n22
5.236 185, 283
Suetonius (Suet.)
Augustus (Aug.)
8 172n17
17.2 158
24.1 253
25 52t
29.4 28
29.6 185n91
34 89
40.3 19
44 180
45.1 180n60
46 88
57.1 160n193
58.2 90, 96
62.1 61n60
62.2 110
63.1 24
64.2 89, 184n84
65 52t, 66
65.4 61, 89, 100n85
72 30
72.3 38

Index Locorum

Suetonius (Suet.) (cont.)
73.1 89
89 86
94.12 126
100 173n25
100.2 123n19
100.4 173n25
101 173n24
101.2 149n135

Caesar (Caes.)
6.1 172n16
26 172n16
74 82n157

Caligula (Calig.)
7 88n26, 195n135
7.7 151n144,
188n104, 202
8 261, 261n66
8.3 262n67
10 174
14.1 60n57
15.1 174
15.2 25, 40, 151, 180
15.3 160, 160n189,
161n195
23.1 119n2
23.2–3 174n31
24.1 38
24.1–2 121
24.3 53t, 72
24.4 160
25 63, 257
25.1 62n62
25.3 80n149, 256
29 60
33 62
39.1 30n101
45 135n85

Claudius (Claud.)
2.1 261
11.2 148n127, 159n86,
182n71

17.2 135n85, 167n2,
179
21 89n32
23 89n32
26 74
26.2 75n123
26.3 60, 64n72
29.1 41, 54t, 72
29.3 75n123
32 89n30, 183n77
33.1 183n76
36 75n123
39.1 75n123
44.2 183n76
45 145n109, 149n137

*de Grammaticis et
rhetoribus (De
gramm.)* 21 187n97

Domitian (Dom.)
1.3 47
3, 14 55t
3.1 47, 48, 64
8.3 48n5
10.2 47
12.3 114n149
13.1 48, 64, 181n67
13.2 60
14 48
22 48n5, 55t

Galba (Galb.)
1 26
5.1 13n13
5.2 4n9, 29
18 151n144, 188n104,
202

Nero
5.2 73n114
6.3 38n135, 38n137,
58n43, 72n111
6.4 72n111
6.20 6n15
7.1 41, 53t, 73

9 101n93, 219n33
9.1 181n68
10.1 58n43
20 6n15
25.2 126
28 181n68
28.1 113n143
28.2 27
34.1 22, 38
34.1–4 54t, 73n115,
241
34.2 39
34.5 53t
35.1 62
35.1–3 64
35.2 54t
37.2 60n55
38 218n24
39.3 54t, 73n115
49.2 79n143

Otho
1.1 4n9, 29, 40
10.3 80n150

Tiberius (Tib.)
5 38n136
6.2 259n51
7.3 260
10.1 63n68, 66n81
11.4 63n68, 66n81
26.2 34n110
27 19
49.1 14
50 25n70
50.2 12
50.2–3 15n26
50.3 29n93, 34, 45,
184
51.2 98n77
53.1 11
53.2 78n138, 127n50,
184n86
58 78n138, 78n141

Index Locorum

61.3 74n121
62 73
62.1 74n120
74 187n101

Vespasian (Vesp.)
3 114n149
7.2 165n216
9 152n148, 200,
   200n164, 216, 218
14.1 80n150
21 114
23 165n215
25 103

Supplementum
   epigraphicum Graecum
   (SEG)
8.794 29n96
11.922–3 158n179

Tabula Siarensis 95,
   173n27, 187–188

Tacitus (Tac.)
Agricola (Agr.)
2–3 60
16 17
Annales (Ann.)
1.4 14, 94n53
1.7 159n187
1.8 149n135
1.8.3 173n25
1.10 100n88
1.13.4–6 19
1.14 149n135
1.14.1 29n93,
   100n86, 112
1.14.3 32, 34
1.32 202
1.34 159n187
1.40–44 261
1.40.3 96n67,
   262n67
1.44.1 262n67

1.53 66n82
1.69 262
1.69.3–4 254n29
1.73 78n141, 151
1.73.3 182n72
1.73.4 147n124
1.74 221n41
2.12 185
2.29.1 14
2.34 10, 11
2.34.2 10, 19, 50
2.41.4 178
2.43 7n17
2.50 52t, 57, 82
2.54.1 263
2.55.6 254n29, 255,
   263n74
2.70–72 263
2.71 255
2.71.4 88n26
2.75 263
2.87 99n84
2.89 35
3.2.4.1–3 52t
3.2.4.2–3 52t
3.3.3 173n27
3.9.2 173n28
3.15.1 44n165
3.17 44n165
3.22–23 52t, 68, 71
3.22–24 14
3.22–30 67
3.22.1 71
3.22.2 68n88, 71
3.23.1 71
3.24 69
3.24.1 66
3.24.1–2 51
3.24.1–3 82
3.24.2 11n8
3.24.2–3 66, 67,
   67n86

3.24.3 67n87
3.25 23n63, 58
3.25–28.2 68
3.28 23n63
3.33 88n29, 254
3.33–34 249n9, 252
3.33–35 254
3.34 261
3.34.1 254
3.34.2 255
3.34.2–5 254
3.34.6 254, 259, 263,
   277
3.36 78n138
3.55 220
3.56–57 73
3.56.2 22
3.63.3 78n138
3.64 151n143,
   161n199, 180
3.64.2 7, 188, 283
3.64.3 37, 128
3.69.6 59n54
3.70 78n141
3.71 123n17
3.76.2 172n17
4.3 54t, 73n119
4.9.2 188n106
4.10 54t, 73n119
4.12 22n59
4.15 158n179
4.16.4–6 180
4.16.6 37n132
4.17.1 161
4.20.4 255n31
4.21 11
4.21.1 11
4.21.2 11n5
4.37–38 158n179
4.39–40 63n67
4.42.3 159n187
4.52 52t, 71

Index Locorum

Tacitus (Tac.) (*cont.*)

4.52.2 96n67, 119n2
4.53 63n67
4.66.1 52*t*, 71, 71n106
4.67.3 22
4.67.4 184n84
4.67.6 78n138
4.70 161n200
4.71 66
4.71.4 29, 52*t*
5.1.1 259n51
5.1.4 174
5.2.1 174n29
5.2.2 29
5.4.2 53*t*
6.2.1 74n120, 186n93, 218n27
6.5.1 156n169, 161
6.8 45n168, 94
6.10 80n148
6.15.1 39n140
6.25 53*t*, 72, 127n50
6.26 255
6.29.4–7 74n121
6.40.4 53*t*, 72n112
11.1 7n17
11.2.1 20, 41
11.3 7n17
11.5.1 45n169
11.12.1 41n153
11.26 183n77
11.26–38 54*t*, 74, 75n123
11.28.2 20
11.32.2 14
11.32.3 14
11.34.3 14
11.37–38 74n122
11.38.3 75
12.2 62
12.3 45n169

12.5 4n8, 60
12.5–7 64
12.6 62
12.6.2 64n72
12.7 11n9
12.7.1 64n72
12.8 41, 72n111
12.22 53*t*
12.22. 73n113
12.22–23 41, 73
12.26.1 34
12.27.1 261n64
12.36–37 167
12.37.1 167n4
12.37.4 35, 168, 236, 241
12.40.2–3 17n32
12.41.6–42.1 248n2
12.42 41, 179n57, 241
12.42.2 169, 286
12.56 170n7
12.56–57 183n77
12.56.3 181n67
12.57.2 170
12.59 41
12.64–65 41, 73
12.68 161
12.68.2–3 39
12.69 152, 165n214, 219n32
13.2 101n93, 152
13.2.3 34n117
13.2.6 32, 152n147, 214, 215n14
13.3.3 149n133
13.4 5
13.4.2 20, 41
13.5.1–2 41
13.5.3 170
13.9 7n18, 12n10
13.11.1 159n187
13.13.1 30

13.13.4 27
13.14.3 152n149
13.14.5 248n2
13.18 5n10, 38
13.18.3 22, 32n107
13.32.2–3 118n171
13.32.3 20n47, 41, 41n152, 72n112
13.42.3 72n111
13.43.2 41, 72n112
13.45.1–2 26n78
13.56.3 30
14.1 41, 64
14.1–13 54*t*, 73n115, 241
14.1.2 62n63
14.3 39n138
14.4–5 39
14.6.1 26n76
14.7.5 248n2
14.8 80n149
14.9 173n24
14.10.3–11.2 73n115
14.11.1 170, 248n2
14.11.1–2 42
14.12 73
14.12.1 217
14.12.4 41
14.12.6 174n32
14.13.2 75
14.27.1 102n95
14.28.2 27
14.29–39 17
14.34 251n14
14.60 30, 39, 75n126
14.60–61 41, 64
14.60–64 75
14.61.1 186n93, 219
14.62–64 54*t*
14.63.1–2 72n110
15.10.3 256n40, 277n154

Index Locorum

15.23 35, 161n199,
    180, 251n15
15.38.2 218n24
16.6 98n78, 174
16.21.2 185n90
16.22.1 161n200,
    162n201
Germania (Germ.)
  7.3–4 251
  19.5 88n27
Historiae (Hist.)
  1.16 94, 106
  1.48 253n21
  1.48.2 255n36
  2.12.2 252n19
  2.56.1 252n19
  2.60 264n80
  2.60.2 5n13
  2.63–64 256
  2.64 80n150,
    264n80
  2.77 103n97
  2.89 178
  2.89–90 264n81

3.32 251n15
3.69 256n38
3.70 264n80
3.77.6–7 256
4.1.3 252n19
Tituli Ulpiani 17,1
    58n43
XII Tables 23n62

Ubi Erat Lupa (UEL)
  6694–6696 233n90
  14766 233n90

Valerius Maximus
    (Val. Max.)
  1.8.4 199n157
  3.5.3 253
  3.8.6 252n18
  4.3.3 38
  5.2.1 199n157
  5.4.7 57n35
  6.3.7 56n33
  9.1.3 15n23, 249n9
  9.15.2 21

Velleius Paterculus
    (Vell. Pat.)
  2,130.5 17
  2.75.2–3 40n148
  2.75.3 150, 150n139
  2.89.3 1n2
  2.100.3–5 65
  2.100.4–5 11n8, 20
  2.100.5 52t, 66
  2.130.5 40n148, 174
Vergil, *Aeneid*
  1.340 16
  1.364 16
  1.421–38 16
  4.50 17
  8.685–88 17n31
Vitruvius, *de Architectura*
    (De arch.)
  1 praef. 2–3 29,
    187n102
  6.5.2 38

Zonaras 7.12 179n56
Zosimus 1.11.2–3 41

Index

Page numbers in *italics* indicate illustrations. Page numbers with an italic *t* appended indicate a table. Place names are indexed by ancient toponym. Church buildings mentioned by name are all alphabetized at "Saint."

Abdera (now Adra, Spain), 98

Acerronia, 26n76

Acilius Attianus (Publius), 175, 264n84

Acte, 30, 113n143

Actium, battle of, 160, 262

adultery. *See also specific women*; as crime in Roman law, 56–58; gladiator, purported adultery of Faustina the Younger with, 55*t*, 75, 117; imperial women accused of, 11n8, 51, 52–55*t*, 65–69, 71–78; *lex Iulia de adulteriis coercendis*, 23, 47, 57, 65, 68; *maiestas* and, 66–69; private/domestic punishment of women for, 39, 56

adventus and triumph processions, 167–69, 171, 175, 177–79, 207

Aelius Aristides, 267, 278, 279

Aelius Aurelius (Titus), 111n133

Aelius Caesar (Lucius), 148n128

Aelius Lamia (Lucius Aelius Lamia Plautius Aelianus), 47, 50, 62n64

Aemilia Lepida (child of Julia the Younger), 25, 50n18

Aemilia Lepida (fiancee of L. Caesar), 52*t*, 70, 71, 116

Aemilia Lepida (former wife of Drusus Caesar), 53*t*, 72, 116

Aemilia Lepida (subject of senatorial trial), 14, 67–68, 116

Aemilius Lepidus (Marcus), 72, 120, 121, 174

Aemilius Paullus (Lucius), 25, 66n83

Aemilius Scaurus (Mamercus), 74n121

Aenatores (Brass-Wind Instrument Players), 200, 218n24, 221, 238–31, *239*, 246

Aequum (Dalmatia), 245

aerarium, 27n79

Afranius Burrus, 5n12, 30

agency of imperial women, 281–82, 286–87, 288

Agrippa (Marcus Vipsanius), 28, 92, 94, 172nn18–19, 173n24, 190, 260, 278, 283

Agrippa Postumus, 89, 158–59

Agrippina the Elder, 290–91; banishment of, 38; on coins, 100–101, *101*, 119, 130, 134, 222; funeral for, 174; imperial family and, 88, 95, 96, *101*; jealousy attributed to, 7n17; law, crime, and punishment, 53*t*, 71–72; provinces and the military, association with, 260, 261–63, 267, 276n151, 277, 278; Rome, public presence in, 184n84, 187–88, 196; security guard of, 22n59; Suetonius' attribution of desire for power to, 11; Tiberius on exposure of corpse on Gemonian Stairs, 184n86

356   *Index*

Agrippina the Younger, 291; as *Augusta*, 33*t*, 34–35; *carpentum,* right to ride in, 169, 179n57; on coins, 101–2, *102, 103*, 119–22, *120*, 130, 132, 139n98, 142*t*; death of emperors and, 78; deity/abstraction, on coin paired with, 142*t*; as heir of companion Acerronia, 26n76; homes/houses maintained by, 38–39; imperial family and, 93, 101–2, *102, 103*; isolation of, 12n10; jealousy attributed to, 41, 70, 72–73, 285, 286; law, crime, and punishment, 30n101, 53*t*, 54*t*, 70, 72–73, 75, 121, 122; *lictor,* accompaniment by, 32, 215n14; Livia compared, 31; Livia emulated by, 214–15, 219; local priestesses for imperial cult of, 156; marriage to uncle Claudius, 4n8, 11n9, 60, 62, 122; murder of, 73, 102, 165; Nero, relationship with, 4n9, 5n10, 7n18, 22, 30, 38–39, 75, 102, 122, 152, 217, 241; power/politics and, 11n9, 12n11, 20, 22, 30–35, 41–42, 46; as priest/*flaminica* of *divus* Claudius, 32, 146, 150, 152, 165, 179, 214–15; provinces and the military, association with, 261, 263n78; rehabilitation under Flavian emperors, 200, 218; religious cult and, 119–22, *120*, 146, 150; reputation of, 1; residing with Livia as teenager, 38; Rome, public presence in, 167–71, 174n29, 178, 181n67, 182, 183n77, 184–85, 189–90, 195, 196, 200–201, 206–8, 284, 285; statues/portraits of, 211–20, *212, 213*, 221, 228, 234, 235–41, *239*, 246–47; theaters, seating in, 37, 180

Albanum (now Albano Laziale, Italy), 270n114

Alexander Severus (emperor). *See* Severus Alexander

Alexandria (Egypt), 262, 271, 272, 274

alimenta, 106, 118, 183–84

Alta Semita (Rome), 174n33

Altar of the Magistri Vici Sandaliari (Rome), 153n157

Annia Faustina/Fundania, 33*t*, 64n73, 266n92, 295

Annius Verus (Marcus), 111

Antinous, 113–16, 164n213

Antioch, 263, 264n84, 271, 272

Antonia the Elder, 290; on Ara Pacis, 90n38; on *aureus* of Caligula, 100–101, *101*; on coin paired with deity/ abstraction, 142*t*; Rome, public presence in, 185; statues/portraits of, 151n146; theaters, seating in, 180

Antonia the Younger, 290; on Ara Pacis, 90n38; as *Augusta,* 33*t*, 34, 40; Caenis (concubine of Vespasian) and, 114; on coins, *131*, 151; funeral and interment of, 174n31; as heir of Berenice, mother of Agrippa I, 26n76; imperial family and, 90n38, 95, 96–97, 101; *ius trium liberorum* ("right of three children"), 25; law, crime, and punishment, 60; Livia compared, 31; Livilla, death of, 39n142, 40n149, 74; local priestesses for imperial cult of, 156; as priest of imperial cult, *131*, 150, 151, 179; provinces and the military, association with, 260–61, 277–78; religious cult and, *131*; residing with Livia, 38; Rome, public presence in, 182n74, 185, 187–88, 189–90, 208n210; statues/portraits of, 236, 237, 238, 241; as *univira,* 88, 96–97

Antonine plague, 117, 171

Antoninus Pius (emperor); adoption by Hadrian/adoption of successors by, 83, 106; burials arranged by, 176; coinage under, 133*t*, 138; as *divus,* 148, 313; imperial family and,

Index 357

83, 110–11, 113–16; law, crime, and punishment, 59; *Ludi Saeculares* of, 153n156; Lysistrate (imperial concubine) and, 40n149, 84, 113–16; Marcus Aurelius' imperial status and, 5, 83; marriage vows before statue of, 179; Matidia the Younger and, 245; never leaving Italy while emperor, 266; power/politics and imperial women, 26, 35–36; public monuments in Rome and, 193–94, *194*, 201, 203–4; unmarried concubines, living with, 61

Antonius (Iullus). *See* Iullus Antonius

Aphrodisias (near modern Geyre, Turkey), 150n140

Apicata, 74

Aponia Montana of Augusta Firma, 157

apotheosis. *See* consecration

Appuleia Varilla, 52*t*, 57, 69n99, 70–71

Aquileia (in modern northern Italy), 260, 278

Ara Pacis (Rome), 90, *91*, 124, 161, 179, 190, 195, 225, 237

Arch at Lepcis Magna, 153, *155*, 178n55

Arch of Constantine (Rome), 200, 239

Arch of Gallienus (Rome), 196

Arch of Germanicus (Rome), 188, 202

Arch of the Argentarii (Rome), 153–54, *154*, 179

Arch of Trajan (Ancona), 108

architectural patronage, 28, 170, 186–87, 208, 225, 245, 283

Arco di Portogallo (Rome), 176, 192–93, *193*, 195

Argentocoxus (Caledonian chieftain), wife of, 271, 279

Argiletum (Rome), 174–75

Armenia/Armenians, 170, 262, 285

Arrecina Tertulla, 61n60

art, imperial women in. *See* statues and portraits of imperial women

Arval Brethren, 33n1, 34n113, 93n50, 116, 123, 145n110, 156n166, 161, 162, 175n39, 180, 263, 272n123

Asinius Gallus (Gaius), 72

Assos (now Behramkale, Turkey), 262

asylum status and imperial cult, 77–78, 218

Athens, 208–9, 245, 258, 259n53, 262, 264n84, 265, 278n160, 279

Atia, 172n17, 172n19

Augusta, designation of, 2, 20, 31, 32–36, 33*t*, 129, 284

Augusta Vindelicum (Raetia), 245

Augustalia, 182

Augustus Caesar (Octavian; emperor); birth rate, efforts to encourage, 23–24, 85–86, 88–89; Caligula and, 119, *120*, 121; on coins, 119, *120*, 130; as *divus,* 7, 119, 121, *131*, 148, 283, 313; funeral of, 123n19, 173, 207; funeral orations by, 172; imperial family and, 1, 3, 88–92, 93–95, 118, 284; law, crime, and punishment of daughter and granddaughter, 61, 65–69, 89; Livia adopted into *gens Iulia* by, 31, 33*t*, 94, 97; *Ludi Saeculares* of, 153; marriage prohibited to active military by, 89n33, 251, 253; marriages/divorces of, 47n1, 61n60, 62, 63n70, 110; oaths and, 158, 159, 160, 161; as *pater patriae,* 69, 89–90, 96, 100n86, 161; power/politics and imperial women, 12, 13, 19, 21, 22, 24, 28, 31, 34, 39; provinces and the military, imperial women's association with, 259, 260, 261, 278; public monuments in Rome and, 7, 151, 186–87, 188, 198; social legislation of, 23, 56–58, 68, 89, 94n55, 282, 284; Spanish wars, *adventus* following, 177–78; statues and portraits of, 220, 240, 241; statues and portraits of imperial women and, 223–24, 225n65, 226, 244

Aulus Vitellius (emperor). *See* Vitellius (Aulus)

Aura body type, *242*, 243

Auzia (now Sour El-Ghozlane, Algeria), 111

Avidius Cassius (Gaius), 75, 117, 267, 268, 285, 286

Baetica, 83n1, 98n75

Balbilla (Julia), 232, 265–66, 279

banquets and feasts, 182–84, 207, 260

barbarian/non-Roman/foreign queens, 16–17, 251

Basilica Julia (Rome), 202

basilica of the two Antoniae (Rome), 185

basilicas of Matidia and Marciana (Rome), 175n36, 177, 190–92

Baths of Agrippina (*Lavacrum Agrippinae*; Rome), 27n88, 196, 282

Baths of Neptune (Ostia), 228–29, *229*

Bedriacum (near Calvatone, Italy), 264

beneficia, 45, 125, 209n213

Berenice (Julia; daughter of Herod Agrippa I), 15n26, 114n147, 163n206

Berenice (mother of Herod Agrippa I), 26n76

birth control, 87

birth rate, efforts to encourage, 23–24, 85–89, 144, 284

Bithynia, 115, 272

body types for statues of imperial women, 214, *215*, *216*, 222–23, 228–32, *229–31*, *242*, *243*, 244, 246

Bonna (now Bonn, Germany), 249

Boudicca, 17, 251

brickyards *(figlinae)* owned by imperial women, 27, 48, 283

Britain, imperial women in, 257, 265, 271. *See also specific locations*

Britannic Arch of Claudius (Rome), 151, 167n1, 190, 236, 237

Britannicus, 34, 72n111, 74, 190, 238

British revolt against Rome, 17, 251

British triumphs of Claudius in Rome, 167–69, 179, 237

Brundisium (now Brindisi, Italy), 253, 264n84, 271

Brutus, 13

Burrus. *See* Afranius Burrus

Byzantium, 262

caduca, 58n43, 59n52

Caecilia Metella, 13, 252n18

Caecilius Metellus (Lucius), funeral speech for, 88n24

Caecilius Metellus (Quintus), 85–86

Caecina Severus (Aulus), 88n29, 254

Caenis (Antonia; imperial concubine), 40n149, 113–16

Caesennius Paetus (Lucius), 256, 277n154

Caesonia. *See* Milonia Caesonia

Calama (now Guelma, Algeria), 31n102

Caligula (emperor); assassination of, 51, 60, 80, 148; coinage under, 100–101, *101*, 119–22, *120*, 130, 134, 222; Drusilla and, 45n170, 72, 121, 148n130; funerals arranged by, 174; imperial family and, 100–101, *101*; law, crime, and punishment under, 60, 70, 72; marriages of, 64; oaths, imperial women in, 160; power/politics and imperial women, 20, 25, 26, 30, 34, 37, 38, 40, 45n170; provinces and the military, association of imperial women with, 80n149, 256, 261, 266n94; public monuments in Rome and, 202; publicity for sisters at beginning of reign of, 119–22, *120*, 182; religious cult and, 119–22, *120*, 151; statues and portraits of imperial women and, 232

Calpurnia (wife of Pliny the Younger), 85n10

Index

Calpurnius Piso (Gaius), 62, 173, 254n29, 255

Calpurnius Piso (Gnaeus), 42, 43, 69, 96

Calpurnius Piso (Lucius), 10–11, 19

Calvisius Sabinus, 255

cameos depicting imperial women, 95n57, 107–8, *108*, 150n142, 219n31

Campania, 26, 38, 66, 73, 214n126, 217, 244n126

Campus Martius (Rome), 173, 174, 175n36, 176, 185, 186–95, 207, 236, 237, 283

Canopus (Egypt), 262

Capitoline (Rome), 102, 151n144, 153, 169, 177–80, 182–83, 200, 202, 203, 256n38, 285

Cappadocia, 262, 267, 272

Capri (Italy), 38n137, 76, 119

Caracalla (emperor); assassination of, 165, 272, 273n130; on coin of Septimius Severus, *134*; coinage under, 134; correspondence, Julia Domna's supervision of, 18, 46, 270, 279; as *divus*, 313; imperial family and, 111, 112; incest of, 60n57, 273; influence of imperial women on, 4; law, crime, and punishment, 60n57, 76–77; oaths, imperial women included in, 162; Plautilla's dowry, control of, 25n74; power/politics and imperial women, 18, 23, 40; provinces and the military, imperial women's association with, 269–73; public monuments in Rome and, 198, 199; religious cult and, 153, 154

Caratacus, 167, 207

Carnuntum (now Petronell, Austria), 263n79, 268n100, 271n119

carpentum, right to ride in; Claudius' British triumphs in Rome, Messalina and Agrippina the Younger in, 167,

169, 179, 180, 237; coins depicting imperial women in *carpentum,* 130, *135*, 135–37, *136*, 174; imperial family and, 103, *104*; power/politics and imperial women, 37, 41, *135*; in public religious ceremonies, 179–82; religious cult and, *135*, 135–37, *136*

Carrhae (now Harran, Turkey), 272

Carthage (Africa Proconsularis), 94

Carthago Nova (now Cartagena, Spain), 113n141, 252

Cassia Longina, 50n18

Cassius (murderer of Julius Caesar), 13

Cassius Dio, on restricted access to information about principate, 6n14

Cassius Longinus (Lucius), 120

Catana (now Catania, Sicily), 188

Catiline, 13, 41n152

Cato the Elder, 223, 224

Ceionia, 266

ceremonial/sacred fire carried before imperial women, 32, 181

Ceres (deity), imperial women associated with, 140–41t, 144, 145, 150n142, 228

Ceres body type, for statues, 222, 228, *229*

charitable expenditures, 28–29. *See also Novae Puellae Faustinianae; Puellae Faustinianae; Puellae Mammaeanae* and *Mammaeani*

chastity, Roman preoccupation with, 62, 63

Christianity and Judaism, imperial women associated with, 162–64, 165, 288

Cicero; Catiline, private trials of followers of, 13, 41n152; Terentia as wife of, 13, 14, 41n152

Cillium (now Kasserine, Tunisia), 233n90

Cinna (Gnaeus Cornelius Cinna Magnus), 4, 19, 40, 259, 279

Circus Flaminius (Rome), 95, 173, 185, 186–88, 202, 208, 225, 233

Circus Maximus (Rome), 179

Cirta, Numidia (now Constantine, Algeria), 112

clarissima femina and *clarissima puella* honorifics, 36, 272n129

Claudia (daughter of Poppaea and Nero), 292; as *Augusta,* 33*t*, 35; on coin paired with deity/abstraction, 142*t*; death of, 180; as *diva,* 145, 148, 149, 180, 306; oaths, imperial women named in, 161, 162

Claudia (stepdaughter of Mark Antony), 61n60

Claudia et Iulia domus, 94, 95

Claudia Pulchra, 52*t*, 70, 71

Claudia Severa, 257

Claudium (Rome), 149n137, 200–201, 211–20, *212, 213,* 239, 241

Claudius (emperor); adoption of Nero, 34, 132; banquets and feasts hosted by, 183nn76–77; British triumphs of, 167–69, 179, 237; as *divus,* 32, 147, 148–49, 152, 313; imperial family and, 89n30, 89n32, 95, 101; imperial women's behavior as reflection on, 6; law, crime, and punishment under, 70, 72, 74–75, 122; *Ludi Saeculares* of, 153n156; marriage to Messalina, 74–75; marriage to niece Agrippina the Younger, 4n8, 11n9, 60, 62, 63–64, 122; oaths, imperial women in, 160; Plautia Urgulanilla as first wife of, 10n2; power/politics and imperial women, 14, 25, 32, 34, 37, 39, 45n169; public monuments in Rome and, 188, 189–90, 200–201; public presence of imperial women in Rome and, 167–70, 179, 208; religious cult and, *131,* 151; residing with Livia as child, 38; statues and portraits of, 236, 238, 240; statues and portraits of imperial women and, 232, 236–38

Claudius Marcellus (Gaius; first husband of Octavia), 21, 63n69

Claudius Nero (Tiberius; first husband of Livia), 24, 63, 259n51

Claudius Pompeianus (Tiberius), 36n123, 63n65, 79, 111n131, 266n92

Cleopatra (Egyptian ruler), 16, 17n31, 19n43, 30, 92n41, 206n200, 222n46, 259

Cleopatra (wife of Gessius Florus), 42

Clodius Albinus (Decimus; emperor), 79n143, 257, 271n116

Clodius Pulcher (Publius), 198, 253

Cloelia, equestrian statue of, 224

Cnidus (freedman of Livia), 150

coins, 124–27. *See also specific imperial women and emperors; carpentum,* women riding in, 130, *135,* 135–37, *136,* 174; centralized versus provincial, 125; "female coin" as percentage of all coin, 132, 133*t*; as historical evidence for imperial women, 125–29, *128;* idealized portraits on, 126–27; imperial family and, 84n8, 100–105, *102–5,* 108–10, *109,* 112n138; pairings of imperial women and deities on, 139–45, 140–43*t*; "portrait types" or "empress coins," 129–39, *131,* 133*t*, *134–39,* 222; religious cult, as evidence of imperial female involvement in, 119–22, *120,* 127–29, 133, 164; terms for, 9

coins depicted; *aurei* of Nero with portraits of Agrippina the Younger, 101–2, *102, 103,* 132; *aureus* of Caligula with portrait of Agrippina the Elder, 100–101, *101,* 130, 133, 174; *aureus* of Hadrian with Sabina's apotheosis, 138, *139,* 192n126; *aureus* of Marcus Aurelius with Faustina the Younger as Mother of the Camps, 267–68,

268; aureus of Septimius Severus with Julia Domna, Caracalla, and Geta, *134*, 164; *aureus* of Trajan with Matidia the Elder and (possibly) Matidia the Younger and Sabina, 108–9, *109*; *denarius* of Augustus with portrait of imperial woman, possibly Julia the Elder, *91*, 91–92, 121n9, 164, 250; *denarius* of Claudius with Antonia the Younger as priest of *divus* Augustus, *131*, 151; *denarius* of Trajan for Marciana with *carpentum, 136*, 136–37; *denarius* of Trajan for Marciana's consecration, 137–38, *138*; *dupondii* of Caligula with brothers Nero and Drusus, 119–20; *dupondius* of Domitian with portrait of Domitia, 104–5, *105*; *dupondius* of Tiberius with SALVS AVGVSTA, *128*; *sestertius* of Caligula with Agrippina, Drusilla, and Julia Livilla, 119–22, *120*, 130, 139n98; *sestertius* of Elagabalus with Julia Maesa, *137*; *sestertius* of Hadrian with Temple of Matidia, *191*; *sestertius* of Tiberius with Livia in *carpentum,* 130, *135*, 135–36; *sestertius* of Titus honoring memory of Domitilla, 103–4, *104*, 135

Colophon (near Ephesus), 262

Colosseum (Rome), 201, 211, 236

Colossi of Memnon (Egypt), 265, 278

Column of Antoninus Pius (Rome), 177n46, 193–94, *194*

Column of Marcus Aurelius (Rome), 177n46, 190

Column of Trajan (Rome), 175, 176, 206

Commagene (in modern south-central Turkey), 262

Commodus (emperor); assassination of, 257; coinage under, 133*t*; as *divus,* 313; as *hostis publicus,* 79n143; imperial family and, 84, 116–17; imperial women

overshadowed by, 1; law, crime, and punishment under, 75–76; Marcia (imperial concubine) and, 48n9, 113n144, 164n213, 181; palace of, 218; provinces and the military, association of imperial women with, 266n92, 268n102; on Sabratha dedication, 80–81; sister Fadilla living with, 39n140

Concordia (deity/abstraction), 121, 197

Concordia (in modern northwest Italy), 157

concubines, imperial, 40n149, 48n9, 61, 75n123, 84, 113–16, 286

Conobaria (Baetica; now Las Cabezas de San Juan, Spain), 158–59

consecration; imperial males, consecrated, list of, 8, 313; of imperial women as *divae,* 145–49, 165, 284, 303–13

consularis femina, 36

contraception, 87

Corfinium (now Corfinio, Italy), 156n165

Corinth (Greece), 93n48, 94, 98

Coriolanus, 199

Cornelia (mother of the Gracchi), 13, 88n25, 93, 187, 222, 224–25

Cornelia (wife of Calvisius Sabinus), 255

Cornelia Paula, 33*t*, 64n73, 295

Cornificia, 84, 85n9, 179n56

Cremona, battle of, 251n15

Crepereia Tryphaena, 220n35

crime and punishment. *See* law, crime, and punishment

Crispina (Bruttia), 294; as *Augusta,* 33*t*; on coins, 268n102; death of, 177; deity/abstraction, coins paired with, 141*t*, 143*t*; indistinctness of, 1; law, crime, and punishment, 55*t*, 76; provinces and the military, association with, 266n92, 268n102; on Sabratha dedication, 80–81; theaters, seating in, 181

362   *Index*

Cuicul (now Djémila, Algeria), 245
cult. *See* religious cult
Cybele (deity), imperial women
    associated with, 140–41*t*, 144
Cyprus, 159
Cyrrhus (in modern northern Syria), 262

Dacia, 263
Dacian Wars, 264n83
Dalmatia/Dalmatians, 183n76,
    245n128, 262
damnatio memoriae; adultery, as
    punishment for, 66n84; of Agrippina
    the Younger, 73n115, 217; of
    Commodus, 81; deliberate damage to
    statues and, 214, 218–19; of Domitian,
    48–49, 60; of Elagabalus, 274; of Julia
    Maesa, 269, 275; of Julia Mamaea,
    269, 276; of Julia Soaemias, 269,
    274; of Livilla, 217; of Plautilla, 269; of
    Severus Alexander, 276
death of emperor, fates of imperial
    women at, 78–81
Delphi, 245, 259n53
Demeter (deity), and Greater
    Herculaneum Woman body type, 228
Diana (deity), imperial women associated
    with, 140–41*t*, 144
Didia Clara, 33*t*
Dido, in *Aeneid,* 16–17
divorce. *See* marriage, divorce, and
    remarriage
dolls, Roman, modeled on imperial
    women, 220n35
Domitia Europe, 49
Domitia Lepida, 292; house of,
    38n135; law, crime, and punishment,
    53*t*, 70, 73, 74n122, 285; power/politics
    and, 38n135, 41
Domitia Longina (Domitia Domitiani
    or Domitia Augusta), 293; as *Augusta,*

33*t*, 35, 47; on coins, 104, *105,* 141*t*,
    142*t*; criminality attributed to, 47–51,
    55*t*, 75, 77; death of Domitian and, 48,
    50, 51, 80; deity/abstraction, paired on
    coins with, 141*t*, 142*t*; as *divi Caesaris
    Mater,* 47; *figlinae* (brickyards) owned
    by, 27, 48, 81; Gabii, shrine at, 48–49,
    146, 247n131; imperial family and,
    102; marriage/divorce with Domitian,
    47–48, 62, 63n68, 64; oaths, imperial
    women included in, 162; Paris
    (pantomime), rumored affair with,
    48, 50, 60, 181n67; provinces and
    the military, association with,
    263; religious cult and, 165; wealth,
    control of, 25n74
Domitia Lucilla, 27
Domitia Paulina, 116n159
Domitian (emperor); assassination of, 48,
    50, 51; *damnatio memoriae* of, 48–49,
    60; Earinus and, 113n143; funeral for Julia
    Titi, 174–75; imperial family and, 103–5,
    105; imperial women's behavior viewed
    as reflection on, 5n13; Julia Titi, alleged
    incestuous relationship with, 48, 55*t*,
    60, 64n72, 272n128; *Ludi Saeculares* of,
    153n156; marriage/divorce with Domitia,
    47–48, 62, 63n68, 64; murder of Paris,
    48, 60; oaths, imperial women included
    in, 162; provinces and the military,
    imperial women's association with, 263
Domitilla (wife or daughter of
    Vespasian), 292; as *Augusta,* 33*t*, 35; on
    coins, 103–4, *104,* 136, 142*t*, 174n34; as
    diva, 306; Rome, public presence in,
    195, 196, 208
Domitilla (unidentifiable Flavian
    family member), association with
    Christianity, 163
Domitius Ahenobarbas (Gnaeus),
    72n109, 73n114, 120

Domitius Corbulo (Gnaeus), 49, 50n18, 263
Domitius Polycarp (Gnaeus), 49
domus, imperial. *See* imperial family
domus Augusta, 93n47, 94–96, 118, 188, 202, 224n56, 226, 233, 284
domus divina, 98–99, 105, 121, 134, 149, 154, 162, 174, 284
domus Iuliorum Claudiorumque, 94, 95
"dowager empresses," status of, 79
drinking cup from Vetera with Augustus and Livia, 250n10
Drusilla, 291; Caligula and, 45n170, 72, 121, 148n130; on coin of Caligula, paired with deity, 119–22, *120,* 139n98; on coin paired with deity/ abstraction, 142t; as *diva,* 124, 137, 147, 148, 164, 303–4; Domitia Longina and, 50n18; golden statues of, 186; in oaths, 160; provinces and the military, association with, 261n66; public funeral of, 174; Rome, public presence in, 178, 180, 182; theaters and games, seating at, 180, 182; Tiberius choosing husband for, 39n140
Drusus (Drusus Caesar; son of Agrippina the Elder), 61n58, 119–20
Drusus the Elder (son of Livia); imperial family and, 95; power/politics and imperial women, 7, 23, 25, 37, 38; provinces and the military, imperial women associated with, 226n68, 236, *250,* 259, 260–61; public presence of imperial women in Rome and, 172, 182n74, 188, 190; statues/ portraits and, 226n68, 236
Drusus the Younger (Drusus Caesar; son of Tiberius); imperial family and, 95, 96, 97n73; law, crime, and punishment, 54t, 72, 73; power/ politics and imperial women, 39,

43; provinces and the military, association of women with, 254, 259, 260, 261; public presence of imperial women in Rome and, 188; statues/ portraits and, 236, 241
Dusmia Numisilla, 98

Earinus, 113n143
Eboracum (York, England), 270n110, 271, 272
Edessa (now Urfa, Turkey), 272
Egypt, 106, 111, 117, 212, 232, 233, 257, 262, 265, 267, 277, 279, 287. *See also specific locations*
Elagabalus (emperor); adoption of Severus Alexander, 274; assassination of, 51, 248, 274; coinage under, 134, *137; damnatio memoriae* of, 274; Hierocles and, 113n144; imperial family and, 112; marriages of, 62–63, 64, 113n144; power/politics and imperial women, 36; provinces and the military, imperial women's association with, 248, 260n57, 273–75, 277; public monuments in Rome and, 201; as purported son of Caracalla, 273
Emesa (now Homs, Syria), 26, 270n113, 271, 273n130
emperors. *See also specific emperors by name*; deaths of, fates of imperial women at, 78–81; eminence of imperial women contingent upon relationship to, 1, 3–6; as *hostis publicus,* 79n143; identification of imperial women with, 80–81; law, relationship of emperor, imperial family, and imperial women to, 10–11, 50–56, 58–61, 77–78; as *primus inter pares,* 1, 60, 288; statues/portraits of, 220–21, 223–24
"empress coins" or "portrait types," 129–39, *131,* 133t, *134–39,* 222

364 Index

Ephesus (near modern Selçuk, Turkey), 111, 245, 266

Epicureans of Athens, Plotina's appeal to Hadrian for, 209–10, 265, 279

equestrian class; Augustus urging to procreate, 89; at banquets and feasts hosted by imperial women, 182–83; Fortuna Equestris, 123; funerals, wives of equestrians at, 123n19; honorifics for, 36n127; *ius trium liberorum* ("right of three children") for, 24n66; *Ludi Saeculares* and, 153; provinces and the military, women associated with, 256

Euboia (Greece), 262

Eumachia, Building of (Pompeii), 198

exemplarity of imperial women, 9n23, 14, 40–41, 220–23, 226, 251

Fadilla, 39n140, 179n56

family. *See* imperial family

Faustina the Elder, 293; as *Augusta*, 33*t*, 35; on coins, 126n43, 133, 138, 141*t*, 143*t*; death of emperors and, 79; deity/abstraction, paired with, 141*t*, 143*t*; as *diva*, 133, 148, 149, 310–11; dolls, Roman, modeled on, 220n35; funeral of, 176–77; imperial family and, 111, 115; indistinctness of, 1; law, crime, and punishment, 59, 75–76; local priestesses for imperial cult of, 157; marriage vows before statue of, 179; *Puellae Faustinianae,* 29, 176, 183–84; Rome, public presence in, 188–89, 193–94, *194*, 203; statues/portraits of, 193–94, *194*; wealth inherited by, 26

Faustina the Younger, 294; as *Augusta*, 33*t*, 36, 83; Avidius Cassius, revolt of, 75, 117, 267, 268, 285, 286; betrothal to Lucius Verus, 83; children borne by, 84–85, 267; on coin paired with

deity/abstraction, 141*t*, 143*t*; on coins, 126n43, 127n44, 133; death of, 177, 267; as *diva,* 311; dolls, Roman, modeled on, 220n35; *figlinae* (brickyards) owned by, 27; gladiator, purported adultery with, 55*t*, 75, 117; imperial family and, 83–85, 102, 111, 112n138, 116–17; law, crime, and punishment, 55*t*, 77; local priestesses for imperial cult of, 157; marriage to Marcus Aurelius, 5, 64, 77n136, 83, 88, 116; marriage vows before statue of, 179; provinces and the military, association with, 78–279, 249n7, 264, 267–68, *268*, 276; *Puellae Faustinianae,* 29, 176, 183–84; reputation of, 85, 116–17; Rome, public presence in, 201, 203, 204; statues/portraits of, 233n90; theaters, seating in, 181

Faustinopolis (formerly Halala; near Cilician Gates, Turkey), 267

Fayum portrait type, 233, *234*

feasts and banquets, 182–84, 207, 260

fertility/fecundity; birth rate, efforts to encourage, 23–24, 85–89, 144, 284; high rates of/lack of control over, 87, 284

figlinae (brickyards) owned by imperial women, 27, 48, 283

fire; firefighters, in Rome, 184n85, 276; Great Fire of 64 CE, 200n164, 201, 218, 239, 240; presence of imperial women at fires in Rome, 184; sacred/ceremonial fire carried before imperial women, 32, 181; at shrine of Vesta, 184, 204n186

fiscus, 27

Flavia Titiana, 33*t*

Flavius Celsus (Titus), 263n79

foreign/barbarian/non-Roman queens, 16–17, 251

Index

Fortuna (divinity), 121

Fortuna Equestris (divinity), 123

Forum Augustum (Rome), 69n94, 185n90, 197

Forum Julium (Forum of Caesar; Rome), 186, 189, 204

Forum of Trajan (Rome), 176n42, 205, 206, 208

Forum Romanum (Rome), 13, 56, 65, 89, 115, 148, 155n161, 171–76, 184–86, 189n109, 198n150, 201–4, 207, 208, 224, 259n50, 285

Forum Transitorium (Rome), 175

friendships between women; Agrippina the Younger's isolation, 12n10; within imperial family, 117–18; Livia's friendships, 10–11, 12n10, 29n96, 50; of Poppaea and Cleopatra, wife of Gessius Florus, 42; provinces and the military, 265–66, 279; in provinces and the military, 257; sources obscuring, 7

Frieze of the Vicomagistri (Rome), 148n125, 157n177, 192n126

Fucine Lake, 30, 169–70, 181n67, 183n77

Fufius Geminus (Gaius), 29

Fulvia, 13, 92n41, 93, 253, 258, 273

funerals, 123, 171–77, 207, 219

Gabii (east of Rome), 48–49, 146, 247n131

Galatia, 272

Galba (Servius Sulpicius; emperor), 29, 61, 79, 106, 263

Galeria Fundana, 80n150, 264, 292

Galerius Trachalus, 5n13

Gallia Lugdunensis, 270n109

Gallitta, 256

games and theaters, imperial women at, 37, 41, 180–82, 207, 244

Gaul, 26, 30n101, 158, 259, 260, 263n78, 272n122, 278. *See also specific locations*

Gaulus (now Ghawdex, Malta), 144

Gemonian Stairs (Rome), 184n86

gender norms; political power, barring women from, 2, 9, 14–19, 45–46, 287–88; provinces and the military, discomfort with women associated with, 249–58, 268, 276, 277, 279; public presence of women in Rome, disapproval/discouragement of, 167–71, 184–86, 207–10

genealogical trees, 8, 297–301

gens Augusta, 94–95, 118

gens Iulia, 31, 33t, 73n117, 90n38, 93–94, 97, 100, 118

Germanicus; death of, 42–44, 255; imperial family and, 88, 89, 95, 96, 97n73; power/politics and imperial women, 25, 38, 42–44; provinces and the military, association of imperial women with, 261–63; religious cult and, 119n2; Rome, city of, 169, 178, 185, 188, 190, 195, 202; statues/portraits of, 236, 238, 241

Germany, 96n67, 182n74, 257, 263, 272, 278. *See also specific locations*

Gessius Florus, 42

Gessius Marcianus, 63n65

Geta (emperor); imperial family and, 76n132, 79n143, 111; provinces and the military, association of imperial women with, 240n111, 270nn109–10, 271n120; public presence of imperial women in Rome and, 198, 200; religious cult and, *134,* 153, 162, 155n163

gladiators; Claudius gesturing to children of, 89n32; Faustina the Younger's supposed affair with, 55t, 75, 117; at games for Matidia the Elder's death, 175; women as, 251n15; women's seating at games of, 180

366   *Index*

Golden House of Nero (Rome), 218

Gracchi, 13, 88n25

Grand Cameo of France, 95n57

Granius Marcellus, 221n41

Great Fire of 64 CE, 200n164, 201, 218, 239, 240

Greater Herculaneum Woman, 222, 223n50, 228, *230*, *231*, 231–32

guardianship, 15–16, 20–21, 23, 29n93

Gytheion (now Gytheio, Greece), 158

Hadrian (emperor); adoption of successors by, 83, 106; Antinous and, 113–16, 164n213; childlessness of, 88; coins/coinage under, 126, 132–33, *133t*, *139*; as *divus*, 313; funerals and, 175–77; imperial family and, 109–10, 113–16; law, crime, and punishment, 59; Marcus Aurelius residing with, 39n139; marriage and relationship with Sabina, 5, 20, 64, 79, 109, 110, 265, 266; Matidia the Younger and, 245; miracles associated with, 165; mother-in-law Matidia the Elder, respect for, 63, 79; Plotina and, 79, 109–10, 264–65, 285; power/ politics and imperial women, 17– 18, 42; provinces and the military, association of imperial women with, 208–10, 265–66, 277, 278, 279; public monuments in Rome and, 188–89, 190–93, *193*, 195, 204–5, 206; statues and portraits of, 220, 245

Hadrianeum (Rome), 177, 192

Hadrianus of Tyre, 278n160

Halala (renamed Faustinopolis; near Cilician Gates, Turkey), 267

Haterius (Quintus), 19

Herculaneum (now Ercolano, Italy), 72n108, 101

Herod Agrippa I of Judaea, 218n27

Herod Agrippa II of Judaea, 114n147

Herodes Atticus (Tiberius Claudius), 267, 279

Hierocles, 113n144

Hip-Swath type statues, 214, *216*, 222–23, 228

homes/houses maintained by imperial women, 25–26, 38–39

honorifics granted to imperial women, 2, 20, 29, 31, 90n34, 100, 112–13. *See also specific honorifics*

Hortensia, 13

Horti Agrippinae (Rome), 196n139

hostis publicus, 79n143, 80n148

Ilium (Troy; Ilion; now Hisarlik, Turkey), 259n53, 260, 262

Illyricum (Balkans), 245n128, 254, 260, 263, 271n119

images of imperial women. *See* statues and portraits of imperial women

imperial cult. *See* religious cult

imperial family, 3, 83–118, 284; adoptive emperors, 83–84, 97, 105–13; Augustus Caesar, dynasty established by, 1, 3; birth rate, efforts to encourage, 23–24, 85–89, 144, 284; centrality of women to dynastic setup of principate, 14, 83–85, 97–98, 110–11, 118; coins/coinage and, 84n8, 100–105, *102–5*, 108–10, *109*, 112n138; fertility, high rates of/lack of control over, 87, 88; genealogical trees, 8, 297– 301; honorifics granted to imperial women, 90n34, 100, 112–13; imperial mother, figure of, 99–105; importance to principate, 4, 85–93; mortality rates and, 84–88, 117; motherless imperial households, 105–13; nontraditional imperial "families," 113–16; portraits/ statues of imperial women and, 233–35, *234*, *235*; provinces and the military, association of imperial women with, 261, 278; special designations for, 93–99; *univira,* ideal of, 63, 87–88, 96–97, 198

imperial fora (Rome), 185, 204–6. *See also specific fora*

Index

imperial home/palace, residence in, 39–40
imperial mother, 99–105
imperial women, 1–9, 281–88. *See also*
coins; imperial family; law, crime,
and punishment; power and politics;
provinces and the military; religious
cult; Rome, public presence of women
in; statues and portraits of imperial
women; *specific women*; agency of, 281–
82, 286–87, 288; *Augusta,* designation
of, 2; changes over time in presentation
of, 3, 9, 281, 284; criticisms of, 5–6,
7, 41–42, 116–17, 184–85; defined,
2; emperor and imperial house,
eminence contingent upon relationship
to, 1, 3–6; exemplarity of, 9n23, 14,
40–41, 220–23, 226, 251; exploring lives,
activities, and visibility of, 1–3; gender
norms for, 2, 9; genealogical trees, 8,
297–301; jealousy attributed to, 7, 41,
72–73, 76n128, 77, 181, 285, 286; list of
women and their life events, 8, 289–
95; mapping of, *ix–x,* 7, *168, 169,* 170–
71; naming and dating conventions,
7, 8; relationships between, 7; from
senatorial elite versus imperial family,
232; sources of information about, 6–7,
8–9, 281; time span addressed, 1, 3
imperium maius, 45
in flagrante delicto, 57n38
incest; between Caligula and Drusilla,
45n170, 72, 121, 148n130; of Caracalla,
60n57, 273; Claudius' marriage to
niece Agrippina the Younger, 4n8,
11n9, 60, 62, 63–64, 122; Julia Titi
and Domitian, alleged incestuous
relationship between, 48, 55t, 60,
64n72, 272n128; in Roman law, 57
infamis, 48n5, 57n38
inheritances and bequests, 7, 23n62, 24–
26, 59, 95, 115n153, 117–18, 197, 284
Isaeum (Rome), 218n24
Isis (deity), imperial women associated
with, 140–41t, 144, 218

Italia (deity), imperial women associated
with, 140–41t
Iullus Antonius, 65, 67
ius trium liberorum (right of three
children), 7, 23–25, 30, 37, 282–83

Judaism and Christianity, imperial
women associated with, 162–64,
165, 288
Julia (daughter of Drusus the Younger),
118n171, 291
Julia (daughter of Titus). *See* Julia Titi
Julia Antonia (mother of Mark
Antony), 13
Julia Aquilia Severa, 33t, 62–63,
64n73, 295
Julia Berenice, 15n26, 114n147, 163n206
Julia Domna, 294; as *Augusta,* 33t; on
coins, 133, *134,* 141t, 143t, 144n104,
164; death of, 26, 40, 165, 177,
272; death of emperors and, 78; deity/
abstraction, paired with, 141t, 143t,
144n104; as *diva,* 312; dolls, Roman,
modeled on, 220n35; emperor's
correspondence, supervision of, 18, 46,
270, 279; honorifics beyond *Augusta*
for, 36n129; imperial family and, 111,
112; incest with Caracalla, suspected
of, 60n57; influence on emperor,
4; law, crime, and punishment, 55t,
60n57, 76, 77; literary patronage of,
29; oaths, imperial women included
in, 162; power/politics and, 18, 23,
29, 46; provinces and the military,
association with, 208n211, 248–49,
269–72, 276, 277, 279; religious
cult and, 150, 152–55, *154, 155,* 157,
165; reputation of, 1; Rome, public
presence in, 178n53, 178n55, 179, 198–
200, 204, 205, 208; statues/portraits
of, 153–54, *154, 155,* 178n55, 179, 221,
249, 272n124, 272n129
Julia Drusilla (daughter of Caligula), 51,
62, 80, 292

368 Index

Julia Helias of Lugdunum, 156n167

Julia Laeta, 98

Julia Livilla (sister of Agrippina the
Younger), 291; on coin of Caligula,
paired with deity, 119–22, *120*,
139n98; imperial family and, 95; law,
crime, and punishment, 30n101, 53*t*,
54*t*, 70, 72, 121–22; provinces and
the military, association with, 262–
63; residing with Livia as teenager,
38; Rome, public presence in,
195; theaters and games, seating at, 37,
180, 182; Tiberius choosing husband
for, 39n140

Julia Maesa, 294; as *Augusta*, 33*t*; on
coins, 133, *137*, 141*t*, 143*t*; *damnatio
memoriae* of, 269, 275; death of,
177, 275; death of Julia Domna and,
272; deity/abstraction, paired with,
141*t*, 143*t*; as *diva*, 165, 312–13; imperial
family and, 112; imperial home/palace,
residing in, 40; provinces and the
military, association with, 260n57, 269,
270, 272–75, 277; Severus Alexander
and, 80n152; statues/portraits of,
272n129; wealth accumulated by,
26, 283

Julia Mamaea, 295; as *Augusta*,
33*t*; Caracalla, purported incest
with, 60n57, 273; Christianity,
association with, 163; on coins, 133,
141*t*, 143*t*; *damnatio memoriae* of,
269, 276; deity/abstraction, paired on
coins with, 141*t*, 143*t*; imperial family
and, 112; jealousy attributed to, 41,
77; marriages of, 63n65; murder of, 3,
46, 51, 77, 80, 165, 177, 249, 277; palace
of Severus Alexander, private rooms
named for, 185n90; power/politics
and, 15n24, 41–42; provinces and
the military, association with,

248–49, 258, 269, 270, 272–77,
279; *Puellae Mammaeanae* and
Mammaeani, 184n83

Julia Soaemias, 294–95; as *Augusta,*
33*t*; Caracalla, purported incest with,
60n57, 273; on coin paired with deity/
abstraction, 141*t*, 143*t*; *damnatio
memoriae* of, 269, 274; imperial family
and, 112; murder of, 51, 77, 80, 177,
248, 274; provinces and the military,
association with, 248, 269, 270,
271n121, 272–75, 277; Rome, public
presence in, 179

Julia the Elder, 290; adultery attributed
to, 11n8, 51, 52*t*, 61, 63n68, 65–69,
89, 184; architectural patronage of,
208n210; *Augusta,* never designated
as, 30; coin, possibly depicted on,
91, 91–92, 121n9, 164; divorce from
Tiberius before exile, 62, 66; imperial
family and, 89, 119; *ius trium
liberorum* ("right of three children"),
25; marriages of, 62; Mausoleum
of Augustus, barred from burial
in, 173n24; power/politics and,
25, 30, 39n140; provinces and the
military, association with, 260, 277,
278; reputation of, 1; Rome, public
presence in, 182, 184; statues/portraits
of, 233n89

Julia the Younger, 290; adultery
attributed to, 11n8, 51, 52*t*, 61, 65–69,
89; *Augusta,* never designated as,
30; house torn down by Augustus due
to extravagance, 30, 38, 39; imperial
family and, 89, 100n85, 119; *ius trium
liberorum* ("right of three children"),
25; Mausoleum of Augustus, barred
from burial in, 173n24

Julia Titi, 293; as *Augusta,* 33*t*,
35; on coins, 104, 141*t*, 142*t*; deity/

abstraction, paired with, 141*t*, 142*t*; as *diva,* 138n95, 165, 306–7; Domitian, alleged incestuous relationship with, 48, 55*t*, 60, 64n72, 272n128; *figlinae* (brickyards) owned by, 27; funeral of, 174–75; law, crime, and punishment, 55*t*, 77; living in palace of Domitian, 39; miniature chalcedony bust possibly showing apotheosis of, 138n95; oaths, imperial women included in, 161n197, 162; power/politics and, 5n13, 35, 42

Julius Caesar; as *divus,* 313; imperial family and, 86, 93; law, crime, and punishment, 60, 82; power/politics and imperial women, 13, 22; public presence of imperial women in Rome and, 172n16, 198; religious cult and, 130, 148, 150, 158n181

Julius Spartiaticus (Gaius), 42n156, 98

Julius Ursus (Lucius; consul), 5n13, 42

Junia, funeral of, 172n17

Junia Silana, 7n18

Junius Silanus (Decimus), 66, 67n86

Juno (deity), imperial women associated with, 140–41*t*, 144, 153, 177, 179

Klaros (in modern Izmir province, Turkey), 262

Kore (deity), and Lesser Herculaneum Woman body type, 228

Lambaesis, Numidia (near modern Batna, Algeria), 269, 271

Laodicea (now Latakia, Syria), 272

Largo Argentina (Rome), 188, 189

Lavacrum Agrippinae (Baths of Agrippina; Rome), 27n88, 196, 282

law, crime, and punishment, 3, 47–82, 285–87. *See also* adultery; incest; *maiestas;* sexual behavior; asylum status and imperial cult, 77–78,

218; charges, imperial women facing, 69–78; death of emperor, fates of imperial women at, 78–81; Domitia Longina, criminality attributed to, 47–51; guardianship of women under law, 16; imperial autocracy, growth of, 77; inheritances and bequests, 7, 23n62, 24–26, 59, 95, 115n153, 117–18, 197, 284; intercession on behalf of condemned, by imperial women, 19–20; involvement of imperial women with, 51–58, 52–55*t*; Julia the Elder and Julia the Younger, crimes and punishment of, 52*t*, 65–69; magic, as crime, 52*t*, 53*t*, 71, 73; marriage, divorce, and remarriage, 61–64; poisonings, 52–55*t*, 56, 71; power/control under law, women barred from, 2, 9, 14–19, 45–46; private initiation of prosecutions, 58; private/domestic punishment of women, 39, 56, 74, 77; relationship of emperor, imperial family, and imperial women to, 10–11, 50–56, 58–61, 77–78; social legislation of Augustus, 23, 56–58, 68, 89, 94n55, 282, 284; trials, imperial women's interference with, 20, 41

lead pipes, stamped with names of imperial women, 27n88, 38n136, 39, 196

lenocinium, 57n38

Lepcis Magna (now Khoms, Libya), 153, 155, 178n55, 271

Lepidus (triumvir), 13

Lesbos (now Lesvos, Greece), 262

Lesser Herculaneum Woman, 222, 223n50, 228

lex Cincia, 94n55

lex de flamonio Galliae Narbonensis, 146n115

lex de imperio Vespasiani, 40–41n151

lex Iulia de adulteriis coercendis, 23, 47, 57, 65, 68

lex Iulia de maiestate, 22, 78

lex Iulia de maritandis ordinibus, 23

lex Iulia theatralis, 37, 180

lex Manciana, 98–99

lex Oppia, 15, 16, 254n28

lex Papia Poppaea, 23, 58, 68

lex Voconia, 24n67

lictor, accompaniment by, 31–32, 150, 215n14

literary patronage, 29

Livia (Julia Augusta), 290; Agrippina the Younger emulating, 214–15, 219; on Ara Pacis, 90, *91;* architectural patronage of, 28; as *Augusta,* 31, 32–34, 33*t,* 37; Augustan *Ludi Saeculares* and, 153; banquets and feasts hosted by, 182–83; birthday, public celebration of, 156n169, 161; *carpentum,* right to ride in, 37, *135,* 135–36, 182; Ceres, statue associating Livia with, 144; on coins, *128,* 128–29, 130, *135;* critical attributions of power and political interference to, 10–15, 41–42; death and funeral of, 40n148, 173–74, 259n50; death of emperors and, 78; death of son Drusus, consolations for, 7, 23, 37, 85n10, 226n68; as *diva,* 37, 144, 147, 148, 161n198, 164, 304–6; Egyptian marriage contracts sworn before statue of, 106, 111; enrollment among "mothers of three children," 7; establishment of Augustan dynasty and, 3; Fortuna Equestris, vows for recovery of and gift to, 123; friendships with other women, 10–11, 12n10, 29n96, 50; *gens Iulia,* adoption by Augustus into, 31, 33*t,* 94, 97; homes/houses maintained by, 25–26, 38; honors of 14 CE for, 31–36; imperial family and, 90, 95, 97, 100, 118; influence on imperial men, 4, 38, 40–41, 42, 46; intercession on behalf of condemned, power of, 19–20; *ius trium liberorum* ("right of three children") granted to, 7, 23–25, 30, 37, 282; jealousy attributed to, 7n17; *lictor,* accompaniment by, 31–32, 150, 215n14; local priestesses for imperial cult of, 156, 157, 158; marriages of, 47n1, 62, 63; as *mater patriae,* 29, 90n34, 100; naked men encountered by, pardoning of, 19, 21, 184n84; oaths, imperial women named in, 161, 162; patronage of Galba and Otho, 4n9; as priest of cult of *divus* Augustus, 29n95, 31, 32, 37, 145, 146, 148, 149–51, 173, 179, 214–15; as *princeps femina,* 40; provinces and the military, association with, *250,* 253, 254, 259–60, 261, 278; reputation of, 1; Rome, public presence in, 172–73, 177–78, 180, 182–83, 185n88, 186, 187–88, 195, 196–200, 201–2, 207, 208, 283, 284, 285; *SCPP* on, 42–44; self-restraint in presence of power, praised for, 17, 18; serious illness of (22 CE), 37, 123, 128, 179–80, 182; statues/portraits of, 150, 214–15, *215, 216,* 220, 222, 223, 225–26, *227,* 233–34, *234, 235,* 241, 246, *250,* 282; theaters, seating in, 37, 180, 182; Tiberius, relationship with, 4, 7, 12, 18, 34, 37, 100, 149, 164, 182–83, 184; *tutela mulierum,* freedom from, 23; verbal insult, right of protection against, 20–22; wealth, control of, 25–26, 28–29, 283

Livilla (Claudia Livia Julia, sister of Claudius), 291; on coin paired with deity/abstraction, 142*t;* imperial family and, 95, 97; law, crime, and

Index

punishment, 54*t*, 73–74; power/politics and, 25, 38, 39, 40n149, 41; provinces and the military, association with, 263; Rome, public presence in, 187–88; Sejanus, accused of adultery with, 39, 40n149, 45n168, 54*t*, 73–74, 184n84; statues of, 186n93, 218; statues/portraits of, 186n93, 218

Lollia Paulina, 291; death of Caligula survived by, 80n149; law, crime, and punishment, 53*t*, 70, 72–73, 285; marriages/divorces of, 62, 63, 64n73; power/politics and, 26, 30, 41, 283; provinces and the military, women's association with, 257n42; tomb for ashes of, 174n32

Lollius (Marcus), 30

Lucilla, 294; as *Augusta*, 33*t*, 36, 133; on coin paired with deity/abstraction, 141*t*, 143*t*; on coins, 133; death of, 177; *figlinae* (brickyards) owned by, 27; indistinctness of, 1; jealousy attributed to, 76n128, 181; law, crime, and punishment, 55*t*, 76, 79; marriages of, 63n65, 83, 85, 111n131; provinces and the military, association with, 266, 279; Rome, public presence in, 181, 183–84; theaters, seating in, 181

Lucius Aelius Caesar. *See* Aelius Caesar (Lucius)

Lucius Caesar (adoptive son of Augustus), 71

Lucius Verus (emperor); adopted by Antoninus Pius, 83, 106; betrothal to Faustina the Younger, 83; imperial family and, 83; marriage to Lucilla, 63n65, 83, 85; Panthea as mistress of, 113n144, 243n120; power/politics and imperial women, 36; provinces and the military, imperial women's association with, 266, 278–79; public monuments

in Rome and, 194; residing in the *domus Tiberiana*, 39n139

Lucus Feroniae (north of Rome), 98

Ludi Magni, 179

Ludi Palatini, 148n132, 183

Ludi Saeculares, 123n19, 152–54, 177, 179, 271n121, 272n129, 284

Lugdunum (now Lyon, France), 156n167, 257, 261, 270n109, 271n116

Luna (deity), imperial women associated with, 108, 140–41*t*

Lysistrate (Galeria; imperial concubine), 40n149, 84, 113–16

Macellum Liviae (Rome), 196, 283

Macrinus (emperor), 26, 79n143, 272, 273

magic, as crime, 52*t*, 53*t*, 71, 73

maiestas (treason); adultery and, 66–69; imperial women accused of, 52–55*t*, 70; power/politics and, 11, 22, 30, 36

Malês (*grammateus* in Palmyra), 277

Manlia Scantilla, 33*t*

Marble Plan of Rome, 187, 197, 201

Marbury Hall type for Livia, 226n69

Marcellus (son of Octavia), 21, 94, 172, 186–87

Marcia (concubine of Commodus), 48n9, 113n144, 164n212, 181

Marcia Furnilla, 29n96, 61n60

Marciana, 293; as *Augusta*, 33*t*, 35, 108; on coins, 109, 132, *136*, 136–38, *138*, 141*t*, 142*t*; deity/abstraction, paired with, 141*t*, 142*t*; as *diva*, 137, 165–66, 175, 307–8; funeral of, 175; imperial family and, 107, 109, 111; imperial home/palace, residing in, 39; provinces and the military, association with, 264; Rome, public presence in, 178, 183, 190–92, 206

Marcomannic Wars, 117, 267

372   *Index*

Marcus Aurelius (emperor); adoption by Antoninus Pius, 83, 106; coinage under, 133*t*; as *divus,* 313; funeral of Matidia the Younger arranged by, 177n47; imperial family and, 83–84, 111, 115; law, crime, and punishment under, 77n136; marriage to Faustina the Younger, 5, 64, 77n136, 83, 88, 116; marriage vows before statue of, 179; provinces and the military, imperial women's association with, 266–67, 278–79; public monuments in Rome and, 194, 204; residing with Hadrian, 39n139; on Sabratha dedication, 80–81; triumphs of, 178–79, 181n69

Marius (Gaius), 91

Mark Antony, 13, 16, 21, 39, 92n41, 148n129, 187, 253n23, 258–59

marriage, divorce, and remarriage. *See also* imperial family; *specific persons*; active military, Augustus' prohibition of marriage to, 89n33, 251, 253; age of women at marriage, 83n1, 87; *cum manu* versus *sine manu* marriage, 16, 23, 56; gifts between married couples, 30n101; pontifices, consulting, 63–64; progeny, preoccupation with, 62, 64; in Roman law, 61–64; stability of imperial marriages, concern over, 64; statues of imperial women, vows and contracts before, 106, 111, 179; *univira,* ideal of, 63, 87–88, 96–97, 198

mater castrorum (Mother of the Camps), 112, 153, 162, 205, 249, 267–68, *268*, 269, 270, 274–76, 279, 284

mater patriae, 29, 90n34, 100

Matidia the Elder, 293; as *Augusta,* 33*t*, 108; on coins, 108–10, *109*, 132,

141*t*, 143*t*; deity/abstraction, paired with, 141*t*, 143*t*; as *diva,* 165–66, 175, 308; funerals and, 175–76; Hadrian's respect for (as mother-in-law), 63, 79, 109–10; imperial family and, 107–11, *108*, *109*, 117–18; power/politics and, 17, 33*t*, 35, 39, 282–83; provinces and the military, association with, 264; Rome, public presence in, 190–92, *191*, 203, 206; statues/portraits of, 245; as *univira,* 63, 88

Matidia the Younger, 293; coins and, *109*, 129–30; funeral of, 177n47; Hadrian/Antoninus Pius and, 245; imperial family and, *109*, 111, 117–18; power/politics and, 25n73, 26n76, 30–31, 35, 36, 39–40, 282–83; provinces, imperial women in, 208n211; Rome, public presence in, 184n83; statues/portraits of, 233n87, 235, 241–45, *242*, 247; theater seating for, 244

matronae of Rome, 24n67, 29n96, 56n32, 121, 153, 205, 208

Matronalia/Matralia, 197–98

Mausoleum of Augustus (Rome), 172, 173–74, 195, 207

Mausoleum of Hadrian (Rome), 111n133, 175–77, 192, 207, 272

Maximinus (emperor), 157n177

Mediolanum (now Milan, Italy), 270n109

Memmius Regulus (Publius), 62, 257n42

Memphis (Egypt), 262

Messalina, 292; adultery and sexual misbehavior, accusations of, 1, 6, 54*t*, 65, 74, 183n77; *Augusta* title denied to, 34, 35n119; *carpentum,* use of, 41, 167, 179, 180, 237; emperor/imperial house, reports of behavior as reflection on, 6; Gaius Silius, "marriage" to,

Index

373

74, 183n77; jealousy attributed to, 7n17, 72, 286; Julia Livilla and, 121–22; Junia Silana and, 7n18; law, crime, and punishment, 54t, 72, 74–75, 122; possibly replaced by Agrippina at Arch of Claudius, 237; power/politics and, 20, 41, 45n169; reputation of, 1; Rome, public presence in, 167, 179, 284; theaters, seating in, 37, 41; Vestal Virgin trying to intercede for, 14

military. *See* provinces and the military

Milonia Caesonia, 50n18, 51, 62, 80, 256, 292

Minerva (deity), imperial women associated with, 140–41t

Minturnae (now Minturno, Italy), 245

"Miracle of the Rain God," 267

Moesia, 257n42, 271, 274n133

Mogontiacum (now Mainz, Germany), 80, 249, 276

Monumentum Claudianum (Rome), 190, 237–38

mortality rates, 84–88, 117

Mother of the Army, 275, 276, 279

Mother of the Camps (*mater castrorum*), 112, 153, 162, 205, 249, 267–68, *268*, 269, 270, 274–76, 279, 284

Munatia Plancina. *See* Plancina

naked men encountered by Livia, pardoning of, 19, 21, 184n84

Narbo (now Narbonne, France), 93–94

Narbonensis, 83n1

Narcissus (imperial freedman), 170

Nero (emperor); adopted by Claudius, 34, 106, 132; Agrippina the Younger, relationship with, 4n9, 5n10, 7n18, 22, 30, 38–39, 75, 102, 122, 152, 217, 241; Claudium destroyed by, 200, 215–16; funeral of Poppaea arranged by, 174; as *hostis publicus,* 79n143; imperial

family and, 98n78, 101–2, *102,* *103*; on influence of imperial women, 4–5; law, crime, and punishment under, 60, 70, 75; marriages of, 61, 64; Messalina's plan to assassinate, 72n111; oaths, imperial women named in, 162; Octavia, divorce from, 5n12, 30, 39; provinces and the military, imperial women's association with, 263; public monuments in Rome and, 190, 200, 218; statues and portraits of, 236–37, 238, 240, 241; suicide of, 264

Nero Caesar (son of Agrippina the Elder), 61n58, 119–20, 174

Nerva (emperor), 5, 79, 88, 105–6, 173n24, 186n93, 263, 285, 286, 313t

Nicaea (now Iznik, Turkey), 271

Nicomedia (now Izmit, Turkey), 272n124, 274n133

Nicopolis (near modern Preveza, Greece), 262

non-Roman/barbarian/foreign queens, 16–17, 251

nontraditional imperial "families," 113–16

Norbanus Flaccus, 188

Noricum, 233n90, 271n116

Novae Puellae Faustinianae, 183–84

Numisia Maximilla (Vestal Virgin), 153

numismatics. *See* coins

oaths, imperial women included in, 158–62

Octacilia Severa, 275n146

Octavia (Claudia Octavia; daughter of Claudius/first wife of Nero), 292; birth of, 74; death of, 41; divorce from Nero, 5n12, 30, 39, 64; law, crime, and punishment, 54t, 61n60, 75; statues/portraits of, 189–90, 218–19, 236, 237, 238, 246

374 Index

Octavia (sister of Augustus), 289–90; architectural patronage of, 28, 170, 186–87, 197, 208, 225; as *diva*, 144; divorce of Mark Antony, 39n141, 259; establishment of Augustan dynasty and, 3; interment in Mausoleum of Augustus, 173n24; living in imperial palace, 39, 259; marriages of, 63n69; power/politics and, 13, 15, 19n43, 39, 46, 282, 283; provinces and the military, association with, 253n25, 258–59; public funeral of, 172, 174, 207; Rome, public presence in, 173n23, 177–78, 186–87, 189–90, 195, 207, 283, 284; statues/portraits of, 222, 223, 225, 226n70; *tutela mulierum,* freedom from, 23; verbal insult, right of protection against, 20–23

Octavian (emperor). *See* Augustus Caesar

Oplontis (in modern Torre Annunziata, Italy), 26

Oppidum Ubiorum (now Cologne, Germany), 261

orans type statues, 214, *215*

Orestina/Orestilla (Cornelia Livia), 62, 64n73

Origen, 163, 288

Ostia, 74, 228–29

Otho (Marcus Salvius; emperor), 29, 40, 61, 80n150, 264

Otriculum (now Otricoli, Italy), 150n142, 214

Ovid, addressing Tiberius as *Augustus,* 34n110; exile of, 65, 69n95

Paccia Marciana (first wife of Septimius Severus), 112, 186n93

Paestum (in modern Campania, Italy), 234

Palatine (Rome), 183, 201, 202, 203

Palazzo Verospi (Rome), 237

Palmyra (northeast of modern Damascus, Syria), 112, 266, 272n129, 277, 279n166

Pandateria (now Ventotene, Italy), 66, 71, 72

Pannonia, 183n76, 255, 266, 268n102, 271, 274n133

Panthea (mistress of Lucius Verus), 113n144, 243n120

Pantheon (Rome), 173, 177, 192, 217n17

Paphlagonian Oath, 159

Paris (pantomime), 48, 50, 60, 181n67

Parthian wars, 175, 184n83, 256, 258, 264, 266, 270, 271, 274, 277n154

pater patriae, 35, 69, 89–90, 96, 99, 100n86, 133, 161

patria potestas, 16, 56, 63n68, 92

Peltuinum (in modern Abruzzi region, Italy), 48

Pelusium (in eastern Nile delta), 271, 272

Pergamum (now Bergama, Turkey), 259n53, 272n124

Perge (east of modern Antalya, Turkey), 157, 220, 229–32

Perinthos (on European coast the Propontis), 262, 272

period face or *Zeitgesicht,* 220, 232

Persian War, 276

Pertinax (emperor), 33*t*n5, 36n124, 123n19, 137n90, 177, 257, 289n1, 313*t*

Perusine War, 253

Pescennius Niger (emperor), 79n143, 270

Philip (emperor), 275n146

Piazza Sciarra (Rome), 189

Piso. *See specific entries at* Calpurnius Piso

Plancia Magna of Perge, 157, 230n81, *231*, 231–32, 246

Plancina (Munatia Plancina), 7n17, 43–44, 100, 173n28, 254n29, 255, 263n74

Plautia Urgulania. *See* Urgulania

Plautia Urgulanilla, 10n2

Plautianus (Gaius Fulvius), 25n74, 55*t*, 76, 153, 271

Plautilla (Publia Fulvia), 294; as *Augusta*, 33*t*; on coins, 133n78; *damnatio memoriae* of, 269, 271n121; law, crime, and punishment, 55*t*, 76–77; power/ politics and, 25n74, 271n121; provinces and the military, association with, 271; religious cult and, 154

Plautius (Aulus), 118n171

Pliny the Younger, on adoptions of Tiberius and Nero, 106; on adultery of tribune's wife with centurion, 256; grief over wife's miscarriage, 85n10; imperial statues owned by, 221n41; petitioning Trajan for *ius trium liberorum* for Suetonius, 24n68

Plotina, 293; as *Augusta*, 33*t*, 35; on coins, 109–10, 132, 141*t*, 142*t*; deity/ abstraction, paired with, 141*t*, 142*t*; as *diva*, 309; *figlinae* (brickyards) owned by, 27; funerals and, 175, 176; Hadrian and, 79, 109–10, 264–65, 285; imperial family and, 107–10, *108*; imperial home/palace, residing in, 39; Jews and Judaism, association with, 163n206; law, crime, and punishment, 59; local priestesses for imperial cult of, 157; power/politics and, 17–18, 25, 35, 42; provinces and the military, association with, 208–10, 264–65, 279; reputation of, 1; Rome, public presence in, 178, 183, 206, 208–9

poisoning, imperial women accused of, 52–55*t*, 56, 71

politics. *See* power and politics

Pollentia (now Pollenzo, Italy), 157

pomerium, 167n3, 177, 186, 190, 254n27

Pompeianus. *See* Claudius Pompeianus (Tiberius)

Pompeii, 26, 156n165, 182, 198

Pomponia Graecina, 118n171

Pons Aelius (Rome), 177, 207

Pontia (now Ponza, Italy), 72n109

Popilia, funeral of, 172n16

Poppaea, 292; ancestral property of, 26; as *Augusta,* 33*t*, 35; on coin paired with deity/abstraction, 142*t*; as *diva,* 148, 149, 306; funeral of, 174; imperial family and, 98n78, 105n105; jealousy attributed to, 73n115; Jews and Judaism, association with, 163; marriages of, 62, 64; oaths, imperial women named in, 162, 292; Octavia targeted by, 41, 64, 75; power/politics and, 26, 35, 41, 42; Rome, public presence in, 185n90; statues/portraits of, 186n93, 218–19

Porolissum (now Moigrad, Romania), 249n6

Porta Esquilina (Rome), 196

Porta Fontinalis (Rome), 172, 176, 177

Porta Pia (Rome), 114n150

Porta Triumphalis (Rome), 173, 175

Porticus ad Nationes (Rome), 188–89

Porticus Liviae (Rome), 28, 164, 182n175, 196–98, 208, 216n15, 283

Porticus Octaviae (Rome), 28, 173, 186–87, 197, 208, 225, 259n50, 283

Porticus of Metellus (Rome), 225

Porticus Vipsiania (Via Flaminia, Rome), 28, 283

"portrait types" or "empress coins," 129–39, *131*, 133*t*, *134–39*, 222

portraits of imperial women. *See* statues and portraits of imperial women

Potentia (now Potenza Picena, Italy), 199n161

376 *Index*

power and politics, 3, 10–46, 282–84; actual, legitimate power of imperial women, 19–31; administration of own affairs without guardian, 20–21, 23, 24; architectural patronage, 28, 170, 186–87, 208, 225, 245, 283; attributions of power and political interference to imperial women, 10–15; *carpentum*, right to ride in, 37, 41, *135*; charitable expenditures, 28–29; criticisms of imperial women's greed for power, 18–19; desire for power attributed to imperial women, 11; gender norms and laws barring women from, 2, 9, 14–19, 45–46; guardianship, 15–16, 20–21, 23, 29n93; homes/houses maintained by imperial women, 25–26, 38–39; honorifics granted to women, 2, 20, 31, 32–36, 33*t*; honors granted to Livia in 14 CE, 31–36; imperial home/palace, residence in, 39–40; influence of imperial women on imperial men, 38–42; intercession on behalf of condemned, 19–20; *ius trium liberorum* ("right of three children"), 7, 23–25, 30; joint actions by women, 13, 14; *lictor*, accompaniment by, 31–32, 150, 215n14; literary patronage, 29; non-Roman queens and, 16–17; Republican women and, 12–13; right of public statuary, 20, 282; *SCPP*, evidence of, 4, 19, 42–44, 46; security details assigned to imperial women, 22–23, 32n107; theaters, seating in, 37; tribunician rights, 20–23, 45, 282; verbal insult, right of protection against, 20–23, 282; wealth, women's control of, 16, 25–31, 282–84

Praetorian Camp (Rome), 167–69, 170, 207, 274

priests; imperial women as priests of imperial cults, 29n95, 31, 32, 37, 145, 146, 149–55, *154, 155*, 164–65, 173, 179, 214–15; local priestesses for consecrated imperial women, 155–58, 164, 287–88

Prima Porta (Rome), Livia's villa at, 25–26, 178n55

primus inter pares, emperor as, 1, 60, 288

princeps femina, as title, 40

prostitution and pimping, 57

provinces and the military, 3, 248–80, 284–85; architectural patronage of Matidia the Younger, 245; armor, Milonia Caesonia paraded by Caligula in, 80n149, 256; arrangements for imperial journeys, 277–78; discomfort with women accompanying armed forces, 249–58, 268, 276, 277, 279; imperial family's importance to principate and, 261, 278; Julio-Claudian women and, *250*, 253, 254, 258–64, 278; limited roles of women with, 279–80; maps of empire, *ix–x,* 7; marriage prohibited to active military by Augustus, 89n33, 251, 253; Mother of the Army, 275, 276, 279; Mother of the Camps *(mater castrorum),* 112, 153, 162, 205, 249, 267–68, *268*, 269, 270, 274–76, 279, 284; rape, in war, 252; second-century imperial women and, 264–68, *268*, 278–79; Severan women and, 248–49, 268–76, 279; statues/portraits of imperial women in eastern provinces, 224, 226; women's actual association with, 248–50, 256–58

Prusias ad Hypium (near modern Düzce, Turkey), 274n133

public monuments associated with imperial women, 185–206, *191, 193, 194. See also specific monuments*

public presence of imperial women in Rome. *See* Rome, public presence of women in

Index

Pudicitia body type, 223, 228

Puellae Faustinianae, 29, 176, 183–84

Puellae Mammaeanae and
Mammaeani, 184n83

punishment of imperial women. *See* law, crime, and punishment

Puteoli (now Pozzuoli, Italy), 48, 98, 102n95

Quadi, 267

Quarta Hostilia, 13, 56n31

Quintilius Verus, 71n106

Quintus Metellus. *See* Caecilius Metellus (Quintus)

Quirinius (Publius), 71

Raetia, 245, 271n116

rape, in war, 252

Regium (now Reggio Calabria, Italy), 66

religious cult, 3, 119–66, 287–88. *See also specific imperial women, as* divae; as acceptable extra-domestic activity for Roman women, 123–24; Antinous, hero cult of, 115; asylum status and, 77–78, 218; coins as evidence of, 119–22, *120,* 127–29, 133, 164; consecration of imperial women as *divae,* 145–49, 165, 284; dedication of statue of *divus* Father Augustus at Theater of Marcellus, by Tiberius and Livia, 7, 151; *divus/diva,* as preferred term for deified persons, 3; Judaism and Christianity, imperial women associated with, 162–64, 165, 288; list of consecrated males, 8, 313; list of *divae* and evidence, 8, 303–12; local priestesses for consecrated imperial women, 155–58, 164, 287–88; oaths, imperial women included in, 158–62; pairings of imperial women and deities, on coins, 139–45, 140–43t; "portrait type" or "empress" coins with

apotheosis/consecration, *131,* 136–39, *136–39*; priests of imperial cults, imperial women as, 29n95, 31, 32, 37, 145, 146, 149–55, *154, 155,* 164–65, 173, 179, 214–15; Rome, public presence of women in, 179–82, 185

remarriage. *See* marriage, divorce, and remarriage

Rhodes (Greece), 262

right of three children *(ius trium liberorum),* 7, 23–25, 30, 37, 282–83

Roma (deity), imperial women associated with, 140–41t

Roman imperial women. *See* imperial women

Rome, public presence of women in, 3, 167–210, 284, 285. *See also specific places and structures within Rome; adventus* and triumph processions, 167–69, 171, 175, 177–79, 207; architectural patronage, 28, 170, 186–87, 208, 225, 245, 283; banquets and feasts, 182–84, 207, 260; ceremonial/sacred fire carried before imperial women, 181; Claudius, public displays of wives of, 167–70, 179, 208; *consecratio* rituals, 171; disapproval/discouragement of, 167–71, 184–86, 207–10; *figlinae* (brickyards) owned by imperial women in and around, 27; funerals, 123, 171–77, 207; gendered aspect of, 198, 208; maps, early 3rd c. CE, *168, 169*; population size/density, 171; public monuments, 185–206, *191, 193, 194*; religious ceremonies, public, 179–82, 185; sacred/ceremonial fire carried before imperial women, 32, 181; theaters and games, 37, 41, 180–82, 207, 244

Rostra (Forum Romanum, Rome), 65, 172, 173, 174, 184

Rubellius Plautus, 30

378 Index

runners *(viatores)* of Treasury of Saturn (Rome), 204, 208

Sabina, 293; as *Augusta,* 33t, 35, 116n159; burial of, 176; on coins, *109,* 138, *139,* 141t, 143t, 144n104, 192n126; deity/abstraction, paired with, 141t, 143t, 144n104; as *diva, 139,* 165, 176, 192–93, *193,* 309–10; *figlinae* (brickyards) owned by, 27; houses/homes maintained by, 39; imperial family and, *109,* 110, 111; imperial home/palace, residing in, 40; indistinctness of, 1, 281; marriage and relationship with Hadrian, 5, 20, 64, 79, 109, 110, 265, 266; power/politics and, 20, 31, 31n102, 39, 283; provinces and the military, association with, 265–66, 277, 278, 279; Rome, public presence in, 170n9, 188–89, 190, 192–93, *193,* 195, 204–5, 207; statues/portraits of, 192–93, *193,* 195, 228–31, *229, 230,* 245, 246
Sabratha/Sabrathans (now Sabratah, Libya), 80–81, 189, 204, 208
sacred/ceremonial fire carried before imperial women, 32, 181
SS. Apostoli (Rome), 189n108
S. Ignazio (Rome), 191
S. Lorenzo in Panisperna (Viminal Hill, Rome), 196
Santa Maria Antiqua (Rome), 202
Santa Susanna, Church and Largo di (Rome), 174n33
Sallustia Orbiana, 33t, 55t, 77, 275n142, 295
Sallustius Crispus Passienus (Gaius), 122
Salome (sister of Herod), 26, 259n53
same-sex relationships, 51n23, 113–16
Samos (Greece), 40, 259n53
Samothrace (Greece), 262
Sardinia, 158

Sarmizegetusa (now Varhely, Romania), 113n141
Scipio Africanus, 161n195, 225, 252
Scribonia, 61n60, 63n70, 66, 110
Sebasteion, Aphrodisias, 150n140
Securitas (divinity/abstraction), 121
security details assigned to imperial women, 22–23, 32n107
Sejanus, 39, 40n149, 45n168, 54t, 73–74, 184n84
Selinous (now Gazipaşa, Turkey), 175, 264, 265
senatorial class; at banquets and feasts hosted by imperial women, 182–83; funerals, wives of senators at, 123n19; honorifics for, 36; imperial women mainly from, 232; *ius trium liberorum* ("right of three children") for, 24n66; *Ludi Saeculares* and, 153; provinces and the military, women's association with, 256; women from senatorial families, senatorial status for, 24n65
Seneca the Younger, exile of, 41, 72
Septicius Clarus, 5, 265, 266
Septimius Severus (emperor); coinage under, 133–34, *134;* as *divus,* 177, 313; funeral of, 177; imperial family and, 111–12; law, crime, and punishment under, 76; oaths, imperial women included in, 162; power/politics and imperial women, 40; provinces and the military, imperial women's association with, 269–73, 279; public monuments in Rome and, 198, 199, 204; public presence of imperial women in Rome and, 179; religious cult and, 153
Sergia Plautilla (mother of Nerva), 106, 186n93
Servilia, 13, 93
Severus Alexander (emperor); adoption by Elagabalus, 274; assassination

of, 3, 51, 80, 249, 276; coinage under, 134; *damnatio memoriae* of, 276; as *divus,* 313; imperial family and, 112; law, crime, and punishment under, 77; military, imperial women's association with, 248–49; power/politics and imperial women, 15n24, 41–42, 46; private palace rooms named for Julia Mamaea, 185n90; provinces and the military, imperial women's association with, 275–76; public monuments in Rome and, 201; *Puellae Mammaeanae* and *Mammaeani,* 184n83; as purported son of Caracalla, 273; on weakness of women as guardians, 15

Sextani Arelatenses (Arles, France), 189

Sextilia (mother of Vitellius), 33*t*, 35, 178, 292

sexual behavior. *See also* adultery; incest; Caligula's desire for sister Drusilla, 45n170; Claudia Pulchra, 52*t*; concubines, dependents, and slaves, sexual relations with, 113–16; depictions of/charges against imperial women for, 1, 52–55*t*, 56–57, 63, 71, 72; Livilla's affair with Sejanus, 39, 40n149, 45n168, 54*t*; of Messalina, 1, 6, 54*t*, 65, 74, 183n77; prostitution and pimping, 57; Roman versus British, 271; same-sex relationships, 51n23, 113–16; senatorial status and scrutiny of, 24n65; Vestal Virgins accused of unchastity, 57

Shoulder-Swath body type, 223, 228

shrine of Aenatores (Brass-Wind Instrument Players; Rome), 200, 218n24, 221, 238–31, *239*, 246

shrine of Concordia (Rome), 197–98

shrines of Pudicitia Patricia and Pudicitia Plebeia (Rome), 185n88

shrine of Vesta (Rome), 152n152, 203, 204n186

Sicily, 158, 188, 259n51, 259n53

Silius (Gaius), 41, 54*t*, 74, 75n124, 183n77

Sinuessa (now Mondragone, Italy), 245

Sirmium (now Sremska Mitrovica, Serbia), 267

Smyrna (now Izmir, Turkey), 265n88, 267, 278

social legislation of Augustus, 23, 56–58, 68, 89, 94n55, 282, 284

Spain, 42, 83n1, 90n38, 102n94, 157, 158, 159, 249n6, 261n61, 293n15. *See also specific locations*

Spanish wars, *adventus* of Augustus Caesar following, 177–78

Sparta, 40, 158, 259n53

Sporus, 113n143

Stabiae (near modern Castellammare di Stabia, Italy), 26

Statilia Messalina, 33*t*, 62, 63n68, 80, 162, 263, 292

Statilius Taurus, 41

statues and portraits of imperial women, 3, 211–47. *See also specific objects, structures, and sites*; Agrippina the Younger, 211–20, *212, 213*, 221, 228, 234, 235–41, *239*, 246–47; Antonia the Elder, 151n146; Antonia the Younger, 236, 237, 238, 241; Ara Pacis (Rome), 90, *91*, 124, 161, 179, 190, 195; asylum status and statues of imperial family, 77–78, 218; body types, 214, *215, 216*, 222–23, 228–32, *229–31, 242, 243, 244, 246*; coloration of statues, 221n42, 244; deliberate damage to statues, 214, 218; dolls, Roman, 220n35; in eastern provinces, 224, 226; exemplarity of imperial women and, 220–23, 226; facial features of, 220, 232, 233–35, *234, 235*; Faustina the Elder, 193–94, *194*; Faustina the Younger, 233n90; hairstyles, 220n35, 223; historical public portraits and statues, 223–28, *227*; imperial family and, 233–35, *234, 235*; Julia Domna, 153–54,

380   *Index*

statues and portraits of imperial women (*cont.*)
154, 155, 178n55, 179, 221, 249, 272n124, 272n129; Julia Maesa, 272n129; Julia the Elder, 233n89; Livia, 150, 214–15, *215, 216,* 220, 222, 223, 225–26, *227,* 233–34, *234, 235,* 241, 246, *250,* 282; Livilla, 186n93, 218; marriage contracts and vows sworn before, 106, 111, 179; Matidia the Elder, 245; Matidia the Younger, 233n87, 235, 241–45, *242,* 247; modifications of statues, 212–14, 217, 218–19; Octavia (daughter of Claudius; first wife of Nero), 218–19, 236, 237, 238, 246; Octavia (sister of Augustus), 222, 223, 225, 226n70; Poppaea, 186n93, 218–19; in public versus private spaces, 221; right of public statuary, 20, 223–24, 225n65, 259, 282; Sabina, 192–93, *193,* 195, 228–31, *229, 230,* 245, 246; *Zeitgesicht* or period face, 220, 232
stepmothers, conventional disparagement of, 115
Suessa Aurunca (now Sessa Aurunca, Italy), 111, 208n211, 241–45, 247
Suetonius; Pliny the Younger petitioning Trajan for *ius trium liberorum* for, 24n68; Sabina, close relationship with, 5, 265, 266
Sufetula (now Sbeitla, Tunisia), 111
Sulla, 13, 146n113, 224n58, 252n18
Sulpicia Lepidina, 257
Superaequani (now Castelvecchio Subequo, Italy), 199n161
sword sheath possibly with Livia, Drusus, and Tiberius, *250,* 259
Syria, 40, 96, 117, 248, 255, 259n53, 262, 264n84, 267, 270n113, 271, 273, 279, 283. *See also specific locations*
Syria Palaestina, 271

Tanusia, 13
Tarracina (now Terracina, Italy), 256

Tarsus (in modern south-central Turkey), 272
Teate Marrucinorum (now Chieti, Italy), 98
Tellus (deity), imperial women associated with, 140–41*t*
Temple of Antoninus and Faustina (Rome), 115, 148, 203–4
Temple of Bona Dea (Rome), 28, 198, 208, 283
Temple of Castor (Rome), 189n108, 202
Temple of Concord (Rome), 28, 204, 283
Temple of *diva* Faustina the Elder (Rome). *See* Temple of Antoninus and Faustina
Temple of *diva* Matidia the Elder (Rome), 27n88, 177, *191,* 191–92, 203
Temple of *divus* Augustus (Rome), 180n59, 182, 183n76, 201–2, 283
Temple of *divus* Claudius (Rome). *See* Claudium
Temple of Faustina the Younger (Rome), 201, 203
Temple of Fortuna Muliebris (Rome), 198–200, 208, 233n88
Temple of the Gens Flavia (Quirinal Hill, Rome), 174, 175
Temple of Julius (*divus* Julius Caesar; Rome), 172
Temple of Juno Lucina (Rome), 197–98
Temple of Jupiter Optimus Maximus (Capitoline, Rome), 182
Temple of Mars Ultor (Rome), 69n94
Temple of Venus (Capitoline, Rome), 202
Temple of Venus and Roma (Velia, Rome), 179
Temple of Venus Genetrix (Forum Julium, Rome), 186, 204, 206n200
Temple of Vespasian (Rome), 204
Terentia (wife of Cicero), 13, 14, 41n152
Terentia Flavola (Vestal Virgin), 153
Thamugadi (east of modern Barna, Algeria), 271

Index

Theater of Marcellus (Rome), 7, 151, 186–87, 188

theaters and games, imperial women at, 37, 41, 180–82, 207, 244

Thebes (Egypt), 262

Thespiae (now Thespies, Greece), 233n89, 260

Thrace, 271, 274n133

Tiberius (emperor); adoption by Augustus, 106; banquets and feasts hosted by, 183n76; effigy, sacredness of, 78n141; imperial cult and, 147n124; imperial family and, 93, 95–98, 100; influence of imperial women on, 4; law, crime, and punishment under, 59n54, 70–72, 73–74; Livia, relationship with, 4, 7, 12, 18, 34, 37, 100, 149, 164, 182–83, 184; in oaths, 159; power/politics and imperial women, 11, 12, 13n14, 14, 15n26, 17, 19, 32, 34, 39, 42–44, 45; provinces and the military, imperial women's association with, 250, 254, 259, 260, 276n151, 277, 278; public monuments in Rome and, 188, 196–97, 202; in *SCPP*, 42–44; statues and portraits of, 234, 238

Tiberius Gemellus, 195

Ticinum (now Pavia, Italy), 259

Titus (emperor), 47, 50, 103–5, *104*, 114n147, 195, 313

Tower of the Winds, Roman Agora (Athens), 209

Trajan (emperor); adoption by Nerva, 106; *adventus* of, 178; childlessness of, 88, 107; coins/coinage under, 126, *136*, *138*; as *divus*, 313; imperial family and, 88, 98–99, 106–10; Pliny the Younger petitioning Trajan for *ius trium liberorum* for Suetonius, 24n68; power/politics and imperial women, 17, 35, 39–40, 46; provinces and the military, association of

imperial women with, 256, 264–65, 278, 279; public monuments in Rome and, 197, 206; religious cult and, *136*, *138*, 165–66; Rome, ashes returned to, 175; same-sex relationships, 114n148; statues and portraits of, 245

travelers, imperial women as. *See* provinces and the military

treason. *See maiestas*

Treasury of Saturn (Rome), runners of, 204, 208

Treviri (on lower Moselle River, Germany), 261n66

Triaria (in modern Isole Tremiti, Italy), 256

tribunician rights granted to imperial women, 20–23, 45, 282

Trimerus, 66

triumphs and *adventus* processions, 167–69, 171, 175, 177–79, 207

Tucci (now Martos, Spain), 98

Turin (Italy), 157

tutela mulierum, 16, 23

Tyana (now Kemerhasar, Turkey), 271

Ulcisia Castra (now Szentendre, Hungary), 276

Ulpian, 2, 15, 24–25, 27n80, 36, 50–51, 58n47, 81, 81n156

Ummidia Quadratilla, 40n150

univira, ideal of, 63, 87–88, 96–97, 198

Upper Germany, 162, 271n116

Urgulania (Plautia), 10–11, 19, 46, 50, 232

Valerius (Lucius), 13n16, 15, 16

Valerius Messalinus, 254

Valerius Messalla Corvinus (Marcus), 90

Vedius Pollio, 197

Veleia (now Velleia, Italy), 214, 225

Venus (deity), imperial women associated with, 140–41*t*, 14'4, 205, 228

verbal insult, right of protection against, 20–23, 282

Index

Verulania Gratilla, 256n38
Verus (emperor). *See* Lucius Verus
Vespasian (emperor); Caenis (imperial concubine) and, 40n149, 113–16; clemency towards imperial women compared to Vitellius, 80n150; deathbed quip of, 165n215; as *divus,* 313; imperial family and, 102–4, 113–16; marriage of Domitian to Domitia Longina and, 47, 50; miracles associated with, 165; public monuments in Rome and, 200, 216, 218; unmarried concubines, living with, 61
Vesta (deity); imperial women associated with, 140–41*t,* 144; shrine of, 152n152, 203, 204n186
Vestal Virgins; Antonia the Younger granted privileges of, 151; *carpentum,* right to ride in, 37; imperial cult of *diva* Julia Augusta (Livia) entrusted to, 148n127; *ius trium liberorum* ("right of three children") granted to, 23n62, 24; *lictor,* accompaniment by, 32; in *Ludi Saeculares,* 153; power/politics and, 14, 16, 32, 41n151; religious cult, as active officiants in, 123; social norms and family ties, connection to, 46n171; as *sui iuris,* 16; Tacitus on womanly deference of, 10n1; at theaters and games, 180, 207; at triumphs and *adventus* processions, 178n52; unchastity, accusations of, 57
Vetera (now Xanten, Germany), 250n10, 262
Vettulenus Civica Barbarus (Marcus), 266
Veturia. *See* Volumnia
Via Appia (Rome), burial place for household dependents of Livia on, 26
Via del Seminario (Rome), 191
Via dell'Impresa (Rome), 190
Via Flaminia (Rome), 151, 172, 175n38, 189, 190, 192, 195, 207, 236, 237

Via Lata (Rome), 28n89, 189n111
Via Latina (Rome), 26n75, 198, 199
Via Nazionale (Rome), 196
Via Recta (Rome), 176, 177
viatores (runners) of Treasury of Saturn (Rome), 204, 208
Vibia Aurelia Sabina, 266n94
Vibidia (Vestal Virgin), 14
Vicetia (now Vicenza, Italy), 184n83, 245
Vicolo dello Sdrucciolo (Rome), 190
Vicolo dello Spado d'Orlando (Rome), 191
"Victory of the Symmachi" statue, 211n2, 218n26
Vicus Iugarius (Rome), 202
Vicus Longus (Rome), 175
Vicus Tuscus (Rome), 202
Vigna Barberini (Palatine, Rome), 201
Villa Adriana (in modern Tivoli, Italy), 39n139
Viminacium (near modern Kostolac, in eastern Serbia), 271n119
Vindolanda (near modern Bardon Mill, England), 251, 257
Vinicius (Marcus), 72n109, 120, 263
Vinius (Titus), 13
Vipsania Agrippina, 90n38
Vipsania Polla, 28, 283
Virgilia, 199
Vitellius (Aulus; emperor); *adventus* of, 178; imperial women's behavior as reflection on, 5n13; on marriage within imperial family, 4n8; provinces and the military, association of imperial women with, 256, 264; violent death of, 80n150
Vitellius (Lucius), 64, 256
Volumnia (Veturia), 199

wealth, women's control of, 16, 25–31, 282–84

Zeitgesicht or period face, 220, 232